1996
The Supreme Court Review

199
Th

"Judges as persons, or courts as institutions, are entitled to
no greater immunity from criticism than other persons
or institutions . . . [J]udges must be kept mindful of their limitations and
of their ultimate public responsibility by a vigorous
stream of criticism expressed with candor however blunt."
—*Felix Frankfurter*

". . . while it is proper that people should find fault when
their judges fail, it is only reasonable that they should recognize the
difficulties. . . . Let them be severely brought to book,
when they go wrong, but by those who will take the trouble
to understand them."
—*Learned Hand*

THE LAW SCHOOL

THE UNIVERSITY OF CHICAGO

upreme Court Review

EDITED BY

DENNIS J. HUTCHINSON
DAVID A. STRAUSS
AND GEOFFREY R. STONE

 THE UNIVERSITY OF CHICAGO PRESS

CHICAGO AND LONDON

INTERNATIONAL STANDARD BOOK NUMBER: 0-226-36313-9

LIBRARY OF CONGRESS CATALOG CARD NUMBER: 60-14353

THE UNIVERSITY OF CHICAGO PRESS, CHICAGO 60637

THE UNIVERSITY OF CHICAGO PRESS, LTD., LONDON

© 1997 BY THE UNIVERSITY OF CHICAGO, ALL RIGHTS RESERVED, PUBLISHED 1997

PRINTED IN THE UNITED STATES OF AMERICA

The paper used in this publication meets the minimum requirements of American National Standard for Information Sciences–Permanence of Paper for Printed Library Materials, ANSI Z39.48-1984. ⊗

TO

PHILIP B. KURLAND

IN MEMORIAM

il miglior fabbro.

CONTENTS

DANIEL J. MELTZER

THE SEMINOLE DECISION AND STATE SOVEREIGN IMMUNITY

In recent years, the Eleventh Amendment has emerged from relative obscurity to become a major focus of constitutional controversy. A few crude statistics evidence this development:

- The Amendment was cited in only ten Warren Court decisions (over sixteen Terms), but has been mentioned in 125 decisions in the twenty-seven Terms since.[1]
- Virtually all of the Rehnquist Court's Eleventh Amendment decisions of any significance were decided by 5–4 margins.[2]
- The Amendment occupies fewer than eleven pages in each of the first two editions of the *Hart and Wechsler* casebook

Daniel J. Meltzer is Professor of Law, Harvard Law School.

AUTHOR'S NOTE: I am grateful to Dick Fallon, Willy Fletcher, Phil Frickey, Charles Fried, Vicki Jackson, Larry Kramer, Bernard Meltzer, Ellen Semenoff, David Shapiro, Joe Singer, and Elizabeth Warren for very helpful suggestions; to Miriam Hechler, Meredith Kotler, and Scott Selby for excellent research assistance; and to the Harvard Law School Summer Research Program for financial support.

[1] The figures result from a search in July, 1996, of the Westlaw "SCT" database during the specified periods for "Eleventh Amendment" or "11th Amendment."

[2] The 5–4 decisions are: *Seminole Tribe of Florida v Florida*, 116 S Ct 1114 (1996); *Hess v PATH Corp.*, 115 S Ct 394 (1994); *Hoffman v Connecticut Dept. of Income Maintenance*, 492 US 96 (1989); *Pennsylvania v Union Gas Co.*, 491 US 1 (1989); *Dellmuth v Muth*, 491 US 223 (1989); and *Welch v Texas Dept. of Highways & Pub. Transp.*, 483 US 468 (1987). Two other closely divided decisions were *Missouri v Jenkins*, 491 US 274 (1989) (5–3) and *Blatchford v Native Village of Noatak*, 501 US 775 (1991) (6–3).
Only two decisions lacked a dissent: *PATH Corp. v Feeney*, 495 US 299 (1990), where four Justices joined a separate opinion favoring the same result but disagreeing sharply with the Court's reasoning; and *Hafer v Melo*, 502 US 21 (1991), which merely reaffirmed the long-established proposition that damages actions against state officials personally raise no Eleventh Amendment concern. See also *Puerto Rico Aqueduct & Sewer Auth. v Metcalf & Eddy, Inc.*, 506 US 139 (1993) (holding, 8–1, that a sovereign may take an immediate appeal from a district court's denial of immunity).

(published in 1953 and 1973), but more than sixty pages in both the third and fourth editions (published in 1988 and 1996).[3]

The latest, though surely not the last,[4] chapter in this unfolding story was written last Term in *Seminole Tribe of Florida v Florida*.[5] Again dividing 5–4, the Court held that the federal courts were powerless to entertain the plaintiff tribe's suit alleging that the state had violated the federal Indian Gaming Regulatory Act.[6] Overruling its 1989 decision in *Pennsylvania v Union Gas Co.*,[7] the Court held that Congress lacks constitutional power, when acting under Article I, to directly overcome a state's immunity from suit in federal court. That ruling forecloses an important enforcement technique that Congress had sought to employ under a range of federal statutes, and raises broad questions about whether Congress can assure adequate enforcement of federal rights against the states.

The Court also ruled that the tribe could not obtain prospective injunctive relief against the Governor of Florida. That conclusion has generated doubts about the vitality of the long-standing and relatively stable tradition that sovereign immunity creates no barrier to federal suits seeking such relief against government officials alleged to be violating federal law.

This article attempts to take stock of the decision and its implications. Part I discusses the statutory framework at issue in *Seminole* and the Court's opinion. Part II sketches the scholarly debate about the Eleventh Amendment, considering in particular whether the Court has correctly viewed it as recognizing a general immunity of the states from federal court suit by private individuals.

---

[3] See Henry M. Hart, Jr., and Herbert Wechsler, *The Federal Courts and the Federal System* 810–20 (1953); Paul M. Bator, Paul J. Mishkin, David L. Shapiro, and Herbert Wechsler, *Hart and Wechsler's The Federal Courts and the Federal System* 926–37 (2d ed 1973); Paul M. Bator, Paul J. Mishkin, Daniel J. Meltzer, and David L. Shapiro, *Hart and Wechsler's The Federal Courts and the Federal System* 1159–1221 (3d ed 1988); Richard H. Fallon, Jr., Daniel J. Meltzer, and David L. Shapiro, *Hart and Wechsler's The Federal Courts and the Federal System* 1041–1105 (4th ed 1996).

[4] See pp 45–46, discussing *Coeur D'Alene Tribe of Idaho v Idaho*, 42 F3d 1244 (9th Cir 1994), cert granted, 116 S Ct 1416 (1996).

[5] 116 S Ct 1114 (1996).

[6] Pub L No 100-497, 102 Stat 2467 (Oct 17, 1988), codified at 25 USC §§ 2701 et seq.

[7] 491 US 1 (1989).

Part III turns to the central question presented in *Seminole*—the vulnerability of state sovereign immunity to congressional override. Part IV examines the Court's dismissal of the tribe's claim against the Governor. Finally, Part V considers what methods for the judicial enforcement of federal law against the states remain open to Congress—a question that requires locating the *Seminole* decision within broader developments concerning constitutional federalism.

I. The Seminole Decision

The origins of the *Seminole* dispute lie in rulings, culminating in the Supreme Court's 1987 decision in *California v Cabazon Band of Mission Indians*,[8] that the states lack authority to regulate gambling on Indian reservations. *Cabazon Band* reaffirmed, however, that state regulation is valid when authorized by Congress.[9] That decision gave more urgency to ongoing congressional consideration of gambling on Indian lands, which resulted in passage of the Indian Gaming Regulatory Act (IGRA).[10]

IGRA was designed to restore to the states a role in regulating gaming operated by Indian tribes. It establishes differing regulatory regimes for each of three classes of gaming. The *Seminole* case involved class III gaming, which includes casino games, slot machines, lotteries, and banking card games. IGRA permits such gaming only where it (1) is authorized by the tribe and the National Indian Gaming Commission (an agency within the Interior Department), (2) takes place in a state that "permits such gaming for any purpose by any person, organization, or entity," and (3) is "conducted in conformance with a Tribal-State compact entered into by the Indian tribe and the State."[11] The Act specifies the permissible scope of such compacts and makes them effective only when approved by the Secretary of the Interior.[12]

IGRA establishes a detailed procedure for forming such a com-

---

[8] 480 US 202 (1987).

[9] Id at 207.

[10] Pub L No 100-497, 102 Stat 2374 (1988), codified at 25 USC §§ 2701 et seq.

[11] 25 USC § 2710(d)(1).

[12] Id § 2710.

pact.[13] After a request by a tribe, "the State shall negotiate with
the Indian tribe in good faith to enter into such a compact."[14] The
section of the Act at issue in *Seminole* provides:

> The United States district courts shall have jurisdiction over
> (i) any cause of action initiated by an Indian tribe arising from
> the failure of a State to enter into negotiations with the Indian
> tribe for the purpose of entering into a Tribal-State compact
> . . . or to conduct such negotiations in good faith.[15]

In such an action (which may not be brought until 180 days after
the tribe's request)[16] the district court, if it finds that the state failed
to negotiate in good faith, "shall order the State and Indian tribe
to conclude such a compact" within sixty days.[17] If no compact is
reached within that period, each party shall submit its best offer
to a court-appointed mediator, who shall select the one that
"best comports" with the Act, other federal law, and the court's
findings.[18] The mediator is then to submit the proposed compact
to the state: if the state accepts it, the compact is submitted to the
Secretary of the Interior for (presumably rather routine) approval;
if the state does not accept it within sixty days, the Secretary
may prescribe regulations (in accordance with statutory criteria)
under which class III gaming may be conducted on the tribe's
lands.[19]

The *Seminole* dispute arose when negotiations about the tribe's
request to conduct class III gaming broke down over the state's
unwillingness to negotiate about forms of gaming (notably casino
gambling) prohibited by Florida law. The tribe argued both
(1) that the state in fact "permits" such gaming within the meaning
of the Act by failing to enforce its prohibition of casino games
against charities that sponsor casino nights, and (2) that IGRA required the state, because it clearly permitted some types of class
III gaming, to negotiate about all types of class III gaming, including casino gambling. Florida disputed both arguments, and hence

---

[13] See id.

[14] Id § 2710(d)(3)(A).

[15] Id § 2710(d)(7)(A).

[16] Id § 2710(d)(7)(B)(i).

[17] Id § 2710(d)(7)(B)(iii).

[18] Id § 2710(d)(7)(B)(iv).

[19] Id §§ 2710(d)(7)(B)(vi–vii), 2710(d)(8)(A–B).

in 1991 the tribe sued the state and its Governor in federal court, alleging that the defendants had failed to negotiate in good faith. The tribe sought a declaratory judgment that Florida was required to negotiate about casino gambling, an order requiring the state to conclude an agreement within sixty days, and the appointment of a mediator.

The district court denied the defendants' motion to dismiss based on state sovereign immunity,[20] but on interlocutory appeal, the Eleventh Circuit reversed.[21] There was no dispute that the claim against Florida *eo nomine* counted as a suit against a state, from which it was at least presumptively immune; the question was whether that presumption could be overcome by a congressional enactment, like IGRA, that clearly purported to subject the state to federal court suit. The key precedent was *Pennsylvania v Union Gas Co.*,[22] where five Justices ruled that federal environmental legislation, enacted under the commerce power, validly abrogated state sovereign immunity. But the Eleventh Circuit held *Seminole* distinguishable from *Union Gas*, reasoning that IGRA was an exercise of congressional authority under the Indian Commerce Clause but not under the Interstate Commerce Clause,[23] and that Congress lacks power under the former provision to abrogate immunity. The court added that *Union Gas* was distinguishable because there the state, as the "owner or operator" of land subject to environmental controls, was undertaking action typical of private individuals; this case, by contrast, involved a state's traditional sphere of activity, as to which Congress lacked power to abrogate immunity.[24] Finally, the court of appeals held the claim against the Governor barred because it was really one against the state and because it improperly sought to command the exercise of discretionary functions by a state official.[25]

By a 5–4 vote, the Supreme Court affirmed, though on a different rationale. Rather than distinguishing this case from *Union Gas*, or contrasting the Interstate and Indian Commerce Clauses, the

---

[20] 801 F Supp 655 (SD Fla 1992).

[21] 11 F3d 1016 (11th Cir 1994).

[22] 491 US 1 (1989).

[23] US Const, Art I, § 8, cl 3.

[24] 11 F3d at 1025–28.

[25] Id at 1028–29.

Court simply overruled *Union Gas*. Although Chief Justice Rehnquist's opinion reaffirmed that Congress does have power, when legislating under Section 5 of the Fourteenth Amendment, to abrogate sovereign immunity and thus to subject states to federal court suit, the Court ruled that Congress lacks such power when acting under Article I's grants of legislative authority.[26]

That ruling alone might have had little practical effect on the tribe's lawsuit, because the suit also named Governor Chiles as a defendant. For sovereign immunity has never been a complete bar to relief against illegal government action; any such bar has always been limited, and the very idea of governmental immunity has been made tolerable, by the permissibility of at least some suits against government officers.[27] Though the line between permissible and impermissible claims has shifted and is often blurry,[28] the relief sought by the tribe rather plainly fell on the permissible side of the line. Nonetheless, the Court dismissed the claim against Governor Chiles—although not because of state sovereign immunity. The Chief Justice noted that IGRA established an intricate but limited remedial scheme for suits against the state as such. Whatever the merits in general of suits to enjoin state officials from violating federal law—of which *Ex parte Young*[29] is the most celebrated example—here the federal courts should not "cast[] aside [the limitations in the Act] and permit[] an action against a state officer based upon *Ex parte Young*."[30] Thus, the Act's express remedies against the state as such were held to be exclusive, precluding any claim against state officials.

Justices Stevens dissented, as did Justice Souter (joined by Justices Breyer and Ginsburg). Each dissent took issue with the Court's treatment of both the claim against the state and the claim against Governor Chiles. Never before, the dissenters argued, had

---

[26] 116 S Ct at 1126–32.

[27] See Louis L. Jaffe, *Suits Against Governments and Officers: Sovereign Immunity*, 77 Harv L Rev 1, 1–2, 18–19, 28–29 (1963).

[28] See generally Richard H. Fallon, Jr., Daniel J. Meltzer, and David L. Shapiro, *Hart and Wechsler's The Federal Courts and the Federal System* 1066–76 (Foundation, 4th ed 1996) ("*Hart and Wechsler*"); David P. Currie, *Sovereign Immunity and Suits Against Government Officers*, 1984 Supreme Court Review 149, 159–67.

[29] 209 US 123 (1908).

[30] 116 S Ct at 1132.

the Court held Congress constitutionally powerless to subject a state to suit in federal court, and nothing in the Eleventh Amendment or in the Court's precedents required such a result. Equally unwarranted, they contended, was the refusal to permit suit against Governor Chiles to proceed.

II. The Eleventh Amendment and State Sovereign Immunity

Does the Eleventh Amendment have anything to do with state sovereign immunity? That question, although not the focus of the opinions in *Seminole*, must be addressed in order to understand the Justices' positions.

The brief text of the Eleventh Amendment reads:

> The Judicial power of the United States shall not be construed to extend to any suit in law or equity, commenced or prosecuted against one of the United States by Citizens of another State, or by Citizens or Subjects of any Foreign State.

In the midst of controversy, three points of agreement are widely shared.

First, the Amendment does not apply in suits brought by other states or by the United States.[31] (At present it is also settled, though far more controversially, that suits by Indian tribes are no different, for purposes of sovereign immunity, from suits by private individuals.[32])

Second, while sovereign immunity has never barred all suits against government officials, it must be deemed to bar some. Since governments can act only through their officers, immunity could otherwise be too easily evaded; and, as David Currie has noted, "[p]eople are not likely to amend constitutions just to change cap-

---

[31] See, for example, *Monaco v Mississippi*, 292 US 313, 330 (1934).

[32] *Blatchford v Native Village of Noatak*, 501 US 775 (1991) (6–3). The Court reasoned that a tribe's suit against a state is like a suit brought by a foreign sovereign, which *Monaco v Mississippi* held to be barred; although the Constitution embodies a mutual surrender by each state of its immunity from suit by another, there is no such mutuality—and hence no surrender—when suit is brought by a foreign government or by an Indian tribe. But compare *Cherokee Nation v Georgia*, 30 US (5 Pet) 1, 15–19 (1831) (holding that a tribe is not a foreign nation for purposes of party-based jurisdiction under Article III).

tions on complaints."[33] The jurisprudence elaborating which types of officer suits are permissible is shifting and complex.[34]

Third, the Amendment was designed to overrule *Chisholm v Georgia*,[35] where the Supreme Court upheld jurisdiction over an assumpsit action against Georgia brought by a South Carolina citizen. But efforts to spell out the implications of this last point generate sharp disagreement. No doubt the Amendment withdraws jurisdiction in a case just like *Chisholm*—a suit based on nonfederal law that is within federal court jurisdiction only because the plaintiff was a citizen of a state other than the defendant. But how should the Amendment apply when federal jurisdiction exists not because of party status but rather because the suit arises under a federal statutory or constitutional provision?[36] Should it matter whether the plaintiff is a citizen of the defendant state, and thus falls outside the Amendment's literal wording? Whether Congress has indicated, as it had not in *Chisholm*, that it seeks to extend federal court jurisdiction over the suit in question?

A. HANS V LOUISIANA

The traditional answer to at least the first two of these three questions was set forth a century ago in *Hans v Louisiana*.[37] That case, like *Chisholm*, revolved around a private person's claim of contractual breach by the state (specifically the failure to pay interest due on state bonds). But because Hans contended that state legislation impaired his contractual rights in violation of the Contract Clause of the federal Constitution, the case might be viewed as falling within the federal question jurisdiction.[38] Justice Brad-

---

[33] Currie, 1984 Supreme Court Review at 151 n 11 (cited in note 28).

[34] See generally authorities cited in notes 27–28.

[35] 2 US (2 Dall) 419 (1793).

[36] See Alan D. Cullison, *Interpretation of the Eleventh Amendment (A Case of the White Knight's Green Whiskers)*, 5 Houston L Rev 1 (1967) (stressing the significance of the source of the right of action).

[37] 134 US 1 (1890).

[38] For exploration of why the dispute in *Chisholm* would not have been viewed as implicating the Contract Clause, see William A. Fletcher, *A Historical Interpretation of the Eleventh Amendment: A Narrow Construction of an Affirmative Grant of Jurisdiction Rather Than a Prohibition Against Jurisdiction*, 35 Stan L Rev 1033, 1055 n 97 (1983); Akhil Reed Amar, *Of Sovereignty and Federalism*, 96 Yale L J 1425, 1470 n 188 (1987).

Professor Burnham suggests that Hans's claim was based on the common law and that the opinion's recognition of federal question jurisdiction referred only to possible federal

ley's opinion skipped over that feature of the case by declaring that prior decisions established that a state cannot be sued, under the federal question jurisdiction, by a citizen of another state or of a foreign country.[39] Those rulings were at best implicit, however, and the Court did not give the point the attention that it deserves.

Unlike Chisholm, however, Hans was a citizen of the state he sued, a seemingly important distinction in view of the Amendment's text and its interpretation by Chief Justice Marshall, in *Cohens v Virginia*,[40] as not reaching suits by citizens of the defendant state. But it would be anomalous, the Court argued in *Hans*, to hold Louisiana immune from suit by noncitizens but not by citizens. Justice Bradley assumed that the adoption of the Eleventh Amendment vindicated Justice Iredell's dissent in *Chisholm*. Although Iredell's principal argument had been statutory—that the jurisdiction granted by the Judiciary Act of 1789 did not extend to unheard of remedies like a suit against a state—Justice Bradley emphasized Iredell's brief dictum expressing doubts that Congress could constitutionally enact a statute subjecting the states to federal court suit. Those doubts were supported, Justice Bradley contended, by statements made by Hamilton, Madison, and Marshall during the ratification debates. Thus, in *Hans* the Court concluded that "the cognizance of suits and actions unknown to the law, and forbidden by the law, was not contemplated by the constitution when establishing the judicial power of the United States."[41]

And so the Eleventh Amendment was seen, if not as establishing, at least as restoring (after the false step in *Chisholm*) an immunity

---

defenses and replies, at a time when the "well-pleaded complaint rule" was not yet clearly established. The Contract Clause, in his view, does not give rise to an implied right of action but merely renders unavailing any reliance on the impairing legislation as a defense to a claim for breach. The plaintiff's claim, he contends, thus remains subject to common law defenses like sovereign immunity. See William Burnham, *Taming the Eleventh Amendment Without Overruling Hans v. Louisiana*, 40 Case W Res L Rev 931, 946–48 (1989–90). See also Martha A. Field, *The Eleventh Amendment and Other Sovereign Immunity Doctrines: Congressional Imposition of Suit Upon the States*, 126 U Pa L Rev 1203, 1266 (1978). The argument may be beside the point, because a case containing a federal defense or reply arises under federal law for purposes of the *constitutional* grant of jurisdiction in Article III.

[39] 134 US at 10, citing *Louisiana v Jumel*, 107 US 711 (1883); *Hagood v Southern*, 117 US 52 (1886); *In re Ayres*, 123 US 443 (1887).

[40] 19 US (6 Wheat) 264, 293 (1821) (alternative holding).

[41] 134 US at 15.

far broader than the provision's text. Subsequent decisions have extended that immunity to actions by foreign countries,[42] and to maritime suits as well as actions at law or equity.[43]

B. THE DIVERSITY VIEW

The question posed by the *Hans* majority—why would the Constitution immunize Louisiana from suit by citizens of another state but not by citizens of Louisiana itself?—is a fair one. Although the Amendment's text can easily be read to support such a distinction, existing efforts to supply a supporting rationale strike me as unpersuasive.[44] But the apparent textual oddity disappears under an interpretation of the Amendment given in superb articles by William Fletcher and Judge John Gibbons.[45] They note that Article III defines federal court jurisdiction both by subject matter (like admiralty and federal question) and party status (like diversity of citizenship or suits to which the United States is a party). *Chisholm* held that a state could be sued when the only jurisdictional basis was "diversity" between the state and the plaintiff. The Eleventh Amendment, in turn, eliminated party-based jurisdiction when the state was a party defendant, but did not alter the states' amenability to suit where jurisdiction was based on subject matter—as with cases in admiralty or those arising under federal law. On this view,

---

[42] See *Monaco v Mississippi*, 292 US 313 (1934).

[43] See, for example, *Ex parte New York*, 256 US 490 (1921). See generally Fletcher, 35 Stan L Rev at 1078–83 (cited in note 38).

[44] See, for example, Lawrence C. Marshall, *Fighting the Words of the Eleventh Amendment*, 102 Harv L Rev 1342 (1989) (the amendment effectively barred suit on most state obligations, which were disproportionally held by out-of-staters, while leaving justiciable the core of individual rights claims); Martin H. Redish, *Federal Jurisdiction: Tensions in the Allocation of Judicial Power* 192–93 (Michie, 2d ed 1990) (mutual political compact between a state and its citizens precludes immunity to suit, but no such compact governs relations with noncitizens); Calvin R. Massey, *State Sovereignty and the Tenth and Eleventh Amendments*, 56 U Chi L Rev 61 (1989); see also *Employees v Department of Pub. Health*, 411 US 279, 313–15 (1973) (Brennan dissenting). For a persuasive response, see William A. Fletcher, *The Diversity Explanation of the Eleventh Amendment: A Reply to Critics*, 56 U Chi L Rev 1261, 1275–89 (1989).

[45] See Fletcher, 35 Stan L Rev (cited in note 38); John J. Gibbons, *The Eleventh Amendment and State Sovereign Immunity: A Reinterpretation*, 83 Colum L Rev 1889 (1983). See also John V. Orth, *The Judicial Power of the United States: The Eleventh Amendment in American History* (Oxford University, 1987); Vicki C. Jackson, *The Supreme Court, the Eleventh Amendment, and State Sovereign Immunity*, 98 Yale L J 1 (1988); Amar, 96 Yale L J 1425 (cited in note 38).

then, the question whether federal courts may entertain a suit against a state depends not on the citizenship of the plaintiff but on the basis of federal subject-matter jurisdiction.

This "diversity" interpretation of the Eleventh Amendment makes sense of the textual limitations to suits by noncitizens (for suits by in-state citizens could not come into federal court on the basis of party status alone) and to suits in law and equity but not those in admiralty (where jurisdiction necessarily rests on subject matter).[46] Although it would go too far to suggest that the Framers of the Constitution or the Eleventh Amendment sharply distinguished between subject matter and party-based jurisdiction when contemplating sovereign immunity, that distinction is generally consistent with early immunity decisions following the ratification of the Amendment;[47] only after the Civil War, when Southern and border states faced debt claims that the federal courts would have been powerless to enforce, did the Court launch the Amendment on the nontextual odyssey that has continued ever since.[48] The diversity view resonates with my own doubts about the desirability of sovereign immunity generally, particularly in a constitutional republic vesting sovereignty in the people.[49] In addition, this view—because it preserves the full reach of federal court power to enforce federal law—averts a collision with Hamilton's axiom of government that the judicial and legislative power should be coextensive.[50]

Moreover, this interpretation explains the settled rule that the Amendment does not bar Supreme Court review of state court judgments that depend upon federal issues, even when a state is a party. After all, the Court's appellate jurisdiction is just as much a

---

[46] Today, admiralty is often treated as governed by federal common law, see, for example, *Hart and Wechsler* at 797–801 (cited in note 28), though originally it was understood more as part of the law of nations. See Fletcher, 35 Stan L Rev at 1078–83 (cited in note 38). But for the founding generation, no head of federal jurisdiction was more important. See Daniel J. Meltzer, *The History and Structure of Article III*, 138 U Pa L Rev 1569, 1578, 1595, and sources cited (1990).

[47] See Fletcher, 35 Stan L Rev at 1078–87 (cited in note 38).

[48] See especially Orth, *Judicial Power* (cited in note 45).

[49] See generally Samuel H. Beer, *To Make a Nation: The Rediscovery of American Federalism* 146–53, 249–55 (Belknap, 1993); Amar, 96 Yale L J at 1429–66 (cited in note 38).

[50] See Jackson, 98 Yale L J at 3–4 and sources cited (cited in note 45); Fletcher, 35 Stan L Rev at 1074 and sources cited in n 170 (cited in note 38).

part of the "judicial power" defined by Article III and the Eleventh Amendment as is original trial court jurisdiction.[51] Efforts to explain this "exception" to state sovereign immunity on the ground that Supreme Court review is not a "suit," or that the state consented to Supreme Court review, have been shown to be unpersuasive[52]—most notably in suits seeking affirmative monetary relief against the state (like those for refunds of unconstitutionally exacted taxes).[53]

Under the diversity theory, although *Hans* was wrong to have found a federal constitutional barrier to the suit in question, states would not necessarily be subject to federal court suit, or to the imposition of some forms of relief, as routinely as private citizens are. Claims based on state law (such as those brought under the federal courts' supplemental jurisdiction) could be defeated by state-created defenses.[54] Claims based on federal judge-made law—for example, *Bivens* actions[55] or certain admiralty suits—would not be barred by the Eleventh Amendment, but the concerns about federal judicial interference with state governments that underlie many judge-made doctrines (for example, the various abstention doctrines, or restrictions on the scope of remedies) might limit or shape the relief available against a state.[56] Those concerns could also lead courts to presume that statutes of general applicability do not substantively regulate the states (just as courts presume that congressional statutes do not preempt state law)[57] ab-

---

[51] The difficulty of any effort to distinguish, for purposes of sovereign immunity, appellate from original jurisdiction is perhaps clearest in the case of removal of a case from state to federal district court. Today we treat removal as an aspect of original district court jurisdiction, and thus fully subject to the Eleventh Amendment, see, for example, *Gorka v Sullivan*, 82 F3d 772 (7th Cir 1996), but Justice Story, in *Martin v Hunter's Lessee*, 14 US (1 Wheat) 304, 348–49 (1816), viewed removal as an aspect of appellate jurisdiction.

[52] See Jackson, 98 Yale L J at 32–39 (cited in note 45).

[53] See, for example, *McKesson Corp. v Division of ABT*, 496 US 18, 31 (1990) (stating broadly that "the Eleventh Amendment does not constrain the appellate jurisdiction of the Supreme Court over cases arising from state courts"); cases cited in Jackson, 98 Yale L J at 14 nn 59, 61 (cited in note 45).

[54] See, for example, *Zeidner v Wulforst*, 197 F Supp 23 (EDNY 1961).

[55] See *Bivens v Six Unknown Named Agents of Fed. Bureau of Narcotics*, 403 US 388 (1971).

[56] See note 284.

[57] See, for example, *Maryland v Louisiana*, 451 US 725, 746 (1981); *Rice v Santa Fe Elevator Corp.*, 331 US 218, 230 (1947).

sent a clear statement by Congress.[58] But any such limitations would pose no constitutional barrier to Congress's action in IGRA, which clearly conferred a "private" right to sue a state in federal court under the federal question jurisdiction. And IGRA's clear indication that specified relief is available would be significant not because it would override any constitutionally based immunity, but because it would prevail over any hesitance that courts might otherwise exhibit about providing such relief against a state.

The diversity view remains, in my opinion, the most convincing interpretation of the Eleventh Amendment (though this brief summary of a complex set of arguments may not suffice to convince the uninitiated, much less a skeptic).[59] But the *Seminole* opinions spent little time discussing that view's merits, which had been debated in a number of decisions in the 1980s, beginning with *Atascadero State Hospital v Scanlon*.[60] In each of those decisions, Justices Brennan, Marshall, Blackmun, and Stevens embraced the diversity view but could not garner the crucial fifth vote. Those four Justices constituted the plurality in *Union Gas*, where they relied on a quite different rationale in upholding the constitutionality of a statute that, like IGRA, subjected an unconsenting state to suit in federal court. And while in *Seminole* the four dissenters endorsed the diversity view[61] and criticized *Hans*, their primary contention was not that the Eleventh Amendment had nothing to do with sovereign immunity, or that *Hans* should be overruled, but rather that Congress had power to abrogate the sovereign immunity recognized in *Hans*.[62] I turn now to that argument.

III. State Sovereign Immunity and Congressional Abrogation

Both *Union Gas* and *Seminole*, unlike *Hans*, involved statutes purporting to regulate the states and to subject them to federal

[58] See, for example, *Gregory v Ashcroft*, 501 US 452 (1991).

[59] For elaboration, see sources cited in note 45; Fletcher, 56 U Chi L Rev 1261 (cited in note 44).

[60] 473 US 234 (1985). See also *Green v Mansour*, 474 US 64 (1985); *Papasan v Allain*, 478 US 265 (1986); *Welch v Texas Dep't of Highways & Pub. Transp.*, 483 US 468 (1987).

[61] 116 S Ct at 1136 (Stevens dissenting); id at 1149–52 (Souter dissenting).

[62] Id at 1134, 1137 (Stevens dissenting); id at 1159, 1173 (Souter dissenting).

court suit.[63] The significance of congressional authorization of suit was the critical issue in both cases.

A. UNION GAS

In *Union Gas*, Justice Brennan's plurality opinion offered two distinct lines of argument, with somewhat differing implications, to support congressional power to abrogate state sovereign immunity. The first line of argument relied primarily on the 1976 decision in *Fitzpatrick v Bitzer*,[64] holding without dissent that the 1972 amendments to Title VII of the Civil Rights Act of 1964[65]—which extended the prohibition of employment discrimination to state and local governments—had validly authorized federal court suit for money damages against an unconsenting state. Justice Rehnquist's opinion for the Court in *Fitzpatrick* reasoned that when Congress takes action under Section 5 of the Fourteenth Amendment, "not only is it exercising legislative authority that is plenary within the terms of the constitutional grant, it is exercising that authority under one section of a constitutional Amendment whose other sections by their own terms embody limitations on state authority. We think that Congress may, in determining what is 'appropriate legislation' for the purpose of enforcing the provisions of the Fourteenth Amendment, provide for private suits against States or state officials which are constitutionally impermissible in other contexts."[66]

In *Union Gas*, Justice Brennan's first line of argument treated the Interstate Commerce Clause—under which the environmental statutes at issue had been enacted—as indistinguishable from the Fourteenth Amendment: the Commerce Clause, too, grants legislative authority to Congress, while it simultaneously (under the dormant Commerce Clause) directly regulates the states.[67] Nor was *Fitzpatrick* distinguishable on the ground that the Commerce

---

[63] Four dissenters in *Union Gas* disputed that the statutes there at issue indicated with adequate clarity an intention to subject the state to federal court suit. See 491 US at 45 (White concurring in the judgment in part and dissenting in part). In *Seminole*, no Justice expressed doubt on this score.

[64] 427 US 445 (1976).

[65] Equal Employment Opportunity Act of 1972, 86 Stat 103, codified at 42 USC §§ 2000e et seq.

[66] 427 US at 456.

[67] 491 US at 15–17.

Clause, unlike the Fourteenth Amendment, predated the Eleventh Amendment; for *Hans* was based on the principle of sovereign immunity that the Eleventh Amendment merely reaffirmed, and that principle predated the Commerce Clause.[68]

This first line of argument might permit abrogation of immunity only when Congress acts under constitutional provisions that also embody a self-executing limit on the states. Not so Justice Brennan's second line of argument in *Union Gas:* "By empowering Congress to regulate commerce, . . . the States necessarily surrendered any portion of their sovereignty that would stand in the way of such regulation."[69] This surrender idea applies equally to every constitutional grant of legislative power—including, for example, the power to regulate bankruptcy or to protect inventions through patent or copyright laws.

The fifth vote in *Union Gas* to uphold abrogation was Justice White's; among the unusual features of his opinion[70] was its incompleteness in indicating his views about "the question whether Congress has the constitutional power to abrogate the States' immunity." Justice White said only this: "I agree with the conclusion reached by Justice Brennan . . . that Congress has the authority under Article I to abrogate the Eleventh Amendment immunity of the States, although I do not agree with much of his reasoning."[71] The nature of his disagreement remained undisclosed.

---

[68] Id at 17–18.

[69] Id at 19–23.

[70] Not the least unusual was his vote. His opinion, concurring in the judgment in part and dissenting in part, first contended (here joined by three Justices) that the environmental statutes at issue did not express an intention to abrogate state immunity with the clarity demanded by the Court's precedents. Id at 45–56. Though that position should have led him to vote against the exercise of federal court jurisdiction, he voted the other way, on the ground that (i) a majority of the Justices disagreed with him about the statute's clarity, and (ii) if they were right, Congress has constitutional power to abrogate immunity.
Traditionally American judges vote for the ultimate disposition that they think is correct; the judgment depends on the number of such votes, rather than on the outcome that would be dictated if, on each issue, the view of the majority prevailed. See generally Lewis A. Kornhauser and Lawrence G. Sager, *The One and the Many: Adjudication in Collegial Courts,* 81 Cal L Rev 1 (1993). In *Union Gas,* different majorities thought that (*a*) the statutory abrogation of immunity satisfied the clear statement rule, and (*b*) Congress had constitutional power to abrogate. Had Justice White's colleagues followed his approach, all nine would have voted to uphold federal court jurisdiction. See generally Kornhauser and Sager (suggesting that the tradition has been unreflective and that issue-by-issue voting in some instances (including *Union Gas*) may be preferable); Colloquium, *Appellate Court Voting Rules,* 49 Vand L Rev 993 (1996).

[71] 491 US at 57.

So *Union Gas* created some uncertainty about the scope of Congress's authority to abrogate. (In the end, the lower courts almost universally ruled, before *Seminole*, that Congress could abrogate when acting under any of its powers.)[72] But Justice White's cryptic opinion, whatever its shortcomings, was not the chief source of any uncertainty, for he declared (without explaining why) that Congress has authority to abrogate "under Article I"—presumably in the exercise of *any* of its powers under that Article.[73] Thus, had he joined Justice Brennan's opinion to make a Court, the scope of congressional abrogation power would not, I believe, have been much clearer.

B. THE VULNERABILITY OF ABROGATION THEORY

Justice Scalia's dissent in *Union Gas* (joined by the Chief Justice and Justices Kennedy and O'Connor) contended that to uphold abrogation would violate the rationale of *Hans* and gut the constitutional immunity it conferred. In response, Justice Brennan devoted rather little attention to *Hans* and dodged the question whether the immunity it had recognized was constitutional in nature, simply noting that since any immunity had validly been abrogated, there was no need to decide whether *Hans* should be overruled.[74]

This response was rather incomplete. If *Hans* recognized a constitutional immunity from suit, then how could Congress overcome it? Justice Brennan himself had offered a different, though partial, response some years earlier: the Eleventh Amendment confers a *constitutional* immunity only in suits by noncitizens; any immunity recognized in suits by citizens is nonconstitutional and hence subject to congressional override.[75] This textual argument suffers, as noted earlier,[76] from the lack of a plausible reason for such a constitutional differentiation. In any event, by the time of the *Union Gas* decision, Justice Brennan appears to have turned

---

[72] See p 29.

[73] Of course, the modern breadth of the commerce power might well support statutes abrogating immunity in, for example, copyright or bankruptcy matters.

[74] 491 US at 23.

[75] See, for example, *Edelman v Jordan*, 415 US 651, 687–88 (1974) (Brennan dissenting).

[76] See note 44.

away from this approach, and his opinion in the case does not even mention the citizenship of the Union Gas company.

A broader version of this approach—advanced by Martha Field[77]—argues that *Chisholm* treated Article III as having displaced state sovereign immunity altogether; the Eleventh Amendment rejected *Chisholm*'s approach, restoring sovereign immunity in all private suits, regardless of the plaintiff's citizenship; but the immunity restored was only a common law doctrine, and therefore can be overcome by federal legislation. This argument eliminates any anomalous distinction between citizens and noncitizens, but at the cost of inability to explain the Amendment's textual limit to suits by noncitizens or aliens—or, for that matter, to suits at law or equity but not in admiralty. Moreover, if the language of the Amendment—"the Judicial Power of the United States shall not be construed to extend"—is viewed as an immunity-based prohibition, its ring is more absolute than qualified.[78] Also problematic is the somewhat peculiar idea of express constitutionalization of a common law doctrine: although major aspects of the Bill of Rights were meant to constitutionalize protections that many thought were implicit at common law, neither those nor any other constitutional provisions are viewed as merely establishing a constitutional default position from which Congress is free to depart.[79] The peculiarity is accentuated if one adds, as Field does, that "in an era of freewheeling federal common law, the federal judiciary might itself make desired modifications" in sovereign immunity.[80] For then the Eleventh Amendment would protect sovereign immunity only to the extent that federal judges—the authors of *Chisholm*—thought desirable.[81]

---

[77] Martha A. Field, *The Eleventh Amendment and Other Sovereign Immunity Doctrines: Part I*, 126 U Pa L Rev 515 (1977).

[78] Professor Field is forced to read the quoted language to mean that the judicial power "should not be deemed *affirmatively to allow* the prosecution of those cases, as it had been deemed to do in *Chisholm*." Id at 543.

[79] The dormant Commerce Clause does create limitations on state power that Congress can brush aside, see *Prudential Ins. Co. v Benjamin*, 328 US 408 (1946), but those limits are meant to benefit the nation (and the other states), of which Congress is the representative; thus, Congress's power is in the nature of a waiver. By contrast, any state sovereign immunity recognized by the Constitution would be meant to benefit each state, and thus only that state should be able to waive it.

[80] Field, 126 U Pa L Rev at 545 n 98 (cited in note 77). But compare Field, 126 U Pa L Rev at 1262–65 (cited in note 38) (federal courts may modify immunity but judicial abrogation is not to be expected).

[81] See *Hart and Wechsler* at 1052 (cited in note 28).

A different account of abrogation power—sketched by Laurence Tribe[82] and John Nowak[83]—draws on Herbert Wechsler's classic discussion of the political safeguards of federalism.[84] The argument is that unelected federal judges pose a threat to state sovereignty not posed by Congress, in which state interests are represented.[85] Thus, they contend that the Amendment confers an immunity "against the federal judiciary [rather than] . . . against Congress,"[86] which may subject the states to federal court suit when acting under any of its powers.

The argument is not without appeal; indeed, where plaintiffs assert congressional rights of action, the result—that federal courts may exercise jurisdiction—is the same as under the diversity theory (where judicial power would turn on the presence of federal question jurisdiction rather than on a congressional override).[87] Still, I have always found this account of abrogation power hard to root in constitutional text, history, or structure. The textual argument[88] that the Amendment speaks only of the "Judicial Power" and thus does not limit Congress is unconvincing: the limits on Article III's "judicial Power" have always been understood not to be subject to congressional expansion, whether in suits arising under federal statutes or otherwise.[89] Nor can this view explain the

[82] Laurence H. Tribe, *Intergovernmental Immunities in Litigation, Taxation, and Regulation: Separation of Powers Issues in Controversies About Federalism*, 89 Harv L Rev 682, 683–99 (1976).

[83] John E. Nowak, *The Scope of Congressional Power to Create Causes of Action Against State Governments and the History of the Eleventh and Fourteenth Amendments*, 75 Colum L Rev 1413 (1975).

[84] Herbert Wechsler, *The Political Safeguards of Federalism: The Role of the States in the Composition and Selection of the National Government*, 54 Colum L Rev 543 (1954).

[85] Professor Nowak adds the claim—for which the evidence seems to me scanty—that the Framers of both Article III and the Eleventh Amendment feared life-tenured federal judges but not politically accountable legislators. Nowak, 75 Colum L Rev at 1430, 1441–42 (cited in note 83).

[86] Tribe, 89 Harv L Rev at 693 (cited in note 82).

[87] The theories diverge in their implications for federal question cases based on judicially created federal rights of action, which the diversity approach would not bar—though principles of comity and remedial discretion might warrant judicial hesitance in allowing at least certain kinds of remedies against the states absent congressional action, see Jackson, 98 Yale L J at 72–104 (cited in note 45); note 284.

[88] See Tribe, 89 Harv L Rev at 694 (cited in note 82); accord *Union Gas*, 491 US at 18 (plurality opinion).

[89] See, for example, *Marbury v Madison*, 5 US (1 Cranch) 137 (1803); *National Mutual Ins Co. v Tidewater Transfer Co., Inc.*, 337 US 582, 604 (1949) (opinion of Rutledge), 626 (opinion of Vinson), 646 (opinion of Frankfurter); *Lujan v Defenders of Wildlife*, 504 US 555 (1992).

distinctive textual limits in the Amendment itself. Finally, this account cannot easily explain why a state is immune from the exercise of original jurisdiction by the district courts but not from Supreme Court appellate jurisdiction to review state court judgments.

In sum, any position that reads Article III and/or the Eleventh Amendment as recognizing state sovereign immunity but that affirms Congress's power to overcome that immunity faces grave difficulties. By contrast, the diversity interpretation can explain the Amendment's text while leaving room for a judge-made doctrine (whether labeled sovereign immunity or principles of statutory interpretation and remedial discretion) calling for hesitation, absent clear legislative or constitutional mandate, in awarding relief against a state. Such a doctrine does not require the awkward prospect of congressional override of a *constitutional* protection in order to preserve federal legislative power to subject states to suit.

If the diversity view is the most attractive interpretation of the Eleventh Amendment, how can one explain Justice Brennan's failure, despite his earlier endorsement of that view, to invoke it in *Union Gas?* Efforts to read a judge's mind are always hazardous, but I would note that Justice White had rejected the diversity view several times within the preceding four years.[90] Perhaps Justice Brennan hoped to obtain five votes for a different approach, or feared that Justice White would not vote to uphold judicial power if the plurality rested on a view with which he squarely disagreed.

In any event, there was some force to Justice Scalia's denunciation of the result in *Union Gas* as "an unstable victory," because "the astounding principle that Article III limitations can be overcome by simply exercising Article I powers . . . is too much at war

---

Justice Souter's dissent in *Seminole* tried to turn a similar point to his advantage. Noting the accepted rule that a state may consent to suit, he argued that *Hans* cannot have recognized a constitutional limitation on federal judicial power, for another accepted rule holds that cases outside the federal courts' subject matter jurisdiction cannot be heard simply because the parties consent. 116 S Ct at 1158. But, as I have argued in a different context, "subject matter jurisdiction is not a self-defining term, and the tradition that defects cannot be waived is not an unshakable axiom but a purposive doctrine." Daniel J. Meltzer, *Legislative Courts, Legislative Power, and the Constitution*, 65 Ind L J 291, 303 (1990). *If* a constitutional doctrine limits exercise of federal judicial power against the states, it would be odd to treat the limits as nonwaivable—especially when the sovereign immunity of the United States may be waived. See also Redish at 183 (cited in note 44) (arguing that if the judicial power excludes only suits against unconsenting states, then state consent, rather than waiving any limitation, simply makes the exclusion inapplicable).

[90] See cases cited in note 60.

with itself to endure. We shall either overrule *Hans* in form as well
as in fact, or return to its genuine meaning."[91] *Seminole* proved
him prophetic.

C. SEMINOLE AND THE REACH OF ABROGATION

The opinions in *Seminole*, rather than starting with *Union Gas*,
went back to more basic questions about the justification for and
meaning of *Hans*. The Court reaffirmed that Article III did not
eliminate the states' sovereign immunity; *Chisholm*'s contrary and
mistaken view had been overridden by the Eleventh Amendment.
The Chief Justice did about as well as one can in explaining the
textual limitation to suits by noncitizens or by aliens; he contended
that the Amendment was directed only at the exercise of party-
based jurisdiction because no general federal question jurisdiction
then existed. (The shortcomings of that explanation would have
been highlighted had the Chief Justice discussed the Amendment's
limitation to law and equity but not admiralty, for the federal
courts have had a general, and exclusive, grant of admiralty jurisdiction since 1789.) Rejecting "blind reliance upon the text" of
the Eleventh Amendment as a "straw man,"[92] the Court (including
its prominent textualists, Justices Scalia and Thomas) rested instead on its view of constitutional background assumptions. The
Chief Justice quoted one of his predecessors, Charles Evans
Hughes, whose opinion in *Principality of Monaco v Mississippi*[93] held
a state immune from federal court suit by a foreign state (a category of lawsuit not mentioned in the Amendment). Hughes declared: "Behind the words of the constitutional provisions [Article
III, § 2 and the Eleventh Amendment] are postulates which limit
and control"—one of which is that "States of the Union, still pos-
sessing attributes of sovereignty, shall be immune from suits, without their consent, save where there has been a 'surrender of this
immunity in the plan of the convention.' "[94]

The internal quotation is from Hamilton, in Federalist 81, and
his notion of surrender is, in a way, the source of abrogation the-

---

[91] *Union Gas*, 491 US at 45.

[92] 116 S Ct at 1130.

[93] 292 US 313 (1934).

[94] Id at 322–23, quoted in *Seminole*, 116 S Ct at 1129.

ory. Although Justice Rehnquist's opinion in *Fitzpatrick* did not invoke this phrase, he could easily have said that the states, in ratifying the Reconstruction Amendments, surrendered any immunity from suit authorized thereunder. And in Justice Brennan's plurality opinion in *Union Gas*, the marriage of Hamilton's idea of surrender to the abrogation power was explicit.[95]

In *Seminole*, the Chief Justice cast no doubt on the continuing force of his opinion in *Fitzpatrick*, reasoning instead that its holding was quite limited. "*Fitzpatrick* was based upon a rationale wholly inapplicable to the Interstate Commerce Clause, *viz.*, that the Fourteenth Amendment, adopted well after the adoption of the Eleventh Amendment and the ratification of the Constitution, operated to alter the pre-existing balance between state and federal power achieved by Article III and the Eleventh Amendment."[96] No such rationale extended to *Union Gas*, which had improperly upset that balance and must therefore be overruled.[97]

The Court's distinction, though it draws on some language in the *Fitzpatrick* opinion,[98] is not well supported. The temporal argument—that the Fourteenth Amendment postdates the Eleventh—fails on its own terms: on the one hand, as Justice Brennan noted in *Union Gas*, proponents of sovereign immunity view the principle underlying it as predating the Commerce Clause;[99] on the other hand, the Reconstruction Amendments cannot have had the purpose of overruling the sovereign immunity recognized by the Eleventh Amendment, as that recognition was given only in subsequent decisions.[100] Moreover, there is a deeper objection to the temporal argument: our practice when construing a positive enactment that has been amended—whether a Constitution or a statute—is not ordinarily to treat the later-added provision as trumping any predecessor. (Recall the familiar canon of statutory interpretation disfavoring repeals by implication.) Rather, we seek to make sense

---

[95] See p 15.

[96] 116 S Ct at 1128.

[97] The Court also criticized *Union Gas* as permitting Congress improperly to expand federal judicial power beyond the limits of the Constitution. 116 S Ct at 1128. That objection applies equally, of course, to *Fitzpatrick*.

[98] See p 14.

[99] See pp 14–15.

[100] See p 11.

of the amended enactment as a whole. Suppose that Congress, fearing jury nullification, enacted a law providing that all federal court suits seeking damages for racial discrimination by state or local officials should be tried to a judge rather than a jury. If a defendant objected that the law denied the right to jury trial guaranteed by the Seventh Amendment, the response that the Fourteenth Amendment postdated the Seventh surely would not be adequate.

Indeed, the stylistic convention of reproducing constitutional amendments after the text of the original document—rather than interlineating them in the original text, as we do in statutory codes—may have subtly affected our interpretive practice.[101] Suppose that the Fourteenth Amendment had been interlineated in the original Constitution—with Section 1's Equal Protection, Due Process, and Privileges and Immunities Clauses added to Article I, Section 10, and Section 5's grant of legislative authority added to Article I, Section 8. Would it not have been harder to distinguish the authority conferred under Section 5 from "other" Article I powers? (Incidentally, interlineation of the Eleventh Amendment into Article III might well have resulted in a rewriting of Article III's party-based clauses, thus making the force of the diversity interpretation more apparent.)

To be sure, it may be particularly difficult to make sense of the power conferred by Section 5 without viewing it as permitting Congress to subject states to federal court suit. But that conclusion merely confirms our belief that states are not fully "sovereign";[102] if they were, then even the most pressing need (for example, combating official racial discrimination) could not overcome immunity. That being so, if Congress also believes it important to subject states to federal court suit under IGRA, why should that judgment be more suspect constitutionally?

The Court is surely correct that the Civil War and the Reconstruction Amendments constitute a profound shift in relations between nation and state.[103] But the *Seminole* Court's implicit, and undefended, assumption that that shift can be cabined off into the

[101] This point was suggested to me in a communication from Edward Hartnett.

[102] See, for example, Andrzej Rapaczynski, *From Sovereignty to Process: The Jurisprudence of Federalism After Garcia*, 1985 Supreme Court Review 341, 346–59.

[103] See, for example, Bruce A. Ackerman, *We the People: Foundations* 82 (Belknap, 1991).

areas specifically regulated by the Thirteenth, Fourteenth, and Fifteenth Amendments—without radiation to other constitutional matters—is highly controversial, to say the least.[104] By the same token, the numerous respects in which the Constitution deprives the states of "sovereignty" as traditionally understood, together with the vast expansion of federal regulatory power in this century, casts doubts upon the continuing force, or even coherence, of appeals to state sovereignty.[105] One need not endorse in full Professor Ackerman's view of Reconstruction and the New Deal as "constitutional moments"[106] to believe that the legal and socioeconomic transformations that they symbolize bear importantly on the interpretation of provisions like the Eleventh Amendment. Thus, even if that Amendment had been understood, before the Civil War, as a general grant of sovereign immunity—a proposition the Court makes little effort to defend and that has been powerfully disputed[107]—any such understanding may be of little contemporary force in view of intervening social, political, and constitutional developments.[108]

Finally, an effort to treat legislation under the Reconstruction Amendments as sui generis seems particularly inapt in a case involving federal action under the Indian Commerce Clause. A key defect in the Articles of Confederation was their division of authority over Indian affairs between the states and the central government. The Constitution responded by making Indian affairs "the exclusive province of federal law."[109] (That Florida's power to regulate Indian gaming existed only by virtue of the permission granted by IGRA is only one illustration of the states' limited sov-

---

[104] See, for example, Ronald M. Dworkin, *Law's Empire* (Belknap, 1986). Though Dworkin's discussion of constitutional law focuses on individual rights rather than government structure, his interpretive approach is clear from the following quotation: "The adjudicative principle of integrity instructs judges to identify legal rights and duties, so far as possible, on the assumption that they were all created by a single author—the community personified—expressing a coherent conception of justice and fairness." Id at 225.

[105] See Rapaczynski, 1985 Supreme Court Review at 346–59 (cited in note 102).

[106] See Bruce Ackerman, *Constitutional Politics/Constitutional Law*, 99 Yale L J 453 (1989).

[107] See Fletcher, 35 Stan L Rev at 1078–87 (cited in note 38).

[108] See Larry Kramer, *What's a Constitution For Anyway? Of History and Theory, Bruce Ackerman and the New Deal*, 46 Case W Res L Rev 885, 907–08 (1996) (stressing that the Framers viewed the Constitution's structural arrangement as tentative and organic).

[109] *County of Oneida v Oneida Indian Nation*, 470 US 226, 234 (1985); see also *Worcester v Georgia*, 31 US (6 Pet) 515, 561 (1832).

ereignty in Indian affairs.)[110] Moreover, Supreme Court authority
had recognized that "the people of the States where [the tribes]
are found are often their deadliest enemies. From their very weakness and helplessness, so largely due to the course of dealing of
the federal government with them, and the treaties in which it has
been promised, there arises the duty of protection, and with it the
power."[111] That federal responsibility is not unlike the federal responsibility for protecting the newly freed slaves that the Reconstruction Amendments gave the federal government.[112] In the end,
the scope of national power (or, put differently, of the state's surrender of sovereignty) seems at least as "plenary" in regulating
Indian affairs as when legislating under the Fourteenth Amendment.

D. THE SEMINOLE DISSENTS

Justices Stevens and Souter, in dissent in *Seminole*, fired off numerous objections to the majority's approach. They did not, however, begin with Justice Brennan's effort in *Union Gas* to assimilate
the commerce power to Section 5, or with an argument that legislative authority under the Indian (or the Interstate) Commerce
Clause was especially "plenary." Rather, they contended that state
sovereign immunity is only a common law doctrine, and thus can
be overcome by *any* exercise of federal legislative power.

The primary dissent by Justice Souter is an erudite but meander-
ing amalgam of arguments found in a large body of recent scholarship. He offered, among others, the following points: (1) It is uncertain whether the Framers assumed that the states enjoyed
immunity in their own courts; (2) The ratification debates contained conflicting statements about whether any such immunity
would survive in party-based cases but no statement that it would
survive in federal question cases; (3) *Hans* was mistaken in recognizing immunity in a federal question case; (4) That mistake was
perhaps explicable by the withdrawal of federal power in the South

---

[110] See generally *Blatchford v Native Village of Noatak*, 501 US 775, 790–92 (1991) (Blackmun dissenting).

[111] *United States v Kagama*, 118 US 375, 384 (1886).

[112] Although the *Blatchford* decision held that suits against states by Indian tribes, unlike
those by sister states, are barred by sovereign immunity, not until *Seminole* did the Court
limit *Congress*'s power to use the federal courts to protect the tribes vis-à-vis the states.

after 1877, after which any judgment purporting to require Louisiana to honor her bonds could not have been enforced; (5) In any event, the immunity that *Hans* recognized in federal question cases is only a nonconstitutional one, which Congress can override; and (6) The general theory of sovereignty underlying the Constitution does not permit a claim of state sovereignty to trump an exercise of congressional authority.

Chief Justice Rehnquist declined to be drawn into a lengthy debate about these points. Writing with the freedom given by five votes, he dismissed the primary dissent as resting on "a theory cobbled together from law review articles and its own version of historical events."[113] In addition to his effort to distinguish *Fitzpatrick* (discussed above) and to explain why stare decisis did not prevent overruling *Union Gas* (discussed below), the Chief Justice argued primarily that *Hans* was indeed a constitutional holding, and had been so treated by more recent decisions.

And so disagreement about the meaning of *Hans* was central to the division on the Court. The dissenters' view of *Hans* began, as Justice Bradley had in *Hans*, with the meaning of Justice Iredell's dissent in *Chisholm*. But Justice Stevens highlighted Justice Iredell's express limitation of his opinion to the "particular question . . . will an action of assumpsit lie against a State?"—a question Iredell said must be "abstracted from the general one, viz. Whether, a State can in any instance be sued?"[114] And Justices Stevens and Souter both emphasized that Iredell rested on the view that the Judiciary Act of 1789, following the principles of the common law, did not purport to confer jurisdiction over an action in assumpsit against an unconsenting state.[115] A case like *Seminole*, resting as it did on a federal cause of action and an express congressional grant of jurisdiction, was for the dissenters easily distinguishable.

All of that is true. On the other hand, as Justice Scalia had noted in his *Union Gas* dissent, Iredell's dissent ended in two sentences—dismissed as dictum by the *Seminole* dissenters but heavily emphasized by the Court in *Hans*[116]—in which Justice Iredell saw fit to

---

[113] 116 S Ct at 1129–30.

[114] *Chisholm*, 2 US at 430 (Iredell dissenting); see 116 S Ct at 1135 (Stevens dissenting).

[115] 116 S Ct at 1134–35 (Stevens dissenting), citing 2 US at 434; 116 S Ct at 1148–49 (Souter dissenting).

[116] 116 S Ct at 1135 n 4 (Stevens dissenting); id at 1149 n 6 (Souter dissenting).

"intimate that my present opinion is strongly against any construction of [the Constitution], which will admit, under any circumstances, a compulsive suit against a State for the recovery of money."[117] Although the Seminole Tribe did not sue Florida for money, that dictum, read in light of Iredell's protestations that suits against unconsenting states were unknown to the common law, does suggest that he doubted the constitutionality of any federal court suit against an unconsenting state. In the end, the battle for Justice Iredell's legacy was a standoff.

The *Seminole* dissenters' next claim—that *Hans*, like *Chisholm*, rested on a lack of statutory jurisdiction—is hard to square with much of the language in the *Hans* opinion. Consider these excerpts:

> Suppose that Congress, when proposing the Eleventh Amendment, had appended to it a proviso that nothing therein contained should prevent a State from being sued by its own citizens in cases arising under the Constitution or laws of the United States: can we imagine that it would have been adopted by the States? The supposition that it would is almost an absurdity on its face.
>
> The truth is, that the cognizance of suits and actions unknown to the law, and forbidden by the law, was not contemplated by the Constitution when establishing the judicial power of the United States.
>
> * * *
>
> "It may be accepted as a point of departure unquestioned," said Mr. Justice Miller, in *Cunningham v. Macon & Brunswick Railroad*, 109 U.S. 446, 451, "that neither a State nor the United States can be sued as defendant in any court in this country without their consent, except in the limited class of cases in which a State may be made a party in the Supreme Court of the United States by virtue of the original jurisdiction conferred on this court by the Constitution."
>
> * * *
>
> It is not necessary that we should enter upon an examination of the reason or expediency of the rule which exempts a sovereign State from prosecution in a court of justice at the suit of individuals. This is fully discussed by writers on public law. It is enough for us to declare its existence.[118]

---

[117] 2 US at 449–50, quoted in *Union Gas*, 491 US at 37–38 (Scalia dissenting). See generally John V. Orth, *The Truth about Justice Iredell's Dissent in Chisholm v Georgia*, 73 NC L Rev 255 (1994).

[118] 134 US at 15, 17, 21.

Justice Stevens sought to dismiss statements like these as historical background for a narrow statutory holding that the grant of federal question jurisdiction in the Judiciary Act of 1875 did not extend to suits against states.[119] Here is Justice Bradley's key language: "But besides the presumption that no anomalous and unheard of proceedings or suits were intended to be raised up by the Constitution—anomalous and unheard of when the Constitution was adopted—an additional reason why the jurisdiction claimed for the Circuit Court does not exist, is the language of the act of Congress by which its jurisdiction is conferred."[120] To my ear, those words confirm that the preceding discussion is an alternative constitutional holding rather than an introductory essay.[121]

How can one explain the dissenters' decision to rest on the vulnerable premise that *Hans* was only a common law decision, rather than simply to argue that *Hans* was wrong and should be overruled?[122] That choice would be understandable if it might have secured a fifth vote for congressional power to enlist the federal courts. But the four dissenters in *Union Gas* remained on the

---

[119] 116 S Ct at 1137–38 (Stevens dissenting); accord 116 S Ct at 1154 n 15 (Souter dissenting).

[120] 134 US at 18.

[121] Justice Stevens reads the concluding language in *Hans*—"Whilst the State cannot be compelled by suit to perform its contracts, any attempt on its part to violate property or rights acquired under its contracts, may be judicially resisted; and any law impairing the obligation of contracts under which such property or rights are held is void and powerless to effect their enjoyment"—as confirming that suit was barred because the federal Contract Clause claim depended on a threshold state law claim (whether there was a contract) as to which sovereign immunity was relevant. See 116 S Ct at 1141 n 14, discussing 134 US at 20–21. See also Burnham, 40 Case W Res L Rev at 965–69 (cited in note 38). I read the first clause rather as tracking the distinction, in nineteenth-century actions against officers, between those for interference with property rights—that is, tort-like claims—which generally were cognizable, see, for example, *Virginia Coupon Cases*, 114 US 269 (1885), and those that sounded in contract, which generally were not, see *In re Ayers*, 123 US 443 (1887). The second clause suggests only that an official's effort to defend a tort suit on the ground that a state statute authorized the action may be defeated if the statute is invalid under the Contract Clause. See, for example, *Smith v Greenhow*, 109 US 669 (1884).

[122] In support of a "common law" interpretation, William Burnham suggests that *Hans* understood the Constitution neither to eliminate sovereign immunity (as *Chisholm* had held) nor to preserve it but merely to be neutral. See Burnham, 40 Case W Res L Rev at 957 (cited in note 38), quoting 134 US at 11 (" '[The Eleventh Amendment] did not in terms prohibit suits by individuals against the States, but declared that the Constitution should not be construed to import any power to authorize the bringing of such suits.' "). To me, that statement connotes not constitutional neutrality, but rather that Article III (or the Constitution generally), as construed *in light of* the Eleventh Amendment, prohibits such suits.

Court, and Justice Thomas was almost certain to uphold state sovereign immunity against any competing theory.[123]

One explanation for the dissenters' approach relates to stare decisis, a doctrine to which Justice Souter did advert.[124] Having criticized the majority for overruling *Union Gas*, perhaps he sought to foreclose the response that he, too, sought to overrule precedent, and so instead argued that congressional abrogation power can co-exist with *Hans* and, more generally, with a constitutionally rooted sovereign immunity. Or perhaps he felt somewhat bound by the Court's past rejections of the diversity view. In any event, the problem of stare decisis was an important and complicated one, for majority and dissent alike.

E. SELECTIVE STARE DECISIS

The battle about stare decisis began with offsetting accusations. The majority treated *Union Gas* as an outlier—the only decision holding that Congress could abrogate immunity when acting under a provision other than the Fourteenth Amendment.[125] Justice Souter responded that "the Court today holds for the first time since the founding of the Republic that Congress has no authority to subject a State to the jurisdiction of a federal court at the behest of an individual asserting a federal right."[126] Both claims were accurate, for the Court had not, before *Union Gas*, squarely ruled on Congress's power to abrogate outside of the Fourteenth Amendment context.[127]

The Chief Justice offered three principal justifications for over-ruling *Union Gas*. The first was the absence of "an expressed rationale agreed upon by a majority of the Court."[128] A second and

---

[123] See, for example, his broad defense of state sovereignty in *US Term Limits, Inc. v Thornton*, 115 S Ct 1842, 1875 (1995).

[124] 116 S Ct at 1159, 1173 (Souter dissenting).

[125] Id at 1128–29 (majority opinion).

[126] Id at 1145 (Souter dissenting).

[127] Of course, as the dissenters noted, see 116 S Ct at 1140 (Stevens dissenting); id at 1159 (Souter dissenting), several rulings that Congress had not expressed its intention to abrogate with sufficient clarity, see, for example, *Atascadero State Hosp. v Scanlon*, 473 US 234 (1985); *Hoffman v Connecticut Dept of Income Maintenance*, 492 US 96 (1989), must have assumed that Congress had that power, or at least that the question was open.

[128] 116 S Ct at 1127.

related contention—that the fractured decision had confused the
lower courts[129]—is a familiar justification for departing from precedent,[130] but was thinly supported. The Court referred only to the
Eleventh Circuit's opinion below (which stated that Justice
White's "vague concurrence renders the continuing validity of
Union Gas in doubt")[131] and to one other court of appeals decision
(which stated that his concurrence "must be taken on its face to
disavow" the plurality's theory).[132] But the lower court decisions
had virtually unanimously read *Union Gas* to permit Congress to
abrogate immunity when acting under not only its commerce
power but any of its enumerated powers; the only court of appeals
to rule otherwise was the Eleventh Circuit in *Seminole*.[133] The
Court's final justification was that *Union Gas* "deviated sharply
from our established federalism jurisprudence and essentially evis-
cerated our decision in *Hans*."[134] As noted, while that contention
had some force, *Union Gas* was not technically inconsistent with
any precedent.

Little had changed in the seven years between *Union Gas* and
Seminole. The only intervening Supreme Court authority concerning abrogation had found that the statutes in question failed to
satisfy the clear statement requirement, and thus that Congress
had not effectively exercised whatever power to abrogate it has.
That requirement, though enforced with undue strictness,[135] did
not appear to present serious difficulties in application. The only
other change of significance since *Union Gas* was in the Court's
membership. Justices Brennan, White, Marshall, and Blackmun,
all supporters of abrogation in *Union Gas*, had been replaced by
Justices Souter, Ginsburg, and Breyer, who were like-minded on

---

[129] Id.

[130] See, for example, *Swift & Co. v Wickham*, 382 US 111, 116 (1965); *Planned Parenthood
v Casey*, 505 US 883, 854 (1992) (opinion of O'Connor, Kennedy, and Souter).

[131] 116 S Ct at 1127, quoting 11 F3d at 1027.

[132] Id, quoting *Chavez v Arte Publico Press*, 59 F3d 539, 543–45 (5th Cir 1995).

[133] See the survey in *In re Merchants Grain*, 59 F3d 630, 635–36 (7th Cir 1995), vacated
and remanded sub nom. *Ohio Agric Commodity Depositors Fund v Mahern*, 116 S Ct 1411
(1996).

[134] 116 S Ct at 1127.

[135] See, for example, William N. Eskridge, Jr., and Philip P. Frickey, *Quasi-Constitutional
Law: Clear Statement Rules as Constitutional Lawmaking*, 45 Vand L Rev 593, 621–23, 629–
45 (1992); David L. Shapiro, *Continuity and Change in Statutory Interpretation*, 67 NYU L
Rev 921, 958–59 (1992).

this issue, and by Justice Thomas, who was not; in *Seminole* he joined the four *Union Gas* dissenters to constitute a new majority.

Justices have frequently stated that "[a] basic change in the law upon a ground no firmer than a change in our membership invites the popular misconception that this institution is little different from the two political branches of the Government. No misconception could do more lasting injury to this Court and to the system of law which it is our abiding mission to serve."[136] But recently Justice Scalia has taken on the proposition frontally: in a dissent urging that *Booth v Maryland* [137](which prohibited a jury from considering a victim impact statement at a capital sentencing hearing) be overruled, he said: "I doubt that overruling *Booth* will so shake the citizenry's faith in the Court. Overrulings of precedent rarely occur without a change in the Court's personnel."[138] *Booth* was in fact overruled two Terms later in *Payne v Tennessee*.[139] Whether or not a majority of Justices would agree with Justice Scalia's declaration, in his separate opinion in *Payne*, that a decision may properly be overruled simply because it is wrong,[140] one may doubt how significant a policy this Court finds stare decisis to be. For even in constitutional cases, where it is common ground that stare decisis carries less weight,[141] overruling simply to correct a perceived mistake would drain stare decisis of any force whatsoever.

To be sure, the public is unlikely to view a change of course in the arcane world of the Eleventh Amendment, unlike one concerning abortion rights, as "a surrender to political pressure."[142] Any effort to explain the overruling of *Union Gas* to the person on the street would generate more bewilderment than outrage. Still, there

---

[136] *Mitchell v W.T. Grant*, 416 US 600, 636 (1974) (Stewart dissenting), quoted in *Planned Parenthood v Casey*, 505 US at 864 (opinion of O'Connor, Kennedy, and Souter). See also, for example, *Mapp v Ohio*, 367 US 643, 677 (1961) (Harlan dissenting).

[137] 482 US 496 (1987).

[138] *South Carolina v Gathers*, 490 US 805, 824 (1989) (Scalia dissenting).

[139] 501 US 808 (1991).

[140] Id at 834 (Scalia, joined by O'Connor and Kennedy, concurring). Compare id at 835 (Souter, joined by Kennedy, concurring) (suggesting that an erroneous precedent should not be overruled absent "special justification," which he found to be present).

[141] See, for example, *United States v Scott*, 437 US 82, 101 (1978); Jerold H. Israel, *Gideon v. Wainwright: The "Art" of Overruling*, 1963 Supreme Court Review 211, 215–16, and sources cited.

[142] *Planned Parenthood v Casey*, 505 US at 867 (opinion of O'Connor, Kennedy, and Souter).

remains a point stressed by Professor Monaghan—that "the real focus of rule of law theories about the Supreme Court in the main is elites, at least 'the reasoning classes.' "[143] In the end, any attempt to persuade "the reasoning classes" that *Union Gas* did not deserve respect as a precedent drew important support from the cryptic quality of Justice White's opinion. The point is not that a majority opinion in *Union Gas* might not also have been overturned, but that the absence of such an opinion, and of any explanation for Justice White's vote, gave at least a fig leaf of cover to what otherwise looked like a naked shift resulting from new appointments.

Of course, *Seminole* presented a second question about stare decisis—whether to overrule *Hans* and subsequent cases viewing the Eleventh Amendment as supporting a general policy of sovereign immunity.[144] Though *Union Gas* was the only Supreme Court decision squarely ruling on the power to abrogate outside of the Fourteenth Amendment area, a long line of cases had followed *Hans*. Nonetheless, there remained an aroma of inconsistency in the Court's fervent insistence that it was respecting stare decisis (by adhering to *Hans*) while overruling a recent decision. The question whether stare decisis called for adhering to *Hans* was not much discussed in *Seminole*—for the dissenters chose to argue that *Hans*, even if wrong, could be distinguished—but had been addressed in Justice Scalia's dissent in *Union Gas*. There he acknowledged that the question of *Hans*'s correctness was a close one, but contended that *Hans* had pervasively affected statutory law, by "automatically assuring that private damages actions created by federal law do not extend against the States."[145] Congress, he suggested, had enacted many statutes with that understanding, and to overturn it now would upset congressional reliance interests.

That argument fails to persuade. For beginning in 1973, the Court made plain that no federal court suit against a state by private parties would be permitted unless Congress had satisfied a clear statement rule,[146] which succeeding cases applied with a ven-

---

[143] Henry P. Monaghan, *Stare Decisis and Constitutional Adjudication*, 88 Colum L Rev 723, 753 (1988).

[144] The petitioner's brief concluded by referring to the diversity view and suggesting that the Court, if it failed to rule for the tribe either on abrogation grounds or under *Ex parte Young*, should overrule *Hans* (at least in suits brought by Indian tribes).

[145] 491 US at 35.

[146] See *Employees of the Department of Public Health & Welfare v Department of Public Health & Welfare*, 411 US 279 (1973).

geance.[147] In that legal environment, it is chimerical to suppose that overruling *Hans* would suddenly subject the states to liability not fairly contemplated by Congress. In fact, the only lower court decisions since *Union Gas* holding the clear statement rule to have been satisfied involved statutory provisions enacted since 1973,[148] most of which were designed either (i) to override a Supreme Court decision holding that the unamended statute had not subjected the state to suit with adequate clarity,[149] or (ii) to eliminate doubt, created by the clear statement decisions, that Congress did intend to subject the states to federal court suit under the particular program in question.[150]

The preceding discussion assumes, of course, the clear statement rule would operate even were *Hans* overruled. There would be powerful arguments for maintenance of the rule even if *Hans* were discarded (although I would not defend the severity with which the Court has enforced its rule).[151] And the Court, even were it to

---

[147] See, for example, cases cited in note 127; *Dellmuth v Muth*, 491 US 223 (1989).

[148] This statement is based on results of a June, 1996, Westlaw search of the "ALLFEDS" database using the words "abrog!" and "*Union Gas.*"

[149] Thus, for example, § 1003 of the Rehabilitation Act Amendments of 1986, 100 Stat 1807, 1845, codified at 42 USC § 2000d-7, sought to override the holding of *Atascadero State Hosp. v Scanlon*, 473 US 234 (1985), that the Rehabilitation Act did not state its intention to subject the states to federal court suit with adequate clarity. (That provision also abrogated immunity under Titles VI and IX of the Civil Rights Act, the Age Discrimination Act of 1975, and any other federal statute prohibiting discrimination by the recipients of federal funds.) Similarly, after the Court in *Dellmuth v Muth*, 491 US 223 (1989), found insufficient clarity in the Education of the Handicapped Act (now known as the Individuals with Disabilities Education Act), Congress amended the Act to clearly abrogate as to future violations, see Pub L No 101-476, Title I, § 103 (Oct 30, 1990), codified at 20 USC § 1403. Section 113 of the Bankruptcy Reform Act of 1994, Pub L No 103-394 (Oct 22, 1994), codified in relevant part at 11 USC § 106, sought to override *United States v Nordic Village, Inc.*, 503 US 30 (1992), and *Hoffman v Connecticut Dept of Income Maintenance*, 492 US 96 (1989)—decisions finding the bankruptcy laws insufficiently clear. An earlier example is found in §§ 6(a)(1), 6(d)(1) of the Fair Labor Standards Amendments of 1974, 88 Stat 55, 56, 61, codified at 29 USC §§ 203, 216(b), which sought to override the *Employees* decision and permit private federal court suit against a state under that Act.

[150] Although the question whether states were immune from suit under the patent, copyright, and trademark acts never reached the Supreme Court, Congress enacted measures clearly indicating its intention to abrogate. See Copyright Remedy Clarification Act, Pub L No 101-553 (Nov 15, 1990), codified at 17 USC §§ 501(a), 511(a); Trademark Remedy Clarification Act, Pub L No 102-542 (Oct 27, 1992), codified at 15 USC § 1122; Patent and Plant Variety Protection Remedy Clarification Act, Pub L No 102-560 (Oct 27, 1992), codified in relevant part at 35 USC §§ 271(h), 296. The Americans with Disabilities Act, Pub L No 101-336 (July 26, 1990), contains a provision, codified at 42 USC § 12202, expressly abrogating immunity.

[151] See, for example, Shapiro, 67 NYU L Rev at 958–59 (cited in note 135); Jackson, 98 Yale L J at 110–11 (cited in note 45); Tribe, 89 Harv L Rev at 695–96 (cited in note 82).

dispense with the rule as to future enactments, could continue to require that statutes enacted during the ascendancy of *Hans* contain a clear statement. (The Court follows a similar practice when deciding whether to imply a private right of action under federal regulatory statutes: the restrictive standards for implication first announced in 1975 have not been applied to statutes enacted from 1964 to 1975, when Congress may have been relying on the more liberal approach that the Court followed during that period.)[152]

Thus, the Court's implicit conclusion that stare decisis permitted overruling *Union Gas* but not *Hans* seems to me open to question. To be sure, as the Court stressed, *Hans* has been followed repeatedly, and *Union Gas* is weakly reasoned. But those weaknesses arise from its acceptance of *Hans*, and thus the two stare decision questions are hardly distinct. In the end, *Seminole* provides further confirmation (if any were needed) that stare decisis is honored "with the predictability of a lightning bolt."[153]

IV. WHITHER EX PARTE YOUNG?

After ruling that the state could not be sued in federal court, the Court turned to the question whether suit against Governor Chiles was also barred. A long tradition permits private suits against state officials alleged to be violating federal requirements—at least where the relief sought is "prospective" in nature. The standard citation remains *Ex parte Young*,[154] which upheld an order restraining the state's attorney general from bringing suit under a statute alleged to trench on constitutional rights.[155] The principle

---

[152] See, for example, *Merrill, Lynch, Pierce, Fenner, & Smith, Inc. v Curran*, 456 US 353, 381 (1982); *Morse v Republican Party of Virginia*, 116 S Ct 1186 (1996).

[153] Henry P. Monaghan, *Our Perfect Constitution*, 56 NYU L Rev 353, 390 (1981).

[154] 209 US 123 (1908).

[155] The *Seminole* Court characterized officer suits under *Young* as an "exception" to the general rule of the Eleventh Amendment, 116 S Ct at 1133—a characterization that first surfaced in *Milliken v Bradley*, 433 US 267, 289 (1977), and has been followed since only in *Pennhurst State School & Hospital v Halderman*, 465 US 89, 102 (1984), *Green v Mansour*, 474 US 64, 67 (1985), and *Puerto Rico Aqueduct & Sewer Auth. v Metcalf & Eddy, Inc.*, 506 US 138, 146 (1993). (This statement is based on a July, 1996, Westlaw search of the "SCT" database for decisions including "Eleventh Amendment," "*Ex parte Young*," and "exception.") A characterization I find more congenial views officers' suits as an integral part of the development of remedies for official misconduct—remedies that were sufficiently broad to make sovereign immunity an abstract idea with limited impact on an individual's right to relief. See, for example, Jaffe, 77 Harv L Rev at 28–29 (cited in note 27); David L. Shapiro, *Wrong Turns: The Eleventh Amendment and the Pennhurst Case*, 98 Harv L Rev 61, 71–72 (1984).

of *Young* has been extended to suits alleging violations of federal statutes.[156] And although the prospective/retrospective line can be more than a little hazy,[157] there was little doubt that an order requiring a state official to cease an ongoing violation of IGRA fit comfortably on the prospective side of the line.

A. THE ELEVENTH CIRCUIT'S APPROACH

The Eleventh Circuit had nonetheless found relief against the Governor unavailable, for two distinct reasons. The first—that "if a suit in reality is against the state itself, the *Ex parte Young* doctrine is inapplicable"[158]—reflected a rather fundamental misunderstanding, for the permissibility of suit against government officials has never rested on any such functional distinction.[159]

The Eleventh Circuit's second ground was that a state executive official cannot be enjoined to perform a "discretionary task"[160]— a category within which the duty to bargain was held to fall. Although the ministerial/discretionary distinction, central to the scope of mandamus, "spilled over into sovereign immunity analysis" in some older decisions,[161] we have come to realize that gov-

---

[156] See, for example, *Edelman v Jordan*, 415 US 651 (1974); *Quern v Jordan*, 440 US 332 (1979); *Worcester County Trust Co. v Riley*, 302 US 292, 297 (1937) (dictum).

[157] See, for example, sources cited in note 28.

[158] 11 F3d at 1029.

[159] See, for example, Ann Althouse, *When to Believe a Legal Fiction: Federal Interests and the Eleventh Amendment*, 40 Hastings L J 1123, 1134 (1989); Jaffe, 77 Harv L Rev at 4 (cited in note 27). The Eleventh Circuit may have been confused by a statement in *Pennhurst State School & Hosp. v Halderman*, 465 US 89, 102 (1984), that "a suit against state officials that is in fact a suit against a State is barred regardless of whether it seeks damages or injunctive relief." That statement was made in holding that federal courts lack authority to issue specific relief against officials for violations of *state* law, without calling into question the availability of relief for violations of *federal* law. The mere fact that a federal cause of action may require some interpretation of state law—as under IGRA, which obliges a state to negotiate about only such class III gaming as state law permits—does not bring *Pennhurst* into play. For example, a suit to enjoin a state official from depriving the plaintiff of liberty or property without due process is not barred simply because it may require interpretation of state law to determine whether a state-created liberty or property interest exists. See, for example, *Kentucky Dept of Corrections v Thompson*, 490 US 454, 463–64 (1989); compare *Geis v Board of Educ. of Parsippany-Troy Hills*, 774 F2d 575 (3d Cir 1985) (permitting relief against state officials for noncompliance with state-law requirements in a federally approved plan for ensuring a disabled child the right to a free public education, even though the state's requirements exceeded those imposed by federal law).

[160] 11 F3d at 1028.

[161] Shapiro, 98 Harv L Rev at 75 (cited in note 155). See, for example, *Philadelphia Co. v Stimson*, 223 US 605, 619–20 (1912); *Board of Liquidation v McComb*, 92 US 531, 541 (1875).

ernment action does not fall into separable categories labeled "discretionary" and "ministerial"; rather, the law generally leaves officials with discretion in some respects but not others.[162] Official action or inaction in violation of a legal requirement is not immune from judicial process, even if related aspects of the official's duties are highly discretionary—a point made in *Young* itself.[163]

There remains the question, however, whether IGRA imposes an enforceable requirement at all. The statute requires the state to negotiate in good faith, and authorizes a federal court, if it finds that the state failed to do so, to order the state and the tribe to conclude a compact within 60 days.[164] The latter provision is a clumsy one, for the Act establishes no mechanism to compel agreement; indeed, other provisions—for mediation, and ultimately for regulation by the Secretary of the Interior—contemplate that agreement may not be forthcoming. A Holmesian bad man might contend that the state (and its officials) are not obliged to negotiate but rather may consider whether to negotiate until sixty days have passed from the order's entry—which merely marks time along the way.

But a court should hesitate before treating an explicit federal cause of action as devoid of any relief of consequence. The order to reach an agreement, predicated as it is on the state's failure to negotiate in good faith, could be construed as in effect requiring the state to fulfill its duty to bargain in good faith—much like bargaining orders entered for violations of the federal labor laws.[165] The court has viewed such a duty as important even though no tribunal has power to impose an agreement[166] and effective sanctions for recalcitrance may be wanting.[167] As the Court noted when approving an injunction to enforce an employer's duty, under the Railway Labor Act, to "treat with" the union, the mere "meeting

---

[162] See, for example, *Work v United States ex rel Rives*, 267 US 175, 177–78 (1925); Louis L. Jaffe, *Judicial Control of Administrative Action* 181 (Little, Brown, 1965).

[163] See *Ex parte Young*, 209 US at 159.

[164] See 25 USC §§ 2710(d)(3)(A), 2710(d)(7).

[165] See 29 USC § 158(d) (National Labor Relations Act); 45 USC § 152 (Railway Labor Act).

[166] See *HK Porter Co. v NLRB*, 397 US 99 (1970).

[167] See Bernard D. Meltzer and Stanley D. Henderson, *Labor Law: Cases, Materials and Problems* 850 (Little, Brown, 3d ed 1985). Moreover, where (as in *Seminole*) discord rests in part on disputes about the law's requirements, judicial intervention may eliminate those areas of disagreement.

of employers and employees at the conference table is a powerful aid to industrial peace" and might "result in agreement, or lead to successful mediation or arbitration."[168] To be sure, that description of labor relations may be on the hopeful side, and the parties in the Indian gambling context may not be under comparable economic pressures to reach agreement. But on the other hand, several factors suggest that productive negotiation may nonetheless be more likely under IGRA than in the labor context: (1) IGRA's authorization, only sixty days after the court's order, of mediation followed by resort to the Secretary of the Interior, reduces the benefits of delay; (2) the "best-offer" mediation creates incentives to narrow differences; and (3) if no agreement is reached, the Secretary (unlike the NLRB) may impose final terms.[169]

B. THE SUPREME COURT'S ANALYSIS

The Supreme Court did not question the existence of an enforceable duty. But it found relief unavailable under *Ex parte Young* for a reason not advanced by the Eleventh Circuit (or by the

---

[168] *Virginian Ry Co. v System Fed'n No. 40*, 300 US 515, 551–52 (1937). The Railway Labor Act applies to a state-owned railroad, *California v Taylor*, 353 US 553 (1957)—a holding unanimously reaffirmed, even during the ascendancy of *National League of Cities v Usery*, 426 US 833 (1976), see *United Transp. Union v LIRR Co.*, 455 US 678 (1982).

[169] In a somewhat lame effort to limit the Court's ruling, Justice Stevens suggested that a suit under IGRA fails to satisfy the Case or Controversy requirement, because if both parties are adamant, the court's only option is to refer the matter to the Executive Branch for resolution. 116 S Ct at 1144–45. Two questions must be distinguished. The first is whether the Court is exercising judicial power. The argument in text suggests that the duty to negotiate is not an empty requirement even if agreement cannot be guaranteed—much as an action seeking only a declaration that a patent is valid, but not a damage award or an injunction, is justiciable. Moreover, a declaratory judgment resolving a legal dispute— for example, whether the state "permitted" casino gaming within the meaning of IGRA— might have preclusive effect in subsequent litigation (for example, a challenge by the state to regulations issued by the Secretary of the Interior). See generally Note, *Nonmutual Issue Preclusion Against States*, 109 Harv L Rev 792 (1996). (The dictum in *United States v Lee*, 106 US 196, 222 (1882), that a judgment against officers does not bind the government can hardly to taken to be authoritative.)

The second issue is whether the exercise of judicial authority is inappropriate on the ground that the Secretary of the Interior can "revise" the judgment. While the exact contours of, and purposes served by, the prohibition on executive revision have never been perfectly clear, IGRA does not give the Secretary any authority to review a federal court's decision. Compare *Chicago & Southern Air Lines, Inc. v Waterman SS Corp.*, 333 US 103 (1948). Nor does the Secretary control the extent of compliance with the judgment, which runs against the state rather than against the federal government or its officials. Compare *Hayburn's Case*, 2 US (2 Dall) 408 (1792); *United States v Ferreira*, 54 US (13 How) 40 (1851). See generally Note, *Executive Revision of Judicial Decisions*, 109 Harv L Rev 2020, 2028–29 (1996).

briefs): "the intricate remedial scheme set forth in § 2710(d)(7)"[170] by its terms ran only against the state, and thus, the Court concluded, implicitly precluded suit against an official under *Ex parte Young.* The Court relied primarily on *Schweiker v Chilicky*,[171] which refused to imply a *Bivens* remedy[172] under the Due Process Clause when reasonably detailed statutory remedies had been provided for the wrongful conduct in question. "Here, of course," the Court stated, "the question is not whether a remedy should be created, but instead is whether the Eleventh Amendment bar should be lifted";[173] but by analogy the same approach applied. The cause of action afforded by IGRA against the state was hedged with intricate restrictions. By contrast, the Chief Justice stated, "an action brought against a state official under *Ex parte Young* would expose that official to the full remedial powers of a federal court, including, presumably, contempt sanctions"[174]—which, the Court assumed, were not available under IGRA in a suit against the state itself.[175] Thus, to permit suit against an official under *Ex parte Young* would contravene the Act's purpose.

In fact, the initial question in *Seminole* was precisely "whether a remedy should be created" (perhaps "awarded" would be more apt). The Court failed to recall that *Ex parte Young* concerned not only the Eleventh Amendment but also implied remedies for violations of federal law.[176] A suit like *Young*—to enjoin enforcement by state officials of a statute alleged to be unconstitutional—is second nature today. But the nineteenth-century tradition from which *Young* grew—that of suits against officers—rested essentially on tort concepts; an official who committed a wrong under the general law could, like other tortfeasors, be held accountable. If the officer defended by claiming authority to act under a state statute, the plaintiff would reply that the Constitution rendered the statute

---

[170] 116 S Ct at 1132.

[171] 487 US 412 (1988).

[172] See *Bivens v Six Unknown Named Agents of Fed. Bureau of Narcotics*, 403 US 388 (1971).

[173] 116 S Ct at 1132.

[174] Id at 1133.

[175] That assumption, though hardly ineluctable, is plausible in view of the inherent vagueness of the duty, the provision of alternative remedies when no agreement is reached, and the sensitivities involved.

[176] Justice Souter's dissent also missed this point. See 116 S Ct at 1182 (Souter dissenting).

invalid, leaving the officer without any defense of statutory authority and thus liable as a tortfeasor.

In *Ex parte Young*, however, the Attorney General's conduct—threatening to bring suit under a state statute alleged to be unconstitutional—was probably not tortious under traditional common law understandings.[177] By nonetheless authorizing suit, *Young* in effect recognized an implied federal cause of action for an injunctive remedy against state officials whose conduct violates the Fourteenth Amendment.[178] That federal remedy could be provided, *Young* held, even though the state court was presumptively competent to adjudicate the due process issue should the threatened enforcement action be filed. Thus, *Young* did not merely articulate a jurisdictional rule about sovereign immunity. There would have been no occasion for *Young*'s Eleventh Amendment holding absent the prior determination that federal law gave the railroad a right of action for injunctive relief.

In *Seminole*, then, the key question was whether federal law gave the tribe a right to declaratory or injunctive relief when state officials refuse to bargain in violation of IGRA. Even remaining within the four corners of IGRA, there is strong reason to think that the answer is yes. Admittedly, the fact that *Seminole* involved violation of a federal statute rather than a constitutional provision makes the argument for an implied remedy somewhat less strong. For the Constitution itself is remarkably bare of remedial specification. "To the framers, special provision for constitutional remedies probably appeared unnecessary, because the Constitution presupposed a going legal system, with ample remedial mechanisms, in which constitutional guarantees would be implemented."[179] Thus, it is a fair assumption in a case like *Young* that standard legal and equitable remedies would be available for constitutional violations. By contrast, the detailed remedial specification often found in stat-

---

[177] See Clyde E. Jacobs, *The Eleventh Amendment and Sovereign Immunity* 138–42 (Greenwood, 1972).

[178] See *Hart and Wechsler* at 1065 (cited in note 28). Though some have argued that federal courts derive power to confer implied remedies from general grants of jurisdiction like 28 USC § 1331, I prefer to view the remedies as implied from the substantive provision being enforced—so that *Young* recognizes an implied remedy required, or at least inspired, by the Due Process Clause. See *Hart and Wechsler* at 876 and n 16 and sources cited.

[179] Richard H. Fallon, Jr., & Daniel J. Meltzer, *New Law, Non-Retroactivity, and Constitutional Remedies*, 104 Harv L Rev 1731, 1779 (1991).

utes (particularly modern statutes) may well argue against judicial supplementation.

Nonetheless, the Court's conclusion that no relief against Governor Chiles could be ordered is in the end very doubtful. There is a long tradition of judicial provision of specific relief (initially via mandamus,[180] and in more modern cases via injunction[181]) against government action that violates statutory requirements—even when the statute in question fails expressly to authorize such relief.[182] Although recent decisions have sharply contracted the scope of implied remedies under federal statutes,[183] those rulings have ordinarily been premised on the ground that when Congress has spelled out who may initiate suit, courts should not give private actors a right to sue not conferred by statute. That ground is inapplicable in *Seminole*, as IGRA expressly authorized plaintiffs like the Seminole Tribe to bring suit.

The conclusion that the tribe should have been afforded a declaratory or injunctive remedy against Governor Chiles, even were it thought problematic when looking only at IGRA, becomes irresistible when one recalls the statutory remedy in 42 USC § 1983. That provision authorizes suit against any person who, while acting under color of state law, deprives another of rights secured by federal law. Under *Maine v Thiboutot*,[184] which interpreted that provision as reaching violations of *any* federal statute by state offi-

---

[180] See, for example, *United States ex rel Kansas City Southern Ry Co. v ICC*, 252 US 178 (1920).

[181] See, for example, *Shields v Utah Idaho Central RR*, 305 US 177, 182–84 (1938).

[182] This tradition remains particularly vibrant in suits seeking declaratory or injunctive relief against state regulation alleged to be preempted. See, for example, *Shaw v Delta Airlines*, 463 US 85 (1983); *Lawrence County v Lead-Deadwood School Dist. No. 40–1*, 469 US 256, 259 n 6 (1985); *Lake Carriers' Assn v MacMullan*, 406 US 498, 506–08 (1972). (Today such suits, or at least some of them, could be brought under the express remedy provided by 42 USC § 1983, as interpreted in *Golden State Transit Corp. v City of Los Angeles*, 493 US 10 (1989).) Although Henry Monaghan, in *Federal Statutory Review Under Section 1983 and the APA*, 91 Colum L Rev 233 (1991), has raised doubts about the Court's approach, I believe it follows comfortably from *Ex parte Young*, which can, after all, fairly be characterized as a case in which state law was preempted by the Due Process Clause. Moreover, where federal law is alleged to preempt state duties, putative dutyholders have an important interest in obtaining anticipatory relief from the duty's threatened enforcement. See generally *Hart and Wechsler* at 1285–86 (cited in note 28); Douglas Laycock, *Federal Interference with State Prosecutions: The Need for Prospective Relief*, 1977 Supreme Court Review 193.

[183] See, for example, *Touche, Ross & Co. v Redington*, 442 US 560 (1979); *California v Sierra Club*, 451 US 287 (1981); see generally *Hart and Wechsler* at 839–46 (cited in note 28).

[184] 448 US 1 (1980).

cials, the tribe had a good argument that Congress, in enacting § 1983, *expressly* created a private right of action (permitting, inter alia, declaratory and injunctive relief) against Governor Chiles for violation of IGRA's duty to bargain in good faith. Regrettably, the *Seminole* opinion failed even to advert to the pertinence of § 1983 (a failure attributable in part to the tribe and the amici in its support, whose briefs failed to mention that provision).[185]

The Court did limit *Thiboutot* with its holding in *Middlesex County Sewerage Authority v National Sea Clammers Association*[186] that a federal statute's comprehensive remedial scheme may leave no room for supplementation by the § 1983 remedy. Just as *Schweiker v Chilicky* ruled that a judicially implied remedy may be precluded by a specific statutory scheme, so *Middlesex* provides that the express statutory remedy generally available under § 1983 may be precluded by a particular enactment.

But the contention that IGRA should be understood to preclude private suit against state officials is unpersuasive. Even accepting the Court's assumption that IGRA did not contemplate imposition of the contempt sanction in a suit against the state, the § 1983 cause of action against state officials can be accommodated to respect that limitation, while permitting, for example, at least declaratory relief. Put differently, if federal statutes can preclude resort to § 1983 in toto (as in *Middlesex*), they can equally well do so in part. (The Court has taken just that approach at the intersection of § 1983 and the Tax Injunction Act.)[187] The question, after all,

---

[185] Although the tribe's complaint similarly failed to mention § 1983, that shortcoming does not justify the Court's failure to consider that provision's implications—which are sufficiently evident to those experienced in dealing with suits against state officials that one doubts that all nine Justices (and their considerably more numerous law clerks) simply overlooked § 1983's pertinence. The case came up on review of a decision on a motion to dismiss the complaint under the Eleventh Amendment. The Court's disposition of the claim against the Governor effectively held that it should have been dismissed under Fed R Civ Proc 12(b)(6), for failure to state a claim on which relief can be granted. To ignore § 1983 merely because the complaint included no reference to it would not have been faithful to Fed R Civ Proc 8(f)'s injunction that "[a]ll pleadings shall be construed as to do substantial justice." See generally 5, 5A Charles A. Wright and Arthur R. Miller, *Federal Practice and Procedure: Civil 2d* §§ 1286, 1363 (West, 1990).

[186] 453 US 1 (1981).

[187] 28 USC § 1342. The Act precludes federal courts from enjoining state tax collection so long as the state courts afford a plain, speedy, and efficient remedy. The Court has read the Act, and the broader federal policy behind it, as a partial preclusion of relief under § 1983 (in state as well as federal court lawsuits); no such relief is available where the state courts provide a plain, speedy, and adequate remedy. *National Private Truck Council, Inc. v Oklahoma Tax Comm'n*, 115 S Ct 2351 (1995).

is one of congressional intent,[188] and there is no reason why a Congress that intended IGRA to be enforceable at the instance of a tribe, in federal court—and was thwarted by an unanticipated Supreme Court ruling—should be understood to have foreclosed a suit by the tribe, against a state official, that has that same purpose and effect.[189]

The remedial issue in *Seminole* thus differed significantly from that in *Schweiker v Chilicky*, on which the Court relied. In *Chilicky*, a suit alleging wrongful termination of federal benefits, the supplemental remedy sought (an implied damages remedy under *Bivens* for a denial of due process) was precluded because it differed in significant respects from the remedy prescribed by the federal statute: a *Bivens* remedy would have (i) been administered by courts (the statutory remedy was administrative), (ii) provided broader damages than Congress had authorized, and (iii) been awarded against federal officials (the statutory remedy was against the government itself). By contrast, supplementation of IGRA's now-invalid action against a state with one against an official would neither conflict with any statutory definition of appropriate relief (indeed, unlike damages, an injunction against the state and against its Governor are functionally indistinguishable) nor shift enforcement authority from an agency to the courts. Indeed, *Seminole* was the unusual case in which, because the specific statutory remedy had been frustrated, maintenance of a "supplemental" remedy was essential to promote the statute's purposes.

All in all, the Court's preclusion of the claim against Governor Chiles rests on a mischaracterization of *Ex parte Young*, a disregard of § 1983, and a misapplication of familiar principles of congressional primacy in shaping remedies for federal statutory violations.

C. THE FUTURE OF EX PARTE YOUNG

Does *Seminole* cast a cloud over the doctrine of *Ex parte Young*—which, Justice Souter declared, "is nothing short of 'indispensable to the establishment of constitutional government and the rule of

---

[188] See *Smith v Robinson*, 468 US 992, 1012 (1984).

[189] Compare id at 1021 (in holding relief under the Rehabilitation Act unavailable as to conduct also governed by the detailed remedial scheme of the Education for the Handicapped Act, stressing that "[w]e do not address a situation where the EHA is not available").

law' "?[190] On its face, the opinion's discussion of *Young* is quite narrow, resting not on the broad concerns voiced in some opinions about judicial incapacity or illegitimacy when implying remedies,[191] but on the particulars of IGRA. Indeed, at the end of its opinion the Court, while refusing to "rewrite" IGRA to permit suit against the Governor, added: "If that effort is to be made, it should be made by Congress, and not by the federal courts."[192] Earlier on, the Court declared that the dissent's contention that the overruling of *Union Gas* impaired vindication of national interests "disregards other methods of ensuring the States' compliance with federal law"—one of which was a suit to "to ensure that [a state] officer's conduct is in compliance with federal law, see, e.g., *Ex parte Young*."[193]

There has, of course, been considerable contraction of private remedies for violations of federal law: cases like *Chilicky* and *Middlesex* are part of a larger restriction of implied rights of action and of the § 1983 remedy, particularly in cases under federal statutory programs.[194] Still, I do not view *Seminole* as a significant step in a general assault on private enforcement of federal law against state officials except where specifically authorized by Congress. One can overstate the recent trend. *Thiboutot* has been limited, not overruled, by *Middlesex:* absent *Thiboutot,* the (virtually irrebuttable) presumption would have been that a federal statute may not be enforced by private parties absent express congressional authorization; *Thiboutot* creates a quite different presumption, requiring affirmative reason to preclude private enforcement under § 1983.[195]

Of course, *Thiboutot* is not immune from overruling. Yet the recent history of congressional overrides of decisions narrowly

---

[190] 116 S Ct at 1180 (quoting Charles A. Wright, *Law of Federal Courts* 292 (West, 4th ed 1983)).

[191] See, for example, *Texas Industries, Inc. v Radcliff Materials, Inc.*, 451 US 630, 638–47 (1981); *Cannon v University of Chicago*, 441 US 677, 730–31, 742–49 (1979) (Powell dissenting); *Thompson v Thompson*, 484 US 174, 191–92 (1988) (Scalia concurring in the judgment).

[192] 116 S Ct at 1133.

[193] Id at 1131 n 14.

[194] See generally *Hart and Wechsler* at 830–46, 1133–37 (cited in note 28).

[195] See, for example, *Wilder v Virginia Hosp. Assn*, 496 US 498 (1990); *Wright v Roanoke Redevelopment & Hous. Auth.*, 479 US 418 (1987).

construing federal civil rights laws[196] may make the Court (not-withstanding recent shifts in Congress) hesitate before taking the more dramatic step of overruling *Thiboutot* to curtail so pivotal a provision as § 1983.[197] Finally, as Henry Monaghan has noted,[198] § 1983 and the Administrative Procedure Act[199] can be seen as parallel provisions, each standing for a broad presumption that the intended beneficiaries of constitutional or statutory provisions may obtain a judicial determination whether official action comports with federal law—a presumption long implemented, before those statutes assumed centrality, by nonstatutory mechanisms.[200] If the Court seeks completely to preclude private suit against officials except where specifically authorized by Congress, it will have to take many large steps beyond *Seminole*, and to uproot broadly and deeply established traditions, in order to reach that destination.

But how else can one explain the Court's singularly unpersuasive treatment of *Ex parte Young?* Assuming that the members of the *Seminole* majority were eager to overrule *Union Gas*, their objective could have been frustrated by a conclusion that an injunctive action against Governor Chiles could go forward. To proceed to determine whether the separate claim against the state *eo nomine* was

---

[196] See, for example, Civil Rights Act of 1991, Pub L No 102-166 (overruling *Patterson v McLean Credit Union*, 491 US 164 (1989), *Lorance v AT&T Technologies, Inc.*, 490 US 900 (1989), *Martin v Wilks*, 490 US 755 (1989), *Wards Cove Packing Co. v Atonio*, 490 US 642 (1989), *Price Waterhouse v Hopkins*, 490 US 228 (1989), *EEOC v Arabian American Oil Co.*, 499 US 244 (1991), *West Virginia University Hosps, Inc. v Casey*, 499 US 83 (1991), and *Library of Congress v Shaw*, 478 US 310 (1986)); Civil Rights Restoration Act of 1987, Pub L No 100-259 (March 22, 1988) (overruling *Grove City College v Bell*, 465 US 555 (1984)).

[197] See generally William N. Eskridge, Jr., & Philip P. Frickey, *The Supreme Court, 1993 Term—Foreword: Law as Equilibrium*, 108 Harv L Rev 26, 38 (1994).

In *Blessing v Freestone*, 68 F3d 1141 (9th Cir 1995), the Ninth Circuit held that custodial parents may sue a state official under § 1983 to enforce federal requirements associated with federal grants to state child support enforcement programs. The Supreme Court has granted the official's petition for certiorari, 116 S Ct 1671 (1996), and the petitioner's brief urges the Court, inter alia, to overrule *Thiboutot*. But much of the concern about *Thiboutot* has arisen in cases, like *Blessing*, where plaintiffs seek to use § 1983 to enforce conditions on federal grants. The Court could reverse the Ninth Circuit, without squarely overruling *Thiboutot*'s holding that § 1983 is available to enforce federal statutes unrelated to civil or equal rights, by following the approach of *Suter v Artist M*, 503 US 347 (1992), which held that the particular requirements relating to the use of federal grants did not create private rights enforceable under § 1983.

[198] See Monaghan, 91 Colum L Rev 233 (cited in note 182).

[199] 5 USC § 701 et seq.

[200] See *Hart and Wechsler* at 995–99 (cited in note 28).

barred by sovereign immunity might have been seen as an inappropriate exercise of remedial discretion, because any relief against the state would have been no broader than that available against Governor Chiles. The policy of constitutional avoidance would only reinforce the argument for a discretionary refusal to decide. Thus, the Court may have strained, consciously or unconsciously, to find the claim against the Governor precluded in order to clear the path to overruling *Union Gas*.[201]

Another feature of the case may help explain the Court's handling of *Young*. The state's brief contended that IGRA ran afoul not only of state sovereign immunity but also of the anticommandeering principle announced in *New York v United States*.[202] The Act was somewhat unusual; it required a state not to take (or refrain from) specific substantive action, but to enter into a negotiating process. For many, the open-endedness of that obligation might be seen as more constitutional virtue than vice. (Indeed, the *Seminole* decision itself may actually have reduced the states' autonomy: for if, as the Eleventh Circuit held,[203] IGRA's authorization of suit is severable, the Act may permit direct federal authorization of Indian gaming without any state participation in shaping the terms.) Nonetheless, the duty to bargain may have struck some Justices as perilously close to a federal takeover of state political

---

[201] One might question this account by pointing to *Alabama v Pugh*, 439 US 781 (1978) (per curiam). There the lower courts had approved injunctions against both the state and state officials, and the Supreme Court granted certiorari for the sole purpose of vacating the injunction against the state, reasoning that Alabama had an interest in not being vulnerable to a contempt citation. (In *Seminole*, the Court noted an additional interest in such a case—that of avoiding " 'the indignity of subjecting a State to the coercive process of judicial tribunals at the instance of private parties.' " 116 S Ct at 1124, quoting *Puerto Rico Aqueduct & Sewer Auth. v Metcalf & Eddy, Inc.*, 506 US 139, 146 (1993) (internal quotation marks omitted).) But on the Court's assumption that contempt sanctions were not contemplated under IGRA, the concern underlying *Pugh* was not present in *Seminole*. Moreover, it is one thing to relieve a state of an extant order that, though unnecessary, is deemed inappropriate; it is another to reach out to decide whether relief neither previously ordered nor necessary could constitutionally be provided.

[202] 505 US 144 (1992); see Brief for Respondents at 33–34, 1995 WL 271443.

[203] Emphasizing IGRA's severability clause (25 USC § 2721), the court of appeals concluded that "[o]ne hundred and eighty days after the tribe first requests negotiations with the state, the tribe may file suit in district court. If the state pleads an Eleventh Amendment defense, the suit is dismissed, and the tribe, pursuant to 25 U.S.C. § 2710(d)(7)(B)(vii), then may notify the Secretary of the Interior of the tribe's failure to negotiate a compact with the state. The Secretary then may prescribe regulations governing class III gaming on the tribe's lands." 11 F3d at 1029.

processes. I do not share that view;[204] indeed, to accept that view would raise broad questions about congressional power to employ alternative dispute resolution when federal law regulates state action. Though in the end the Court treated the question as not before it,[205] some Justices may have hesitated to impose on state officials an obligation that seemed at least unusual and perhaps even unconstitutional.[206]

But fears that the *Seminole* decision may signal the demise of *Ex parte Young* were fueled by the Court's action less than three weeks later granting the state of Idaho's petition for certiorari in *Coeur d'Alene Tribe of Idaho v State of Idaho.*[207] There the tribe sued state officials about property rights within the tribe's reservation; the tribe's claim is based in part on a federal executive order, later

---

[204] My view does not depend on uncertainty whether *New York* was correctly decided or whether it extends to commandeering state executive rather than legislative officials, see Saikrishna B. Prakash, *Field Office Federalism*, 79 Va L Rev 1957 (1993) (arguing against that extension). (On the latter point, the Brief for the National Governors Association et al as Amici Curiae at 20 n 11 stated that "[e]xcept for Kansas, we are aware of no evidence casting doubt on the complete authority of the Governor in each State, not only to negotiate, but to enter into compacts under IGRA." But see *New Mexico v Johnson*, 120 NM 562, 904 P2d 11 (1995) (holding that the Governor lacks authority to enter into compacts with Indian tribes under IGRA).) To be sure, the Act may put Governors in a difficult political bind, requiring them to bargain in the shadow of whatever regulations the Secretary could be expected, absent agreement, to impose, and to take the heat for either (i) agreeing to a compact authorizing gambling or (ii) failing to forestall federal intervention and authorization. But *New York* precludes Congress from blurring the lines of accountability, not from making state officials accountable for difficult choices. See Richard E. Levy, *New York v. United States: An Essay on the Uses and Misuses of Precedent, History, and Policy in Determining the Scope of Federal Power*, 41 Kan L Rev 493, 525 (1993).

Nor does IGRA turn states into arms of the federal government. The Act requires only negotiation; agreement cannot be compelled, and no federal substantive policy must be enforced. This is little different from the federal statutory directive upheld in *FERC v Mississippi*, 456 US 742, 765 (1982), requiring that state regulatory agencies consider (but need not adopt) federally specified regulatory standards. Though the provision in *FERC* merely invited states to adopt federal standards, while IGRA requires negotiation in good faith, surely it is noteworthy that violation of IGRA's obligation was not, in the Court's view, enforceable by contempt, and hence may not have been genuinely enforceable at all.

Thus, if the Court was seized of an anticommandeering itch, I believe it should have waited for it to pass. And in any event, in holding that the statute foreclosed suit against officers (or, for that matter, that Congress lacks power under Article I to subject a state to federal court suit), the Court was scratching in the wrong place.

[205] See 116 S Ct at 1126 n 10.

[206] It is also possible that a number of Justices, though not prepared to overrule *Thiboutot*, are hardly enthusiastic partisans—as the recent, closely divided decisions in *Suter v Artist M*, 503 US 347 (1992) and *Wilder v Virginia Hosp. Assn*, 496 US 498 (1990), reveal—and thus are receptive to arguments in particular cases about statutory foreclosure.

[207] 42 F3d 1244 (9th Cir 1994), cert granted, 116 S Ct 1415 (1996).

ratified by Congress, and in part on unextinguished aboriginal title (which the Supreme Court has viewed as based on federal law[208]). The Ninth Circuit ruled that sovereign immunity barred a quiet title remedy but not an injunction against the officials' interference with the tribe's possession; the state's petition for certiorari challenges the latter holding.

Here, too, I do not read the Court's action as evidence that *Ex parte Young* is on its deathbed. The suit presents difficult questions along existing doctrinal axes in suits against officers. A state-created right of action challenging officials' continuing possession of disputed land would be barred by the holding of *Pennhurst State School & Hospital v Halderman*[209] that sovereign immunity precludes federal courts from awarding specific relief against state officials for a violation of state law.[210] The Court might be reluctant to permit the tribe to escape that rule because its state law action incorporates a claim to title based upon *federal* law. There is, moreover, the further question whether, even were the suit viewed as sufficiently "federal," the relief sought—which requires adjudication of the state's property rights and may effectively eliminate the state's capacity to continue in possession—falls on the prohibited side of the line between prospective and retrospective relief.[211] The Court could easily rule for the state without casting doubt on *Young*. Thus, although one cannot possess great confidence about prophecies in this volatile corner of constitutional interpretation, I see no strong basis to fear *Young*'s demise.[212]

---

[208] See *Oneida Indian Nation v County of Oneida*, 414 US 661 (1974).

[209] 465 US 89 (1984).

[210] Except, possibly, in the unusual case in which the official acts entirely outside the scope of any delegated authority. See id at 114 n 25.

[211] Compare *Florida Dept of State v Treasure Salvors, Inc.*, 458 US 670 (1982), where four Justices held that a federal court exercising in rem admiralty jurisdiction may arrest objects possessed by state officials who lack a colorable claim that they belong to the state. The plurality did not decide whether the court could proceed to determine title to the property, while four dissenting Justices objected that a suit against officials who (in the dissenters' view) did have a colorable claim of right was effectively one against the state and was therefore barred.

[212] The early decisions following *Seminole* have continued to entertain suits for prospective relief against state officials. See, for example, *Thiel v State Bar of Wisconsin*, 94 F3d 399 (7th Cir 1996); *NRDC v California Dep't of Transp.*, 96 F3d 420 (9th Cir 1996); *Death Row Prisoners of Pennsylvania v Ridge*, 1996 US Dist LEXIS 15540 (ED Pa).

V. The Impact of Seminole: Congress and the Enforcement of Federal Law

A. THE NEED FOR RETROSPECTIVE STATE GOVERNMENT LIABILITY

The majority and dissent divided over not only the nature of sovereign immunity but also the significance of the *Seminole* decision itself. Justice Stevens proclaimed that "[t]he importance of the majority's decision to overrule [*Union Gas*] cannot be overstated," because it "prevents Congress from providing a federal forum for a broad range of actions against States,"[213] while Justice Souter asked, rhetorically, whether it was plausible that the Constitution left the national government "without any way to render individuals capable of enforcing their federal rights directly against an intransigent state."[214] The Court's response stressed the mechanisms that remain to enforce federal law against the states: suit by the United States, private suit for prospective relief under *Ex parte Young*, and Supreme Court review of state court decisions.[215]

There is something to the majority's observation that "the Nation survived for nearly two centuries without the question of the existence of [power to abrogate] ever being presented to this Court."[216] Still, experience for much of that time, when both federal regulatory power and state governmental activity were far more constricted, may not be highly pertinent to today's problems. Indeed, Congress has seen fit in recent years to enact a number of statutory provisions seeking to subject the states to federal court suit, for retrospective as well as prospective relief, under a range of federal programs. These include the copyright,[217] trademark,[218] and patent laws;[219] the Individuals with Disabilities Education Act;[220] the Fair Labor Standards Act;[221] the bankruptcy laws;[222] the Vet-

---

[213] 116 S Ct at 1134 (Stevens dissenting).

[214] Id at 1173 (Souter dissenting).

[215] Id at 1131 n 14 (majority opinion).

[216] Id at 1131.

[217] 17 USC §§ 501(a), 511 (added by Pub L No 101-553 (Nov 15, 1990)).

[218] 15 USC § 1122 (added by Pub L No 102-542, § 3(b) (Oct 27, 1992)).

[219] 35 USC § 296 (added by Pub L No 102-560, § 2(a)(2) (Oct 28, 1992)).

[220] 20 USC § 1403 (added by Pub L No 101-476, Title I, § 103 (Oct 30, 1990)).

[221] 29 USC §§ 203, 216 (added by §§ 6(a)(1), 6(d)(1) of the Fair Labor Standards Amendments of 1974, Pub L No 93-259 (April 8, 1974)).

[222] See note 149.

eran's Reemployment Rights Act;[223] and provisions barring discrimination on the basis of race, sex, age, and disability.[224] The
reasons that Congress might view retrospective relief against state
governments as important are straightforward—to compensate individuals for harm suffered and to reduce the likelihood of
noncompliance.[225]

Those purposes can be pursued, without encountering any sovereign immunity barrier, by awarding retrospective relief (ordinarily damages) against individual state officials personally. That
approach might prove feasible in certain contexts—for example,
some suits for copyright infringement. But over the broad range
of cases, this approach suffers obvious defects. The responsible officials may be hard to identify, have left the jurisdiction, or be
judgment-proof. When the scope of substantive duties is uncertain,
personal liability may impair effective government decision making
and unfairly penalize individuals;[226] alleviating these concerns by
conferring official immunity correspondingly impairs achievement
of the posited congressional purposes. And in some cases, imposition of personal liability would require changing long-standing legal conceptions; for example, a bankrupt estate could not recover
damages, caused by breach of a state contract, from responsible
state officials without a basic shift in agency principles.

There is precedent in American law, especially in the nineteenth
century, for a rather harsh regime of personal official liability,
which may have the salutary effect of pressuring states to waive
sovereign immunity or indemnify officials in order to alleviate
hardship.[227] But in today's world of high litigation costs, massively
complex federal requirements, and erratic but sometimes punishing jury verdicts, such an approach seems neither very practical,
politically feasible, nor likely to contribute to harmonious
federalism.

---

[223] 38 USC §§ 4301, 4303(4) (added by Pub L No 93-508 (Dec 3, 1974)).

[224] See notes 149–50.

[225] See, for example, *Edelman v Jordan*, 415 US 651, 692 (1974) (Marshall dissenting);
Fallon and Meltzer, 104 Harv L Rev at 1787–97 (cited in note 179).

[226] See generally Peter H. Schuck, *Suing Government* (Yale University Press, 1983).

[227] See Fallon and Meltzer, 104 Harv L Rev at 1822–24 and sources cited (cited in note
179).

B. CONGRESSIONAL OPTIONS AFTER SEMINOLE

How might Congress, should it wish to impose state governmental liability under a federal regulatory program,[228] do so consistently with *Seminole?*[229] A statutory drafter confronting that question has a number of options, each of which raises difficult constitutional questions.

1. *Reliance on Section 5 of the Fourteenth Amendment.* One option is to try to justify a measure as an exercise of legislative power under Section 5 of the Fourteenth Amendment, thereby permitting outright abrogation under the *Fitzpatrick* decision. The feasibility of that strategy plainly varies statute by statute: it would be hard to execute as to the Fair Labor Standards Act,[230] but looks far more promising as to Title VII's prohibition of employment practices that have a disparate impact, even absent the proof of intentional discrimination necessary to establish a violation of the Equal Protection Clause.[231] But there will be many hard cases, of which I will suggest just two for purposes of illustration: (1) Are

---

[228] Following the *Seminole* decision, the Court vacated lower court decisions that had upheld federal court jurisdiction against unconsenting states under the copyright and bankruptcy laws. *Ohio Agric Commodity Depositors Fund v Mahern,* 116 S Ct 1411 (1996) (bankruptcy), vacating *In re Merchants Grain,* 59 F3d 630 (7th Cir 1995); *University of Houston v Chavez,* 116 S Ct 1667 (1996) (copyright), vacating *Chavez v Arte Publico Press,* 59 F3d 539 (5th Cir 1995).

[229] IGRA itself, which never sought to impose retrospective liability on the states, could be fixed relatively easily (bracketing possible Tenth Amendment objections) by an express legislative authorization of suit against state officials.

[230] Vicki Jackson suggested to me that one could view the Act as giving employees a property interest (in premium pay for overtime), whose deprivation by a state employer denies due process. Though the logic is clear, most any statutory right of action could be similarly characterized: the Union Gas Company could claim a property interest in recovering damages from a state under federal environmental laws; the Seminole Tribe could claim a liberty interest in negotiating with the state. I doubt the Supreme Court would accept an argument that would so sharply limit the effective scope of *Seminole,* see note 233, and the argument was rejected in one post-*Seminole* decision, see *Chauvin v Louisiana,* 937 F Supp 567 (ED La 1996), while a second, though not addressing this particular argument, ruled that the FLSA could not be upheld as an exercise of congressional power under § 5, see *Wilson-Jones v Caviness,* 99 F3d 203 (6th Cir 1996); see also *Close v New York,* 1996 US Dist LEXIS 12330 (NDNY) (dismissing suit without even considering whether the FLSA was an exercise of congressional power under § 5).

[231] For an affirmation of a similar exercise of power under § 2 of the Fifteenth Amendment, see *City of Rome v United States,* 446 US 156 (1980), upholding a preclearance requirement for electoral changes that have a discriminatory effect—even on the assumption that the Amendment itself prohibits only purposeful discrimination. The decision relied heavily on a demonstrated history of intentional discrimination, which the Title VII example would thus require to be on all fours.

prohibitions against discrimination on the basis of age or disability a valid exercise of power to prevent invidious discrimination prohibited by the Equal Protection Clause? (Is it tenable to suggest that general practices satisfying the "rational basis test" under Section 1 of the Fourteenth Amendment can be prohibited by Congress under Section 5—either because those practices, in particular cases, may be irrational,[232] or because Congress may authorize use of a different standard to evaluate their legality?) (2) Can patent or copyright infringement actions be justified as efforts to prevent the taking (or deprivation) of property without just compensation (or due process)?[233] However one might decide these or other cases, *Seminole* brings to the fore difficult and unsettled questions (with which courts already have been grappling[234]) about the scope of Section 5.

2. *Conditional spending power.* A second technique involves con-

---

[232] In *EEOC v Wyoming*, 460 US 226 (1983), the Court upheld application of the Age Discrimination Act to the states under the commerce power, without reaching the question whether § 5 also provided a valid source of authority. But Chief Justice Burger's dissent (joined by Justices Powell, Rehnquist, and O'Connor) did address that question and gave a negative answer. He argued that age was not a suspect classification, and that the decisions in *Massachusetts Bd of Retirement v Murgia*, 427 US 307 (1976), and *Vance v Bradley*, 440 US 93 (1979), had upheld mandatory retirement statutes as rational. See also *MacPherson v University of Montevallo*, 938 F Supp 785 (ND Ala 1996), a post-*Seminole* decision that followed Chief Justice Burger in ruling that the Age Discrimination in Employment Act was not an exercise of congressional power under § 5, and hence dismissed a suit under the Act against a state entity.

As to disability, compare *City of Cleburne v Cleburne Living Center*, 473 US 432 (1985), holding a zoning ordinance requiring a special permit for a proposed group home for the mentally retarded to be invalid under the Fourteenth Amendment. *Cleburne* was a particularly aggressive application of the minimum rationality test, see id at 458–60 (Marshall concurring in the judgment in part and dissenting in part), and one from which at least some Justices complain that the Court has retreated, see *Heller v Doe*, 509 US 312, 337 (1993) (Souter dissenting); but compare *Romer v Evans*, 116 S Ct 1620 (1996) (robustly applying rational basis scrutiny to invalidate a state constitutional provision purporting to preclude laws or policies prohibiting discrimination on the basis of sexual orientation). Moreover, in many contexts to which the Americans with Disabilities Act applies—for example, employment—differential treatment based on disability may seem less irrational than the ordinance at issue in *Cleburne*. But in *Mayer v University of Minnesota*, 940 F Supp 1474 (D Minn 1996), the court upheld its jurisdiction over a suit against a state entity under the ADA and the Vocational Rehabilitation Act, viewing those Acts as valid exercises of power under § 5 to combat arbitrary discrimination.

[233] See *College Savings Bank v Florida Prepaid Postsecondary Educ. Expense Bd.*, 1996 WL 728173 (DNJ) (holding abrogation of immunity valid as to a claim for infringement of a patent, which the court viewed as property, but invalid as to a false advertising claim under the Lanham Act, finding the latter claim to be merely a right of action and arguing that if Congress could treat such a right of action as property, it could effectively circumvent *Seminole*). See generally Jack M. Beermann, *Government Official Torts and the Takings Clause: Federalism and State Sovereign Immunity*, 68 BU L Rev 277, 301–29 (1988).

[234] See, for example, notes 230, 232–33.

gressional use of the spending power to condition a state's receipt of federal funds upon its waiver of sovereign immunity. Suppose that congressional legislation provides unambiguously that state universities accepting federal funds for student financial assistance, or for research grants, will be deemed to have waived sovereign immunity with respect to claims that they discriminate on the basis of age or disability, or that they have engaged in copyright infringement.[235] A state might object that such a statute creates an unconstitutional condition, by making the availability of funds depend upon waiver of the state's "constitutional right" to immunity in the federal courts.[236] There is, however, no single unconstitutional conditions doctrine: sometimes conditions on the enjoyment of constitutional rights are tolerated and sometimes not, and no simple formula tells us which is which.[237]

The closest precedent is *South Dakota v Dole*,[238] where Chief Justice Rehnquist's opinion for the Court upheld a statutory provision that withheld a fraction of highway construction funds from states whose drinking age was lower than twenty-one. Positing that the Twenty-First Amendment would prohibit direct congressional regulation of the drinking age, the state argued that Congress could not circumvent that prohibition through use of the conditional spending power. The Court accepted arguendo the state's premise but rejected its conclusion, viewing prior decisions as holding that "a perceived Tenth Amendment limitation on congressional regulation of state affairs [does] not concomitantly limit the range of conditions legitimately placed on federal grants."[239]

Dole is a particularly broad precedent. For although the Court

---

[235] An analogous technique would have Congress amend IGRA to permit only those states that had expressly waived immunity from suit under that Act to regulate class III gaming. In *Seminole*, the Court rejected the tribe's argument that the statute could be upheld as if it had so provided, ruling that "[t]he Eleventh Amendment immunity may not be lifted by Congress *unilaterally* deciding that it will be replaced by grant of some other authority." 116 S Ct at 1125 (emphasis added).

[236] See Tribe, 89 Harv L Rev at 692 (cited in note 82).

[237] See generally Cass R. Sunstein, *Why the Unconstitutional Conditions Doctrine Is an Anachronism (With Particular Reference to Religion, Speech, and Abortion)*, 70 BU L Rev 593 (1990); Kathleen M. Sullivan, *Unconstitutional Conditions*, 102 Harv L Rev 1413 (1989); Richard A. Epstein, *The Supreme Court, 1987 Term—Foreword: Unconstitutional Conditions, State Power, and the Limits of Consent*, 102 Harv L Rev 1 (1988); Albert J. Rosenthal, *Conditional Federal Spending and the Constitution*, 39 Stan L Rev 1103, 1121 (1987).

[238] 483 US 203 (1987).

[239] Id at 210.

spoke of a Tenth Amendment limitation, in fact the Twenty-First Amendment is, on the state's premise, a more potent restriction of federal power, since it limits congressional action that would otherwise fall within, for example, the commerce power. In this respect, the Twenty-First Amendment resembles the Eleventh Amendment as interpreted in *Seminole*. Thus, *Dole*'s conclusion that the conditional spending power can be exercised within such enclaves of state authority strongly supports the validity of the hypothetical statute.[240]

A different precedent supports the view that Congress may condition the availability of a federal "gratuity" on the state's relinquishment of sovereign immunity. *Petty v Tennessee-Missouri Commission*[241] involved a federal court suit against a bi-state commission approved by Congress as an interstate compact. The commission was governed by a statutory proviso that, in the Court's view, made it "clear that the States accepting it waived any immunity from suit which they otherwise might have,"[242] and the Court accordingly ruled that the states had thereby consented to suit. Justice Frankfurter's dissent read the proviso differently, but agreed with the Court's premise that "Congress could have insisted upon a provision waiving immunity from suit in the federal courts as the price of obtaining its consent to the Compact."[243]

---

[240] An interesting feature of the Court's federalism jurisprudence is that Chief Justice Rehnquist authored both *Seminole* and *National League of Cities v Usery*, 426 US 833 (1976), on the one hand, and *Dole* on the other. For him, at least, the notion that the state, in a conditional spending case, is "waiving" any constitutional objection by accepting funds appears to carry great force. See *Dole*, 483 US at 210 (stressing that the state could adopt the "simple expedient" of not yielding to the alleged federal coercion). More generally, the Chief Justice has often been attracted to arguments that the greater power includes the lesser—a standard riposte to a claim of unconstitutional conditions. See Lynn A. Baker, *Conditional Federal Spending After Lopez*, 95 Colum L Rev 1911, 1915 n 13 (1995). See also *New York v United States*, 505 US 144, 167–69 (1992), where the Court, while holding unconstitutional a federal statute that "commandeers" a state's regulatory power, distinguished as ordinarily permissible federal spending conditioned on the state's exercising regulatory power. Thus, the conditional spending cases may feature an alliance of "liberals" who favor broad federal power and "conservatives" who favor the greater includes the lesser argument. (That only Justice Brennan agreed with Justice O'Connor's dissent in *Dole* might be explicable in similar fashion: though generally a supporter of broad national power, he may have been wary of validating any greater includes the lesser argument.)

[241] 359 US 275 (1959).

[242] Id at 280.

[243] Id at 285 (Frankfurter dissenting). See also *Edelman v Jordan*, 415 US at 672 (describing *Petty* as a case where consent turned on whether Congress intended to abrogate immunity and on whether the state had consented to that abrogation).

By contrast, in *New York v United States*, 505 US 144, 182 (1992), the Court rejected

To be sure, commentators express considerable unease about the conditional spending cases.[244] Citizens cannot escape the federal government's taxing powers, and the state's choice under federal conditional spending programs—either accepting funds and the attached strings, or getting nothing in return for the applicable tax contributions from its citizens—may seem to be no choice at all.[245] Arguments have also been made that the power to spend for the general welfare is particularly insidious because the desire for federal funds may blunt state and local governments' objections to conditions on the funds—objections they would voice more forcefully if Congress sought to impose the conditions directly.[246] It may be unwise to view the Court—notwithstanding its dismissive reference in *Seminole* to theories "cobbled together from law review articles"[247]—as unreceptive to these commentators' concerns.

Moreover, even the *Dole* opinion purported to recognize some limits on the spending power. The first two—that the exercise of spending power must promote the general welfare, and the conditions must be clearly stated—can be satisfied relatively easily. But

---

the argument that an otherwise unconstitutional federal statute, directing state regulation, could be validated by the consent of state officials. Viewing the aspect of state sovereignty it was protecting as an implicit limitation on the reach of the commerce power, the Court ruled that congressional action exceeding its authority cannot be validated by state consent. One could imagine the following parallel argument: state sovereign immunity implicitly limits the exercise of Congress's Article I powers, and state officials cannot ratify federal statutes exceeding that limit. Justice White's dissent in *New York*, citing the *Petty* decision, accused the Court of making unjustified distinctions about which aspects of sovereignty could be waived. Id at 200 (White dissenting). Whoever had the better of the argument, not only *Petty* but the entire history of sovereign immunity as a protection only of *unconsenting* states counsels strongly against extending this aspect of *New York* to the Eleventh Amendment context.

[244] See, for example, Baker, 95 Colum L Rev 1911 (cited in note 240); Thomas R. McCoy and Barry Friedman, *Conditional Spending: Federalism's Trojan Horse*, 1988 Supreme Court Review 85; Rosenthal, 39 Stan L Rev 1103 (cited in note 237); Lewis B. Kaden, *Politics, Money, and State Sovereignty: The Judicial Role*, 79 Colum L Rev 847, 871–83, 983–97 (1979); Richard B. Stewart, *Federalism and Rights*, 19 Ga L Rev 917, 951–59 (1985).

[245] Baker, 95 Colum L Rev at 1935–39 (cited in note 240); McCoy and Friedman, 1988 Supreme Court Review at 124 (cited in note 244).

[246] Rosenthal, 39 Stan L Rev at 1141 (cited in note 237); McCoy and Friedman, 1988 Supreme Court Review at 123–25 (cited in note 244). See also Baker, 95 Colum L Rev at 1939–47 (cited in note 240) (offering additional, not entirely convincing, arguments why the political safeguards of federalism are especially subject to failure in this context). But see Jesse H. Choper, *Federalism and Judicial Review: An Update*, 21 Hastings Const L Q 577, 580 n 27 (questioning the argument); Deborah Jones Merritt, *Three Faces of Federalism: Finding a Formula for the Future*, 47 Vand L Rev 1563, 1577 (1994) (elaborating an "autonomy" model of federalism drawn from *New York v United States*, and stating that it imposes no special constraints on the Spending Power).

[247] 116 S Ct at 1129–30; see p 25.

the Court added in dictum that "our cases have suggested (without significant elaboration) that conditions on federal grants might be illegitimate if they are unrelated 'to the federal interest in particular national projects or programs.' "[248] The majority, in finding the drinking age requirement sufficiently related to the purpose of safe interstate travel, did not scrutinize the relationship strictly[249]—as Justice O'Connor's dissent demonstrated. Yet the idea that spending conditions must be germane, though it presents impressive practical and theoretical difficulties,[250] is still floating about,[251] and may at some point limit aggressive use of the spending power. (May a statute condition provision of tuition grants to graduate students in mathematics on the mathematics department's waiver of immunity from suit under the copyright, patent, and minimum wage laws? On a similar waiver by the entire university? By every other agency or department in the state as to all federal statutes?)[252]

---

[248] 483 US at 207–08 (quoting *Massachusetts v United States*, 435 US 444, 461 (1978) (plurality opinion)).

[249] The *Dole* Court, though warning that some financial inducements might "pass the point at which 'pressure turns into compulsion,' " 483 US at 211 (quoting *Steward Machine Co. v Davis*, 301 US 548, 590 (1937)), concluded that the condition was not unconstitutional simply because Congress had succeeded in inducing states to accept the funds. 483 US at 211. The Court added that the state would sacrifice only 5% of its funds by not complying—without explaining why losing 5% of a $100 million grant imposed less pressure than losing 100% of a $5 million grant. See also *New York v United States*, 505 US 144, 166–67 (1992) (distinguishing conditional spending generally from "outright coercion"); *South Carolina v Baker*, 485 US 505, 511 n 6 (1988) (in a passing reference to *Dole*, mentioning the coercion limitation). For exploration of the analytical problems posed by the idea of coercion, see generally Sullivan, 102 Harv L Rev at 1428–56 (cited in note 237).

[250] See generally Sullivan, 102 Harv L Rev at 1456–76 (cited in note 237); McCoy and Friedman, 1988 Supreme Court Review at 120–23 (cited in note 244); David E. Engdahl, *The Spending Power*, 44 Duke L J 1, 56–62 (1994). Also problematic is a distinction, proposed by some commentators, between those conditions specifying the purpose for which funds will be spent (which are valid) and those seeking to purchase compliance with a regulatory objective (which are invalid insofar as they regulate the states in a fashion that Congress could not undertake directly). See McCoy and Friedman at 103; Baker, 95 Colum L Rev at 1954 (cited in note 240). Does a federal requirement that grants to a state university for biological research not be used to subsidize action infringing valid patents specify how funds shall be spent or purchase a regulatory objective? Can the grants also be conditioned on the university's not infringing the copyright laws in its preparation of course materials for students—on the theory (well known to university fundraisers) that money raised for one activity (biological research), by freeing up funds in the general budget, may indirectly support other activities (operation of the copy center)? Compare *Grove City College v Bell*, 465 US 555 (1984) (holding that only the particular college program that benefited from federal funds was required to comply with federal conditions prohibiting discrimination), overridden by the Civil Rights Restoration Act of 1987, Pub L No 100-259.

[251] See *New York v United States*, 505 US 144, 167 (1992). Compare *Nollan v California Coastal Comm'n*, 483 US 825, 837 (1987).

[252] See note 250.

Finally, quite apart from any constitutional or political barriers to its use, the conditional spending power is not a cure-all for the practical concerns voiced by the *Seminole* dissenters. For some of the recent statutory provisions purporting to abrogate sovereign immunity—for example, in bankruptcy proceedings[253]—are not now, and could not easily be, associated with federal spending programs.

3. *Suit by the United States.* A third option for Congress is to empower the federal government—whose lawsuits against the states are not limited by sovereign immunity—to enforce federal law. A first, seemingly unobjectionable, step would be to authorize the Attorney General to bring federal court suit in the name of the United States against state governments engaging, for example, in copyright infringement, and to specify that one authorized remedy is a fine equal to the damage suffered by the copyright holder.[254] Although such a provision would help promote compliance, it would afford no compensation to the copyright holder, and would shift enforcement from private to public hands.

But an ingenious argument by Jonathan Siegel responds to these objections.[255] As a second step, he suggests that Congress provide that any fine collected by the United States be paid to the injured party. That approach is found in the Fair Labor Standards Act, which authorizes the Secretary of Labor to bring suit for unpaid minimum wages or overtime compensation on behalf of employees, and provides that any recoveries be held in a separate account to be paid to the employees in question.[256] In *Employees of the Department of Public Health & Welfare v Department of Public Health & Welfare*,[257] the Court, while refusing to permit private enforcement of the FLSA against a state agency, referred explicitly to the Secretary's authority as falling within the rule that states have no immunity in suits by the United States.[258]

---

[253] See note 149.

[254] See *United States v California*, 297 US 175, 188 (1936) (suit for penalties for violation of Federal Safety Appliance Act); *EEOC v Wyoming*, 460 US 226 (1983) (suit for damages on behalf of victims of age discrimination).

[255] Jonathan R. Siegel, *The Hidden Source of Congress's Power to Abrogate State Sovereign Immunity*, 73 Tex L Rev 539 (1995).

[256] 29 USC §§ 216(c), 217.

[257] 411 US 279, 285–86 (1973).

[258] Compare *United States v Minnesota*, 270 US 181, 193–95 (1926) (permitting the United States, as guardian of the interests of Indians, to sue the state on their behalf, and rejecting

The third step is for the statute to authorize a private lawyer (with the consent of the injured party) to bring suit in the name of the United States—not unlike a qui tam action. Voilà—federal court suits against a state for retrospective relief, paid ultimately to the injured private litigant, who has power to institute the suit (albeit nominally on behalf of the United States). Siegel's coup de grace—step four—is to contend that, having come that far, one might as well permit private suits without the fiction that they are on behalf of the United States. (Variations on Siegel's theme could address particular concerns: for example, Congress could give the United States some control over the litigation, as it has in qui tam actions under the False Claims Act;[259] or Congress could require the state to pay 110% of the damages suffered, with the extra 10% going into the federal treasury to defeat objections that the United States is not the real party in interest.)[260]

If there is no obvious place to stop between Siegel's starting point (that the United States can sue the states in federal court) and his conclusion (that private parties can do likewise when authorized by Congress), then his argument is another way to highlight the difficulties of the prevailing interpretation of the Eleventh Amendment. Of course, five Justices might well find a stopping point, though just where it would be or how it would be justified is far from clear.[261] Still, Siegel's approach may prove useful at least in some settings. For example, suppose the United States were appointed trustee or co-trustee in bankruptcy (with a trustee's normal power to employ agents) whenever there are claims against a

---

the argument that suit was barred because the United States was not the real party in interest).

[259] See Siegel, 73 Tex L Rev at 561 n 125, 569 n 147 (cited in note 255).

[260] Compare *New Hampshire v Louisiana*, 108 US 76 (1883), where the plaintiff states sued on defaulted bonds, as assignees for collection only, on behalf of certain of their citizens. The Court held the suits barred by sovereign immunity, finding that the bondholders controlled the litigation, paid its expenses, and would receive the proceeds, while the state was acting merely as a collecting agent. But some of the reasoning—that there cannot be both a direct remedy for a private party and an indirect one brought by the state—seems overbroad and hard to square with much contemporary enforcement activity.

[261] In *Blatchford v Native Village of Noatak*, 501 US 775, 785–86 (1991), the Indian plaintiffs argued that 28 USC § 1362, which confers federal jurisdiction over suits arising under federal law brought by recognized Indian tribes or bands, constitutes a delegation of the United States's exemption from state sovereign immunity. The Court expressed doubt that that exemption can be delegated, even to persons on whose behalf the United States itself might sue, but rested on the ground that § 1362 did not so delegate.

state. Since trustees by their nature act on behalf of beneficiaries,[262] there would be no need to provide specially that proceeds collected by the United States be paid to the bankrupt estate. And established practice permits the United States Trustee to participate in bankruptcy proceedings from which it does not stand to gain anything.[263] Thus, perhaps authorizing suit by the United States would alleviate the serious problems otherwise posed by *Seminole* for the administration of bankruptcy.[264]

4. *Suit in state court.* A last possibility is for Congress to rely upon the state courts to require state governments to provide retrospective relief authorized by federal law. (In some instances, existing grants of exclusive federal jurisdiction would have to be made concurrent.)[265] For the Eleventh Amendment by its terms regulates only *federal* judicial power, and this is one textual limitation that the Supreme Court has observed.[266]

Suppose that a state, when sued in its own courts, sought to invoke a state law defense of sovereign immunity. There is an easy syllogism to offer in response: federal law trumps state law under the Supremacy Clause; thus, so long as Congress clearly indicates that state courts must entertain a federal cause of action, any contrary rule of state law is invalid. Many recent congressional enactments seeking to extend federal power over the states have had two parts: one purporting to abrogate the states' immunity from federal court suit, and a second providing that a state is substantively liable like any other defendant.[267] *Seminole* casts doubt on only the first of those provisions.

No decision, however, holds unambiguously that the states may

---

[262] See 11 USC § 323 (granting the trustee the power to sue and be sued as the "representative of the estate").

[263] See 28 USC §§ 581, 586,

[264] For discussion of those problems, see *Special Report—Seminole: What It Means/Possible Defenses*, 29 Bankruptcy Ct Decisions # 8 (Aug 13, 1996). Siegel suggests that his approach may be inapt in bankruptcy, as ordinarily the bankrupt estate's claim against a state does not rest on federal law. See 73 Tex L Rev at 569 n 146 (cited in note 255). But since the bankruptcy power authorizes federal legislation governing the administration of state law claims in bankruptcy, I don't see any distinctive constitutional difficulties in this area.

[265] See, for example, 28 USC § 1333 (suits in admiralty), § 1334 (bankruptcy), § 1338 (patent, copyright, and plant variety cases).

[266] See, for example, *Reich v Collins*, 115 S Ct 547, 549 (1994); *Hilton v South Carolina Pub. Rys Comm'n*, 502 US 197, 204–05 (1991); *Nevada v Hall*, 440 US 410, 420 (1979).

[267] See, for example, statutes cited in notes 150, 220.

not invoke sovereign immunity to resist enforcement of federal law in their own courts. To be sure, a number of decisions voice a broad supremacy argument.[268] But some were suits against private parties or local governments rather than the state itself, or rested on state court discrimination against federal rights of action;[269] others, involving only prospective injunctive relief against officers, may not clearly implicate sovereign immunity.[270]

The strongest support for a state court obligation is found in a recent ruling that a state court's refusal to provide a refund remedy for taxes exacted under an unconstitutional statute violates the Fourteenth Amendment, "the sovereign immunity States traditionally enjoy in their own courts notwithstanding."[271] But the reference to sovereign immunity was dictum, as the state court's refusal rested on a different ground.[272] Moreover, the taxpayer's claim was constitutionally based; if a state's claim of immunity in its courts is similarly viewed as constitutional (or as quasi-constitutional), then perhaps, under an implicit form of balancing, it matters whether the federal law being enforced is of constitutional status.

I have always thought that the better argument favors upholding the state courts' obligation.[273] *Seminole* does not address this question directly, but the opinion, in discussing constitutional means of ensuring the states' compliance with federal law, stated that "this Court is empowered to review a question of federal law arising from a state court decision *where a State has consented to suit.*"[274]

---

[268] See, for example, *Mondou v New York, NH & H RR*, 223 US 1, 57–58 (1912); *Howlett v Rose*, 496 US 356, 367–75 (1990); *Testa v Katt*, 330 US 386, 393 (1947).

[269] See, for example, the decisions cited in the preceding footnote.

[270] See *General Oil v Crain*, 209 US 211 (1908).

[271] *Reich v Collins*, 115 S Ct 547, 549 (1994). See also *Atascadero State Hosp. v Scanlon*, 473 US 234, 239–40 n 2 (1985) (dictum); *Employees of the Department of Public Health & Welfare v Department of Public Health & Welfare*, 411 US 279, 297–98 (1973) (Marshall concurring in the result).

[272] See *Reich v Collins*, 437 SE2d 320 (Ga 1993), rev'd, 115 S Ct 547 (1994).

[273] See, for example, Louis E. Wolcher, *Sovereign Immunity and the Supremacy Clause: Damages Against States in Their Own Courts for Constitutional Violations*, 69 Cal L Rev 189 (1981); Nicole A. Gordon and Douglas Gross, *Justiciability of Federal Claims in State Court*, 59 Notre Dame L Rev 1145, 1171–77 (1984); Jackson, 98 Yale L J at 38 nn 157–58, 74 n 304, 99 & n 394 (cited in note 45).

[274] 116 S Ct at 1131 n 14 (emphasis added, citation omitted). Note that one argument in *Hans* itself for immunity from federal court suit was that federal and state jurisdiction were concurrent, and "[t]he state courts have no power to entertain suits by individuals against a state without its consent." 134 US at 18.

That qualification, mentioned only in passing, hardly squares with cases in which, for example, a tax refund was required of a recalcitrant state. If it were to take hold, it would constitute an important restriction on not only federal judicial but also federal legislative power—for then (absent state consent) substantive regulation passed by Congress could not be fully enforced in *any* court.[275]

An opponent of any state court obligation might contend that Congress lacks power to commandeer the state courts to award retroactive relief against unconsenting states. That phrasing is designed, of course, to echo *New York v United States*,[276] where the Court ruled that Congress could not require state officials to enact and enforce, as state law, regulations specified by federal law. The *New York* Court expressly distinguished cases upholding the state *courts'* obligation to enforce federal law on the ground that that obligation is specifically set forth in the Supremacy Clause.[277] Whether or not that distinction can be justified under that Clause[278] or on some other basis,[279] the anticommandeering principle might be seized upon to raise doubts about Congress's consti-

---

[275] See *Hilton v South Carolina Pub. Rys Comm'n*, 502 US 197, 203–04 (1991). Compare *General Oil v Crain*, 209 US at 211 ("If a suit against state officers is precluded in the national courts by the Eleventh Amendment to the Constitution, and may be forbidden by a state to its courts, . . . without power of review by this court, . . . an easy way is open to prevent the enforcement of many provisions of the Constitution . . . .").

[276] 505 US 144 (1992).

[277] Id at 177–79.

[278] See David L. Shapiro, *Federalism: A Dialogue* 112–13 n 18 (Northwestern University Press, 1995). The Clause reads: "This Constitution, and the Laws of the United States which shall be made in Pursuance thereof; and all Treaties made, or which shall be made, under the Authority of the United States, shall be the supreme Law of the Land; and the Judges in every State shall be bound thereby, any Thing in the Constitution or Laws of any State to the Contrary notwithstanding." The specific direction that state judges are bound by federal law in their action is compatible with, but need not entail, a federal obligation to take jurisdiction of particular cases. Moreover, the Clause's opening phrase could be viewed as addressed to all state officials (judges included), with the language after the semicolon primarily for emphasis. In any event, the question is not whether the Clause addresses state judicial, executive, or legislative officials (it does) but rather just what does it require.

[279] See Prakash, 79 Va L Rev 1957 (cited in note 204) (arguing that the original understanding contemplated federal power to avail itself of state magistracies—i.e., state judges and executive officials—to enforce federal law); H. Jefferson Powell, *The Oldest Question of Constitutional Law*, 79 Va L Rev 633, 687–88 (1993) (making prudential argument based on revitalization of participatory politics). Of course, in *FERC v Mississippi*, 456 US 742 (1982), the Court relied on, and extended, the obligation of state *judges* to enforce federal law in upholding a federal requirement that state *regulatory officials* adjudicate certain disputes.

tutional power to require the states courts to enforce federal law against the states.[280]

Even if such power exists, the resulting system of enforcement would be at once imperfect and peculiar. To permit resort to state but not federal court in order to recover against a state would impair specific federal policies in some areas—for example, the pursuit of uniform and expert patent adjudication by excluding state jurisdiction and centralizing federal appeals in a single circuit,[281] or the prompt resolution of bankruptcy matters in a single, unified proceeding. Beyond such concerns lies a broader oddity. Sovereign immunity is ordinarily a substantive defense, not a forum choice provision; the United States, for example, is immune in state and federal courts alike. States hardly enjoy a true immunity if their own courts can be obliged to award plenary relief under federal law.[282] And if Congress may force state courts to entertain federal actions against unconsenting state governments, why can it not obtain such enforcement in federal courts—which it might prefer for all the standard reasons?[283] To return to IGRA: if Congress has power to subject a state to suit at all, why should the Constitution permit such a suit, brought by an Indian tribe, to be heard only in the state's own courts rather than by a more neutral federal forum—particularly when federal Indian policy has long deemed state courts not to be a viable venue for adjudication of sensitive Indian claims.[284]

---

[280] See Powell, 79 Va L Rev at 643 n 50 (cited in note 279) (suggesting that Justice O'Connor finds the established obligation of state courts to enforce federal law anomalous).

[281] See 28 USC §§ 1338, 1295.

[282] Justice Scalia's dissent in *Union Gas*—the seed from which *Seminole* flowered—analogized a state's sovereign immunity to that of the United States, finding no reason that private remedies against the states must be broader than those against the United States. Moreover, as noted earlier, he argued that overruling *Hans* would upset Congress's longstanding assumption that private damage actions it creates do not extend to the states. In *Hilton v South Carolina Pub. Rys Comm'n*, 502 US 197 (1991), however, the Court held that the FELA "creates a cause of action against a state-owned railroad, enforceable in state court," id at 199, and emphasized that the Eleventh Amendment does not apply in state courts, id at 204–05. In dissent, Justice O'Connor (joined by Justice Scalia) argued only that the FELA lacked the necessary clear statement to require a state to entertain damage actions against itself in its own courts. But because the state court's refusal to hear the case had rested on its construction of the FELA rather than on state sovereign immunity, the decision does not resolve whether states are obliged to entertain federal causes of action.

[283] Accord Amar, 96 Yale L J at 1476–78, 1483 (cited in note 38). See also *Hilton*, 502 US at 210 (O'Connor dissenting).

[284] See pp 23–24. See also Ann Althouse, *Tapping the State Court Resource*, 44 Vand L Rev 953, 967–73 (1991).

* * *

Thus, a variety of techniques *may* permit Congress to come rather close to achieving what, in my view, it should have constitutional power to achieve directly—the imposition of plenary liability upon the states for violation of federal law, in federal (or, alternatively, in state) court. But none of them is legally or practically unproblematic, and all require careful attention to subtle if not opaque constitutional concerns. Also required will be the political resolve to revisit statutory programs in order to work around the *Seminole* decision.

The dramatic results of the 1994 election symbolize a broader shift in the national political climate. In a small way, *Seminole* itself may contribute to that shift when the rather arcane question arises of whether or how to provide retrospective relief against states that violate federal law. For the decision provides, if not a clear argument that any particular alternative technique is unconstitutional, at least as a federalist totem, a constitutional argument with a small "c," that Congress should not so impose on the states. In that way, the political safeguards of federalism may be ideologically reinforced by the strong reaffirmation in *Seminole* of one aspect of state autonomy.

C. SEMINOLE AND CONSTITUTIONAL FEDERALISM

Insofar as *Seminole* is significant as a reminder that judicially enforceable limits on national power do remain, that message is a bit curious when viewed against a snapshot of today's constitu-

---

Jackson, 98 Yale L J at 72–118 (cited in note 45), while endorsing the diversity interpretation, argues for a federal common law of remedial discretion that disfavors federal court provision of retrospective relief. She contends that such relief, when compared to prospective relief, (i) confers fewer general benefits on the entire citizenry, (ii) risks improperly monetizing constitutional rights, (iii) more directly implicates state fiscal interests, and (iv) poses greater risks of nonenforcement. Insofar as those arguments are cogent, they strike me as calling for hesitation by *any* court, state or federal, in awarding such relief absent clear constitutional or statutory mandate—a view Jackson at times seems to embrace. She also advances, more tentatively, the narrower argument that such relief may be better handled by state courts, on the ground that they more typically hear damage actions and that their involvement may decrease hostility to adverse fiscal consequences. Id at 98–102. But federal courts may entertain damage actions under most of these statutory schemes against local governments, state and local government officials, and private parties; and insofar as state courts engender less hostility because they less faithfully enforce federal law, one may doubt their preferability—a point Jackson herself notes. See also Nowak, 75 Colum L Rev at 1443–44 (cited in note 83) (arguing that it is healthier for states to oppose federal mandates through political than legal processes).

tional terrain. Not only has the Court failed significantly to restrict the reach of congressional power to regulate private conduct, but it has (at least for the moment) abandoned the effort of *National League of Cities v Usery*[285] to limit substantive regulation of the states themselves. Subject only to the rules that it must articulate its intention with adequate clarity[286] and may not commandeer state legislatures,[287] Congress may regulate the states directly,[288] and the resulting obligations may be enforced in part if not in full by a variety of judicial mechanisms. The *Seminole* decision creates, as the only generally applicable rule of state immunity, a freedom from unconsented federal court suit by private individuals seeking retrospective relief—and then only if the statute cannot be viewed as enforcing one of the Reconstruction Amendments. Two centuries after the Founding, that is a curious and unstable place for the last stand of state sovereignty.[289]

But perhaps *Seminole*'s relation to broader currents of constitutional federalism should be viewed not through still photography but as part of a motion picture whose conclusion has yet to appear.[290] The day after the *Seminole* decision, the *New York Times* opined: "It is evident now that the *Lopez* decision was a signal that the current majority is in the process of revisiting some long-settled assumptions about the structure of the Federal Government and the constitutional allocation of authority between Washington and the states."[291] If a new federalist script is being written, the principal cinematographers are the Chief Justice and Justice O'Connor. Both dissented in *Garcia v San Antonio Metropolitan Transit Authority*,[292] where Justice Rehnquist predicted that the

---

[285] 426 US 833 (1976).

[286] See *Gregory v Ashcroft*, 501 US 452 (1991).

[287] *New York v United States*, 505 US 144 (1992).

[288] See *Garcia v San Antonio Metropolitan Transit Auth.*, 469 US 528 (1985).

[289] Compare Rapaczynski, 1985 Supreme Court Review at 346 n 21 (cited in note 102) (viewing state sovereign immunity as "by and large[] irrelevant" to the broader problems of federalism in view of a state's susceptibility to suit by sister states or by the United States).

[290] Compare Shapiro, 98 Harv L Rev at 61–62 (cited in note 155) (discussing the Eleventh Amendment as exemplifying Dworkin's description of the judge as one contributor to a chain novel).

[291] Linda Greenhouse, *Justices Curb Federal Power to Subject States to Lawsuits*, New York Times (March 28, 1996), p A1. For a collection of similar statements, see Robert F. Nagel, *The Future of Federalism*, 46 Case W Res L Rev 643, 643–44 (1996).

[292] 469 US 528 (1985).

principle of *National League of Cities* (an opinion he wrote) "will . . . again command the support of a majority of this Court." Justice O'Connor has advocated stricter limits on the conditional spending power and wrote *New York v United States*.[293] And both voted, in *United States v Lopez*,[294] to strike down legislation (for the first time in sixty years) as beyond the limits of the commerce power.[295]

These decisions, like *Seminole*, are reminders that the constitutional dialogue about the relation of nation and states remains with us.[296] Yet the critical question is not whether there are competing views about federalism or competing strains within any single view (there are), but rather whether determination of the limits on national authority will occur in a political or a judicial forum. In addressing that question, one may be wise to exhibit the caution shown by Chinese Premier Zhou En-Lai when asked his view of the French Revolution; he reportedly answered, "It's too soon to tell."[297] But at present, I am inclined to view *Lopez* less as a fundamental recasting of relations between nation and state than as a warning shot across the bow—to remind Congress that there may be a price to pay when it cavalierly fails to "make out even a minimally plausible case for utilizing the commerce power to undergird a new regulatory scheme, especially one that deals with problems historically regarded as chiefly of state and local concern."[298] If so, *Lopez* will prove to be a narrow decision about a question of great moment—the scope of congressional power to regulate. *Seminole*, by contrast, is a broader decision about a question of less significance—the liability of states to federal court suit for retrospective relief at the instance of private individuals.

---

[293] 505 US 144 (1992).

[294] 115 S Ct 1624 (1995).

[295] Also noteworthy is Justice Thomas's broad defense of state sovereignty, joined by the Chief Justice and Justices O'Connor and Scalia, in his dissent in *U.S. Term Limits, Inc. v Thornton*, 115 S Ct 1842 (1995).

[296] For a marvelous examination of the dialogic quality of debates about federalism, see Shapiro, *Federalism: A Dialogue* (cited in note 278).

[297] Simon Schama, *Citizens: A Chronicle of the French Revolution* xiii (Vintage, 1989).

[298] Louis H. Pollak, *Foreword*, 94 Mich L Rev 533, 552 (1995). For other commentary viewing *Lopez*'s significance as limited, see Charles R. Fried, *The Supreme Court, 1994 Term—Foreword: Revolutions?* 109 Harv L Rev 13, 34–45 (1995); Deborah Merritt Jones, *Commerce!*, 94 Mich L Rev 674 (1995); Nagel, 46 Case W Res L Rev 643 (cited in note 291); H. Jefferson Powell, *Enumerated Means and Unlimited Ends*, 94 Mich L Rev 651, 652 (1995). See also Philip Bobbitt, *Constitutional Fate: Theory of the Constitution* 194 (Oxford University, 1982) (viewing *National League of Cities* as a judicial reminder that Congress should "renew its traditional role as protector of the states").

In thinking about *Seminole*'s wider implications, one must recall that the Chief Justice not only authored *Lopez* but broadly upheld conditional spending in *South Dakota v Dole;* that Justice O'Connor's efforts to preserve aspects of state sovereignty are tempered by a general acceptance of the reach of modern national power,[299] and by a fundamental moderation[300] that Justice Kennedy shares.[301] But, as Justice Scalia reminded us,[302] changes in constitutional doctrine tend to follow changes in Court personnel; and one or two new Justices whose agenda includes restoration of constitutional limits on national power could cause us, some years from now, to view *Seminole* as the herald of more significant changes.

Whatever the makeup of the Court in the years to come, history tells us that significant constitutional limits on the scope of federal legislative power have proven difficult to erect and impossible to sustain.[303] The point is most familiar with respect to the constitutional crisis in the 1930s and the dramatic post-1937 withdrawal of serious limits on the reach of federal power.[304] But Professor Rapaczynski reminds us that three other constitutional amendments have been precipitated by judicial efforts to enforce constitutional limits on the scope of federal power regarding such diverse subjects as slavery in the territories, the federal income tax, and the voting age in state elections.[305] And during the brief ascendancy of *National League of Cities,* from 1976 to 1985, the Court was unable to apply the principle of state sovereignty there announced with any bite.[306]

The rule laid down in *Seminole* suffers from no similar history of frustration; indeed, the frustration lies with its opponents, whose efforts to establish a plenary basis for the exercise of federal judicial

---

[299] See Powell, 79 Va L Rev at 645–46 (cited in note 279).

[300] See, for example, *Planned Parenthood v Casey,* 505 US 833, 844 (1992) (opinion of O'Connor, Kennedy, and Souter).

[301] See *United States v Lopez,* 115 S Ct at 1634 (Kennedy concurring).

[302] See p 30.

[303] See Powell, 79 Va L Rev at 669–70 (cited in note 279).

[304] See Nagel, 46 Case W Res L Rev at 654 (cited in note 291) ("the Court's history [in trying to enforce the principle of enumerated powers] is littered with one failed and discarded doctrine after another").

[305] See Rapaczynski, 1985 Supreme Court Review at 342–43 (cited in note 102).

[306] See *EEOC v Wyoming,* 460 US 226 (1983); *FERC v Mississippi,* 456 US 742 (1982); *United Transp. Union v LIRR Co.,* 455 US 678 (1982); *Hodel v Virginia Surface Mining & Recl. Ass'n,* 452 US 264 (1981).

power against the states have (outside of the Fourteenth Amendment area) seen no lasting victories. Because the Court here is
dealing with a quite specific provision (albeit one whose current
interpretation requires disregarding its text), the impulse to enforce the Amendment's limits, as the Court understands them, may
be stronger than any parallel impulse to enforce broader notions
of limited federal power or of state autonomy. And in the area of
sovereign immunity, the Court has had better success in constructing a doctrine that, however complex, fictional, and difficult
to justify, is yet capable of relatively stable application.[307]

The meaning of a precedent (or of a series of precedents) is
given not only by the language of judicial opinions but also by
interpretations of that language in subsequent decisions. Only the
future will tell us the meaning of the present. Still, there remain
reasons to think that the decision in *Seminole* is not one of a
mounting series of blows to the reach of national power, but rather
a gesture in the direction of a diffuse conception of state sovereignty that in the end will not be generally enforced by the
Court.[308] If that is so, the *Seminole* decision may come to be seen
not only as regrettable but also as quixotic.

---

[307] One might also suggest that the Court is more enthusiastic about enforcing the Eleventh Amendment because that provision limits the power not of the political branches but
of unelected federal judges. But the suggestion lacks force insofar as the Amendment bars
the federal courts from exercising judicial power that Congress clearly bestowed, as was
true under IGRA and as would generally be the case so long as a clear statement rule is
maintained.

[308] It may be worth remarking that the statutory provisions struck down in both *Lopez*
and in *Seminole* could be viewed as not especially important. The Gun-Free School Zones
Act of 1990 was a species of the congressional crime of the month; forty states had similar
laws, and in any event other common prohibitions (for example, on carrying a concealed
weapon or on possession of a firearm by a convicted felon) may have been thought to
suffice. See Pollak, 94 Mich L Rev at 552 (cited in note 298). Moreover, the invalidated
statute was plainly reparable with little loss of efficacy, and Congress has already sought
to cure the problem found in *Lopez*, see § 657 of Pub L No 104-208, 1996 HR 3610 (Sept
30, 1996) (amending 18 USC § 922(q) by adding findings about the relationship of firearms
to interstate commerce and by making criminal only the possession of a firearm that has
moved in, or otherwise affects, interstate commerce).

Although judicial enforcement of IGRA's duty to bargain is not insignificant, it is hardly
essential—especially if, as the Court assumed, no contempt sanctions are available. Without
such enforcement, the Act effectively provides that if no agreement has been reached within
180 days of the tribe's request to negotiate with the state, the Secretary of the Interior is
empowered to prescribe terms for class III gaming. A state, though no longer obliged to
negotiate or to participate in mediation, might still choose to do so—particularly if it feared
that a refusal might result in the Secretary's granting the tribe unduly broad authority to
conduct gaming.

LOUIS MICHAEL SEIDMAN

ROMER'S RADICALISM: THE UNEXPECTED REVIVAL OF WARREN COURT ACTIVISM

If there is ever a final reckoning of twentieth-century constitutionalism, *Romer v Evans*[1] will stand as a monument to the transformative possibilities of constitutional law. Yet the opinion also suggests ways in which the very possibility of transformation serves to reenforce existing categories and relationships.

In a powerful 6–3 decision, the Court boldly invalidated "Amendment 2" to the Colorado Constitution, which prohibited the state or any of its subdivisions from granting to homosexuals "any minority status, quota preferences, protected status or claim of discrimination."[2] By handing gay people their first major Su-

Louis Michael Seidman is Professor of Law, Georgetown University Law Center.

AUTHOR'S NOTE: I am grateful to William Eskridge, Chai Feldblum, Judith Mazo, Roy Schotland, Mark Tushnet, and participants in the Georgetown University Law Center Summer Workshop Series and the University of Virginia Constitutional Law Symposium for providing helpful comments on an earlier version of this article. Alfonso Moreno, Darren Hultman, and Rebecca Kamp provided excellent research assistance. The Georgetown University Law Center provided financial support through its Summer Writer's Grant program.

[1] 116 S Ct 1620 (1996).

[2] The amendment states:

Neither the State of Colorado, through any of its branches or departments, nor any of its agencies, political subdivisions, municipalities or school districts, shall enact, adopt or enforce any statute, regulation, ordinance or policy whereby homosexual, lesbian or bisexual orientation, conduct, practices or relationships shall constitute or otherwise be the basis of or entitle any person or class of persons to have or claim any minority status, quota preferences, protected status or claim of discrimination. This Section of the Constitution shall be in all respects self-executing.

Col Const, Art II, § 30b.

preme Court victory in the history of the republic,[3] the opinion substantially alters the legal landscape.

The day before *Romer* was announced, many gay-rights advocates viewed the Supreme Court as an implacable foe—its decisions to be feared, its jurisdiction at all cost to be avoided.[4] Now, it seems, the Court has switched sides. To be sure, it remains too early to know what future Justices will make of *Romer*. It is (barely) possible to read the opinion so narrowly as to change very little. Still, at a minimum, the opinion gives litigants new ammunition to challenge a range of practices previously thought permissible, including the exclusion of gay people from a variety of antidiscrimination and social welfare measures,[5] the military's "don't ask/don't tell" policy,[6] and the prohibition on gay marriage.[7]

As significant as this immediate impact is, the opinion is still more notable for its surprisingly anachronistic tone and intellectual style. Like stories of Isaac Bashevas Singer, bravely using a forgotten language to recreate a dead society, *Romer* rekindles a way of thinking and writing about constitutional law that had long gone out of fashion. The opinion recaptures the moral drama and ambiguity of Warren Court activism years after the culture had seemingly discarded it. Produced in the teeth of an intellectual environment extraordinarily hostile to its core assumptions, it nonetheless renews promises long repudiated and anxieties long repressed.

Romer resembles the products of the Warren Court in several

---

[3] During the Warren Court period, the Court extended First Amendment protection to some gay pornography in decisions that were arguably of significant value to the gay community. See, for example, *Manual Enterprises, Inc. v Day*, 370 US 478 (1962) (holding that material in question, which appealed to prurient interests of homosexuals, did not violate contemporary community standards). But cf *Mishkin v New York*, 383 US 502 (1966) (material designed for "deviant sexual group" can be suppressed even if it fails to appeal to prurient interest of "average" person so long as it appeals to prurient interest of members of that group). *Romer* marks the first occasion on which the Court has recognized a claim of discrimination brought by gay people.

[4] See, for example, Sue Chrisman, *Evans v. Romer: An "Old" Right Comes Out*, 72 Denver U L Rev 519, 521 (1995) ("[f]ear rippled through the gay community" when Supreme Court granted review in *Romer*).

[5] See, for example, Americans with Disabilities Act of 1990, 42 USC § 12211(a) (1988 ed, Supp V) (excluding homosexuals from coverage).

[6] See National Defense Authorization Act for Fiscal Year 1994, Pub L No 103-160, 107 Stat 1670, codified at 10 USC § 654 (codifying "don't ask/don't tell" policy).

[7] See, for example, Defense of Marriage Act, Pub L No 104-199, 110 Stat 2419 (1996), to be codified at 1 USCA § 7 (defining marriage for federal purposes as only "a legal union between one man and one woman.").

respects. In tone, Justice Kennedy's opinion for the Court seems far out of place in current volumes of the U.S. Reports. The opinion is short, sweeping, and direct. It contains not a single footnote, and a bare minimum of legal analysis. Reflecting the casual attitude toward precedent for which the Warren Court was famous, it fails so much as to mention *Bowers v Hardwick*,[8] which many had thought dispositive. In place of technical discussion of precedent and doctrine, Kennedy relies upon sweeping moral generalities— some might say bromides—concerning "transactions and endeavors that constitute ordinary civic life in a free society"[9] and "our constitutional tradition."[10]

As if to emphasize the fact that the opinion declares simple and powerful moral truths, the five other Justices who joined the Kennedy opinion remain uncharacteristically silent. One looks in vain for the separate opinions partially dissenting from footnote 63 or joining all but paragraph three of Part IV A. The opinion stands alone and with quiet dignity against the backdrop of Justice Scalia's vigorous dissent.

Of course, Justice Scalia has a style all his own. Yet his opinion also evokes memories of the powerful emotions triggered by Warren Court activism. The second Justice Harlan would surely have been more civil in dissent (and, indeed, might not have dissented at all), but Scalia's opinion mimics Harlan's disgust with the supposed lack of technical competence of his colleagues and dismay at their failure to appreciate the limits of their role. The opinion differs from Warren-era dissents only because it combines this Harlanesque critique of judicial activism with two other styles of Warren Court bashing that, for the most part, found expression only off the bench: the sarcastic and condescending laments of the "scholastic mandarins"[11] who criticized the Court in the law reviews, and the angry, spasmodic responses to the Court's perceived assault on conventional mores voiced in tabloid editorials and on highway billboards.

---

[8] 478 US 186 (1986).

[9] 116 S Ct at 1627.

[10] Id at 1628.

[11] See J. Skelly Wright, *Professor Bickel, the Scholarly Tradition, and the Supreme Court*, 84 Harv L Rev 769, 777–78 (1971) (criticizing "scholastic mandarins" for their "haughty derision of the [Warren] Court's powers of analysis and reasoning").

If one looks beyond these surface similarities, *Romer*'s reproduction of 1960s jurisprudence is still more striking. Whereas much of modern constitutional law seems narrow and crabbed, *Romer* is deliberately generative. The Court injects itself into one of the great social, political, and moral issues of our time. Moreover, it does so with creative generality and ambiguity, opening many new avenues for litigation and raising far more questions than it answers.

All this is accomplished through the revival of doctrinal techniques that had been thought long discredited. Like the Warren Court, the *Romer* majority might have more comfortably used the law of substantive due process to support its conclusions. Like the Warren Court (albeit for only partially similar reasons), it found access to this body of doctrine blocked and responded to this difficulty through inventive, if awkward, resort to the Equal Protection Clause. And like the Warren Court, *Romer* used equal protection doctrine to attack constitutional law's traditional conservative bias in favor of negative rights. In the hands of both Courts, equality is a lever that can be used to force affirmative government action that redistributes power and affords positive protection for vulnerable groups. Both Courts accomplished this result by destabilizing the baseline from which constitutional violations are traditionally measured.

Yet for all its implicit radicalism, *Romer* is also profoundly conservative. Here, too, there are deep links to antecedents from thirty years ago. The sustained right-wing assault on the Warren Court caused many to lose sight of the fact that Earl Warren, himself, was hardly a revolutionary. His roots were within the Republican Party's moderate wing, which was middle class, pragmatic, and only mildly reformist.[12] In recent years, right-wing populists have

---

[12] See Bernard Schwartz, *Super Chief: Earl Warren and His Supreme Court—A Judicial Biography* 7 (New York Univ Press, 1983).

> Warren's outstanding feature [as California Governor] remained the image of bland competence that he projected. "Earl Warren is honest, likable, and clean," wrote John Gunther in 1947. Gunther listed his outstanding characteristics as "decency, stability, sincerity, and lack of genuine intellectual distinction. . . . he will never set the world on fire or even make it smoke."

See also G. Edward White, *Earl Warren: A Public Life* 19 (Oxford Univ Press, 1982) (arguing that Warren was well suited to "[a]ppeals to honesty, to nonpartisanship, to decisive 'forward-looking' government, and to the 'white light' of public opinion" that dominated California political rhetoric). But compare id at 127 (arguing that the characterization of

shouted down Republicans of this stripe, but it seems clear that
the four Republican appointees who joined the *Romer* majority
nonetheless view themselves as part of this now endangered
tradition.

At its best, moderate Republicanism was characterized by the
kind of genial openness and sensible good will exemplified in the
personality of Earl Warren himself. But paradoxically, this tolerance and empathy were rooted in the confidence that comes from
deep-seated, unshakable certainty as to the rightness of American
values and mores. Once again, Earl Warren perfectly captures the
tensions inherent in this mix. Although he supported some of the
most destabilizing movements of his time, he nonetheless embraced without embarrassment "corny" and "old fashioned"
American values.[13] Although he was prepared to redefine "Ameri-
canism" in new and surprising ways, he was unwilling to let go of
the category itself, and this unwillingness inevitably meant that
there were limits to his taste for social upheaval.[14] As good-hearted
and progressive as it was, there was also an exclusionary underside
to the Warren Court revolution that left the Court open to
charges of hypocrisy and elitism.[15]

With the collapse of that revolution, these tensions and contradictions were mostly forgotten. *Romer*'s astonishing return to Warren Court activism revives not only the promise of the period, but
the tensions and contradictions as well. At bottom, these uncer-
tainties have to do with the ability of the Court to give a convinc-

---

Warren as "'middle-of-the-road' " or "'moderate' Republican" is "superficial" and "highly
misleading.").

[13] See Schwartz, *Super Chief* at 139 (cited in note 12) ("According to Justice Stewart,
'Warren's great strength was his simple belief in the things which we now laugh at—
motherhood, marriage, family, flag, and the like.' ").

[14] See, for example, *Street v New York*, 394 US 576, 605 (1969) (Warren dissenting) (arguing that "the States and the Federal Government [have] the power to protect the flag
from acts of desecration and disgrace"); *United States v O'Brien*, 391 US 367 (1969) (Warren,
CJ) (upholding statute prohibiting destruction of draft cards); *Roth v United States*, 354 US
476, 496 (1957) (Warren concurring) (upholding right of government to prosecute defendants who were "plainly engaged in the commercial exploitation of the morbid and shameful
craving for materials with prurient effect."); Schwartz, *Super Chief* at 139–43 (cited in note
12) (recounting Warren's defense of "the place of family in our civilization" and attack on
legislation authorizing "consensual divorces" after six-week residence).

[15] For representative criticism along these lines, see Alexander M. Bickel, *The Supreme
Court and the Idea of Progress* 137 (Harper & Row, 1970) (attacking the Court for requiring
"integrated education . . . willy-nilly for the poor, but a matter of choice for the well-to-
do").

ing account of individual rights—an account that transcends the narrow biases of the Justices themselves. Thus, if *Romer* stands as a monument to the constitutional hopes of our era, it also reminds us of the reasons why those hopes have often been disappointed.

The rest of this essay explores the double-edged quality of *Romer* and of the tradition it revives. In Part I, I explore *Romer*'s transformative potential. I defend an interpretation of Justice Kennedy's opinion that reads it as pushing the boundaries of traditional constitutional discourse in surprising and creative ways. By reworking traditional categories so as to include what was previously excluded, the opinion opens possibilities for significant change.

Parts II and III discuss the problems with the majority's approach. Many of these are identified in Justice Scalia's dissent. Yet for all its vituperation, the dissent shares a common premise with the Court's opinion. Part II argues that, like the majority, Justice Scalia embraces important components of Warren Court jurisprudence. His dissenting opinion evidences a willingness to give up on the traditionally conservative vision of limits on state coercion premised on the requirements of neutrality and objectivity. I argue that the collapse of the ideal of government neutrality has contributed to the divisive and hyperbolic quality of some modern constitutional rhetoric.

In Part III, I argue that although Justice Scalia fails to see that his insights apply to his own position, he is surely right when he insists that in a world without such neutral and objective limits, the Court's conclusions will inevitably be biased and elitist. Paradoxically, the very act of expanding and redefining social categories draws our attention to what remains outside the protected enclave. Inclusionary efforts have meaning only so long as things remain excluded; liberal tolerance of lifestyles we find abhorrent necessarily implies authoritarian intolerance of lifestyles that are more abhorrent still.

The difficulties identified in Parts II and III raise more fundamental questions about the function of constitutional law. Throughout our history, we have argued about whether the Constitution serves primarily to entrench and legitimate the status quo or to promote social change. In a brief, concluding section, I argue that Warren Court activism paradoxically accomplished both effects simultaneously. Constitutional progress occurred when the Court took advantage of the plasticity of social categories to break down settled understandings; yet the progress was justified by insistence on the rigidity of the same categories. The upshot is that for all its radicalism, the Warren Court was also deeply conservative. The legitimating force of the sort of controlled transformation perfected by the Warren Court helps explain why its techniques remain attractive even in this conservative era.

I. Romer's Radicalism

Part of the genius of *Romer* is that the opinion is written in a deliberatively generative fashion. Instead of trying to control future doctrinal developments and shut down lines of argument, it clears away obstacles and opens up possibilities. One consequence of this jurisprudential style is that it makes for difficulty of interpretation and prediction. No one can write confidently about what *Romer* "means" because its ultimate meaning is yet to be determined by future judges and litigants.[16]

It would be a mistake, then, to attempt a definitive analysis of the opinion. In what follows, I attempt something more modest. My aim is to advance one of several possible interpretations of *Romer*—what I call the "radical" interpretation. I do not claim that this is the only way the Court's opinion can be interpreted, although I do think it makes the best sense of what the Court has in fact said and done.

Many readers will nonetheless want to reject my interpretation out of hand. Confident of the Court's deep conservatism, they will insist that these Justices could not possibly have intended the results I argue for. And perhaps they are right. But my claim is not about intent. It is instead about the radical possibilities offered by a brand of constitutionalism that even the cautious and conservative Justices who currently populate the Court are unwilling to repudiate. Perhaps future Courts will ignore these possibilities. Perhaps they ought to be ignored. But the time to think seriously about the advantages and disadvantages of the future that *Romer* opens for us is now, before its meaning becomes fixed.

---

[16] Of course, there is a sense in which this is true of every opinion. No opinion can control its own precedential force. For a discussion, see Mark V. Tushnet, *Following the Rules Laid Down: A Critique of Interpretivism and Neutral Principles*, 96 Harv L Rev 781, 804–18 (1983). Still, the feel of open texture is more apparent and, perhaps, more intentional in *Romer* than in many other Supreme Court opinions.

A. PATHS NOT TAKEN

A defense of the radical reading begins by focusing on lines of argument the Court chose not to pursue. Consider, first, the opinions of the Colorado Supreme Court.[17] That Court had also invalidated Amendment 2, but under a very different theory. The Amendment had been adopted by state-wide referendum after several localities had enacted ordinances extending antidiscrimination protection to gay people in a variety of contexts.[18] The Colorado court reasoned that Amendment 2 not only repealed these ordinances, but also prevented municipalities from enacting new measures protecting gay people unless they and their supporters first went through the arduous process of securing the Amendment's repeal. This additional hurdle, imposed upon gay people but no other group, denied them equal access to the political process and, therefore, had to be subjected to heightened scrutiny[19]—scrutiny that it could not survive.[20]

There are several reasons why the Colorado court may have been attracted to this line of analysis. An important strand of revisionist history has attempted to assimilate Warren Court radicalism into the mainstream constitutional tradition by treating its decisions as requiring no more than a fair political process.[21] On this theory, the Warren Court was not attempting to effect radical social change by judicial decree. It was not motivated by a substantive theory of justice and made no effort to promote a particular set of values. On the contrary, it was insisting on no more than democracy.[22]

---

[17] In *Evans v Romer*, 854 P2d 1270 (Colo 1993) ("*Evans I*"), the state supreme court held that Amendment 2 was subject to strict scrutiny under the Equal Protection Clause. The court remanded the case for a determination as to whether this standard could be met. The trial court held that it could not, and the state supreme court affirmed in *Evans v Romer*, 882 P2d 1335 (Colo 1994) ("*Evans II*").

[18] See Denver Rev Mun Code, Art IV §§ 28-91 to 28-116 (1991); Aspen Mun Code § 13-98 (1977); Boulder Rev Code §§ 12-1-1 to 12-1-11 (1987).

[19] *Evans I* at 1285.

[20] *Evans II* at 1341–50.

[21] See John Hart Ely, *Democracy and Distrust* (Harvard Univ Press, 1980).

[22] See id at 73–74 (Warren Court decisions were "certainly interventionist, . . . but the interventionism was fueled not by a desire on the part of the Court to vindicate particular substantive values it had determined were important or fundamental, but rather by a desire to ensure that the political process—which is where such values *are* properly identified weighed, and accommodated—was open to those of all viewpoints on something approaching an equal basis.").

In a conservative era, it is easy to see why the Colorado court would want to evoke this least threatening version of judicial activism. Confronted with the undeniable fact of *Bowers v Hardwick*, it was especially important to proceed in a fashion that avoided endorsement of a substantive right to engage in homosexual conduct. Moreover, a line of Supreme Court precedent had utilized a political process argument analogous to that invoked by the Colorado court to invalidate a variety of seemingly similar measures that created special obstacles for African-Americans seeking legislation favoring their cause.

For example, the Supreme Court had struck down state measures creating a constitutional right to engage in racial housing discrimination;[23] prohibiting localities from adopting voluntary bussing plans to promote racial integration;[24] and requiring supermajorities before a municipality could enact racial antidiscrimination legislation.[25] In each of these cases, the Court insisted that the state had no constitutional obligation to enact antidiscrimination measures in the first place or to refrain from repealing them once enacted.[26] The problem with the laws in question, according to the Court, was not that they dismantled prior protections, but that they biased the political process in a fashion that made it more difficult for racial minorities than for other groups to enact the legislation they favored. This precedent allowed the Colorado court to argue that it, too, was insisting on no more than a level playing field without either protecting an affirmative right to engage in gay sex or insisting on the enactment or nonrepeal of laws barring discrimination against gay people.

To be sure, there were problems with this argument. For one thing, the precedent itself was shaky. The decisions in question were rendered by sharply divided courts,[27] and only one currently sitting Justice had voted with the majority in the earlier cases.[28]

---

[23] See *Reitman v Mulkey*, 387 US 369 (1967).

[24] See *Washington v Seattle School Dist. No. 1*, 458 US 457 (1982).

[25] See *Hunter v Erickson*, 393 US 385 (1969).

[26] See *Hunter*, 393 US at 390 n 5; *Reitman*, 387 US at 380–81; *Seattle School Dist. No. 1*, 458 US at 483.

[27] Although only Justice Black dissented in *Hunter*, the Court divided 5–4 in *Reitman* and *Seattle School District*.

[28] Of the Justices voting in the majority in *Hunter*, *Reitman*, and *Seattle School District*, only Justice Stevens remains on the Court. Justices Rehnquist and O'Connor dissented in *Seattle School District*.

Moreover, even when announced, the political process decisions struck many commentators as anomalous.[29] The Court never satisfactorily explained the difference it saw between unfairly *biasing* the political process on the one hand and simply *using* the process on the other. For example, when opponents of bussing schoolchildren in order to promote racial balance secured passage of a state-wide initiative prohibiting the practice, they used a process that was equally open to all. Bussing proponents could have used the same process to require programs they favored and, even with passage of the initiative, were not prevented from using the process to secure its repeal. Although the state-wide initiative created a more difficult political task for bussing proponents than for advocates of other public policy measures, this was true only because bussing opponents had already achieved the more difficult political task of erecting this barrier.[30]

Nor were the decisions obviously on point. Each of the prior cases had arisen in a racial context. Racial discrimination, of course, is inherently suspect and triggers heightened scrutiny. *Bowers*, in contrast, made discrimination based on sexual orientation an unlikely candidate for heightened review. Broadening the Court's holding to apply in situations not involving inherently suspect classifications yields highly implausible results. Whenever a matter is decided on a state-wide basis, the losers are placed at the political disadvantage of having to secure a state-wide repeal before they can realize victories on a local basis. A general holding that this effect amounts to an unconstitutional biasing of the political process would put state governments out of business. Indeed, for just this reason, the Supreme Court has expressly declined to extend the "political process" argument to discrimination against public policy outcomes that were not racially based.[31] The Colorado

---

[29] See, for example, David Strauss, *Discriminatory Intent and the Taming of Brown*, 56 U Chi L Rev 935, 981 (1989) and sources cited therein; Mark Tushnet and Jennifer Jaff, *Why the Debate Over Congress' Power to Restrict the Jurisdiction of the Federal Courts Is Unending*, 72 Georgetown L J 1311, 1323 n 53 (1984).

[30] For some characteristically tendentious questions raising these points, see Geoffrey Stone, Louis Michael Seidman, Cass Sunstein, and Mark Tushnet, *Constitutional Law* 647–48 (Little Brown, 3d ed 1996).

[31] See *James v Valtierra*, 402 US 137, 141 (1971) (upholding California constitutional prohibition against state entities constructing low rental housing unless approved by majority of those voting in local election on ground that provision was racially neutral and not "aimed at a racial minority.").

court's effort to distinguish this line of authority might charitably be described as awkward.[32]

Perhaps these obstacles could have been overcome. In *Washington v Seattle School District No. 1*,[33] the most recent Supreme Court decision relying on the political process approach, the Court invalidated a state-wide initiative prohibiting school bussing designed to achieve a level of racial integration not required by the United States Constitution. Although the initiative did not facially categorize on a racial basis (blacks and whites favor and oppose racial desegregation),[34] the Court nonetheless subjected it to strict scrutiny, holding that it unfairly disadvantaged advocates of desegregation. To be sure, the provision had a discriminatory *effect* on racial minorities, since a greater percentage of blacks than whites favor desegregation.[35] But the Court has made clear that discriminatory effect alone is not sufficient to trigger heightened scrutiny in the absence of a purpose of disadvantaging a protected group,[36] and the Court did not find that there was such a purpose in *Seattle School District.*[37]

---

[32] The Colorado court disposed of *James* in a footnote. See *Evans I*, 854 P2d at 1282 n 21. It correctly observed that the *James* majority expressly declined to extend the political process cases to provisions that are not "aimed at a racial minority," but attempted to circumvent this language by noting that all the Justices in the *James* majority later joined the Supreme Court's decision in *Gordon v Lance*, 403 US 1 (1971). *Gordon*, too, declined to invalidate a supermajority requirement, in this case requiring a 60% majority for approval of increases in bonded indebtedness. However, the Colorado court emphasized language in *Gordon* that distinguished *Hunter* on the ground that the *Gordon* supermajority requirement did not "[fence] out [a sector of the population] from the franchise because of the way they will vote." 403 US at 5. The Colorado court implausibly read the negative implication of this language as countermanding *James*'s refusal to extend the political process argument to nonracial contexts.

[33] 458 US 457 (1982).

[34] The Court noted that it was "undoubtedly . . . true . . . that the proponents of mandatory integration cannot be classified by race: Negroes and whites may be counted among both the supporters and opponents of Initiative 350. And it should be equally clear that white as well as Negro children benefit from exposure to 'ethnic and racial diversity in the classroom.' " Id at 472.

[35] The Court found implicit in its prior cases the suggestion that "desegregation of the public schools . . . at bottom inures primarily to the benefit of the minority, and is designed for that purpose." Id at 472.

[36] *Washington v Davis*, 426 US 229 (1976).

[37] Although the Court found that the initiative was "effectively drawn for racial purposes," 458 US at 471, it did not find that it was drawn for the purpose of disadvantaging a racial minority. Instead, the Court thought that it was enacted because of, rather than in spite of, " 'its adverse effects upon' busing for integration." Id. Passing a measure because it discourages a public policy outcome beneficial to a racial minority is not the same thing as passing it because the measure harms the minority. Compare *Personnel Administrator of*

Seattle School District contains at least a hint, then, of a middle ground that would neither apply the political process argument across the board nor restrict it to racial classifications. Perhaps shifts in the political process that obstruct ordinary majoritarian mechanisms are impermissible when they discriminate against identifiable groups that are not "suspect" in the usual sense, but that are not defined solely by their position on a contested public policy question either. Perhaps advocates of gay rights constitute such a group.

If all of this sounds implausible, a second avenue was also open to the Supreme Court: It might have reversed the Colorado court and upheld Amendment 2, either by distinguishing the *Seattle School District* line of authority or by overruling it. Certainly, many commentators anticipated this outcome.[38] An opinion along these lines might have repudiated at least the more fanciful extensions of *Seattle School District*, while leaving the Court free in future cases to pursue any path it chose with regard to discrimination against gay people.

A third possibility would have avoided the hard questions entirely by focusing on the fact that plaintiffs had mounted a facial assault against the Amendment. The Court had previously stated that such attacks must fail unless "no set of circumstances exists under which the Act would be valid."[39] The Court might have pointed to a relatively uncontroversial application of the Amendment (for example, its use to invalidate quotas favoring gay people) and saved for another day problems posed by more controversial applications.

If the Court was intent upon striking down the Amendment, still a fourth possibility was available. The Amendment was susceptible to a very broad construction, which would have not only prevented municipalities from passing legislation specifically designed to benefit gay people, but also prevented them from applying to

---

Massachusetts v Feeney, 442 US 256 (1979) (applying low level scrutiny to state veterans' preference in civil service hiring although legislature knew that preference would disproportionately harm women applicants).

[38] See, for example, Michael J. Gerhardt and Tracey Maclin, *Mock Arguments in Romer v. Evans*, 4 Wm & Mary Bill of Rights J 639, 670 (1995); Chrisman, *Evans v. Romer*, 72 Denver L Rev at 520–21 (cited in note 4).

[39] *United States v Salerno*, 481 US 739, 745 (1987).

gay people more general protections available to everyone else. For example, a Colorado statute prohibits public servants from knowingly, arbitrarily, and capriciously refraining from performing a duty imposed on the official by law.[40] Municipal officials who, pursuant to this statute, required police to investigate criminal assaults upon gay people in the same way that they investigated assaults on heterosexuals might be seen as enforcing a "policy" recognizing a "claim of discrimination" against gay people in violation of Amendment 2.

Although there was some language in the Colorado court's opinion suggesting that it did not interpret the Amendment in this fashion,[41] Justice Kennedy states that this language was not dispositive.[42] Had the Court read the Amendment in such a broad way, it could have invalidated the Amendment by holding simply that the state may not except gay people from generally applicable statutes for arbitrary reasons. Instead, the Court assumed *arguendo* that the Amendment had a much narrower scope—prohibiting only

---

[40] Colo Rev Stat § 18-8-405 (1988).

[41] The Colorado Court made the following observation:

> [I]t is significant to note that Colorado law currently proscribes discrimination against persons who are not suspect classes, including discrimination based on age; marital or family status; veterans' status; and for any legal, off-duty conduct such as smoking tobacco. Of course Amendment 2 is not intended to have any effect on this legislation, but seeks only to prevent the adoption of antidiscrimination laws intended to protect gays, lesbians, and bisexuals.

Evans II, 882 P2d at 1346 n 9 (citations omitted).

[42] The Court asserted that "[t]he state court did not decide whether this amendment has this effect, and neither need we." 116 S Ct at 1626.

In his dissenting opinion, Justice Scalia argued that "The clear import of the Colorado court's conclusion . . . is that 'general laws and policies that prohibit arbitrary discrimination' would continue to prohibit discrimination on the basis of homosexual conduct as well. . . . This analysis, which is fully in accord with (indeed, follows inescapably from) the text of the constitutional provision, lays to rest such horribles . . . as the prospect that assaults upon homosexuals could not be prosecuted." Id at 1630.

Justice Scalia's argument appears to conflate two possible interpretations of the Amendment. One interpretation (clearly rejected by the Colorado court) is that the Amendment excluded gay people from coverage they would otherwise enjoy when they are discriminated against on a basis having nothing to do with homosexuality. For example, on this interpretation an African-American homosexual could not bring a claim of racial job discrimination if he was fired from a government job because of race. The other interpretation (not squarely addressed by the Colorado court) is that the Amendment prevents gay people from relying on statutes of general applicability when the ground of their exclusion from coverage is their homosexuality. For example, on this interpretation, a gay person discharged from a government job because of his homosexuality could not advance a claim that the discharge was arbitrary under a state statute prohibiting arbitrary discharge.

legislation that singled out gay people for protection—and held that, even as so read, it was unconstitutional.[43]

B. THE RADICAL INTERPRETATION

Of course, the effect of assuming that the Amendment had a narrow scope was to give the holding invalidating it a broad reach. Indeed, the effect of each choice made by the Court was to broaden the impact of the decision. Instead of using any of the other possible rationales, the Court relied upon the substantive inequality inherent in denying gay people the protection of antidiscrimination laws when so many other groups are protected. The crucial step was the Court's premise that "the structure and operation of modern anti-discrimination laws"[44] provided the baseline against which Colorado's treatment of gay people had to be measured. These laws, which the Court describes in some detail,[45] provide protection against discrimination in a wide variety of contexts to a wide variety of groups.[46] Against this backdrop, there was

> nothing special about the protections Amendment 2 withholds. These are protections taken for granted by most people either because they already have them or do not need them; these are protections against exclusion from an almost limitless num-

---

[43] The Court stated:

> In any event, even if, as we doubt, homosexuals could find some safe harbor in laws of general application, we cannot accept the view that Amendment 2's prohibition on specific legal protections does no more than deprive homosexuals of special rights. To the contrary, the amendment imposes a special disability upon those persons alone.

116 S Ct at 1626–27.

[44] Id at 1625.

[45] See id at 1625–26.

[46] The Court noted that at common law, innkeepers, smiths, and certain others were prohibited from refusing to serve a customer without a good reason. These laws did not provide specific protection for particular groups, however, and, when the Court held that the Fourteenth Amendment failed to give Congress power to prohibit discrimination in public accommodations, Civil Rights Cases, 109 US 3 (1883), most states enacted detailed statutory schemes. See 116 S Ct at 1625. The Court observed that these statutes typically went beyond the common law by covering additional entities and "by enumerating the groups or persons within their ambit of protection." Id. Colorado had chosen not to limit this protection to groups that have been given heightened scrutiny under the Equal Protection Clause. Instead, it "set forth an extensive catalogue of traits which cannot be the basis for discrimination, including age, military status, marital status, pregnancy, parenthood, custody of a minor child, political affiliation, physical or mental disability of an individual or of his or her associates—and, in recent times, sexual orientation." Id at 1626.

ber of transactions and endeavors that constitute ordinary civic life in a free society.[47]

Because Colorado had in effect declared that "in general it shall be more difficult for one group of citizens [gay people] than for all others to seek aid from government,"[48] it had denied equal protection of the laws.

The potential scope of this holding is breathtaking. Note first that the Court's rationale does not depend upon the fact that there had been a state-wide nullification of local antidiscrimination measures or on the greater difficulties gay people might have in achieving repeal of the state-wide nullification. These factors are relevant to the political process argument, which the Court rejects; they have no relevance to an argument premised on differential protection against discrimination between gay people and other groups. Indeed, the Court itself drew attention to this point when, shortly after *Romer*, it vacated and remanded for reconsideration the Sixth Circuit's decision in *Equality Foundation of Greater Cincinnati, Inc. v City of Cincinnati*,[49] a case where the lower court had upheld a *local* charter amendment barring *local* antidiscrimination measures favoring gay people.[50]

The Court's rationale also seems to make irrelevant the vexed distinction between constitutional measures barring or discouraging antidiscrimination statutes on the one hand and mere repeal of such statutes on the other. This distinction played a prominent role in the Court's political process cases, where the argument was that constitutional measures biased ordinary political processes against certain groups.[51] In contrast, Justice Kennedy's argument is about substance rather than process. His complaint is that gay people have been excepted from the general baseline of antidis-

---

[47] Id at 1627.

[48] Id at 1628.

[49] 116 S Ct 2519 (1996).

[50] See *Equality Foundation of Greater Cincinnati v City of Cincinnati*, 54 F3d 261 (6th Cir 1995). Although the remand was only for reconsideration in light of *Romer*, it takes on added significance in light of Justice Scalia's dissent from the remand, which argued that the case was distinguishable on the ground that the bar to measures favoring gay people was enacted on the local level. See 116 S Ct at 2519 (Scalia dissenting).

[51] Compare *Seattle School Dist. No. 1*, 458 US 457 (invalidating state initiative because it restructured the political process by barring certain school desegregation techniques) with *Crawford v Board of Education*, 458 US 527 (1982) (upholding state constitutional amendment because it merely repealed state created right to desegregation measures).

crimination. Of course, this unequal treatment can be achieved as effectively by the repeal of ordinary legislation as by a constitutional measure barring such legislation in the future.

Nor is it possible to restrict the Court's rationale to repeals of previously enacted measures. It makes no sense to say that a jurisdiction that enacts measures protecting gay people but then decides to repeal the measures is more constitutionally vulnerable than a jurisdiction that never enacts them in the first place.[52] In both cases, gay people are denied rights afforded to other groups and, on the Court's rationale, in both cases this differential treatment violates the Constitution's promise of equality.

The upshot is that *Romer* seems to impose an affirmative constitutional requirement on jurisdictions to protect gay people from private discrimination, at least so long as they maintain comprehensive protection for other groups.[53] Moreover, if gay people are entitled to affirmative protection, then surely they are entitled to negative freedom from government persecution as well. It is therefore difficult to see how *Bowers*'s validation of same-sex sodomy laws survives the Court's analysis. The sound of the Court's silence regarding *Bowers* is deafening.

To be sure, these remarkable conclusions require some qualification. Although the Court's rationale supports these results, not all of its language does.[54] A future court determined to read the

---

[52] The Court has stated that "the Equal Protection Clause is not violated by the mere repeal of . . . legislation or policies that were not required by the Federal Constitution in the first place." *Crawford*, 458 US at 535. It would seem to follow that if a repeal does violate the Constitution, this must be because the measure *was* "required by the Federal Constitution in the first place." Compare Cass Sunstein, *Public Values, Private Interests and the Equal Protection Clause*, 1982 Supreme Court Review 127, 160–61 (arguing that risk of improper motivation may be greater in case of repeal than in case of failure to enact).

[53] The opinion is vague as to how comprehensive the protection for other groups must be to trigger an equal protection violation. The Court notes that Amendment 2 withholds "protections taken for granted by most people, either because they already have them or do not need them." 116 S Ct at 1620. Yet as comprehensive as Colorado's antidiscrimination policy is, there are many who remain excluded—for example, obese people, ugly people, people with low intelligence, people who have committed felonies. Perhaps the point is that these groups do not "need" protection or that adverse treatment of them should not count as "discrimination." These justifications for excluding groups from the regime of nonprotection bring to the surface the normative questions that Justice Kennedy's opinion begs. For a discussion, see pages 101–02, 113–14.

[54] At various points in the opinion, the majority hints that the result is influenced by political process considerations. See, for example, 116 S Ct at 1625 ("The amendment withdraws from homosexuals but no others, specific legal protection from injuries caused by discrimination, *and it forbids reinstatement of these laws and policies*") (emphasis added); id

opinion narrowly could point to the Court's refusal to elevate sexual orientation classifications to the "suspect" category[55] and to its emphasis on the unusual breadth of Amendment 2.[56] The Court implies that more discrete measures disadvantaging gay people, having a more obvious connection to some legitimate government purpose, might survive rational basis review.[57]

---

at 1627 ("Homosexuals are forbidden the safeguards that others enjoy *or may seek* without constraint") (emphasis added). Other passages are open to more than one interpretation. For example, the Court states that "A law declaring that in general it shall be more difficult for one group of citizens than for all others to seek aid from the government is itself a denial of equal protection of the laws in the most literal sense." Id at 1628. The most natural reading of this passage is that the failure to protect gays from discrimination in the context of a general regime of nondiscrimination makes it more difficult for them to "seek aid from the government" and therefore violates equal protection "in the most literal sense." Yet the reference to seeking "aid from government" might also be read as referring to the increased difficulty in securing passage of legislation rather than to the increased difficulty in preventing discrimination.

Against these isolated passages must be weighed the overall structure of the Court's opinion. The Court begins by characterizing the Colorado Supreme Court as relying upon the argument that Amendment 2 "infringed the fundamental right of gays and lesbians to participate in the political process" and resting on prior precedent outlawing "discriminatory restructuring of governmental decisionmaking." Id at 1624. The Court then states that it affirms the state court's judgment, "but on a rationale different from that adopted by the State Supreme Court." It is in support of this "different" rationale that the Court describes the general regime of nondiscrimination and the "special" exclusion of gays from this regime. See id at 1625–27. It concludes by holding that "Amendment 2 . . . in making a general announcement that gays and lesbians shall not have any particular protections from the law, inflicts on them immediate, continuing, and real injuries that outrun and belie any legitimate justifications that may be claimed for it." Id at 1628–29. The passage seems to say that it is this substantive withdrawal of protection, rather than the procedural obstacles that prevent its reinstatement, that inflicts the "immediate, continuing and real injuries" the Constitution prohibits.

[55] The Court states that it is deciding the case against the backdrop of the principle that "if a law neither burdens a fundamental right nor targets a suspect class, we will uphold the legislative classification so long as it bears a rational relation to some legitimate end." 116 S Ct at 1627. It invalidates Amendment 2 because it "fails, indeed defies, even this conventional inquiry." Id.

[56] The Court emphasizes that "the amendment has the peculiar property of imposing a broad and undifferentiated disability on a single named group, an exceptional . . . form of legislation," id, and notes that "[t]he resulting disqualification of a class of persons from the right to seek specific protection from the law is unprecedented in our jurisprudence." Id at 1628.

[57] Colorado argued that the Amendment served the legitimate purpose of protecting freedom of association, respecting the liberty of landlords and employers with personal or religious objections to homosexuality, and conserving resources to fight discrimination against other groups. Id at 1629. The Court's response indicated that it might be more receptive to arguments along these lines if the measure had been more narrowly drawn:

> The breadth of the Amendment is so far removed from these particular justifications that we find it impossible to credit them. We cannot say that Amendment 2 is directed to any identifiable legitimate purpose or discrete objective. It is a status-based enactment divorced from any factual context from which we could

It does not even necessarily follow that *Bowers* is doomed. At first blush, it seems anomalous to say that the state has the constitutional authority to jail people who engage in same-sex sodomy, but not to exempt them from antidiscrimination laws. In other contexts, however, the Court has sometimes rejected analogous "greater power includes the lesser power" arguments. For example, the Court has sometimes held that although the government might withhold funding from a program altogether, the conditions it attaches to funding must rationally relate to the program's purpose.[58] Similarly, it might be argued that the state's theoretical power to criminalize conduct[59] does not mean that it can use unrelated programs to discourage the activity. Theoretically, the state can make smoking cigarettes a criminal offense; but it might be unconstitutional for the state simply to deny drivers licenses to people who smoke.

These arguments favoring a narrow reading of the opinion are surely fair, but it would also be wrong to make too much of them. Although the Court purports to use rational basis review, it is worth remembering that the modern assault on gender discrimination began in this fashion as well.[60] Only later did the Court acknowledge that its insistence on "rational basis" really amounted to heightened scrutiny.[61]

Moreover, even if the Court never elevates sexual orientation to

---

discern a relationship to legitimate state interests; it is a classification of persons undertaken for its own sake, something the Equal Protection Clause does not permit.

Id.

[58] See, for example, *South Dakota v Dole*, 483 US 203, 207 (1987) ("[O]ur cases have suggested . . . that conditions on federal grants might be illegitimate if they are unrelated 'to the federal interest in particular national projects or programs.' " (quoting *Massachusetts v United States*, 435 US 444, 461 (1978) (plurality opinion))). Compare *Harris v McRae*, 448 US 297, 317 n 19 (1980) ("A substantial constitutional question would arise if Congress had attempted to withhold all Medicaid benefits from an otherwise eligible candidate simply because that candidate had exercised her constitutionally protected freedom to terminate her pregnancy by abortion."). This line of authority rests on the ability somehow to determine abstract "purposes" for programs that are independent of the statutory provisions that define them.

[59] In Colorado's case, the power is only theoretical. Colorado has chosen not to criminalize same-sex sodomy. See *Romer v Evans*, 116 S Ct at 1633 (Scalia dissenting).

[60] See *Reed v Reed*, 404 US 71 (1971) (invalidating gender classification regarding persons entitled to administer decedent's estate because it failed to bear "rational relationship" to state's objective).

[61] See *Craig v Boren*, 429 US 190 (1976) (establishing intermediate scrutiny for gender classifications).

suspect class status, the kind of "rational basis" review *Romer* uses has potentially far-reaching consequences. The Court relies upon the strand of rational basis precedent holding that it is impermissible to base a classification upon mere dislike of an unpopular group.[62] The breadth of Amendment 2 is relevant because it demonstrates such dislike.[63] It is for just this reason that the Court did not follow the practice of rejecting a facial challenge if any application of the measure would be constitutional. Here, no application would be constitutional because the Amendment's indiscriminate assault on gay people demonstrated that *any* application would be infected by the pervasive dislike that the Constitution prohibits.[64]

It follows that less comprehensive measures—for example, laws banning gay marriages, the failure to include gay couples within state-sponsored health plans, or the don't ask/don't tell policy—would also be invalid if they were infected by similar animosity. To be sure, proof of such animosity might be more difficult with respect to measures that are narrower in scope. Perhaps some such measures might be supported on instrumental grounds unrelated to mere disapproval of gay sex. The fact remains, however, that most discrimination against gay people rests at bottom on moral disapproval, which the Court has now recharacterized as irrational animosity. Indeed, the *Bowers* Court acknowledged as much when it upheld state laws banning homosexual sodomy on this basis,[65] and Justice Scalia implicitly makes a similar point when he argues in dissent that moral disapproval provides the necessary justification for Amendment 2.[66] The contemporary justification for the ban on gay marriage ultimately rests on moral grounds.[67] Exclusion

---

[62]

> [L]aws of the kind now before us raise the inevitable inference that the disadvantage imposed is born of animosity toward the class of persons affected. "[I]f the constitutional conception of 'equal protection of the laws' means anything, it must at the very least mean that a bare . . . desire to harm a politically unpopular group cannot constitute a *legitimate* governmental interest."

116 S Ct at 1628 (quoting from *Department of Agriculture v Moreno*, 413 US 528 (1973) (emphasis in original)).

[63] See 116 S Ct at 1629.

[64] Id.

[65] 478 US at 195 (cited in note 8).

[66] See 116 S Ct at 1633 (Scalia dissenting).

[67] See, for example, 142 Cong Rec H7277 (July 11, 1996) (remarks of Congressman Hoke) (arguing for Defense of Marriage Act on ground that "[i]t is through the law that we as a nation express the morals and the moral sensibilities of the United States.").

of gay people from the military poses more complex issues, but to the extent that it rests upon arguments about "unit cohesion," it too might be vulnerable to challenge.[68]

C. LIBERAL AND CONSERVATIVE ACTIVISM

These are remarkable outcomes. Perhaps it bears emphasis that *Romer* invites, but does not demand them. The ultimate meaning of *Romer* is likely to remain contested for the foreseeable future. Still, even if future courts reject the radical reading of *Romer*, few would have predicted that the Rehnquist Court would have produced a document fairly open to this interpretation. Moreover, if one broadens the focus from the decision's particular doctrinal implications to its more general jurisprudential approach, *Romer's* radicalism becomes still more apparent. To see why, we need to examine with some care the very first words of the Court's opinion:

> One century ago, the first Justice Harlan admonished this Court that the Constitution "neither knows nor tolerates classes among citizens." *Plessy v Ferguson* . . . (dissenting opinion). Unheeded then, those words now are understood to state a commitment to the law's neutrality where the rights of persons are at stake.[69]

The Court's dramatic invocation of the Harlan dissent, coming almost precisely one hundred years to the day after *Plessy* was decided, is doubly ironic. First, in important respects, *Romer* actually repudiates the jurisprudential presuppositions of Harlan's *Plessy* dissent. Second, that repudiation makes hash out of the "law's neutrality," which the Court also seeks to invoke.

These problems become apparent when we consider the fault lines around which modern constitutional argument has been organized. One division has been between supporters of judicial ac-

---

[68] Arguably, exclusion of gay people from military service is distinguishable because it rests only indirectly on animus toward homosexuals. The government's interest is in "unit cohesion," rather than in morality. The interest is threatened because private individuals (other soldiers), rather than the government officials, are motivated by dislike of or discomfort with homosexuals. The Court has rejected a similar argument in the racial context, however. See *Palmore v Sidoti*, 466 US 429 (1984) (equal protection prohibits reliance on private prejudice as ground for divesting divorced mother of custody of child when she remarries man of different race).

[69] 116 S Ct at 1623 (quoting *Plessy v Ferguson*, 163 US 537, 559 (1896) (Harlan dissenting)).

tivism and restraint. Judicial activists favor relatively uninhibited judicial intervention to enforce the norms that judges find in the Constitution. Advocates of restraint, in contrast, counsel against judicial interference with political outcomes. If one views *Romer* through this lens, the Court's invocation of the *Plessy* dissent is entirely appropriate. Both opinions reflect a willingness to use judicial power to invalidate political decisions thought to violate constitutional norms. The Warren Court is conventionally thought to represent a high point—or low point, depending upon one's perspective—of this tradition. On this view, then, *Romer*, the *Plessy* dissent, and Warren Court jurisprudence are all linked.

The trouble with this way of organizing constitutional argument is that it fails to capture the disagreement that animates modern discussion of judicial review. Today, no sitting Justice is a consistent advocate of judicial restraint. Within the last several years, the Court has regularly invalidated many political outcomes in areas as diverse as affirmative action,[70] federalism,[71] separation of powers,[72] free speech rights,[73] reproductive autonomy,[74] gender discrimination,[75] property rights,[76] and political districting.[77] Nor is there a significant difference between "liberal" and "conservative" Justices with regard to the frequency with which they support "activist" results. Both liberals and conservatives can regularly be found arguing for activism and for restraint in various contexts.

It would be a mistake, however, to suppose that the Court has reached consensus on these issues. On the contrary, the Justices

---

[70] See *Adarand Constructors, Inc. v Pena*, 115 S Ct 2097 (1995); *City of Richmond v J.A. Croson Co.*, 488 US 469 (1989).

[71] See *United States v Lopez*, 115 S Ct 1624 (1995); *New York v United States*, 505 US 144 (1992).

[72] See, for example, *Metropolitan Washington Airports Authority v Citizens for the Abatement of Aircraft Noise*, 501 US 252 (1991); *Bowsher v Synar*, 478 US 714 (1986); *INS v Chadha*, 462 US 919 (1983).

[73] See, for example, *44 Liquormart, Inc. v Rhode Island*, 116 S Ct 1495 (1996); *Denver Area Educational Telecommunications Consortium, Inc. v Federal Communications Commn*, 116 S Ct 2374 (1996); *Colorado Republican Federal Campaign Comm. v Federal Election Commn.*, 116 S Ct 2309 (1996).

[74] See *Planned Parenthood of Southeastern Pennsylvania v Casey*, 505 US 833 (1992).

[75] See *United States v Virginia*, 116 S Ct 2264 (1996).

[76] See *Lucas v South Carolina Coastal Council*, 505 US 1003 (1992); *Nollan v California Coastal Commn*, 483 US 825 (1987).

[77] See *Miller v Johnson*, 115 S Ct 2475 (1995); *Shaw v Reno*, 113 S Ct 2816 (1993). Cf *Davis v Bandemer*, 478 US 109 (1986).

have sharply divided over many of the cases cited above. This is so because the real dispute in modern constitutional law is not between advocates of activism and restraint, but between advocates of liberal and conservative activism. Whereas constitutional liberals, who remember the Warren Court nostalgically, favor judicial activism in order to force the rest of the government to become more activist, constitutional conservatives, who revile the Warren Court, favor judicial activism in order to keep the rest of the government passive.

The majority of the Court's recent "activist" decisions have been of the conservative variety. These decisions treat market outcomes achieved in a private sphere as presumptively free and government intervention as potentially coercive and inherently suspect. On this view, the judiciary must be activist so as to provide the space that individuals need to conduct their lives free of government coercion. For example, the Court's recent hostility to affirmative action[78] seems premised on the assumption that racial disproportions produced by private activity are simply "there" and require no justification, whereas government action to correct these disproportions violates core constitutional values. Similarly, the Court's revived interest in free speech rights[79] assumes that people are "free" to speak when "Congress makes no laws" and that private interference with speech markets poses no threat to liberty.

Viewed from this perspective, the link between *Romer* and the *Plessy* dissent dissolves. The issue in *Plessy* was the constitutionality of state regulation of privately owned systems of transportation. While the majority was prepared to permit such regulation, Justice Harlan's dissent argued for the autonomy of private market outcomes. The opinion therefore reflects conservative activism.

In this sense, the true descendant of Justice Harlan's *Plessy* dissent is not the *Romer* majority, but the *Bowers v Hardwick* dissent. The *Bowers* dissent treated homosexual activity in the same way that Justice Harlan treated decisions by private railway companies concerning integrated seating: within a private sphere that was not subject to government control.

Advocates of gay rights did not prevail in *Bowers*, however. In-

---

[78] See note 70.

[79] See note 73.

stead, they prevailed in *Romer*, where the issue was not the government's obligation to remain outside the private sphere, but its obligation to expand the public sphere. Instead of holding that the government must refrain from coercion, the Court's *Romer* holding means that Colorado is now required to use the coercive power of the state to prevent private parties from discriminating against gay people.[80] There is precedent for this sort of use of judicial power, but the precedent is not the *Plessy* dissent. It is, instead, the line of cases that developed during the Warren Court period. These cases, in turn, were rooted in a version of American Legal Realism, the development of which—ironically—was motivated by the desire to refute positions analogous to that taken in Harlan's *Plessy* opinion.

To be sure, realism is conventionally treated as developing in response to *Lochner v New York* and the Court's invalidation of social and economic legislation during the first part of the twentieth century.[81] Justice Harlan, himself, dissented in *Lochner*,[82] as well as in *The Civil Rights Cases*,[83] where he indicated a willingness to permit (although not compel) government coercion to enforce a regime of racial nondiscrimination. These opinions are consistent with the judicial restraint position. But although Harlan's own views were complex and not altogether consistent, there can be no doubt that at least some of his contemporaries saw a connection between his stand in *Plessy* and the rise of substantive due process.

The roots of substantive due process lie in legal formalism—a strongly libertarian jurisprudential position that takes as its project the limitation of the state's power.[84] Formalism treats the private sphere as prepolitical and presumptively free. People who remain within this sphere are juridically equal and free to choose their own life plans and values. The state, in turn, must be rigorously

---

[80] Of course, this requirement holds only so long as Colorado continues to provide protection for other vulnerable groups. For a discussion of the Warren Court's use of equal protection methodology to force government action, see pages 92–94.

[81] See, for example, Elizabeth Mensch, *The History of Mainstream Legal Thought*, in David Kairys, ed, *The Politics of Law* 26 (Pantheon, 1982) ("realism was . . . a reaction against Supreme Court decisions . . . which had invalidated progressive regulatory legislation favored even by many business leaders.").

[82] 198 US 45, 65 (1905).

[83] 109 US 3, 26 (1883).

[84] See, for example, Gary Peller, *The Metaphysics of American Law*, 73 Cal L Rev 1151, 1193–1207 (1985).

neutral as between these different life plans and goals. Its sole justification is to prevent individuals from interfering with other individuals. It achieves this goal by strictly adhering to formal equality
between citizens and by not interfering with the rights of these
citizens unless they interfere with the rights of others.

This conception of law, celebrated most famously in *Lochner*,
emerged much earlier as part of the ideological base of the abolitionist movement.[85] The cry of free labor and free contracts was
an important component of abolitionist rhetoric.[86] It is not a coincidence that the Republican party, born in the fight against slavery,
reached maturity as the party of free market capitalism. Legal formalism was far more congenial to the rapidly industrializing north
than to the rural south. It was therefore natural for Justice Harlan
to insist upon formal equality—color blindness—and to resist government regulation in the form of state-imposed segregation. Nor
was it an accident that when Harlan and his colleagues took the
first hesitant steps to distinguish *Plessy* and whittle away at Jim
Crow, they relied upon theories grounded in the rights of private
property, freedom of contract, and substantive due process.[87]

By the time legal academics began their assault on formalism in
the first part of the twentieth century, the political valence of the
formalist position had shifted. Government neutrality, protection
for private property, and freedom of contract were now seen as

[85] For a discussion, see William E. Nelson, *The Impact of the Antislavery Movement Upon Styles of Judicial Reasoning in Nineteenth Century America*, 87 Harv L Rev 513, 547–58 (1974).

[86] See Eric Foner, *Free Soil, Free Labor, Free Men: The Ideology of the Republican Party Before the Civil War* (Oxford Univ Press, 1970).

[87] For example, in *Berea College v Commonwealth of Kentucky*, 211 US 45, 67–68 (1908), Justice Harlan, writing in dissent, used substantive due process principles in an attempt to distinguish *Plessy* and defend the right of a private college to operate on an integrated basis. Although only Justice Day joined the dissent, the majority failed to engage him on this crucial point. Whereas the state court had relied primarily on the argument that the state had a constitutionally adequate interest in preventing even voluntary intermixing of the races, the Supreme Court affirmed the judgment on the narrow ground that the College, as a corporation created by the state, lacked the rights that an individual would have. Nine years later, the seeds planted by Justice Harlan's dissent ripened into a holding when the Court, in an opinion by Justice Day, struck down a segregation statute, making it unlawful for members of one race to occupy a residence on a block upon which the majority of houses were occupied by members of another race, on substantive due process grounds. See *Buchanan v Warley*, 245 US 60 (1917).

For a modern argument associating the struggle against Jim Crow with free market capi-
talism, see Jennifer Roback, *The Political Economy of Segregation: The Case of Segregated Street-cars*, 46 J Econ Hist 893 (1986); Jennifer Roback, *Southern Labor Law in the Jim Crow Era: Exploitative or Competititive*, 51 U Chi L Rev 1161 (1984).

cementing existing social relations instead of undermining them. The realists, political liberals who were interested in redistribution, developed two sorts of critiques of the formalist position. First, they disputed the proposition that there was a coherent line between public and private spheres. The private sphere itself was constituted by background principles of law that were not "natural" or "pre-political," but reflected public decisions.[88] The goal of state neutrality was therefore incoherent. Whether by acting or by failing to act, the state was always taking some position with regard to the distribution of resources.

Second, they disputed the association between freedom and the private sphere. State passivity often left individuals at the mercy of other individuals, who obstructed their freedom.[89] State intervention that curbed private power was sometimes a prerequisite to true freedom.

Originally, these critiques served as the basis for the replacement of judicial activism with judicial restraint. With the effective overruling of *Lochner*, the Roosevelt Court stood passively by as Congress enacted sweeping regulatory legislation.[90] Realists of the 1930s argued that because there was no "neutral" position that validated judicial intervention, public policy should be left to the political process.

By the 1950s, however, the Warren Court began to use realism as a basis for a new form of judicial activism. The transformation was first apparent in the law of race. Whereas the *Plessy* dissent equated racial equality with the withdrawal of government power, the Warren Court understood that Jim Crow could not be dismantled without government intervention.

Sometimes, the Court merely permitted such intervention. For example, its validation of the 1964 and 1965 Civil Rights Acts[91] was compatible with the older judicial restraint version of realism.

---

[88] See, for example, Morris R. Cohen, *Property and Sovereignty*, 13 Cornell L Q 8 (1927).

[89] See, for example, Robert Hale, *Coercion and Distribution in a Supposedly Non-Coercive State*, 38 Pol Sci Q 470 (1923).

[90] See, for example, *NLRB v Jones & Laughlin Steel Corp.*, 301 US 1 (1937) (upholding National Labor Relations Act); *Wickard v Filburn*, 317 US 111 (1942) (upholding Agricultural Adjustment Act); *Steward Machine Co. v Davis*, 301 US 548 (1937) (upholding Social Security Act).

[91] See *Heart of Atlanta Motel v United States*, 379 US 241 (1964) (upholding 1964 Act); *Katzenbach v McClung*, 379 US 294 (1964) (same); *South Carolina v Katzenbach*, 383 US 301 (1966) (upholding 1965 Act).

The Court did no more than "get out of the way" of the political branches when Congress used federal authority against the states and private actors who were engaged in discrimination.

It was obvious, however, that Congress could not be relied upon to do all that needed to be done. Consequently, the Court's most important and dramatic decisions—in particular *Brown v Board of Education,*[92] and the cases that followed—do not fit within the judicial restraint pattern. Instead, the Court crafted a new version of activism that forced government to intervene.

To be sure, *Brown*'s attack on racial classifications is compatible with the formal equality that Justice Harlan had insisted upon in *Plessy. Brown* can be understood as starting from Justice Harlan's premise that formal distinctions between whites and blacks are constitutionally suspect. Even in the beginning, though, the Court's approach was significantly different. Whereas Justice Harlan failed to go beyond the formal requirement, Chief Justice Warren emphasized the effect of segregation on black children and the government's affirmative obligation to do something about this effect.[93] In the cases that followed *Brown*, the Court made clear that "neutrality" and formal equality regarding integration were insufficient. Instead, the government had an affirmative obligation to implement integration plans that "promise[d] realistically to work, and promise[d] realistically to work now."[94] The upshot was an insistence that desegregation plans be race-conscious—the reversal of Justice Harlan's color-blind requirement.[95] Moreover, the Warren Court's state action cases emphasized public responsibility for racial oppression that existed in the "private" sphere. Instead

---

[92] 347 US 483 (1954).

[93] In perhaps the most famous passage in the opinion, Chief Justice Warren wrote that "[t]o separate [African-American children] from others of similar age and qualifications solely because of their race generates a feeling of inferiority as to their status in the community that may affect their hearts and minds in a way unlikely ever to be undone." 347 US at 494.

[94] See *Green v County School Board of New Kent County,* 391 US 430, 439 (1968).

[95] For example, in *North Carolina State Board of Education v Swann,* 402 US 43 (1971), the Court invalidated a North Carolina statute providing that no student should be assigned to a school on the basis of race. The Court wrote that "[j]ust as the race of students must be considered in determining whether a constitutional violation has occurred, so also must race be considered in formulating a remedy. To forbid, at this stage, all assignments made on the basis of race would deprive school authorities of the one tool absolutely essential to fulfillment of their constitutional obligation to eliminate existing dual school systems." 402 US at 46.

of accepting the prepolitical character of this sphere and equating it with freedom, the Court directed attention to the ways in which the government action influenced supposedly private conduct and the oppression that this conduct created.[96]

In the waning days of the Warren era, the Court began to extend its new version of judicial activism beyond race. Much of this expansion developed under the rubric of "substantive equal protection"—a doctrine that required "strict scrutiny" of government measures unequally impinging on constitutional rights.[97]

At first blush, this doctrine seems mysterious. If a measure in fact infringes a constitutional right, why is it not simply invalid under the constitutional provision that establishes that right? What additional work is done by the Equal Protection Clause? The doctrine makes more sense against the backdrop of the Court's experience with conservative judicial activism. In part, equal protection rhetoric allowed the Court to avoid the distasteful label of "substantive due process." The difference between substantive due process and substantive equal protection was not simply verbal, however. Historically, due process analysis was tied to libertarian theories of constitutional rights. This vocabulary did not permit the Court to require extensions of government power. In contrast, heightening the level of scrutiny under the Equal Protection Clause permitted the Court to require government intervention. It is hard to see how X's liberty is invaded if the government extends a benefit only to Y, but X can claim that his right to equality is violated. Although in theory the government can remedy this violation by withdrawing the benefit from Y, in practice it will often extend the benefit to X. Hence, equality, unlike liberty, provided a tool to implement the goals of liberal judicial activism by requiring an expansion of governmental authority.

---

[96] See, for example, *Evans v Newton*, 382 US 296 (1966) (state implicated in administration of racially segregated park); *Burton v Wilmington Parking Authority*, 365 US 715 (1961) (state implicated in segregatory policies of private restaurant operating in government-owned building).

[97] See, for example, *Harper v Virginia State Board of Elections*, 383 US 663 (1966) (poll tax violates equal protection); *Griffin v Illinois*, 351 US 12 (1956) (failure to provide transcript for indigent defendant violates equal protection); *Douglas v California*, 372 US 353 (1963) (failure to appoint counsel for indigent for first appeal of right violates equal protection). Compare *Shapiro v Thompson*, 394 US 618 (1969) (waiting period for welfare benefits subject to strict scrutiny because it penalizes constitutionally protected right to travel).

In a series of cases dealing with welfare and poverty, the Warren Court began to explore some of the possibilities of liberal activism.[98] The process was cut short by the 1968 election, Chief Justice Warren's retirement, and the rapid appointment of four conservative Justices.[99] The end of the Warren Court era was effectively announced in *San Antonio Independent School District v Rodriguez*,[100] where the Court sharply limited the substantive equal protection doctrine by proclaiming its refusal to heighten the level of equal protection scrutiny to protect nontextual rights.

The *Rodriguez* Court purported to justify this refusal in terms of judicial restraint. The majority claimed that the Court lacked legitimate authority to protect rights not specified in the text of the Constitution.[101] But this explanation will not do. In the same term that Justice Powell authored *Rodriguez*, he joined the Court's majority in *Roe v Wade*,[102] one of the most important activist decisions of the century and a decision that plainly gave protection to nontextual rights.

In fact, instead of shifting the court from activism to restraint, *Rodriguez* and *Roe* announced the movement from liberal to conservative activism. Significantly, the *Roe* Court relied upon substantive due process rather than equal protection to invalidate abortion laws. Its decision narrowed, rather than broadened, the public sphere.

This shift from equality to liberty was linked to a return to a formal conception of rights. For example, Justice Marshall's *Rodri-*

---

[98] See note 97.

[99] Some of the most eloquent statements of the liberal activist position came in dissenting opinions delivered after the liberals no longer controlled a working majority of the Court. See, for example, *San Antonio Independent School District v Rodriguez*, 411 US 1, 70–72 (1973) (Marshall dissenting). For an even more sweeping assertion of liberal activist views, see *Board of Regents of State Colleges v Roth*, 408 US 564, 588–89 (1972) (Marshall dissenting):

> In my view, every citizen who applies for a government job is entitled to it unless the government can establish some reason for denying employment. This is . . . liberty—liberty to work—which is the 'very essence of the personal freedom and opportunity' secured by the Fourteenth Amendment.

[100] 411 US 1 (1973).

[101] See id at 33 ("It is not the province of this Court to create substantive constitutional rights in the name of guaranteeing equal protection of the laws. . . . [T]he key to discovering whether education is 'fundamental' . . . [is] whether there is a right to education explicitly or implicitly guaranteed by the Constitution.").

[102] 410 US 113 (1973).

guez dissent argued for a constitutional requirement to make free speech rights truly meaningful by affirmative government intervention through the provision of adequate education.[103] In contrast, the majority held that the government had no obligation to make the exercise of rights effective. The Constitution was satisfied so long as the government did not formally obstruct that exercise.[104] Similarly, a few years after *Roe*, the Court rejected a substantive equal protection challenge to the failure to fund abortions.[105] *Roe* required a withdrawal of government coercion, not the provision of a government subsidy.

Four years after *Rodriguez*, the Court effectively extended this analysis to the race problem. In *Washington v Davis*,[106] the Court held that the Fourteenth Amendment required no more than the formal equality espoused in the *Plessy* dissent. So long as the government did not intervene to make things worse for African-Americans, it had no constitutional responsibility to make things better.[107] Their actual status in society was located within a private sphere that was not a product of government action.

Standing alone, *Washington v Davis* might be read as a manifestation of judicial restraint. *Washington v Davis* goes no further than to say that the Constitution did not mandate government action to improve the status of African-Americans. However, the Court's more recent affirmative action holdings make clear that it has adopted a conservative activist stance with regard to race. Now

---

[103] 411 US at 112 (Marshall dissenting).

[104] According to Justice Powell:

The Court has long afforded zealous protection against unjustifiable governmental interference with the individual's rights to speak and to vote. Yet we have never presumed to possess either the ability or the authority to guarantee to the citizenry the most *effective* speech or the most *informed* electoral choice. That these may be desirable goals . . . is not to be doubted. . . . But they are not values to be implemented by judicial intrusion into otherwise legitimate state activities.

411 US at 36 (emphasis in original).

[105] See *Maher v Roe*, 432 US 464 (1977). See also *Harris v McRae*, 448 US 297 (1980).

[106] 426 US 229 (1976).

[107] The narrow holding of *Washington v Davis* was that in the absence of an impermissible purpose, government programs that have a disproportionately negative impact on racial minorities are not subject to heightened scrutiny under the Equal Protection Clause. See 426 US at 239. The holding means that so long as the government does not go out of its way deliberately to make things worse for African-Americans, it has no affirmative obligation to adjust its programs so as to make things better.

federal courts stand ready to intervene so as to prevent the government from going beyond formal equality.[108] In effect, the Constitution protects the integrity of a private sphere within which the fate of African-Americans will be decided.

D. ROMER AND LIBERAL ACTIVISM

Viewed against this backdrop, *Romer*'s radicalism becomes apparent. With liberal activism in full retreat everywhere else, the Court has suddenly revived it with respect to gay rights. Few would have predicted such a revival. Now that it has occurred, however, the setting for it seems especially appropriate.

Recall that realists rejected the idea of an autonomous private sphere and argued that even if such a sphere existed, it was wrong to assume that individuals were free when they remained within it.[109] These arguments have special bite in the context of discrimination against gay people. It is obvious to anyone willing to look that the supposedly private sphere within which people make choices about sexual relations is publicly constituted. Indeed, opponents of gay rights concede as much when they argue that changes in government policy regarding homosexuality will lead to more of it. This empirical claim may or may not be right, but whether or not individuals respond to incentives regarding sexual orientation, few can doubt that the incentives are present. Even if one puts to one side the criminalization of some gay sex, the government offers very substantial subsidies for those willing to participate in heterosexual marriage, subsidies that are not available to those who choose to engage openly in gay behavior.

It is obvious as well that even if the government were entirely passive—indeed, especially when it remains entirely passive—gay people do not lead lives that are free. In fact, direct government coercion plays a secondary role in the subjugation of gay people, and the impact of criminal statutes such as the one validated in *Bowers* is trivial. Instead, the subjugation is accomplished through a system of private violence, social ostracism, and ostentatious in-

---

[108] See *Adarand Constructors, Inc. v Pena*, 115 S Ct 2097 (1995) (applying strict scrutiny to affirmative action program); *City of Richmond v J.A. Croson Co.*, 488 US 469 (1989) (same).

[109] See page 91.

difference—attitudes and conduct that the government tolerates even when it does not promote them.

To its great credit, the *Romer* Court built its opinion on these realist insights. The Court refused to accept the myth of laissez-faire as the baseline against which constitutional rights are measured. Instead, it acknowledged that the web of antidiscrimination laws defines the supposedly "private" space within which individual choices about sexual relations are made.[110] The Court also refused to equate government nonintervention with individual freedom. On the contrary, it recognized that it is antidiscrimination law that makes possible "an almost limitless number of transactions and endeavors that constitute ordinary civic life in a free society."[111]

The Court deserves credit as well for the moral imagination necessary to see that this treatment of gay people is constitutionally problematic. Discrimination against gay people would be untroubling if they were definitionally outside the political community. Only a decade ago, the Court endorsed something like this view. For the *Bowers* majority, it was obvious that there was "[n]o connection between family, marriage, or procreation on the one hand and homosexual activity on the other."[112] Not content with the majority's expulsion of gay people from the affective community, Chief Justice Burger insisted on their expulsion from the moral community as well. Condemnation of homosexuality was "firmly rooted in Judeo-Christian moral and ethical standards." To grant it constitutional protection "would be to cast aside millennia of moral teaching."[113]

Instead of excluding gay people from the community, the new majority built empathic connections to them.[114] All claims from equality depend upon analogies between the benefited and bur-

---

[110] See 116 S Ct at 1626.

[111] Id at 1627.

[112] *Bowers v Hardwick*, 478 US 186, 191 (1986).

[113] Id at 197 (Burger concurring).

[114] Compare *Bowers v Hardwick*, 478 US at 191 ("No connection between family, marriage, or procreation on the one hand and homosexual activity on the other has been demonstrated") with *Romer v Evans*, 116 S Ct at 1629 ("We must conclude that Amendment 2 classifies homosexuals not to further a proper legislative end but to make them unequal to everyone else. This Colorado cannot do. A State cannot so deem a class of persons a stranger to its laws.").

dened group. It is precisely because gay people are relevantly similar to other groups protected by antidiscrimination laws that the state's failure to provide such protection to gay people violates the Constitution. The *Romer* Court's willingness to see these similarities—to hold itself open to the suffering of people whose sexual practices may seem alien, but who are nonetheless deemed fundamentally the same—is in the best tradition of Warren Court activism.

It bears emphasis that this reading of *Romer* is supported, but not mandated, by the text of the opinion. The ultimate "meaning" of *Romer* will depend upon what future courts make of the decision, rather than on anything inherent in the opinion itself. Deciding whether *Romer* protects gay marriages or invalidates "don't ask/don't tell" is therefore a little like speculating about Hamlet's childhood. The opinion provides new grounds for challenging old ways of thinking, but it cannot determine whether those challenges will ultimately succeed. For now, the only thing that is certain is that the opinion is open to a broad construction if future courts are disposed to so construe it. Whether they will be so disposed depends upon future political and social developments that we cannot reliably predict.

II. Activism and Neutrality

Precisely because *Romer*'s future is indeterminate, now is the time to resume the conversation, interrupted a quarter century ago, about the potential advantages and disadvantages of Warren Court activism. The advantages are obvious. The Court's willingness to expand social categories so as to include ostracized groups has the potential of building connections between people who previously envisioned themselves as hopelessly divided. The result is a society that is more inclusive and empathetic with fewer individuals who bear unnecessary pain and isolation.

What of the disadvantages? In recent years, it has become fashionable to attack the Court's actual ability to bring about the state of affairs promised by liberal activists. It is said that the Court's political capital is extremely limited, that judicial decisions seldom produce social change, and that judicial intervention sometimes di-

verts energy from, or even obstructs, the kind of political organizing more likely to produce lasting and meaningful reform.[115]

These are serious charges, but for now, I want to put them to
one side. Instead, in this Part and the one that follows, I will focus
on two interrelated problems: the difficulty Warren Court activism
poses for the defense of constitutional neutrality, and the implicit
exclusionary implications of such activism. In the final Part, I will
argue that these problems, although real enough on their own
terms, nonetheless also provide a means by which the Court can
overcome its political weakness and succeed in implementing its
agenda.

A. THE ELUSIVE GOAL OF NEUTRALITY

To see the first problem, we need to return to the quotation
from Justice Harlan's *Plessy* dissent with which the *Romer* majority
begins its opinion. We have already seen that *Romer* stands in opposition to Harlan's conservative activism. Yet the *Romer* majority
nonetheless seeks to invoke Harlan's defense of "the law's neutrality where the rights of persons are at stake." How are we to make
sense of this "neutrality" once it is disengaged from Harlan's jurisprudential stance?

The goal of neutrality makes some sense from the perspective of
judicial restraint. A court determined not to interfere with political
outcomes is neutral in the sense that it neither requires nor prohibits those outcomes. For example, Justice Harlan's dissent in
Lochner[116] would neither require nor prohibit labor legislation.
Similarly, modern dissenters from the Court's affirmative action
jurisprudence would leave the political branches free either to enact or reject measures favoring minorities.[117]

There is a sense in which conservative activists also defend neu-

---

[115] See, for example, Gerald Rosenberg, *The Hollow Hope: Can Courts Bring About Social Change?* (Univ of Chicago Press, 1991); Michael Klarman, *Rethinking the Civil Rights and Civil Liberties Revolution*, 82 U Va L Rev 1 (1996).

[116] 198 US 45, 65 (1905).

[117] See, for example, *Adarand Constructors, Inc. v Pena*, 115 S Ct 2097, 2134 (1995) (Ginsburg dissenting) ("[I]n view of the attention the political branches are currently giving the
matter of affirmative action, I see no compelling cause for the intervention the Court has
made in this case. . . . [I]n this area, large deference is owed by the Judiciary to
[Congress].").

trality. They believe that certain matters should be left in a private sphere precisely because the government should remain neutral with regard to them. Justice Harlan's *Plessy* dissent left railways free to adopt or reject racist seating arrangements. Similarly, not all advocates of abortion rights believe that abortion is a good thing. They favor judicially enforced government neutrality respecting abortion so that people can decide for themselves whether it is a good thing or not.[118]

It is far less clear what liberal activists could possibly mean by neutrality. Recall that liberal activism began with the realist critique of the supposed neutrality of conservative activism. Once one sees that the boundaries of the private sphere are, themselves, the result of public choice, the neutrality of conservative activism evaporates. Thus, when the Court invalidated wage and hour legislation during the *Lochner* period, it was not being neutral. By choosing this particular location for the boundary between private and public, it favored employers who possessed the power to coerce employees into accepting harsh conditions of employment.

Nor, of course, can liberal activism accept the idea that neutrality consists of judicial restraint and upholding political decisions. The Court's inaction leaves in place a state of affairs for which it bears some responsibility: the *Plessy* court was responsible for failing to dismantle a regime that was strikingly nonneutral.

In short, once one recognizes that there is no "natural" state of affairs, departures from which (associated with government changes in the "private" status quo) are nonneutral, the "commitment to the law's neutrality where the rights of persons are at stake" evaporates. Government choices can be legislative or judicial, and they can take the form of feasance or nonfeasance, but whatever their form and institutional structure, they always take some side in a contested, public debate.

The collapse of the ideal of constitutional neutrality is painfully obvious on even a superficial reading of *Romer*. Because government nonintervention is not a natural state of affairs, the Court, in good liberal activist fashion, takes the general regime of government-mandated antidiscrimination as a baseline. It claims that it

---

[118] See, for example, *Planned Parenthood of Southeastern Pennsylvania v Casey*, 505 US 833, 853 (1992) (abortion right protected because it involves "personal decisions concerning not only the meaning of procreation but also human responsibility and respect for it.").

is enforcing the neutrality requirement by insisting that gay people receive the same benefits from antidiscrimination policy accorded to other groups.

There is a sense in which this stance does indeed require neutrality. But there is an obvious sense in which it does not. The failure to protect gay people from discrimination is nonneutral only to the extent that homosexuality is an irrelevant characteristic that does not justify different treatment. Moral conservatives who oppose gay rights deny precisely this point, and by dismissing their objection, the Court plainly allies itself with the enemies of moral conservatism—a fact that it cannot obscure by rhetorically equating moral disapproval with irrational animus.

The Court acknowledges the state's argument that the Amendment is designed to protect "other citizens' freedom of association, and in particular the liberties of landlords or employers who have personal or religious objections to homosexuality,"[119] but asserts that "[t]he breadth of the Amendment is so far removed from these particular justifications that we find it impossible to credit them."[120] The Court's position ignores the possibility that the Amendment is based upon broader respect for, and agreement with, persons who have generalized "personal or religious objections to homosexuality" and, therefore, object to the recognition or encouragement of the practice in any context. The breadth of the Amendment is completely consistent with the government objective of favoring this view. Indeed, it is hard to imagine why else the Amendment would have been adopted.

Similarly, although the Court asserts that the statute involves "a classification of persons undertaken for its own sake,"[121] this claim will not withstand analysis. The classification is not undertaken "for its own sake" but rather to express disapproval of homosexuality. Imagine, for example, a statute that precluded municipalities from enacting measures recognizing claims of discrimination against spouse abusers. This statute would not discriminate "for its own sake." Rather, it would "discriminate" for the purpose of discouraging spouse abuse. An advocate of the measure could rightly claim that spouse abusers are different from, say, African-

---

[119] 116 S Ct at 1629.

[120] Id.

[121] Id.

Americans, the physically handicapped, or other groups protected by antidiscrimination law because spouse abusers have done something "wrong." Of course, this is precisely the claim made by moral conservatives with respect to homosexuality. By treating Amendment 2 as if it were no more than "a classification of persons undertaken for its own sake," the Court implicitly rejects that claim and, therefore, acts nonneutrally with respect to the moral conservatives who advance it.

If the Court had merely overruled *Bowers*, it might have been able to hang on to its claim of neutrality by pointing out that it was allowing individuals to decide for themselves the moral questions raised by homosexuality, much as individuals now make their own decisions about the morality of abortion or the truth of Christianity. Of course, even this outcome is not "neutral" as to people who believe that the question should be collectively decided, and it is vulnerable to attack by people who accept realism's critique of the feasance/nonfeasance distinction. In any event, the important point is that the Court went beyond a mere overruling of *Bowers*. Its decision has the effect of reviving local antidiscrimination measures, thus injecting the question into the public sphere instead of keeping it private. It is just this effect that locates *Romer* within the liberal activist tradition, and it is this effect as well that makes the Court's claim to neutrality implausible. This is so because by making the question public, the Court vindicates one set of individual choices (for example, the choice to engage in homosexual sex) at the expense of another (for example, the choice not to rent one's property to a homosexual).[122]

B. NEUTRALITY AND JUSTICE SCALIA

One would expect Justice Scalia to capitalize on this problem for the majority, and, indeed, the dissent, like the majority, attempts to

---

[122] The Court implies that a measure limited to protecting discrete groups, like landlords not wishing to rent their property to gay people, or employers not wishing to hire gay people, might be constitutional. See 116 S Ct at 1629 ("The breadth of the Amendment is so far removed from these justifications [i.e., the individual claims of landlords and employers] that we find it impossible to credit them."). The difficulty with this disintinction is that every successful claim of discrimination brought by a gay person limits the freedom of some defendant who wishes to discriminate. If the state may legitimately recognize individual claims to freedom by individual defendants, why is it unconstitutional to recognize such claims in general?

wrap itself in the mantle of neutrality. Yet surprisingly, the dissent, like the majority, ultimately denies the possibility of neutrality.

Some passages in Justice Scalia's opinion suggest that he accepts the premises of conservative activists concerning a natural, prepolitical baseline from which departures of neutrality can be measured. Thus, Justice Scalia characterizes Amendment 2 as prohibiting "special treatment"[123] for homosexuals and accuses the majority of "terminal silliness" for insisting that the denial of "preferential" treatment amounts to an equal protection violation.[124]

If one takes as a baseline a world without government intervention, then government protection of homosexuals does indeed amount to "special treatment." The treatment of homosexuals is "special" in the sense that it goes beyond the baseline formed by the government's general passivity. A conservative activist who believed in an autonomous private sphere and natural limits on the powers of government could coherently hold this view.

But conservative activism—the view that the Court should protect an autonomous private sphere from government intervention—is not Justice Scalia's true position. If it were, he would be receptive to the arguments of the *Bowers* dissent, which, of course, he is not.[125] On the contrary, he is an opponent of fixed baselines demarcating a prepolitical private sphere. He therefore believes that Colorado could, if it wished to, intervene either to prohibit gay sex or to prohibit discrimination against gay people.[126] Once this much is conceded, though, it is hard to know what to make of Justice Scalia's complaint that the Court is insisting on special treatment for gay people. As the majority points out, Colorado had shifted the baseline by insisting on a regime of nondiscrimination for many other groups. Justice Scalia's opinion provides no answer to the argument that, as measured against this baseline,

---

[123] See 116 S Ct at 1630 (Scalia dissenting) ("The amendment prohibits *special treatment* of homosexuals, and nothing more.") (emphasis in original).

[124] See id.

[125] Justice Scalia asserts that the *Bowers* holding is "unassailable, except by those who think that the Constitution changes to suit current fashions." 116 S Ct at 1631 (Scalia dissenting).

[126] Justice Scalia states that he should not be understood as being critical of "[the] legislative successes [of homosexuals]; homosexuals are as entitled to use the legal system for the reinforcement of their moral sentiments as are the rest of society." 116 S Ct at 1634.

which the state was free to adopt, the failure to protect gay people denies them equal treatment.[127]

C. NEUTRALITY IN TIME OF WAR

As if to concede the inadequacy of his claim that Amendment 2 is neutral, Justice Scalia devotes the bulk of his opinion to a demonstration that neutrality with respect to homosexuality is not constitutionally required. The point is made most dramatically in the opening sentence of his opinion: "The Court has mistaken a Kulturkampf for a fit of spite."[128]

This sentence emphatically repudiates conservative activism. It must also rank among the most disturbing statements ever to appear in the U.S. Reports. Its clear meaning is that if the majority had only understood that Colorado was engaged in a "Kulturkampf," it would have been forced to uphold Amendment 2. Could Justice Scalia conceivably understand the implications of this view?

The original Kulturkampf was an effort by the German government to rid the country of Catholic influence. At the height of this effort, the government attempted to close Catholic educational

---

[127] Oddly, in a different context, Justice Scalia has relied upon precisely this point. When the Court recognized a liberty interest protected by the Due Process Clause in the right to die, see *Cruzan v Director, Mo. Dept. of Health*, 497 US 261 (1990), Justice Scalia's concurring opinion paralleled his *Romer* objection to the Court's use of judicial power to withdraw the question from the political process. See 457 US at 293 (Scalia concurring) ("even when it *is* demonstrated by clear and convincing evidence that a patient no longer wishes certain measures to be taken to preserve her life, it is up to the citizens of Missouri to decide, through their elected representatives, whether that wish will be honored.") (emphasis in original). In the right to die context, however, Justice Scalia went on to ask whether there were "no reasonable and humane limits that ought not be exceeded in requiring an individual to preserve his own life?" He responded as follows:

> There obviously are, but they are not set forth in the Due Process Clause. What assures us that those limits will not be exceeded is the same constitutional guarantee that is the source of most of our protection—what protects us, for example, from being assessed a tax of 100% of our income above the subsistence level, from being forbidden to drive cars, or from being required to send our children to school for 10 hours a day, none of which horribles is categorically prohibited by the Constitution. Our salvation is the Equal Protection Clause, which requires the democratic majority to accept for themselves and their loved ones what they impose on you and me.

497 US at 300.

[128] 116 S Ct at 1629 (Scalia dissenting).

institutions, license priests, and jail clergy who dissented from government policy.[129]

What are we to make of Justice Scalia's invocation of these historical events? Presumably, he does not personally approve of culture wars directed against Catholics, gay people, or, for that matter, any other group. Apparently, though, he thinks that it is no business of courts to stop them once they have begun.

This is a truly radical position, which, properly understood, denies the very possibility of constitutionalism. The more traditional view, which Justice Scalia seems to reject, is that we have a constitution precisely so as to insure that our country never has a Kulturkampf. On this view, the Constitution insures that the government will remain a neutral arbiter in the struggle between contending forces. The government can demand each citizen's allegiance because it stands above sectarian squabbling and extends equal concern and respect to everyone. Constitutional restrictions on state power protect each individual against the possibility that other citizens will use government coercion to wage war against a politically vulnerable group to which she belongs.

Perhaps these are old fashioned notions, yet the continuing hold they have on us is demonstrated by the unease with which many Americans reacted to Patrick Buchanan's call to arms in a "culture war"—rhetoric with which the Scalia dissent also resonates in jarring fashion. Although Justice Scalia is often referred to as a conservative, his willingness to associate himself with Buchanan's rhetoric is not conservative at all. As I have said,[130] judicial conservatives argue for an inviolate private sphere in order to enforce a regime of government neutrality. Justice Scalia's rejection of these views is rooted not in conservatism, but in legal realism, the lessons of which he seems to have absorbed with a vengeance. Justice

---

[129] For a good, recent account of the Kulturkampf, see Helmut W. Smith, *German Nationalism and Religious Conflict* 19–49 (Princeton Univ Press, 1995). Smith emphasizes the factors that made the German struggle especially bitter:

> Divided by confession, the rhetoric of Germany's conflict was reinforced by the vocabulary of religious antagonism, the fronts between the two adversaries hardened by a history of civil wars between Catholic and Protestant powers, their antipathy tempered by a long and tenacious memory of mutual intolerance.

Id at 19–20.

[130] See page 88.

Scalia seems to understand that because the "private" sphere is publicly constructed, there can be no neutral ground in the war between opposing cultural forces. The government must be captured by one side or the other, and if the Court reverses the results of this political struggle, then it, too, is taking sides in a culture war.

Perhaps, then, Justice Scalia understands better than the majority just how destabilizing realist methodology is. For all that it unsettles us, perhaps we need to learn the truth that realism has to teach us. Perhaps it would be bracing to have on the Court a Justice—the first since Holmes—willing to tell us this truth with all its uncompromising and delegitimating force.

The difficulty is that Justice Scalia is hardly uncompromising and could not be less interested in delegitimation. He uses the rhetoric of realism when it serves his purpose, yet tries to disguise his realist inclinations when it does not. Thus, as a good realist, he powerfully attacks the notion that the political branches can remain neutral as between opposing sides in a culture war. Yet he wants to claim the role of neutral for himself. Indeed, on his view, it is precisely to preserve judicial neutrality that the Court should refrain from attempting to enforce a regime of political neutrality.[131]

If the realists are right, though, Justice Scalia's claim to neutrality is bound to fail. And fail it does. It fails first on the rhetorical level. A sensitive reading of Justice Scalia's dissent makes clear that he is far from neutral where homosexuality is concerned. For example, in the course of his argument supporting Amendment 2, Scalia quotes the following passage from a century-old Supreme Court opinion:

> [C]ertainly no legislation can be supposed more wholesome and necessary in founding of a free, self-governing common-wealth, fit to take rank as one of the co-ordinate States of the Union, than that which seeks to establish it on the basis of the idea of the family, as consisting in the springing from the union for life of one man and one woman in the holy estate of matrimony; the sure foundation of all that is stable and noble in our civilization; the best guaranty of that reverent morality which

---

[131] See 116 S Ct at 1629 (Scalia dissenting).

is the source of all beneficent progress in social and political improvement.[132]

To be sure, in the very next sentence, Justice Scalia distances himself from these sentiments: "I would not myself indulge in such official praise for heterosexual monogamy, because I think it no business of the courts (as opposed to the political branches) to take sides in this culture war."[133] But it is an ancient and hackneyed rhetorical technique coyly to deny what one in fact asserts,[134] and it is difficult to believe that Justice Scalia would have quoted, for example, racist language from an old Supreme Court opinion in a case in which he called for the rejection of an antidiscrimination claim brought by an African-American.

In fact, Justice Scalia's own characterization of homosexuals reveals the dark underside of realism's rejection of state neutrality. For Scalia, gays are an elite group that has a "high disposable income."[135] They "possess political power much greater than their numbers"[136] and are able to control the policies of powerful, intellectual institutions like the nation's law schools.[137] Gays enjoy "enormous influence in American media and politics."[138] Once

---

[132] *Murphy v Ramsey*, 114 US 15, 45 (1885), quoted at 116 S Ct at 1636–37 (Scalia dissenting).

[133] 116 S Ct at 1637 (Scalia dissenting).

[134] For perhaps the most famous example, see William Shakespeare, *Julius Caesar* Act III, sc ii.

[135] 116 S Ct at 1634 (Scalia dissenting).

[136] Id.

[137] Justice Scalia accuses the Court of reflecting the values of the "lawyer class from which [its] Members are drawn."

> How that class feels about homosexuality will be evident to anyone who wishes to interview job applicants at virtually any of the Nation's law schools. The interviewer may refuse to offer a job because the applicant is a Republican; because he is an adulterer; because he went to the wrong prep school or belongs to the wrong country club; because he eats snails; because he is a womanizer; because she wears real-animal fur; or even because he hates the Chicago Cubs. But if the interviewer should wish not to be an associate or partner of an applicant because he disapproves of the applicant's homosexuality, *then* he will have violated the pledge which the Association of American Law Schools requires of all its member-schools to exact from job interviewers: "assurance of the employer's willingness" to hire homosexuals. . . . This law-school view of what "prejudices" must be stamped out may be contrasted with the more plebeian attitudes that apparently still prevail in the United States Congress, which has been unresponsive to repeated attempts to extend to homosexuals the protections of federal civil rights laws.

116 S Ct at 1637 (Scalia dissenting).

[138] Id.

confined to cosmopolitan centers "such as New York, Los Angeles, San Francisco, and Key West,"[139] their influence is now spreading to the heartland where they threaten "traditional American moral values."[140]

These stereotypes about gay people, like the reference to the Kulturkampf, have historical antecedents. They are precisely the stereotypes used to justify the second, more violent Kulturkampf that gripped Germany fifty years after Bismarck had finished his work—a Kulturkampf that linked homosexuals to Jews, Gypsies, and other "cosmopolitan" forces supposedly threatening German culture. One wonders, once again, whether Justice Scalia can be unaware of the historical overtones his rhetoric evokes. Is he merely tone deaf, or does he have perfect pitch?

More than a half century ago, some Catholic intellectuals railed against the divisive consequences of legal realism. At a time when it seemed possible that the Third Reich would indeed rule for a thousand years, they argued for a link between realism and fascism. Once the law's neutrality was debunked and natural limits on the state's power abandoned, they warned, nothing separated the courtroom from the gas chambers.[141]

From today's perspective, many of these arguments seem hyperbolic, perhaps even hysterical. Yet one does not have to endorse all of these claims to see that there is a link between the acceptance of the realist attack on neutrality and the resort to polarizing rhetoric—as demonstrated not only by Justice Scalia's dissent but, perhaps, by the preceding paragraphs of this essay as well.

139

> By the time Coloradans were asked to vote on Amendment 2, their exposure to homosexuals' quest for social endorsement was not limited to newspaper accounts of happenings in places such as New York, Los Angeles, San Francisco, and Key West. Three Colorado cities—Aspen, Boulder, and Denver—had enacted ordinances that listed "sexual orientation" as an impermissible ground for discrimination. . . . The phenomenon had even appeared statewide.

116 S Ct at 1634 (Scalia dissenting).

[140] Justice Scalia accuses the Court of employing "a constitutional theory heretofore unknown to frustrate Colorado's reasonable effort to preserve traditional American moral values." 116 S Ct at 1636.

[141] See, for example, Francis E. Lucey, *Jurisprudence and the Future Social Order*, 16 Soc Sci 213, 214 (1941) (realism "sounds very much like what must have been the theme song of the Nazi storm troopers"). For a summary of the relevant literature, see Edward Purcell, Jr, *The Crisis of Democratic Theory: Scientific Naturalism and the Problem of Value* 164–72 (Univ Press of Ky, 1973).

For this reason, some modern politicians have tried to control the centrifugal forces in our society and paper over our most destabilizing disagreements through rhetoric that emphasizes our common civic culture. No doubt, the majority's struggle to assimilate gay people into the general culture of nondiscrimination is motivated by a similar impulse. The difficulty with such efforts is that once realist deconstructive techniques have been disseminated, they are not easily ignored or controlled. In some sense, realism is simply true, or at least so it seems to people who received their legal education in our era. As much as it would be nice if things were different, there is not a common ground between gay people and moral conservatives, and there is no way for the state to remain neutral between their competing claims. This realization, in turn, inevitably raises the stakes and produces the sort of divisive rhetoric that has become Justice Scalia's hallmark.

D. THE CLOSETED REALISM OF JUSTICE SCALIA

Precisely because the realists were right, Justice Scalia's claim to judicial neutrality must fail on an analytic, as well as a rhetorical level. The dissent associates neutrality with judicial restraint and claims that it is exhibiting such restraint by refusing to interfere with Colorado's decision to enact Amendment 2. Whereas judicial conservatives, like the Catholic opponents of legal realism, associated legitimacy with a willingness by the political branches to respect natural limits on state power, Justice Scalia associates neutrality with a willingness of the judicial branch to respect democratic outcomes.[142]

There are many reasons why this stance is unconvincing. First, it ignores the realist insight that nonfeasance does not guarantee neutrality. On the political level, Justice Scalia seems to understand that when the government tolerates gay sex, it aligns itself against the position of moral conservatives. On the judicial level, he fails to understand that when the Court tolerates gay repression, it aligns itself against the position of homosexuals.

---

[142]

Since the Constitution of the United States says nothing about [homosexuality], it is left to be resolved by normal democratic means. . . . This Court has no business imposing upon all Americans the resolution favored by the elite class from which the Members of this institution are selected . . . .

116 S Ct at 1629 (Scalia dissenting).

Some passages in Justice Scalia's opinion suggest that democracy provides the neutral justification for judicial nonfeasance: although the Court's failure to act leaves nonneutral political outcomes intact, these nonneutral outcomes are justified because they reflect the views of all the people, instead of the elite "lawyer class" from which judges are drawn.[143] But this view founders on the fact that Amendment 2 overturned democratic decisions—the decisions of the localities that adopted laws forbidding discrimination against gay people. So democracy alone is not enough; Justice Scalia must defend a particular conception of democracy.

Justice Scalia himself draws attention to this difficulty. He asserts that the election victories gay people won in the various Colorado municipalities that passed gay-rights ordinances were not truly democratic:

> [B]ecause those who engage in homosexual conduct tend to reside in disproportionate numbers in certain communities, . . . have high disposable income, . . . and of course care about homosexual-rights issues much more ardently than the public at large, they possess political power much greater than their numbers, both locally and statewide. . . .
>
> That is where Amendment 2 came in. It sought to counter both the geographic concentration and disproportionate political power of homosexuals by (1) resolving the controversy at the statewide level, and (2) making the election a single-issue contest for both sides.[144]

Apparently Justice Scalia would not use judicial power to countermand these local victories by gay people despite the flaws in the democratic process that he identifies.[145] But if he would indeed uphold them, and if they are indeed as undemocratic as he claims, then he can no longer assert that democracy legitimates his judicial stance. On the other hand, if he were to invalidate the local measures because they were undemocratic, he would have to defend a particular, contested theory of democratic decision making.

For example, defenders of federalism, with whom Justice Scalia is frequently allied, have sometimes argued against larger units of

---

[143] See id at 1637 (Scalia dissenting).

[144] Id at 1634 (Scalia dissenting).

[145] Scalia asserts that he does "not mean to be critical of these legislative successes; homosexuals are as entitled to use the legal system for reinforcement of their moral sentiments as are the rest of society." Id.

aggregation. They have insisted that local decision making is more democratic because it allows for more direct participation,[146] because only those directly affected by the measures in question are granted the franchise,[147] and because losers can more readily exercise the exit option.[148] Similarly, some political theorists have pointed out that "single-issue" elections fail to measure intensity of preference and therefore distort outcomes in undemocratic ways.[149]

Of course, any judicial choice between these competing democratic theories—defending, respectively, larger and smaller units of aggregation or single-issue and multiple-issue elections—would itself be made by a court and therefore would not be subject to a democratic check. Paradoxically, then, the attempt to ground judicial restraint on democratic theory ends up being antidemocratic. Either it leaves intact political outcomes despite their undemocratic character, or it chooses between competing theories of democracy in undemocratic fashion.

Perhaps all this could be forgiven if Justice Scalia were a true advocate of judicial restraint. But he is not. When it suits his purposes, Justice Scalia can be every bit as activist as the Justices he regularly attacks. Sometimes, he presents himself as an originalist, willing to invalidate political outcomes that conflict with the Constitution's text as understood at the founding.[150] More recently, he has tended to emphasize the ambiguity of the Constitution's commands and has argued that the Court ought to read them as if they prohibited political outcomes that conflict with our country's

---

[146] See Andrzej Rapaczynski, *From Sovereignty to Process: The Jurisprudence of Federalism After Garcia*, 1985 Supreme Court Review 341, 400–08.

[147] Compare Michael McConnell, *Federalism: Evaluating the Founders' Design*, 54 U Chi L Rev 1484, 1494 (1987).

[148] See, for example, Prichard, *Securing the Canadian Economic Union: Federalism and Internal Barriers to Trade*, in Michael A. Trebilcock, ed, *Federalism and the Canadian Economic Union* 17–18 (Univ of Toronto Press, 1983).

[149] For a good discussion, see Lynn Baker, *Direct Democracy and Discrimination: A Public Choice Perspective*, 67 Chi Kent L Rev 707, 721–25 (1991).

[150] See, for example, *California v Hodari D.*, 499 US 621, 626–27 (1991) (analyzing text of Fourth Amendment); *County of Riverside v McLaughlin*, 500 US 44, 60 (1991) (arguing that as to "questions on which a clear answer already existed in 1791 . . . it is the function of the Bill of Rights to *preserve* that judgment, not only against the changing views of Presidents and Members of Congress, but also against the changing views of Justices whom Presidents appoint and Members of Congress confirm to this Court.") (emphasis in original).

traditions. For example, in the equal protection context, he recently wrote that

> [The] function of this Court is to preserve our society's values;
> . . . regarding (among other things) equal protection, not to
> revise them; to prevent backsliding from the degree of restriction the Constitution imposed upon democratic government,
> not to prescribe, on our own authority, progressively higher
> degrees. For that reason it is my view that, whatever abstract
> tests we may choose to devise, they cannot supersede—and indeed ought to be crafted so as to reflect—those constant and
> unbroken national traditions that embody the people's understanding of ambiguous constitutional texts.[151]

This position is not easily reconciled with Justice Scalia's willingness on other occasions to invalidate political outcomes—for example, regarding regulatory takings[152] and affirmative action[153]—that contradict neither text nor tradition.[154] Whether or not he is a consistent textualist or traditionalist, however, it is clear that he is not a neutral. On the contrary, he is a passionately engaged combatant in our culture wars. When he invalidates statutes in the teeth of both text and tradition, as he has in defense of property rights and the rights of white males, he engages in the sort of "act[s] . . . of political will"[155] for which he has vigorously attacked

---

[151] *United States v Virginia*, 116 S Ct 2264, 2292 (1996) (Scalia dissenting).

[152] See *Lucas v South Carolina Coastal Council*, 505 US 1003 (1992) (Scalia, J).

[153] See *City of Richmond v J.A. Croson Co.*, 488 US 469, 520–28 (1989) (Scalia concurring); *Adarand Constructors, Inc. v Pena*, 115 S Ct 2097, 2118–19 (1995) (Scalia concurring in part and concurring in the judgment).

[154] There is no indication that the framers meant to require compensation when government regulation destroyed the value of land without physically taking possession of it. See William Treanor, *The Original Understanding of the Takings Clause and the Political Process*, 99 Colum L Rev 782 (1995); William Treanor, *The Origins and Original Significance of the Just Compensation Clause of the Fifth Amendment*, 94 Yale L J 694, 711 (1985); Joseph Sax, *Takings and the Police Power*, 74 Yale L J 36, 56–59 (1964); *Lucas v South Carolina Coastal Council*, 505 US 1003, 1055–59 (1992) (Blackmun dissenting). As Justice Scalia acknowledges, see *Lucas v South Carolina Coastal Council*, 505 US at 1014, the "tradition" of compensating such takings did not begin until 1922 when the Court required such compensation in *Pennsylvania Coal Co. v Mahon*, 269 US 393 (1922). Similarly, there is no reason to think that the framers of the Fourteenth Amendment intended to heighten the level of scrutiny for measures that benefited African-Americans. On the contrary, the original impetus for the amendment was the desire to expand the scope of congressional power to enact the nineteenth-century analogues of affirmative action measures. See Eric Schnapper, *Affirmative Action and the Legislative History of the Fourteenth Amendment*, 71 Va L Rev 753 (1985). The "tradition" of invalidating such measures began in 1978. See *University of California v Bakke*, 438 US 265 (1978).

[155] *Romer v Evans*, 116 S Ct at 1637 (Scalia dissenting).

his colleagues. Even when his decisions rest on text or tradition
that transcends his personal predilections, he is plainly taking sides.
For what is a culture war if not a struggle between traditional and
emerging values? Justice Scalia's insistence on respect for text and
tradition amounts to nothing less than an attempt by one side in
this struggle to appropriate constitutional law for use as a weapon
against the other side.

The short of the matter, then, is that Justice Scalia believes in
neither judicial conservatism nor judicial restraint. He is instead a
closet realist, who deserves to be "outed." He is quite ready to
take sides on the issues that divide us, but unready to acknowledge
that he is doing so. If the realists were right, he can hardly be
condemned for taking sides, for realism teaches us that there is
ultimately no refuge from choice. He can and should be condemned for the side that he has chosen to take and for hypocriti-
cally denying that he has taken it.

III. Missing in Action in the Culture Wars

Yet for all the moral and intellectual failings of Justice
Scalia's dissent, he is on to an important truth. Although he fails
to see that his critique applies to his own position, he nonetheless
hits pay dirt when he accuses the majority of elitism and partiality.
Justice Scalia is on target, for example, when he points out that
although the majority's analysis would apply to polygamy as well
as homosexuality, the majority is plainly unwilling to follow the
uncomfortable logic of its own argument.[156]

---

[156] Justice Scalia relies upon *Davis v Beason*, 133 US 333 (1890), where the Court upheld
the constitutionality of a territorial statute that prohibited polygamists and individuals who
advocated polygamy from voting in any election or holding public office. The majority
deals with *Davis* as follows:

> To the extent *Davis* held that persons advocating a certain practice may be denied
> the right to vote, it is no longer good law. . . . To the extent it held that the
> groups designated in the statute may be deprived of the right to vote because of
> their status, its ruling could not stand without surviving strict scrutiny, a most
> doubtful outcome. . . . To the extent *Davis* held that a convicted felon may be
> denied the right to vote, its holding is not implicated by our decision and is
> unexceptionable.

116 S Ct at 1628.

This response serves to dispose of *Davis*, but does not deflect the main thrust of Justice
Scalia's attack. Although changes in the Court's First Amendment and voting rights jurisprudence make *Davis*'s narrow holding obsolete, the Court is plainly unwilling to disavow
the proposition that government policy can legitimately be shaped by moral opposition to

For Justice Scalia, the argument from polygamy operates as a reductio ad absurdum demonstrating that the majority's position is untenable. As with all reductios, however, the argument has the potential to cut in the opposite direction. A historical perspective, once again, helps illuminate the point. The passage quoted by the majority from Justice Harlan's *Plessy* dissent has been repeated so frequently as to have become a constitutional cliche. Consider the implications of another passage from the same opinion—a passage almost always omitted when the dissent is celebrated:[157]

> There is a race so different from our own that we do not permit those belonging to it to become citizens of the United States. . . . I allude to the Chinese race. But by the statute in question, a Chinaman can ride in the same passenger coach with white citizens of the United States, while citizens of the black race in Louisiana, many of whom, perhaps, risked their lives for the preservation of the Union, who are entitled by law, to participate in the political control of the State and nation, who are not excluded, by law or by reason of their race, from public stations of any kind, and who have all the legal rights that belong to white citizens, are yet declared to be criminals, liable to imprisonment, if they ride in a public coach occupied by citizens of the white race.[158]

Many years after these words were written, when the Warren Court took its first tentative steps toward granting constitutional protection to sexual nonconformists, the first Justice Harlan's grandson had this to say:

> "[T]he family . . . is not beyond regulation," and it would be an absurdity to suggest either that offenses may not be committed in the bosom of the family or that the home can be made a sanctuary for crime. The right of privacy . . . is not an absolute. Thus, I would not suggest that adultery, homosexuality, fornication and incest are immune from criminal enquiry, however privately practiced. . . . But not to discriminate between what is involved in this case [i.e., contraception] and either the traditional offenses against good morals or crimes which,

---

polygamy when that policy does not trench upon independently protected constitutional rights.

[157] I must acknowledge that the passage was omitted from the version of *Plessy* appearing in the first two editions of the constitutional law casebook of which I am a coauthor. The passage is included in the third edition. See Geoffrey Stone, Louis Michael Seidman, Cass Sunstein, and Mark Tushnet, *Constitutional Law* 515 (Little Brown, 3d ed 1996).

[158] 163 US at 561.

though they may be committed anywhere, happen to have been committed or concealed in the home, would entirely misconceive the argument that is being made.[159]

These examples illustrate an important and disturbing lesson. In both cases, the authors struggle to include previously excluded groups within the Constitution's protection. The logic of these inclusionary arguments rests on analogy. Blacks are really just like whites and, therefore, deserve to be so treated. Users of contraceptives are really just like other married persons, and therefore deserve to be accorded the respect that married persons have traditionally been granted. Yet in both cases, the argument for inclusion is advanced by emphasizing what the newly included group is not. Blacks are not, after all, "Chinamen." Married couples using contraception are not, after all, homosexuals. And, one might add, homosexuals are not, after all, polygamists.

Nor are polygamists the only group left outside the *Romer* Court's empathic boundaries. For example, Justice Scalia is probably right when he complains that the Court's disparagement of the position of moral conservatives is "nothing short of insulting,"[160] and that the Court's failure to consider their welfare relates to their marginal status in the world inhabited by Supreme Court Justices.

The welfare of still other groups is apparently so insignificant that they are not even on the Court's radar screen. Consider this: Justice Kennedy's majority opinion holds that Colorado violated the Constitution when it created a structural obstacle to legislation protecting gay people against the backdrop of measures protecting many other groups. Yet in an ironic reversal of the first Justice Harlan's empathic hierarchy, Justice Kennedy does not seem to have noticed that this argument precisely parallels the argument the Court has recently and emphatically rejected in the racial dis-

---

[159] The quoted text appears in Justice Harlan's dissent to the Court's decision in *Poe v Ullman*, 367 US 497 (1961), dismissing on justiciability grounds a challenge to Connecticut's prohibition against birth control. See 367 US at 552–53 (Harlan dissenting). Four years later, Justice Harlan incorporated the dissent by reference into his concurring opinion when the Court invalidated the same prohibition. See *Griswold v Connecticut*, 381 US 479, 500 (1965) (Harlan concurring). See also id at 498–99 (Goldberg concurring) ("[T]he Court's holding today . . . in no way interferes with a State's proper regulation of sexual promiscuity or misconduct.").

[160] 116 S Ct at 1637 (Scalia dissenting).

tricting[161] and affirmative action[162] contexts. Whereas the Court chastizes Colorado for erecting barriers preventing gay people from enjoying an equal chance to secure legislation favoring their interests, the Court itself has erected such barriers for African-Americans.

For example, legislatures regularly draw district lines so as to insure some representation for a wide variety of groups, such as Republicans, suburbanites, and various ethnic minorities.[163] Yet when legislatures attempt to provide similar protection for African-Americans, the Court itself has erected a structural bar to prevent this equal treatment.[164]

There is a similar difficulty at the heart of the Court's affirmative action jurisprudence. Imagine a state-run university that adjusts admission standards for students whose grade and test scores do not accurately reflect their potential because of various types of disadvantage. The program benefits students whose disadvantage stems from physical disability, or poverty, or unfamiliarity with the dominant culture or language. There is no constitutional obstacle to the establishment of such a program. Yet if an African-American student tries to claim parallel disadvantage because of a long history of slavery and race discrimination, he must overcome the special obstacle of strict scrutiny, which the Court uses to evaluate "affirmative action" measures.[165] This special barrier, established by the Court itself, is precisely analogous to the special barrier, established for homosexuals, by Amendment 2.[166]

---

[161] See *Shaw v Reno*, 113 S Ct 2816 (1993); *Miller v Johnson*, 115 S Ct 2475 (1995).

[162] See *City of Richmond v J.A. Croson Co.*, 488 US 469 (1989); *Adarand Constructors, Inc. v Pena*, 115 S Ct 2097 (1995).

[163] The Court has upheld the power of jurisdictions to engage in nonracial gerrymandering so long as the scheme does not "consistently degrade a voter's or a group of voters' influence on the political process as a whole." *Davis v Bandemer*, 478 US 109, 132 (1986). To the extent that jurisdictions have an affirmative constitutional duty to avoid degradation, they are not only permitted, but required to consider group identification when drawing district lines.

[164] According to the Court, race may not be the "dominant and controlling rationale" for drawing district lines even when the districting produces a number of African-American representatives proportionate to their percentage of the population. *Miller v Johnson*, 115 S Ct at 2486.

[165] See note 162.

[166] The cases might be formally distinguished on the ground that whereas the Court's affirmative action jurisprudence creates a barrier to measures favoring any race, Amendment 2 applies to only one sexual orientation. The cases could be made parallel if Colorado rewrote Amendment 2 so as to prevent recognition of claims of discrimination by either

It might be thought that the cases can be distinguished on the ground that our history of race discrimination should make us suspicious about whether special treatment of African-Americans really works to their benefit. "Strict scrutiny" might be appropriate so as to determine whether or not such special treatment, supposedly designed to help, is really demeaning and based on racist stereotypes.[167]

But this distinction does not survive the *Romer* opinion. The *Romer* Court's central point was that protecting gay people from discrimination against the backdrop of antidiscrimination laws that protect most other groups is *not* special treatment.[168] Similarly, it would seem, recognizing the disadvantage suffered because of racism against a backdrop of protection for other groups who have been similarly disadvantaged by other causes amounts to no more than equal treatment. Yet the equal treatment that the state *must* provide for gay people, it *may not* provide for African-Americans.

One natural reaction to these observations is to praise *Romer's* inclusionary effort, while lamenting the failure to carry the project far enough. On this view, the Court is right to protect homosexuals, but wrong not to protect polygamists, moral conservatives, and African-Americans as well.

But this approach oversimplifies the problem. One difficulty is immediately apparent: for reasons explored in the previous section, the Court cannot remain neutral between the conflicting claims of gay people and moral conservatives. The zero-sum nature of conflicts of this sort means that the inclusion of one group must always lead to the exclusion of another.

Moreover, even when the inclusionary effort does not have this zero-sum characteristic, it is still hampered by more subtle difficulties. As noted above, Warren Court equal protection methodology rests on the force of analogy. Thus, the *Romer* Court came to

---

homosexuals or heterosexuals. None of the Court's analysis suggests that this change would affect the result in the case.

[167] See *City of Richmond v J.A. Croson Co.*, 488 US at 493 ("Absent searching judicial inquiry into the justification for such race-based measures, there is simply no way to determine what classifications are 'benign' or 'remedial' and what classifications are in fact motivated by illegitimate notions of racial inferiority or simple racial politics.").

[168] See 116 S Ct at 1626–27 ("we cannot accept the view that Amendment 2's prohibition on specific legal protections does no more than deprive homosexuals of special rights. To the contrary, the amendment imposes a special disability upon those persons alone. Homosexuals are forbidden the safeguards that others enjoy or may seek without constraint.").

see that gay people are really "just like" other groups that have suffered from discrimination and received protection from the state. But a claim that one group is "just like" another must always be measured against some standard, and it will seem natural to use the standard provided by the dominant group.

For example, within a few weeks of the Court's decision in *Romer*, it held that the Equal Protection Clause prohibited the Virginia Military Academy from categorically excluding women applicants.[169] As in *Romer*, the Court used the force of analogy to remake existing categories. It violates the Equal Protection Clause to exclude all women because some women are "just like" the men admitted to VMI. Yet the very act of reconceiving the category also reenforces it. Women benefit from the decision only to the extent that they are in fact "just like" men. Although they will no longer be subject to categorical exclusion, their admission to VMI will continue to be determined on the basis of criteria that rest on male values and behavior.[170]

It is likely that *Romer* will have a similar impact on homosexuals. The antidiscrimination law that *Romer* requires takes hold only so long as the claimant's behavior is close enough to the dominant norms to make the analogy plausible. *Romer* is likely to provide little comfort for individuals who truly challenge those norms instead of mimicking them.

This implicit, exclusionary impact of Warren Court activism suggests still a third way in which it reenforces existing norms: A judgment that two groups are similar to each other must always be made against the backdrop of some other group that is not like the first two at all. Without this contrasting backdrop, it would

---

[169] *United States v Virginia*, 116 S Ct 2264 (1996).

[170] The Court recognized that admission of women to VMI would entail minimal adjustments "primarily in arranging housing assignments and physical training programs for female cadets." 116 S Ct at 2279. However, the main thrust of its opinion was that the categorical exclusion of women was unconstitutional only because some women could satisfy criteria designed to accommodate men.

> It may be assumed, for purposes of this decision, that most women would not choose VMI's adversative method. . . . The issue, however, is not whether "women—or men—should be forced to attend VMI"; rather, the question is whether the State can constitutionally deny to women who have the will and capacity, the training and attendant opportunities that VMI uniquely affords.

116 S Ct at 2280.

not be possible to notice the similarity between the two favored groups.

It follows that every attempt to expand empathic boundaries must have an exclusionary underside and that there are inevitable limits to the project of liberal tolerance. Perhaps the second Justice Harlan was wrong to exclude homosexuals from constitutional protection, but he may have been right to exclude adulterers, and, if not adulterers, then surely those who practice incest or spousal abuse. If we were truly to include everyone under some gargantuan "big tent," there would be no point in having the tent in the first place, for then the community "covered" by the tent would lose its moral significance.

These insights create a difficult dilemma for advocates of gay liberation. Gay people have made tremendous strides by emphasizing their commonality with mainstream culture. In an odd, but nonetheless effective inversion, they have insisted that gay marriage is about "family values." Gay sex is "just like" heterosexual sex but for the insignificant fact that the partners happen to be identically gendered.

As effective as this strategy has been, it is not without costs. It serves to further isolate gay people whose lifestyles bear little resemblance to those of heterosexuals and to obscure the ways in which gay sex might be valued precisely to the extent that it is *not* like heterosexual sex. Consider, for example, the argument that gay sex presents a model of what heterosexual sex could become if only it were freed from gender hierarchy.[171] This is a complex claim that may or may not be correct, or may be correct in some contexts but not others. A Supreme Court decision with truly radical pretensions might have explored and built upon these ways in which homosexuality differs from heterosexuality. But whatever else *Romer* is about, and whatever its other virtues, it does not articulate a radical critique of mainstream sexual practices. It reworks existing categories to include some people who were previously excluded. Yet this very reworking strengthens the categories by implicitly contrasting what is now included with what remains excluded.

---

[171] For a discussion, see Lee C. Rice, *Homosexuality and the Social Order* in *The Philosophy of Sex: Contemporary Readings* 263–67 (Alan Soble ed 1980).

IV. Radicalism and Restraint

If this analysis is correct, it may help to explain the continuing attraction of Warren Court activism a quarter century after its apparent demise. Decisions like *Romer* have a double effect. Warren Court activism serves to stabilize the system even as it destabilizes individual components of it. This carefully controlled loss of control promotes an overall equilibrium, all the more stable because it is dynamic.

Viewed from this perspective, the supposed problems Warren Court activism poses for the constitutional ideals of neutrality and inclusiveness are actually advantages. It is true that the realist critique, upon which Warren Court activism rests, replaces the ideal of neutrality with the inevitability of choice. It is also true that this substitution produces insecurities that lead to more divisive and apocalyptic rhetoric on all sides. Finally, it is true that if we ever fully accepted the logic of the realist position, we would see that the categories through which we filter constitutional judgments are infinitely malleable and that constitutional law involves nothing but pure and unmediated choice. This realization would be destabilizing indeed.

But many realists also understood that as a matter of social fact, if not abstract logic, the choice always is mediated. As Justice Scalia reminds us, it is filtered through elite perceptions of what is and is not "sensible" and criteria of judgment drawn from the dominant culture. This filtering process undeniably denigrates and isolates the groups that are left out, at least for a while. Yet it also allows for change, which, in turn, makes still further change suddenly seem possible. Warren Court activism gradually expands our social categories, but as they expand, they are also reenforced, thereby coupling radical transformation with the illusion of continuity.

This double effect, in turn, is closely tied to broader legitimating forces within our society. American exceptionalism rests generally on our society's unusual ability to incorporate and "mainstream" radical impulses and to transmute explosive issues of race and class into manageable issues of culture and lifestyle. Sooner or later, most American revolutionaries show up on Nike and Levi commercials. They succeed in changing the culture even as they are swallowed up and destroyed by it.

Feared and reviled by conservatives, Warren Court activism

nonetheless contributed to this profoundly conservative process. The Warren Court succeeded in preserving American mores through the turbulent '60s, even as those mores were transformed. True conservatives might have valued the stability that was thereby achieved. *Romer*'s radicalism suggests that a few modern conservatives may finally be getting the message.

KATHLEEN M. SULLIVAN

CHEAP SPIRITS, CIGARETTES, AND FREE SPEECH: THE IMPLICATIONS OF 44 LIQUORMART

Left for dead after the Court's decision a decade ago in *Posadas de Puerto Rico Associates v Tourism Co.*,[1] the protection of commercial speech under the First Amendment has enjoyed a remarkable revival. *Posadas* upheld a ban on the advertisement of casino gambling to residents of Puerto Rico, reasoning that the greater power to ban gambling entailed the lesser power to suppress gambling advertising in order to reduce demand. Because government, since the demise of *Lochner*, may ban most economic transactions—all those that are not independently constitutionally protected, such as sales of abortions or rosary beads—*Posadas* suggested a wide berth for permissible advertising regulation.[2] *Posadas* thus appeared to signal a rollback of the Court's decision a decade earlier in *Virginia Board of Pharmacy v Virginia Citizens Consumer Council*,[3] which struck down a ban on price advertising of prescription drugs, and

Kathleen M. Sullivan is Stanley Morrison Professor of Law, Stanford University.

AUTHOR'S NOTE: The author thanks Ed Baker for his insights, Jay Wexler for his research assistance, and the Roberts Program in Law and Business and the Robert E. Paradise Fellowship Fund at Stanford Law School for financial support.

[1] 478 US 328 (1986).

[2] See Philip B. Kurland, *Posadas de Puerto Rico v Tourism Company:* "'Twas Strange, 'Twas Passing Strange, 'Twas Pitiful, 'Twas Wondrous Pitiful,'" 1986 Supreme Court Review 1, 12–13 (noting that, if "advertising of any economic activity that was not itself constitutionally protected activity, however legal that activity might be, was properly subject to government censorship . . . , then, under *Posadas*, there is no advertising that is not subject to government censorship").

[3] 425 US 748 (1976).

so for the first time admitted commercial speech to the protection of the First Amendment.[4]

In recent terms, however, the Court has granted repeated victories to advertisers in First Amendment challenges. It has struck down a ban on the placement of commercial newsracks on city streets,[5] a ban on cold calls to potential customers by certified public accountants,[6] a restriction on the professional designations that accountants may use in their advertising,[7] and a federal law barring beer makers from stating the alcohol content of their beer on their labels.[8] Along the way, the Court noted that commercial speech may not be given an automatic discount in the scale of First Amendment values.[9]

On the other hand, government continued to win a few against commercial speakers. In *United States v Edge Broadcasting Co.*,[10] the Court upheld against First Amendment challenge a federal law prohibiting a radio station licensed to a nonlottery state from broadcasting ads for another state's lottery. And in *Florida Bar v*

---

[4] For a historical overview, see Alex Kozinski and Stuart Banner, *The Anti-History and Pre-History of Commercial Speech*, 71 Tex L Rev 747 (1993).

[5] *City of Cincinnati v Discovery Network, Inc.*, 507 US 410 (1993).

[6] *Edenfield v Fane*, 507 US 761 (1993).

[7] *Ibanez v Florida Bd. of Accountancy*, 512 US 136 (1994).

[8] *Rubin v Coors Brewing Co.*, 115 S Ct 1585 (1995).

[9] *Discovery Network*, 507 US at 428 ("In the absence of some basis for distinguishing between 'newspapers' and 'commercial handbills' that is relevant to an interest asserted by the city, we are unwilling to recognize Cincinnati's bare assertion that the 'low value' of commercial speech is a sufficient justification for its selective and categorical ban on newsracks dispensing 'commercial handbills.' ").

Contrast this approach with the one the Court has taken to another area of "less protected" speech: sexually explicit but nonobscene speech. In that area, Justice Stevens, author of the opinion in *Discovery Network*, was quite willing to apply a categorical discount, relieving the city of any strong obligation to demonstrate that adult movie theaters caused problems the city could not solve some other way. See, for example, *Young v American Mini Theatres, Inc.*, 427 US 50, 70 (1976) ("[F]ew of us would march our sons and daughters off to war to preserve the citizen's right to see 'Specified Sexual Activities' exhibited in the theaters of our choice."). While that approach never captured a clear majority, the Court has reached similar results by upholding laws as aimed at the content-neutral "secondary effects" of sexually explicit but nonobscene speech, see *City of Renton v Playtime Theatres, Inc.*, 475 US 41 (1986), without regard to whether other unregulated activities (bars, pool halls, adult bookstores) cause the same problems. *Discovery* followed the path not of *Renton*, but rather of *Police Dept. v Mosley*, 408 US 92 (1972), which held subject matter underinclusion (only nonlabor speech barred) fatal in a law claimed to serve content-neutral ends (quiet near a school). This suggests that the Court in *Discovery* saw commercial speech as more like political than like sexual speech.

[10] 509 US 418 (1993).

Went for It, Inc.,[11] the Court upheld a state bar rule making lawyers wait thirty days before soliciting legal business from accident victims or their families by direct mail.

Thus, before last Term, advocates and opponents of robust protection for commercial speech each could claim some measure of victory. Those who favored broad freedom for commercial speech could plausibly claim that the Court was becoming increasingly libertarian in this area—except when it came to regulation of lawyers and vice.[12] Those who believed that commercial speech protection was misbegotten in the first place could view *Edge* and *Florida Bar* hopefully as showing that the Court would still defer to sensible advertising regulations, striking down only those that were excessively silly.[13]

44 Liquormart, Inc. v Rhode Island[14] gave credence to the first of these views. The decision unanimously struck down a state ban on the truthful advertisement of liquor prices. For the last four decades, Rhode Island law had prohibited manufacturers and sellers of alcoholic beverages from advertising their prices "in any manner whatsoever" except on price tags or signs inside liquor stores and invisible from the street.[15] It likewise had prohibited publication of liquor prices in Rhode Island–based media.[16] The state supreme court twice upheld these laws as directly promoting "temperance" among Rhode Islanders.[17] In *Liquormart*, two discount liquor re-

---

[11] 115 S Ct 2371 (1995).

[12] The Court's earlier treatment of regulations of lawyer advertising had been equivocal. It struck down a total ban on price advertising by lawyers, *Bates v State Bar of Arizona*, 433 US 350 (1977), a bar against the use of pictures in a legal advertisement, *Zauderer v Office of Disciplinary Counsel*, 471 US 626 (1985), and a ban on solicitation of legal business by mail, *Shapero v Kentucky Bar Assn.*, 486 US 466 (1988), but upheld a ban on in-person solicitation of legal business, *Ohralik v Ohio Bar Assn.*, 436 US 447 (1978), and state sanctions for lawyers' misleading omissions in advertisements, *Zauderer*.

[13] On this view, *Coors* merely struck down for "overall irrationality" a regulatory scheme that barred disclosure of alcohol content on beer labels but permitted or required it on wine and spirit labels, and which allowed beer manufacturers to hook macho drinkers anyway with the term "malt liquor." See *Coors*, 115 S Ct at 1592–93. And on this view, the commercial newsrack ban in *Discovery Network* was just too small a drop in the bucket: You cannot cure the problem of ugly newsracks by eliminating 62 commercial newsracks and leaving 1,500 to 2,000 noncommercial newsracks in place. See *Discovery*, 507 US at 417–18.

[14] 116 S Ct 1495 (1996).

[15] *Liquormart*, 116 S Ct at 1501 n 2, quoting RI Gen Laws § 3-8-7 (1987).

[16] Id at 1502 n 3, quoting RI Gen Laws § 3-8-8.1 (1987).

[17] Id at 1502, citing *S & S Liquor Mart, Inc. v Pastore*, 497 A2d 729 (RI 1985) and *Rhode Island Liquor Stores Assn. v Evening Call Pub. Co.*, 497 A2d 331 (RI 1985).

tailers challenged the statutes in federal district court. One of them had been assessed a $400 fine for running a newspaper ad that did not print any liquor prices, but that did print low prices for snacks and mixers while running the word "WOW" beside pictures of rum and vodka bottles.[18] The district court declared the advertising ban invalid under the First Amendment, finding that it " 'has no significant impact on levels of alcohol consumption in Rhode Island.' "[19] The First Circuit reversed, holding that the advertising ban necessarily would reduce liquor purchase and consumption by discouraging price competition that would lower prices and so increase the volume of sales.[20]

The Supreme Court reversed unanimously, invalidating the ban. The Justices fragmented messily on the appropriate standard of scrutiny, but all of the principal opinions expressed strong skepticism toward state regulation of advertising as a device for preventing consumers from knowing about a product in order to induce them not to buy it—the very rationale that had easily sustained the regulation in *Posadas*. They likewise found the state's goal (less bibulous Rhode Islanders) inadequately met by means that should have seemed sensible, not silly, by the lights of previous decisions. *Liquormart* is thus the Court's most libertarian decision on commercial speech since *Virginia Board*.[21]

After *Liquormart*, it is unclear why "commercial speech" should continue to be treated as a separate category of speech isolated from general First Amendment principles. Since *Virginia Board*, the Court has treated commercial speech as protected speech, but not as fully protected speech. The principal differences are (1) that regulation of false or misleading commercial speech is subject to no First Amendment scrutiny,[22] (2) that advertisements of illegal transactions may be banned even if they fall short of otherwise proscribable incitement,[23] and (3) that all commercial speech regu-

---

[18] Id at 1503, quoting *44 Liquor Mart, Inc. v Racine*, 829 F Supp 543, 549 (DRI 1993).

[19] Id.

[20] *44 Liquormart, Inc. v Rhode Island*, 39 F3d 5, 7 (1st Cir 1994).

[21] Or maybe since *Linmark Associates, Inc. v Willingboro*, 431 US 85 (1977), in which the Court, following *Virginia Board*, held that a town may not stem white flight, a laudable end, by means of banning the display of "For Sale" and "Sold" signs. *Linmark*, like *Virginia Board*, held it impermissible to stop advertising on the ground that it "will cause those receiving the information to act upon it." Id at 93.

[22] See *Virginia Board*, 425 US 771 n 24.

[23] See id.

lations are subject to a form of intermediate rather than strict scrutiny, even if they are aimed squarely at an advertisement's message or communicative impact.[24] The Court rested these distinctions upon what it called "commonsense differences": commercial speech allegedly has "greater objectivity and hardiness" than other kinds.[25]

Such categorization of commercial speech into a lower order in the First Amendment hierarchy recalls, in diluted form, the Court's excision of incitement, fighting words, libel, obscenity (and indeed, once upon a time, commercial speech) from all First Amendment protection on the ground that on average the costs of such speech predictably outweigh its benefits.[26] But there is another way of carving up the free speech universe more typical of recent cases, and that is to look at the aim of the regulation rather than at the nature of the speech, or as John Ely once put it, at "teleology" rather than "ontology."[27] Regulations aimed at viewpoints, subject matters, or the communicative impact of speech on its audience get strict scrutiny, even if the ideas aimed at are not very good or valuable ideas; laws aimed at harms from speech unrelated to ideas get some scrutiny, but a lot less. On this approach, the form of a regulation—content-specific or content-neutral—matters mostly as evidence of its purpose, but purpose is the dominant consideration.

After *Liquormart*, it looks like teleology is making a comeback in this area of law, whether or not a majority of the Justices admits it. The Court would appear to view suppressing commercial speech by reason of its message or communicative impact as suspicious, even though suppressing commercial speech for other rea-

---

[24] This standard of review was crystallized in *Central Hudson Gas & Elec. v Pub. Serv. Commission*, 447 US 557, 566 (1980). Additional differences include the exclusion of commercial speech from certain First Amendment procedural benefits, such as the presumption against prior restraint, see *Virginia Board*, 425 US at 771 n 24, and the overbreadth doctrine, see *Bates v State Bar of Arizona*, 433 US 350, 379–81 (1977).

[25] *Virginia Board*, 425 US at 771 n 24.

[26] See, for example, *Chaplinsky v New Hampshire*, 315 US 568, 571–72 (1942) (holding that fighting words "are no essential part of any exposition of ideas, and are of such slight social value as a step to truth that any benefit that may be derived from them is clearly outweighed by the social interest in order and morality"); Harry A. Kalven, *The Metaphysics of the Law of Obscenity*, 1960 Supreme Court Review 1.

[27] John Hart Ely, *Flag Desecration: A Case Study in the Roles of Categorization and Balancing in First Amendment Analysis*, 88 Harv L Rev 1482, 1496 (1975).

sons (preserving professionalism and privacy in *Went for It* or federalism in *Edge Broadcasting*, for example) is allowable if it does not go too far. This dichotomy resembles the general distinction in First Amendment practice between review of content-based and content-neutral laws.[28] Nominal intermediate scrutiny for all commercial speech regulations is fatal in fact for laws aimed at suppressing ideas, but a toss-up for laws aimed at advertising's associated material harms. Thus, what is crucial is not whether we are in the world of commercial speech, but what aspects of commercial speech—its message or its harms—government seeks to regulate.

So why does the Court not simply dissolve the category of commercial speech and assimilate advertising to the general run of First Amendment law? Six Justices have suggested that the Court move openly in this direction, but they have not all sat on the Court at the same time.[29] For now, only a plurality would formalize this approach, and would expressly apply strict scrutiny to some commercial speech regulations that are aimed at message or communicative impact. Even these Justices, however, would apply "less than strict review" to regulations aimed at false or deceptive commercial speech—regulations that would at least in many instances be held impermissibly content-based if applied to noncommercial speech.[30]

Why does a majority not join this view, or go farther and assimilate commercial to other speech? The answer cannot be that the Court views commercial speech as generally less valuable than other speech, or its regulation as generally less problematic than other speech restrictions. There are plausible arguments for such a view as a matter of First Amendment theory, but the Court has

---

[28] See *United States v O'Brien*, 391 US 367 (1968), which upheld a law aimed at draft card destruction as substantially even if not compellingly justified, after determining that its purpose was "unrelated to the suppression of free expression." The intermediate scrutiny called for in *O'Brien*, as modified in later decisions, see *Ward v Rock Against Racism* 491 US 781 (1989), has been generalized to cover all content-neutral regulations, not only those applied to symbolic conduct such as burning a draft card. See, for example, *Turner Broadcasting System, Inc. v FCC*, 114 S Ct 2445 (1994) (applying *O'Brien* test to law requiring cable operators to carry broadcasters).

[29] In addition to Justices Stevens, Kennedy, and Ginsburg in *Liquormart*, Justices Brennan, Marshall, and Blackmun at various times endorsed such a view. See, for example, *Central Hudson*, 447 US at 573–79 (Blackmun joined by Brennan concurring); *Posadas*, 478 US at 350–51 (Brennan, joined by Marshall and Blackmun dissenting); *Discovery Network*, 507 US 431–38 (Blackmun concurring); *Fane*, 508 US 777 (Blackmun concurring).

[30] See *Liquormart*, 116 S Ct 1495, 1507 (Stevens, joined by Kennedy and Ginsburg).

expressly rejected them. The answer might be that commercial speech doctrine is simply a pragmatic compromise between the view that regulating advertising is more like regulating sales and the view that it is more like regulating speech, and is thus doomed to the kind of doctrinal incoherence that normally accompanies such analogical crisis—compare the law of gender discrimination. A third possibility is that the current majority is concerned that escalating review of commercial speech regulations will have bad consequences. Applying intermediate scrutiny to laws regulating false or misleading advertising or ads that promote illegal products might hobble the state and federal consumer protection apparatus, as might applying strict scrutiny to all commercial speech regulations aimed at the advertisers' message. Tobacco advertising regulations recently promulgated by the Clinton administration furnish a useful test case for exploring these issues.

I. COMMERCIAL SPEECH AND FIRST AMENDMENT THEORY

It is commonly remarked that extending the First Amendment to commercial speech has diverse ideological appeal: conservatives like it because it favors markets; liberals like it because it favors speech.[31] It is true that commercial speech advocates span the spectrum from Ralph Nader to Philip Morris. But still, this picture of strange but harmonious bedfellows oversimplifies the matter. On the conservative side, some who generally favor free markets favor broad freedom for commercial speech,[32] while others have questioned whether commercial speech requires any robust constitutional protection at all.[33] And particular commercial inter-

---

[31] Compare Alex Kozinski and Stuart Banner, *Who's Afraid of Commercial Speech?* 76 Va L Rev 627, 652 (1990) ("The commercial speech doctrine is the stepchild of first amendment jurisprudence: Liberals don't much like commercial speech because it's commercial; conservatives mistrust it because it's speech.").

[32] See generally id.

[33] See Richard A. Posner, *Free Speech in an Economic Perspective*, 20 Suffolk U L Rev 1, 19–20, 39–40 (1986). Posner argues that speech worthy of First Amendment protection is that which operates as a public good. Speech, like clean air or the national defense, will be underproduced to the extent that its producers cannot fully internalize the benefits of producing it. An idea, once circulated, or information, once public, may be used by those who have not paid for it. Thus, ideas and information will be underproduced by rational speakers, and laws restricting speech will only further reduce an inadequate supply. The benefits of commercial speech, in contrast, are more readily captured by its producer through sale of the underlying product. And "in an information market that operates without substantial externalities, regulation is not so apt to carry us far away from the optimal level of production of information." Id at 40. See also Ronald A. Cass, *Commercial Speech,*

ests sometimes favor and sometimes disfavor advertising regulation, depending on their market position. Mom-and-pop liquor stores liked the regulation in *Liquormart*;[34] big liquor discounters such as Liquormart did not.

Liberals likewise divide on the matter. True, commercial speech protection was pioneered by progressive consumer advocates, who were suspicious of advertising limitations favored by an industry or profession. In cases of professional monopolies (such as those held by pharmacists, lawyers, and accountants), they saw commercial speech deregulation as a mini Sherman Act, protecting consumers by increasing competition, undercutting monopoly rents, and bringing price levels down. On the other hand, those same advocates have switched sides when they see advertising bans themselves as a form of consumer protection.[35]

If commercial speech protection has had its supporters from left and right, it has likewise had bipartisan critics. The critics have found such protection difficult to square with standard theories justifying special protection of speech from majoritarian politics. Strikingly, however, none of these critiques seems to have moved the Court since *Virginia Board*. While *Virginia Board* maintained some distinctions between commercial and other protected speech, it and later cases expressly rejected the global arguments of its critics.

1. *Self-government.* On the view that the Free Speech Clause is meant to protect only or principally political speech, and to prevent government from entrenching itself by suppressing political dissent, shampoo ads don't rate protection. On this view, selling products and services serves private interest in profit, not public interest in government. And on this view, the content of advertise-

---

Constitutionalism, Collective Choice, 56 U Cin L Rev 1317, 1364–69 (1988); Daniel A. Farber, *Free Speech Without Romance: Public Choice and the First Amendment*, 105 Harv L Rev 554, 565–66 (1991).

[34] The Rhode Island Liquor Stores Association intervened on the government side below. See *Liquormart*, 116 S Ct at 1503.

[35] For example, consider the policy positions of the Public Citizen Litigation Group, founded by Ralph Nader and Alan Morrison. Morrison and the Group invented the modern doctrine of commercial speech when they litigated and won *Virginia Board*. They were also prime movers in the cases lifting some of the restrictions on lawyer advertising. See note 12 above. On the other hand, Public Citizen submitted a comment in support of the Clinton administration tobacco regulations, including legal commentary arguing that the tobacco advertising restrictions were nearly entirely consistent with the First Amendment. *Comments of Public Citizen, Inc. Regarding the FDA's Proposal to Regulate the Sale and Promotion of Tobacco Products to Minors*, Before the Food and Drug Administration, Docket No 95N-0253 (Jan 2, 1996).

ments or other invitations to engage in commercial transactions has low value in comparison with speech about ideology and public policy commitments. No one would march his or her sons or daughters off to war to protect the right to hear which shampoo gives most body. "For in a democracy, the economic is subordinate to the political."[36]

The standard response to such arguments begins by denying the plausibility of a solely political account of the First Amendment. What about art, science, literature? It's a bit of a stretch to say that reading modernist novels enhances one's perspicacity at the polls, though some have tried.[37] Yet the Court has assimilated the arts, humanities, and sciences to the political core of the First Amendment without blinking. Still, proponents of the self-government model argue, it's a much bigger stretch to suggest that product advertising informs political deliberation. Ideas and worldviews, they would say, gain far less stimulus from information about the price and availability of economic goods than they do from the products of even nonpolitical thought or research about the human condition.

Replies to this argument conceive self-government more broadly than as deliberation by enlightened voters. One version links economic self-interest to formal politics. "It's the economy, stupid," said the sign in the war room of the 1992 Clinton campaign. Thus, advertising might be closer to the phenomena that drive political elections than the entire Modern Library put together. A second

---

[36] *Central Hudson Gas & Elec. v Pub. Serv. Commission*, 447 US 557, 599 (1980) (Rehnquist dissenting). For other examples of the argument that self-government is a primary value in speech protection and that commercial speech does not serve it, see Cass R. Sunstein, *Democracy and the Problem of Free Speech* 130–44 (1993); Thomas H. Jackson and John Calvin Jeffries, Jr., *Commercial Speech: Economic Due Process and the First Amendment*, 65 Va L Rev 1, 9–12, 15 (1979). For the countervailing view that at least some commercial speech is relevant to political dialogue, see Steven Shiffrin, *The First Amendment and Economic Regulation: Away from a General Theory of the First Amendment*, 78 Nw U L Rev 1213, 1225–39 (1983).

Some have suggested that advertising laws do not aim at speech at all, political or not, but rather simply at conduct. See, for example, Daniel A. Farber, *Commercial Speech and First Amendment Theory*, 74 Nw U L Rev 372, 389 (1979) (arguing that regulation of commercial speech amounts to regulation of contracts); Ronald K. L. Collins and David M. Skover, *Commerce and Communication*, 71 Tex L Rev 697, 699 (1993) (arguing that "modern mass advertising is . . . . speech in the service of selling").

[37] See Alexander Meiklejohn, *The First Amendment Is an Absolute*, 1961 Supreme Court Review 245, 255–57 ("Literature and the arts must be protected by the First Amendment. They lead the way toward sensitive and informed appreciation and response to the values out of which the riches of the general welfare are created.").

version regards formal politics as a small fraction of self-governing activity. A speech doctrine centered on politics and grudgingly extended to art and science may befit a republic, but a democracy ought countenance political oratory and pushpin alike.[38]

In this debate, the Court has plainly joined in the more capacious view, depicting self-government as the aggregate of individual economic decisions rather than as collective deliberation on the public good. As Justice Blackmun wrote for the Court in *Virginia Board*,

> So long as we preserve a predominantly free enterprise economy, the allocation of our resources in large measure will be made through numerous private economic decisions. It is a matter of public interest that those decisions, in the aggregate, be intelligent and well informed. . . . Therefore, even if the First Amendment were thought to be primarily an instrument to enlighten public decisionmaking in a democracy, we could not say that the free flow of information does not serve that goal.[39]

So much for the primacy of the political conception of First Amendment. Of course, drawing such a loose chain of causation between unregulated advertising and self-government might appear in effect to substitute general social welfare for self-government as the First Amendment value that is being protected.[40]

Advertising might be defended as serving the end of self-government, finally, because it facilitates the institution of the press. The inclusion of the press clause alongside the speech clause contemplated institutional speech, not merely the clash of individual opinion. In other contexts, the Court has emphasized the importance of activities that facilitate speech beneficial to the political process,

---

[38] Compare R. H. Coase, *The Economics of the First Amendment: The Market for Goods and the Market for Ideas*, 64 Am Econ Rev Proc 384, 386 (1974) ("Self-esteem leads the intellectuals to magnify the importance of their own market. . . . [S]elf-interest combines with self-esteem to ensure that, while others are regulated, regulation should not apply to them."). Coase here argued not for constitutional parity in reviewing advertising and other speech regulation, but more broadly for constitutional parity in reviewing speech regulation and regulation of economic transactions.

[39] *Virginia Board*, 425 US at 765 (citations and footnotes omitted).

[40] See Jackson and Jeffries, 65 Va L Rev at 29–31 (cited in note 36) (criticizing *Virginia Board* for substituting the economic due process values of competition in trade for the free speech values of self-government and self-expression).

even if those activities would have questionable First Amendment value apart from that instrumental function.[41] Advertising finances publication in print, broadcasting and cable media, and increasingly on the internet, enabling the dissemination of more speech than subscribers alone would pay for in its absence. Arguments that all social value from advertising may be captured by the producer of the advertised good or service ignore this important form of surplus.

2. *Truth.* The Millian notion that the unregulated clash of individual expression will produce truth in the long run would seem at first glance utterly unrelated to the advertising business. The goal of advertising is sales, not knowledge, and the time frame is short-run, not long. But again, the Court appeared in *Virginia Board* to assimilate commercial speech to the truth-seeking justification for First Amendment review broadly construed. Justice Blackmun's opinion for the Court portrayed the clash of competing pitches for products as the rough equivalent of good counsel driving out bad: If the channels of communication remain open, "nothing prevents the 'professional' pharmacist from marketing his own assertedly superior product, and contrasting it with that of the low-cost, high-volume prescription drug retailer."[42] The individual, not the government, is the most reliable judge between them. On the Court's view, government ought not pronounce false consciousness any more than false ideas.

Of course, *Virginia Board*, like *Liquormart*, involved suppression solely of true price data, so the connection to the truth-seeking function of free speech was virtually tautological. The exception carved out in *Virginia Board* for regulation of false or misleading speech departs from the rest of Mill's premise that "[e]ven a false statement may be deemed to make a valuable contribution to pub-

---

[41] See, for example, *Buckley v Valeo*, 424 US 1 (1976) (political expenditures); *Meyer v Grant*, 486 US 414 (1988) (paid solicitation of petition signatures); *New York Times v Sullivan*, 376 US 254, 270 (1964) (negligently false and injurious statements of fact, which though not protected in themselves, afford necessary breathing room to the "uninhibited, robust, and wide-open discussion" of matters of public concern).

[42] *Virginia Board*, 425 US at 770. Compare *Whitney v California*, 274 US 357, 375 (1927) (Brandeis concurring) (noting that free discussion "affords ordinarily adequate protection against the dissemination of noxious doctrine" and that "the fitting remedy for evil counsels is good ones"). *See Linmark*, 431 US at 97 (citing *Whitney*, 274 US at 377 (1927) (Brandeis concurring)).

lic debate, since it brings about 'the clearer perception and livelier impression of truth, produced by its collision with error.' "[43] Government may save individual listeners the trouble of unearthing the factual falsity of commercial data.

3. *Self-determination or autonomy.* Unlike self-government and truth theories, the theory that free speech promotes human autonomy depends not on its social consequences but on its realization of human personality. Advocates of speaker autonomy as the central value underlying the Free Speech Clause reject heightened protection for commercial speech because it is generally engaged in by corporations, which lack a human personality or an interest in expressive self-fulfillment.[44] It is for this reason that the protection of corporate speech under the First Amendment has been justified solely on the basis of its social consequences.[45] Corporate speech may be instrumental to full public debate on issues that affect corporate interests, but no one supposes that such speech is intrinsically fulfilling to the corporate agents who engage in it or the corporate owners whose interests its serves.

The Court nonetheless emphasized a kind of autonomy as one driving principle of *Virginia Board*—not the autonomy of the *speaker* to fulfill his rational capacities, but the autonomy of the *listener* in making up his own mind.[46] *Virginia Board* deemed keeping citizens in ignorance of drug prices an impermissible technique for regulating pharmacy practices. The constitutionally required "alternative to this highly paternalistic approach" was "to assume

---

[43] *New York Times v Sullivan*, 376 US at 279 n 19, quoting John Stuart Mill, *On Liberty.*

[44] See C. Edwin Baker, *Human Liberty and Freedom of Speech* 194–224 (1989); C. Edwin Baker, *Turner Broadcasting: Content-Based Regulation of Persons and Presses*, 1994 Supreme Court Review 57, 62–80; Jackson and Jeffries, 65 Va L Rev at 14–15 (cited in note 36) ("Whatever else it may mean, the concept of a first amendment right of speaker autonomy in matters of belief and expression stops short of a seller hawking his wares.").

[45] See *First National Bank v Bellotti*, 435 US 765, 775–86 (1978).

[46] See David Strauss, *Persuasion, Autonomy, and Freedom of Expression*, 91 Colum L Rev 334 (1991) (arguing that listener autonomy—the freedom to be persuaded rather than coerced—may be understood as animating much First Amendment jurisprudence, and that "government may not suppress speech on the ground that the speech is likely to persuade people to do something that the government considers harmful," id at 335). See also Burt Neuborne, *The First Amendment and Government Regulation of Capital Markets*, 55 Brooklyn L Rev 5 (1989) (defending "hearer-centered" approaches to free speech); Martin Redish, *The First Amendment in the Marketplace: Commercial Speech and the Values of Free Expression*, 39 Geo Wash L Rev 429, 441–44 (1971) (arguing that providing consumers with information on the competing merits of products enhances their rational self-fulfillment).

that this information is not in itself harmful, that people will perceive their own best interests if only they are well enough informed, and that the best means to that end is to open the channels of communication rather than to close them."[47]

An obvious reply to such arguments from listener autonomy is that freedom *from* regulation may not automatically entail a condition of freedom *to* choose autonomously.[48] A citizen's autonomy in acting upon an unregulated advertisement can be constrained as a descriptive matter by, for example, lack of education or resources, lack of access to further information that would illuminate or discredit the advertisement,[49] or a condition of addiction to a product that creates a physiological dependence.[50] In addition, it can be argued, the Court's account of listener autonomy ignores the role of commercial speech in taste creation. Advertising is not just information to be applied to preexisting wants and needs; it is designed to implant or alter consumer desires. On this view, autonomy might be promoted by limiting ads that themselves manipulate taste. Finally, corporations and consumers will frequently have asymmetric information about a product, with little likelihood of correction by competitors.[51] A choice made with such incomplete information might again be less than fully autonomous.[52]

While relying heavily on listener autonomy in *Virginia Board*, the Court qualified its holding in partial answer to such problems. *Virginia Board* confined its holding to truthful and nonmisleading

---

[47] *Virginia Board*, 425 US at 770.

[48] See Isaiah Berlin, *Two Concepts of Liberty*, in *Four Essays on Liberty* 118 (1969); Richard H. Fallon, Jr., *Two Senses of Autonomy*, 46 Stan L Rev 875 (1994).

[49] For this reason, advertisers may sometimes be compelled to add state-mandated speech to their own. Consider, for example, proxy statements and pharmaceutical warning labels.

[50] See Sylvia A. Law, *Addiction, Autonomy and Advertising*, 77 Iowa L Rev 909 (1992) (arguing that advertising promoting psychoactive products that cause harmful dependence and likely to cause such dependence in a substantial portion of users should be more regulable than other forms of commercial speech).

[51] See Posner, 22 Suffolk U L Rev at 40 (cited in note 33) ("competing producers of goods and services (unlike competing scientists in the market for scientific ideas) may have weak incentives to unmask the lie to the consumers"). And consumers, being diffuse and holding low individual stakes, will be unlikely to fill this gap unless well organized.

[52] The baseline question here is profound: What constitutes "full" autonomy? One might argue that autonomy is always the exercise of choice under imperfect information, or one might insist that there are some minimal preconditions for its exercise. Supplying those preconditions thus would not violate but enhance autonomy.

commercial speech, leaving intact vast state and federal regulatory schemes for the protection of consumers and markets through the suppression of false and misleading commercial speech. In dictum, the Court explained that commercial speech is "more easily verifiable by its disseminator" than by its audience.[53] Given this asymmetry of information known to speaker and listener, the Court suggested, government should be freer to police commercial speech than other kinds for fraud.[54]

4. *Negative theories.* Some theories of the First Amendment tend to refer not to the underlying value of speech, but to the danger that government regulation in this area will tend systematically to misfire.[55] One such negative theory supposes that government will tend to regulate speech—more than other human activities—for reasons unconnected to legitimate public goals. On this view, the preferred constitutional status of speech follows from history and experience suggesting that it will be especially vulnerable to exercises of official corruption, bias, or self-dealing.[56] This danger is thought to be self-evident in the case of political dissent: Incumbent governments, who have a self-interest in maintaining power, have strong incentives to quash opposition. Suppressing dissenters' speech preserves political rents.

It might appear to follow, on this view, that commercial speech needs less protection than political speech because in a predominantly private-enterprise economy, government actors do not generally compete against commercial producers. No tyrannous politician lies awake scheming to suppress shampoo ads, but silencing the opposition is another matter. *Virginia Board* may be read, however, to reject such a sharp distinction, at least tacitly. Politicians might not compete directly with drug discounters, but they do serve constituents, such as the pharmacy profession, whose politi-

---

[53] 425 US at 772 n 24 ("The truth of commercial speech . . . may be more easily verifiable by its disseminator than, let us say, news reporting or political commentary, in that ordinarily the advertiser seeks to disseminate information about a specific product or service that he himself provides and presumably knows more about than anyone else.").

[54] For vigorous counterargument, see Kozinski and Banner, 76 Va L Rev at 634–38 (cited in note 31).

[55] See Strauss, 91 Colum L Rev at 349–50 (cited in note 46).

[56] See Vincent Blasi, *The Pathological Perspective and the First Amendment*, 85 Colum L Rev 449, 459 (1985) ("Most constitutional commitments are fragile in the sense that they embody ideals that are easily abandoned or tempered in times of stress. Certain distinctive features of the commitment to free speech enhance that fragility.").

cal power might be disproportionate to their numbers.[57] To the extent that government is captured by private interest groups, it might well have an incentive to suppress the speech of those groups' competitors. In this respect, the dangers of official content bias lurk near both political and commercial speech.[58]

The Court's acknowledgment of this problem, though, is subject to two qualifications. First, *Posadas* ignored a particularly glaring version of it. If suppressing the speech of competitors of powerful constituents is bad, suppressing the speech of competitors with government's own businesses is worse. There could be no more literal commercial analogue to the suppression of political dissent. And yet the Court upheld Puerto Rico's ban on casino gambling ads directed at local residents despite the fact that its most plausible explanation was to suppress private competition with the Commonwealth's own lucrative public lottery.

Second, the Court in *Virginia Board* appeared to view the danger of official bias or content-based hostility as minimal when government regulates false and misleading commercial speech, for "the truth of commercial speech . . . may be more easily verifiable" than that of political speech.[59] In other words, the Court assumed that official judgments in this area would be sufficiently objective to avoid controversial disagreements over values that would mar any comparable effort to identify false or misleading political speech.

A second kind of negative free speech theory would suggest that speech regulation will misfire by overdeterring speech because it is more fragile or easily chilled than conduct in instances outside the intended scope of regulation.[60] The focus here is on the speak-

---

[57] See generally Mancur Olson, *The Logic of Collective Action: Public Goods and the Theory of Groups* (1965); Daniel A. Farber and Philip P. Frickey, *Law and Public Choice: A Critical Introduction* (1991).

[58] Of course, it might be objected that this argument fails to distinguish factional capture of speech regulation from similar capture of economic regulation. See Jackson and Jeffries, 65 Va L Rev at 29–30 (cited in note 36) ("The Court [in *Virginia Board*] seems to have viewed Virginia's law as nothing more or less than a classic case of special interest legislation inconsistent with any disinterested understanding of the public good. . . . It is surprising to discover, however, that these economic considerations add up to a *constitutional* impediment to legislative control of the marketplace [and that the] source of that constitutional restraint is the first amendment.").

[59] 425 US at 772 n 24.

[60] The fragility of speech can be redescribed in economic terms: Speech will be more readily deterred by regulation than other activities because it most often functions as a public good, whose benefits cannot be fully captured by its producer. See note 33 above.

er's motivations rather than the government's. This view helps explain, for example, the special procedural First Amendment doctrines against vagueness, overbreadth, and prior restraint. The Court in *Virginia Board* viewed commercial speech as fragile enough to warrant inclusion in the First Amendment, but not fragile enough to require such special procedural protections. Noting that commercial speech is "hardi[er]" or "more durable than other kinds" of speech because "advertising is the sine qua non of commercial profits," Justice Blackmun also wrote that it might be "less necessary to tolerate inaccurate statements for fear of silencing the speaker."[61]

* * *

In sum, the Court in *Virginia Board* rejected all the major wholesale theoretical objections to the protection of commercial speech under the First Amendment. It diluted the notion of deliberative self-government to encompass decentralized exercises of consumer sovereignty; it reconceived truth-seeking as a relativistic individual rather than an objective social quest; it endorsed a robust notion of listener autonomy, erasing concern that corporate advertisers are not themselves bearers of autonomy; and it acknowledged at least implicitly that governmental suppression of commercial speech can misfire through official favoritism and bias. It qualified the protection of commercial speech only by observing two "commonsense differences" from other kinds of speech: its supposedly greater objectivity and its hardiness, or inelasticity of supply.

II. Liquormart: Virginia Board v Central Hudson

Under *Virginia Board, Liquormart* should have been an easy case for invalidation. Rhode Island, just like Virginia, had suppressed truthful price data in order to stop consumers from acting on it in ways the state presumed harmful to their health and social interests. The identical state technique was held impermissible in *Virginia Board* as paternalistic. Even if preventing a race to the bottom among pharmacists or promoting temperance are good things in the abstract, *Virginia Board* holds that the state may not serve such goals by removing information in order to change behavior rather than by regulating behavior directly.

---

[61] 425 US at 772 n 24.

Why, then, did it take the Supreme Court four different opinions to reach a judgment of invalidation, rather than a per curiam opinion saying simply "reversed, by reason of *Virginia Board*"? The stumbling block was the Court's earlier decision in *Central Hudson Gas & Electric Corp. v Public Service Commission*,[62] and its offspring, which had set up a deep tension with *Virginia Board*. In *Central Hudson*, the Court reviewed a New York ban on promotional advertising by an electric utility. The state defended the ban as promoting energy conservation. The Court held this interest substantial and held further that the advertising ban directly advanced it. The Court demanded very little factual proof of this connection, suggesting that a simple presumption would do: "There is an immediate connection between advertising and demand for electricity. Central Hudson would not contest the advertising ban unless it believed that promotion would increase its sales."[63] The Court went on to strike down the ban anyway because it swept too far, reaching even promotion of substitute energy products whose use would not increase total energy consumption. But a crucial line had been crossed: As Justice Blackmun noted, this was the first time the Court had stated that advertising might be suppressed in order to "'dampen' demand for or use of the product" advertised.[64]

From this aspect of *Central Hudson* it was a short step to the ruling in *Posadas*. Puerto Rico deemed gambling a substantial harm to its residents and so aimed to reduce their demand for gambling. Advertising gambling would stimulate demand (as in *Central Hudson*), and in addition might increase price competition among casinos and so lower prices and increase sales to the extent that they were price-elastic (a possibility irrelevant to the monopoly seller in *Central Hudson*). Thus, the Court held, a ban on advertising would directly advance the state's interest in decreasing gambling purchases by local residents, q.e.d. *Edge Broadcasting* followed similar logic in upholding a gambling broadcast ban. North Carolina had a policy against lotteries, and wished to discourage demand

---

[62] 447 US 557 (1980).

[63] Id at 569.

[64] Id at 574 (Blackmun joined by Brennan concurring in judgment). In *Linmark*, the Court previously had suggested nearly the opposite, striking down a ban on residential "for sale" signs on the ground that government may not try to stop panic selling by manipulating the flow of information between buyers and sellers.

for lottery participation among its own residents. Presuming that advertising increases demand and hence consumption, the Court held that the federal government could permissibly lend support to North Carolina's antilottery policy by barring North Carolina broadcasters from running ads for the Virginia lottery.[65] The laws in *Posadas* and *Edge* fared better than the utility regulation in *Central Hudson*, as the Court found them adequately narrowly tailored to their ends. But the core premise was consistent across the three cases: government was free to stop advertising in order to prevent the audience from acting on the information by buying more of the advertised product than they otherwise might—so long as it did not sweep in too much speech in doing so.

By the logic of *Central Hudson, Posadas*, and *Edge, Liquormart* should have been an easy case the other way. Rhode Island sought to suppress demand for alcoholic beverages. Its legislature presumed that advertising increases demand and lowers prices, increasing sales and consumption. Its lawyers went further than the mere presumptions that had sufficed in the earlier cases, presenting experts and statistical evidence at trial to demonstrate the price sensitivity of alcohol consumption. Surely the First Circuit may be forgiven for taking *Central Hudson* and its progeny at their word, and finding it adequate justification for Rhode Island's liquor advertising ban that price advertising would lower prices and increase demand.

But the *Central Hudson* trilogy was fundamentally at odds with the anti-paternalism premise of *Virginia Board. Virginia Board* had held that suppressing information to keep people from acting on it in undesirable ways smacked of impermissible motive, amounting to a kind of thought control. *Central Hudson* and its heirs said this was fine, as long as it was relabeled the suppression of demand. Surely it would be implausible to distinguish *Virginia Board* and *Liquormart* as cases about price and *Central Hudson, Posadas, and Edge* as cases about promotion.[66] *Virginia Board* clearly assumed that price data were promotional, in the sense that advertis-

---

[65] Technically, the federal government interest in *Edge* was not suppressing demand but furthering federalism by conforming federal broadcast policy to state lottery policy, whichever way state lottery policy went. But this expressive or structural interest depends on the underlying premise that broadcast ads will increase demand in nonlottery states.

[66] Tellingly, no justice suggested such a distinction in *Liquormart*.

ing of low prices would induce people to buy the lower-priced products. Thus the tension between the two lines of cases over the permissibility of the government interest is irreducible.

The Court's indifference to alternative means of regulation in the *Central Hudson* line of cases and *Posadas* was also at odds with *Virginia Board*. If suppressing demand is the goal, the state always has available to it alternative methods that do not involve suppressing any speech. If the state wants to keep prices high to discourage consumption, assuming some degree of consumer responsiveness to price, it could impose a sales or excise tax or a minimum price floor. For a more direct approach, it could regulate consumption itself by prohibiting or rationing the product. Finally, government is free to propagandize against a product or practice on its own nickel—variations on "just say no."[67] Viewed in this light, all suppression of advertising in order to suppress demand suppresses speech unnecessarily. Ordinarily, in review of laws aimed at communicative impact—as of any other content-based law—the availability of such alternatives is dispositive against the government. Moreover, *Central Hudson, Posadas,* and *Edge* each involved a total ban on a particular message, not the channeling of a permitted message into alternative channels—a factor that in typical review of even content-neutral laws strengthens the case for putting the state to alternative, less speech-restrictive methods.[68]

Thus the trick in *Liquormart* was how to invalidate the price advertising ban under *Virginia Board* while getting around the logic of the *Central Hudson* line of cases. The three major opinions found three ways to do this, differing only in their degree of explicitness. Taking them in descending order of radicalism:

1. *Thomas: per se impermissible.* Justice Thomas's concurrence rejected the pro-paternalism premise of *Central Hudson* most explicitly. Justice Thomas would hold that suppressing advertising is always an impermissible means of suppressing demand for a good or service. He would declare "*per se* illegitimate" any asserted state interest in keeping "users of a product or service ignorant in order

---

[67] *Posadas* considered and rejected the alternative of "a 'counterspeech' policy" by Puerto Rico to discourage gambling, 478 US at 344, but did not consider whether the First Amendment compelled Puerto Rico to try banning local residents from the gaming tables before banning casinos' speech.

[68] See, for example, *City of Ladue v Gilleo*, 512 US 43 (1994).

to manipulate their choices in the marketplace."[69] No balancing ought apply, in his view, to a regulation that proceeds by "keeping would-be recipients of the speech in the dark."[70]

2. *Stevens: strict scrutiny.* Justice Stevens, joined by Justices Kennedy and Ginsburg only on this point, took the second sharpest departure from the pro-paternalism premise of *Central Hudson.* In a portion of his majority opinion that the other six Justices did not join, Justice Stevens wrote that bars against "dissemination of truthful, nonmisleading commercial messages for reasons unrelated to the preservation of a fair bargaining process" should receive strict scrutiny.[71] Justice Stevens and his two colleagues would abandon across-the-board intermediate scrutiny for commercial speech and instead substitute two-tier review: regulations whose purpose is "to protect consumers from misleading, deceptive, or aggressive sales practices" or to ensure "disclosure of beneficial consumer information" should receive "less than strict" scrutiny, while laws aimed at the content of an advertiser's truthful, nonmisleading message should receive strict scrutiny under general First Amendment principles.[72] Like Justice Thomas, Justice Stevens urged strong skepticism toward "regulations that seek to keep people in the dark for what the government perceives to be their own good,"[73] without quite declaring that such regulations are inherently void.

In the alternative, Justice Stevens wrote for himself and Justices Kennedy, Souter, and Ginsburg that the Rhode Island law would in any event fail the traditional *Central Hudson* test because the state had not shown that "its speech prohibition will *significantly* reduce market-wide consumption."[74] He lost Justice Thomas on this point because Thomas regarded this argument as contradicting the anti-paternalism premise driving the other portions of the Stevens opinion: the alternative holding "seems to imply that if the State had been *more successful* at keeping consumers ignorant

---

[69] *Liquormart,* 116 S Ct at 1515–16 (Thomas concurring in part and in judgment).

[70] Id at 1518.

[71] Id at 1507 (Stevens joined by Kennedy and Ginsburg).

[72] Id.

[73] Id at 1508.

[74] Id at 1509 (Stevens joined by Kennedy, Souter, and Ginsburg).

and thereby decreasing their consumption, then the restriction might have been upheld."[75]

3. *O'Connor: direct regulation as alternative means.* The group of Justices giving the third sharpest repudiation to *Central Hudson* were those who nominally reaffirmed its mode of scrutiny.[76] Justice O'Connor, joined by Chief Justice Rehnquist and Justices Souter and Breyer, wrote separately, concurring in the judgment, to reiterate that the *Central Hudson* intermediate scrutiny standard was still the law, but that Rhode Island had simply flunked it.[77] Why? Because Rhode Island "has other methods at its disposal—methods that would more directly accomplish this stated goal without intruding on sellers' ability to provide truthful, nonmisleading information to customers."[78] What methods? Increasing sales taxes, limiting per capita purchases and conducting educational campaigns—all of which would be more direct and as or more effective.

The O'Connor concurrence suggests that the Rhode Island law was thus not narrowly tailored enough, as if some other law banning ads in order to depress demand and consumption might someday pass that test. But surely Justice Thomas was correct to note that such a law is hard to imagine: "it would seem that directly banning a product (or rationing it, taxing it, controlling its price or otherwise restricting its sale in specific ways) would virtually always be at least as effective in discouraging consumption as merely restricting advertising regarding the product would be, and thus virtually all restrictions with such a purpose would fail the fourth prong of the *Central Hudson* test" as the O'Connor concurrence construed it.[79] It is no answer to suggest that, since *Posadas,*

---

[75] Id at 1518 (Thomas concurring and concurring in part).

[76] Justice Scalia concurred in the judgment, acquiescing in the *Central Hudson* test in the absence of demonstrated evidence of original intent toward advertising protection. Id at 1515.

[77] Justice Stevens's opinion, joined by Kennedy, Souter, and Ginsburg on this point, agreed that, even if strict scrutiny were not employed, the Rhode Island law would still not survive *Central Hudson* because Rhode Island had "failed to establish a 'reasonable fit' between its abridgement of speech and its temperance goal." Id at 1510.

[78] Id at 1521 (O'Connor joined by Rehnquist, Souter, and Breyer).

[79] Id at 1519 (Thomas concurring in part and in judgment). Justice Thomas himself had used similar analysis to invalidate a federal ban on stating beer alcohol strength on labels. See *Coors Brewing,* 115 S Ct at 1593–94 (finding that the availability of other options, "such

intermediate scrutiny of commercial speech regulation generally has gotten stricter and the Court has required a "closer look" at the facts underlying a state's claims about the efficacy of its advertising ban.[80] Perhaps it takes a battle of experts at trial to establish whether or not an advertising ban would decrease consumption. Price elasticities and market shares are matters open to empirical debate. But it does not take a single expert to prove that taxes, price floors, rationing and government speech exist as plausible alternatives. Indeed, the O'Connor concurrence itself treats the existence of alternative, non-speech-restrictive methods for demand suppression as entirely intuitive.

* * *

In sum, *Liquormart*'s several opinions treated a ban on a commercial message designed to stop listeners from acting on it much the way they might have treated any other ban on speech by reason of its communicative impact.[81] As with any such law, the harm that

as directly limiting the alcohol content of beers," indicated that the law "is more extensive than necessary").

[80] *Liquormart*, 116 S Ct at 1522 (O'Connor concurring in judgment). See, for example, *Edenfield*, 507 US at 770–73 (holding that a ban on solicitation by certified public accountants did not advance directly enough state interests in preventing fraud, overreaching or compromised independence); *Went for It*, 115 S Ct at 2384 (Kennedy dissenting) (describing the state's evidence of the damage solicitation does to professionalism as bad science, "noteworthy for its incompetence").

[81] Some have suggested that interference with communicative impact is the defining characteristic of all content-based laws. See, for example, John Hart Ely, *Flag Desecration: A Case Study in the Roles of Categorization and Balancing in First Amendment Analysis*, 88 Harv L Rev 1482 (1975); Laurence H. Tribe, *American Constitutional Law* 790 (2d ed 1988). Others have treated laws aimed at communicative impact as a subspecies of content-based laws, belonging to but not exhausting the category. See Geoffrey R. Stone, *Content Regulation and the First Amendment*, 25 Wm & Mary L Rev 189, 207–17 (1983). Either way, laws aimed at communicative impact generally draw strict scrutiny.

In *Virginia Board*, *Linmark*, and *Liquormart*, the Court was concerned with one type of communicative impact regulation—laws that restrict speech because government expects people to act unwisely or harmfully if they have access to the restricted information. This paternalism concern surfaces occasionally outside the area of commercial law. See, for example, *Barnes v Glen Theatre, Inc.* (White dissenting) ("It is only because nude dancing performances may generate emotions and feelings of eroticism and sensuality among the spectators that the State seeks to regulate such expressive activity, apparently on the assumption that creating or emphasizing such thoughts and ideas in the minds of the spectators may lead to increased prostitution and the degradation of women. But generating thoughts, ideas, and emotions is the essence of communication."). But other types of interference with the communicative impact of speech have also triggered the Court's concern. See, for example, *Boos v Barry*, 485 US 312 (1988) (invalidating law prohibiting display of any sign within 500 feet of a foreign embassy if the sign would bring the foreign government "public odium or disrepute"); *Texas v Johnson*, 491 US 397 (1989) (invalidating ban on destruction of venerated objects so as to cause "serious offense"); *Forsythe County v Nationalist Movement*, 505 US 123 (1992) (invalidating a parade permit fee whose amount was to be calibrated to the amount of hostility the parade was expected to evoke).

the state is seeking to avert arises from "the way people can be expected to react to [the] message"[82]—here, by being moved to go out and stock up on cases of cheap spirits and beer. Whether or not Rhode Island aimed ultimately at excessive drinking, that harm was only implicated by liquor price advertising by virtue of what liquor ads say and how the reader or listener will respond to that content. Thus, under standard First Amendment analysis, the governmental interest behind a liquor price advertising ban would trigger strict scrutiny. The opinions of Justices Stevens and Thomas favor such review explicitly, and Justice O'Connor's concurrence replicates strict scrutiny without saying so by treating the availability of less restrictive alternatives as dispositive without any further balancing.

III. Abandoning the Category "Commercial Speech"

Liquormart might simply have reaffirmed the anti-paternalism principle set forth in *Virginia Board* with respect to truthful, nonmisleading price data. The Court would thus have avoided any question of how to review commercial speech regulations aimed at false or misleading claims or promotion of unlawful products. In other words, it might have left intact the commercial speech status quo, except for overruling the pro-paternalism aspects of *Central Hudson, Posadas,* and *Edge.* Such a hypothetical narrow opinion might have held that stopping advertising in order to stop people from acting on its message is a cardinal First Amendment sin, and thus that it matters not that it is committed against a lower form of First Amendment life, commercial speech. Such an opinion would have resembled structurally Justice Scalia's opinion for the majority of the Court in *RAV v City of St. Paul,*[83] which held that discriminating against race-centered or racist speech committed the sins of subject matter and viewpoint discrimination, even if the speech targeted amounted to otherwise unprotected fighting words.

But *Liquormart* did not take that narrow road. Instead, the Justices skirmished over the appropriate standard of scrutiny of commercial speech regulations across a range far broader than the total

---

[82] See Ely, 88 Harv L Rev at 1497.
[83] 505 US 377 (1992).

price publication ban at issue in the case. Four Justices in *Li-quormart*—Justices Stevens, Kennedy, Thomas, and Ginsburg—in various ways avoided the usual force of the category "commercial speech" as an analytic device, at least for paternalistic laws aimed at truthful, nonmisleading commercial messages. To these Justices, the Rhode Island law tried to stop advertisers from persuading people to buy their product, and so was per se or presumptively impermissible. That it operated in a commercial context was beside the point. The four Justices did not attract a fifth, although they would have done so if Justice Blackmun had still been on the Court.[84]

It is unclear whether this plurality would apply strict scrutiny to *all* laws aimed at the content of a commercial advertisement, or only to those that are paternalistic. Justices Stevens, Kennedy, and Ginsburg suggest that all laws that "single out certain messages for suppression" should receive strict scrutiny, even when directed at commercial speech.[85] Yet even this trio would withhold strict scrutiny "[w]hen a State regulates commercial messages to protect consumers from misleading, deceptive, or aggressive sales practices, or requires the disclosure of beneficial consumer information"—in which case they would apply "less than strict review" even though such regulations would ordinarily be considered content-based.[86] This little-noticed dictum did call for a departure from conventional commercial speech law in one respect: The Court had previously suggested that fraudulent or misleading commercial speech is altogether unprotected, and thus that regulation of such speech triggered no First Amendment review.[87] Any review, even if "less than strict," is thus a novelty. And there is reason to believe these three Justices intended full-fledged intermediate scrutiny here: Elsewhere they describe the *Central Hudson* test itself as employing a "less than strict standard."[88] But the Stevens opinion still hedges a bit against applying the ordinary First

---

[84] Blackmun, the author of *Virginia Board*, increasingly took the same view in his later commercial speech decisions. See, for example, *Central Hudson*, 447 US at 573–79 (Blackmun concurring); *Discovery Network*, 507 US at 431–38 (Blackmun concurring); *Fane*, 508 US at 777 (Blackmun concurring). Justice Blackmun's replacement, Justice Breyer, in contrast, joined the concurrence in *Liquormart*.

[85] *Liquormart*, 116 S Ct at 1507.

[86] Id.

[87] See *Virginia Board*, 425 US at 771 n 24.

[88] *Liquormart*, 116 S Ct at 1510.

Amendment distinction between review of content-based and content-neutral laws. Justice Thomas declined to comment on how far he might extend the super-strict scrutiny he would apply to commercial speech regulations that are driven by paternalism.[89] And the majority, through their concurrences, took pains not to endorse the plurality's approach.

What would the world look like if the plurality's approach were taken to its logical conclusion, and all distinctive First Amendment treatment of commercial speech eliminated? For starters, it is not clear that laws could permissibly single out commercial speech from other speech without running afoul of the presumption against subject matter discrimination.[90] *Discovery Network* might be read as a precursor of such an approach: That decision invalidated a ban on commercial but not on noncommercial newsracks. Because there was no showing that commercial newsracks caused any greater sidewalk clutter than their noncommercial counterparts, the city was left trying to justify its law on the ground that commercial speech was less valuable than noncommercial speech. The Court rejected that justification as impermissibly content-based.[91] *Discovery* left open the possibility of singling out commercial speech for regulation when such regulation is directed at distinctively commercial harms. But the difference in "value" under the First Amendment between commercial and noncommercial speech was not in itself sufficient to justify a difference in treatment.[92]

A second consequence of assimilating commercial speech to general First Amendment principles would be, well, truth in advertising, so to speak. At the moment, intermediate scrutiny under *Central Hudson* is a doctrinal anomaly: intermediate in theory but

---

[89] Id at 1519 n 5 (Thomas concurring and concurring in judgment).

[90] See, for example, *Police Department v Mosley*, 408 US 92 (1972). On laws that discriminate on the basis of subject matter, see generally Geoffrey R. Stone, *Restrictions of Free Speech Because of Its Content: The Peculiar Case of Subject-Matter Restrictions*, 46 U Chi L Rev 81 (1978).

[91] 507 US at 429–30.

[92] It is conceivable that government could still single out advertisements for content-neutral purposes—for example, by applying industry-specific economic policies. The Court has treated laws favoring or disfavoring specific speakers as content-neutral if they have a justification entirely divorced from any hostility to ideas. See, for example, *Turner Broadcasting, Inc. v FCC*, 114 S Ct 2445, 2458–62 (1994) (requirement that cable operators carry over-the-air broadcasters); *Leathers v Medlock*, 499 US 439 (1991) (tax on cable but not other media).

often fatal in fact.[93] To be sure, the Court may be shifting toward a more interventionist brand of intermediate scrutiny in various areas of content-neutral speech regulation also,[94] but as a practical matter, it has long applied intermediate scrutiny with extra bite to regulations of commercial speech—a trend with which the governing opinions in *Liquormart* are consistent. This may be driven by an unarticulated sense that commercial speech regulations are content-based—all of them in the sense that they single out the subject matter of proposals of economic transactions, and many of them in the additional sense that they aim, as in *Liquormart*, at the message or the predicted listener response. Routing content-based commercial speech regulations directly to strict scrutiny would promote clarity on this point, reconciling the Court's stated standard with the predominant results.

But something must be holding the Court back from heading in this direction—or even as far as the approach of the Stevens three would take it.[95] What are the possible downsides, or per-

---

[93] *Central Hudson* set forth the now-canonical test, requiring a substantial government interest that is advanced directly by regulations no more extensive than necessary. This test closely resembles the equally canonical *O'Brien* test for review of content-neutral regulations. Just as later cases made clear that *O'Brien* didn't mean what it said, and that "no more extensive than necessary" actually meant "more effective than not," see *Ward v Rock Against Racism*, 491 US 781, 796–802 (1989); so the Court clarified in *Board of Trustees, SUNY v Fox*, 492 US 469 (1989), that the *Central Hudson* test required "a fit that is not necessarily perfect, but [merely] reasonable," id at 480. However grammatically similar these formulations, the Court rarely invalidates a content-neutral regulation of noncommercial speech, but has found a number of commercial speech regulations wanting.

[94] See, for example, *Turner*, 14 S Ct at 2470–72 (remanding for the development of a "more thorough factual record" to determine if cable must-carry rules in fact advance the government's asserted interests in protecting the viability of broadcasting and fair competition in video programming); *Madsen*, 114 S Ct at 2524–25 ("When evaluating a content-neutral injunction, we think that our standard time, place, and manner analysis is not sufficiently rigorous. We must ask instead whether the challenged provisions of the injunction burden no more speech than necessary to serve a significant government interest.").

[95] In some cases it is no doubt general skepticism toward commercial speech protection. Chief Justice Rehnquist, for example, dissented vigorously in *Virginia Board* and *Central Hudson*, and wrote in *Posadas* that the greater power to ban gambling includes the lesser power to discourage it by suppressing ads—a position expressly rejected by Justices Stevens, Kennedy, Thomas, and Ginsburg in *Liquormart*, see 116 S Ct at 1512–13. In light of this history, he must be presumed to have joined Justice O'Connor's concurrence in *Liquormart* only with some regret. Similarly, Justice O'Connor has consistently favored restrictions on professional advertising to promote professionalism. See *Edenfield*, 507 US at 778–81 (O'Connor dissenting); *Ibanez*, 114 S Ct at 2092–94 (O'Connor concurring in part and dissenting in part). In other cases, such as Justice Souter's, the question is more open. Justice Souter joined Justice Kennedy's vigorous dissent in *Florida Bar*, and joined most of Justice Stevens's opinion in *Liquormart*, but notably declined to join the portion of that opinion calling for revision of the standard of review.

ceived bad consequences, of assimilating commercial speech to the Court's existing approaches to fully protected speech? Three areas of current law deserve attention:

1. *Advertisement of illegal transactions.* Commercial speech law currently treats advertisement of an illegal product or transaction as unprotected speech, and its regulation as therefore subject to no First Amendment review.[96] It would appear that Justices Stevens, Kennedy, and Ginsburg would be willing to see such speech governed by ordinary First Amendment rules, for they do not include it in the categories of commercial speech that they would subject to "less than strict review": Such deference to government is warranted, in their view, only "[w]hen a State regulates commercial messages to protect consumers from misleading, deceptive, or aggressive sales practices, or requires the disclosure of beneficial consumer information."[97]

Why might one want to review ads for what is illegal under ordinary First Amendment principles? Under Justice Stevens's general analysis, it might be because there are no distinctively "commercial harms"[98] involved in solicitations to illegal acts. "Hit man wanted for job next week, good salary guaranteed," is plainly proscribable as solicitation to murder, but so is "Volunteer hit man wanted; job to be done next week for love of God and country." Solicitation to murder is proscribable not because it may involve an exchange of money for services in some or even most cases, but because of its obvious close connection to serious harm. Nor has the First Amendment generally been thought to proscribe solicitation to engage even in less serious crimes than murder: The person who says "steal that bicycle," "climb over that 'no trespassing' sign," or "torch that building" may be found guilty of complicity or solicitation even if those words were his only contribution to the crime—or of attempt in the event the encouragement doesn't work.

Of course, First Amendment limitations on the regulation of subversive advocacy that took half this century to develop would bar government from punishing a political speech advocating the desirability of assassinating the President, or the undesirability of

---

[96] See *Virginia Board*, 425 US at 772; *Central Hudson*, 447 US at 563–64.

[97] *Liquormart*, 116 S Ct at 1507.

[98] Id at 1508 (quoting *Discovery Network*, 507 US at 426).

the ownership of private property—even if a specific death threat or solicitation to trespass may be made a crime.[99] Commercial advertising of illegal products, however, is unlikely to resemble such protected advocacy, and thus unlikely to trigger any rigorous scrutiny under ordinary First Amendment principles. Even without special rules for commercial speech, "Grass for sale, $1 a joint" would be regulable without the scrutiny that would attach to a bar on saying "Legalize marijuana."

Thus treating advertisements for illegal transactions as commercial speech gains the government an advantage over conventional First Amendment analysis only if it extends to a broader class of advertisements than those expressly soliciting illegal acts. *Pittsburgh Press Co. v Human Relations Commission*,[100] a case decided before *Virginia Board*, suggests as much, to the extent that it retains any vitality. *Pittsburgh Press* held proscribable as sex discrimination the publication of gender-specific "help wanted" ads. Such ads did not literally propose transactions in violation of civil rights laws, but they certainly increased their likelihood. Under conventional First Amendment law, such loose probabilistic connection to harms is not enough; "every idea is an incitement,"[101] but that does not mean the state may punish the teaching of Marx or the objectification of women in pornography.[102] If *Pittsburgh Press* still governs advertisements of unlawful transactions, it represents a significant departure from usual principles.

But it is hardly clear that such a departure is warranted. Consider the case of the tobacco advertising regulations promulgated by the Food and Drug Administration in late 1996.[103] Among other regulations treating cigarettes as a nicotine-delivery device and limiting their sales, the regulations would bar cigarette manufacturers or distributors from placing any tobacco advertisements within 1,000 feet of a playground or school,[104] would permit only "tombstone" advertising (black-and-white, text only, no color or

---

[99] See *Brandenburg v Ohio*, 395 US 444 (1969); *Rankin v McPherson*, 483 US 378 (1987); *Whitney v California*, 274 US 357, 377–78 (1927) (Brandeis concurring).

[100] 413 US 376 (1973).

[101] *Gitlow v New York*, 268 US 652, 673 (Holmes dissenting).

[102] See *American Booksellers Ass'n. v Hudnut*, 771 F2d 323 (7th Cir 1985), aff'd mem, 475 US 1001 (1986).

[103] See 61 Fed Reg 44396, 44615–18 (Aug 28, 1996).

[104] 21 CFR § 897.30(b), quoted in 61 Fed Reg 44617 (1996).

graphics) on billboards elsewhere and in any magazine whose read-ership consists of more than 15% children,[105] and would bar spon-sorship of athletic or artistic events in the brand name of tobacco products.[106] The principal stated purpose of the regulations is to prevent encouragement of children and teenagers to begin smok-ing. Accordingly, the regulations seek to eliminate widespread public display of images with special appeal to children—in partic-ular, the cartoon figure of "Joe Camel," whose campaign is said to be correlated with a marked increase in Camel's share of the market among minors who smoke.

One possible defense of these regulations against First Amend-ment challenge by tobacco advertisers is that they are aimed at preventing illegal transactions—namely, the sale of tobacco prod-ucts to minors. No tobacco ad, however, literally says, "Kids, buy our smokes—for you a special introductory price of $1 a pack." If they did, they would be regulable as solicitation of illegal trans-actions, with or without any special commercial speech doctrine. Joe Camel is a subtler beast—disproportionately appealing to younger sensibilities, perhaps, but also as an easily recognizable brand symbol for legal adult purchasers. Accordingly, the illegality rationale for these regulations is tenable only if advertising illegal transactions is understood as facilitating them in the loosest sense—looser, even, than in *Pittsburgh Press*. Many advertisements depict products lawful to sell in some circumstances but not in others. Those advertisements might increase the probability of un-lawful transactions. Promotions of prescription drugs, which by definition are illegal to sell without a prescription, might increase attempts by buyers to forge prescriptions or seek out corrupt phar-macists for illegal sales. Ads for nonobscene adult entertainment might increase the probability that persons under 21 will forge identification papers or otherwise attempt illegally to slip in. But much other speech that might increase the probability of unlawful acts is permitted because that is not its only effect, and because unlawful acts may be directly regulated.[107]

If such loose applications of the illegality rationale appear unten-

---

[105] 21 CFR § 897.32, quoted in 61 Fed Reg 44617 (1996).

[106] 21 CFR § 897.34, quoted in 61 Fed Reg 44617–18 (1996).

[107] See, for example, *American Booksellers Ass'n v Hudnut*, 771 F2d 323 (7th Cir 1985), aff'd mem, 475 US 1001 (1986).

able, then there is no case for a special commercial speech doctrine regarding illegal ads. Ordinary First Amendment principles already permit government to punish solicitation to engage in illegal transactions, whether or not the solicitor is commercially motivated. To that extent, current commercial speech doctrine regarding illegal transactions is redundant. And as to merely increasing the probability of illegal acts, it is not clear why commercial speech poses any distinctive harm as compared with other types of speech.

2. *False and misleading advertising.* Current law treats regulation of false or misleading commercial speech as exempt from the heightened scrutiny called for in *Central Hudson*, and thus in effect as a mini-species of unprotected speech. Justices Stevens, Kennedy, and Ginsburg would escalate review of such regulations to something that sounds like the *Central Hudson* test. Here, they would still give some discount from strict review because of distinctive features of commercial speech: Presumably they mean, following *Virginia Board*, that it is easier to segregate false statements of fact (because commercial data are "more easily verifiable"), and regulation of their falsity is less likely to chill commercial speech beyond the precise scope of the regulation (because the profit motive makes commercial speech "more durable than other kinds").[108]

What would it mean to apply ordinary First Amendment principles in this context? Many false statements of fact in commercial advertisements would still appear easily proscribable. As *Virginia Board* stated, "Untruthful speech, *commercial or otherwise*, has never been protected for its own sake."[109] Protecting false statements may serve an instrumental function, such as affording "breathing room" to true statements.[110] This is why politicians may be allowed to lie about some facts in electoral campaigns without facing actions for fraud.[111] And that is why false statements of fact may be

---

[108] For criticisms of these generalizations about commercial speech, see Kozinski and Banner, 76 Va L Rev at 635–38 (cited in note 31).

[109] 425 US at 771 (emphasis added). See also *Gertz v Robert Welch, Inc.*, 418 US 323, 340 (1974) ("there is no constitutional value in false statements of fact"); *Garrison v Louisiana*, 379 US 64, 75 (1964) ("the use of the known lie as a tool is at once at odds with the premises of democratic government"; the First Amendment does not protect "calculated falsehood").

[110] See *New York Times v Sullivan*, 376 US 254 (1964).

[111] Compare *Brown v Hartlage*, 456 US 45 (1982) (holding that state may not invalidate election on ground candidate had promised voters falsely that he would serve for a salary less than that fixed by law).

protected if insegregable from a protected political diatribe.[112] But false statements of fact in commercial advertisements are not likely to be similarly intertwined with protected speech.[113]

Of course, the norm against false statements of fact is underenforced, as daily claims in supermarket tabloid headlines demonstrate. Government bothers to regulate falsity only when it causes harm. Injury to reputation through libel, impairment of trials or the congressional oversight process through perjury, and impairment of elections through misrepresentation of the vote count provide obvious examples. False statements of fact about products that will cause people to injure themselves would likewise appear to be readily proscribable without any special consideration of their commercial context. "Product safe for children" is not protected speech when it promotes a product causing widespread infant death. Snake oil is a harder question; It is not clear that the claim "product cures baldness forever" causes more harm than the supermarket tabloid headlines.

Thus, treating knowingly false statements of fact in advertising like other false speech would appear to have little impact on government's latitude for regulation in this area. Not so, however, for misleading commercial speech. A vast regulatory apparatus in both the federal government and the states has developed to control not only knowingly false statements of fact, but also potentially misleading or deceptive speech.[114] For government, this is the turf

---

[112] But see *Beauharnais v Illinois*, 342 US 250 (1952) (permitting action for libel of a racial group).

[113] Compare *Board of Trustees, SUNY v Fox*, 492 US 469 (1989) (sales pitch for tupperware not inseverable from homilies about domestic frugality).

[114] See, for example, 15 USC § 45 (1996) (authorizing Federal Trade Commission to limit deceptive practices); 21 USC § 343 (providing that a food is misbranded when its label is false or misleading); 21 USC § 352 (same for drugs and devices); 21 CFR § 1.21 (1996) (authorizing Food and Drug Administration to require disclosure of material facts to avoid misleading labeling of food, drug, or device); 15 USC § 77K (making it illegal to file misleading registration statement with the Securities Exchange Commission). Substantially similar provisions appear in state "printer's ink" laws, which prohibit untrue, misleading, or deceptive advertising, see, for example, Colo Stat § 6-1-105 (1996), and "blue sky" laws, which prohibit the buying or selling of securities in connection with any misleading statement, see, for example, Cal Corp Code § 25401 (1995).

The definitions of false and misleading statements in these laws sweep broadly. For example, the FTC sanctions material representations that are "likely to mislead consumers acting reasonably under the circumstances." *Federal Trade Commission Policy Statement on Deception*, 103 FTC 174 (1994). The FDA has promulgated extensive regulations that govern in minute detail the labeling of food and drug packages to ensure that they are not misleading. See, for example, 21 CFR § 105.66 (requiring that foods purporting to be low calorie must meet specific criteria); 21 CFR § 104.20 (listing acceptable label claims for vitamin or minworth fighting over in considering whether to abandon special rules for false and misleading commercial speech. Under current conceptions of misleading commercial speech as wholly unprotected by the First Amendment, the fit of the law to the harms it seeks to prevent need not be tested for reasonable fit,[115] injunctions or other prior restraints are permissible,[116] and speech of particular content may be freely compelled.[117] Broad prophylactic measures may sweep in significant amounts of nondeceptive or at least ambiguous speech. For example, because the FDA authorizes promotion of pharmaceutical products only for agency-approved uses, companies that manufacture contraceptive pills declined to advertise the undisputed efficacy of such pills as an abortifacient when

---

eral additives to food); 21 CFR § 152.126 (requiring that a frozen cherry pie label may not bear any misleading pictorial representation of the cherries in the pie). And the SEC is permitted to treat as misleading even speech that is exaggerated or hyperbolic: "What might be considered innocuous 'puffery' or mere statement of opinion standing alone may be actionable as an integral part of a representation of material fact when used to emphasize and induce reliance upon such a representation." *Casella v Webb*, 883 F2d 805, 808 (9th Cir 1989).

[115] FTC determinations are subject only to deferential review for substantial evidence, see *Kraft, Inc. v FTC*, 970 F2d 311, 316 (7th Cir 1992), cert denied, 507 US 909 (1993), though courts sometimes review FTC orders to ensure that they are "no broader than reasonably necessary to prevent the deception," *FTC v Brown & Williamson Tobacco Corp.*, 778 F2d 35, 170 (DC Cir 1985). FDA determinations whether a label is misleading are reviewed quite deferentially. See, for example, *Henley v FDA*, 77 F3d 616 (2d Cir 1996) (holding that FDA's determination not to include estrogen warning label was warranted given FDA's expertise in interpreting scientific studies).

[116] Preclearance or licensing requirements for speech are common in consumer protection regulation. See, for example, 21 CFR § 101.14(c) ("FDA will promulgate regulations authorizing a health claim only when it determines, based on the totality of publicly available scientific evidence (including evidence from well-designed studies conducted in a manner which is consistent with generally recognized scientific procedures and principles), that there is significant scientific agreement, among experts qualified by scientific training and experience to evaluate such claims, that the claim is supported by such evidence.").

[117] The FTC, FDA, and SEC are authorized to treat as misleading material omissions from advertisements. See 15 USC § 55 (authorizing FTC to determine falsity based on "the extent to which the advertisement fails to reveal facts material in light of representations" made); 21 USC § 321(n) (authorizing FDA to determine misbranding based on "the extent to which the labeling fails to reveal facts material in the light of . . . representations" made); 15 USC § 77l (providing for liability when securities prospectus knowingly or negligently "omits to state a material fact necessary in order to make the statements [made], in the light of the circumstances under which they were made, not misleading"). Under First Amendment principles applicable to noncommercial speech, such requirements would trigger strict review, either because they have the effect of compelling the speech that otherwise would have been omitted, or by deterring statements that otherwise might be made lest they later be found to contain material omissions. See, for example, *Pacific Gas & Electric Co. v Public Utilities Commission*, 475 US 1 (1986).

used in higher doses, at least in the absence of specific FDA authorization.[118] For another example, one argument that has been made for the constitutionality of tobacco advertising bans—more prominent in the days before Joe Camel had eclipsed the Marlboro Man—holds that cigarette ads are inherently deceptive because "[s]moking is portrayed as not harmful, by associating it with traditionally young, healthy, athletic, and virile activities. . . ."[119]

Applying ordinary First Amendment principles—or even the "less than strict" review advocated by the Stevens three in *Liquormart*—would work a sea change in this area of regulation. It is possible that in some cases the government might ultimately prevail even under heightened or strict scrutiny[120] on the ground that unchecked misleading commercial speech would have catastrophic consequences (the product might kill or seriously injure you), and because more speech is unlikely to intervene to correct that harm (the manufacturer or advertiser is uniquely in a position to know that the product might kill or seriously injure you, and competitors will decline to unmask the problem to preserve their own sales of similar products). But putting the government to such a particularized showing would make current consumer protection laws much harder to defend.

These considerations no doubt help explain the lack of interest in abandoning the category commercial speech on the part of the five Justices who concurred in *Liquormart* on narrow grounds—as well as the reluctance of even Justices Stevens, Kennedy, and Ginsburg to subject regulations of false and misleading ads to full-bore strict scrutiny. But it is worth noticing that deference to such regulations raises considerable tension with the normative premises of *Virginia Board* that were resuscitated in *Liquormart*. *Liquormart* held that government may not regulate true and nonmisleading

---

[118] See Tamar Lewin, *U.S. Agency Wants the Pill Redefined*, New York Times A1, A1 (July 1, 1996).

[119] Vincent Blasi and Henry P. Monaghan, *The First Amendment and Cigarette Advertising*, 250 JAMA 502, 506 (1986).

[120] Strict scrutiny is not always fatal in fact. See, for example, *Burson v Freeman*, 504 US 191 (1992) (upholding ban on political signs near polling place); *Denver Area Telecommunications Consortium v FCC*, 116 S Ct 2374, 2432 (1996) (Thomas concurring in part and dissenting in part) (arguing that regulation requiring cable operators to segregate and scramble indecent material triggered but satisfied strict scrutiny).

commercial speech on the ground that it does not trust people to deal appropriately with the information. Any correction to the bad effects of reliance on such speech must lie elsewhere—for example, in the counterspeech of competitors or of the government itself. The underlying model of the listener is one of a robust, self-determining agent fully capable of placing true information in whatever context might be necessary in order to decide whether or not to act upon it. The image of the listener confronted with misleading commercial speech is radically different: Here, the consumer is not expected to have the competence or access to information needed to question the advertiser's claim, and correction is not to be left to competitors and mere government counterspeech.[121]

The Court has not made clear why government paternalism in the case of true speech is abhorrent while government paternalism in the case of misleading speech is entirely permissible. Both turn on preventing the listener from being persuaded by the speech to his own or society's peril. Misleading commercial speech does not amount to the kind of fraud that warrants government intervention under standard libertarian theory. Nor is it the case that true commercial speech is restricted only to prevent individual self-destruction, whereas misleading commercial speech is restricted to prevent the listener who acts upon it from causing external social harm. After all, Virginia was concerned with preventing a race to the bottom among pharmacists, and Rhode Island was concerned with preventing the social harms of excessive drinking. In contrast, a law regulating what foods may be labeled "low-calorie" is designed mostly to protect the consumer from herself.

3. *Content-based regulation of commercial speech.* In addition to deference to regulations of ads of illegal transactions and false or misleading ads, the principal remaining advantage to the government from segregating commercial speech from mainstream First Amendment jurisprudence is that it may sustain content-*based* commercial speech regulations under less than strict scrutiny. *Li-*

---

[121] See, for example, *US Articles of Drugs, etc.*, 263 F Supp 212, 215 (D Neb 1967) (noting that FDA regulations assess whether labels are misleading from the perspective of "prospective purchasers to whom the claims are addressed," and that "[i]t would defeat the obvious intent of the Act to hold such persons to special knowledge or ability. Nor should the Court assume that the buying public will exercise great selectivity and caution in what they choose to believe of what they hear and read.").

quormart would appear to eliminate one type of content-based commercial speech regulation—namely, laws motivated by paternalistic concern that the listener will act wrongly on true factual information. But other types of content-based commercial speech regulations (apart from those aimed at false or misleading ads) receive intermediate scrutiny, with mixed results.[122]

What would change if the Court were to generalize from *Liquormart* and subject to strict scrutiny under conventional First Amendment principles all regulations of advertising that are aimed at its message or its communicative impact? For example, consider regulations designed to prevent advertisers from conveying particular images that they seek to associate with their product or service. While *Liquormart*, like *Virginia Board*, concerned only the provision of true price information, most of what Madison Avenue sells is product image. Even under the existing notion that the government has broad leeway to control misleading commercial speech, it is not generally claimed that such imagistic associations are deceptive. Some regulations might nonetheless aim to stop positive associations of a product with an advertising image for the same reason Rhode Island aimed to keep discount liquor price information from consumers: simply to stop them from buying the product, or more of the product than they otherwise would. This is in large part the theory underlying the FDA's tobacco advertising restrictions insofar as they implicitly target Joe Camel and like images.

As a practical matter, subjecting all such regulations to strict scrutiny would eliminate a lot of trial and discovery work for lawyers and experts. *Central Hudson* itself rested on a presumption that advertising caused harmful effects, but later cases have demanded far more searching and fact-intensive adjudication of whether an advertising restriction directly advances the state's ends and does not infringe too much speech in the process.[123] Where demand

---

[122] Compare, for example, *Carey v Population Services International*, 431 US 678 (1977) (invalidating a ban on contraceptive advertising on the ground that audience offense was an insufficient justification), and *Bolger v Youngs Drug Products Corp.*, 463 US 60 (1983) (same for ban on unsolicited mailings of condom ads), with *Ohralik v Ohio State Bar Association*, 436 US 447 (1978) (upholding bar disciplinary sanction against face-to-face solicitation of legal business in part because of overbearing impact on listener), and *Florida Bar v Went for It* (upholding moratorium on direct mail solicitation of legal business from accident victims in part because of intrusion on the sensibilities of accident victims and their families).

[123] See, for example, *Edenfield*, 507 US at 776 (holding that government is obligated "to demonstrate that it is regulating speech in order to address what is in fact a serious problem

reduction is the state's goal, such a showing could entail complex evidence about market structures, income distribution, and price elasticities—the very kinds of evidence Rhode Island tried to marshal before the district court in *Liquormart*.

Such intensive review of facts under flexible standards or balancing tests creates a host of familiar institutional problems: For example, it collapses the legislative and adjudicative functions, and creates fluctuating precedent that gives uncertain guidance to lower courts and parties.[124] But it also has a perverse substantive effect in cases of content-based regulation of commercial speech: The more effectively government thwarts the comunicative effect of the advertising, the more directly it advances its ultimate goal and satisfies the now-dominant stringent version of *Central Hudson*. As Justice Stevens noted for the *Liqormart* plurality, the Rhode Island law failed even under *Central Hudson* because "the State has presented no evidence to suggest that its speech prohibition will *significantly* reduce market-wide consumption" of alcohol.[125] Justice Thomas correctly noted the inconsistency of this argument with the central premise of *Virginia Board:* it "seems to imply that if the State had been *more successful* at keeping consumes ignorant and thereby decreasing their consumption, then the restriction might have been upheld."[126] All these problems are avoided if laws aimed at the commercial message are treated as content-based and subjected to conventional strict scrutiny, which is much more susceptible to summary decision.

For example, to return to the FDA tobacco regulations, review under the currently demanding version of *Central Hudson* would involve courts in intensive review of voluminous evidence on the alleged links between cigarette advertising and cigarette consumption, and in particular between cigarette advertising and the inculcation of the smoking habit in children. The administrative record is immense and filled with opposing findings, whose conflicts the

---

and that the preventative measure it proposes will contribute in a material way to solving that problem").

[124] See *Liquormart*, 116 S Ct at 1520 (Thomas concurring) (criticizing the *Central Hudson* test as "very difficult to apply" because of "the inherently nondeterminative nature of a case-by-case balancing 'test' unaccompanied by any categorical rules). See generally Kathleen M. Sullivan, *Foreword: The Justices of Rules and Standards*, 106 Harv L Rev 22 (1992).

[125] 116 S Ct at 1509.

[126] 116 S Ct at 1518 (Thomas concurring).

FDA has worked at great length to resolve. Judicial review of facts here is not meant to be *de novo*,[127] but it is not to be entirely deferential either.[128] For all the FDA's herculean efforts, it may nonetheless be difficult to satisfy the Court that advertising causes people to begin smoking, controlling for other influences.[129] Review under the current approach would also call for detailed demonstration by the state that alternative means of direct market regulation—such as restrictions on vending machines, free samples, and so forth contained elsewhere in the new regulation—have been tried and failed persistently. This showing too would be fraught with factual detail and disagreement.[130]

These complex disputes would be avoided if the regulations were subject to strict scrutiny on the ground that, whatever their ultimate end, they aim at speech for its communicative impact, and if the plurality view in *Liqormart* were extended from paternalistic regulations of true factual representations to all regulations of commercial speech for its communicative impact. Such scrutiny would be virtually inevitably fatal. The FDA distinguishes the tobacco regulation from other demand-suppressive advertising bans such as the one in *Liquormart* on the grounds that it is aimed at keeping messages from children, who lack the autonomy ascribed to listeners in *Virginia Board*, and that it is a channeling (place or manner) regulation rather than a total ban.[131] These distinctions may or may not persuade the Court, but they do not erase the regulations' content basis. While the distinction between content and manner regulation is sometimes elusive,[132] there can be no doubt that restriction of particular political advertisements to certain media, or to black-and-white formats, would be held content-based if justified on the ground that people would make undesir-

---

[127] See *Turner*, 114 S Ct at 2471–72.

[128] See *Hurley v Irish-American Gay, Lesbian and Bisexual Group of Boston*, 115 S Ct 2338, 2344 (1995).

[129] See Law, 77 Iowa L Rev at 918 (cited in note 50).

[130] For a detailed argument that the tobacco advertising regulations should fail under such *Central Hudson* review, see Martin H. Redish, *Tobacco Advertising and the First Amendment*, 81 Iowa L Rev 589 (1996).

[131] See 61 Fed Reg 44469–74 (Aug 28, 1996).

[132] See, for example, *ISKCON v Lee*, 505 US 672, 703–07 (Kennedy concurring) (reasoning that a ban on face-to-face solicitation of immediate payment in an airport terminal was a regulation of manner, not content, because it permitted asking for money by mail).

able positive associations with the unrestricted ads.[133] Only if commercial speech is categorically subordinate can the tobacco ad restrictions be treated differently.[134]

The question remains what legislatures and agencies would do in response to such curtailment of their powers to regulate advertisements for their content or communicative impact. They might achieve the same consumer protection goals through direct regulation of production and sales, shifting means but not altering ends. Or it might prove more difficult to implement direct regulation as a substitute, for all sorts of political reasons. These are complicated empirical questions, but it is hardly clear that the shift would render consumer protection agencies powerless.

IV. Conclusion

Liquormart would be a relatively trivial case if all it had done was to reaffirm the precise holding of *Virginia Board*, that a state may not completely ban the publication of true prices of legal products. What makes it seem a good deal more significant is the division it elicited among the Justices on the proper approach to commercial speech regulation overall. A plurality, at least, are willing to move commercial speech somewhat closer to the core of the First Amendment, applying strict scrutiny to paternalistic interventions between speaker and listener for the listener's own good. It remains to be seen whether this group of Justices would extend that approach to all content-based commercial speech regulations, whether a fifth or more will join them, and whether such a move would prompt any change in the Court's currently exceptional treatment of false and misleading commercial speech.

To be sure, commercial speech protection raises serious institutional questions about the power of corporations in relation to government. For example, tobacco advertising expenditures

---

[133] Again, strict scrutiny of such content-based channeling regulations would not necessarily be fatal. See *Burson v Freeman*, 504 US 191 (1992) (upholding under strict scrutiny a ban on political signs near polling places).

[134] Unless, of course, the Court gives an implicit discount to such speech despite its nominal protection, which is arguably what it has done, for example, with sexually explicit but nonobscene speech. See, for example, *City of Renton v Playtime Theatres, Inc.*, 475 US 41 (1986) (upholding content-based zoning of adult theaters on the ground that it was justified by content-neutral secondary effects of speech).

amount to $6 billion a year industry-wide, a sum that dwarfs any plausible countervailing educational efforts by government. But the structure of communications industries raises profound questions well beyond the context of advertising, as recent cases on regulation of cable illustrate.[135] The First Amendment may have to take more account of institutional theory generally. But treating commercial speech more like other speech produced for profit will not impede this inquiry.

---

[135] See *Turner*, 114 S Ct at 2470–72; *Denver Area Educational Telecommunications Consortium, Inc. v FCC*, 116 S Ct 2374 (1996).

MARK TUSHNET

"THE KING OF FRANCE WITH FORTY
THOUSAND MEN": FELKER v TURPIN
AND THE SUPREME COURT'S
DELIBERATIVE PROCESSES*

I. Introduction

When the Supreme Court granted certiorari in *Felker v Turpin* on May 3, 1996, and ordered an expedited briefing and argument schedule,[1] it seemed that a major constitutional decision might be in prospect. On April 24, the President had signed the Anti-Terrorism and Effective Death Penalty Act of 1996, amending the federal habeas corpus statute. One section of the Act dealt with successive habeas corpus petitions. According to the Act, a habeas petitioner filing a second or successive petition must satisfy certain requirements dealing with the nature of the claim. Initial habeas petitions can be filed directly in the district court. Under the Act, however, second or successive petitions may not. Instead,

Mark Tushnet is Carmack Waterhouse Professor of Constitutional Law, Georgetown University Law Center.

Author's note: Part II of this article is adapted from *Making Constitutional Law: Thurgood Marshall and the Supreme Court, 1961–1991* (Oxford, 1997). The author would like to thank Vicki Jackson, Daniel Meltzer, and Larry Yackle for comments on a draft of this article.

* "The King of France, with forty thousand men, marched up the hill, and then marched back again." Quoted in *Florida v Royer*, 460 US 491, 520 (Rehnquist, J, dissenting).

[1] 116 S Ct 1588 (1996). It may be worth noting that the Court granted certiorari even though one of the questions it had to decide was whether Congress had precluded review by writ of certiorari. The Court ultimately dismissed the petition for certiorari "for want of jurisdiction." 116 S Ct 2333, 2341 (1996).

the court of appeals acts, as the Court put it, as a "gatekeeper" for such petitions: The prospective habeas petitioner must apply to the court of appeals for leave to file the petition in the district court.[2] The court of appeals may grant leave to file only if the petitioner "makes a prima facie showing that the application satisfies" the statute's requirements regarding the nature of the claim. The statute also provides that the court of appeal's "grant or denial" of leave to file "shall not be appealable and shall not be the subject of a petition for rehearing or for a writ of certiorari."[3]

Felker was convicted of murder and sentenced to death. After exhausting his appeals and filing a first unsuccessful habeas petition, he filed a motion for leave to file a second petition, in which he would assert a colorable claim of innocence, based on new forensic evidence that the victim had died while Felker was under police surveillance, and a claim that the trial court had given an unconstitutional instruction defining the term "beyond a reasonable doubt." The court of appeals denied leave to file, and Felker applied to the Supreme Court for a writ of certiorari and for an original writ of habeas corpus. The Court directed counsel to submit briefs limited to three questions, one of which was whether the preclusion of review was "an unconstitutional restriction" of the Supreme Court's jurisdiction.[4] The question of the scope of Congress's power to restrict the Court's jurisdiction is one of the most difficult in the law of the federal courts. To Justice Stevens, expediting review was "unnecessary and profoundly unwise," for the Court should consider such questions "with the utmost deliberation, rather than unseemly haste."[5]

And the haste was indeed great. The Court gave the parties two weeks to prepare and file their briefs, and set oral argument for two weeks after that. In 1990 the Court accelerated its consideration of a challenge to the constitutionality of the federal Flag Protection Act of 1989.[6] The statute itself specified that appeals should

---

[2] The Court in *Felker* described those seeking leave to file "prospective applicants" because they had no right to file a habeas petition until they received leave to file.

[3] Pub L No 104-132, 110 Stat 1217, §§ 106(b)(1), (b)(2), (b)(3), amending 28 USC § 2244 (b).

[4] 116 S Ct 1588.

[5] Id. Justice Stevens's dissent was joined by Justices Souter, Ginsburg, and Breyer.

[6] *United States v Eichman*, 494 US 1063 (1990).

be expedited,[7] and even so the Court gave the lawyers three weeks to write, and another three weeks to prepare for argument. In 1974 when the Court chose to decide whether President Richard Nixon had to turn over audiotapes from his office, it also gave the lawyers three weeks to write and three more weeks to prepare.[8]

Some expedition might have been appropriate. Had the case been put on a normal briefing and argument schedule, it would not have been heard by the Court until October or November 1996. A decision might not have been rendered before June 1997. Every well-advised person on death row with a nonfrivolous successive claim who did not welcome execution would of course file an application in the court of appeals for leave to file a successive petition in the district court. After leave was denied, as it ordinarily would be, the prospective habeas applicant would then file a petition for review in the Supreme Court raising the constitutional questions pending in *Felker*. And, under the Court's sensible practice, it would hold all those applications until it decided *Felker*. After all, the Court might hold the preclusion of review unconstitutional. If so, each prospective applicant would then be entitled to file a petition for certiorari in the normal course. And, finally, there was some chance, small though it might be, that one of these applicants would actually present a case worthy of Supreme Court attention on the merits of the claims presented.[9] Executions would be effectively suspended until the Court decided *Felker*.[10]

Although Congress did not expressly direct the Court to expedite review, as it had in the Flag Protection Act, its aim in enacting the Anti-Terrorism and Effective Death Penalty Act was clear enough: to reduce what Congress and the President regarded as excessive delays in carrying out lawful executions.[11] It would have

---

[7] The statutory provision is quoted in *United States v Eichman*, 496 US 310, 313 n 2 (1990) ("The Supreme Court shall, if it has not previously ruled on the question, accept jurisdiction over the appeal and advance on the docket and expedite to the greatest extent possible").

[8] *United States v Nixon*, 417 US 927 (1974).

[9] For a discussion of what those claims might be, see text accompanying notes 68–70.

[10] The suspension of executions would not be complete because it would affect only those who filed successive petitions.

[11] The "gatekeeper" provision expedites litigation if the court of appeals denies leave to file a successive petition. It slows litigation down by inserting an additional step when the court of appeals grants leave to file. The provision's theory must be that district courts would take too long to deny successive petitions under the statute's new standards.

been deeply ironic had a statute designed to expedite executions had the effect of imposing a year-long moratorium on them instead.[12]

The moratorium would have resulted from the Court's application of its internal rules of scheduling, opinion-writing, and, notably, holding cases pending the disposition of related ones that the Court was already considering. From 1981 to 1991, the Court experienced a fair amount of internal turmoil over the application of the Court's rules in death penalty cases. Those who believed the death penalty to be generally constitutional came to believe that their opponents were manipulating the Court's internal rules simply to delay executions. The Court's experience from 1981 to 1991 sheds additional light on its decision to order an expedited hearing in *Felker*, no matter how justified that decision might have been by the policies underlying the 1996 Act.

II. The Death Penalty and the Court's Internal Rules

A. THE BACKGROUND

When the Supreme Court upheld the constitutionality of modern death penalty statutes in 1976,[13] capital punishment's supporters might have believed that executions would resume after a relatively brief shakedown period. They were wrong. To adopt a military analogy, death penalty abolitionists continued to fight even as they were forced to retreat. They fought in two ways: relatively large-scale fixed battles over whether the death penalty was administered in a racially discriminatory manner, whether those who were mentally retarded or juveniles at the time they murdered others could be executed, and the like; and guerilla campaigns against the execution of almost anyone sentenced to death, on the ground that particular problems in the defendant's trial invalidated either the conviction or the death sentence.

The big stories about the death penalty were the fixed battles,

---

[12] It is worth noting that every major statutory innovation requires litigation to resolve novel interpretive questions. The justices might have taken the position that Congress's purposes to expedite litigation in all future habeas corpus cases would not be impaired by following the normal schedule in one early case.

[13] *Gregg v Georgia*, 428 US 153 (1976).

which death penalty abolitionists regularly lost.[14] Inside the Court, however, the guerilla actions proved to be more irritating, in part because the justices who found the death penalty constitutional in principle sometimes fractured over these individual challenges.

The legal bases for the fixed battles covered a large number of cases. Until the Court resolved them, it would be unfair to execute someone who might benefit from a ruling against the death penalty, just as it would have been unfair while *Felker* was pending to execute someone whose application for leave to file a successive habeas petition had been denied. Even after the death penalty abolitionists lost the fixed battles, the individual claims of each defendant still remained.

The slow pace of execution may have accurately reflected divisions in the country. Some observers suggested that a large majority of Americans approved of the death penalty in the abstract but were much more divided over how frequently it should be administered, and in which cases. Personal relations became strained when that ambivalence was reflected inside the Court. Two justices, Marshall and Brennan, always voted against capital punishment. In nearly every case, the Court's rules made it possible for them to delay executions if they found one or two allies. The Court's conservatives only gradually discovered that the rules contributed to the guerilla war against capital punishment.

The conservatives' problems arose from the "rule of four." Before 1925, the Supreme Court had to hear argument in almost every case brought to it. The justices found the burden of deciding all those cases nearly impossible, and persuaded Congress to give the justices discretion to hear only the cases they wanted to. Some members of Congress were concerned that this might close the Court's doors too tightly. To allay those fears, the justices promised Congress that a minority on the Court would always have the power to force the majority to hear a case. The "rule of four" means that it takes only four justices to get a case heard, even though it takes five votes to get a decision.[15]

The "rule of four" itself contributed to delay because scheduling

---

[14] See, for example, *McCleskey v Kemp*, 481 US 279 (1987); *Stanford v Kentucky*, 492 US 361 (1989).

[15] David O'Brien, *Storm Center: The Supreme Court in American Politics* 246–55 (Norton, 3d ed 1993).

argument and drafting opinions can put off the announcement of a judgment for almost a year. But the "rule of four" had other consequences. Suppose a capital defendant applies for review after the state has set a date for his execution. Four justices can get the Court to grant review. But the execution date might fall before briefs were due, before argument is scheduled, or before a Court decision could be expected. Ordinarily the state could go ahead with the execution. Letting a state execute someone whose case was being considered by the Supreme Court struck many justices as peculiarly unfair. They had a procedural device to prevent that. The state would have to wait if the Supreme Court itself issued a stay of execution. But, under the Court's rules, it took *five* justices to issue a stay.[16]

The position taken by Marshall and Brennan made the question of when to issue stays of execution particularly difficult for justices who did not think capital punishment was unconstitutional. Perhaps two other justices thought a capital defendant presented a serious claim about his individual case, whose merits the Court should consider, but, the conservatives thought,[17] Marshall and Brennan voted to grant review because they opposed capital punishment completely. Often, then, the four votes to grant review on the merits of a particular challenge seemed almost insincere. Should a justice in the majority join the four others to issue a stay of execution?

There was an even more arcane issue that caused problems. In many areas, not limited to death penalty cases, several cases arrive at the Court presenting similar though not quite identical issues. Sometimes the Court decides to hear a group of related cases. Sometimes, however, it decides to "hold" the related cases until it decides the lead case. Then the justices take a look at the cases they have held in light of the decision they have made. The decision might have nothing to say about the issues in the related cases, and the Court will deny review. Or the decision might have some bearing on the related cases. The Court could decide to hear argu-

---

[16] The Court's internal rules are written but not published. In this article I refer to them as "rules," in contrast to the published Supreme Court Rules.

[17] I use the term *conservatives* to refer to justices who did not believe the death penalty to be unconstitutional in general or in most of its applications. The term is not entirely accurate, but I have been unable to come up with a better short-hand term.

ment in one of them. More commonly, the Court remands the case, sending it back to the lower courts for them to consider how the new case affects the one that was held.

How many votes should it take to hold a case pending a decision in the related one? For most of Marshall's tenure, the Court's rules said that a case would be held if three justices thought it related to one in which the Court was hearing argument. The argument for that rule was simple: No one could tell whether the decision in the primary case would affect the related ones until the justices wrote opinions in the primary case. If three justices thought a case was related to the primary one, they might be able to persuade a fourth to grant review in light of the decision, once it was handed down. Until then, it was prudent to let three justices hold a case, almost as insurance against the possibility that something surprising might happen in the primary case.

Holding cases was not a real problem when the primary case raised a broad-based challenge to the death penalty. If the Court was considering whether the Constitution allowed states to execute people who were minors when they committed their crimes, the Court would hold all cases involving such minors. Once those broad-based challenges were disposed of, the question of which cases to hold became more difficult inside the Court. For, by that time, Marshall and Brennan had been joined by Justices Blackmun and Stevens as reasonably consistent opponents of capital punishment. Too frequently, the conservatives thought, either Blackmun or Stevens became the third vote to hold a case as related when it really had little to do with the primary case.

The problem was exacerbated after the justices heard argument and voted on the principal case. They knew, although the public did not, what the result was going to be. But the justices felt they had to follow what Marshall once called "the fiction that a case is not 'decided' until it is officially announced."[18] If the Court was going to uphold the death penalty in the principal case, the conservatives found it particularly galling that three justices could nonetheless delay executions in cases only tangentially implicating an issue that they knew was about to be rejected.

---

[18] TM to conference, probably March 20, 1986, William J. Brennan Papers, Manuscript Division, Library of Congress, box 719, file 16.

B. THE FIRST STIRRINGS OF DIFFICULTY

In the long run, the conservatives believed themselves most disadvantaged by what they saw as the liberals' manipulation of the Court's rules. But the conservatives themselves took the first steps that divided the Court.

In 1981, five years after the Court again authorized capital punishment, Justice Rehnquist became impatient. He used two cases involving murders committed in 1973 and 1976 as vehicles for a proposal he believed would break the "stalemate" he saw in administering the death penalty. The Court, Rehnquist proposed, should grant review in *every* capital case, even if the claims presented would not ordinarily be treated as worth the Court's time. In one of the cases, for example, the defendant argued that a state procedural rule made it difficult for him to show in the state postconviction proceeding that jurors at his trial were affected by adverse pretrial publicity. Marshall wrote an opinion showing that the defendant's argument was not frivolous, but it was unlikely to win because the procedural limits in state postconviction proceedings would not affect the defendant's ability to get a federal court to decide in a habeas corpus proceeding whether the pretrial publicity made his trial unconstitutional.[19]

Stevens called Rehnquist's bluff. With Marshall and Brennan voting to grant review, Rehnquist's vote in the two cases left the petitioners only one vote short of getting Supreme Court review. Stevens looked at the cases and chose to vote to grant review—satisfying the rule of four—in the case where the defendant made the stronger constitutional claim. Rehnquist was now faced with the prospect of having the Court hear a case showing that careful examination of constitutional claims in death penalty cases was desirable. To avoid that, he withdrew his vote to grant review in that case. He did publish a dissent from the denial of review in the other case. Stevens responded with an opinion explaining that Rehnquist's proposal was "an improper allocation of the Court's limited resources" because hearing all death penalty cases "would consume over half of [the] Court's argument calendar" on issues of no national significance. He tweaked Rehnquist in observing that death penalty issues "have not been difficult for three Mem-

---

[19] *Coleman v Balkcom*, 451 US 949 (1981).

bers of the Court"—Marshall and Brennan, of course, but also Rehnquist: Stevens wrote, "[I]f my memory serves me correctly, Justice Rehnquist has invariably voted to uphold the death penalty."[20]

Three years later, tensions within the Court increased as the possibility of more executions grew. The problems seemed minor at first. Early in 1984, Justice Powell noted that defendants' efforts to stay their executions disrupted the Court. He pointed out that the Court's staff had to stay in the building through the night because they could not be sure whether a stay would be sought. Soon after that, the Court accepted Powell's suggestion that it establish procedures to keep the justices informed of the status of death penalty cases.[21]

The justices were notified when a court of appeals was considering a stay of execution, then after it decided whether to issue or deny the stay, then about counsel's plans to seek review and a stay from the Supreme Court. Sometimes, of course, the cases never reached the Court—a lower court, sometimes a state court, would delay the execution. The overall effect was to increase the flow of paper inside the Court, and to heighten the justices' awareness of the details of death penalty cases. The justices became almost micro-managers in death penalty cases. Memos like one from Justice White saying "The state is apparently making some noises about trying to do something about the stay" in one case became almost routine. It became more difficult to see the Court's role as resolving large questions of constitutional law when the justices had to think about what to do in every case where a murderer faced execution.[22]

Again, the conservatives made an already difficult situation worse. In May 1984, James Adams faced execution in Florida. On May 8 he persuaded the federal court of appeals to stay his execution, arguing that his federal habeas corpus petition presented issues that the appeals court was already considering in two other cases. Florida's attorney general immediately went to the Supreme

---

[20] Id at 451 US 949, 951 n 2 (1981). The shifting votes are shown in Brennan Papers, box 549, file 4.

[21] Powell to Burger, Jan 31, 1984, Brennan Papers, box 640, file 4.

[22] White to conference, May 19, 1986, Thurgood Marshall Papers, Manuscript Division, Library of Congress, box 378, file 3.

Court, arguing that Adams was barred from presenting his claim at such a late date because he failed to present it in an earlier federal proceeding. On May 9, the justices agreed, voting 5 to 4 to vacate the stay. Marshall was outraged. In a memo to his files he noted that the discussion of the case had taken only 18 minutes, and that his motion to be given 24 hours to write a dissent had been denied. In a published dissent, Marshall chastised the majority for its "indecent desire to rush to judgment in capital cases," which was "especially egregious" when the Court overrode a lower court's decision to issue a stay: "Caution has been thrown to the winds with an impetuousness that is truly astonishing." The Court "appears to have . . . forgotten here . . . that we are not dealing with mere legal semantics; we are dealing with a man's life." Adams was executed on May 10.[23]

C. TENSION ESCALATES: THE PROBLEM OF STAYS OF EXECUTION

The next year, Willie Darden's case produced "real bitterness."[24] Darden was convicted of murdering the owner of a furniture store. Darden was on a furlough from prison at the time of the murder. Shortly after it occurred, his speeding car slid off a wet road and crashed, a few miles from the furniture store. The car matched the description the police had of a car that had been at the store, and the police searched the crash area, discovering a gun that turned out to be of the type used in the murder (although it was never identified as the murder weapon). The store owner's wife identified Darden as the killer when she saw him at the preliminary hearing at which he was charged with murder.

Darden's main claim was that his trial was unfair because the prosecutor engaged in serious misconduct. As Powell wrote, the prosecutor's closing argument to the jury "deserves the condemnation it has received from every court to review it." Violating well-established standards, the prosecutor called Darden "an animal," said that he should not "be out of his cell unless he has a leash

---

[23] *Wainwright v Adams*, 466 US 964, 965–66 (1984); TM memo to files, May 9, 1984, Marshall Papers, box 330, file 3. Details on Adams's crime are provided in David von Drehle, *Among the Lowest of the Dead: The Culture of Death Row* 241–51 (Times Books, 1995).

[24] Tony Mauro, *Courtside: Reading Between Blackmun's Lines*, The Recorder (March 2, 1994), p 7 (quoting Blackmun law clerk Pamela Karlen).

on him," said "I wish that I could see him sitting here with no face," criticized the prison authorities for giving Darden a furlough, and stated his personal belief that Darden was guilty. Darden claimed he was innocent; as his lawyer put it, "They took a coincidence and magnified that into a capital case."[25]

The Supreme Court considered Darden's claims serious enough to justify review. In its first consideration of the case in 1977, however, the Court decided it had made a mistake in attempting to review what was so clearly a fact-bound decision with few implications for national law, and dismissed the case "as improvidently granted." After eight years of habeas corpus proceedings, in which the appeals court was severely divided, the case came back to the Supreme Court.[26]

Darden's lawyers had to stay his execution if they were to get the Supreme Court to consider his claims. On September 3, 1985, the Court received an application for a stay. The Court voted to deny the application by a 5–4 vote, and notified the lawyers. Around 9 P.M., the Court received a letter from Darden's lawyers asking that the application for a stay be treated as a request for review of the lower courts' decision that Darden's trial has not been unfair. Without further discussion, the four justices who voted to grant the stay—Brennan, Marshall, Blackmun, and Stevens—voted to grant review. Powell then joined them to stay Darden's execution, despite his evident belief that Darden's case did not deserve any further consideration. Burger was so upset at what happened that he published an unprecedented dissent from a *grant* of review. Noting that Darden's claims "have been passed upon no fewer than 95 times by federal and state court judges," Burger said that the Court was wrong to "accept meritless petitions presenting claims that we rejected only hours ago."[27]

---

[25] *Darden v Wainwright*, 477 US 168, 179–80 (1986).

[26] *Darden v Florida*, 430 US 704 (1977).

[27] Powell to Colleagues, Sept 4, 1985, Brennan Papers, box 700, file 7; *Darden v Wainwright*, 473 US 928, 929 (1985) (Burger, CJ, dissenting). Blackmun wrote that he "knew of no other recent case in which a Justice has dissented [from a grant of review] on the ground that the claims raised by the petitioner—which at least four Justices must have found worthy of full consideration—were meritless." *Darden v Wainwright*, 477 US 205 n 9 (Blackmun, J, dissenting). After hearing argument, the Court rejected Darden's claims by the same 5 to 4 vote that occurred earlier. Darden was executed on March 15, 1988. Blackmun sent a statement on the execution (published as *Darden v Dugger*, 485 US 943 (1988) (Blackmun, J, dissenting)) to Brennan, Marshall, and Stevens with a cover note say-

The justices discussed what to do over the next few weeks. Powell wrote that the "experience" with granting review in *Darden* "disturbs me." He called what Brennan and the other justices in the minority had done "more than a little unusual," and was "not at all sure it was done in accordance either with our Rules or precedent." As he saw it, they had "exploited" the rule of four. But he had broader concerns as well. The case, he said, "illustrates how easily the system is manipulated in capital cases." Perhaps writing too hastily under time pressure, Powell mistakenly said that "[n]o one suggests that [Darden] is innocent—a fact that all too often under our law is irrelevant." He continued, "Unless the habeas corpus statute is substantially changed, . . . the states should rescind their capital punishment laws."[28]

Brennan replied, agreeing that the Court's procedures should be reexamined because they "exposed the Court to criticism that its own decisions are arbitrary." The real problem, he suggested, was the tension between the rule of four and the requirement of five votes to stay an execution. "We are all indebted to Lewis," he wrote, "for twice sparing the Court and the petitioner" the fate of being executed even though four Justices thought he presented serious claims. He proposed that the rule of four be extended to applications for stays, at least in cases like Darden's, where the defendant was trying to get review of his first habeas corpus action. Blackmun agreed. "The Court as an institution would surely appear intellectually and morally bankrupt if we were to announce that a petitioner's claims are worthy of review but that we would abandon our responsibility to perform such review if the state chooses to execute in the meantime."[29]

Justice Rehnquist equably said that "we have been living in reasonable peace and harmony for several years" requiring five votes for a stay, although he thought it might make sense to have a rule of four for stays if there was a "reasonable prospect of success on the merits." Burger set Stevens on edge with his observation that the Court's dismissal of Darden's case in 1977 "should have re-

---

ing, "For what it is worth (and it will not be worth very much). . . ." Blackmun to Brennan et al, Jan 21, 1988, Marshall Papers, box 435, file 6.

[28] Powell to Colleagues, Sept 4, 1985, Brennan Papers, box 700, file 7.

[29] Brennan to conference, Sept 6, 1985, Marshall Papers, box 355, file 10; Blackmun to conference, Sept 10, 1985, id.

moved any doubt . . . as to our view of the merits"; as Stevens correctly said, the Court's dismissal was the equivalent of a denial of review, which ought to suggest nothing about the Court's view of the merits.[30]

The Court considered changing its rules at the end of September. It had one suggestion—Powell's, to require five votes to grant review—and one formal proposal—Brennan's, to allow a stay with four votes. Brennan wrote a long memo supporting his proposal. Because the "use of capital punishment by the states is only beginning to hit full stride," the Court could expect "the difficulties we experienced" in *Darden* "to recur." And, because "the law in this area continues to develop and as the views of each of us continue to evolve,"—perhaps here alluding to the positions Blackmun and Stevens were taking—"we must expect more close cases in which at least four Justices are not prepared to make a final decision based only on the papers accompanying a stay application under the staggering time pressures we have experienced." As Brennan saw it, the issue was whether the Court or the states determined when the Court decided to hear cases. He agreed with Blackmun "that this Court should refuse to be pushed into premature review . . . by the states' scheduling of execution dates."[31]

Brennan was clearly concerned that Powell's memorandum expressed a troubling attitude about divisions within the Court. He tried to allay concern that some justices were using the rule of four "in bad faith" by noting that four justices might vote to grant review if "forced to make a last minute decision under great time pressure," but that "with a little more time, there might have been fewer votes." He rejected Powell's claim that anyone had " 'exploit[ed]' anything," saying that "four members of the Court honestly felt that an issue warranting plenary review was presented, and they voted accordingly." After that, Brennan believed, the law and even more strongly the Court's traditions meant that a stay should "automatically" be granted, to avoid the "unpalatable" result that the state could moot the case by executing the defendant.

Brennan continued to defend his proposal, but nothing came of it. Indeed, it seems likely that he offered his proposal at least as

---

[30] Rehnquist to conference, Sept 9, 1985, id; Burger to conference, Sept 10, 1985, id; Stevens to conference, Sept 12, 1985, id.

[31] Brennan to conference, Sept 19, 1985, id.

much to forestall action on Powell's suggestion—to show that changing the rules would divide the Court once again—as to accomplish a change in the rules.

Frustration over the rules continued. Just before the formal discussion of Brennan's proposal, for example, Burger objected to a request from Brennan. Sometimes, after the justices make their initial decision to deny review in a case, one justice will request that the case be "relisted," to give time to prepare a memorandum that might change a vote or two. When Brennan requested relisting a capital case, Burger saw the request as merely another tactic to delay execution because the relisting would extend the Court's consideration of the case beyond the scheduled execution date. Brennan replied that he was "entitled" to relist a case. A few months later Marshall wrote his colleagues about a petition for rehearing. He pointed out that the petition showed that the case was related to one on which review had already been granted, and he hoped that someone who had voted to deny the original request for review would at least request a response from the state to the petition for rehearing.[32]

Procedural irritants continued to disturb relations among the justices. Aubrey Adams was convicted of murdering an eight-year-old girl in 1978. Florida scheduled his execution for early March 1986. By that time death penalty litigators had managed to persuade some courts that it was unconstitutional to try defendants with "death-qualified" juries, whose members said they had no objections in principle to imposing a death sentence. Other courts disagreed, and the Supreme Court had already agreed to decide the question when Adams's application for a stay of his execution arrived at the Court. It had also already voted to reject the challenge, but the decision had not been announced.

Four justices voted to hold the case until the "death-qualification" decision was announced. A majority thought, however, that Adams's case was different, because no potential juror had actually been removed from the jury in the process of death qualification. What should be done about Adams's application for a stay of execution? Powell made it a practice "solely for institutional reasons"

---

[32] Burger to Brennan, Sept 29, 1985, Marshall Papers, box 354, file 6; Brennan to Burger, Sept 28, 1985, id; TM to conference, Nov 29, 1984, box 355, file 8, id.

to provide the fifth vote for a stay when four justices voted to grant review. Burger occasionally did so as well.[33]

Powell was confused about the state of the votes in Adams's case. At first he thought that four justices had voted to grant review, and therefore he voted for the stay even though he believed that "Adams and his counsel are 'playing games with us.'" When he realized that the four justices had voted only to hold the case until the death-qualification decision was announced, he told his colleagues that he felt "differently about votes to hold," and now voted to deny the stay.

Marshall told his colleagues that the issues needed a full discussion "because these unresolved disputes invite confusion, changes of mind, and strategic behavior when a person's life is at stake." He believed that "whether the vote is a grant or a hold, the power given to four or three by our rules is nugatory if an execution is permitted to moot the case." He said that "the power to issue a stay under these circumstances simply should not depend on an *ad hoc* act of generosity by some fifth Justice." As Marshall saw it, "the fate of each prisoner . . . seems to depend primarily upon whim and accident." Marshall called the Court's own "contribution to the arbitrariness of the death penalty" itself "alarming."[34]

Brennan may have illustrated the problem of strategic behavior when he responded to Powell's vote change by asserting that his first choice was to grant review, and that his alternative vote was to hold the case.[35] This meant that there might be four votes to grant review, which would trigger Powell's policy. Although Powell continued to believe that the Court was "simply being exploited," he grudgingly voted to grant the stay. But, he wrote, "[t]he effect of the Court's action will not be misunderstood" by anti-death penalty litigators. Pointing to the fact that Adams's lawyers had filed three petitions for review and four applications for

---

[33] Powell to conference, March 6, 1986, Brennan Papers, box 719, file 16; Burger to conference, March 4, 1986, id. After Burger and Powell retired, Kennedy and White continued the practice. Kennedy to conference, Sept 14, 1988, Marshall Papers, box 436, file 7; White to Conference, Nov 29, 1989, box 492, file 7 ("Since there are four votes to grant . . . I shall change my vote and make a fifth to grant a stay"), id.

[34] TM to Burger, March 4, 1986, Marshall Papers, box 395, file 4.

[35] Powell to conference, March 3, 1986, Brennan Papers, box 719, file 16; Brennan to conference, March 3, 1986, id.

stays of execution within the prior week, Powell told his colleagues that "there has been a gross abuse of the processes of our Court." He would not "criticize counsel for taking advantage of us if we permit it," but he thought that the Court should change its rules to avoid "indefinite delay in enforcing the law of the law."[36]

Burger backed Powell up. He said he was "not prepared to adopt the novel proposition that 'four to hold' should automatically constitute a stay in a capital case." He too derided some "counsel's protestations" that their cases were related to the death-qualification case; the "mere ritualistic invocation" of that case "cannot be enough to justify a stay of a lawfully imposed death sentence."[37]

Marshall replied to Burger's concerns about death-penalty lawyers by saying that if "lawyers are routinely able to hoodwink three Justices into voting to hold a case that is actually unrelated" to a pending case, "the Court's problems . . . far exceed" the procedural matters the justices were considering. As he saw it, "when this Court has chosen to give some number of Justices less than a majority certain powers," such as to grant review or hold a case, "the majority may not take action to void the exercise of such powers," as denying stays of execution would.[38]

In the end, Adams could not get four votes to grant review. Brennan drafted a dissent from the denial of review describing the Court's processes, including a statement that the justices "internally agreed" that once four justices voted to grant review, a fifth would join them to stay an execution. That statement set Burger off. That decision, he said, "must have taken place when I was in Moscow or Peking." He and Powell gave "a 'comity' vote twice," but that did not "establish an 'agreement.'" He also criticized Brennan for proposing to publicize internal discussions. Burger was annoyed at Brennan's assertion that "the only reason that Adams' petition has not been granted is that [the lawyer in the pending death-qualification case] beat him in the race to the Clerk's office." The issues in the cases were different, Burger said; "Adams' lawyer 'raced' to raise the claims only at the eleventh hour." He suggested

---

[36] Powell to conference, March 6, 1986, Brennan Papers, box 719, file 16.

[37] Burger to conference, March 20, 1986, Brennan Papers, box 719, file 16.

[38] Marshall to conference, probably March 20, 1986, Brennan Papers, box 719, file 16.

that Brennan "may well want to alter his draft in light of the facts
. . . I have pointed out."[39]

Brennan took out the draft's statement about an "agreement"
to provide a fifth vote for a stay, but he continued to describe the
Court's practices as a "rule that the five [voting against review]
will give the four an opportunity to change at least one mind."
One justice who voted against review "will nonetheless vote to
stay." Burger replied that he had "never heard of such a 'rule.'
. . . " He again mentioned his "practice," but, he wrote, "If that
'practice' does not make an 'agreement,' it certainly does not make
a 'rule.' " Brennan had had enough. Mildly and mistakenly
tweaking Burger for misunderstanding the difference between using "three periods rather than four" when quoting from a text,
Brennan told Burger that "if you read again" the draft dissent, he
would find that the word "rule" referred to the "Rule of Four,"
rather than the practice of voting to stay an execution. After further delays, Adams was executed on May 4, 1989.[40]

Burger repeatedly fulminated against what he called "the 'phoni-
ness' of this eleventh hour business" and "spurious claims of 'rush
to judgment.' " Those on the other side, however, hardly thought
the claims spurious. As they saw it, the Court itself was rushing to
judgment. In a memo he never sent to his colleagues, for example,
Brennan replied to Burger's observation about the rush to judgment by noting that "at the time the Chief voted in this case, no
papers had been filed by counsel, and therefore the Chief voted
on the merits . . . without having had the opportunity to read the
papers. Spurious indeed!"[41]

By the late 1980s, the majority's impatience led to occasional
sloppiness. Once in 1987 the conservatives voted to grant a state's
petition for review of a state court decision vacating a death sentence before the prisoner's response was even due. Marshall
drafted what Blackmun called a "devastating dissent" criticizing
the Court's action. Referring to comments of some of his col-

---

[39] Burger to conference, March 25, 1986 (two memos), Brennan Papers, box 719, file 16.

[40] The procedural history is laid out in *Dugger v Adams*, 489 US 401 (1989).

[41] Burger to Powell, Jan 13, 1984, Marshall Papers, box 334, file 1; Burger to Powell, March 20, 1986, Brennan Papers, box 700, file 10; Brennan to conference, March 20, 1986, id (marked "not circulated—for histories").

leagues that they would vote to review the case "even though the opposition material had not yet been seen," Blackmun observed, "the Spring rush to judgment is really bad this year." Marshall's dissent led the Court to wait, and in the fall the Court denied the state's application for review.[42] In a 1986 case, the Court was prepared to deny review, but a proposed dissent led the justices to hold the case until another one was decided. After that decision was handed down, the Court vacated the death sentence without hearing argument.[43]

D. PRACTICES CHANGE

Cases like these were too rare to overcome the conservatives' view that the Court was interfering with the fair administration of justice. Under Chief Justice Rehnquist, they adopted the practice of scheduling arguments in capital cases as soon as possible "where it appears that there will be a fair number of 'holds' for the case, because of the desirability of getting the 'lead' case decided and disposing of the 'holds.'" Marshall objected in vain, saying that he saw "no reason to *rush* in death cases unless it is to save a life."[44]

The practice of granting stays when four justices wanted to grant review eroded as well. In June 1990, four members of the Court indicated they would grant certiorari in *Hamilton v Texas* to consider Hamilton's claim that her son James Smith was mentally incompetent and should not be allowed to withdraw his appeal from his death sentence.[45] Smith's execution date had already been

---

[42] TM dissent, *Texas v Williams*, May 11, 1987, Marshall Papers, box 408, file 1; Blackmun to conference, May 12, 1987, id; *Texas v Williams*, 484 US 816 (1987).

[43] Draft dissent, Nov 7, 1986, Marshall Papers, box 410, file 6; *Truesdale v Aiken*, 480 US 527 (1987). In *Turner v Murray* the Court stayed an execution and then, over the dissent of four justices, denied the state's motion to vacate the stay. After the case was argued, O'Connor and White, who had initially voted to deny review, voted to overturn Turner's death sentence because the trial judge had barred his lawyer from questioning jurors about racial prejudice. White was influenced by the fact that this was a capital case involving a white victim and an African-American defendant. Powell responded that "Virginia is not Texas or Florida," being more restrained in administering death sentences. The prosecutor, Powell said, had "never hinted at" the racial questions, and the trial, he pointed out, had been "changed from [a] racial bias county to [Virginia's] eastern shore." O'Connor decided not to dissent from the reversal. Conference notes, *Turner v Sielaff*, Brennan Papers, box 698, file 5; *Turner v Murray*, 476 US 28 (1986). Turner was sentenced to death once again and was executed on May 25, 1995.

[44] Rehnquist to conference, Feb 14, 1990, Marshall Papers, box 493, file 2; TM to conference, Nov 15, 1990, box 523, file 4, id.

[45] 498 US 908 (1990).

set. Only the four justices who voted to grant review voted for a stay. As a result, Smith was executed in late June. Hamilton's petition for certiorari came up in the normal course in October, and, unsurprisingly, the Court denied review because the case was mooted by Smith's death. Marshall expressed his "frustration" at this outcome, saying that "the Court's willingness . . . in this case to dispense with the procedures that it ordinarily employs to preserve its jurisdiction only continues the distressing rollback of the legal safeguards traditionally afforded."[46]

After Brennan retired, the conservatives had the votes not only to deal with cases on the merits but to change the Court's rules. On May 23, 1991, a month before Marshall himself retired, the justices voted to require four votes to hold cases. It was a fitting conclusion to the Court's internal battles, an unpublicized change in procedures designed to restore what Rehnquist had almost a decade earlier called "reasonable peace and harmony." For Marshall, however, it was purchased at the cost of the decent consideration that people sentenced to death ought to receive from the nation's highest court.[47]

With this in the background, it is not surprising that the Court decided to expedite its hearing in *Felker*, nor that there were four dissenters. The Court's experience created an atmosphere in which pursuing the normal course had come to take on a mild smell of manipulation. Whether or not anyone had ever relied on the Court's internal rules in a bad faith effort to delay executions, the Court's majority was in a position to invoke those rules, expedite the hearing in *Felker*, and avoid any possibility of manipulation to an end the majority might have believed improper.

III. The Costs of Expedition

In the end, the decision to expedite the hearing in *Felker* did not matter. The Court unanimously held that the statute barred review by writ of certiorari but did not cut off the possibility of review by a writ of original habeas corpus in the Supreme

---

[46] Id.

[47] Rehnquist to conference, May 23, 1991, Marshall Papers, box 525, file 1.

Court.[48] Congress's attempt to speed up executions was rendered almost entirely toothless: Every prospective habeas applicant denied leave to file a second or successive petition by a court of appeals now can file an application for leave to file an original writ in the Supreme Court, instead of filing a petition for certiorari.[49] At least until the Court changes its internal rules, those applications are handled on the same schedule inside the Court as petitions for certiorari. The preclusion of review did nothing to expedite executions.[50]

Did the decision to expedite briefing and argument in *Felker* affect the quality of the Court's opinion? The tight schedule meant that all parties had to file their briefs simultaneously. They had to guess what their opponents would say. Perhaps that led everyone to be quite cautious in their claims about the statute's scope. Notably, there was essentially unanimous agreement in the briefs that the statute did not bar the Court from hearing original habeas petitions.

Chief Justice Rehnquist's opinion for the Court has all the characteristics readers have come to expect of his recent work. It takes up and answers the questions presented in crisp and largely conclusory paragraphs. The opinion in *Felker* answers all the questions except two: Why *should* the preclusion of review provision be interpreted in a way that makes it a failed effort to achieve its evident aim of speeding up executions by expediting litigation? And what exactly does the new statute as interpreted in *Felker* really do?[51]

Chief Justice Rehnquist's opinion deals with the statutory limitation on review by directing us to the Court's last major confrontation with congressional efforts to restrict its jurisdiction. After the Civil War, Congress expanded the scope of habeas corpus and simultaneously authorized appeals from circuit court habeas decisions to the Supreme Court. Concerned that a pending case would

---

[48] Justices Stevens and Souter wrote concurring opinions and joined each other's, as did Justice Breyer.

[49] The statute does expedite review by eliminating the possibility of a rehearing en banc by the court of appeals on a panel's denial of leave to file a successive petition.

[50] For a discussion of what the statute might have accomplished with respect to review in the Supreme Court, see text accompanying notes 56–70.

[51] The limitation of the questions to be addressed in the briefs may have deprived the Court of the aid it needed on this question, although Chief Justice Rehnquist's opinion for the Court does at least make some gestures in the direction of answering it.

produce a Court holding that congressional reconstruction was un-constitutional, Congress repealed the provision authorizing appeals in 1868. *Ex parte McCardle* upheld the repeal against a constitu-tional challenge, the Court carefully noting that the repeal did not affect the jurisdiction the Court had previously had to issue writs of habeas corpus in cases involving those held pursuant to federal authority.[52] When presented with such a case in *Ex parte Yerger*, the Court held that the 1868 repeal did not affect the Court's power to issue an original writ of habeas corpus.[53] The 1868 Act did not refer to the Court's own jurisdiction, and, the Court said, repeals by implication were not favored.

For the Chief Justice, *Yerger* resolved the question of preclusion of review in *Felker*. Like the 1868 statute, the 1996 one does not "mention[ ] our authority to entertain original habeas petitions." Because the Court retained the power to hear habeas cases, "there can be no plausible argument that the Act has deprived this Court of appellate jurisdiction" in violation of the Constitution.[54]

Crisply done, though it guts the main purpose of limiting re-view.[55] More problematic, perhaps, the Court's interpretation of the Act makes one wonder what exactly the Act did. The 1868 repeal had some effect even after *Yerger:* It barred Supreme Court review of appeals court decisions in cases involving those seeking habeas with respect to detentions under *state* authority. What, however, does the 1996 Act do?

A. CHANGING THE STANDARD FOR SUPREME COURT REVIEW

Perhaps the 1996 Act changes the standard for obtaining Su-preme Court review. Without the Act, a prospective habeas peti-tioner denied leave to file by a court of appeals would file a petition for certiorari. In considering the petition the Court would apply its Rule 10, which states that certiorari is a matter "of judicial dis-cretion," and "will be granted only for compelling reasons."[56] Rule

---

[52] 74 US (7 Wall) 508 (1868).

[53] 75 US (8 Wall) 85 (1869).

[54] 116 S Ct at 2339.

[55] Richard Fallon et al, eds, *Hart and Wechsler's The Federal Courts and the Federal System, 1996 Supplement* 71 (Foundation, 1996), raises the interesting question of how a custodian may obtain Supreme Court review of a court of appeals decision *granting* leave to file a successive petition.

[56] US Sup Ct Rule 10.

20(4)(a), which deals with the original writ of habeas corpus, requires the petitioner to "show that exceptional circumstances warrant the exercise of the Court discretionary powers," and states that "[t]his writ is rarely granted."[57]

Perhaps there is a difference between "compelling reasons" and "exceptional circumstances," though the Court's opinion does not make that difference apparent.[58] Felker had filed a petition for an original writ of habeas corpus, which the Court denied. It noted that his claims did not "materially differ" from claims by other habeas petitioners that the Court had reviewed "on stay applications." The claims, the opinion said, did not satisfy "the relevant provisions of the [1996] Act, let alone the requirement that there be 'exceptional circumstances' justifying the issuance of the writ."[59] It is not clear that this says anything that would not be equally appropriate in noting that a petition for certiorari failed to establish "compelling circumstances" for granting review.[60]

The Court's reference to "the relevant provisions of the Act" suggests another possibility. The Court's interpretation might mean that the 1996 Act directed the Court to substitute the Act's requirements for the unstructured discretionary decision the Court would make in considering either a certiorari petition or an application for an original writ of habeas corpus. For example, a prospective habeas petitioner denied leave to file a successive writ might seek review on the ground that the court of appeals had misinterpreted the Act's requirement that "the factual predicate for the [new] claim could not have been discovered previously through the exercise of due diligence,"[61] in conflict with some other circuit's interpretation of that requirement. In addition to

---

[57] US Sup Ct Rule 20(4)(a).

[58] The standards in Rules 10 and 20 are each discretionary. Perhaps the Court will come to treat the standards differently: Rule 20 as less stringent than Rule 10 if the justices come to believe that review in some cases is important, or Rule 20 as more stringent if they come to find the burdens of processing applications for leave to file petitions for an original writ of habeas corpus burdensome.

[59] 116 S Ct 2341.

[60] The Court might examine the petition for leave to file an original writ to see if it made out a prima facie case that the new statutory standards for filing a successive writ were satisfied. If the Court concluded that the petition did so, presumably it could transfer the petition to the appropriate district court to determine whether the standards were in fact satisfied. Query whether the Court will have less, or less usable, information in making such an assessment than it would have in a petition for certiorari.

[61] Section 106(b)(2)(B)(i).

asking whether the Court's usual discretionary standards were satisfied, the Act might direct the Court to ask as well whether "the
facts underlying the claim, if proven and viewed in light of the
evidence as a whole, would be sufficient to establish by clear and
convincing evidence that, but for constitutional error, no reasonable fact-finder would have found the applicant guilty of the underlying offense."[62]

Chief Justice Rehnquist's summary of the Court's holding asserts that "the Act does impose new conditions on our authority
to grant relief,"[63] but the supporting analysis, if it can be called
that, is terse to the point of obscurity. The Act's new requirements,
the opinion says, "*inform* our authority to grant relief."[64] "Inform"
does not mean "dictate" or "constrain," as the opinion made clear
in its next paragraph: "Whether or not we are bound by these
restrictions, they certainly inform our consideration of original habeas petitions."[65]

Why so cagey? Perhaps out of concern that interesting separation of powers questions would arise if Congress purported to dictate the Court's standards for exercising jurisdiction conferred on
it by statute. The "rule of four," for example, is an internal Court
rule, not enacted into law in part because of such concerns.[66] Could
Congress require that all decisions invalidating state statutes be
supported by seven justices? By five (even if there are two vacancies
on the Court)? Or, as Justice Souter wondered, could Congress
require the Court to write long opinions?[67]

The 1996 Act could properly "inform" the Court's exercise of
discretionary authority, however. Recent decades saw the Court
itself refashioning the writ of habeas corpus in part on the ground
that the courts ought to elaborate statutory details in light of contemporary circumstances. So too with the original writ of habeas
corpus: Contemporary circumstances, evidenced by congressional
action, bear on the appropriate structure of the writ even if Con-

---

[62] Section 106(b)(2)(B)(ii).

[63] 116 S Ct 2337.

[64] Id at 2339 (emphasis added).

[65] Id.

[66] For a discussion of the rule's background, see John Paul Stevens, *The Life Span of a
Judge Made Rule*, 58 NYU L Rev 1, 10–14 (1983).

[67] *United States v Lopez*, 115 S Ct 1624, 1656 (Souter, J, dissenting).

gress did not—and perhaps cannot—dictate that structure to the Court.

Chief Justice Rehnquist's opinion thus does not demonstrate that the 1996 Act changes the standards for granting review, although that remains the best candidate for an explanation of what the Act as interpreted in *Felker* does.

B. CHANGING THE ISSUES THE COURT CONSIDERS

A second way to make the 1996 Act meaningful would be to hold that shifting review from certiorari to the original writ changes the issues the Court will consider. On certiorari the Court would consider whether the court of appeals properly applied the statutory standards for granting leave to file a successive petition. Perhaps on original habeas the Court would consider only the merits of the underlying petition. So, in Felker's case, the Court would consider not whether the federal court of appeals properly denied leave to file but whether the state trial court gave unconstitutional jury instructions.

Felker said nothing about this question, but the two concurring opinions did. Justice Stevens asserted that review of "gatekeeping" decisions remained available through the All Writs Act, and that in the course of exercising original habeas jurisdiction, the Supreme Court could "consider earlier gatekeeping orders entered by the court of appeals to inform our judgment and provide the parties with the functional equivalent of direct review."[68] Justice Souter was a bit more circumspect, saying only that Felker had not sought anything other than certiorari or original habeas, but that "if it should later turn out that statutory avenues other than certiorari for reviewing a gatekeeping determination were closed, the question of whether the statute exceeded Congress's . . . powers would be open."[69]

As Justice Souter suggested, the question of the issues open to Supreme Court review would be important "if the court of appeals adopted divergent interpretations of the gatekeeper standard."[70] We are accustomed to thinking that one important role for the

---

[68] 116 S Ct 2341 (Stevens, J, concurring).

[69] Id at 2342 (Souter, J, concurring).

[70] Id.

Supreme Court is to ensure that federal statutes have the same meaning in Georgia that they have in North Carolina. If the 1996 Act required the Supreme Court on habeas corpus to consider only the merits of Felker's unconstitutional instruction claim, and ruled out other ways of obtaining review of questions about interpreting the gatekeeper provision, the possibility of lack of uniformity would be real.

Yet interpreting the 1996 Act to leave open review of gatekeeper decisions would increase the puzzle about what the preclusion of review provisions in the Act actually accomplished. Not only would it have failed to expedite the capital punishment process; it would have failed as well to direct attention away from technicalities and toward the merits of the capital defendant's constitutional claims.

C. AVOIDING CONSTITUTIONAL QUESTIONS

A standard explanation for some interpretations that render statutes meaningless is that such interpretations are necessary to avoid deciding difficult constitutional questions. Would preclusion of review of court of appeals' gatekeeper decisions raise such a question? Notably, Chief Justice Rehnquist's opinion says not a word about construing statutes to avoid constitutional questions, although he invoked that canon in another case involving congressional restrictions on the jurisdiction of the federal courts.[71] Here I do not intend to go into highly contested issues about congressional power to preclude Supreme Court review with an eye to offering a resolution. Instead, I sketch the problems to see whether the Court in *Felker* properly said nothing about them.

Justice Scalia, for one, thinks that principle and precedent make it clear that Congress has plenary authority to preclude judicial review of federal questions.[72] Even if Congress's power is not as absolute as Justice Scalia believes, however, would precluding review in *Felker* raise a difficult constitutional question?

The standard account is that if Congress's power is limited, it is because our constitutional system requires that the Supreme

[71] *Webster v Doe*, 486 US 592, 603 (1988).
[72] 486 US 611–15 (Scalia, J, dissenting).

Court's "essential functions" be preserved.[73] Unhappily for scholars, it has proven quite difficult to specify what those essential functions are. The best candidates are that we need the Supreme Court to ensure the supremacy and uniformity of federal law.[74]

It is not clear, however, that ensuring supremacy requires *Supreme Court* jurisdiction. Professor Akhil Amar has forcefully argued, for example, that the Constitution assumes that all Article III courts are equivalent for these purposes, so that supremacy concerns are satisfied if Congress confers jurisdiction on courts of appeals to consider questions of federal law.[75] Of course, some federal court—the court of appeals—had decided the gatekeeper questions in *Felker*.

What about uniformity? On the level of constitutional policy, the question is whether lack of uniformity in the interpretation of federal law is a constitutional value of sufficient force to override a congressional determination that other values are more important. Could Congress decide, for example, that there would be no Supreme Court review of court of appeals decisions interpreting the Carriage of Goods by Sea Act, or the Longshore and Harbor Workers Compensation Act, believing that the time consumed on deciding whether to grant review could be better spent, and that the loss to the nation's law of a tiny bit of uniformity is worth the gain in time for other cases?[76]

I find it hard to see why not.[77] Justice Souter noted the argument

---

[73] Henry Hart, *The Power of Congress to Limit the Jurisdiction of Federal Courts: An Exercise in Dialectic*, 66 Harv L Rev 1362, 1364–65 (1953).

[74] Leonard Ratner, *Congressional Power Over the Appellate Jurisdiction of the Supreme Court*, 109 U Pa L Rev 157 (1960).

[75] Akhil Amar, *The Two-Tiered Structure of the Judiciary Act of 1789*, 138 U Pa L Rev 1499 (1990); Akhil Amar, *A Neo-Federalist View of Article III: Separating the Two Tiers of Federal Jurisdiction*, 65 BU L Rev 205 (1985).

[76] I use these examples because Professor Sturley has cogently argued that the Supreme Court has exercised its discretionary certiorari power perversely, leaving the interpretation of COGSA up to the courts of appeals, even though uniformity is quite important in that essentially commercial context, while aggressively reviewing LHWRA cases, where lack of uniform interpretation is less important because of the cases' tort-like nature. Michael Sturley, *Observations on the Supreme Court's Jurisdiction in Intercircuit Conflict Cases*, 67 Tex L Rev 1251 (1989).

[77] The situation would arguably be different if Congress precluded review not for the administrative reasons I have described but because it believed that precluding review would systematically skew outcomes in a desired direction. Then, however, the objection is not to a lack of uniformity in results but rather to a uniformity accomplished through subterfuge. Compare *United States v Klein*, 80 US (13 Wall) 128 (1872).

that denying Supreme Court review might be inconsistent with the constitutional provision that courts of appeals must be "inferior" to the Supreme Court: The "lower" courts are inferior to no one with respect to questions as to which there is no possibility of Supreme Court review.[78] I think that argument, while ingenious, is a bit too precious. I would think that a court generally subject to Supreme Court review was inferior to the Supreme Court in the constitutional sense even if some of its decisions were not reviewable.

Perhaps one might distinguish between the Carriage of Goods by Sea Act and the federal habeas corpus statute on the ground that the latter is "connected to" underlying constitutional issues in a way the former is not, and that uniformity is truly essential when constitutional questions are involved. But if the Supreme Court reviews court of appeals gatekeeper decisions to see if they are consistent with the statutory standards, it is not saying anything about the underlying constitutional questions. And, of course, as the preceding section has suggested, the constitutional questions might be open on original habeas anyway.

I have suggested that it is not easy to know whether preclusion of Supreme Court review is itself a difficult constitutional question. The path *Felker* took is hard to justify unless there is a "meta-principle" of statutory interpretation directing the courts to interpret statutes to avoid deciding whether a statute, if interpreted in a particular way, would raise a difficult constitutional question.

IV. Conclusion

The Anti-Terrorism and Effective Death Penalty Act of 1996 is a mess.[79] Congress and the President wanted to make a public statement about capital punishment. The preclusion of review provision expresses a mood. Whether it actually accomplishes anything is another question.[80] Given the Supreme Court's inter-

---

[78] 116 S Ct 2342 n 2, citing Evan Caminker, *Why Must Inferior Courts Obey Supreme Court Precedents?* 46 Stan L Rev 781, 828–37 (1994).

[79] For more extensive discussion of problems with the Act, see Mark Tushnet and Larry Yackle, *Symbolic Statutes and Real Laws: The Pathologies of the Anti-Terrorism and Effective Death Penalty Act and the Prison Litigation Reform Act* (forthcoming).

[80] This is not to say, of course, that *other* provisions of the statute might not accomplish something.

pretation of the provision in *Felker*, the provision does no more than slightly tighten the Supreme Court's standard for deciding whether to consider a death penalty case involving someone who has already had two shots at Supreme Court review and restructure the forms in which the Court can consider whether the court of appeals properly interpreted the gatekeeper provision. And it may do much less than that.

It seems to me unlikely that the Court would have done a better job of figuring out what the provision means, and explaining why Congress and the President would want to modify Supreme Court jurisdiction in so modest a way, if it had had more time. If Chief Justice Rehnquist had had six months to write an opinion rather than three weeks, it would have looked almost exactly like *Felker*.

LARRY ALEXANDER

THE SUPREME COURT, DR. JEKYLL,
AND THE DUE PROCESS OF PROOF

I

Almost any American can tell you that in our system of criminal justice, defendants are "presumed innocent" and can only be convicted of crimes upon proof of guilt "beyond a reasonable doubt." Most Americans would be surprised, however, to discover that the requirement of proof beyond a reasonable doubt was not formally announced to be of constitutional status until 1970; and they would be flabbergasted to learn that the courts themselves are uncertain about to which, if any, elements of crimes this requirement applies.

This uncertainty over the scope of the reasonable doubt requirement has nowhere been better illustrated than in the Supreme Court's recent decision in *Montana v Egelhoff*.[1] The five opinions produced by the majority and the dissent illustrate not only contrasting views about the reasonable doubt requirement's scope, but also the variety of issues that bear on the reasonable doubt requirement. Those issues include to what extent the federal Constitution limits the states' definitions of crimes or requires that criminal punishment reflect culpability, and to what extent the rules of admissibility of evidence are affected by the reasonable doubt re-

Larry Alexander is Warren Distinguished Professor of Law, University of San Diego.

AUTHOR'S NOTE: I would like to thank the following people for their very helpful comments: Kevin Cole, Michael Corrado, Evan Lee, Stephen Morse, Dale Nance, Robert Schopp, and Fred Zacharias. The usual disclaimer applies.

[1] 116 S Ct 2013 (1996).

quirement. It is rare that a case that goes virtually unnoticed turns out to be such a rich mine of issues of constitutional magnitude.

II

In 1970, the Supreme Court, in *In Re Winship*, held that "the Due Process Clause protects the accused against conviction except upon proof beyond a reasonable doubt of every fact necessary to constitute the crime charged."[2] The Court based its holding on the extreme disvalue of having the factually innocent suffer loss of liberty and stigmatization and on the insecurity that a lower standard of proof would produce.

Five years after *Winship*, in *Mullaney v Wilbur*,[3] the Court declared Maine's murder statute unconstitutional because it placed on the defendant the burden of rebutting malice through proof of heat of passion stemming from sudden provocation. The Court reasoned that because Maine had made malice an element of the crime of murder and defined it to preclude provoked/heat-of-passion killings, it had violated *Winship*'s requirement that the prosecution bear the burden of proving the crime beyond a reasonable doubt.

Two years later, however, in *Patterson v New York*,[4] the Court upheld a New York murder conviction under a statute that did not make lack of provocation/heat of passion an element of the crime, but that made "extreme emotional disturbance" a partial affirmative defense, reducing murder to manslaughter. The burden of proving the defense was on the defendant, and the standard was the preponderance of the evidence. Defendant argued that New York's murder law was functionally equivalent to the Maine law struck down in *Mullaney*, and that extreme emotional disturbance must be disproved beyond a reasonable doubt by the prosecution. The majority of the Court disagreed. In an opinion authored by Justice White, the majority denied

> that a State must prove beyond a reasonable doubt every fact, the existence or nonexistence of which it is willing to recognize

---

[2] 397 US 358, 364 (1970).
[3] 421 US 684 (1975).
[4] 432 US 197 (1977).

as an exculpatory or mitigating circumstance affecting the degree of culpability the severity of the punishment.[5]

Thus,

> [t]he crime of murder is defined by the statute . . . as causing the death of another person with the intent to do so. The death, the intent to kill, and causation are the facts that the State is required to prove beyond a reasonable doubt. . . . No further facts are either presumed or inferred in order to constitute the crime. . . . [6]

Patterson provoked an outpouring of commentary, most of it critical. The tenor of the criticism was that the Court had, as Justice Powell in his dissent, joined by Brennan and Marshall, had complained, elevated form over substance. The dissenters and academic critics viewed the statutes in *Mullaney* and *Patterson* as functional equivalents, both requiring proof beyond a reasonable doubt of death, intent, and causation, and both reducing the grade of the homicide upon defendant's proof by a preponderance of the evidence of sufficient provocation. Because the Maine and New York statutes were functionally identical, their constitutional status should be the same.

The "form over substance" critics of the *Mullaney/Patterson* tandem were divided into two major camps, the substantivists and the proceduralists.[7] The substantivists argued that *Winship*'s requirement of proof beyond a reasonable doubt of crimes must itself rest on some substantive notion of what a "crime" is for constitutional purposes.[8] If a state can make anything a crime, then *Winship* is of dubious value as a protection against loss of liberty and against

---

[5] Id at 207.

[6] Id at 205–06.

[7] The characterizations "substantivists" and "proceduralists" were Scott Sundby's. See Scott E. Sundby, *The Reasonable Doubt Rule and the Meaning of Innocence*, 40 Hastings L J 457, 505 (1989).

[8] See Ronald J. Allen, *Structuring Jury Decisionmaking in Criminal Cases: A Unified Constitutional Approach to Evidentiary Devices*, 94 Harv L Rev 321, 342–45 (1980); Ronald J. Allen, *The Restoration of In Re Winship: A Comment on the Burdens of Persuasion in Criminal Cases After Patterson v. New York*, 76 Mich L Rev 30, 42–47 (1977); Ronald J. Allen, *Mullaney v. Wilbur, the Supreme Court, and Substantive Criminal Law—An Examination of the Limits of Legitimate Intervention*, 35 Tex L Rev 269, 270, 283–85, 295–97 (1977); John Calvin Jeffries, Jr. and Paul B. Stephan III, *Defenses, Presumptions, and Burden of Proof in the Criminal Law*, 81 Yale L J 1325, 1327–28, 1370 et seq (1979). See also William J. Stuntz, *Substance, Process, and the Civil-Criminal Line*, 7 J Contemp Legal Issues 1, 31–34 (1996).

stigmatization. Implicit in the substantivists' "form over substance" criticism was the idea that substantive due process or the Eighth Amendment (Cruel and Unusual Punishments Clause) mandates a constitutional minimum that must be proved by the state beyond a reasonable doubt before conviction of various crimes.[9] For these critics, either *Mullaney* stood for the proposition that the absence of provocation was a constitutionally required element of the crime of murder or its functional equivalent, in which case *Patterson* was incorrectly decided, or else *Mullaney* itself was incorrect and absence of provocation could be entirely eliminated as a precondition to a murder conviction.[10] Moreover, if these critics were right, the Due Process Clauses (or Eighth Amendment) speak to what degree of self-control (voluntariness) and what level of mens rea must be present, and what justifications and excuses must be absent, for each crime or level of punishment, at least as constitutional minima.

It was just this implication of federal constitutional standards for the definitions of crimes to which the proceduralist critics of the Court objected. On their view, the *Mullaney/Patterson* tandem was problematic, not because the federal Constitution imposed minimum requirements on the states' definitions of crimes, but because whatever definitions of crimes the states came up with were themselves matters of substance—on what facts did conviction and punishment turn—not form (the allocation of those facts between the offense and affirmative defenses).[11]

The proceduralists split into several subcamps depending upon whether the definition of a "crime" for proof-beyond-reasonable-doubt purposes included all elements upon which punishment

---

[9] See Allen, *Structuring Jury Decisionmaking* at 342–47 (cited in note 8) (relying on both the Due Process Clauses and the Eighth Amendment as the sources of the federal constitutional minima regarding elements of crimes); Allen, *The Restoration* at 46–47 (cited in note 8) (relying on the Eighth Amendment); Jeffries and Stephan at 1368–69 (cited in note 8) (relying on both the Due Process Clauses and the Eighth Amendment).

[10] Ronald Allen argued that it was *Mullaney*, not *Patterson*, that was incorrect, and that punishing provoked homicide as murder should not be deemed to violate the federal Constitution. See Allen, *Mullaney v. Wilbur* at 284–86 (cited in note 8).

[11] See Donald A. Dripps, *The Constitutional Status of the Reasonable Doubt Rule*, 75 Cal L Rev 1665, 1666, 1680–87 (1987); Dale A. Nance, *Civility and the Burden of Proof*, 17 Harv J L & Pub Pol 647, 687–89 (1994); Scott E. Sundby at 497, 505 (cited in note 7); Barbara D. Underwood, *The Thumb on the Scales of Justice: Burdens of Persuasion in Criminal Cases*, 86 Yale L J 1299, 1317–24 (1977).

turned,[12] all elements which affected stigmatization,[13] or all elements that came within the principle of legality (for which notice was constitutionally required).[14] The proceduralists all agreed, however, that whatever definitions of crimes the states established, *Winship* required that all of the elements of those crimes be proved beyond a reasonable doubt.[15] Because both New York and Maine had defined murder to include the absence of provocation, that element could not be converted into an affirmative defense on

---

[12] This is approximately the position of Sundby and Underwood. See Sundby at 505–09 (cited in note 7); Underwood at 1341–48 (cited in note 11). See also Nance at 687 n 131 (cited in note 11).

[13] This is Nance's position. See Nance at 688 (cited in note 11).

[14] This appears to be Dripps's position. See Dripps at 1680–87 (cited in note 11).

[15] The proceduralists criticized the substantivists' position on three basic grounds. First, they pointed out that the Supreme Court had been quite unsuccessful in specifying constitutionally required elements under both the Due Process Clauses and the Eighth Amendment. See, e.g., Underwood at 1328 (cited in note 11) ("The Court has assiduously avoided the development of doctrine concerning the constitutional limits of substantive criminal law" (citing Herbert L. Packer, *Mens Rea and the Supreme Court*, 1962 Supreme Court Review 107)). Second, they argued that the substantivists' position on the reasonable doubt rule logically extended to other constitutional rights regarding the criminal process, such as the right to counsel. See, e.g., Dripps at 1715–16 (cited in note 11); Underwood at 1329–30 (cited in note 11). Third, they argued that allowing shifting the burden of proof to defendants for elements that are not within the substantivists' constitutionally required minima would lead to having convictions turn on the arbitrary fact of how much evidence in support of the defense happened to be generated. See, e.g., Sundby at 497 (cited in note 7); Underwood at 1322–23 (cited in note 11). (Underwood also argued that substantivism's toleration of affirmative defenses violated the principle that legislatures should engage in truth in labeling when it comes to defining crimes. See Underwood at 1323–24 (cited in note 11).)

The substantivists not only attempted to answer these criticisms—see, e.g., Allen, *The Restoration* at 43–45 n 60 (cited in note 8)—but also attacked the proceduralists on a number of grounds. First, they argued that concern with procedure but not with the substance to which it attaches is illogical. See, e.g., id; Jeffries and Stephan at 1345–52 (cited in note 8). Second, they argued that the proceduralists' position entailed a requirement of proof beyond reasonable doubt for facts adduced at sentencing, directly contrary to the Supreme Court's holding in *Williams v New York*, 337 US 241 (1949). See, e.g., Allen, *Mullaney v. Wilbur* at 291–94 (cited in note 8); Jeffries and Stephan at 1352–53 (cited in note 8). (For Dripps's reply to this criticism, see Dripps at 1697–1700 (cited in note 11).) Third, there is the point raised by the proceduralists themselves that their position entails the constitutional invalidity of a large number of affirmative defenses the burden of proof of which is on the defendant, even though many of these affirmative defenses are time-honored, and some have been upheld against constitutional attack by the Supreme Court. (The most significant example is that of *Leland v Oregon*, 343 US 790 (1952), in which the Supreme Court upheld Oregon's placing the burden of proving defendant's insanity in a criminal case on the defendant and additionally set the standard for proof of insanity as beyond a reasonable doubt.) See, e.g., Underwood at 1303–04 (cited in note 11). See also Harold A. Ashford and D. Michael Risinger, *Presumptions, Assumptions, and Due Process in Criminal Cases: A Theoretical Overview*, 79 Yale L J 165, 202–03 (1969). Of course, *Patterson v New York* itself falls into this group of precedents upholding affirmative defenses. See 432 US at 207–08.

which the burden of proof was borne by the defendant. The *Mullaney/Patterson* tandem was wrong because *Patterson* was wrong.

Despite these two lines of criticism, *Mullaney/Patterson* has remained the constitutional law governing burdens of proof in criminal cases. The state's formal definitions of crimes largely control when the burden of proof beyond a reasonable doubt can be reduced or shifted to the defendant.

III

Montana defines "deliberate homicide" as "purposely" or "knowingly" causing another's death.[16] In 1987 it enacted a law that prohibited the trier of fact from considering a defendant's "intoxicated condition . . . in determining the existence of a mental state which is an element of the offense."[17] Thus, if a defendant denied killing purposely or knowingly because he was too intoxicated to intend to kill, he would not be allowed to present evidence on this point. Presumably he could still deny that he intended the death and testify to that effect, but he could not buttress his bare denial with evidence that he was intoxicated.

Normally in a criminal case, the state has not only the burden of proving the core elements of the offense beyond a reasonable doubt, but also the burden of production of evidence. Thus, in a homicide prosecution, the state must generally introduce evidence of defendant's conduct, the victim's death, and the causal relation between the conduct and death. Moreover, when it charges a state of mind other than the state of mind normally associated with the proved conduct, it must generally introduce evidence on that point, usually in the form of defendant's statements or circumstantial evidence establishing motive.

Nevertheless, the burden of production is not entirely on the prosecution, even when the prosecution bears the burden of proof. For example, if the prosecutor introduces evidence of defendant's conduct, and that conduct in most cases is voluntary, the defendant must introduce evidence of some unusual condition—for example,

---

[16] Mont Code Ann § 45-5-102 (1995).

[17] Mont Code Ann § 45-2-203 (1995).

hypnotism, somnambulance, or automatism[18]—to defeat the inference of voluntariness. Likewise, with respect to mens rea, if the conduct ordinarily suggests knowledge, the defendant may have to produce evidence of a mistake to defeat the natural inference.

Again, in the aforementioned cases, the burden of proof is not shifted from the prosecution to the defendant. Rather, the prosecution is assisted in meeting its burden of proof by what are in effect permissive inferences. If the prosecution proves facts A, B, and C, and if the defendant then offers no evidence to prove not-D, not-E, and not-F, the trier is permitted to infer that D, E, and F as well as A, B, and C have been proved beyond a reasonable doubt.

The constitutional status of such permissive inferences as those just described has been stated by the Supreme Court but never well explained. The principal case on this point is *County Court v Allen*.[19] There the Court said that mandatory presumptions—those that instruct the trier to find the presumed fact if another fact is established beyond a reasonable doubt—even if rebuttable, are unconstitutional if the presumed fact is not correlated with the proved fact so strongly as to make their conjunction generally true beyond a reasonable doubt.[20] On the other hand, permissive inferences, which allow but do not compel the trier to find the inferred fact upon proof of some other fact, are constitutional if the correlation between proved and presumed fact is merely "more likely than not" (>50%).[21]

Now there is a problem here. Why, if the standard of proof is "beyond a reasonable doubt," should the trier be permitted to infer a fact from a proved fact if their correlation in the world is not

---

[18] For example, see Model Penal Code § 2.01(2), listing various conditions that negate voluntariness. Automatism is an altered state of consciousness similar to somnambulance that can be brought about by certain traumas or pathologies.

[19] 442 US 140 (1979).

[20] Id at 157–60. See also *Sandstrom v Montana*, 442 US 510 (1979).

[21] The third category of presumptions is that of mandatory irrebuttable (conclusive) presumptions. Conclusive presumptions in effect change the definition of the crime. Without the conclusive presumption, the crime requires proving the presumed fact. With the conclusive presumption, the crime is now established by proving either the presumed fact or the fact that gives rise to the presumption.

Conclusive presumptions are certainly unconstitutional if the Constitution requires the crime to contain the presumed fact. Even if that is not the case, however, conclusive presumptions appear to violate the *Mullaney/Patterson* holdings in that the state is redefining the crime through tampering with the methods of proof rather than directly.

"beyond a reasonable doubt" but the considerably weaker "more probably than not"? The inference is, of course, not mandatory, and the trier may decline to make the permitted inference. Moreover, the standard of proof formally remains "beyond a reasonable doubt." Nonetheless, the trier is given what appear to be two contradictory instructions: you must be assured beyond a reasonable doubt that all the elements of the crime exist, and you may infer one of those elements from proof of a fact that makes its existence only more likely than not.

Justice Stevens, writing for the *County Court* majority, wrote cryptically on this point:

> There is no more reason to require a permissive . . . presumption to meet a reasonable doubt standard before it may be permitted . . . than there is to require that degree of probative force for other relevant evidence before it may be admitted. As long as it is clear that the presumption is not the sole and sufficient basis for a finding of guilt, it need only satisfy [the weaker] test. . . . [22]

The first sentence, however, seems encumbered by a confusion between the standards for relevancy and the standards for proof. And the second sentence is either a retraction of the Court's blessing of permissive inferences or a misconception of what a permissive inference is, namely, an instruction to the trier that it may find the inferred fact upon proof of the triggering fact(s) *even if it does not find credible any other evidence the prosecution has offered.*[23]

There is a way of squaring *County Court* with *Winship*, however. For suppose that it is legitimate to place the burden of production on the defendant on some issues (such as intoxication as negating intent). Then it might be the case that proved fact F does establish inferred fact I beyond a reasonable doubt when conjoined with a third fact, to wit, that defendant, bearing the burden of production of evidence negating I, failed to produce any credible evidence of I-negating facts N. In other words, the correlation between F

---

[22] 442 US at 167.

[23] The fact that the instructions to the jury appeared to permit it to make the inference even if it disbelieved the prosecution's other evidence was a point seized upon by Justice Powell in his dissent. See 442 US at 173–76. See also Allen, *Structuring Jury Decisionmaking* at 335–36, 364–65 (cited in note 8); Ashford and Risinger at 199–201 (cited in note 15); Note (Collier), *The Improper Use of Presumptions in Recent Criminal Law Adjudication*, 38 Stan L Rev 423, 439, 461 (1986).

and I is only "more likely than not" if we ignore the absence of N; given that absence, however, *in the context of a burden of production on someone facing a prison sentence*, the correlation is "beyond a reasonable doubt."

Thus, by way of illustration, suppose that the permissive inference that most conduct is voluntary is not true "beyond a reasonable doubt" but only "more probably than not." But suppose further that most criminal conduct for which the defendant, on pain of likely imprisonment, offers no credible evidence of hypnosis, somnambulance, and so forth *is* voluntary "beyond a reasonable doubt." If we place the burden of production on defendant with respect to these voluntariness-negating conditions, and he produces no credible evidence to establish them, then the inference of voluntariness would be true beyond a reasonable doubt.[24] It is against this constitutional framework regarding presumptions that Montana's preclusion of intoxication evidence to prove defendant's mental state should be assessed. Interestingly, it does not fit any of the categories the Court has discussed. It is not a mandatory irrebuttable presumption (of intent from the conduct proved) because it is not mandatory. The trier is not forced to find the requisite mental state from the prosecution's proof. On the other hand, it is not a permissive rebuttable inference because the permissive inference established is not rebuttable. One can infer nothing against the defendant from his failure to provide credible proof of intoxication because he is legally precluded from doing so.

In short, what Montana has done is create a permissive but irre-

---

[24] There are three points of note about this analysis of permissive inferences. First, it relies on a notion of burden of production that does not require a directed verdict for the prosecution on the inferred fact if defendant fails to produce credible evidence. Some burdens of production result in directed verdicts if they are not met, but directed verdicts against defendants in criminal cases are not permissible. See *Sandstrom v Montana*, 442 US at 516 n 5 (cited in note 20); Ashford and Risinger at 175 n 21 (cited in note 15).

Second, this analysis of how the burden of production might square permissive inferences with the requirement of proof beyond a reasonable doubt even when the correlation between the inference-triggering fact and inferred fact is only "more probably than not" has some support in the case law and academic commentary. See *Barnes v United States*, 412 US 837, 845–46 (1972); Ashford and Risinger at 181–84 (cited in note 15).

Finally, the burdens of production placed on defendant for Model Penal Code type affirmative defenses—defenses, the negation of which the prosecution bears the burden of proving beyond a reasonable doubt—are entirely inapposite to the analysis here, which is confined entirely to elements of the offense. Failure of defendant to produce credible evidence of Model Penal Code affirmative defenses results in the jury's not being instructed regarding the defenses. See Allen, *Structuring Jury Decisionmaking* at 327–34 (cited in note 8).

buttable inference. And whereas in other jurisdictions the trier may permissibly infer intent beyond a reasonable doubt from the prosecution's evidence added to the defendant's failure to produce evidence of intoxication, the prosecution's evidence in Montana falls short of that strength.

There is, finally, another way to characterize the effect of Montana's preclusion of intoxication evidence, namely, as a change in its definition of murder. Whereas the murder statute defines the crime as intentional (purposeful or knowing) homicide, the murder statute and the intoxication statute when read together define the crime as intentional homicide *or* homicide committed while intoxicated in which there is sufficient evidence to infer intent if intoxication is ruled out as a possibility.[25] I offer this quite complex definition rather than the simpler "intentional or nonintentional by virtue of intoxication" because the trier must still find beyond a reasonable doubt that the killing was intentional and cannot convict merely on a finding of killing while intoxicated.

IV

On July 12, 1992, in Troy, Montana, James Allen Egelhoff and two recent friends, Roberta Pavola and John Christenson, spent the day drinking together in bars and at a party. After leaving the party in Christenson's station wagon, they apparently continued drinking after purchasing beer and perhaps whiskey.

About midnight, Lincoln County, Montana, sheriff's officers, responding to reports of a possible drunk driver, discovered the station wagon in a ditch along a highway. Pavola and Christenson were in the front seat, each dead from a single gunshot to the head. Egelhoff was alive and lying in the back seat of the station wagon. He was yelling obscenities. His .38 caliber handgun was on the floor of the car near the brake pedal, with four loaded rounds and two empty casings. Egelhoff had gunshot residue on his hands and a blood alcohol level of .36 percent when measured one hour later.

Egelhoff was charged with deliberate homicide—purposeful or

---

[25] See also the similar characterization of the Montana statute in an amicus brief submitted in *Montana v Egelhoff*, 116 S Ct 2013 (1996), and referred to approvingly by Justice Ginsburg, id at 2024.

knowing homicide; and at trial the jury was instructed that "[a] person acts purposely when it is his conscious object . . . to cause such a result," and that "[a] person acts knowingly when he is aware . . . there exists the high probability that his conduct will cause a specific result."[26]

Egelhoff denied the killing and claimed that he was too intoxicated to have physically carried it out. He also claimed that he was so intoxicated that he could not recall the events of July 12.

Although the trial court allowed Egelhoff to use evidence of his intoxication in these ways, it instructed the jury, in pursuance of Montana's new statute,[27] that it could not consider evidence of Egelhoff's intoxication in determining the existence of purpose or knowledge.

The jury convicted Egelhoff, but the Montana Supreme Court reversed the conviction.[28] It held that Egelhoff had a right under the Due Process Clause to present all relevant evidence to rebut the state's evidence on all elements of the offense. Because Montana's statute prevented the jury from considering evidence of Egelhoff's intoxication to rebut the state's evidence of his mens rea, and because such evidence was clearly relevant to that issue, the statute had relieved the state of its constitutionally compelled burden to prove the elements beyond a reasonable doubt.

The Montana Supreme Court relied heavily on *Martin v Ohio*,[29] in which the U.S. Supreme Court held that it was not a violation of due process to place the burden of proving self-defense on the defendant, but in which it went on to say that "[i]t would be quite different if the jury had been instructed that self-defense evidence could not be considered in determining whether there was a reasonable doubt about the State's case," which would plainly "relieve the State of its burden and run afoul of the *Winship* mandate."[30]

The Montana Supreme Court reasoned that § 45-2-203, although it did not shift the burden of proving mens rea beyond a

---

[26] Id at 2013, 2016 (1996).

These instructions are quite orthodox. See, e.g., Model Penal Code §§ 2.02(2)(a) and (2)(b) (defining "purposely" and "knowingly").

[27] Mont Code Ann § 45-2-203.

[28] *State v Egelhoff*, 272 Mont 114, 900 P2d 260 (1995).

[29] 480 US 228 (1987).

[30] Id at 233, quoted at 900 P2d at 265.

reasonable doubt, improperly lessened the state's burden.[31] The Court also distinguished between eliminating voluntary intoxication as a (presumably excusing) affirmative defense—which the state was constitutionally free to do—and precluding voluntary intoxication evidence relevant to negating the offense.[32]

V

The U.S. Supreme Court reversed the Montana Supreme Court. Justice Scalia, in an opinion joined by Chief Justice Rehnquist and Justices Kennedy and Thomas, denied that the Due Process Clause entitles defendants to present all relevant evidence.[33] Scalia cited the rules of evidence, which routinely bar all sorts of evidence that meets the standard of relevance. For example, the rules of evidence bar admission of relevant evidence that is privileged, prejudicial, confusing, or cumulative, or that falls within categories of inadmissible evidence such as hearsay or nonauthenticated documents.

Moreover, said Scalia, responding to a point made by the dissent, the fact that the Montana law excludes a category of evidence that tends to prove a particular fact—unlike, for example, the category of hearsay evidence, which could be relevant to any fact—is immaterial. The question is only whether the state has "good and traditional policy support" for excluding this category, as it does for excluding the more traditional forms of inadmissible evidence.[34]

Justice Scalia first turned to whether Montana had "traditional" policy support. The common-law tradition was firmly against allowing intoxication to excuse or mitigate an offense.[35] Scalia inferred that the common law as well precluded the use of intoxication evidence to negate mens rea.[36]

Nonetheless, the common-law position began to erode in the early nineteenth century, and by that century's end, most American jurisdictions allowed the use of evidence of intoxication to ne-

---

[31] 900 P2d at 266.

[32] Id.

[33] 116 S Ct at 2016–17.

[34] Id at 2017 n 1.

[35] Id at 2018.

[36] Id.

gate certain types of mens rea. But despite this erosion of the common law's position, the position that evidence of intoxication should be admissible to negate mens rea was not itself so deeply rooted at the time of the Fourteenth Amendment's adoption to be considered a fundamental principle of due process. Moreover, about one-fifth of the states never adopted that position or, like Montana, had abandoned it.[37]

Scalia next turned to whether Montana had "good" policy reasons for its statute. Because so many serious crimes are committed by intoxicated defendants, "[d]isallowing consideration of voluntary intoxication has the effect of increasing the punishment for all unlawful acts committed in the state, and thereby deters drunkenness or irresponsible behavior while drunk."[38] In other words, like a murder statute that requires *either* intent *or* intoxication, a murder statute that requires intent but disallows relevant evidence of intoxication to negate it raises the risks of criminal conviction for those who drink or take drugs and thus deters that criminogenic conduct.

Scalia concluded his affirmative case for reversal:

> In sum, not every widespread experiment with a procedural rule favorable to criminal defendants establishes a fundamental principle of justice. Although the rule allowing a jury to consider evidence of a defendant's voluntary intoxication where relevant to *mens rea* has gained considerable acceptance, it is of too recent vintage, and has not received sufficiently uniform and permanent allegiance to qualify as fundamental, especially since it displaces a lengthy common-law tradition which remains supported by valid justifications today.[39]

All that remained for Scalia was to deal with the *Winship* line of cases on burden of proof. He seized on the Montana Supreme Court's characterization of § 45-2-203 as a burden reducing rather than a burden shifting rule. Scalia correctly noted that the Montana court had not meant by "burden reducing" that the standard of proof was reduced from beyond a reasonable doubt to some lower standard, but rather that the burden of proving intent be-

---

[37] Id at 2019–20.

[38] Id at 20.

[39] Id at 2021.

yond a reasonable doubt was made easier by the preclusion of evidence of defendant's intoxication.[40] "But," replied Scalia,

> *any* evidentiary rule can have that effect. "Reducing" the State's
> burden in this manner is not unconstitutional, unless the rule
> of evidence itself violates a fundamental principle of fairness
> (which, as discussed, this one does not). We have "reject[ed]
> the view that anything in the Due Process Clause bars States
> from making changes in their criminal law that have the effect
> of making it easier for the prosecution to obtain convictions."[41]

Finally, Scalia turned to the language from its decision in *Martin
v Ohio* upon which the Montana Supreme Court had relied and
dismissed it as a mere dictum. Further,

> [i]f the *Martin* dictum means that the Due Process Clause re-
> quires all relevant evidence bearing on the elements of a crime
> to be admissible, the decisions we have discussed show it to be
> incorrect.[42]

Justice Ginsburg concurred in the judgment of the Court. She
rejected Scalia's characterization of § 45-2-203 as merely an evidentiary rule.[43] Instead, she viewed Montana as having essentially
added a new category of murder, namely, a killing in which the
defendant's voluntary intoxication has reduced his capacity for
self-control.[44] Not only was this the effect of § 45-2-203; the statute itself is located in the "Crimes" title of the Montana Code
rather than in the title dealing with admissibility of evidence.[45] For
her, then, the constitutional question was whether Montana could

---

[40] Id at 2023.

[41] Id (emphasis in original; citation omitted).

[42] Id.

[43] Id at 2024.

[44] Justice Ginsburg recognized that the statute did not actually make intoxicated killings
an alternative to intentional ones but rather had a more complex functional formulation
similar to the one I gave previously. See text at note 25. She quoted approvingly an amicus
brief that described the statute functionally as follows:

> To obtain a conviction, the prosecution must prove only that (1) the defendant
> caused the death of another with actual knowledge or purpose, *or* (2) that the
> defendant killed "under circumstances that would otherwise establish knowledge
> or purpose 'but for' [the defendant's] voluntary intoxication."

116 S Ct at 2024.

[45] Id.

treat this type of "murder" as just as culpable as a fully intentional killing.[46]

Making that question the pivotal one, Justice Ginsburg found the case easy. Given the long common-law tradition against allowing voluntary intoxication to mitigate or excuse criminal acts, no "fundamental principle of justice" was offended by Montana's making killing while intoxicated as serious a crime as intentional homicide.[47] Nor was it of any constitutional significance whether Montana in its definition of murder equated intentional and intoxicated killings or instead, by excluding intoxication evidence relevant to intent, came up with a combination of statutes that produced almost the same result.[48]

There were three dissenting opinions. Justice O'Connor wrote for all four dissenters—Stevens, Souter, Breyer, and herself—and focused primarily on the exclusion of relevant evidence, which she viewed as violative of due process. From O'Connor's point of view, § 45-2-203 was less like the exclusion of the category "hearsay evidence" and, if I may characterize rather than paraphrase, more like the exclusion of the category "exculpatory evidence."[49] The latter would clearly be unconstitutional. And although less draconian, § 45-2-203 likewise deprives a defendant of a fair opportunity to present a defense.

O'Connor cited the dictum in *Martin v Ohio* that the Montana Supreme Court had relied on and that Scalia had rejected.[50] But she also referred to some cases that both Scalia and Ginsburg completely ignored but that were clearly specters haunting their opinions, namely, the *Winship/Mullaney/Patterson* line of cases.[51] O'Connor cited *Patterson* for the proposition that

> a state legislature certainly has the authority to identify the elements of the offenses it wishes to punish, but once its laws are written, a defendant has the right to insist that the State prove beyond a reasonable doubt every element of an offense charged.[52]

---

[46] Id.

[47] Id at 2024–25.

[48] Id at 2025 n 1.

[49] Id at 2026.

[50] Id at 2028. See also text at note 42.

[51] 116 S Ct at 2027.

[52] Id.

And although she did not cite it by name, it was actually *Mullaney*, as glossed by *Patterson*, that O'Connor was thinking of in that statement.

Mullaney was particularly relevant to Justice Ginsburg's concurrence because she relied so heavily on the argument that § 45-2-203 was a legislative redefinition of the crime of murder. The gist of the academic and dissenting justices' criticisms of the *Mullaney/Patterson* tandem was that Maine in *Mullaney* had in essence legislatively redefined murder in the manner that New York had in *Patterson*. If the Constitution forbade Maine's functional redefinition, why did it not also forbid Montana's? If *Patterson* in light of *Mullaney* means that form counts over function, why is Montana permitted to elevate function over form?

There was still a further problem with Justice Ginsburg's "redefinition" approach that Justice O'Connor noted. The Montana Supreme Court had ruled that § 45-2-203 was *not* a legislative redefinition of the crime of murder, and under ordinary principles of federalism, the Court is bound by the Montana Supreme Court's interpretation of Montana law.[53] This latter point was also central to Justice Souter's separate dissenting opinion:

> I have no doubt that a State may so define the mental element of an offense that evidence of a defendant's voluntary intoxication at the time of commission does not have exculpatory relevance and, to that extent, may be excluded without raising any issue of due process. I would have thought the statement at issue here . . . had implicitly accomplished such a redefinition, but I read the opinion of the Supreme Court of Montana as indicating that it had no such effect, and I am bound by the state court's statement of its domestic law.[54]

Justice Souter went on to opine that had Montana redefined its murder statute to make voluntary intoxication irrelevant to exculpation—by making it a substitute for *mens rea*—he would have no problem with its constitutionality. Only the state court's holding that murder had not been so redefined kept him from voting to uphold the constitutionality of the conviction.[55] Significantly, Justice Souter nowhere mentioned *Mullaney*, much less suggested that

---

[53] Id at 2031.

[54] Id at 2032.

[55] Id.

it might pose a problem for a redefinition of murder accomplished by excluding otherwise relevant evidence.

Justice Breyer also wrote a separate dissent in which Justice Stevens joined. Breyer agreed that the Montana Supreme Court's holding that murder had not been redefined foreclosed upholding the law on that basis.[56] Justice Breyer, however, and presumably Justice Stevens, was much more skeptical about the constitutionality of Montana's scheme even had the Montana court decided that the state *had* redefined murder.[57] Breyer noted that, viewed as a redefinition of murder, the scheme did not amount to murder as intentional *or* intoxicated killings. Rather, it amounted to murder as intentional killings or as nonintentional killings that would look intentional (beyond a reasonable doubt) if one did not know of defendant's intoxication. And Justices Breyer and Stevens were unwilling to endorse the constitutionality of such an odd hypothetical law.

VI

It is time now to take stock of what the various opinions in *Egelhoff* add up to or suggest. Justice Scalia's opinion for the plurality appears to boil down to this: A state may exclude an entire category of exculpatory evidence if it is based on conduct that the state (1) wishes to deter and (2) could punish without violating a "fundamental principle of justice" supported by tradition. Montana's exclusion of otherwise relevant intoxication evidence served the legitimate policy of making voluntary intoxication itself punishable whenever it led either to criminal conduct or to conduct that would be criminal if accompanied by mens rea. Tradition did not foreclose such a policy.

Scalia never mentioned, much less dealt with, *Mullaney*, or more precisely, *Mullaney* as glossed by *Patterson*. Scalia was obviously seeking to avoid characterizing § 45-2-203 as a redefinition of murder given the Montana Supreme Court's holding to the contrary and the apparently ironclad argument that the U.S. Supreme Court was bound by that holding. If it is not a redefinition of murder, however, then, unlike the typical exclusions of relevant

---

[56] Id at 2034–35.
[57] Id at 2035.

evidence, it must be an exclusion designed to lessen the prosecution's burden of proof. It does so, as the Montana Supreme Court correctly noted, not by lowering the burden to something less than beyond a reasonable doubt, but by deliberately making the reasonable doubt standard easier for the prosecution to meet.[58] It is difficult to see, however, why that course is less subject to *Mullaney*'s strictures than shifting the burden of proof to the defendant on an element of the offense. Indeed, an intoxicated defendant would prefer bearing the burden of persuasion on whether his intoxication negated his intent rather than having the prosecution nominally bear the burden but himself be precluded from introducing evidence of intoxication. *Mullaney* seems an a fortiori case for overturning Egelhoff's conviction if the Montana Supreme Court's holding that murder had not been redefined sets the parameters of the discussion.[59]

Suppose § 45-2-203 is viewed as a redefinition of murder. This was Justice Ginsburg's position in her concurrence. Justice Ginsburg appeared completely untroubled by the Montana Supreme Court's holding to the contrary. Indeed, despite the fact that all of the dissenting opinions expressly relied to some extent on the proposition that the federal courts are bound by the interpretation of state law of a state's highest court, Justice Ginsburg's opinion completely ignores that point. For Justice Ginsburg, this *was* a redefinition of murder, the Montana Supreme Court's holding to the contrary notwithstanding.

I think Justice Ginsburg must be correct here, and the dissenters wrong, not about the general proposition that state court interpretations of state law bind the federal courts, which is true, but about that proposition's application to *Egelhoff*. For there was no uncertainty over the meaning of § 45-2-203 or over its effects. Had there been, the Montana Supreme Court's resolution of the uncer-

---

[58] 900 P2d at 266.

[59] Neither Justice Scalia, any other justice, nor the Montana Supreme Court discussed a different policy that might justify Montana's exclusion of relevant evidence, namely, excluding evidence whose probative value is low and potential to confuse is high. For example, if the Montana legislature believed that intoxication almost never negates purpose or knowledge, but believed also that juries will overestimate intoxication's probative strength, it might have premised its statute on those beliefs rather than on the need to deter unintended killings by the intoxicated.

tainty would have been definitive. Rather, the question whether § 45-2-203 redefined the crime of murder was merely one of characterization. And there is no reason why the state court's characterization of state law should bind the federal courts when it only affects the application of federal law and does not affect state law in any way. Put differently, when the only effect the Montana Supreme Court's "interpretation" of state law will have is how the federal Due Process Clause applies to state law, that court should have no power to bind the federal courts to its interpretation.

But if Justice Ginsburg was correct to ignore the Montana Supreme Court's holding that murder had not been redefined, was she also correct in concluding that Montana's redefinition of murder was constitutionally unproblematic? The first problem with her position is, as mentioned previously,[60] *Mullaney*. *Patterson* appears to make *Mullaney* stand for the proposition that redefinitions of crimes cannot be accomplished functionally through the relatively sub rosa reallocation of evidentiary burdens, but can only be accomplished formalistically through the explicit change in the definition of the crime. If that is so, then Justice Ginsburg could only reach the result she did by ignoring *Mullaney* as so glossed.

Perhaps ignoring *Mullaney* was exactly what both Justice Ginsburg and the plurality were consciously doing. *Patterson* had left *Mullaney* a formalistic shell, and perhaps Ginsburg and Scalia were eliminating the shell, albeit sub silentio. If the criticism of *Mullaney* as glossed by *Patterson* is that it elevated form over substance, the majority was returning substance to primacy over form by making *Mullaney* a dead letter.

The difficulty with overruling *Mullaney* is that it forces the Court to rethink the basic *Winship* requirement of proof beyond a reasonable doubt. Without *Mullaney*, *Winship* is toothless unless the Court now sides with either the substantivists' or the proceduralists' criticism of *Mullaney/Patterson*.

For the substantivists, there are federally defined core elements of each crime that cannot be eliminated, functionally as well as formally, or made into defenses, the burden of proving which is on the defendant. A federal law of substantive crimes, developed

---

[60] See ¶ following note 52.

under the Due Process Clause, or the Eighth Amendment, is the substantivists' *Winship*-preserving alternative to *Mullaney/Patterson*.[61]

Egelhoff can be viewed as the case that threw off the formalism of *Mullaney/Patterson* and began developing such a federal law of substantive crimes. The general question that it decided was whether a killing committed because of intoxication could be treated as equally culpable—or at least equally punishable—as an intentional killing. At least seven Justices answered that question affirmatively. Justices Breyer and Stevens seemed also to endorse that position. Because § 45-2-203 did not make all intoxicated killings punishable as murder, but only those that otherwise appeared intentional—and because Justices Breyer and Stevens were troubled by that aspect of the statute—their endorsement of the more general proposition that intoxicant-induced killings can be treated like intentional ones is less certain, though highly likely.

Alternatively, *Egelhoff* might signal the Court's embrace of the proceduralists' criticism of *Mullaney/Patterson*. The proceduralists argue, not for developing a federal constitutional law of substantive crimes, but for making the constitutional law of criminal procedure—including *Winship*'s requirement of proof beyond a reasonable doubt—applicable to all elements that the *state* has made material for conviction and punishment.[62] Although the proceduralists are much more deferential to the states than the substantivists when it comes to deciding what shall be punished, they are much less deferential to the states than the substantivists when it comes to creating defenses that must be proved by the defendant.

There are no indications that any of the justices in *Egelhoff* would endorse the proceduralist position. Every proceduralist rejects some traditional affirmative defenses, and the most far-reaching versions of proceduralism would require overturning vast amounts of state criminal law in addition to Supreme Court precedents like *Patterson* and *Leland v Oregon*.[63] And while the substanti-

---

[61] See also text at notes 7–10.

[62] See also text at notes 11–15.

[63] See Underwood at 1303–04 (cited in note 11). See generally note 15. Even the Model Penal Code, which comes closest to the proceduralists' ideal of never shifting the burden of persuasion to defendant, even on affirmative defenses, does shift that burden on some defenses that will affect conviction, punishment, and stigma. See, e.g., Model Penal Code § 2.04(3)(b), (4) (creating a new mistake of law defense but placing the burden of proving it on the defendant).

vist position has its own difficulties—such as explaining if or why federal constitutional constraints on criminal procedures other than the reasonable doubt rule should apply to elements of crimes and defenses beyond the constitutionally mandated core[64]—the difficulties with the proceduralist position, like its sweep, are greater. Most fundamentally, and despite valiant justificatory efforts by skilled proceduralists, its divorce of a federal concern for procedure from a federal concern for substance remains highly problematic.[65] Additionally, proceduralists have never convincingly justified the inapplicability of *Winship* to matters proved at the sentencing stage.[66]

I am going to assume in the remaining sections that the Court, if it is indeed repudiating *Mullaney/Patterson*, will not adopt the proceduralist position in its place. Although the substantivist position will not be attractive to many of the justices, the proceduralist position is both too radical in its handling of precedent and too shaky theoretically to attract the Court.

VII

If *Egelhoff* means the Supreme Court now adheres to the pre-*Patterson* understanding of *Mullaney*, namely, that there is a federal constitutional law of mandatory elements of crimes, then the Court's presumption jurisprudence will have to be rethought. If an element is constitutionally mandatory—if a state may not punish for a particular crime at a particular level of severity without proving the element beyond a reasonable doubt—the existing constitutional jurisprudence regarding presumptions remains intact. The state may not establish a conclusive (mandatory irrebuttable) presumption of that element based on proof of some other fact beyond a reasonable doubt because invoking the conclusive

---

[64] See Dripps at 1715–16 (cited in note 11); Underwood at 1329–30 (cited in note 11). For a response, see Allen, *The Restoration* at 43–45 n 60 (cited in note 8).

[65] See Allen, *The Restoration* at 42–47 (cited in note 8); Jeffries and Stephen at 1345–52 (cited in note 8). For analyses of other areas of constitutional law haunted by the question whether "the greater power includes the lesser," see *Unconstitutional Conditions Symposium*, 26 San Diego L Rev 175–345 (1989); Larry Alexander, *Constitutional Theory and Constitutionally Optional Benefits and Burdens*, 11 Const Comm 287 (1994).

[66] See Allen, *Mullaney v. Wilbur* at 291–94 (cited in note 8); Jeffries and Stephan at 1352–53 (cited in note 8). For a response, see Dripps at 1697–70 (cited in note 11).

presumption eliminates the constitutionally required element from the definition of the crime and replaces it with the presumption-triggering fact. Nor may the state prove the element through a mandatory rebuttable presumption because doing so is inconsistent with *Winship*'s requirement of proof beyond a reasonable doubt. Permissive rebuttable inferences remain available, however, if the connection between the triggering fact (proved beyond a reasonable doubt) and the inferred fact—when coupled with a fairly placed burden of production on defendant—is "beyond a reasonable doubt" whenever defendant fails to produce credible rebuttal evidence.[67]

If an element is *not* constitutionally required, however, then the existing jurisprudence of presumptions should be eliminated. A conclusive presumption is unproblematic because it is merely a re-definition of the crime that eliminates the presumed fact as a re-quired element and makes the triggering fact an alternative to it. Because the presumed fact is by hypothesis constitutionally op-tional, dealing with it in this manner is unobjectionable in a post-*Mullaney/Patterson* regime.

If conclusive presumptions are permissible for constitutionally optional elements, then mandatory rebuttable and permissive pre-sumptions will be as well. Here, the greater power of establishing a conclusive presumption should surely entail the lesser power of establishing presumptions that the defendant can more easily rebut.[68]

What does not follow straightforwardly is that the strange per-missive but irrebuttable presumption of intent established by Mon-tana's § 45-2-203 is constitutional. That would depend first on whether as a general matter the Constitution allows intoxication to substitute for intent in a crime as serious as murder, the topic

---

[67] See text at note 24.

[68] The proceduralist position on presumptions would track the substantivist position set forth in this section, except that optional affirmative defenses would be few in number, and there would be no reason whatsoever to preclude use of conclusive presumptions. Because the latter are functionally tantamount to redefinitions of crimes—and because the procedur-alists would allow the states unbridled freedom to define crimes as they choose—procedur-alists would have no objection to conclusive presumptions, at least so long as they were understood by the public and engendered no confusion over how much stigma convictions merited. On the other hand, in keeping with their position's rejection of "the greater power includes the lesser," proceduralists would not allow mandatory rebuttable presumptions because they do not redefine the crime but merely (improperly) affect the burden of proof.

of the next section. Even if the Constitution does so allow, however, the constitutionality of § 45-2-203 would depend additionally on whether a State could punish as murder, not all intoxicant-induced killings, but only those committed in circumstances that would indicate intent beyond a reasonable doubt to a jury uninformed of the intoxication. That was the question that troubled Justices Breyer and Stevens in *Egelhoff,* and they were right to be troubled. The Equal Protection Clause limits the state's ability to define crimes even within the domain unconstrained by the Due Process Clause, and it precludes making arbitrary distinctions among those who kill. Thus, even if the Constitution grants Montana the greater power of punishing as murder all killings by the voluntarily intoxicated, it may well not grant the "lesser" power of doing what Montana did in *Egelhoff.*

VIII

If the real message of the Court in *Egelhoff* is that *Mullaney* is dead and that the Constitution permits intoxicant-induced killings to be punished as severely as intentional ones, what should be our verdict on that message?

If there was a good case for overruling *Mullaney* after *Patterson*— and I side with the overwhelming weight of commentary in thinking there was—then the only objection remaining to the Court's doing so in *Egelhoff* was the manner in which it was done. As far as thousands of lawyers, judges, law professors, and law students know, the *Mullaney/Patterson* tandem is still good law. If it is not, the Supreme Court should tell us directly and not force us through complex inferences to ascertain what can easily be stated.

Of course, for overruling *Mullaney* to be a good thing, the Supreme Court will have to do a decent job in deciding what *are* the core elements of crimes that due process (or the Eighth Amendment) requires be proved beyond a reasonable doubt. And that leads to asking how well the Court did on the question of whether intoxication can be an alternative to intent in the most serious of all crimes, murder.

Because the Justices overwhelmingly expressed support for allowing states to substitute voluntary intoxication for intent in murder statutes, it is instructive to look at the much more common practice among the states, namely, substituting voluntary intoxication for the mens rea of recklessness. The Model Penal Code's approach to voluntary intoxication is the prototype for this more common practice.[69] Indeed, prior to 1987, it was the prototype for Montana's approach.[70]

The Model Penal Code allows evidence of voluntary intoxication to negate purpose or knowledge when these are the mental states that must be proved to convict.[71] On the other hand, where recklessness or negligence suffice, the Model Penal Code states that

> [w]hen recklessness establishes an element of the offense, if the actor, due to self-induced intoxication, is unaware of a risk of which he would have been aware had be been sober, such unawareness is immaterial.[72]

In other words, recklessness, which ordinarily requires consciousness of a substantial and unjustifiable risk,[73] can be established in the absence of such consciousness if the absence is produced by voluntary intoxication.[74]

The Model Penal Code approach to intoxication can be viewed as one in which voluntary intoxication is treated like a culpable but nonpunishable act that enters the actor in a punishment lottery. If he is lucky and does not commit the actus reus of any crime, nothing happens. If, however, he is unlucky and commits the actus reus of some crime, he is punished for whatever crime he happens to commit at the level that he would have been punished had he committed the crime recklessly, including reckless homicide. The approach bears similarities to felony-murder statutes, where the underlying felony can be upgraded to murder if a death occurs even if the mens rea required for murder is otherwise absent.[75]

---

[69] See Wayne R. LaFave and Austin W. Scott, Jr., *Substantive Criminal Law § 4.10* (West, 1986).

[70] See *State v Egelhoff*, 272 Mont 114, 900 P2d 200, 264 (1995).

[71] Model Penal Code § 2.08(1).

[72] Model Penal Code § 2.08(2).

[73] See Model Penal Code § 2.02(2)(c).

[74] If negligence is the mens rea required for the crime, and the question is whether defendant failed to advert to a risk to which the reasonable person would have adverted—see Model Penal Code § 2.02(2)(d)—defendant's voluntary intoxication as the explanation for his not recognizing the risk would establish his inadvertence as unreasonable.

[75] See Kevin Cole, *Killings During Crime: Toward a Discriminating Theory of Strict Liability*, 28 Am Crim L Rev 73 (1990).

The Model Penal Code approach to voluntary intoxication can be contrasted with an alternative that is less lottery-like. A state could make voluntary intoxication itself a crime on the ground that it produces an unreasonable risk of uncontrollable harmful conduct. The seriousness of the crime and the severity of its punishment could be based on the average social harm voluntary intoxication leads to, or they could be based on the greatest social harm for which voluntary intoxication is a substantial and unjustifiable risk. In either case, the punishment for homicide committed by an intoxicated actor unaware of what he was doing would probably be much lower than the standard punishment for reckless homicide. On the other hand, the great majority of intoxicated actors who harm no one would all be criminally punishable at that level.

Montana has taken the Model Penal Code's penal lottery approach to voluntary intoxication, but it has upped the stakes. Now if the actor kills someone while intoxicated and possesses neither the purpose to kill, the knowledge that he is killing, nor even an awareness that he is risking death, he can be convicted of a crime that is the equivalent of intentional homicide.

We might appreciate the draconian nature of Montana's approach by contrasting the culpability of two Dr. Jekylls. The first Dr. Jekyll realizes that whenever he drinks the potion, he becomes the maniacal, homicidal, and morally nonculpable (because nonresponsible) Mr. Hyde. If after that realization Dr. Jekyll again drinks the potion, *he*, if not "Mr. Hyde," is surely as culpable as an ordinary murderer.

The second Dr. Jekyll is aware that there is a finite but very tiny risk that if he drinks the potion, he will become Mr. Hyde. The far greater probability is that he will do nothing of note, or perhaps turn into a less destructive Mr. Hyde. If he is culpable at all for drinking the potion—which we shall assume is a legal substance whose consumption is widespread, of longstanding, and pleasurable—his culpability is surely *not* that of an ordinary murderer.

Montana treats the voluntarily intoxicated defendants who kill as if they were the first Dr. Jekyll. And the Justices of the Supreme Court appeared to have no difficulty, at least as a constitutional matter, with either the lottery nature of Montana's approach or the severity of the consequences that befall the losers in such a lottery, as Egelhoff himself could well have been.

If *Egelhoff* is a preview of what the Court will find to be the constitutionally required components of the states' criminal laws, we should expect then that the Constitution will turn out to be rather toothless in this area, and that the states will be able to define crimes and set punishments pretty much as they want. That is an unsurprising outcome given the Court's prior efforts under the Due Process Clause(s) and Cruel and Unusual Punishments Clause with respect to limitations on the definitions of crimes and the severity of punishments.[76] If the *Mullaney/Patterson* tandem are

---

[76] There are three principal lines of Supreme Court decisions suggesting the development of federal constitutional restrictions on the states' definitions of crimes. One line consists of but one case—*Robinson v California*, 370 US 660 (1962). In *Robinson* the Court held that the Eighth Amendment barred California's making addiction to narcotics a crime. The Court's rationale was that "being" addicted was not a voluntary act, and that the Eighth Amendment required that punishment not be based on a status that could be acquired involuntarily.

Robinson was limited in *Powell v Texas*, 392 US 514 (1968), in which the Court held that the Eighth Amendment did not bar a state's punishing an alcoholic for public drunkenness. The Court reasoned that unless alcoholics were unable to control their actions—a proposition for which it found no evidence—their punishment for public drunkenness was punishment for their voluntary conduct, not punishment for their status as alcoholics. Justice Black in his concurring opinion would have limited *Robinson* to punishment for mere status and would have upheld Powell's conviction even if his conduct was involuntary given his alcoholism.

Finally, in *United States v Moore*, 486 F2d 1139 (DC Cir 1973), the Court of Appeals for the District of Columbia followed *Powell*, not *Robinson*, in upholding the conviction of a narcotics addict for possession of heroin.

The second line also consists of Eighth Amendment cases, this time cases dealing with disproportionality between the culpability manifested by a crime and the punishment the state imposes. The proportionality line of inquiry arguably began with *Weems v United States*, 217 US 349 (1910), was severely restricted in *Rummel v Estelle*, 445 US 263 (1980), and then appeared to blossom again three years later in *Solem v Helm*, 463 US 277 (1983). In *Solem*, the Court confronted a case in which a punishment of life imprisonment was imposed under South Dakota's recidivist sentencing statute on someone convicted of writing a bad check. Although the Court claimed it was not overruling *Rummel* (id at 288 n 13), the test the Court proposed specifically considered the two factors rejected by the *Rummel* Court as being too subjective to be the basis of an Eighth Amendment Claim. According to the *Solem* Court, the proper analysis of an Eighth Amendment claim should consider the sentence imposed on other criminals in the same jurisdiction, as well as the penalties imposed for the commission of the same crime in other jurisdictions. Id at 291–92. The gravity of the offense together with the harshness of the penalty should also form a third leg of the analysis. Id. In its factual analysis, the *Solem* Court distinguished *Rummel* by showing that Rummel, sentenced under the Texas recidivist statute, would be eligible for parole after twelve years, while Helm would only be eligible if he received a grant of clemency from the governor of South Dakota. Id at 297.

Seven years later the Court stepped away from proportionality. In a fractured opinion the Court stated that a mandatory lifetime punishment for a first time offender's possession of 657 grams of cocaine was neither cruel nor unusual. *Harmelin v Michigan*, 501 US 957 (1991). Announcing the decision of the Court, Justice Scalia denied that the Eighth Amendment contained any prohibition on disproportionate punishment at all. Speaking for the plurality, Justice Kennedy agreed that Harmelin's punishment was not violative of the Eighth Amendment, but reached that decision through a reworking of the three-part test

now gone, however, leaving *Winship* applicable only to the constitutionally required minima, then *Egelhoff* suggests that *Winship* will have precious little scope. The majestic constitutional principle of proof beyond a reasonable doubt in criminal cases may turn out to be more like the Wizard of Oz—the little man behind the curtain rather than the awesome projection on the screen.

IX

The task of developing a constitutional law of substantive crimes is a daunting one, whether one views it in terms of constitutional jurisprudence, basic moral principles, or wise public policy. The Supreme Court appeared to embark on that task in *Mullaney*, only to quickly withdraw from it in *Patterson*. In *Egelhoff*, although the matter is uncertain due to its neglect of *Mullaney* and to its typical multiplicity of opinions, the Court once again appears to have taken a step down that road. Whether it will once again abandon the task, or whether it will proceed with it and do it well, is a story as yet untold.

---

that the Court had formally accepted in *Solem*. Claiming to reconcile *Rummel* and *Solem*, Justice Kennedy stated that if the criminal offense committed was serious enough, there was no need to compare the sentence to that imposed for other criminal offenses, or for comparable criminal offenses in other jurisdictions. Id at 1005. These other two comparisons are only relevant if the initial comparison of the seriousness of the crime and the degree of punishment leads to an "inference of gross disproportionality." Id. Because possession of over one and a half pounds of cocaine was a serious offense, there was no need to advance to any other stage of the analysis.

The third line of cases consists of cases decided under—or in the shadow of—the Due Process Clauses. In *Morisette v United States*, 342 US 246 (1952), the Court read an intent requirement into a statute dealing with the taking of government property, intimating that due process would preclude imposition of serious punishment in the absence of mens rea. And in *Lambert v California*, 355 US 225 (1957), the Court held that due process prohibited extension of the principle that ignorance of the law is no excuse to the crime of failing to register as a convicted felon.

The *Morisette/Lambert* line of due process cases never flowered into a full-fledged constitutional jurisprudence of mens rea. Echoes of those cases can still be heard, however, in the Court's interpretation of criminal statutes. For example, in 1985 and again in 1994, the Court read criminal statutes to require knowledge of illegality as an element of the offense. See *Liparota v United States*, 471 US 419 (1985); *Ratzlaff v United States*, 114 S Ct 655 (1994). Although these decisions were based on statutory interpretation rather than directly on the Constitution, it is quite possible that the Court believes there are due process constraints on the definitions of crimes, and that this belief influenced its reading of the statutes.

MARCEL KAHAN AND

LINDA SILBERMAN

MATSUSHITA AND BEYOND:

THE ROLE OF STATE COURTS

IN CLASS ACTIONS INVOLVING

EXCLUSIVE FEDERAL CLAIMS

I. The Matsushita Decision

Toward the start of 1996, two independent developments occurred that profoundly affect the litigation of securities class actions. One was the enactment of the Private Securities Litigation Reform Act in December 1995;[1] the other—two months later—was the Supreme Court's decision in *Matsushita Electric Industrial Co. v Epstein.*[2]

Marcel Kahan and Linda Silberman are Professors of Law, New York University School of Law.

Authors' note: Our thanks to Stephen Burbank, John Coates, Ed Cooper, Rochelle Dreyfuss, Fred Dunbar, Eleanor Fox, Ronald Gilson, Victor Goldberg, Helen Hershkoff, Reinier Kraakman, Andreas Lowenfeld, Larry Kramer, Geoffrey Miller, Alan Morrison, Judith Resnik, Roberta Romano, Helen Scott, David Shapiro, and the participants at the George Washington Law Center faculty workshop for their helpful comments. A special debt of gratitude to Stephen Burbank and Ronald Gilson, who carefully reviewed the article and provided extensive comments, and to Chancellor William Allen and Judge Edward Becker, who offered us the benefit of their practical experience. Counsel for both sides provided us with briefs, documents, and background information from the *Matsushita* litigation and shared their views of the case with us. Steven Cottreau, a second-year student at NYU, provided valuable research assistance and became in effect a third collaborator. The Filomen D'Agostino and Max E. Greenberg Research Fund provided generous financial support.

[1] Pub L No 104-67, 109 Stat 737, codified in scattered sections of 15 USC.

[2] 116 S Ct 873 (1996).

© 1997 by The University of Chicago. All rights reserved.
0-226-36313-9/97/1996-0009$02.00

The Act represented the temporary resolution of a bitter debate over the role of securities class litigation.[3] While securities class litigation has been recognized as an important private enforcement device, class lawyers have been accused of bringing nonmeritorious claims in order to extort a settlement and of selling out meritorious claims for low settlements and high attorneys' fees. The Private Securities Litigation Reform Act was an attempt to remedy these perceived abuses.[4] The Act contains a number of provisions making it more difficult for plaintiffs' lawyers to bring securities class actions.[5] Most importantly for our purposes, the Act creates a presumption that the class member with the greatest financial stake in a securities class action be appointed "lead plaintiff"[6] and gives the lead plaintiff the right to select class counsel.[7]

---

[3] For press accounts discussing the need for reform, see, for example, Ed McCracken, *The New Threat to High-Tech Firms*, San Francisco Chronicle A19 (June 28, 1995); George F. McGunnigle and Michael J. Wurzer, *Reform Needed to Limit Securities Fraud Suits*, Minneapolis Star Tribune 3D (Apr 24, 1995); Andrew E. Serwer, *What to Do about Legal Blackmail*, Fortune 136 (Nov 15, 1993); *Shareholder Suits: Class Acts*, The Economist 95 (Mar 19, 1994, US ed). Other accounts, however, cautioned against reform. See Penni Crabtree, *Look Out, Little Guy: Demons Abound in Battle over Shareholder Suits*, San Diego Union-Tribune I-1 (Oct 29, 1995); Frank Lalli, *Congress Aims at Lawyers and Ends up Shooting Small Investors in the Back*, Money 9 (Sept 1995); Gene Marlowe, *Securities Fraud Victims out of Luck?* Tampa Tribune 1 (Aug 6, 1995); Anne Kates Smith, *Some Call It Securities Reform*, US News & World Report 117 (Nov 13, 1995).

[4] See Private Securities Litigation Reform Act of 1995, S Rep No 104-98, 104th Cong, 1st Sess (1995); Securities Litigation Reform, HR Rep No 104-369, 104th Cong, 1st Sess (1995).

[5] The Private Securities Litigation Reform Act amended the Securities Act and the Securities Exchange Act by raising the pleading burden for fraud (Pub L No 104-67 at sec 101(b) § 21D(b)), imposing mandatory sanctions for frivolous pleadings and motions (id at sec 101(a) § 27(c); id at sec 101(b) § 21D(c)), creating a "safe-harbor" from securities fraud liability for certain projections and forecasts (id at sec 102), and cutting back on joint and several liability for violations of the securities laws (id at sec 201). The state of affairs that these provisions seek to remedy has been characterized as one where actions are brought by "figurehead plaintiffs who are essentially hired by class action lawyers." *In re California Micro Devices Securities Litig.*, 1996 US Dist LEXIS 1361, *31 (ND Cal).

[6] "Lead plaintiff" is a term used by the Act to refer to the class member that is the most adequate plaintiff under the criteria established by the Act and that is entitled to select class counsel. See, for example, id at sec 110(a) § 27(a)(3)(B)(i) ("the court . . . shall appoint as lead plaintiff the member or members of the purported plaintiff class that the court determines to be most capable of adequately representing the interests of class members").

[7] Id at sec 101(a) § 27(a)(3); id at sec 101(b) § 21D(a)(3). There are some initial indications that the lead plaintiff provisions of the Act are effective. See, for example, Karen Donovan, *New Securities Law May Squeeze Out Milberg Weiss*, Natl L J A7 (Aug 12, 1996) (discussing *Gluck v Cellstar Corp.*, a federal securities action, and attempt by Wisconsin Investment Board, holder of 1.6 million shares, to be appointed lead plaintiff). But see *Greebel v FTP Software, Inc.*, 1996 US Dist LEXIS 13510, *24 (D Mass) (appointing moving parties as lead plaintiff as no other persons have sought such appointment and approving appointment of Milberg, Weiss as lead counsel). Indeed, the Act may have also influenced state practice

The Supreme Court's holding in *Matsushita*—that state court class action settlements can release exclusive federal claims—has the potential to undermine some of these reforms. As we will show, the ability to settle exclusive federal claims in state courts may exacerbate the very conflicts of interests between class lawyers and class members that the lead plaintiff provision of the Private Securities Litigation Reform Act was designed to reduce.

The *Matsushita* case grew out of the 1990 acquisition of MCA, Inc., a Delaware corporation, by Matsushita. State plaintiffs filed a shareholder class action against MCA and its directors in Delaware Chancery Court on September 26, 1990, one day after the announcement that MCA and Matsushita were negotiating a possible acquisition.[8] They alleged that MCA and its directors had breached their fiduciary duties to MCA shareholders in failing to maximize shareholder value.[9] Matsushita was not named as a defendant in the initial complaint.[10]

With the state claims pending, MCA and Matsushita proceeded to negotiate the terms and structure of MCA's acquisition. On November 26, Matsushita commenced a tender offer for MCA stock, offering MCA shareholders $66 in cash and $5 worth of stock in WWOR-TV per share of MCA stock.[11] Lew Wasserman, MCA's chairman and CEO and owner of about 5 million shares (approxi-

---

regarding derivative suits. See Bill Alden, *Intervenors Given Role in Derivative Suit*, NY L J 1 (Sept 11, 1996) (describing addition of CalPERS as co-counsel in New York state derivative action after CalPERS successfully argued that previous settlement agreement negotiated by individual investors was inadequate).

[8] 116 S Ct at 885.

[9] Id at 876. To succeed on such a claim, plaintiff would have to show either (i) that MCA's directors failed to take steps reasonably designed to maximize the price at which MCA would be acquired, for example, by exclusively dealing with Matsushita without a basis for concluding that no other party would be willing to pay more for MCA (see, for example, *Revlon, Inc. v MacAndrews & Forbes Holdings, Inc.*, 506 A2d 173 (Del 1986)), or (ii) that the directors were "grossly negligent" in determining that the price Matsushita was willing to pay was a beneficial price (see, for example, *Smith v Van Gorkom*, 488 A2d 858 (Del 1985)). Obviously, any such claims were premature at the time they were brought since MCA had just started negotiations. Even at the time negotiations had been concluded, the claims were highly unlikely to succeed. As to the first showing, no second party interested in acquiring MCA ever came forward—a fact that usually dooms claims under *Revlon*. As to the second showing, the negotiations lasted two months; and even once a merger agreement was entered into, MCA preserved its right to accept a higher offer should one be made before the merger was consummated. The length of the negotiations and the presence of the market check made it extremely unlikely that a court would find that the directors were "grossly negligent."

[10] 116 S Ct at 876.

[11] See *Epstein v MCA, Inc.*, 50 F3d 644, 647 (9th Cir 1995).

mately 5%) of MCA's stock, did not participate in the tender offer.[12] Instead, on the morning of November 26, he and Matsushita agreed to exchange his shares of MCA for preferred stock in a Matsushita subsidiary.[13] Whether Wasserman and Matsushita were obligated to perform this exchange and how many shares of preferred stock Wasserman would receive depended on whether Matsushita's public tender offer was successful and whether Matsushita raised the tender offer price.[14] The transaction with Wasserman was designed to help him avoid the payment of capital gains tax on his shares. (Wasserman's basis in the MCA shares was 3 cents per share and his capital gains would have been about $350 million.)[15]

On December 3, 1990, a second set of plaintiffs (the Epstein plaintiffs) filed suit in federal court in California against Matsushita and certain other defendants.[16] The Epstein plaintiffs alleged violations of the Securities Exchange Act of 1934—claims over which the federal courts have exclusive jurisdiction—and sought class certification. The thrust of the federal claims was that Matsushita had given Wasserman preferential treatment in its tender offer for MCA stock contrary to the SEC's "all-holder best-price" rule.[17] If successful, these claims would expose Matsushita to po-

---

[12] Id.

[13] Id at 653.

[14] Id.

[15] Id at 647.

[16] 116 S Ct at 885.

[17] Id at 885–86. Rule 14d-10(a)(2) requires that "the consideration paid to any security holder pursuant to the tender offer is the highest consideration paid to any security holder during such tender offer"; Rule 14(d)-10(c) provides that the previous section does "not prohibit" the payment of more than one type of consideration "provided that security holders are afforded equal rights to elect . . . . "

The Epstein plaintiffs also asserted that Matsushita gave preferential treatment to Sheinberg, MCA's chief operating officer. Sheinberg tendered his shares in the public tender offer, but also received $21 million in cash. Plaintiffs claimed that cash payment was part of the consideration for his shares, while defendants claimed it was given in exchange for unexercised MCA stock options. See *Epstein v MCA, Inc.*, 50 F3d 644, 657 (9th Cir 1995).

The main issues with respect to the federal claims were (i) whether there was a private right of action (with two circuits having found one to exist); (ii) whether the consideration paid to Wasserman was paid during the tender offer, and whether the $21 million paid to Sheinberg was paid for the tendered shares; and (iii) whether the consideration paid to Wasserman was higher than the consideration paid to public shareholders or, in any case, whether the mere failure to permit the public shareholders to elect such consideration violated Rule 14d-10.

tentially staggering liability in the several hundred million dollars range.[18]

Eight days after the federal claims were filed, on December 11, 1990, the parties in the Delaware action announced a settlement in principle which released all federal and state claims arising out of the tender offer, provided for a modification of a "poison pill" in the corporate charter of an MCA subsidiary to be spun off to MCA shareholders, and granted the state class counsel $1 million in attorneys' fees.[19] With the settlement terms negotiated, the state plaintiffs, on December 14, 1990,[20] amended their complaint by alleging that the preferential treatment of Wasserman created a conflict of interest that had not been properly disclosed and adding Matsushita as a defendant for aiding and abetting the breach of fiduciary duty involved in the preferential treatment of Wasserman.[21]

On April 22, 1991, the Delaware Chancery Court rejected the settlement. Though the court characterized the state-law claims as "at best extremely weak," it found that the federal claims had "substantial merit."[22] The proposed settlement, however, offered only "illusionary" value to class members and conveyed "no real monetary benefit," whereas the proposed attorneys' fees amounted to a "generous payment."[23] Despite these hints as to the Chancery

---

[18] We are not aware of any reported decision on the proper measure of damages for violations of Rule 14d-10. One possible measure of damages would be the value of the preferential treatment to Wasserman, who avoided payment of $20 capital gains tax (at a 28% rate) per share of MCA stock. At $20 a share, damages to MCA shareholders would amount to $1.7 billion. Alternatively, damages could be measured by the additional value MCA shareholders would have received had they been given the opportunity to receive preferred stock (and not pay capital gains tax) rather than cash (and pay capital gains tax). In this case, damages would be substantially lower than $1.7 billion (since most MCA share-holders presumably had a higher basis in MCA shares than did Wasserman and would thus have benefited less by avoiding capital gains tax). But even assuming that the average basis in MCA stock was $34 (MCA's September share price before negotiations with Matsushita were announced) and average capital gains tax thus $10 per share, damages would exceed $700 million.

[19] *Epstein v MCA, Inc.*, 50 F3d at 660.

[20] The chronology supports the contention of the federal plaintiffs that the second state complaint was written for settlement purposes. See Brief for Respondants at 4, *Matsushita Elec. Indus. Co. v Epstein*, 116 S Ct 873 (1996).

[21] *In re MCA, Inc. Shareholders Litig.*, 598 A2d 687, 690 (Del Ch 1991).

[22] Id at 694, 696.

[23] Id at 695–96.

Court's view of the state claims, defendants did not seek to have these claims dismissed. Nor was there any other litigation activity in the state court for the next eighteen months.[24]

In the federal action, the district court, after rejecting the Epstein plaintiffs' motions for class certification and summary judgment, granted summary judgment in favor of Matsushita and the other defendants on February 10, 1992.[25] The Epstein plaintiffs appealed to the Ninth Circuit.

In October 1992, while the dismissal of the federal claims was on appeal, a second settlement agreement was submitted to the Delaware Chancery Court. The settlement called for a $2 million fund that would afford MCA's shareholders 2 to 3 cents per share in exchange for release of all federal and state claims and provided for an opt-out for class members who wanted to reject the settlement.[26] A fairness hearing was held in January 1993.[27] On February 16, 1993, the Chancery Court approved the settlement as being in the best interest of the class. Though the recovery provided to class members was "meager," the federal claims—having been dismissed by the federal district court—now had "minimal economic value" and the state claims remained "extremely weak."[28] Responding to several objectors to the settlement, the court ruled that there was "no evidence of any collusion" even though "suspicions abound."[29] (The Epstein plaintiffs did not object or opt out in the Delaware proceeding.) The court also reduced counsel fees from the requested $691,000 to $250,000.[30] The Delaware Supreme Court affirmed the Chancery Court's ruling in September 1993.[31]

Following the Delaware settlement, proceedings in the dismissed federal securities case reached the Ninth Circuit.[32] There,

---

[24] *Epstein v MCA, Inc.*, 50 F3d at 660.

[25] *In re MCA, Inc. Shareholders Litig.*, 1993 WL 43024, *2 (Del Ch), reprinted in 18 Del J Corp L 1053, 1059, aff'd, 633 A2d 370 (Del 1993).

[26] 116 S Ct at 886.

[27] 598 A2d at 692.

[28] 1993 WL 43024 at *1, *4.

[29] Id at *5.

[30] Id at *5–6.

[31] 633 A2d 370.

[32] The appeal was argued on August 2, 1993. It was reargued on October 12, 1993.

in addition to pressing for an affirmance on the merits, Matsushita argued that the Delaware settlement barred litigation of claims by all shareholders who had failed to opt out of the Delaware class settlement.[33] The court of appeals first found that the Epstein plaintiffs had asserted valid Exchange Act claims and were entitled to summary judgment on the issue of liability.[34] It also instructed the district court to certify the case as a class action, finding that the suit fit the requirements of Rule 23 "like a glove."[35] On the preclusion point, the court held that a state settlement could release exclusive federal claims only if the claims rested on an "identical factual predicate," where issue preclusion could operate as a bar if the state case were litigated.[36] In the case at bar, the state and federal claims turned on different facts (though they arose from the same transaction). The court therefore ruled that the Delaware settlement did not bar the federal claims.[37]

The Supreme Court reversed the Ninth Circuit on the preclusive effect of a state court settlement encompassing exclusive federal claims.[38] Relying on the Court's earlier decision in *Marrese v*

[33] *Epstein v MCA, Inc.*, 50 F3d at 659. Certain plaintiffs did opt out, and their claims were obviously not barred by the Delaware release. See id at 659 n 22. Of course, it may not be worthwhile for these few individual plaintiffs to proceed with the federal litigation. See, for example, *De Angelis v Salton/Maxim Housewares, Inc.*, 641 A2d 834, 839–40 (Del Ch 1993) (recognizing that litigation by members who opt out may be "uneconomically feasible"), rev'd on other grounds, *Prezant v De Angelis*, 636 A2d 915 (Del 1994).

[34] 50 F3d at 648. Summary judgment on liability was granted with respect to the claim that Wasserman's treatment violated Rule 14d-10 and the case was remanded for the determination of damages. As to the treatment of Sheinberg, the Court of Appeals remanded to the district court for determination of the purpose of the $21 million fee.

[35] Id at 668. The Court also described the performance of the Epstein plaintiffs and their counsel in pursuing this litigation as "exemplary." Id at 669.

[36] Id at 664–65.

[37] Id at 665–66. State court global settlements encompassing exclusive federal claims can result from two situations. First, the same alleged wrongdoing by the defendant might be the basis of the state and the federal claim. For example, a materially false statement in a proxy statement would give rise to an exclusive federal claim (for violation of Rule 14d-9) and to a state law claim (for breach of the duty of candor). In such cases, the Ninth Circuit test would presumably permit a state court to release exclusive federal claims in a global settlement. Second, the state and the federal claims might be based on different alleged wrongdoings (as in *Matsushita*, where the federal claim was based on an alleged violation of the "all-holder best-price" rule and the initial state claim was for breach of fiduciary duties based on different activities). In such cases, the Ninth Circuit test would ordinarily not permit a state court to release exclusive federal claims in a global settlement.

[38] This continued a trend of having state law dictate federal preclusion doctrine. See, for example, *Allen v McCurry*, 449 US 90 (1980); *Kremer v Chemical Constr. Corp.*, 456 US 461 (1982); *Migra v Warren City School Dist. Bd. of Educ.*, 465 US 75 (1984); *Marrese v American Academy of Orthopaedic Surgeons*, 470 US 373 (1985). These cases interpret 28 USC § 1738 (the Full Faith and Credit statute) as requiring a federal court adjudicating a matter of

American Academy of Orthopaedic Surgeons,[39] Justice Thomas, in an opinion unanimous on this point, wrote that the Full Faith and Credit statute (28 USC § 1738) applied to class actions (just as to individual actions) and to settlements (just as to litigated actions). As the product of a "judicial proceeding" within the meaning of 28 USC § 1738, a state class action settlement is entitled to the same effect that it would have under the law of that state.

What effect that might be is not always clear. As the Supreme Court itself pointed out in *Marrese,* "a state court will not have occasion to address the specific question whether a state judgment has issue or claim preclusive effect in a later action that can be brought only in federal court."[40] In *Matsushita,* however, the Court concluded that under Delaware law, state courts have power to approve a global settlement that encompassed exclusive federal claims[41] (even though it appears that the Delaware courts have

---

federal substantive law to apply the preclusion law of the state whose judgment is claimed to have preclusive effect. That approach has been criticized by Professor Stephen Burbank, who argues that Section 1738 requires the application of the law that would be applicable in the rendering state, which might well be federal preclusion law. See Stephen B. Burbank, *Interjurisdictional Preclusion: Full Faith and Credit and Federal Common Law: A General Approach,* 71 Cornell L Rev 733, 797–816 (1986).

[39] 470 US 373 (1985).

[40] 470 US at 381–82. On remand, the district court in *Marrese* characterized its task of ascertaining state law on the question as "nearly metaphysical" and an "exercise in extrapolation." 628 F Supp 918, 919 (ND Ill 1986). Professor Burbank is particularly critical of the Supreme Court's approach to Section 1738 in the context of exclusive federal claims. See Burbank, 71 Cornell L Rev at 822–29 (cited in note 38).

[41] See, for example, *Nottingham Partners v Dana,* 564 A2d 1089 (Del 1989) (asserting that a state has power through a non-opt-out class action settlement to release individual shareholder's claim within federal court's exclusive jurisdiction).

In explaining the scope of its settlement power, the Delaware Supreme Court in *Nottingham* opined that a state settlement could release exclusively federal claims so long as the state and federal actions "arose under the same set of operative facts." Id at 1107. The Delaware Supreme Court relied on *TBK Partners, Ltd. v Western Union Corp.,* 675 F2d 456, 461–62 (2d Cir 1982), an early case which upheld the power of a federal court to settle a class action releasing *state* appraisal claims (previously dismissed without prejudice in New York state court) where the released claims were said to be based on the "identical factual predicate as that underlying the claims in the settled class action."

Extending this holding to reach exclusive federal claims in *Nottingham,* the Delaware Supreme Court observed that it was simply ratifying a practice already adopted by the Delaware Chancery Courts, citing to *Shingala v Becor Western, Inc.,* 1988 WL 7390 (Del Ch), reprinted in 13 Del J Corp L 1232 (Delaware class action settlement releasing later-filed federal action alleging state and exclusive federal claims); and *Tabas v Crosby,* 1982 WL 17835 (Del Ch) (Delaware court approving settlement in derivative and class action that contained general release despite pending derivative action in state court and unspecified claim in federal court and permitting individual plaintiffs in the other actions to opt out), aff'd sub nom *Geller v Tabas,* 462 A2d 1078 (Del 1983).

never focused on the problems of state settlements that release exclusive federal claims pending as a federal class action).[42]

The Court thus ruled that the exclusive jurisdiction provisions of the Securities Exchange Act did not operate as a partial repeal of 28 USC § 1738[43] or evidence of an intent to contravene the common-law rules of preclusion. The Court drew a distinction between the jurisdictional provisions of the Exchange Act, which provide for exclusive jurisdiction to "enforce" rights or obligations under the Act, and approval of a settlement which merely "released" those rights in the exercise of the state's judicial power over state claims.[44]

Justice Ginsburg, joined by Justice Stevens, dissented on the issue of Delaware law, arguing that the content of Delaware preclusion law was for the Ninth Circuit on remand and not for the Supreme Court to decide.[45] The dissenters (joined on this point

---

[42] The problem of releasing exclusive federal class action claims is that even when an opt-out right is afforded in the state class action, it is unlikely to produce a viable federal class. Thus federal class action for these exclusively federal claims is, as a practical matter, destroyed. When the released federal claim is an individual one, an opt-out right in the state action protects the ability of the opt-out plaintiff to pursue the claim. Delaware courts, however, have also approved settlements releasing exclusive federal claims for monetary damages *without* affording opt-out rights, thus precluding individual claims. See, for example, *Nottingham Partners v Trans-Lux Corp.*, 564 A2d 1089 (Del 1989) (non-opt-out state settlement released individual securities claim action pending in federal court) (for the application of this settlement as a bar to later-asserted exclusive federal claims, see *Nottingham Partners v Trans-Lux Corp.*, 925 F2d 29 (1st Cir 1991)); and *In re Vitalink Communications Corp. Shareholders Litig.*, 1991 WL 238816 (Del Ch) (approving non-opt-out state settlement that released unasserted federal claims), aff'd sub nom *Grimes v John P. McCarthy Profit Sharing Plan*, 610 A2d 725 (Del 1992) (for the application of this settlement as a bar to later-asserted exclusive federal claims, see *Grimes v Vitalink Communication Corp.*, 17 F3d 1553 (3d Cir 1994)).

[43] The "implied repeal" argument has been made and rejected in numerous cases. See, for example, *Allen v McCurry*, 449 US 90 (1980); *Migra v Warren City School Dist. Bd. of Educ.*, 465 US 75 (1984).

[44] *Matsushita Elec. Indus. Co. v Epstein*, 116 S Ct 873, 881–82 (1996). Another explanation for the Court's conclusion that exclusive federal claims can be settled even if they can't be litigated is that a settlement, as a kind of contract, can cover claims over which the court has no jurisdiction. When approved by a court, a settlement acquires the force of a binding judgment. As in other class action contexts, nonparticipating members of the class are bound by a judgment if due process requirements such as the adequacy of notice, the opportunity to opt out, and the adequacy of representation are satisfied in the proceedings leading up to the settlement and its final approval. See Richard H. Fallon, Daniel J. Meltzer, and David L. Shapiro, *Hart & Wechsler's The Federal Courts and the Federal System* (Foundation, 4th ed), 1996 Supp at 74–75.

[45] Id at 887–88. As Justice Ginsburg points out, the majority may have overestimated the breadth of Delaware preclusion law. See id at 888 n 4 (observing that "the Court appears to have blended the 'identical factual predicate' test applied by the Delaware Supreme Court in *Nottingham Partners v Dana* with the broader 'same transaction' test advanced by Matsushita" (citation omitted)). The *Nottingham* opinion is difficult to decipher on this point.

by Justice Souter) also maintained that the Ninth Circuit remained free to consider the due process issue of whether the Delaware courts fully and fairly litigated the adequacy of class representation.[46]

Both *Marrese* and *Matsushita* can be criticized for undermining the "exclusivity" policies of federal jurisdiction by allowing state law to determine the preclusive effect of state court litigation and settlement of claims within the federal courts' exclusive jurisdiction.[47] However, the impact of *Marrese* is mitigated by state preclusion law's recognition of a "prior jurisdictional competency" standard; under that standard, state preclusion law does not purport to bar a later-filed federal court claim over which the state court did not have jurisdiction.[48] In *Marrese*, the Supreme Court left

---

Most of the textual references to the scope of preclusion accorded to settlement releases refer to "identical operative factual predicate," "same factual predicate," or "same set of operative facts." See 564 A2d at 1105–07. The Delaware Supreme Court, however, left room for doubts in two footnotes. In the first, the court, citing a case in support of approving general releases, noted that the released litigation was based on the "same transaction." Id at 1105 n 35. Later, the court supported its conclusion that the released claims "arose under the same set of operative facts" by citing to the settlement hearing transcript in which the counsel for the objectors admitted that the claims were based on the "same transaction." Id at 1107 n 37. The court may have failed to fully understand the import of its language on this matter. See note 37 for the differing results produced by the two formulations. Or the Delaware court may have consciously adopted the "identical factual predicate" language in the belief that the Second Circuit in *TBK Partners* had set forth a federal test for when federal claims that were part of a state court's general release would be precluded. See note 41.

Interestingly, although the Supreme Court in *Matsushita* quotes language from the Delaware Chancery opinion approving the *MCA* settlement which refers to a release of claims "which arise out of the challenged transaction," it does not expressly delineate what limits there are on a state court release for preclusion to attach. Looking to state law under Section 1738, preclusion would not normally attach to a claim that did not, at minimum, meet a "transactional" nexus. As for Delaware law in particular on the scope of a release, confusion abounds in the rulings following *Nottingham*. See *In re Union Square Associates Securities Litig.*, 1993 WL 220528, *3–5 (Del Ch) (citing *Nottingham* and Second Circuit cases and then holding that "same factual predicate" test was met by factual finding that the "claim arises (at least partially) out of the same transaction").

[46] 116 S Ct at 888–90. Justice Thomas's majority opinion did not address the due process claim, observing in a footnote that "[w]e need not address the due process claim, however, because it is outside the scope of the question presented in this Court. While it is true that a respondent may defend a judgment on alternative grounds, we generally do not address arguments that were not the basis for the decision below." 116 S Ct at 880 n 5 (citation omitted).

In the same footnote, Justice Thomas also made the following observation about the due process contention, possibly suggesting his predisposition on the issue: "Respondents make this claim in spite of the Chancery Court's express ruling, following argument on the issue, that the class representatives fairly and adequately protected the interests of the class." Id.

[47] See Burbank, 71 Cornell L Rev at 797–816 (cited in note 38).

[48] 470 US at 382, citing Restatement (Second) of Judgments § 26(1)(c) (1982).

open the possibility that a grant of exclusive jurisdiction to federal courts could justify an exception to Section 1738 if state preclusion law did *not* incorporate such a prior jurisdictional competency standard.[49] Since *Marrese*, this "prior competency" standard appears to operate in most state courts as a limit on the preclusive effect of their judgments.

The "prior jurisdictional competency" standard in litigated cases serves to accommodate federal interests: because an exclusive federal claim could not be brought as part of a state proceeding, the interest in finality is outweighed by the federal interest in having such a claim proceed in federal court. Similar accommodation may occur in determining whether factual findings by state courts are entitled to preclusive effect in federal litigation of exclusive federal claims.[50] Section 86 of the Restatement of Judgments 2d indicates that determination of an issue by a state court will usually preclude relitigation of that issue in federal court, unless preclusion is "incompatible with a scheme of federal remedies which contemplates that the federal court may make an independent determination of the issue in question."[51] The Restatement Comments suggest that relitigation may be appropriate where the determination of the federal issue depends on a legal frame of reference which involves federal law.[52]

A prior jurisdictional competency requirement in the settlement

---

[49] "Only if state law indicates that a particular claim or issue would be barred, is it necessary to determine if an exception to § 1738 should apply." 470 US at 386. Compare *Kremer v Chemical Constr. Corp.*, 456 US 461 (1982) (finding no exception to Section 1738 in Title VII) with *Brown v Felsen*, 442 US 127 (1979) (making no reference to Section 1738 and finding congressional intent that state judgments should not have claim preclusive effect on dischargeability issue in bankruptcy).

[50] See, for example, *Becher v Contoure Labs., Inc.*, 279 US 388 (1929). See also Restatement (Second) of Judgments § 86(2) (1982).

[51] See Restatement (Second) of Judgments § 86(2) (1982). This distinction is made more concrete by illustrations in the Restatement Comments: A finding in a state contract action, P v D, that D's agent made certain statements would bind D in a subsequent federal antitrust action between the parties. But a determination in D's favor that the contract was not part of a scheme to violate the federal antitrust laws might not be given preclusive effect. (The issue arises because state courts, although without jurisdiction over antitrust claims, do have jurisdiction to hear a defense based on the antitrust laws.)

[52] Arbitration of exclusive federal claims has also been upheld by the Supreme Court. See, for example, *Shearson/Am. Exp., Inc. v McMahon*, 482 US 220 (1987) (permitting arbitration of Securities Exchange Act claims); *Mitsubishi Motors Corp. v Soler Chrysler-Plymouth, Inc.*, 473 US 614 (1985) (permitting arbitration of exclusive federal antitrust claims in Japan under Swiss law). Arbitration awards which turn out to violate public policy, however, may not be enforced. See id.

context would be inconsistent with *Matsushita:* such a requirement would prevent state courts from releasing exclusive federal claims as part of a global class settlement.[53] Yet some mechanism is necessary to protect federal interests in the global settlement context. By permitting state courts to approve global settlements, the Supreme Court in *Matsushita* decided, in our view correctly, to enable states to settle exclusive federal claims. Missing at this stage, however, is a mechanism for accommodating the federal interests connected to the Congressional grant of exclusive jurisdiction to federal courts[54] and, perhaps more significantly, to Congress's recent judgment—in the Private Securities Litigation Reform Act—that the class member with the largest financial stake should be presumptively entitled to act as class representative and to appoint class counsel in federal securities actions.[55]

Two possibilities exist. State courts themselves can supply this missing element by taking account of federal interests in their own settlement structures. Alternatively, an independent federal check may operate by way of a federal collateral attack, as suggested in Justice Ginsburg's opinion. Whether, on the facts of *Matsushita,* the Delaware court made a sufficient inquiry into the adequacy of representation, and whether an affirmative finding by the state court is binding on the federal court,[56] are issues now before the Ninth Circuit on remand.

The remainder of the paper explores these two options in greater detail. Part II presents an analysis of the problems and benefits of state court global settlements encompassing exclusive fed-

---

[53] The Epstein plaintiffs conceded that, outside the class action context, jurisdictional allocations would not impede a state court settlement that released both state and exclusive federal claims. They argued, however, that the jurisdictional limitations should play a more significant role with respect to settlements in the class context. Brief for Petitioner at 67–71, *Matsushita Elec. Indus. Co. v Epstein,* 116 S Ct 873 (1996).

[54] In light of the grant of concurrent jurisdiction to federal and state courts over claims under the Securities Act of 1933, one may wonder about the rationale for exclusive jurisdiction by federal courts over claims under the Securities Exchange Act of 1934. See *Murphy v Gallagher,* 761 F2d 878 (2d Cir 1985). Of course, if exclusive jurisdiction under the Securities Exchange Act does not make sense here, it is for Congress to change it.

[55] The provisions dealing with the appointment of class counsel are found at Pub L No 104–67 at sec 101(a) (appending § 27(a)(3) to Title I of the Securities Act of 1933 (15 USC § 77a et seq)) and sec 101(b) (adding § 21D(a)(3) to the Securities Exchange Act of 1934 (15 USC § 78a et seq)). For a discussion of these provisions, see text accompanying notes 75–79.

[56] For a discussion of these issues, see text accompanying notes 141 to 191.

eral claims. Part III offers a prescription for how state courts can balance these deficiencies and benefits in determining the scope of their settlements. Part IV examines, in general and specifically with respect to the *Matsushita* remand, when collateral attack on state court settlements should be permitted. Part V discusses the implications of our proposal for other types of class action settlements.

II. AN ANALYSIS OF STATE COURT GLOBAL SETTLEMENTS ENCOMPASSING EXCLUSIVE FEDERAL CLAIMS

Now that *Matsushita* requires that preclusive effect be given to state court settlements that release exclusive federal claims and allows states broad latitude in defining the scope of such settlements, state courts should take special care in structuring global settlements. State court class action settlements of exclusive federal claims raise issues of fairness and process that go beyond the concerns present in ordinary class action settlements; in addition, such settlements affect federal interests in the proper handling of federal claims subject to the exclusive jurisdiction of federal courts. We first briefly review the process concerns with respect to ordinary class action settlements. We then address state court settlements encompassing exclusive federal claims.

A. CLASS ACTION SETTLEMENTS IN GENERAL

Even ordinary class action settlements can be disconcerting from a process perspective.[57] The rights of absent members of the class

---

[57] The benefits of the class action have been extolled elsewhere. See, for example, Kenneth W. Dam, *Class Actions: Efficiency, Compensation, Deterrence, and Conflict of Interest*, 4 J Legal Stud 47 (1975); Harry Kalven, Jr. and Maurice Rosenfield, *The Contemporary Function of the Class Suit*, 8 U Chi L Rev 684 (1941). In short, by consolidating the claims of similarly situated parties in one proceeding, they can result in reduced litigation expenditures and help avoid inconsistent verdicts. The concerns resulting from the fact that class attorneys, rather than the class members, control the litigation are alleviated through a variety of mechanisms: controlling the types of cases that may be brought as class actions, ensuring adequate representation, and providing class members with rights to receive notice and, in claims for monetary damages, to opt out of the class. See Arthur R. Miller, *Of Frankenstein Monsters and Shining Knights: Myth, Reality, and the "Class Action Problem,"* 92 Harv L Rev 664 (1979). Nonetheless, criticisms of class actions have been legion. See, for example, Samuel Estreicher, *Federal Class Actions After 30 Years*, 71 NYU L Rev 1, 3 (1996) (summarizing contemporary criticisms of class actions). See generally Herbert B. Newberg and Alba Conte, *Newberg on Class Actions* [hereinafter Newberg, *Class Actions*] § 5 (3d ed 1992) (describing benefits and drawbacks of class actions).

may be compromised without their consent by agents whom they have not selected. The class action attorney—not the class members whose rights are at stake—makes all important decisions: whether to file a claim, how much time and effort to invest in pursuing it, what litigation strategy to employ, and finally whether and on what terms to settle.[58] This discrepancy in power and information creates the danger that unscrupulous class counsel will settle a class claim for a generous attorney fee, but a paltry recovery to class members.[59]

These process deficiencies require an enhanced role for the court in ensuring that the class representatives, and the class attorney, adequately represent the class, and that any settlement is fair to all class members. Specifically, class action settlements trigger special procedural safeguards not present in ordinary litigation. The court must approve all settlements of class actions,[60] and a practice has evolved of holding "fairness hearings" on the propriety of proposed settlements. In these hearings, courts make an independent evaluation of the fairness of the settlement to class members, including an assessment of the relationship between the

[58] See John C. Coffee, Jr., *Understanding the Plaintiff's Attorney: The Implications of Economic Theory for Private Enforcement of Law Through Class and Derivative Actions*, 86 Colum L Rev 669 (1986); Jonathan R. Macey and Geoffrey P. Miller, *The Plaintiffs' Attorney's Role in Class Action and Derivative Litigation: Economic Analysis and Recommendations for Reform*, 58 U Chi L Rev 1 (1991). For a discussion of ethical problems facing class action attorneys, see Nancy Morawetz, *Bargaining, Class Representation and Fairness*, 54 Ohio St L J 1 (1993).

[59] See *Mars Steel Corp. v Continental Ill. Nat'l Bank & Trust*, 834 F2d 677, 681–82 (7th Cir 1987) (Posner, J) ("Ordinarily the named plaintiffs are nominees, indeed pawns, of the lawyer, and ordinarily the unnamed class members have individually too little stake to spend time monitoring the lawyer—and their only coordination is through him. The danger of collusive settlements . . . make[s] it imperative that the district judge conduct a careful inquiry into the fairness of a settlement to the class members before allowing it to go into effect and extinguish, by the operation of res judicata, the claims of class members who do not opt out of the settlement."). See also John C. Coffee, Jr., *The Unfaithful Champion: The Plaintiff as Monitor in Shareholder Litigation*, 48 L & Contemp Probs 5 (Summer 1985).

[60] See, for example, FRCP 23(e); *In re California Micro Devices Securities Litig.*, 1996 US Dist LEXIS 1361, *12 (ND Cal) ("courts have developed monitoring techniques designed to make themselves 'surrogate clients' "). Surprising as it seems, Federal Rule 23 (and state class actions analogues) provides no standards to govern judicial approval of class action settlements. See William W. Schwarzer, *Settlement of Mass Tort Class Actions: Order Out of Chaos*, 80 Cornell L Rev 837, 841–42 (1995). For example, Rule 23(e) provides "[a] class action shall not be dismissed or compromised without the approval of the court, and notice of the proposed dismissal or compromise shall be given to all members of the class in such manner as the court directs." Rule 23(d) authorizes the court to "make appropriate orders" in the conduct of class action. State and federal courts have developed a variety of procedures in supervising class action settlements. See *Manual for Complex Litigation, Third* § 30.4 (1995).

recovery obtained by class plaintiffs and the fees for the class attorney. Class actions certified for litigation and followed by a settlement will necessarily have been found to meet the numerosity, commonality, typicality, and adequacy requirements imposed by class action rules.[61] In "settlement class actions," however, the settlement is tentatively approved at the same time the class is conditionally certified for settlement purposes.[62] Because inadequate prosecution, attorney inexperience, and collusion are "paramount concerns" in precertification settlements,[63] the need for a judicial determination of adequacy of representation finding in this context is "particularly acute."[64] Finally, class action settlement practice provides class members with notice of the settlement terms, a right to object to the settlement, and in most actions involving money damages, the right to opt out of the class.[65] With these safeguards

---

[61] See FRCP 23. Many states, including Delaware, have adopted class action rules based on FRCP 23; see, e.g., Del Ch Ct R 23. See also Note, *Due Process and Equitable Relief in State Multistate Class Actions After Phillips Petroleum Co. v Shutts*, 68 Tex L Rev 415, 425 n 84 (1989).

[62] See *Manual for Complex Litigation, Third* § 30.212, § 30.45 (1995). For a discussion of "settlement classes" of this type, see *In re General Motors Corp. Pick-Up Truck Fuel Tank Litig.*, 55 F3d 768 (3d Cir 1995), cert denied sub nom *General Motors Corp. v French*, 116 S Ct 88 (1995); *Mars Steel Corp. v Continental Ill. Nat'l Bank & Trust*, 834 F2d 677, 681–82 (7th Cir 1987).

The Federal Judicial Center's study of class action litigation (based on activity in four federal judicial districts between July 1, 1992 and June 30, 1994) showed that in several districts, at least a quarter of the certified class actions settled within two months after certification; a large number of those actions were settlement classes which were certified simultaneously with the preliminary approval of a proposed settlement. See Thomas E. Willging, Laural L. Hooper, and Robert J. Niemic, *An Empirical Analysis of Rule 23 to Address the Rulemaking Challenges* [hereinafter *FJC Study*], 71 NYU L Rev 74, 146 (1996).

[63] See *In re General Motors Corp. Fuel Tank Litig.*, 55 F3d at 795. See also *In re California Micro Devices Securities Litig.*, 1996 US Dist LEXIS 1361 (ND Cal) (Walker, J). The *Manual for Complex Litigation, Third* § 30.45 (1995) recognizes a role for settlement classes, but expressly notes some of their troubling aspects, including conflicts between class counsel and class members and the release of other claims.

[64] See 55 F3d at 795. Some courts have made formal findings of adequacy of representation, recognizing the Rule 23(a) and (b) requirements as the source of legitimacy for settlement classes, while other courts appear to collapse the "adequacy of representation" finding into one which evaluates the fairness of the settlement. See 55 F3d at 795. Judge Becker criticized the latter approach as inadequate to assure that the named plaintiffs and their counsel are suitable representatives of the absentees' claims. Id at 795–96.

In *Prezant v De Angelis*, 636 A2d 915 (1994), the Delaware Supreme Court held that mere evaluation of the settlement merits is insufficient, and that state trial courts are "required to make an explicit determination on the record of the propriety of the class action according to the requisites of Rule 23(a) and (b)." Id at 925. (Del Ch Ct R 23 is modeled on FRCP 23.)

[65] See *Manual for Complex Litigation, Third* §§ 30.212, 30.4 (1995). In settlement class actions where certification is conditioned on settlement, certification and settlement notices are often combined. Id.

properly employed, class action settlements are, for certain types of cases, a tolerably fair and efficient way to resolve claims.

To be sure, even in ordinary class action settlements, these protections are far from foolproof. In many instances, substantial conflicts of interest between class counsel and class members remain,[66] opt-out rights may not afford effective protection to class members, and a court's evaluation of the substantive fairness of the settlement may be insufficiently informed and excessively deferential.[67] To address these concerns, both courts and commentators have advocated reform of the class action mechanism in general[68] and of settlement class actions in particular.[69]

However effective the procedures for settlement class actions are as a general matter (and however effective they may become if some of the proposed reforms are adopted), they work less well when a state court settlement also releases exclusive federal

---

[66] See In re California Micro Devices Securities Litig., 1996 US Dist LEXIS 1361, *11–12 ("This danger of class counsel self-dealing . . . is present in every situation where class counsel is allowed to prosecute an action and negotiate settlement terms without meaningful oversight by the class representative."); Mars Steel, 834 F2d at 681 ("the negotiator on the plaintiffs' side, that is the lawyer for the class, is potentially an unreliable agent of the principals").

[67] Curiously, while judges appear to have played an active role in assessing the fairness of settlements in mass tort cases, judicial investigation in securities cases seems substantially more passive. For a counterexample in the securities field, see In re California Micro Devices Securities Litig., 1996 US Dist LEXIS 1361 (refusing to approve proposed settlement of securities class action because it was negotiated under "quasi-collusive circumstances" and because putative class representatives, in failing to monitor adequately class counsel, were unable "fairly and adequately" to represent the interests of the class).

[68] An overwhelming literature on class actions exists. Two recent symposiums canvased a myriad of issues, including the scope of the rules, notice and opt-out provisions, attorney-class conflicts, fees, and parallel actions. See Symposium, The Institute of Judicial Administration Research Conference on Class Actions, 71 NYU L Rev 1 (1996); Symposium, Mass Torts: Serving Up Just Deserts, 80 Cornell L Rev 811 (1995). See also Robert G. Bone, Rule 23 Redux: Empowering the Federal Class Action, 14 Rev Litig 79 (1994); John C. Coffee, Jr., The Regulation of Entrepreneurial Litigation: Balancing Fairness and Efficiency in the Large Class Action, 54 U Chi L Rev 877 (1987); Macey and Miller, 58 U Chi L Rev 1 (cited in note 58); Elliot J. Weiss and John S. Beckerman, Let the Money Do the Monitoring: How Institutional Investors Can Reduce Agency Costs in Securities Class Actions, 104 Yale L J 2053 (1995).

[69] See Roger C. Cramton, Individualized Justice, Mass Torts, and "Settlement Class Actions": An Introduction, 80 Cornell L Rev 811 (1995); Schwarzer, 80 Cornell L Rev 837 (cited in note 60); In re Wells Fargo Securities Litig., 156 FRD 223 (ND Cal 1994) (describing court use of competitive bid to select class counsel); In re California Micro Devices Securities Litig., 1996 US DIST LEXIS 1361 (criticizing settlement class action in securities case).

For a view that present Rule 23, properly construed, does not authorize settlement classes, see Note, Back to the Drawing Board: The Settlement Class Action and Limits of Rule 23, 109 Harv L Rev 828 (1996).

claims. In Section B, we discuss why and how the class action settlement process is impaired in these situations. In Section C, we examine the benefits of state court settlements of exclusive federal claims.

B. PROBLEMS IN STATE COURT GLOBAL SETTLEMENTS

1. *Reduced state class attorney bargaining power.* By definition, state court settlements of exclusive federal claims involve claims that could not have been tried in the state court had they not been settled. Thus, the options of the state class attorney with respect to these claims are fundamentally different from the options with respect to state or nonexclusive federal claims. The latter claims can be either settled or tried in the state court. Exclusive federal claims can only be settled in state court (though the state class attorney could try to assert them in a parallel federal class action).

The fact that the state class attorney may lack the power to litigate the exclusive federal claims can substantially reduce her bargaining power relative to a state class attorney with the power to litigate state and federal claims in state court.[70] To see why, assume for the moment that the state class attorney could not assert the federal claims in a federal class action (for example, because a different attorney has already been appointed class counsel). Thus, for the state class attorney, the only option is to settle the federal claims in state court.

The outcome of a negotiation, such as a settlement negotiation, is circumscribed by each party's best alternative to a negotiated agreement. The alternative to a negotiated settlement is to continue litigation. A party will only agree to a settlement if settlement is preferable to (or, at a minimum, as good as) continuing litigation. We will refer to the settlement terms that are just as good as continuing litigation as the "minimum acceptable settlement terms." (Of course, a party may engage in strategic bargaining and refuse to accept a settlement offer above the minimum acceptable terms in order to obtain even better terms.) In the context of a

---

[70] See *Prezant v De Angelis*, 636 A2d 915, 919 (Del 1994) (overturning state class settlement releasing state and federal claims for failure of Chancery Court to make explicit findings on adequacy of representation and noting state counsels' "weaker bargaining position").

class action, the relevant parties are generally the class attorney and the defendant.[71]

Compare now the state class attorney's alternatives to litigation in two instances: where the class attorney maintains two claims (A and B), both of which can be litigated in state court, and where she maintains one claim (A) which can be litigated in state court and another claim (B) which is within the exclusive jurisdiction of the federal courts. In the first case, the class attorney's alternative to settlement is to litigate both claims in state court and to obtain potential attorneys' fees related to any ultimate recovery on claims A and B (and incur litigation costs). In the second case, the alternative to settlement is to litigate claim A in state court and to obtain potential attorneys' fees related to any ultimate recovery on claim A alone.[72] If the expected recovery on claims A and B exceeds the expected recovery on claim A alone—either because asserting claim B increases plaintiffs' likelihood of winning or because it increases the amount of recoverable damages—the alternative to settlement is worse when the class attorney cannot litigate claim B in state court than if she can. The inability to litigate claim B therefore lowers the minimum acceptable settlement terms and thereby weakens the state class attorney's bargaining power. Other things being equal, therefore, a class attorney is likely to settle for a lower amount if she can litigate only claim A in state court than she would if she could litigate both claims in state court.

The degree to which the inability to litigate the federal claims lowers the minimum acceptable settlement terms depends on two factors. One factor, of course, is the litigation value—the "merits"—of the federal claim.[73] Weak federal claims will reduce the

---

[71] For a more in-depth analysis of bargaining, see, for example, Howard Raiffa, *The Art and Science of Negotiation* (Harv U Press, 1982), and Eric Rasmusen, *Games and Information* (Basil Blackwell, 1989). See also Geoffrey P. Miller, *Some Agency Problems in Settlement*, 16 J Legal Stud 189 (1987).

[72] From the perspective of the defendant, the alternative to settlement is approximately equal in both cases. In the first case, failure to settle involves the risk of liability on claims A and B (and litigation costs); in the second case, if a different attorney has brought claim B in federal court, failure to settle claim A involves the risk of liability on claims A and B (and litigation costs). If claims A and B are pursued in two separate proceedings (for example, claim A in a state court proceeding and claim B in a federal court proceeding) rather than in a single proceeding, litigation costs may increase.

[73] Some commentators have claimed that certain types of federal securities claims tend to have little merit. See, for example, James Bohn and Stephen Choi, *Fraud in the New-Issues Market: Empirical Evidence on Securities Class Litigation*, 144 U Pa L Rev 903 (1996) (finding that most suits relating to IPOs are frivolous). For other empirical studies on the

minimum acceptable settlement terms less than strong federal claims. The second factor is the extent to which the addition of the federal claim increases defendant's exposure beyond the level of exposure on the state claim alone. Defendant's exposure can increase either because it is possible for the plaintiff to prevail on the federal claim *without* prevailing on the state claim (for example, because the two claims are different in nature, as in *Matsushita*, or because the federal claim is easier to prove) or because the plaintiff can recover higher damages (or obtain additional remedies) if she prevails on both claims than if she prevails on the state claim alone. If the federal claim neither increases plaintiff's likelihood of winning nor her damages if she wins, the ultimate recovery on both claims would not exceed the ultimate recovery on one claim—and the attorney's bargaining power would not be impaired by the inability to assert one of the claims.

Let us now revisit the assumption that the state class attorney could not be appointed class counsel in federal court. If the class attorney is sure to be appointed class counsel in a federal class action, the alternative to a settlement would be to litigate both claims—either in federal court (an alternative approximately equivalent to litigating both claims in state court)[74] or, more rarely, in two separate proceedings. In that case, the inability to litigate claim B in state court would not weaken her bargaining power.

---

significance of merits in securities litigation, see, for example, Roberta Romano, *The Shareholder Suit: Litigation without Foundation?* 7 J L Econ & Org 55 (1991) (finding that shareholder class action suits are less likely to be frivolous than derivative suits); Jennifer Francis, Donna Philbrick, and Katherine Schipper, *Determinants and Outcome in Class Action Securities Litigation* (Aug 1994); Frederick C. Dunbar, Todd S. Foster, Vinita M. Juneja, and Denise N. Martin, *Recent Trends III: What Explains Settlements in Shareholder Class Actions?* (National Economic Research Associates, 1995) (concluding that some so-called nuisance suits may be efficient low-value settlements of meritorious cases with high trial costs); Willard T. Carleton, Michael S. Weisbach, and Elliott J. Weiss, *Securities Class Action Lawsuits: A Descriptive Study*, 38 Ariz L Rev 491 (1996) (finding that data on low-value settlements are consistent with the presence of nuisance suits settled on the basis of plaintiffs' attorney's expenses rather than on the economic damages suffered by plaintiffs).

In our view, the empirical evidence on the merits of securities fraud suits is inconclusive. At least some suits are meritorious in that plaintiffs sometimes prevail on the merits after litigation. To the extent that securities litigation is burdensome, inefficient, and unjustified, more dramatic reforms of securities litigation in general are in order. See, for example, Victor P. Goldberg, *Securities Litigation Reform: A Fish Story* (Working Paper 1995); Ralph K. Winter, *Paying Lawyers, Empowering Prosecutors, and Protecting Managers: Raising the Cost of Capital in America*, 42 Duke L J 945 (1993).

[74] If the state and the federal claims grow out the same sets of facts, both claims could be litigated in federal court as a matter of supplemental jurisdiction. See 28 USC § 1367. Indeed, failure to assert such a state claim with the federal claim might result in later preclusion of the state claim.

In a number of circumstances, however, the state class attorney may not be confident that she will be appointed class counsel in federal court.[75] This may be particularly likely for cases filed after the passage of the Private Securities Litigation Reform Act which, in relevant parts, applies to securities class actions brought in federal court, but not to class actions in state court.[76] The Act provides that the court appoint as lead plaintiff, from all those seeking to become lead plaintiff, the class member with the largest financial interest in the claims[77] and empowers the lead plaintiff to select class counsel.[78] The process of selecting the lead plaintiff is meant to proceed expeditiously and be completed no later than 110 days after the complaint is filed.[79] Given this selection mechanism, a state class attorney will frequently know, or be able to predict, whether she is likely to be selected as class counsel.

2. *Defendant's increased ability to engage in plaintiff shopping.* Permitting state court settlements of exclusive federal claims also increases the defendant's ability to engage in "plaintiff shopping." Plaintiff shopping refers to the capacity of the defendant to choose

---

[75] This possibility should be assessed in light of the choice by the class attorney to bring a case in state court rather than in federal court. While there may be other reasons for this choice of forum, the choice may also be explained by the class attorney's belief that she would not be appointed class counsel in federal court.

[76] The provisions on the appointment of lead plaintiff apply only to private actions that are "brought as a plaintiff class action pursuant to the Federal Rules of Civil Procedure." Pub L No 104-67, 109 Stat 737, secs 101(a) § 27(a), 101(b) § 21D(a), codified at scattered sections of 15 USC.

[77] The Act provides that the plaintiff who files the first complaint must publish notices of the action in widely circulated business papers or wire services inviting other class members to move the court to serve as lead plaintiffs. The court is then to select the lead plaintiff from among those that have filed a complaint or made a motion in response to the notice. The court must appoint the plaintiff with the largest financial interest as lead plaintiff unless that plaintiff does not meet the requirements of Rule 23, will not fairly and adequately represent the class, or is subject to certain unique defenses. Moreover, the Act restricts the number of times any person may serve as a lead plaintiff during any three-year period. Id at secs 101(a) § 27(a)(3), 101(b) § 21D(a)(3).

[78] The provisions on the appointment of lead plaintiff are likely to result in closer monitoring of the settlement by the class plaintiff. If the class member appointed as lead plaintiff has a sufficiently large financial claim, she may monitor the class attorney directly and refuse to accept a settlement that is below the litigation value of the claim. For that reason, as well, it is likely that the federal class attorney will be a more faithful advocate of the class members with respect to the exclusive federal claims than the state class attorney would be.

[79] Under the Act, the plaintiff who files the action has 20 days to publish notice. Id at sec 101(a) § 27(a)(3)(A)(i); id at sec 101(b) § 21D(a)(3)(A)(i). No later than 90 days after publication of notice, the court must appoint the class representative(s). Id at sec 101(a) § 27(a)(3)(B)(i); id at sec 101(b) § 21D(a)(3)(B)(i).

the class attorney who negotiates settlement terms from among several attorneys who have filed related class actions. Plaintiff shopping obviously occurs when the defendant induces a particular attorney to file a class action, possibly after having already negotiated a settlement with that attorney. More importantly for our purposes, however, plaintiff shopping can also occur when two or more parallel lawsuits covering the same or related claims proceed. Since the lawsuit that is resolved first (by judgment or settlement) will usually be preclusive of the other suits, the defendant can effectively choose one negotiating partner from among those attorneys who have filed lawsuits by arriving at a quick settlement with that attorney and delaying the proceedings in all other suits.[80]

Plaintiff shopping results in two problems. First, to the extent that plaintiffs' attorneys differ in their assessment of the litigation value of the claims, the defendant will choose the plaintiffs' attorney who has the lowest assessment and is consequently willing to accept the lowest settlement terms. Second, the knowledge by plaintiffs' attorneys that the defendant can engage in plaintiff shopping creates a strong incentive to accept settlement terms favorable to the defendant, even if they are below one's estimate of the litigation value of the claims, in order to maximize the likelihood of being chosen a negotiating partner and of earning attorneys' fees.[81] For these reasons, the class attorney chosen by the defendant is likely not to be the one that would best represent the interests of the class members.

In class actions filed in federal court, there are limits on a defendant's ability to engage in plaintiff shopping. If two or more class actions covering similar claims are filed in federal courts, most courts usually employ one of several mechanisms to consolidate the actions in the most appropriate forum: the general federal transfer statute may be used to transfer a case to a different fo-

---

[80] See generally John C. Coffee, Jr., *Class Wars: The Dilemma of the Mass Tort Class Action*, 95 Colum L Rev 1343, 1369–72 (1995) (describing the "reverse auction" phenomenon in state/federal securities litigation). See also Richard B. Schmitt, *Behind Apple's Class-Action Settlement*, Wall St J B1 (Dec 4, 1996) (reporting Texas state class action settlement on terms previously rejected by different set of plaintiffs' lawyers in earlier-filed Ohio federal court action).

[81] Indeed, *Matsushita* may entice state class attorneys to bring a nonmeritorious state claim for the principal purpose of settling a pending federal claim—and earning a fee in the wake of that settlement.

rum;[82] the case may be referred to the panel on multidistrict litigation, which may transfer the case to a single district for coordinated or consolidated proceedings;[83] or other devices, such as a stay of the later-filed action or informal cooperation, may be adopted. Only rarely will two class actions covering essentially the same case proceed in parallel fashion in federal courts.[84]

The newly adopted Private Securities Litigation Reform Act further diminishes the ability to engage in plaintiff shopping within the federal system. Under the mechanism for the selection of the lead plaintiff established by the Act, the party with the largest financial interest is ordinarily entitled to become the lead plaintiff and selects the class attorney.[85] Thus, the ability of a defendant to influence the choice of the class attorney is practically eliminated.[86]

The ability of state courts to settle exclusive federal claims circumvents these limits on plaintiff shopping. State courts are not subject to the supervisory powers of the Panel on Multidistrict Litigation and have not, to the same extent as federal courts, engaged in self-restraint in dealing with claims that have already been as-

---

[82] See 28 USC § 1404(a) ("For the convenience of parties and witnesses, in the interest of justice, a district court may transfer any civil action to any other district of division where it might have been brought").

[83] 28 USC § 1407(a). The language of the statute refers to transfers "for coordinated or consolidated pretrial proceedings," but the case often is never remanded for trial. See *Manual for Complex Litigation, Third* § 31.133 (1995) (suggesting that cases transferred under Section 1407 may be eligible for consolidation in transferee court under Section 1404 or Section 1406); Newberg, *Class Actions* at § 9.14 (cited in note 57) ("the majority of cases transferred under Section 1407 reach final disposition in the transferee courts"); Comment, *The Judicial Panel on Multidistrict Litigation: Time for Rethinking*, 140 U Pa L Rev 711, 712 (1991) ("through manipulation of other venue statutes, the courts receiving the cases consolidated by the Panel often decide on their own to retain the cases for trial"). See also *In re Coordinated Pretrial Proceedings in Antibiotic Antitrust Actions*, 538 F2d 180, 196 n 31 (8th Cir 1976) (noting that the decision to remand is within the control of the panel and can only be reviewed by extraordinary writ).

[84] See Geoffrey P. Miller, *Overlapping Class Actions*, 71 NYU L Rev 514, 519–20 (1996) ("the problems of conflict and overlap have been handled quite effectively"); *FJC Study* at 87 (cited in note 62) ("[W]e looked at how often courts do not consolidate [class action] cases even though they are related to other litigation . . . . On the federal level, nonconsolidation of related cases occurred in 5% to 21% of the cases in the four districts.").

[85] See text accompanying notes 75–79.

[86] Indeed, the defendant may even lack standing to challenge whether a plaintiff satisfies certain of the criteria for being appointed lead plaintiff. See *Greebel v FTP Software, Inc.*, 1996 US Dist LEXIS 13510, *9–11 (D Mass) (holding that defendant lacks standing to challenge presumption in favor of appointment of plaintiff with largest financial stake as lead plaintiff and has no right to pursue discovery on this issue).

serted in a different forum.[87] Cooperative efforts between state and federal courts occasionally occur, but they rest on the ad hoc efforts of particular judges.[88] Finally, the provisions of the Private Securities Litigation Reform Act do not apply to class actions filed in state court.[89]

Thus, a state court could certify a party as class representative, and her counsel as class counsel, even if they could not represent the class on the federal securities claims in a federal court. Under *Matsushita*, the class representative in the state action could then settle any federal securities claim—even if, under a deliberate scheme adopted by Congress, a different party has been appointed as lead plaintiff in federal court.[90] A defendant thus regains the ability to engage in plaintiff shopping: the defendant can choose a negotiating partner from among the class counsel appointed in

---

[87] See, for example, *In re Union Square Assoc. Securities Litig.*, 1990 WL 212308 (Del Ch) (approving settlement and release of claims and noting that the release will be used to seek dismissal of two later-filed federal actions that asserted exclusive federal claims); *Shingala v Becor Western Inc.*, 1988 WL 7390 (Del Ch) (approving settlement releasing claims asserted in later filed federal class action), reprinted in 13 Del J Corp L 1232.

But see *Prezant v De Angelis*, 636 A2d 915, 919 (Del 1994) (noting the Delaware court will usually stay after-filed suits when previously filed suits stating similar claims are pending in another court, particularly federal claims pending in federal court). Delaware Chancery Courts, however, are divided over whether this stay policy prevents the state case from settling. Compare *Stepak v Tracinda Corp.*, 1989 Del Ch LEXIS 95 (staying state action and indicating that it will not hold future settlement hearings in deference to parallel action) with *De Angelis v Salton/Maxim Housewares, Inc.*, 641 A2d 834, 838 (Del Ch 1993) (noting that because the state action was filed after several federal class actions, the plaintiff in the Delaware action "could have only hoped to settle"), rev'd on other grounds sub nom *Prezant v De Angelis*, 636 A2d 915 (Del 1994).

[88] See *Manual for Complex Litigation, Third* §§ 31.3, 33.23 (1995) (offering possible methods of coordination). See also Judith Resnik, *History, Jurisdiction, and the Federal Courts: Changing Contexts, Selective Memories, and Limited Imagination*, 98 W Va L Rev 171, 203–08 (1996) (citing examples of the "fruits of coordination" that are "beginning to be visible"); William W. Schwarzer, Nancy E. Weiss, and Alan Hirsch, *Judicial Federalism in Action: Coordination of Litigation in State and Federal Courts*, 78 Va L Rev 1689 (1992) (discussing the problems of multiforum litigation and explaining methods of informally coordinating related state and federal cases).

One example is the "Brooklyn Navy Yard" asbestos cases, which featured substantial coordination and joint rulings. Judge Helen Freedman of the New York State Supreme Court and Federal Judges Jack B. Weinstein and Charles P. Sifton of the Eastern District of New York coordinated motion rulings and other pretrial matters and even contemplated a joint trial. See, for example, *In re Joint E. & S. Dist. Asbestos Litig.*, 129 FRD 434 (EDNY, SDNY, & Sup Ct NY 1990); Schwarzer et al, 78 Va L Rev at 1704–05.

[89] See note 76.

[90] In a future case, the Supreme Court could conceivably confine its holding in *Matsushita* to settlements that occurred prior to the Private Securities Litigation Reform Act.

federal court and any other attorneys who have advanced related claims in state court.

"Shopping" of a different variety—to find a state court willing to approve settlements with less than rigorous oversight—is an additional danger created by *Matsushita*. To be sure, forum shopping among state and federal courts is a price one pays for federalism in both class[91] and non-class litigation. But in the disposition of claims subject to the exclusive jurisdiction of the federal courts, firmer limits should be imposed on forum shopping. The Delaware state courts have a substantial nexus with litigation arising under Delaware corporate law, and permitting Delaware state global settlements is consistent with Delaware's interest in disposing of the underlying state claims. However, *Matsushita* itself sets no limit on any state's ability to settle exclusive federal claims in its courts, and greatly expands opportunities for forum shopping in this context.

3. *Court's reduced ability to assess fairness of settlement.* Finally, in state court settlements of exclusive federal claims, the judge's ability to assess the fairness of a settlement is impeded. An independent substantive evaluation of the fairness of a settlement by the judge is an integral part of the procedural safeguards in a class action.[92] To perform this evaluation, a judge must assess the legal and factual strength of the asserted claims from the perspective of a litigant. This requires information about the nature of the claim

---

[91] An egregious example of this type of forum shopping occurred after both the Third Circuit and the Texas Supreme Court refused certification of settlement classes in *In re General Motors Corp. Pick-Up Truck Fuel Tank Litig.*, 55 F3d 768 (3d Cir 1995), cert denied sub nom *General Motors Corp. v French*, 116 S Ct 88 (1995), and *General Motors Corp. v Bloyed*, 916 SW2d 949 (Tex 1996). Although the Third Circuit had remanded the case to the federal district court in Philadelphia for further proceedings consistent with its opinion, the same class plaintiffs represented by the same class counsel brought a similar nationwide settlement class action in Louisiana state court, see *White v General Motors Corp.*, No 42865 (La D Ct, Iberville Parish, order approving notice, Sept 3, 1996), requesting approval of a slightly revamped version of the prior settlement (along with generous attorneys' fees) previously rejected by the Third Circuit. Such blatant attempts to undermine the authority of a court's prior exercise of jurisdiction should be remediable through use of a federal court injunction, the Anti-Injunction Act presenting no barrier when an injunction is issued "in aid of its jurisdiction, or to protect or effectuate its judgments." 28 USC § 2283. See Geoffrey P. Miller, 71 NYU L Rev at 523–25 (cited in note 84). Of course, no such remedy is possible if, in future, plaintiffs and class counsel initially seek approval of a settlement class from a state court willing to bless such a settlement, thus engendering a "race to the bottom." Imposition of a nexus requirement between the forum and the litigation would discourage such court-shopping efforts. See notes 110–11 and accompanying text.

[92] See *Manual for Complex Litigation, Third* § 30.42 (1995) (stressing the importance of the court's role in evaluating proposed settlements and setting forth factors that should be taken into account).

and any factual and legal disputes relevant to the claim.[93] The main sources for this information are the class attorney and the defendant's attorney.[94]

At the time the attorneys for the class and the defendant submit a proposed settlement to the court, neither of them has an incentive to provide the judge with the requisite information. At that point, both the class attorney and the defendant share an interest in having the judge approve the settlement that they negotiated. They will therefore attempt to present only information that shows that the settlement is fair to the class members and try to withhold or downplay any information that would indicate that the settlement is not fair. Both sides can thus be expected to argue that the legal and factual basis of the claims is relatively weak, that the amount of the settlement is high relative to the strength of the claims, that the class members can count themselves lucky to obtain the benefits of such a settlement, and so on.[95]

The only time when the judge is likely to receive information from the parties of record that may indicate that a settlement is not fair is during the adversarial proceedings that precede the settlement: in the complaint, in papers opposing a motion to dismiss or defendant's motion for summary judgment, in the plaintiffs' motion for summary judgment and for class certification, in pretrial conferences, in discovery disputes, and so on. In such proceedings, the class attorney has incentives to present the case in the strongest possible light.[96] Information provided in such proceedings may enable the judge to conclude that the legal and factual strength of the claims is relatively high—and thus that the terms of a relatively low settlement are inadequate.[97]

---

[93] The inherent limitations of making this evaluation are discussed in Judith Resnik, *Judging Consent*, 1987 U Chi Legal F 43, 87–92.

[94] The judge can perform some limited independent research, especially on legal matters, and objectors to a settlement may occasionally present relevant evidence. See text accompanying notes 98–100.

[95] Depicting the settlement terms in this light has the added advantage of justifying a relatively high fee award for the class attorney (who negotiated such a good settlement).

[96] The defendant always has an incentive to present the plaintiffs' case in the weakest possible light, and will thus rarely be a source of information indicating that the substantive terms of a settlement are unfair.

[97] In certain cases, the number of plaintiffs who opt out of a settlement may also be a factor relevant to an assessment of the fairness of the settlement. For example, customers representing over 9% of all lysine sales opted out of the settlement of lysine price-fixing

Class objectors to the settlement, if there are any, may also provide information bearing on the fairness of the settlement.[98] Objectors, however, may be hampered by inadequate incentives to come
forward, lack of information about the merits of a settlement, time
constraints and an inability to conduct discovery,[99] and a dynamic
favoring approval of a settlement once notice has gone out and a
final fairness hearing has been scheduled.[100]

With respect to exclusive federal claims, presettlement adversar-

---

claims against Archer Daniels Midland and others. See Nancy Millman, *ADM Settlement
Approved: Firm to Pay $25 Million 2 Others to Pay $10 Million in Price Suit*, Chicago Tribune
1 (Jul 20, 1996). Other things being equal, opting out should be more frequent if the
settlement amount is low relative to the litigation value of the claims. However, in instances
where the claims of individual plaintiffs are low, it is likely that most would not opt out
even if the settlement amount were substantially below the expected recovery in a class
litigation. Plaintiffs with individually small claims will not bother to expend the effort to
determine the litigation value of their claims and will thus not know that the proposed
settlement is low. Moreover, even a plaintiff who knows that the proposed settlement is
low may decide not to opt out if he believes that most other plaintiffs will fail to opt out,
and that it would not be economical to pursue the claims of the few plaintiffs who do opt
out in individual or class actions.

[98] See *Manual for Complex Litigation, Third* § 30.14 (1995) (suggesting that the judge may
hear at the preliminary hearing from parties not involved in the settlement negotiations,
and that "[o]pportunity should be provided at the [formal] hearing for all objections to the
settlement to be presented to the court"). For examples of objector involvement in settlement approval, see, for example, *Sandler Assoc., L.P. v Bellsouth Corp.*, 818 F Supp 695, 699
(D Del 1993) (noting that the state court allowed objectors to settlement to engage in
discovery), aff'd 26 F3d 123 (3d Cir 1994); *De Angelis v Salton/Maxim Housewares, Inc.*, 641
A2d 834, 839–40 (Del Ch 1993) (stating that discovery undertaken by objectors revealed
class representative's misrepresentations), rev'd on other grounds sub nom *Prezant v De
Angelis*, 636 A2d 915 (Del 1994); *Amsellem v Shopwell*, 1979 WL 2704 (Del Ch) (indicating
objectors conducted a comprehensive review of discovery materials and then voiced specific
objections), reprinted in 5 Del J Corp L 367.

[99] These factors would not apply to a party that has brought an independent suit. See
text accompanying notes 126–31. In federal class actions, the objectors' right to discovery
is within the discretion of the trial court. See, for example, *In re General Motors Corp. Engine
Interchange Litig.*, 594 F2d 1106 (7th Cir 1979) (holding that trial court abused its discretion
by not permitting objectors to class action settlement to engage in discovery regarding the
adequacy of representation during settlement negotiations); *Geller v Tabas*, 462 A2d 1078,
1081 (Del 1983) ("A refusal to delay a settlement to permit objectors to take discovery will
not be overturned unless there was an abuse of discretion on the part of the Vice-Chancel-
lor."). See also Newberg, *Class Actions* at § 11.57 (cited in note 57) ("[T]he objector's request
for discovery should be granted if he or she can demonstrate to the court that the previous
discovery was not adversarial in nature.").

[100] The Federal Judicial Center's study provides additional insight about the role and
effect of objectors at settlement hearings. The data show that nonrepresentative parties
attended the settlement hearing infrequently (14% in one district being the high mark),
but that settlements that were the subject of a hearing did generate at least one objection
in one-half of the cases. The majority of objections concerned the insufficiency of the award
and the amounts of attorneys' fees. Ninety percent of the proposed settlements were approved without changes. See *FJC Study* at 146 (cited in note 62).

ial proceedings never take place in the state court proceedings.[101] Such claims will not be mentioned in the complaint; will not be the subject of motions to dismiss, motions for summary judgment, and motions for class certification; and will not be dealt with in pretrial conferences. The judge may not even learn about the existence and nature of such claims until a proposed settlement encompassing such claims is presented to the court.[102] Presettlement information about the factual basis of these claims would only be available to the judge to the extent that there is an overlap in the factual and legal issues relevant to the state and the federal claims. This information deficiency may render it more difficult for the judge to assess the fairness of a settlement of these claims.[103]

Moreover, apart from the problem that the class attorney and the defendant have no incentive to alert the court to facts suggesting that a negotiated global settlement may not be fair, the class attorney may not even bother to determine whether any substantial federal claims exist that would be released. Ordinarily, parties investigate the strength of their claims for three reasons: first, in order to prepare for litigation; second, in order to guide one's settlement negotiations by assessing one's own bottom line settlement offer (i.e., the value of one's best alternative to settlement); and third, in order to guide one's settlement negotiations by estimating the other side's bottom line settlement offer. But if the class attorney cannot litigate the federal claims in federal court, the first two motives for investigating the claims are absent. Thus, to the extent that the federal claims involve legal and factual questions that differ from the state claims, the state class attorney will tend to investigate the federal claims much less than she would if

---

[101] An action brought in federal court solely to implement a previously agreed-upon settlement also avoids preliminary skirmishing. In this respect, such class actions suffer the same information deficiency as do global state court settlements. See *In re California Micro Devices Securities Litig.*, 1996 US Dist LEXIS 1361 (ND Cal) (Walker, J).

[102] If a federal case covering the exclusive federal claims has been filed, information about the case is also available from the federal plaintiff and from the federal litigation. See text accompanying notes 126–31.

[103] In some cases, the difficulty is further enhanced by the state court judge's lack of expertise with the governing federal law. While a concern about a state court's lack of expertise may be misplaced in the case of the Delaware Chancery Court, see, for example William H. Rehnquist, *The Prominence of the Delaware Court of Chancery in the State-Federal Joint Venture of Providing Justice*, 48 Bus Law 351 (1992)—the court in which the issue of settlement of exclusive federal claims has most frequently arisen—this concern may be more acute in other states.

she could litigate them in state court.[104] It follows that even if the state class attorney fully disclosed to the court all information bearing on the fairness of the proposed global settlement, a state court would be hampered by an information deficiency with respect to any legal or factual questions specific to the exclusive federal claims.

* * *

In the context of state court settlements of exclusive federal claims, the reduced bargaining power of the state class attorney, defendant's increased ability to engage in plaintiff shopping, and the court's difficulty in making an independent assessment of the fairness of a proposed settlement are sufficient to raise a cautionary flag. Such concerns suggest that some limitations should be placed on global state court settlements encompassing exclusive federal claims.

C. BENEFITS OF STATE COURT GLOBAL SETTLEMENTS

The principal benefit of permitting state court settlements to encompass exclusive federal claims is to make it easier for parties to arrive at a settlement, thereby reducing litigation costs and attorneys' fees.[105] It is commonly asserted that a defendant would not be willing to settle a case unless the settlement releases all—state and federal—claims that could be brought. If a state court cannot release the defendant from liability under the federal claims, settlement of a state class action would thus be impeded. Viewed from this perspective, permitting state court settlements of exclusive federal claims promotes settlements (at least in state courts).[106]

---

[104] The class attorney in the state action may also be hampered by an inability to investigate the federal claims. Since the federal claims are never directly presented in the state court, they may be outside the scope of discovery in the state case. Depending upon the relationship between the state and federal claims, the class attorney may not have access to information necessary to assess the strength of the federal claims. However, to the extent that the state and federal claims are transactionally linked, most discovery regimes would be broad enough to provide access to information relevant to both claims.

[105] Making it easier for the parties to settle may not be desirable if ease of settlement is achieved by eroding the procedural and structural protections accorded to class members.

[106] The majority in *Matsushita* noted that recognition of state court settlements serves the "principles of comity and repose embodied in § 1738." See *Matsushita Elec. Indus. Co. v Epstein*, 116 S Ct 873, 883 (1996).

In some instances, a settlement of just the state claims would indeed offer no benefit to a defendant. This would be the case if the defendant's exposure on the federal and the state claim would not exceed its exposure on just the federal claim (i.e., if it is not possible for the plaintiff to prevail on the state claim without prevailing on the federal claim and if the plaintiff cannot recover higher damages if she prevails on both claims than if she prevails on the federal claim alone).[107] In such cases, a settlement of just the state claim would not be rational since it would impose costs on the defendant without reducing its exposure to liability.

Take, for example, shareholders who allege that the price received when their company merged was unfair (for example, $100 million too low) and seek recovery both under state corporate law (for example, for breach of fiduciary duties) and the federal securities laws (for example, for misleading disclosures in the proxy statement). Assume that there is no significant dispute over any of the elements of the state and federal claim except over one: whether the relevant facts as to the fairness of the price were properly disclosed.[108] If the case is litigated, and plaintiffs can show that the facts were properly disclosed, they prevail on both claims; if they cannot, they lose on both claims. But even if plaintiffs win on both claims, they can recover their damages ($100 million) only once. Settling the state claims for, say, $10 million would not make sense for defendants, even if $10 million is much less than the expected liability on the state claims (for example, if plaintiffs' chances of winning $100 million are 30%). The defendant would be better off not having settled the state claim than having settled it for $10 million and still be exposed to a 30% chance of losing the remaining $90 million (and incurring litigation costs) on the federal claim.

In other cases, where exposure on the state and federal claims exceeds exposure on just the federal claim, settlement of just the

---

[107] Another reason why settlement of the state claim only would not reduce the defendant's exposure to liability is that the state claim is frivolous. As we discuss below, lack of merit in the state claim militates against a global state-court settlement.

[108] Under federal law, there is no basis for a claim that a disclosure in a proxy statement is misleading if all material facts are disclosed. See *Virginia Bankshares, Inc. v Sandberg*, 501 US 1083 (1991). Under Delaware corporate law, approval of a transaction by disinterested shareholders after disclosure of all material facts in most circumstances insulates the transaction from subsequent challenges. See *In re Wheelabrator Technologies, Inc. Shareholders Litig.*, 663 A2d 1194 (Del Ch, 1995).

state claim would reduce the defendant's exposure to liability. In such cases, defendant should be willing to settle the state claim by itself on some terms. A global settlement may nevertheless be desirable because it may be easier to negotiate a global settlement than a settlement of just the state claims and because a global settlement would avert the necessity of a separate proceeding disposing of the federal claims.

In either of these cases, of course, it is not necessary for the *state* court to approve a global settlement. In most cases, it is equally possible for a federal court to approve a global settlement. Indeed, since a federal court ordinarily has jurisdiction over all the claims that would be settled,[109] approval of a global settlement by a federal, rather than a state, court would not entail the deficiencies discussed in the preceding section.

Nevertheless, there are some situations in which the state courts may be a preferable forum to entertain a global settlement. First, to the extent that the state claims are stronger than the federal claims, states with a substantial nexus to the parties or the claims[110] have significant interests in supervising settlements of the state claims in their courts.[111] When there is a transactional nexus between the federal and state claims, a global settlement— rather than separate settlements—is still desirable. Therefore, both the state's interest in the matter and the efficiency values in a global settlement tilt toward allowing a state court settlement of the entire matter. Second, no federal claims may have yet been brought in federal court, or the litigation in the state court may have proceeded much further than the litigation in the federal courts (for example, state court discovery may be complete while federal discovery has not even started). But absent such circumstances, the federal court is likely to be at least as good a forum, and will often be a superior forum, for entertaining a global settlement proposal.

---

[109] See note 74.

[110] Such a nexus will exist in these corporate/securities cases when the corporation is incorporated (or headquartered) in a state and its law is likely to govern the transaction, or when large numbers of shareholders are residents of the state and the state has an interest in their protection.

[111] Requiring a nexus between the forum and the litigation will have the benefit of eliminating widespread forum shopping.

III. Beyond Matsushita: When State Courts Should Approve Global Settlements

A. PRESENT STATE COURT PRACTICE

In light of the *Matsushita* decision, and of the problems associated with allowing state courts to enter binding settlements of exclusive federal claims in class actions, the critical question is: Under what circumstances *should* state courts approve the release of exclusive federal claims and give preclusive effect to such judgments? State courts have not always been careful to distinguish settlements that release exclusive federal claims from other settlements: for example, the Delaware cases on class action settlements, which deal almost exclusively with claims based upon corporate duties and securities laws,[112] appear to apply similar criteria when the proposed settlements release claims brought before the court for adjudication and when the release includes other claims not asserted in the action, such as exclusive federal claims.[113]

Delaware courts, like courts in other jurisdictions, articulate a general test of substantive fairness, which applies to all settlements.[114] And in making that evaluation, courts have given addi-

---

[112] See, for example, *Dieter v Prime Computer, Inc.*, 681 A2d 1068 (Del Ch 1996); *In re Dr. Pepper/Seven Up Co., Inc. Shareholders Litig.*, 1996 WL 74214 (Del Ch); *Prezant v De Angelis*, 636 A2d 915 (Del 1994); *In re Amsted Indus. Inc. Litig., Consol.*, 1988 Del Ch LEXIS 116, aff'd sub nom *Barkan v Amsted Indus., Inc.*, 567 A2d 1279 (Del 1989); *In re Beatrice Co., Inc. Litig.*, 1986 WL 4749 (Del Ch), reprinted in 12 Del J Corp L 199, aff'd 522 A2d 865 (Del 1987); *Polk v Good*, 507 A2d 531 (Del 1986).

[113] "[T]he court's function is to consider the nature of the claim, the possible defenses thereto, the legal and factual circumstances of the case, and then to apply its own business judgment in deciding whether the settlement is reasonable in light of these factors." *Polk v Good*, 507 A2d 531, 535 (Del 1986). The main difference that exists in a settlement releasing claims pending in another jurisdiction is that the value of those claims needs to be evaluated as well. See *In re Mobile Communications Corp. of Am., Inc. Consol. Litig.*, 1991 WL 1392 (Del Ch) (evaluating claims pending in federal court that arise under Securities Exchange Act, Securities Act, and RICO), reprinted in 17 Del J Corp L 297, aff'd 608 A2d 729 (Del 1992); *In re First Boston, Inc. Shareholders Litig.*, 1990 WL 78836 (examining pending Securities Exchange Act claims and ultimately approving settlement at 1990 WL 201388). At times, however, this evaluation lacks, to put it mildly, explicitness. See *In re Union Square Assoc. Securities Litig.*, 1990 WL 212308 (Del Ch) (approving settlement that included a general release and only mentioning pending claims in two federal actions in a footnote).
Delaware Chancery Courts also have a history of approving settlements that release claims pending in other state courts. See, for example, *Steiner v Sithe-Energies, L.P.*, 1988 WL 36133 (Del Ch), reprinted in 14 Del J Corp L 413.

[114] For a brief summary of Delaware substantive considerations of settlement approval, see Theresa L. Kelly, *J. L. Schiffman & Co. v. Standard Industries, Inc. and Other Recent Settlement Proposal Cases*, 19 Del J Corp L 447 (1994).

tional scrutiny to settlements on the basis of particular facts that are brought to their attention.[115] Courts are also aware that they need to protect the interests of absent class members by assuring adequacy in representation of the class.[116] The existence of pending claims in other jurisdictions is a factor to be taken into account in protecting the interests of class members, and in the MCA litigation, the Vice Chancellor himself noted that the court "must be particularly careful in reviewing a proposed settlement that has the effect of barring claims of at least arguable merit that are not being asserted in Delaware but are being asserted in another forum."[117]

Certain procedural requirements also characterize settlement class actions. Most courts adopt a two-step process for deciding whether to certify class treatment in a settlement class action.[118] When a proposed settlement is reached between the parties prior to certification of the class, the court holds a preliminary hearing—at which class counsel and defense counsel appear—to review the settlement. If this preliminary evaluation does not suggest doubts as to its fairness or other deficiencies,[119] the court directs

---

[115] Delaware courts have noted several situations in which settlement approval will undergo greater scrutiny. See, for example, *In re Amsted Indus. Inc. Litig.*, 1988 Del Ch LEXIS 116, at *3 (non-opt-out settlements); *In re MCA, Inc. Shareholders Litig.*, 598 A2d 687, 695 (Del Ch 1991) (small benefit offered to the class); *Kahn v Occidental Petroleum*, 1989 Del Ch LEXIS 92, at *9–10 (defects in the bargaining process). See also *In re Advanced Mammography System, Inc., Shareholder Litigation*, No 14831, slip op at 2 (Del Ch, Oct 30, 1996) (refusing to release, in context of claims to be dismissed as moot, any other claims that have not been advanced where there has been no serious discovery regarding such other claims and class members received no consideration).

[116] See, for example, *Prezant*, 197 A2d at 921 ("the settlement of a class action is unique because the fiduciary nature of the class action requires the Court of Chancery to participate . . . to the extent of determining its intrinsic fairness"); *Wied v Valhi, Inc.*, 466 A2d 9, 14 (Del 1983) (Court should "guard against surreptitious buy-outs of representative plaintiffs, leaving other class members without recourse.").

[117] *In re MCA, Inc. Shareholders Litig.*, 1993 WL 43024 (Del Ch) (Hartnett, VC). Particular care may arise in taking note of extreme informational gaps. Where the court lacks information sufficient to value claims pending elsewhere, the court may delay settlement approval. See *In re First Boston, Inc. Shareholders Litig.*, 1990 WL 78836, *9, 1990 Del Ch LEXIS 74 (delaying settlement approval because "the court must know something more in order to evaluate the two claims that remain open in my mind"), settlement later approved 1990 WL 201388. Filling this information gap, however, does not necessarily result in an extensive amount of information. See *In re Mobile Communications Corp. of America, Inc. Consol. Litig.*, 1991 WL 1392, at *12 (Del Ch 1991) (noting that business judgments necessarily are made with imperfect information), reprinted in 17 Del J Corp L 297, aff'd 608 A2d 729 (Del 1992).

[118] See *Manual for Complex Litigation, Third* § 30.4 (1995).

[119] Chancellor William Allen has observed that it is unlikely for a settlement to be rejected at this stage of the process. See *Stepak v Tracinda Corp.*, 1989 Del Ch LEXIS 95, *3:

It is the typical practice in this court, as elsewhere, to set a motion for approval

notice be sent to class members for participation at a formal hearing at which arguments and evidence are presented in support of and in opposition to the settlement.

B. A MORE CONTEXTUAL APPROACH

These general settlement procedures may be adequate when a court is asked to approve the settlement of state claims that could be litigated before it. However, state courts should adopt more exacting standards and procedures before approving a global settlement encompassing exclusive federal claims. As explained above, global settlements in state court may result in three problems: impaired bargaining power of the state class attorney, plaintiff and forum shopping by the defendant, and a reduced ability of the state court to evaluate the fairness of the settlement. The potential for state-court settlements to "hijack" exclusive federal securities claims is particularly troublesome in light of the recently adopted Private Federal Securities Reform Act. The provisions of the Act for the appointment of a lead plaintiff and class counsel would be undermined if state court global settlements could easily terminate securities litigation. State courts need to weigh carefully the benefits of a state court global settlement against these dangers.

Our proposal—which can be implemented for state courts as a matter of statute, court rule, or state practice—offers standards for best accomplishing global settlements. The basic test imposes a set of substantive standards as well as procedural safeguards for settlements encompassing exclusive federal claims that go beyond the general inquiry as to the prerequisites for class certification and the substantive fairness of the settlement. In particular, before approving a state global settlement, a judge should obtain reasonable information about the federal claims to be settled. Specifically, we recommend that counsel for plaintiffs who have filed federal claims be asked to participate in a preliminary fairness hearing on

---

of a settlement of a class action down for hearing on the merits and to defer all consideration of the substance of such proposal until notice has been afforded and a hearing held. This practice has the obvious advantage of efficiency. An alternative technique, although rarely invoked, is authorized. Occasionally, the particulars of a case may warrant the expenditure of judicial time in making a preliminary assessment of the proposed settlement in order to determine whether it meets truly minimum standards sufficient to invoke the mechanism required by Rule 23(e).

the state global settlement that is held before notice is sent to class members.[120] The state judge should weigh the benefits of a state global settlement against the possible dangers posed by the state class counsel's impaired bargaining power and the defendant's ability to engage in plaintiff shopping and against the federal interest in implementing the lead plaintiff scheme of the Private Securities Litigation Reform Act. These considerations play out differently in different contexts.

1. *State court settlement proposed with no federal claims filed.* When no federal claims have yet been asserted by any party, a global settlement in state court involves significant benefits and relatively few drawbacks. As no claims are pending in federal court, the state court is the only court that can entertain a global settlement. Moreover, if no federal claims have been brought, it is relatively unlikely that a state court global settlement would release federal claims with significant litigation value. Finally, in this context, the likelihood that the state court settlement is the product of impaired bargaining power by the state attorney or of plaintiff shopping by the defendant is reduced.

Nonetheless, two concerns remain. First, there is the problem that the state court is not in a good position to evaluate the worth of any unasserted federal claims. Second, in some instances, a speedy state court settlement might be designed to preempt a later assertion of important and substantial exclusive federal claims. (Indeed, the availability of such preemption might encourage a rush to bring a state court settlement class action.) These concerns take on additional importance in light of the Private Securities Litigation Reform Act, which establishes a set of prerequisites for filing a federal securities claim in federal court, thus imposing some lag before these claims can be asserted.[121]

---

[120] In some situations, detailed information about the merits of the federal claims should be made available to the class members as part of the notice procedure. See, for example, *Sandler Assoc., L.P. v Bellsouth Corp.*, 818 F Supp 695, 699 (noting that objectors were allowed by state court to include "a statement of reasons for their objections to the settlement in the hearing notice"), aff'd 26 F3d 123 (3d Cir 1994). For empirical data about the content of notices of proposed settlements, see *FJC Study* at 131–34 (cited in note 62) ("Having read the notices in these cases presses us to make an additional observation. Many, perhaps most, of the notices present technical information in legal jargon. Our impression is that most notices are not comprehensible to the lay reader.").

[121] See Pub L No 104-67, 109 Stat 737, sec 101(b) § 21D(a)(2) (requiring plaintiff to provide sworn certification he has reviewed and authorized complaint); § 21D(b)(1) (requir-

Before approving a global settlement releasing unasserted exclusive federal claims, a state court judge should therefore obtain information about the existence and nature of any federal claims. As an initial matter, the defendant should be required to confirm that in fact no federal claims to be released under the proposed settlement have been filed elsewhere and that the defendant has no notice that any such claims are likely to be brought. Lawyers for the parties should then provide information about the viability of any potential federal claims that would be released as part of the settlement. Plaintiff's lawyer should disclose whether she has investigated the existence of possible federal claims; and both plaintiff and defendant counsel should provide the court with an assessment of their litigation value if any claims exist.

To be sure, where no federal claims have been filed, we expect that plaintiff and defendant counsel will ordinarily agree either that no federal claims are viable, or that they have little value. The imposition of sanctions for misrepresentations to the court and the availability of a legal malpractice claim against the plaintiff class attorney, however, offer some deterrent against unrealistic or sham representations about the nature of these claims.[122]

---

ing complaint to specify each allegedly misleading statement, the reason why statement is misleading, and any facts on which belief that statement is misleading is formed); § 21D(b)(2) (requiring complaint to state with particularity facts giving rise to a strong inference that defendant acted with requisite state of mind). See also *Greebel v FTP Software, Inc.*, 1996 US Dist LEXIS 13510, *14 (D Mass) ("The purpose of requiring certification with the complaint is to slow the race to the courthouse by so-called professional plaintiffs.").

[122] Some global settlements appear to provide for a release of malpractice claims against the class counsel. See *In re MCA, Inc. Shareholders Litig.*, No 11740, at 3–4 (Del Ch Feb 22, 1993) (Order and Final Judgment) (on file with authors) ("All claims, rights and causes of action . . . against any of the Released Persons or *against anyone else* in connection with or that arise now or hereafter out of . . . the Initial Proposed Settlement [or] this Settlement . . . are hereby compromised, settled, released and discharged with prejudice. . . ." (emphasis added)). See also Opening Brief for Appellants at 31, *Epstein v MCA Inc.*, No 92-55675 (9th Cir 1996) (stating that release approved by Delaware Chancery Court "purports to preclude [class] counsel's 'clients' from . . . maintaining even a meritorious malpractice action").

Similar language has been interpreted to bar malpractice claims arising out of settlement. Compare *Wells v Shearson Lehman/Am. Exp., Inc.*, 72 NY2d 11, 16, 526 NE2d 8 (1988) (holding that release in settlement of Delaware class action barred malpractice suit against financial advisors of class members). Our guidelines for state court settlement practice would have courts refuse to approve settlements containing such a release.

A recent decision in the Seventh Circuit, *Kamilewicz v Bank of Boston Corp.*, 92 F3d 506 (7th Cir 1996), invokes the somewhat peculiar *Rooker-Feldman* doctrine (see *Rooker v Fidelity Trust Co.*, 263 US 413 (1923) and *District of Columbia Court of Appeals v Feldman*, 460 US 462 (1983)) to prevent a malpractice claim in federal court against attorneys who had negotiated a state class action settlement. However, as persuasively argued by Judge Easterbrook, writing for five circuit judges dissenting from a denial of a rehearing en banc in *Kamilewicz*,

Equipped with this information, a state court can then proceed to assess preliminarily whether, given the particular context, the value of possible federal claims has been reasonably investigated and whether the settlement is fair with respect to both the state and the federal claims to be released. If the court is satisfied, it can provide for notice and the opportunity to opt out of the settlement class and then conduct a formal hearing on the fairness of the settlement. Since no federal claims are pending, the interest in settling the claims in state court is strong; the likelihood that substantial federal claims exist is reduced; and the concerns over class counsel's impaired bargaining power, the potential for plaintiff shopping, and the undermining of the Congressional lead plaintiff scheme are alleviated.

Even in this context, however, the power of state courts to release exclusive federal claims should not be unlimited. Only a state with a substantial nexus to the litigation should be permitted to approve a global settlement. Such a nexus may exist because the corporation is incorporated in a state and its law would govern the state law claims, or because there are substantial shareholders from the state which is asked to approve a settlement affecting their interests. Such a nexus requirement will have the advantage of discouraging efforts to forum shop for a court that might be too eager to attract settlement business through easy approval of what could be sell-out or collusive settlements.

A state court global settlement should also be limited to federal claims that have a transactional relationship to the state claims. The transactional requirement ensures that the plaintiffs' lawyer's investigation of the basic state claims brings her into contact with the necessary facts and events that might give rise to possible federal claims and helps to assess to what extent the litigation value of such claims should be further explored. Moreover, both from defendant's and the state's perspective, a transactional requirement should satisfy the need to achieve a reasonable and workable settlement of the state claims.[123]

Rooker-Feldman should have no application to a malpractice action. 1996 US App LEXIS 30388. For an elaborate discussion of how malpractice and other remedies can be used in cases of lawyer malfeasance in class action litigation, see Susan P. Koniak and George M. Cohen, *Under Cloak of Settlement*, 82 Va L Rev 1051 (1996).

[123] See, for example, *Nottingham Partners v Dana*, 564 A2d 1089 (Del 1989), which limits the preclusive effect of releases to claims based on the same operative facts. For the debate over the nature of the similarity required in Delaware, see note 45.

One variation on this scenario is a federal claim that is not pending when the state settlement is proposed, but which is filed before the final settlement hearing takes place.[124] As part of the fairness hearing, the court should inquire whether the circumstances with respect to the existence of federal claims have changed. In the usual case, a subsequent "later-filed" federal claim should not per se disturb the balance of equities favoring a global settlement.[125] Otherwise, notice of a proposed global settlement would invite federal "spoiler" claims brought principally as an impediment to an imminent state court settlement. However, if the court determines that there was a "rush to settlement" (leaving no time for a federal court to be filed before the settlement was proposed), or if the federal claim arose after the preliminary settlement hearing was held, the court should treat the claim as if it had been pending when the state court settlement was proposed—the variation we examine in the next section.

2. *State court settlement proposed and federal claims pending.* When a federal claim is pending at the time a global state court settlement is proposed, the state court's actions should be guided by the following considerations. First, the existence of a pending federal claim and of a party pressing that claim increases the information that the court could, and should, obtain. Second, the presence of a pending federal claim makes it more likely that the state counsel's bargaining power in negotiating the settlement was impaired and that the defendant engaged in plaintiff shopping. And third, if the federal claim is a securities claim, a Congressionally sanctioned process for the appointment of lead plaintiff as class representative, which would be undermined by a state court global settlement, has commenced. In this situation, a state court should proceed as follows.

a) Obtaining information about the federal claims. As soon as it appears that a proposed state court settlement would release a pend-

---

[124] See *In re Mobile Communications Corp. of Am., Inc. Consol. Litig.*, 1991 WL 1392, *6 (Del Ch) (noting that federal class action was commenced subsequent to the preliminary fairness hearing), reprinted in 17 Del J Corp L 297, aff'd 608 A2d 729 (Del 1992). Compare *McCubbrey v Boise Cascade Home & Land Corp.*, 71 FRD 62, 69 n 15 (ND Cal 1976) (listing several individual actions that were filed after class notice was sent but before the settlement was approved).

[125] The court, of course, must still evaluate the fairness of the settlement at the settlement hearing in light of all relevant information, including any evidence presented by a federal plaintiff who appears as objector in the state fairness hearing.

ing federal claim, the defendant should be required to inform the state court of the federal claim and of the identity of the federal plaintiffs. To obtain information about these federal claims in the most expeditious manner, the court should invite counsel for the federal plaintiffs, and in particular counsel for the lead plaintiff if one has been appointed, to a *preliminary* fairness hearing.[126] At the preliminary hearing, the federal plaintiffs through their counsel should be given full opportunity to inform the judge about their views of the strength of the federal claims to be released, the fairness of the settlement, and the circumstances in which the settlement was negotiated.[127] The court should also take into account the extent to which the federal and the state plaintiffs' counsel have examined the facts and the law bearing on the strength of the federal claims. Finally, the state court should give substantial weight to the views of a federal lead plaintiff, to whom Congress—through the Private Securities Litigation Reform Act— has entrusted the preliminary responsibility of class representation.

There are two major benefits to inviting representatives of the federal plaintiffs to a preliminary hearing. First, if the court rejects a proposed settlement, it is preferable to do so at a preliminary hearing, before the time and expense of sending notice to class members and holding a final hearing are incurred.[128] Second, it may be easier at the preliminary stage to address deficiencies in the structure of the proposed settlement or to renegotiate its terms.

If a settlement is approved, counsel for federal plaintiffs should in proper circumstances be awarded attorneys' fees even if she does not represent any plaintiffs in the state action and did not participate in the settlement negotiations. Such fees are appropriate whenever the presence of federal claims increased the litigation value of the claims and federal counsel contributed to the develop-

---

[126] If the appointment of a lead plaintiff in the federal action is imminent, the judge should postpone the preliminary hearing until a lead plaintiff is appointed.

[127] If a federal court has issued rulings on the federal claim bearing on the strength of these claims, the state court should also review these rulings.

[128] For the costs of notice, see *FJC Study* at 129–30 (cited in note 62) ("Across the [four] districts, in the cases for which data were available, the median costs of distributing notices exceeded $36,000 per case and in two of the districts, the median costs were reported to be $75,000 and $100,000 per case. [footnote omitted] In at least 25% of the cases in each district, the cost of notice exceeded $50,000 per case and in two of the districts, such costs exceeded $100,000 per case. These data are best viewed as a collection of anecdotes and estimates.").

ment of these claims.[129] The award to the state counsel should correspondingly be reduced.[130]

An award of attorneys' fees to the federal counsel is compelled by considerations of fairness, incentives, and federalism. To the extent that the work product of the federal counsel resulted in an increase in the amount defendant was willing to settle for, the proper party to be rewarded is the federal counsel. Moreover, if the federal counsel could not obtain fees in a state global settlement, such counsel could be placed in a dilemma. When faced with a global settlement proposal that is fair, the counsel would either have to favor the settlement—and forfeit any fees for her work— or oppose the settlement despite its fairness.[131] Finally, due regard for the Congressional scheme for the appointment of a lead plaintiff requires that the counsel selected by the lead plaintiff be compensated to the extent that she contributed to the class recovery.

We expect that this integrated role of a federal plaintiff—in particular, an appointed federal lead plaintiff—at the preliminary hearing stage will, in turn, influence the way in which a proposed

---

[129] Some courts recognize the possibility of awarding attorneys' fees to lawyers other that class counsel. See, for example, *In re Marine Midland Motor Vehicle Leasing Litig.*, 155 FRD 416, 422–23 (WDNY 1994) ("in order for the court to grant the fee petition of [objecting plaintiff's] counsel, counsel must demonstrate that they had performed specific services that have benefited the fund in some tangible way"). Other courts have awarded such fees. In *In re Amsted Indus. Inc. Litig., Consol.*, 1988 Del Ch LEXIS 116, aff'd 567 A2d 1279 (Del 1989), the court awarded such fees to an objecting class member's attorney, even though the value of the settlement to the class was not increased and the counsel "failed to win acceptance of his position." Id at *32. Instead the court noted the counsel's "determined, detailed and highly professional advocacy" which "forced the court to review the proposal most searchingly." Id. The court went on to note the counsel's participation in discovery, id at *33, and stated that "the class has benefitted thereby in just the way it would benefit if the court were to require an additional expert to evaluate a settlement." Id at *34.

The notion of awarding fees to attorneys who made a substantial contribution to the proceeding has been implemented in bankruptcy. See 11 USC § 503(b)(3)(D), (b)(4) (providing for "administrative expense" priority any creditor, indenture trustee, or equity security holder and their attorneys who make a "substantial contribution" to a case).

A more radical approach for using the law on attorneys' fees to enhance the participation of individual litigants and their counsel in the context of mass tort litigation is found in Judith Resnick, Dennis E. Curtis, and Deborah R. Hensler, *Individuals Within the Aggregate: Relationship, Representation, and Fees*, 71 NYU L Rev 296 (1996).

[130] See *In re Amsted*, 1988 Del Ch LEXIS at *32 (noting that settlement agreement provided for legal fees not to exceed $300,000, and granting fees to objector's counsel which necessarily reduced amount available to class counsel).

[131] Conversely, state counsel's incentives to consent to an inadequate settlement for the federal claims are reduced if state counsel has to share fees with federal counsel according to their contributions. See text accompanying notes 72 and 81 (discussing how possibility of obtaining fee award for federal claim may induce state class attorney to assent to inadequate settlement).

global state court settlement is negotiated to start with. As we explain below, the views of the federal plaintiff with respect to the fairness and appropriateness of the proposed settlement are to be accorded substantial weight (at least as far as the federal claims are concerned); thus, a defendant who is not trying to engage in plaintiff shopping has every incentive to involve the federal plaintiff in the settlement negotiations from the start. Finally, our proposal would prevent a federal plaintiff who fails to respond to the state court's invitation to participate in the state court hearing from attacking a state court global settlement collaterally.[132] Thus, our proposal results in incentives to fashion participatory global settlements between the defendant and both the state and the federal plaintiffs.

b) Should the state court approve a global settlement? Even if a state court has access to the additional information we describe, the dangers of impaired bargaining power by the state class attorney and plaintiff shopping by the defendant remain.[133] Moreover, the interest of the state court in disposing of the claims through a settlement and the possibility of a partial (state-claim only) settlement will vary case by case. To illustrate how a state court should proceed, we discuss four different paradigm cases: first, the likelihood of success on the state and the federal claims turns on the same issues and plaintiffs are limited to one recovery[134] (the "single ex-

---

[132] See text accompanying notes 189–93. There are precedents for such "compulsory intervention." For example, the common law practice of "vouching in" allowed a defendant to give timely notice to a third person who had an obligation of indemnification to the defendant and to request that the third party undertake the defense. Whether or not the third party accepted the invitation to participate, the third party was bound by an adjudication of defendant's liability to the plaintiff. See James, Hazard, and Leubsdorf, *Civil Procedure* § 10.18 n 4 (Little Brown, 4th ed 1992). The Civil Rights Act of 1991, Pub L No 102-166, 105 Stat 1071, codified in part at 42 USC § 2000e-2(n), overturned the Supreme Court's decision in *Martin v Wilks*, 490 US 755 (1989) (holding that nonparties who have notice of an action and bypass an opportunity to intervene are not bound by the decree). Under section 108 of the amendments, in federal employment discrimination cases, a person who has notice of a proposed judgment or order and an opportunity to present objections in the action may not later challenge the practice that is resolved by the judgment or order.

[133] *Prezant v De Angelis*, 636 A2d 915, 925 (Del 1994) (noting that apparent fairness of settlement is not sufficient for settlement approval "because an adequate representative, vigorously prosecuting an action without conflict and bargaining at arms-length, may present different facts and a different settlement proposal to the court than would an inadequate representative").

[134] A combination of a state and a federal claim can increase exposure beyond one of the claims by itself if the claims do not turn on the same issues (thus making is possible to prevail on one claim but not on the other if both were litigated) or if recovery if the plaintiff prevails on both claims exceeds recovery if the plaintiff prevails on just one of the claims.

posure" case); second, the state and the federal claims turn on different issues and the state claims are stronger than the federal claims (the "state claims stronger" case);[135] third, the claims turn on different issues and the federal claims are stronger than the state claims (the "federal claims stronger" case); and fourth, the claims turn on different issues and both claims are about equally strong (or equally weak) (the "equal merits" case).

i) The "single exposure" case. As we explained earlier, in the "single exposure" case, a separate settlement of the state claims is not feasible, and a state has an obvious interest in disposing of claims arising under its own law and asserted in its own courts. Moreover, in the "single exposure" case, the bargaining power of the state class attorney is not impaired by her inability to assert the federal claims in state court since the federal claims would not contribute to either the plaintiffs' likelihood of prevailing or to the amount of damages if the plaintiffs prevail.

Two related problems remain, however: the ability of the defendant to engage in plaintiff shopping, and the undermining of the "lead plaintiff" provisions of the Private Securities Litigation Reform Act. If a global settlement is proposed in a state court, the state court should examine the conduct of the respective counsel for indicia of plaintiff shopping. A partial list of relevant factors includes: whether the state attorneys actively prosecuted the state claims or entered settlement negotiations immediately after the claims were filed; whether the federal attorneys actively prosecuted the federal claims; whether the defendant actively defended against the claims in both courts; the type of settlement discussions between the defendant and the different attorneys; the amount of attorneys' fees proposed to be awarded; and the timing of the relevant litigation and settlement activities (for example, whether the state claims were filed after negotiations with the federal plaintiffs broke down).[136]

---

[135] By stronger, we mean that the litigation value is higher. A claim may be stronger than another claim either because plaintiff's chances of obtaining recovery are higher or because damages are higher if plaintiff obtains recovery.

[136] State courts, of course, should also be aware of the opposite problem—the potential for federal claims being asserted for the principal reason of "spoiling" a global state court settlement. The problem of federal "spoiler" claims, however, is ameliorated by several provisions of the Federal Securities Litigation Reform Act. The Act makes it easier for a defendant to have a securities fraud claim dismissed and provides for mandatory sanctions

If the state court concludes that no plaintiff shopping took place and that the terms of the settlement are fair, it should approve a global settlement. The federal class attorney, of course, will have an opportunity to present views on both of these issues in the preliminary hearing.

ii) The "state claims stronger" case. If the state and federal claims turn on different issues or potentially afford different measures of damages, a state's interest in disposing of its claims in its own courts is also strong if the state claims are stronger than the federal claims.[137] Moreover, if the federal claims are weak, the concern that they may not be adequately dealt with in the state proceeding is ameliorated. Thus, a state court can approve a global settlement so long as the settlement meets the ordinary standards necessary for approval.

We caution, however, that the very issue of assessing the relative merits of the state and the federal claims brings into play the concerns discussed in the previous section. That is, a state class attorney has an incentive to play down the federal claims that she cannot litigate, and the defendant has the ability to "shop" for a state attorney that will do so and settle the claims cheaply. The court should take this into account in assessing the relative merits of the state and the federal claims and give particular weight to the views of the counsel for the federal lead plaintiff. Since Congress through the Private Securities Litigation Reform Act has put its trust in lead plaintiffs and their counsel adequately to represent a class of securities claimants, the state court should give proper deference to this mechanism. Nonetheless, the focus should be on the assessment of the relative merits of the claims.[138]

iii) The "federal claims stronger" case. If the federal claims are stronger than the state claims, a global settlement in state court

---

for filing frivolous claims. Moreover, the provisions for the appointment of a lead plaintiff reduce the incentives to file a "spoiler" claim. See notes 76–77 and accompanying text.

[137] The relative strength of the state claims ought to be reflected in the substantive terms of the proposed settlement. A proposed settlement that offers only minimal recovery to class members is unlikely to be based on relatively strong state claims and should not be analyzed under this subsection.

[138] For cases that discuss the relative merits of claims, see, for example, *In re Mobile Communications Corp. of Am., Inc. Consol. Litig.*, 1991 WL 1392, *6–10 (Del Ch) (weighing the strength of several federal and state claims), reprinted in 17 Del J Corp L 297; *Raskin v Birmingham Steel Corp.*, 1990 WL 193326, *5 (Del Ch) (finding that of four sets of claims, federal Securities Exchange Act claims "appear to be the only seriously litigable claims and that they do not appear to be strong").

is not proper. The dangers of a "hijacking" of the federal claims are too high, and the state's interest is too low, to justify state court approval of a global settlement that is opposed by the federal plaintiff.[139] State courts, however, would be free to approve settlements that encompass only state claims, according to their normal procedures.

iv) The "equal merits" case. The case where the federal and state claims turn on somewhat different issues and neither claim can be said to be stronger may be the hardest to evaluate. In this case, there is a concern both about the ability of the defendant to engage in "plaintiff shopping" and about impaired bargaining power of the state class attorney. States have some interest in settling the state claim in state court, but separate settlements are conceivable (though a global settlement may be more efficient).

In the "equal merits" case, as in the "single exposure" case, the court should examine the conduct of the respective counsel for indicia of plaintiff shopping and not approve a settlement if they find that the defendant has engaged in it. Even if they find that there was no plaintiff shopping, state courts should give special weight to the views of a federal class attorney who opposes the settlement. In the "equal merits" case, unlike the "single exposure" case, a settlement of the state claim is not inextricably tied to a settlement of the federal claim; that reduces the state's interest in a global, as opposed to a state-claim only, settlement. Also, even in the absence of plaintiff shopping, the bargaining power of the state class attorney with respect to the federal claims is impaired.

One factor that a state court should consider in deciding whether to approve a global settlement in these circumstances is the progress of the litigation in the two fora. If the federal litigation has progressed significantly, the state court should not approve a settlement encompassing the federal claims. The benefit of settling the federal claims is reduced since the parties have already expended much litigation effort on these claims. Moreover, if there were to be a settlement, the federal court that had overseen the prior litigation would be in a better position to assess its fairness.

---

[139] The first MCA settlement proposal, which the Delaware Chancery Court rejected, presumably falls in this "Federal Claims Stronger" category. See text accompanying note 22.

On the other hand, if the state litigation had progressed significantly and the federal litigation had not, the state court may be the superior forum for entertaining a global settlement.

Finally, the state court needs to remain cognizant that as far as the federal claims are concerned, the positions of the state and the federal class attorney are not equal. Under the timetable provided by the Securities Litigation Reform Act, the appointment of a lead plaintiff will ordinarily either have occurred or be imminent when the state court settlement is proposed. Thus, at least in securities cases, the federal class attorney will have the imprimatur of a Congressional judgment as to who can best represent the class members. The state class attorney not only lacks this imprimatur but lacks any authority to litigate the federal claims and thus has a disadvantage in bargaining over the terms on which they ought to be settled. Given this status gap, state courts should refrain from approving a global settlement opposed by the federal class attorney unless the state court is convinced that its failure to approve a global settlement would be seriously detrimental to the interests of the class members.[140]

IV. Availability of Federal Collateral Attack

In Part III, we proposed a set of safeguards to protect against the dangers in state court global settlements and to take account of federal interests at stake when exclusive federal claims are released as part of such settlements. Another attractive feature of our proposal is that it provides an alternative to collateral attack as a means of protecting federal interests.

A. THE GENERAL PROBLEM OF COLLATERAL ATTACK IN CLASS ACTION SETTLEMENTS

As a matter of due process, class action judgments and settlements can bind absent class members only when there has been adequate representation by the class representatives. Class action procedures in both the federal and state courts generally provide

---

[140] The application of these criteria to the second MCA settlement is discussed in the text accompanying notes 187–91.

for a determination that the representative party will "fairly and adequately protect the interests of the class"[141] to be made as part of the class certification process. Challenges to a finding of adequacy of representation can be reviewed through the appellate process and (as due process issues) ultimately by the Supreme Court of the United States.

What is unclear is whether a determination of adequacy of representation—either in litigation or in a settlement—may be collaterally challenged by class members. In the non-class context, absent fraud and collusion, collateral attacks are generally limited to issues of personal and subject matter jurisdiction, both of which determine a court's power to proceed. Even then, such a challenge is usually authorized only where a defendant defaults in the first action and raises the jurisdictional issue collaterally. This general policy limiting collateral attacks requires parties to litigate and appeal disputed issues in the case as it is being heard, and accords finality to whatever decision is reached. Jurisdiction is an exception because it is thought that the defendant should not have to raise the matter of jurisdiction before a court without the power to proceed.[142]

To some degree, the question of adequate representation in class actions is akin to the question of jurisdiction: both go to the basis of the court's authority over the absent class member, and both implicate due process of law. This suggests that lack of adequate representation—like lack of jurisdiction—may be raised collaterally. On the other hand, a court hearing a class action does have personal jurisdiction over absent class members if there has been

---

[141] Adequate representation under FRCP 23(a)(4) encompasses both the adequacy of the representative plaintiff and the adequacy of class counsel. Newberg, *Class Actions* at § 7.24 (cited in note 57) (stating that adequate representation requires both); see also *Manual for Complex Litigation, Third* § 30.16 (1995) (noting that selection of class counsel has implications for adequacy of representation).

[142] With respect to personal jurisdiction, a defendant may challenge jurisdiction collaterally only if he defaults and does not appear in the action. Otherwise, the defendant must contest jurisdiction in the action (or waive it) and will be bound by the court's determination. Subject matter jurisdiction may get somewhat more favorable treatment in a collateral challenge. If there is no default and the issue of subject matter is raised and decided (or if it could have been raised), collateral attack is usually not permitted. But when a court "lack[s] capability to make an adequately informed determination of a question concerning its own jurisdiction," a party may be given the opportunity to attack the court's subject matter jurisdiction in a collateral challenge. See Restatement (Second) of Judgments § 12 (1982).

notice and a right to opt out;[143] forcing a class member to object to the adequacy of representation in the court entertaining the proposed class suit thus does not undermine the adequacy requirement in the way that forcing a party to raise the lack of personal jurisdiction directly would undermine the personal jurisdiction requirement.

Moreover, a court entertaining a proposed class action is charged with the responsibility of assuring "adequacy" before a class action is permitted. In a contested case, the issue of adequacy will usually be litigated, and the court will have the arguments of counsel to aid it in deciding the matter. In a settlement, where there may be no adversarial litigation of adequacy,[144] the court itself has the obligation to make the finding of adequate representation.[145] The court's determination, like other issues litigated by class representatives, is binding on absent class members.[146] These arguments suggest that, as long as the court entertaining a proposed class action affords class members fair opportunity to raise the issue, adequacy of representation should be raised directly, and not be permitted to be raised collaterally.

The choice of the appropriate model for raising the issue of "adequate representation" in class action *settlements* faces the Ninth Circuit on remand in *Matsushita*.

---

[143] In *Phillips Petroleum Co. v Shutts*, 472 US 797 (1985), the Supreme Court held that absent class members who receive individual notice and fail to opt out of a proposed class action "consent" to the jurisdiction of the court.

[144] Objectors to the settlement may contest the issue; indeed, our proposal invites other counsel who object to the settlement to raise their objections directly in the settlement court.

[145] See, for example, *In re California Micro Devices Securities Litig.*, 1996 US Dist LEXIS 1361, *5–6 (ND Cal) ("A critical factor in determining whether a settlement is worthy of court approval under FRCP 23(e) is whether the class has been 'fairly and adequately' represented by the class representative during settlement negotiations.").

[146] Note, however, that a representative does not bind those for whom he acts as against third parties who are aware of the representative's failure to fulfill his responsibility. This limitation encompasses collusion or other situations where the representative's management of the litigation is so deficient as to be apparent to the opposing party. See generally Restatement (Second) of Judgments § 42(1)(e) (1982):

> (1) A person is not bound by a judgment for or against a party who purports to represent him if:
> . . . .
> (e) The representative failed to prosecute or defend the action with due diligence and reasonable prudence, and the opposing party was on notice of facts making that failure apparent.

B. HINTS FROM THE SUPREME COURT IN MATSUSHITA

At the Supreme Court, the federal due process challenge was avoided by the majority of the Court. Footnote 5 of Justice Thomas's opinion states: "We need not address the due process claim . . . because it is outside the scope of the question presented in this Court."[147] Nonetheless, Justice Thomas's additional observations in that same footnote may be some indication of his predisposition. He wrote that the due process challenge is made "in spite of the Chancery Court's express ruling, following argument on the issue, that the class representatives fairly and adequately protected the interests of the class."[148]

Justice Ginsburg, in her partial dissent, offered an extensive analysis of the due process question, providing a roadmap for a possible constitutional collateral attack on the Delaware judgment. Justice Ginsburg first observed that the Supreme Court's decision in *Kremer v Chemical Construction Corp.*[149] provides a limited exception to 28 USC § 1738 in that a " 'state may not grant preclusive effect in its own courts to a constitutionally infirm judgment, and other state and federal courts are not required to accord full faith and credit to such a judgment.' "[150] She emphasized that due process requires more than notice and an opportunity to opt out—both of which were available in the Delaware proceeding—and stressed that adequate representation is critical in "class action lawsuits, emphatically including those resolved by settlement."[151]

What Justice Ginsburg did not say—and what the Supreme Court heretofore has left unanswered—is whether state rulings on these matters can be second-guessed in a collateral attack. Justice Ginsburg's characterization of the Delaware court proceedings in this case—"the order contains no discussion of the adequacy of the representatives" and the settlement approval "contains only boilerplate language" on adequacy of representation—suggests

---

[147] 116 S Ct at 880 n 5.

[148] Id. The Court drops a "cf" citation to *Prezant v De Angelis*, 636 A2d 915, 923 and quotes language from that decision: "[The] constitutional requirement [of adequacy of representation] is embodied in [Delaware] Rule 23(a)(4), which requires that the named plaintiff 'fairly and adequately protect the interests of the class.' " (alterations in original).

[149] 456 US 461 (1982).

[150] 116 S Ct at 888 (quoting *Kremer*, 456 US at 482).

[151] 116 S Ct at 890.

that she would open the door for some kind of limited check on this issue by the federal court.

C. THE CASE LAW BACKDROP

The leading case permitting a collateral attack for a failure of adequate representation of class members is the well-known early case of *Hansberry v Lee*.[152] (Indeed, plaintiffs have suggested that *Matsushita* is the modern corporate equivalent of *Hansberry*.) In *Hansberry*, a first action was brought in Illinois state court by white landowners to enforce a racially restrictive real property covenant[153] "in behalf of themselves and all others similarly situated."[154] The parties stipulated—falsely, as it turned out—that the requisite number of property owners had signed the covenant, thus making the covenant enforceable.[155] Without definitive procedures, like those under Rule 23, in place, the court in the initial action did not formally designate the action as a class suit and made no finding of adequate representation.[156] The husband of the named plaintiff in the first action, who was a member of the original class, then brought a second action in Illinois state court. The state court held that he was precluded from challenging the stipulation in the first suit.[157] The Supreme Court of the United States reversed, holding that the "procedure and the course of litigation"[158] were insuffi-

---

[152] 311 US 32 (1940).

[153] See *Burke v Kleiman*, 277 Ill App 519 (1934).

[154] 311 US at 45. In its decision reviewing the later action, the Supreme Court described the plaintiffs in this first action as seeking "to compel performance of the agreement in behalf of themselves and all others similarly situated," noting that they "did not designate the defendants in the suit as a class or seek any injunction or other relief against others than the named defendants, and the decree which was entered did not purport to bind the others." Id.

[155] See *Burke*, 277 Ill App 519 (holding the covenant enforceable); *Lee v Hansberry*, 372 Ill 369, 372, 24 NE2d 37, 38 (1939) (noting factual finding that only about 54% had signed, not the requisite 95%).

[156] Although it is sometimes suggested that *Hansberry* may also have been a case about inadequate notice, it should be noted that the class member who challenged the original judgment was the husband of the plaintiff who brought the initial action. See *Hansberry*, 372 Ill at 372. Although as a "common law" class action there were no formal procedures by which class members could object or opt out, the *Hansberry* class, as property owners subscribing to a common covenant, might well fall within a modern Rule 23 (b)(1)(A) class, where opt-outs would not be required. Adequate representation would, of course, still have to be found.

[157] *Hansberry*, 372 Ill 369.

[158] 311 US at 44.

cient to satisfy the requirements of a class suit. The Court acknowledged that members of a class not present as parties to the litigation may be bound by a judgment "where they are in fact adequately represented by parties who are present,"[159] but the Court held that "due process" requires that the "procedure adopted, fairly insures the protection of the interests of absent parties who are to be bound."[160]

Hansberry presents a good fit for the *Kremer*-type exception, which has generally been interpreted to mean that a judgment need not be recognized if there was no full and fair opportunity to raise objections in the initial proceeding. However, it offers little guidance as to the obligations of parties who forgo the opportunity to challenge adequacy in the initial proceeding and later attempt to raise a collateral challenge.[161] Unlike in *Hansberry*, various procedural safeguards for the protection of absent class members were present in the Delaware *Matsushita* proceedings, including formal notice, the right to opt out, and an opportunity to object.[162] (Indeed, objections to the settlement on the basis of possible collusion, unfairness of the settlement, and lack of adequate representation had been raised by several members of the class in the Delaware proceedings, although not by the Epstein plaintiffs.)[163]

---

[159] Id at 43.

[160] Id at 42. See also *Richards v Jefferson County, Ala.*, 116 S Ct 1761 (1996) (where taxpayer plaintiffs in state action did not sue on behalf of a class and the judgment in the action did not purport to bind taxpayers who were nonparties, other taxpayer plaintiffs in federal action were not bound by prior judgment).

[161] The Reporter's Note to Restatement (Second) of Judgments § 42, Comment e (1982), discusses the black letter rule in § 42(d) that a person is not bound by a class representative if there is such a divergence of interest that he could not fairly represent them. The Reporter's Note, citing *Hansberry v Lee*, states: "The finding of divergence of interest may, of course, be made on collateral challenge." However, as we have explained above, *Hansberry* itself was a case where there were no procedures available in the direct proceeding to challenge the alleged conflict between class members.

[162] See *In re MCA, Inc. Shareholders Litigation*, 1993 WL 43024 (Del Ch) and Del Ch Ct R 23.

[163] The Epstein Briefs to the Ninth Circuit on remand insist that the objectors did not raise "adequate representation claims at all," see Reply Brief for Appellants at 18, *Epstein v MCA Inc.*, No 92-55675 (9th Cir 1996), and that "no one focused on adequate representation apart from collusion," Opening Brief at 22 (emphasis removed). However, Matsushita states in its Briefs that the arguments raised by plaintiffs on remand—that the settlement was collusive, that defendants were attempting to purchase immunity for a meager sum, that the Delaware plaintiffs were unable to litigate the federal claims and did not understand their true value, that the settlement benefited the wrong class, that the Delaware representatives did not provide adequate representation, and that the settlement was designed solely

Recent cases dealing with collateral attacks on *federal* class action settlements appear to have interpreted *Hansberry* in precisely this way. Collateral attacks based on inadequacy of representation have not been looked on favorably;[164] and the few courts that have permitted a limited attack rejected the challenge on the merits.[165] A restrictive approach to collateral attack is justified in this context because federal class action procedures in effect appoint the court as guardian of the interests of absent class members to ensure adequate representation and the fairness of any settlement.[166] When class members have an opportunity to object to the settlement and to opt out of it, there is little reason to allow a party who refuses to avail itself of these opportunities to attack the settlement collaterally. In effect, a collateral attack in these circumstances is a post-settlement opt-out that undermines the ability to settle a class action altogether. Moreover, if the court is assessing adequacy of representation at the time the settlement is approved (rather than as a predictor at the start of litigation, as in class actions that go to trial), it has information about the quality of representation at

---

to eradicate the federal claims which the Delaware representatives grossly undervalued, see Defendants' Brief in Response at 7–8—were actually litigated by the Delaware objectors, see Defendants' Sur-Reply Brief at 6.

[164] See, for example, *Thompson v Edward D. Jones & Co.*, 992 F2d 187 (8th Cir 1993) (holding that plaintiff, who received notice of earlier class settlement and failed to opt out, was bound by settlement agreement, and stating that plaintiff should have objected to the settlement or sought direct relief from the judgment in the earlier action); *King v South Cent. Bell Tel. & Tel. Co.*, 790 F2d 524, 530 (6th Cir 1986) ("King had retained her own counsel and there was ample time to challenge the class action settlement by appeal. She chose to attack the settlement collaterally and should not now complain of any inadequacy in representation.").

[165] See, for example, *In re Agent Orange Prod. Liab. Litig.*, 996 F2d 1425, 1437 (2d Cir 1993) (rejecting challenges to class action settlement on adequacy of representation grounds due to conflict between present and future claimants), cert denied sub nom *Ivy v Diamond Shamrock Chems. Co.*, 510 US 1140 (1994); *Brown v Ticor Title Ins. Co.*, 982 F2d 386, 390–91 (9th Cir 1992) ("[T]o avoid the binding effect of a prior class action based on class counsel's error, a party must show not only that the prior representative 'failed to prosecute or defend the action with due diligence and reasonable prudence,' but also that 'the opposing party was on notice of facts making that failure apparent.' " (quoting Restatement (Second) of Judgments § 42 (1982))), cert dismissed *Ticor Title Ins. Co. v Brown*, 511 US 117 (1994).

Compare *Gonzales v Cassiday*, 474 F2d 67 (5th Cir 1973) (collateral attack on class action *judgment* for inadequate representation permitted where class representative secured a better monetary deal for himself than for rest of the class; behavior of class representative *after* certification gave rise to challenge to adequacy of representation).

[166] See generally Note, *Collateral Attack on the Binding Effect of Class Action Judgments*, 87 Harv L Rev 589 (1974).

all relevant times.[167] Finally, the federal appellate courts are available to check abuses by the trial courts with respect to determinations of adequacy of representation.[168]

The equities with respect to collateral attack are somewhat different in the *Matsushita*-type settlement, where a state court is releasing exclusive federal claims. As we have shown, there are institutional process deficiencies in global state court settlement—deficiencies that our proposals seek to remedy. In the absence of safeguards like those we recommend, potential dangers in the settlement process necessarily raise questions about the adequacy of representation. The weaker bargaining power of the state class at-

---

[167] Collateral attack, as a postjudgment election to opt out, makes more sense in the nonsettlement context, where the adequacy of representation may be satisfied at the time of class certification, but the *later* conduct of the representative is actual evidence of "inadequate representation." This was the situation in *Gonzales*, 474 F2d 67, where the court permitted a collateral attack on a class action judgment. The first court's finding of adequacy of representation did not preclude the second court from evaluating the quality of representation with respect to conduct that took place after the initial certification.

[168] In settlement class actions, effective review means giving unnamed class members the right to appeal adequacy of representation and fairness of the settlement, including attorneys' fees. However, both state and federal courts are split on whether absent class members, who do not object or intervene, have standing to appeal. See Note, *Un-Appealing Class Action Settlements: Who No One Has Standing to Challenge Settlements after Haberman v. Lisle*, 49 Ark L Rev 375 (1996); Timothy A. Duffy, *The Appealability of Class Action Settlements by Unnamed Parties*, 60 U Chi L Rev 933 (1993). Federal review is conducted under the abuse of discretion standard. See, for example, *DeGrace v Rumsfeld*, 614 F2d 796, 810 n 12 (1st Cir 1980) ("Where, as here, the district court has not operated under any erroneous legal premises in its application of the requirements of Fed.R.Civ.P. 23, its decision will be overturned only upon a showing that it abused its discretion."); *Harris v Peabody*, 611 F2d 543 (5th Cir 1980) (holding that district court did not abuse its discretion in dismissing party as inadequate representative). See also Newberg, *Class Actions* at § 11.60 (cited in note 57) (noting "when the district court simultaneously certifies a class and approves a settlement, the court [of] appeal 'will more rigorously scrutinize the [d]istrict court's analysis of the fairness, reasonableness and adequacy of both the negotiation process and the proposed settlement.'" (quoting *In re Drexel Burnham Lambert Group, Inc.*, 960 F2d 285, 292 (2nd Cir 1992))).

State courts also seem to conduct a similar review. See *Prezant v De Angelis*, 636 A2d 915, 925 (Del 1994) (stating that challenges to settlements based on noncompliance with Rule 23 requirements will be reviewed only for abuse of discretion).

For the view that adequacy of representation by the attorney should be reviewed de novo, see *In re Asbestos Litig. (Ahearn)*, 90 F3d 963, 1009 (5th Cir 1996) (Smith dissenting) ("We apply a mixed standard of review to a district court's determination that a conflict of interest does not exist. The existence of a particular set of circumstances is a factual determination that we review for clear error. Whether those circumstances amount to a conflict of interest is a legal question that we review de novo."). Compare *FDIC v United States Fire Ins. Co.*, 50 F3d 1304, 1311 (5th Cir 1995) ("[W]e interpret the controlling ethical norms governing professional conduct as we would any other source of law." (quoting In re Dresser Indus., Inc., 972 F2d 540, 543 (5th Cir 1992), "[W]e will perform a 'careful examination,' or de novo review, of the district court's application of the relevant rules of attorney conduct.").

torney, the defendant's ability to engage in plaintiff shopping, the state court's reduced ability to obtain information and evaluate the fairness of the settlement, and (in future cases) the undermining of the lead plaintiff scheme of the Federal Securities Litigation Reform Act[169] make the process of determining adequacy potentially suspect.

If no collateral review is permitted in federal court, federal plaintiffs with exclusive federal claims are forced to raise their objections to the propriety of a state court global settlement in a forum without jurisdiction over the claims themselves. The federal plaintiffs are subject to the vagaries of state court procedures and state court judges who will decide the adequacy of representation and fairness of the settlement of claims that Congress has prohibited state courts from entertaining. While theoretically any due process violation can be remedied through direct Supreme Court review, as a practical matter that check is not a meaningful one.

On the other side, however, stand the strong policies with respect to finality of, and respect for, state court adjudication. By definition, in a court-approved settlement, a state court has determined that the class is adequately represented and that the settlement is fair. Moreover, the state court has at least implicitly determined that it is a proper forum for entertaining a global settlement encompassing exclusive federal claims. Allowing a collateral attack undermines the very authority of the state that is recognized in *Matsushita*. The finality of the state's settlement authority is impaired because there is always the threat of subsequent litigation, however weak the merits of the challenge. Indeed, dissatisfied class members may be encouraged *not* to appear in the state court proceeding, but instead to raise their objections in a collateral attack

---

[169] As noted earlier, the federal interests are even stronger with the enactment of the Private Securities Reform Litigation Act. The new Act expresses a Congressional policy that certain shareholders are the appropriate representatives of shareholders asserting federal claims under the Securities Acts. If the state class plaintiffs and their attorneys are other than those designated in the Congressional scheme, the state court's determination that there has been adequate representation may by incompatible with the federal scheme. In such a situation, the effect of the state court judgment in a subsequent action in federal court may be captured by the provision in Restatement (Second) of Judgments § 86(2) (1982):

> A determination of an issue by a state court does not preclude relitigation of that issue in federal court if according preclusive effect to the determination would be incompatible with a scheme of federal remedies which contemplates that the federal court may make an independent determination of the issue in question.

in federal court. In effect, class members can decide where they have the best opportunity to make the challenge, and engage in their own kind of forum shopping. The result will be a significantly reduced incentive for defendants to enter into a global state class settlement because there will always be the threat of additional litigation to challenge the settlement, even if the attack does not ultimately succeed on the merits. To grant state courts authority to enter global settlements releasing exclusive federal claims but subjecting such settlements to collateral review is the worst of all worlds. If the process by which state court findings about the adequacy of representation and fairness of the settlement is so imperfect that collateral attack is always possible, the better result would be to prohibit states from approving such global settlements in the first place.

To be sure, global settlements can always take place in federal court. But forcing all state claims related to federal securities matters into federal court—even when the federal claims are weak and might not have been asserted in the ordinary course—is hardly an attractive alternative. Multiple settlements with different groups of plaintiffs' counsel are also a possibility, but this alternative encourages duplicative litigation and substantially increases the transaction costs of settlements.

These concerns were sufficiently strong to lead two federal courts to reject federal collateral challenges to global settlements approved by state courts. In *Nottingham* and *Grimes*, the First and Third Circuits found that class members whose federal claims were released by a Delaware settlement (even ones without opt-out rights) could not collaterally attack the propriety of class certification or the fairness of the settlement in a subsequent federal action.[170] In *Nottingham*, the class members seeking to make a collateral attack had objected to the settlement (as well as its non-opt-out nature) in the Delaware Chancery Court and appealed the

---

[170] See *Nottingham Partners v Trans-Lux Corp.*, 925 F2d 29, 33 (1st Cir 1991) ("If, having objected and been overruled, appellants were still dissatisfied with the Delaware judgment, their recourse was to the United States Supreme Court by means of certiorari, not to the lower federal courts in the vain pursuit of back-door relief"); *Grimes v Vitalink Communications Corp.*, 17 F3d 1553 (3d Cir 1994) (holding where class objector pursued adequacy of representation and disclosures issues through the Delaware court system and to the Supreme Court, objector and other represented plaintiffs are barred from relitigating those issues in later-filed federal action). See generally Note, 87 Harv L Rev 589 (cited in note 166).

approval of the settlement to the Delaware Supreme Court. In *Grimes*, one of the class members appeared in Delaware and challenged both the adequacy of the representation and the fairness of the settlement; the other class member did not appear or raise objections in the state proceedings.[171]

As a matter of due process, the decisions in *Nottingham* and *Grimes* might be considered stronger cases for permitting collateral attack than *Matsushita* because the state court settlements in those cases did not provide for opt-outs by class members.[172] But in *Matsushita*, the settlement precluded federal claims brought as a *federal class action*.[173] Although class members in *Matsushita* were able to opt out of the Delaware settlement class, a small-stakes individual

---

[171] See *Grimes*, 17 F3d 1553.

A recent decision in the Seventh Circuit, *Kamilewicz v Bank of Boston Corp.*, 92 F3d 506 (7th Cir 1996), found that the *Rooker-Feldman* doctrine, see note 122, operates to limit a federal court's jurisdiction in an attack on a state court class settlement. In *Kamilewicz*, the court dismissed a complaint by class members who were charged attorneys' fees amounting to more than the amount of their recovery under the Alabama state court settlement and who subsequently brought a federal court action against the class attorneys for malpractice and against the bank for the injury resulting from the settlement. The Seventh Circuit construed *Rooker-Feldman* to bar a federal action that it regarded as an attempt to appeal a state court class action settlement. The court also noted that in these circumstances not even a challenge by absent class plaintiffs on personal jurisdiction grounds was sufficient to overcome the *Rooker-Feldman* bar. On denial of a rehearing en banc, a vigorous dissent by Judge Easterbrook, joined by four other judges, protested the expansion of *Rooker-Feldman* to bar a malpractice action. The dissent further argued that *Rooker-Feldman* should have no bearing on a collateral attack of a judgment based on lack of personal or subject matter jurisdiction. It also suggested that absent class members are not "parties" to a class action and therefore are outside the purview of *Rooker-Feldman*. 1996 US App LEXIS 30388.

Our own view is that traditional preclusion doctrine and not *Rooker-Feldman* is the appropriate analytical framework in the *Matsushita* context where a class member seeks to reassert the very claims released in a state court settlement (rather than claims arising from the settlement). It would be the ultimate irony if *Rooker-Feldman* were used to prevent federal courts from hearing exclusive federal claims.

[172] Because both state actions were suits for injunctive relief, the Delaware courts ruled that no opt-out was necessary, despite the fact that the releases included federal claims for money damages. See also *King v South Cent. Bell Tel. & Tel.*, 790 F2d 524 (6th Cir 1986) (class member in non-opt-out Title VII settlement in federal court precluded from raising adequacy of representation in collateral federal action).

For a contrary view of when opt-outs are required by due process for out-of-state plaintiffs, see *Colt Indus. Shareholder Litig.*, 565 NYS2d 755, 762, 566 NE2d 1160 (1991) (holding out-of-state plaintiff must be given an opportunity to opt out of predominantly equitable action whose settlement "purported to extinguish [plaintiff's] rights to bring an action in damages in another jurisdiction"). See also Note, *State Settlement Class Actions That Release Exclusive Federal Claims: Developing a Framework for Multijurisdictional Management of Shareholder Litigation*, 95 Colum L Rev 1765, 1783–91 (1995) (summarizing the different approaches taken in Delaware and New York).

[173] In *Nottingham*, a pending individual securities action brought on behalf of a large individual shareholder was held precluded by the non-opt-out Delaware class settlement;

federal action was the most likely alternative. A federal class action was viable in these circumstances only if the number of individual opt-outs were extremely high.[174] To the extent that a federal court is precluded from reexamining the issue of the adequacy of representation, the state court controls who "represents" federal class members with respect to the settlement of exclusive federal claims as well as the due process dimensions of such representation. In light of the Federal Securities Litigation Reform Act, federal plaintiffs have an even stronger claim that federal relitigation of the adequacy issue should be permitted. The revised federal standard for the appointment of a "lead plaintiff" to represent class members and to select class counsel now conflicts with the standards used by state courts for the selection of class representative and class counsel.[175] The argument is that the federal court must be free to decide for itself whether state court representatives were "adequate" to release the claims of a potential federal class.

Even here, however, broad collateral attacks are unwarranted. Just as we would reject a strict rule that the new Securities Litigation Reform Act prevents state court settlements from releasing exclusive federal claims, we do not believe it justifies relitigation of state determinations of adequacy made in the course of a global settlement. The more appropriate reform is to ensure that state

---

in *Grimes*, a later-filed federal action brought on behalf of two class members was held barred, and the ability to challenge the adequacy of representation was denied.

The federal district court in *Matsushita* denied class certification and dismissed the claim, but on appeal the Ninth Circuit ruled that the action was properly brought as a class action. Thus in its posture before the Ninth Circuit, the question is whether the Delaware settlement can appropriately release a federal *class* claim within the federal court's exclusive jurisdiction. It should also be noted that several plaintiffs did opt out of the Delaware settlement class, and those claims may proceed in federal court irrespective of the settlement.

[174] See *Prezant v De Angelis*, 636 A2d 915, 924 (Del 1994) (opt-out rights "are infrequently used and usually economically impracticable"). It might be possible to argue that where a federal class has been *certified* in federal court, it is appropriate for the federal class plaintiffs to "opt-out the entire federal class" from the state class settlement. Such a course of action was unavailable to the Epstein plaintiffs in *Matsushita* because class certification had been denied.

Such an approach would moot our proposal in the limited situation where a federal class is actually certified prior to approval of a state settlement. Although we recommend guidelines that would generally lead state courts to refrain from settling federal claims under these circumstances, we do not give the federal action an "absolute right to proceed." A "federal opt-out class" has the danger of offering unrestrained incentives to "spoiler" federal claims.

[175] The argument looks to the Restatement (Second) of Judgments § 86(2) (1982) exception to preclusion which permits relitigation if preclusion would undermine federal interests. See note 169. The point here would be that a federal court must be free to relitigate the issue of whether class representatives in the state class action were "adequate" to release

and federal courts share settlement authority in class actions involving federal and state claims, and that global settlements by state courts fairly and adequately take account of federal interests. Our proposal offers a set of procedures and safeguards to accomplish both of these objectives and thereby reduces the need for a subsequent federal collateral attack.

The arguments for federal collateral attack in a *Matsushita*-type settlement are based on the need to accommodate federal interests that carry with them important due process implications. By providing state courts considering global settlements with a fuller range of information and by enhancing their sensitivity to the federal interests involved in the release of exclusive federal claims, the quality of state settlement procedures is substantially improved. Objecting class members (and their counsel) have incentives to participate in the state proceedings, and as a result, state courts are able to make a realistic appraisal of the competing state and federal interests and accordingly determine the proper scope of a particular settlement.[176] Under such a regime, no collateral attack is warranted. State courts would engage in a genuine balancing of state and federal interests as part of the settlement process, and the settlement approval, like other state court determinations, is entitled to full faith and credit.

D. A RETURN TO MATSUSHITA

The analysis above does not directly speak to the issue of whether a collateral attack is appropriate in *Matsushita* itself. On the one hand, as a state court global settlement, it carries process deficiencies which we have previously discussed. On the other hand, the Private Securities Litigation Reform Act was not yet in place, and thus no express federal standard of "adequacy" determined who should represent a federal class on a federal securities claim.

But even before reaching the question of whether federal concerns, due process or other, override the preclusion required by 28 USC § 1738, there is an initial question as to what preclusion

---

federal *class* claims in light of the new Federal Securities Act provisions of who is an adequate representative of securities claims brought in federal court.

[176] The propriety of releasing the federal claim should be reviewable by the Supreme Court of the United States either as a matter of due process or because an improper release of a federal claim raises an issue of federal law.

Delaware itself would require to be given to the settlement. Under Section 1738, Delaware law, as an initial matter, determines whether or not a collateral attack is available.

In *Prezant v De Angelis*,[177] the Delaware Supreme Court spoke to the collateral attack point in a somewhat different context. In reversing the Chancery Court's approval of a state class settlement releasing federal claims, the Delaware Supreme Court ruled that there must be an explicit determination that the class representatives adequately represent the class before a settlement can be approved. Indeed, it instructed the Chancery Court to articulate on the record its findings regarding the satisfaction of the Rule 23 criteria and supporting reasoning in order to facilitate possible appellate review. The Court further commented:

> Such a determination will include a finding that their due process right to adequate representation has in fact been satisfied. *Defendants will be protected from a possible collateral attack on the validity of the settlement by a class member claiming the settlement did not meet the requirements of Rule 23.* This protection will help insure that the final release sought by defendants in settlements is indeed final.[178]

Thus, to the extent that a state court approving a class settlement made no findings of adequate representation, it seems that Delaware law might itself permit a collateral attack on due process grounds.

The Vice Chancellor's opinion approving the *Matsushita* settlement does not discuss adequate representation per se. It says only that the settlement is "fair," "in the best interests of the class," and that there is "no evidence of collusion."[179] Even though the Delaware Supreme Court (four months prior to *Prezant*) approved the settlement in a one-paragraph conclusory order,[180] the Vice Chancellor's opinion on its face seems to fail to satisfy the requirement to articulate in the record its findings regarding adequacy and supporting reasoning. Whether this suffices as a matter of

---

[177] 636 A2d 915 (Del Ch 1994).

[178] 636 A2d at 925–26 (emphasis added).

[179] *In re MCA, Inc. Shareholders Litig.*, 1993 WL 43024, at *1, *5 (Del Ch). The order and final judgment approving the settlement also contain general language referring to the adequacy of representation, but do not articulate specific findings regarding the satisfaction of the Rule 23 criteria and supporting reasoning. See *In re MCA, Inc. Shareholders Litig.*, No 11740 (Del Ch Feb 22, 1993) (Order and Final Judgment) (on file with authors).

[180] *In re MCA, Inc. Shareholders Litig.*, 633 A2d 370 (Del 1993).

Delaware law to preclude collateral attack raises at least a plausible issue for consideration.[181]

The more likely focus on remand, however, is the argument suggested by Justice Ginsburg—that *federal* due process provides the basis for a collateral attack on the state court settlement.[182] The Epstein plaintiffs contend in the proceedings on remand that they fall within the *Kremer* exception because the Delaware settlement lacked due process, and in particular that it failed to ensure that the class representatives met the adequate representation requirement. They rely specifically, as did Justice Ginsburg, on Section 42(d) of the Restatement (Second) of Judgments, which states that represented persons may avoid being bound when the "representative could not fairly represent them with respect to the matters as to which the judgment is subsequently invoked."[183]

Because they did not appear or participate in the Delaware proceedings, the Epstein plaintiffs contend that they may now challenge the adequacy of representation. As to the Chancery Court's determination that the Delaware plaintiffs "as representatives of the Settlement Class, have fairly and adequately protected the interests of the Settlement Class and that the maintenance of this action as a class action meets all the requirements of Rule 23(a) and (b)(3) of the Court of Chancery,"[184] they argue that no deference is

---

[181] The U.S. Supreme Court's majority opinion in *Matsushita* did forecast Delaware preclusion law to this degree: it stated that the "Delaware Supreme Court has further manifested its understanding that when the Court of Chancery approves a global release of claims, its settlement judgment should preclude on-going or future federal court litigation of any released claims." 116 S Ct at 879. However, since the due process issue was not addressed by the U.S. Supreme Court, Delaware's law on the particular point of if and when adequacy of representation may be challenged collaterally was never explored.

Note also that the Delaware Supreme Court affirmed the settlement in the *Matsushita* case on September 21, 1993; its decision in *Prezant*, requiring an express finding of adequate representation in the Chancery Court, was rendered on February 3, 1994. If Delaware law was not changed by *Prezant*, the mere affirmance of the *MCA* settlement by the Delaware Supreme Court might not prevent the collateral attack that *Prezant* implies; alternatively, a 60(b) proceeding in Delaware might have been possible.

[182] 116 S Ct at 888–90 (Ginsburg concurring in part and dissenting in part).

[183] Restatement (Second) of Judgments § 42(d) (1982).

[184] *In re MCA, Inc. Shareholders Litig.*, No 11740, at 2 (Del Ch Feb 22, 1993) (Order and Final Judgment) (on file with authors). The Epstein plaintiffs resist any characterization of the Delaware order as a "finding" because there is no evidence in the record as to the adequacy of representation and because the order referring to the adequacy of representation was prepared for the Vice Chancellor's signature by Delaware counsel. See Reply Brief for Appellants at 8–9, *Epstein v MCA Inc.*, No 92-55675 (9th Cir 1996).

due because there was no serious consideration or litigation of the issue.[185]

The broad role for collateral attack advocated by the federal plaintiffs in *Matsushita*—that is, that by not participating in the state settlement proceedings they are free to relitigate the issue of adequate representation and fairness of the settlement in their own action—claims too much. It would inhibit class action settlements not just in contexts like *Matsushita*—where the state court approving the settlement lacked jurisdiction over the federal claims—but it many other contexts as well. To be sure, under *Hansberry* and *Kremer*, plaintiffs may show that the *procedures* in place—or lack of them—were deficient as a matter of due process to assure adequacy of representation and fairness of the settlement. But this may be a difficult position for the Epstein plaintiffs to maintain. They appear to have had alternative routes to attack the Delaware settlement. Even if the opt-out route was unlikely to have preserved the viability of a future federal class, they were free (as other objectors did) to appear and object at the fairness hearing before the Chancery Court, and seek further review from the Delaware Supreme Court and ultimately (however unlikely) the Supreme Court of the United States. Indeed, even after the settlement was approved, they might have attempted to open up the judgment in the equivalent of a Rule 60(b) proceeding in Delaware.[186]

The purpose of a federal collateral attack is not to review state court findings of fact but to ensure that state class action settlement structures afford class members a fair opportunity to object to the adequacy of representation and to the substantive fairness of a settlement. When global state court settlements encompass exclusive federal claims, however, settlement structures must go further: they must also take account of the federal interests. Our proposals set forth in Part III are designed to assure that state courts are sensitive to these interests. While we do not suggest that state courts must adopt our proposal in all its details to insu-

---

[185] See Newberg, *Class Actions* at § 11.64 (cited in note 57) (arguing that collateral "relief should be granted . . . only in those rare circumstances in which the complaining party can demonstrate that the defect in proceedings was basic to the validity of the class judgment").

[186] See 116 S Ct at 890 n 11 (Ginsburg concurring in part and dissenting in part) (noting that "[c]ounsel for Matsushita acknowledged that relief from a judgment may be sought in Delaware pursuant to that State's counterpart to Federal Rule of Civil Procedure 60(b)").

late their global settlements against collateral attack, they must take reasonable measures to protect the federal interests—and guard against the deficiencies of global state court settlements that we discussed in Part II—in fashioning their settlement structures.

In *Matsushita*, the Delaware state courts showed some sensitivity to the impact of the release of the federal claims before it. The Chancery Court rejected the first settlement, noting that a state court must "carefully scrutinize" a global settlement in considering whether to release exclusive federal claims; when the second settlement was proposed, the court noted its reluctance "to take any action that could be construed as attempting to interfere with the appellate process in the federal courts"; and it noted that class certification had been denied in the federal action, that the federal claims had been dismissed, and that a motion for expedited appeal to the Ninth Circuit had not been granted. These facts appear to have been important to the Chancery Court's decision to approve the second settlement proposal.

On the other hand, several factors were present in the *Matsushita* settlement that, according to our proposal, should lead a state court to refrain from entertaining a global settlement: the federal claims were actively pursued while the state claims lay dormant; the defendant failed to have the state claims dismissed, even after the Chancery Court characterized them as extremely weak; the circumstances of the first settlement proposal suggest that it was intended to hijack the federal claims; the settlement proposal provided for relatively high attorneys' fees (which the court reduced by 74%); and, given the different nature of the claims, a settlement of just the state court claims was, in principle, possible.[187]

If the Federal Securities Litigation Reform Act had applied to the *Matsushita* claims, the Delaware global settlement would evidence sufficient disregard for the role of a federal plaintiff and of the federal interest to be subject to collateral attack. In *Matsushita* as it is presented to the Ninth Circuit, however, though the issue is close, we would not permit a collateral attack under federal law (though, as noted, we believe Delaware state law might well allow for collateral attack in these circumstances).

---

[187] See text accompanying notes 8–31.

Our conclusion is reinforced by the Epstein plaintiffs' strategic decision not to present their case to the Delaware courts.[188] As we discussed, it is state courts, in the first instance, that should decide whether or not to approve a global settlement, and proper incentives should be provided to all parties to supply information that the state courts need to make this decision. If federal plaintiffs fear that state courts do not take sufficient account of the federal interests, they should appear in state court and argue their case—rather than sit back and attack a state court settlement collaterally. Contrary to some federal courts who seem to regard objections by federal plaintiffs in the state proceedings as a reason not to permit collateral attack,[189] we view such an appearance in the state proceedings as a prerequisite for collateral attack[190]—at least as long as such an appearance in not clearly futile.[191] By forcing federal plaintiffs to raise objections in state courts, but permitting them to attack the settlement collaterally if the structures that state courts employ in settling federal claims do not reasonably protect the federal interests, state courts will have both the requisite information

---

[188] That choice may be the result of a decision like *Nottingham*, in which the First Circuit applied principles of issue preclusion to preclude a collateral attack on a no-opt-out Delaware global settlement where the federal class plaintiffs had previously raised their objections to the settlement in state court. Of course, the Third Circuit in *Grimes* had also barred a collateral attack in a situation where the federal plaintiff had made no objection in the state proceeding and no opt-out right had been afforded. See notes 42 and 170.

[189] See note 170 and accompanying text.

[190] The requirement is similar to a rule of exhaustion of remedies, such as the exhaustion of state remedies doctrine developed by the Supreme Court in the context of habeas corpus, see Charles Alan Wright, *Law of Federal Courts* 354 (West, 1994), and later written into the statute and recently amended, see 28 USC § 2254(b), (c), (d) (1996).

In the context of judicial review of administrative proceedings, exhaustion of "legislative" or "administrative" remedies may be required before certain federal actions can be brought; however, invocation of a state "judicial remedy" can result in preclusion by virtue of 28 USC § 1738, see *Kremer v Chemical Constr. Corp.*, 456 US 461, 470–71 (1982). *Kremer* itself leaves open an exception to preclusion if there was not a "full and fair opportunity" to litigate the claim or issue, id at 480–81, but adds that "state proceedings need do no more than satisfy the minimum procedural requirements of the Fourteenth Amendment's Due Process Clause in order to qualify for the full faith and credit guaranteed by federal law." Id at 481. Our position is consistent with *Kremer* in leaving open a structural challenge to state proceedings that fail to consider federal interests.

[191] Of course, raising objections to a proposed state court global settlement can only be a prerequisite for a collateral attack if the federal plaintiffs receive timely notice of the proposed settlement.

and an added incentive to abstain from settling exclusive federal claims when federal interests so require.

V. Implications for Class Action Settlements More Generally

The proposals we have urged for adoption by state courts are directed to the particular problems of global state court class settlements that release exclusive federal claims. We do not offer these procedures as a remedy for the alleged defects of class action litigation[192] or the claimed process deficiencies in other types of class settlements, such as mass torts[193] or voucher-based settlements.[194] Various reforms, such as improvements with respect to notice to absent class members,[195] broader opt-out rights,[196] and availability of interlocutory appeal of certification decisions,[197] have been advocated to improve the class action, and jurisdiction over absent class members and requirements of opt-out rights in class actions providing limited monetary relief will be issues before the Supreme Court this term.[198] More particularly, in the wake of de-

---

[192] Many of the problems of class action practice are surveyed by Professor Edward Cooper, Reporter to the Advisory Committee on Civil Rules, in *Rule 23: Challenges to the Rulemaking Power*, 71 NYU L Rev 13 (1996). See also Brian Wolfman and Alan B. Morrison, *Representing the Unrepresented in Class Actions Seeking Monetary Relief*, 71 NYU L Rev 439 (1996).

[193] See, for example, Coffee, 95 Colum L Rev 1343 (cited in note 80).

[194] See, for example, Note, *In-Kind Class Action Settlements*, 109 Harv L Rev 810 (1996).

[195] Empirical data relating to notice questions is included in *FJC Study* at 125–34, 146–49 (cited in note 62).

[196] See, for example, George Rutherglen, *Better Late Than Never: Notice and Opt Out at the Settlement Stage of Class Actions*, 71 NYU L Rev 258 (1996).

[197] Proposed amendment FRCP 23(f) permits appeals from an order granting or denying class certification at the discretion of the court of appeals. See FRCP 23(f), 91 F3d CCLXXVI, CCLXXVII (Proposed Draft, published Sept 16, 1996).

[198] See *Adams v Robertson*, 676 S2d 1265 (Ala 1995), cert granted 117 S Ct 37 (1996). In *Adams*, the Alabama Supreme Court approved a settlement in a nationwide state class action on behalf of cancer policy insureds who claimed that their insurer fraudulently caused them to switch cancer insurance policies. The settlement provided for the restitution of benefits available under the prior policies, elimination of monetary limits in the new policies, and reinstatement of lapsed policies without evidence of insurability or payment of back premiums, and released all other claims related to the insurance exchange program. Prior to any settlement being reached, a nationwide class was certified under Alabama Rule 23 (b)(1)(B) and 23(b)(2) without any provision for class members to opt out of the class in order to bring individual lawsuits. When a settlement was reached several months later, court-approved notice was sent to class members, providing class members with a right to object

bate over abuses in the class action settlement practice, class action settlements have been a subject of consideration in the Advisory Committee on Civil Rules, and a revision of Rule 23 has been circulated for notice and comment.[199] Two recent and important federal Court of Appeals decisions—in reaching conflicting decisions about the criteria that must be satisfied in order to have a class action settlement—have sharpened that debate.[200] The Third Circuit's opinion in *Georgine v Amchem Products Corp.*[201] held that the certification requirements of Rule 23—those of both Rule 23(a) and 23(b)(3)—are to be applied to class action settlements in the same way as they would be if the case were to be litigated. Under that standard, the court held that class counsel could not adequately represent both presently injured and futures claimants in class action litigation against asbestos manufacturers.[202] Several months later, in *In re Asbestos Litigation (Ahearn)*,[203] the Fifth Circuit approved a settlement class of extant and latent asbestos victims and expressed its view that the negotiation process and the settlement itself were important factors in determining whether certification of a class in a settlement context was proper. Both of the cases purported to be a construction of the present Rule 23, although there are obviously due process concerns about adequate representation lurking in the background. The issue is likely to be settled shortly by the Supreme Court of the United States, which recently granted certiorari in *Georgine*.[204]

The Advisory Committee on Civil Rules and the Standing Com-

---

to the settlement at a fairness hearing but not to opt out of the settlement because opt-outs "would create a risk of a race to the courthouse by those permitted to opt-out in an effort to obtain for themselves alone the entirety of the consitutionally permissible punitive recovery in one or a few individual actions." Id at 1296. The Alabama Supreme Court affirmed the trial court's findings that no opt-out right was required in this type of class action, and that out-of-state plaintiff class members/objections need not have "minimum contacts" with the State of Alabama in order to be bound by the class action settlement.

[199] See FRCP 23, 91 F3d at CCLXXVII (Proposed Draft) (cited in note 197).

[200] Compare *Georgine v Amchem Prods. Corp.*, 83 F3d 610 (3d Cir 1996) (reversing district court approval of certification and holding that settlement classes must meet the same requirements as classes certified for trial), cert granted sub nom *Amchem Prods. v Windsor*, 117 S Ct 379 (1996) with *In re Asbestos Litigation (Ahearn)*, 90 F3d 963 (5th Cir 1996) (holding that the settlement should be considered when determining whether the requirements of FRCP 23 have been met).

[201] 83 F3d 610 (3d Cir 1996).

[202] Id at 630–31.

[203] 90 F3d 963 (1996).

[204] See *Amchem Prods. v Windsor*, cert granted, 117 S Ct 379 (1996).

mittee on Rules of Practice and Procedure have proposed an amendment to Rule 23 for comment, which addresses the issue of settlement classes.[205] The present Rule 23, in subdivision (b), describes the three types of actions[206] that may be maintained as class actions, provided the prerequisites listed in subdivision (a) are met.[207] The proposed amendment adds a (b)(3) "settlement class" as an additional category (4) along with these requirements:

> (4) the parties to a settlement request certification under subdivision (b)(3) for purposes of settlement even though the requirements of subdivision (b)(3) might not be met for purposes of trial.[208]

No other criteria or procedures are included in the rule, and no specific guidelines for the approval of class action settlements are set forth.[209] As others have suggested,[210] more definite guidance is required.

As we have shown by our close examination of the particular type of class settlement involved in *Matsushita*, different species of class actions may call for specialized procedures that are not necessarily trans-substantive. At the same time, some of the deficiencies

---

[205] See FRCP 23(b)(4), 91 F3d at CCLXXVII (Proposed Draft) (cited in note 197).

[206] FRCP 23(b)(1) actions include those that, if prosecuted as individual actions, would either risk "establish[ing] incompatible standards of conduct" for the defendant or "as a practical matter be dispositive of the interests of the other members not parties to the adjudications or substantially impair or impede their ability to protect their interests." Rule 23(b)(2) actions are maintainable when the defendant "has acted or refused to act on grounds generally applicable to the class, thereby making appropriate final injunctive relief or corresponding declaratory relief with respect to the class as a whole." Rule 23(b)(3) actions require commonality and superiority: "questions of law or fact common to the members of the class predominate over any questions affecting only individual members, and that a class action is superior to other available methods for the fair and efficient adjudication of the controversy."

[207] FRCP 23(a) lists four prerequisites to a class action:

> One or more members of a class may sue or be sued as representative parties on behalf of all only if (1) the class is so numerous that joinder of all members is impracticable, (2) there are questions of law or fact common to the class, (3) the claims or defenses of the representative parties are typical of the claims or defenses of the class, and (4) the representative parties will fairly and adequately protect the interests of the class.

[208] See FRCP 23(b)(4), 91 F3d at CCLXXVII (Proposed Draft) (cited in note 197).

[209] Indeed, there is no express provision in the proposed Rule which authorizes opt-out rights in settlement classes, but the Advisory Committee Note indicates that members of settlement classes do have that right. The omission is criticized by John C. Coffee, Jr., *Class Action "Reform": Advisory Committee Bombshell*, NY L J 1 (May 21, 1996).

[210] See particularly Schwarzer, 80 Cornell L Rev 837 (cited in note 60).

we identify in class settlement practice, such as plaintiff shopping and the conflicts of interest between class counsel and class members, permeate class settlements more generally. Ultimately, we believe that class action settlements require special attention, and that more detailed procedures for class settlements ought to be included as part of the Rule 23 agenda. We hope that our proposals here will serve as a model for continuing efforts in that direction.

MICHAEL H. GOTTESMAN

UNION SUMMER: A REAWAKENED
INTEREST IN THE LAW OF LABOR?

At their peak in 1954, unions represented 38% of this nation's private sector employees.[1] Their role declined steadily over the next four decades, the loss of members accelerating in the 1980s.[2] In 1995, only 11.4% of private sector workers were represented by unions.[3] With the loss of members, the labor movement also lost its political potency: its influence within the Democratic party

Michael H. Gottesman is Professor of Law at Georgetown University Law Center.

AUTHOR'S NOTE: I wish to thank the following Georgetown law students for valuable research assistance: Robert Arreola, Julie Campbell, Jennifer Ness, David Orlin, and Samantha Whitehouse.

[1] Paul C. Weiler, *Promises to Keep: Securing Workers' Rights to Self-Organization Under the NLRA*, 96 Harv L Rev 1769, 1772 n 4 (1983) (hereinafter "Weiler, *Promises*") (citing data sources).

[2] By 1978, the figure had fallen to 24%. Id. By 1989, the figure had dropped to 13.5%. US Department of Commerce, *Statistical Abstract of the United States 1995*, Table No 695.

[3] US Department of Labor, Bureau of Labor Statistics, *Employment and Earnings*, Table No 42 at 212 (Jan 1996), reprinted in BNA, Daily Labor Report 28 (Feb 12, 1996): D-4 (private nonagricultural wage and salary workers). By contrast, 43.5% of public sector workers were represented by unions in 1995. Id. The divergence between the success of unions in the private and public sectors is explainable principally by two factors. First, public employers generally do not resist unionization, whereas most private employers do, and employer resistance is a powerful deterrent to unionization. Weiler, *Promises* (cited in note 1), at 1771–74; see also text accompanying notes 157–59. Second, the mechanisms for resolving negotiation deadlocks are different in the two sectors. The terminal point for public sector negotiations is arbitration or legislation (strikes ordinarily are forbidden by statute), while in the private sector the strike is the workers' only mechanism to induce settlement from a resistant employer, see text accompanying note 33. The advantage of having a professional bargaining representative in complex interest arbitration and/or to lobby the legislature is obvious, and no risk attends the choice. By contrast, the exercise of the right to strike has many costs. It is confrontational, expensive, and may cost the strikers their jobs. See text accompanying notes 33–43.

shriveled, and its lobbying clout in Congress virtually disappeared. In all respects, the labor movement had gone into a deep sleep.

As unions' standing plummeted in the 1980s, so did the Supreme Court's interest in the workplace. Until the 1983 term, labor and employment cases "dominated" the Supreme Court docket,[4] in some years garnering thirty or more decisions.[5] Since then, although the number of workers in the private sector has risen more than 20%,[6] the volume of Supreme Court decisions involving the workplace has steadily declined.[7] The nadir was reached in the 1994 term, when the Court issued only six decisions even remotely touching the workplace and none that involved unions.[8]

These parallel trajectories are not coincidental. Some drop in the volume of labor decisions would be expected, given that the Court now decides only half as many cases as a decade ago.[9] That

---

[4] 53 USLW 3083 (1984) (describing the fall-off in volume of labor and employment cases in the 1983 term).

[5] Id. In the 1981 Term, the Court decided 35 cases involving the workplace, 51 USLW 3087 (1982), and, in the 1982 Term, 30 such cases, 52 USLW 3055 (1983).

[6] There were 71 million nonagricultural wage and salary workers in the US private sector in 1983, US Department of Labor, Bureau of Labor Statistics, *Employment and Earnings* (Jan 1985), and 88 million in 1994. US Department of Labor, Bureau of Labor Statistics, *Employment and Earnings* (Feb 1996).

[7] In the 1983 and 1984 Terms, the numbers of decisions involving the workplace were 23 and 20, respectively. 53 USLW 3083 (1984); 54 USLW 3075 (1985). The number declined gradually thereafter to six in the 1994 term. 64 USLW 3095 (1995).

[8] *McKennon v Nashville Banner Publ'g Co.*, 115 S Ct 879 (1995) (after-acquired evidence of a discharged employee's wrongdoing does not bar all relief for a discharge motivated by age in contravention of the Age Discrimination in Employment Act, albeit it may foreclose reinstatement or front pay); *Hess v Port Auth. Trans-Hudson Corp.*, 115 S Ct 394 (1994) (bistate Compact Clause agency does not enjoy the Eleventh Amendment immunity accorded states, and thus may be sued in federal court by employees for violations of the Federal Employers' Liability Act); *Gutierrez de Martinez v Lamagno*, 115 S Ct 2227 (1995) (Attorney General's certification that a federal employee was acting within the scope of employment when committing a tort—a certification that triggers automatic substitution of the US as the party defendant in the tort suit in place of the employee—is subject to judicial review); *North Star Steel Co. v Thomas*, 115 S Ct 1927 (1995) (limitations period for suits under the Worker Adjustment and Retraining Notification Act is to be determined by most analogous state statute of limitations); *Curtiss-Wright Corp. v Schoonejongen*, 115 S Ct 1223 (1995) (ERISA's requirement that every benefit plan contain "a procedure for amending such plan and for identifying the persons who have authority to amend the plan" is satisfied by a plan provision stating, in its entirety, "the company reserves the right at any time to amend the plan"); *Milwaukee Brewery Workers' Pension Plan v Joseph Schlitz Brewing Co.*, 115 S Ct 981 (1995) (under ERISA's provision that employers withdrawing from multiemployer benefit plans may satisfy their share of the plan's unfunded liabilities by making payments over time, interest on the amortized charge begins to accrue on the first day of the plan year after withdrawal, not on the last day of the plan year preceding withdrawal).

[9] The Court issued signed opinions in 170 cases in the 1981 Term and 174 cases in the 1982 Term. 53 USLW 3028 (1984). By contrast, the Court issued signed opinions in 91

alone, however, cannot explain a drop from more than thirty to six. The decline of the labor movement undoubtedly accounts for much of the rest.

The fall-off in union density has "defederalized" the workplace. The relationship between unions, their members, and employers is governed largely by federal law.[10] But the relationship between unorganized workers and their employers is regulated principally by state law.[11] The decline in union membership has shifted the locus of legal regulation from federal to state law,[12] cutting the Supreme Court out of the loop.

Moreover, in the one area in which federal law most affects unorganized workers—the provision of minimum labor standards—labor's diminished lobbying influence has lightened the Court's workload. The decade between 1964 and 1975, when unions were still politically effective, witnessed the greatest outpouring of protective labor legislation this country has ever seen. Title VII of the Civil Rights Act of 1964, the Age Discrimination in Employment Act (1967), the Occupational Safety and Health Act (1970), and the Employee Retirement Income Security Act (1975) were all vigorously championed by the labor movement, and none likely would have been enacted without a politically powerful labor

---

cases in the 1994 Term, 64 USLW 3094 (1995), and 75 cases in the 1995 Term, 65 USLW 3041 (1996).

[10] Organizing, collective bargaining, and the deployment of economic weapons by each side to induce the other to agree are governed exclusively by the National Labor Relations Act, 29 USC §§ 151 et seq, which effectively preempts all state laws in these areas. Michael H. Gottesman, *Rethinking Labor Law Preemption: State Laws Facilitating Unionization*, 7 Yale J Reg 355, 374–83 (1990). Likewise, enforcement of the end-product of these processes, the collective bargaining agreement, is governed exclusively by federal law. Labor-Management Relations Act § 301, 29 USC § 185; *Textile Workers v Lincoln Mills*, 353 US 448 (1957); *Local 174, Teamsters v Lucas Flour Co.*, 369 US 95 (1962). So, too, is the legal relationship between the individual employee and the union governed principally by federal law—the duty of fair representation in the workplace, *Vaca v Sipes*, 386 US 171 (1967), and the Landrum-Griffin Act in the union hall, 29 USC §§ 401 et seq.

[11] There are a number of federal statutes that prescribe mandated floors for worker terms and conditions of employment, from a minimum wage to a safe and healthy occupational environment, but apart from these, the employment relationship in the private sector is governed by state statutory and common law. Similarly, with the exception of rights conferred by the federal Constitution, state law governs the relationship between states, local governments, and their employees regardless whether they are unionized. (Public employees are excluded from coverage of the NLRA.)

[12] See, for example, Clyde W. Summers, *Labor Law as the Century Turns: A Changing of the Guard*, 67 Neb L Rev 7 (1988) (predicting that the guardian of worker rights in the next century will be the states via common law rulings and statutes protecting individual workers, rather than the federal government via laws protecting collective bargaining).

lobby.[13] Each generated a long list of Supreme Court decisions. But, by the mid-1980s, the number of interpretative issues under these statutes requiring Supreme Court attention began to ebb.[14] Because Congress has not enacted new labor statutes of comparable magnitude since 1975, the Court's interpretative pipeline has not been refilled.[15]

I. Awakenings

The past year has witnessed an apparent reversal of both of these trends. The labor movement has shown signs of reawakening, and the Supreme Court has shown renewed interest in the workplace.

A long and heated campaign for the leadership of the AFL-CIO culminated in the election of an insurgent slate in October 1995. The slate had promised to reinvigorate the labor movement by

---

[13] OSHA and ERISA were proposed initially by the labor movement, and unions were their principal proponents throughout legislative consideration. Unions also lobbied heavily for the enactment of the Civil Rights Act of 1964, including Title VII. One union's role in bringing about an end to the filibuster over that bill—the longest filibuster in Senate history—is described in Rowland Evans and Robert Novak, *Inside Report: Cloture Post Mortem*, Washington Post (June 18, 1964), at A23:

> [E]ssential votes were picked off one by one. . . . Collaborating with Sen. Hubert Humphrey of Minnesota, manager of the bill, the United Steelworkers Union called in 32 activists in its politically potent "Legislative Education Committee" and turned them loose in the Senate office buildings. They latched down needed doubtful votes, including Sen. Howard Cannon, Nevada Democrat, and Ralph Yarborough, the liberal Democrat from Texas, who was fearful his vote would infuriate the conservative forces of Gov. John Connally. Humphrey, working up to the last minute, called the Steelworkers at 7:30 the morning of the cloture vote to get the word on Cannon.

[14] Of these statutes, only ERISA continues to generate any substantial number of Supreme Court opinions, including two in the 1994 Term, see note 8, and four in the 1995 Term, see note 28. The last Term in which the Court decided a significant number of Title VII cases was the 1988 Term, during which three controversial interpretations emerged that were subsequently overturned by the Civil Rights Act of 1991. *Price Waterhouse v Hopkins*, 490 US 228 (1989); *Wards Cove Packing Co. v Antonio*, 490 US 642 (1989); *Martin v Wilks*, 490 US 755 (1989).

[15] The few statutes affecting the workplace that have been enacted in recent years, most notably the Worker Adjustment and Retraining Act (1988) (requiring employers to give advance notice to employees of intended plant closings), the Americans with Disabilities Act (1990) (forbidding discrimination on the basis of physical and mental disability), the Civil Rights Act of 1991 (overturning several Supreme Court opinions construing Title VII, see note 14), and the Family and Medical Leave Act (1993) (requiring employers to permit employees to take leave without pay to attend to certain family crises), were not of the magnitude of those enacted in the 1964–75 era, and none has generated any substantial volume of Supreme Court opinions. In the 1995 Term, for example, only one opinion was issued involving a labor statute enacted after 1975. *Brown v United Food and Commercial Workers*, described infra at note 28.

pouring massive resources into organizing workers and utilizing innovative techniques to rebuilding unions' political clout. Upon taking office, the slate set about tackling both tasks.

On the political front, the AFL-CIO raised its dues and committed $35 million to promoting worker legislation and attempting to influence the 1996 congressional elections.[16] One-fourth of the delegates to the 1996 Democratic convention were union officials.[17] Vast resources were dedicated to a nationwide television advertising campaign supporting legislation to raise the minimum wage[18] and opposing reelection of the Republicans first elected to Congress in 1994. Robert Novak, no fan of the labor movement, expressed awe at the political clout of the "newly awakened sleeping giant of organized labor" and its "tough new leadership."[19]

On the organizing front, the new AFL-CIO leadership committed $20 million to reinvigorating organizing efforts. The program began with "Union Summer," in which 2,000 college students were enlisted to devote their 1996 summer vacations to assisting in high-profile organizing drives—an effort modeled after 1964's "Freedom Summer," during which college students were deployed to support the civil rights movement's efforts in the South.[20]

It remains to be seen, of course, whether these efforts will result in a significant increase in the percentage of workers opting for union representation. At the least, however, some of the conditions that contributed to labor's long slide have ameliorated, rendering a comeback plausible (albeit few believe labor can reclaim the position it held four decades ago):

- There is growing dissatisfaction among employees that they have not shared equitably in the fruits of the strong economy of

[16] BNA, Daily Labor Report 169 (Aug 30, 1996), C-1; Sharon Cohen, *Reawakening the Worker: Fiery AFL-CIO President Strives to Revitalize Labor Movement*, Austin American Statesman (Sept 2, 1996), at A13.

[17] William Serrin, *Is This Really Labor's Day? They Have New Faces in Their Top Ranks and Growing Political Clout, but the Old Problems Remain*, Washington Post (Sept 1, 1996), at C1; BNA Daily Labor Report 169 (Aug 30, 1996): C-1.

[18] The bill was enacted and signed by President Clinton on August 20, 1996. John F. Harris, *Minimum Wage Hiked in High-Profile Signing*, Washington Post (Aug 21, 1996), at A4.

[19] Robert Novak, *GOP Readies for War with Big Labor* (Chicago Sun-Times, May 16, 1966), at 27.

[20] BNA, Daily Labor Report 169 (Aug 30, 1996): C-1; Margot Hornblower, *Labor's Youth Brigade: In 1964 'Freedom Summer' Volunteers Flooded the South. Now, 'Union Summer' Puts Young Activists on the Job* (Time Magazine, July 15, 1996), at 44.

the past few years,[21] and increased anxiety about job security occasioned by the massive dislocations attributable to corporate reorganization and downsizing.

• Recent polls suggest that public esteem for unions is rising.[22]

• A major cause of the decline in unionism was increased competition from foreign companies enjoying lower labor costs, which destroyed the ability of unions to extract a "union premium" by cartelizing all the competitors in an industry and securing wage improvements whose cost was passed on to consumers.[23] But the imbalance in labor costs has moderated in recent years; indeed, hourly labor costs of American employers are now substantially lower than those of their competitors in Western Europe and Japan.[24] Unions thus have an enhanced opportunity to achieve gains for workers at the bargaining table.

• The United States has experienced a sustained period of low unemployment.[25] Employers, therefore, will have greater difficulty finding permanent replacements if their employees strike. If unions regain the capacity to exert economic pressure in support of their bargaining demands, they will be able to proffer tangible improvements for employees choosing union representation.[26]

---

[21] A bipartisan federal advisory panel appointed by the president and Congress recently reported, after a lengthy study, that a substantially greater percentage of workers are working longer hours for less pay than in the past. Competitiveness Policy Council, *Running in Place: Trends in U.S. Living Standards* (published Sept 12, 1996), described in BNA, Daily Labor Report 179 (Sept 16, 1996): A-3.

[22] Marc Levinson, *It's Hip to Be Union*, Newsweek (July 8, 1996), at 44 (citing nationwide poll showing unions with 62% favorable rating). See also John Greenwald, *The Battle to Revive U.S. Unions . . . A New Militancy Is Taking Hold in America's Workplace*, Time Magazine (Oct 30, 1995), at 64.

[23] Samuel Estreicher, *Labor Law Reform in a World of Competitive Labor Markets*, 69 Chi Kent L Rev 3, 12–14 (1993).

[24] BNA, Daily Labor Report 165 (Aug 26, 1996): D-3 (hereinafter DLR 165); BNA, Daily Labor Report 135 (July 14, 1995): D-13. For example, hourly compensation costs in Japan were 47% of those in the United States in 1975, but 138% in 1995. DLR 165. The comparable figures for France were 71% in 1975 and 112% in 1995. Id. Germany's costs were the same as those in the US in 1975, but rose to 185% in 1995. Id. The comparable figures for Korea were 5% in 1975 and 43% in 1995. Id.

[25] The unemployment rate in the past three years consistently has been below 6.1%. In contrast, the rate was above 6.1% in each of the following years: 1980—8.1%; 1981—7.6%; 1982—9.7%; 1983—9.6%; 1984—7.5%; 1985—7.2%; 1986—7%; 1987—6.2%; 1991—6.7%; 1992—7.4%; 1993—6.8%. Bureau of Labor Statistics Data, http://stats.bls.gov/cgi-bin/surveymost (1996).

[26] The significance of permanent replacements to the prospects of unionization is discussed in text accompanying notes 38–43.

These factors led then-Secretary of Labor, Robert Reich, to predict an increase in the number of workers joining unions in coming years.[27]

At the same time as the labor movement shows signs of reawakening, the Supreme Court is showing renewed interest in the workplace. In the 1995 term, the Court issued twelve decisions affecting the workplace.[28] This represents 16% of the seventy-five

---

[27] *Reich Predicts More Unionization*, BNA, Daily Labor Report 171 (Sept 4, 1996): A-2.

[28] *NLRB v Town & Country Elec., Inc.*, 116 S Ct 452 (1995), discussed in text accompanying notes 49–133 (paid union organizers who seek employment with an employer targeted for organization are "employees" entitled to the National Labor Relation Act's protections against discrimination based on union allegiance); *Auciello Iron Works v NLRB*, 116 S Ct 1754 (1996) (employer whose outstanding contract offer is accepted by union cannot refuse to enter into the agreement on the ground that prior to acceptance, the employer acquired a good faith doubt as to whether a majority of the employees continued to desire representation by the union); *Holly Farms Corp. v NLRB*, 116 S Ct 1396 (1996) (live haul crews employed by chicken processors to go to farms of independent contractors and gather up and transport chickens to the processing plant are not agricultural employees exempted from NLRA coverage, and thus enjoy the rights accorded employees by the NLRA); *Brown v Pro Football, Inc.*, 116 S Ct 2116 (1996), discussed in text accompanying notes 134 64 (employers engaged in multiemployer bargaining may agree among themselves on a common wage that all will implement when an impasse is reached with the union; the agreement is protected against antitrust sanction by the nonstatutory labor exemption to the Sherman Act); *United Food and Commercial Workers [UFCW] v Brown*, 116 S Ct 1529 (1996) (union has standing to sue for monetary remedies for its members whose rights under the Worker Adjustment and Retraining Act [WARN] have been violated); *O'Connor v Consolidated Coin Caterers*, 116 S Ct 1307 (1996) (employee states prima facie case of age discrimination violative of the Age Discrimination in Employment Act when replacement is significantly younger, even though the replacement is also above age 40 and thus within the class protected by the ADEA); *Varity Corp. v Howe*, 116 S Ct 1065 (1996) (employer acted as fiduciary, within meaning of ERISA's fiduciary obligations provisions, when it lied to employees about economic prospects of subsidiary in order to induce their withdrawal from the parent's benefit plans and transfer to the subsidiary's benefit plans; employees may sue for personal relief for violation of fiduciary obligations); *Lockheed Corp v Spink*, 116 S Ct 1783 (1996) (plan administrators of benefit plans do not violate the "prohibited transactions" provision of ERISA by implementing a plan provision that accords greater benefits to retirees only if they have waived their right to bring other lawsuits against the employer); *Peacock v Thomas*, 116 S Ct 862 (1995) (ERISA does not create federal cause of action to pierce corporate veil in order to impose liability on company official who diverted corporate assets, rendering the corporation unable to satisfy a judgment against it for breaching its fiduciary obligations under ERISA; *United States v CF&I Fabricators*, 116 S Ct 2106 (1996) (government claim for tax imposed upon company for failing to make contributions to a benefit plan required by ERISA is entitled to the priority of a general unsecured claim); *Brotherhood of Locomotive Eng'rs [BLE] v Atchison, Topeka & Santa Fe R.R.*, 116 S Ct 595 (1996) (time spent by train crew employees awaiting arrival of replacement employees is "limbo time," within the meaning of the Hours of Service Act, to be counted neither toward the twelve-consecutive-hour maximum prescribed by the Act for "on duty" time, nor the ten-consecutive-hour minimum for "off duty" time following completion of duty); *Norfolk & W. Ry. v Hiles*, 116 S Ct 890 (1996) (misalignment of couplers on railroad cars does not constitute a violation of the Safety Appliance Act, and thus does not relieve railroad employee injured while aligning the couplers of the obligation to prove negligence in order to recover damages from his employer for his injury).

decisions issued by the Court,[29] the largest representation of workplace cases since the 1982 term.[30] Of particular interest, five of those decisions involved the rights of unions.[31]

This shift is not explainable by a sudden increase in the number of "*cert*-worthy" labor and employment cases on the Court's docket. To the contrary, several of the Court's workplace decisions in the 1995 term can fairly be described as inconsequential: the stakes were small, and there was no conflict in the circuits.[32] It may be, therefore, that the Court's renewed interest in this area is linked to the revitalization of the labor movement itself.

Be that as it may, what is clear is that two of the Court's decisions in the 1995 term may have a significant impact on the success of the labor movement's current efforts to expand its ranks. It is those decisions that occasion this article.

In *NLRB v Town & Country*, the Court handed the labor movement a vitally needed tool to facilitate its organizing efforts. For

---

[29] 65 USLW 3041 (1996).

[30] In the 1982 Term, there were 30 decisions involving the workplace, 52 USLW 3055, constituting 17% of the 174 signed opinions that term, 53 USLW 3028. A review of the comparable statistics for each subsequent year discloses none in which the ratio was as high as the 1995 Term. In the immediately preceding Term, workplace-related decisions represented 6.6%—six of 91 signed opinions, 64 USLW 3095, 3094.

[31] The following decisions (cited in note 28) directly involved the rights of unions: *Town & Country; Auciello; Holly Farms; Brown v Pro Football; UFCW v Brown.* Two other cases arose in industries that are unionized (indeed, in one a union was the named plaintiff), but involved legal issues that would have been the same even if the employees had been unrepresented: *BLE v Atchison, Topeka; Norfolk & W. Ry. v Hiles.*

[32] *Auciello* (cited in note 28) involved an infrequently arising issue in which there was no circuit conflict; the court of appeals had approved the National Labor Relations Board's interpretation of the Act as amply within its authority, and the Supreme Court unanimously agreed, declaring that "To affirm [the Board's] rule of decision in this case, indeed, there is no need to invoke the full measure of the 'considerable deference' that the Board is due . . . by virtue of its charge to develop national labor policy." 116 S Ct at 1759.

Holly Farms (cited in note 28) posed an issue that affects a single category of employees of a few chicken processing firms, the resolution of which has no transportability to any other employees. The Court divided 5–4 in its resolution, suggesting interest among the Justices, but the choice to hear the case could not have been prompted by conceptions that it had general importance.

Norfolk & W. (cited in note 28), which determined whether employees injured while coupling misaligned railroad cars must establish negligence to recover for their injuries, involved a type of accident that occurs to only one or two dozen employees per year in the United States. Tim Poor, *Court Voids Verdict in Worker's Suit*, St. Louis Post-Dispatch (Feb 28, 1996), at 5A; the ruling has no precedential importance for resolving damage claims arising from any other type of injury.

BLE v Atchison, Topeka (cited in note 28) involved an issue of great interest to railroads and railroad workers, but one which had evoked no circuit conflict and on which the Court affirmed the court of appeals.

the first time in the sixty-year history of the NLRA, the Court
approved a way by which union organizers can secure access to
the workplace to talk to the employees they seek to organize. And
in *Brown v Pro Football*, the Court rejected an interpretation of the
Sherman Act that would have constituted a substantial deterrent
to unionizing. The court of appeals had ruled that employees, by
unionizing, forfeit the protection that the Sherman Act otherwise
affords against their employer conspiring with other employers to
"cap" wages and thereby eliminating a competitive employer market for labor. The Supreme Court rejected that rule, holding instead that only by engaging in *multiemployer* bargaining do unions
license employers to conspire with each other over wages. Because
multiemployer bargaining is consensual, unions need not opt for
it. The Supreme Court's rule, unlike the approach it rejected, will
not chill willingness of workers to unionize.

II. The Historic Link Between the Legal Regime and the Prospects for Regenerating the Labor Movement

Labor's ability to rebound is confounded by structural impediments imposed by existing labor law—impediments not evident on the face of the National Labor Relations Act, but read
into the Act by the Court. Congress enacted the NLRA in 1935
in the midst of the Great Depression. The declared purpose was to
enable workers to increase their bargaining power by unionizing,
bargaining collectively with their employers, and exerting combined economic force in support of their bargaining demands. To
that end, Congress wrote an open-ended statute, declaring its purposes in a few broadly conceived sentences and delegating to the
National Labor Relations Board the task of formulating specific
rules to achieve these objectives. The Board generated just such
rules, but the Court often nullified or weakened them, declaring
that the Act's broad commands had to be "balanced" against employer prerogatives nowhere mentioned in the statute.
Without question, the most important of these interpretations
was the Court's weakening of the right to strike. The ability of
workers to strike was the centerpiece of the Act's design. Workers
could organize into unions and bargain collectively, but still
needed a mechanism that would convince employers to make con-

cessions. The strike was to be that mechanism. Its centrality in the design was explained by Justice Brennan:

> [C]ollective bargaining, under a system where the Government does not attempt to control the results of negotiations, cannot be equated with an academic collective search for truth. . . . The parties . . . proceed from contrary and to an extent antagonistic viewpoints and concepts of self-interest. *The presence of economic weapons in reserve, and their actual exercise on occasion by the parties, is part and parcel of the system. . . . ". . . [C]ollective bargaining is a brute contest of economic power somewhat masked by polite manners and voluminous statistics."*[33]

To enable employees to strike without fear of punishment by their employers, Congress decreed in the Act that employers may not discriminate against employees for exercising the right to strike.[34] Within three years of the Act's passage, however, the Supreme Court ruled that although employers may not *fire* workers who strike, they may *permanently replace* them, that is, they may promise others that if they cross the picket lines and take the strikers' jobs, they will be kept on when the strike ends in preference to the strikers.[35] The Court explained that this interpretation was necessary because if employers could not promise permanent employment, they might not be able to attract workers to cross picket lines, and thus might not be able to continue operating in the face of a strike. The explicit right to strike without fear of job loss was thus subordinated to an employer interest nowhere stated in the Act.[36] Five decades later, the Court abandoned the initial rationale

---

[33] *NLRB v Insurance Agents Int'l Union*, 361 US 477, 488–89 (1960) (emphasis added, quoting Archibald Cox, *The Duty to Bargain in Good Faith*, 71 Harv L Rev 1401, 1409 (1958)).

[34] Section 7, 29 USC § 157, confers upon employees the right, inter alia, to "engage in . . . concerted activities." Section 8(a)(1), 29 USC § 158(a)(1), forbids employers to "interfere with, restrain, or coerce employees in the exercise of the rights guaranteed in Section 7." Section 8(a)(3), 29 USC § 158(a)(3), forbids employers to "discriminat[e] in regard to . . . tenure of employment . . . [to] discourage membership in any labor organization." Section 13, 29 USC § 163, declares: "Nothing in this Act . . . shall be construed so as either to interfere with or impede or diminish in any way the right to strike."

[35] *NLRB v Mackay Radio & Tel. Co.*, 304 US 333 (1938).

[36] The Board subsequently ruled that strikers who have been permanently replaced are entitled to be placed on a preferential waiting list, to be proffered recall opportunities upon departure of the replacements, unless, in the meantime, the strikers have acquired regular and substantially equivalent employment elsewhere. *Laidlaw Corp.*, 171 NLRB 1366 (1968), enf'd 414 F2d 99 (7th Cir 1969). While this mitigates the harshness of permanent replacement, it does not remove the disincentive to striking that *Mackay Radio* created. The wait for recall can be years—and that wait marks the "penalty" for striking. Moreover, the employee will be obliged of necessity to seek other employment, and if substantially equiva-

of this doctrine and held that employers can offer permanent employment to replacements even when such a promise is not necessary to attract them. The Court had come to conceive the permanent replacement of strikers as a "weapon" that employers can freely deploy to defeat strikes.[37]

These rulings, which have been widely criticized as unfaithful to the congressional purpose,[38] explain the virtual abandonment of the strike in the past decade.[39] Although the right of permanent replacement was announced in 1938, it was not often used until the 1980s.[40] Then, employers began invoking the right more fre-

---

lent employment is found prior to the opportunity for recall, the recall right will terminate. The International Paper Strike of 1987, see note 41, ended in 1988, but four years later, only 350 of the 1,200 permanently replaced strikers had been recalled from the preferential recall list, and there were very few recalled in subsequent years. Julius Getman, *The Human Costs of Permanent Strike Replacement*, 40 SLU L J 51, 52 n 17 (1996).

[37] *Trans World Airlines v Independent Fed'n of Flight Attendants*, 489 US 426 (1989). Also important was the Court's decision in *Belknap, Inc. v Hale*, 463 US 491 (1983), holding that the NLRA does not preempt the use of state contract law to award damages to strike replacements whose promise of permanent employment was breached. This meant that employers who had made such promises could not change their minds and accommodate union demands for reinstatement of strikers without confronting a substantial monetary consequence.

[38] See, for example, James B. Atleson, *Values and Assumptions in American Labor Law* 19–34 (U Mass Press, 1983); William B. Gould, *Agenda for Reform* 185–88, 202–03 (MIT Press, 1993); Charles B. Craver, *Can Unions Survive?* 29, 132–34, 143–46 (NYU Press, 1993); Paul C. Weiler, *Governing the Workplace* 264–69 (Harvard Press, 1991).

[39] The number of strikes per year averaged 2,660 in the 1970s, but only 1,250 in the 1980s. Gould at 181 (cited in note 38). The drop in large strikes, 1,000 or more workers, was even more precipitous, from more than 300 per year in the 1960s to only 40 in 1991. Id.

[40] "Before 1980, it was extremely rare for employers to hire permanent replacements during an economic strike." HR Rep No 102–57, at 14 (1991). The House Report cited, inter alia, a study conducted by a Wharton Business School professor and two management labor lawyers in 1982, which concluded that resort to permanent replacements was a "relatively new phenomenon" and that instances prior to 1980 were "rather unique" (employers choosing to operate during strikes, if at all, with managerial and supervisory employees and temporary replacements). Id (quoting Perry, Kramer, and Schneider, *Operating During Strikes: Company Experience, NLRB Policies, and Governmental Regulations*, Labor Relations and Public Policy Series No 23, University of Pennsylvania (1982)). "In the last decade, however, the frequency with which employers use or threaten to use permanent replacements has increased tremendously." HR Rep No 102-57 at 2; see also id at 17–20 (describing the findings of a number of studies conducted in 1991, all concluding that there had been a marked increase in resort to permanent replacements after 1980, including one study by the General Accounting Office, *Report to Congressional Requesters: Strikes and the Use of Permanent Replacements in the 1970's and 1980's*, GAO/HRD-91-2 (1991)).

The House Report cited in this note accompanied a bill to forbid the hiring of permanent replacements which was passed by the House but died in the Senate in the face of a threatened filibuster, see note 43.

The House Report attributed the lack of resort to permanent replacements prior to 1980 to three factors: the desire of employers not to lose the productivity of experienced workers,

quently, and a number of highly publicized strikes ended in disaster with employers permanently replacing the entire workforce.[41] As a result, in many industries, employees no longer dare to strike—they will lose their jobs if they do—and unions cannot conscionably encourage them to do so.[42] Without a meaningful right to strike, unions are unable to promise employees they can materially improve their terms of employment.[43]

Another important area in which the Court has diminished the

---

their desire to be seen in their communities as "good corporate citizens," and the availability to unions of secondary pressures that would prolong the conflict even if the employer resorted to permanent replacements. HR Rep No 102-57 at 15–16. The Report attributed the changed attitude after 1980 to these factors: President Reagan's permanent replacement of the air traffic controllers in 1981, which signaled that it was acceptable to engage in the practice; the change in the structure and mobility of corporate capital in the 1980s represented by the wave of mergers and leveraged buyouts, which brought in new managers who did not have a loyalty to the existing workforce and who were driven by a greater focus on short-term performance to reduce labor costs; and changes in the legal regime which removed the entitlement of unions to resort to secondary pressures as a means to continue exerting pressure on employers after the permanent replacement of strikers. HR Rep No 102-57, at 20–22.

[41] Some of the most prominent incidents were President Reagan's replacement of the air traffic controllers in 1981; Phelps Dodge's replacement of its striking copper workers in 1983; Continental Airlines' replacement of its pilots in 1985; Trans World Airlines' replacement of its flight attendants in 1986; International Paper's replacement of workers at its plant in Jay, Maine, in 1987; Kraft Foods' replacement of the workers in its Boston plant in 1989; and Greyhound Bus' replacement of its nationwide staff of bus drivers in 1990. These and other instances of permanent replacement are described in HR Rep No 103-116, at 3–10, 21 (1993) (hereinafter 1993 House Report). Of the 243,300 employees who participated in strikes in 1990, 11% were permanently replaced. Craver (cited in note 38), at 90.

[42] 1993 House Report at 7 (cited in note 41) (citing union president's testimony about the "many, many situations where we have had to advise our members that they dare not strike because of the risk of permanent replacement").

[43] In 1991, the House of Representatives passed a bill to forbid the hiring of permanent replacements in most circumstances, but the bill died in the Senate in the face of a threatened filibuster. Archibald Cox, Derek Curtis Bok, Robert A. Gorman, and Matthew W. Finkin, Labor Law 531–32 (Foundation Press, 12th ed 1996). In 1995, President Clinton promulgated Exec Order No 12,954, 60 Fed Reg 13,023 (1995), authorizing the Secretary of Labor to terminate federal contracts and to bar future contracts with any employer that anywhere in its operations permanently replaced strikers. The Executive Order was struck down by the D.C. Circuit on the ground that it conflicted with the NLRA, which, in light of the Supreme Court's rulings, "guarantees [employers] the right to hire permanent replacements." Chamber of Commerce of the U.S. v Reich, 74 F3d 1322, 1339 (DC Cir 1996). The Department of Justice announced on September 9, 1996, that it will not seek Supreme Court review of this ruling. BNA, Daily Labor Report 175 (Sept 10, 1996): AA-1. This "right" (in a statute that on its face confers "rights" only on employees) has also been construed to preempt state laws forbidding replacement of strikers. Employers Assn. Inc. v United Steelworkers of Am., 803 F Supp 1558 (D Minn 1992), aff'd, 32 F2d 1297 (8th Cir 1994); discussed in Michael H. LeRoy, The MacKay Radio Doctrine of Permanent Strike Replacements and the Minnesota Picket Line Peace Act: Questions of Preemption, 77 Minn L Rev 843 (1993).

value of unionization concerns the subjects about which employers must bargain with unions. The Act declares that employers must bargain with unions over "wages, hours, and terms and conditions of employment."[44] The Court has held, however, that employers need not bargain with unions over "entrepreneurial decisions" that eliminate jobs (e.g., plant shutdowns or moves), even though such decisions "touch[] on a matter of central and pressing concern to the union and its member employees: the possibility of continued employment and the retention of the employees' very jobs,"[45] unless "the benefit for labor-management relations and the collective bargaining process outweighs the burden placed on the conduct of the business."[46] The Court justified this doctrine on the ground that "[m]anagement must be free from the constraints of the bargaining process to the extent essential for the running of a profitable business."[47]

Here again, the Court has imposed a value not stated in the Act to trump a protection the Act expressly conferred—an approach that has been widely criticized as inconsistent with the congressional purpose.[48] The impact of this doctrine on unionism can be devastating. In an era in which the paramount employee concern has been fear of job loss due to restructuring, the Court has rendered unions impotent even to attempt to persuade employers to retain the employees' jobs.

These rulings stand as formidable obstacles to the efforts of unions to persuade workers to opt for union representation. What is most significant about the 1995 term, however, is that the Court broke through a third obstacle it had previously erected against

---

[44] Sections 8(a)(5) and 8(d) of the NLRA, 29 USC § 158(a)(5) and (d).

[45] *First Nat'l Maintenance Corp. v NLRB*, 452 US 666, 677 (1981).

[46] Id at 679. In the case before it, in which an employer decided to shut down a part of its business, the Court concluded that there was no obligation to bargain, as the harm to the employer occasioned by an obligation to bargain—including the possibilities that the union would delay the shutdown or strike in an effort to forestall it or disclose confidential information—would outweigh the incremental benefits of allowing the union to negotiate. Id at 686. The Court held that the employer would be obliged to bargain with the union following the shutdown over the *effects* of the shutdown on the employees, for example, whether there should be severance pay. Id at 681–82. Of course, once a shutdown occurs, the union and employees are unlikely to have bargaining power that could be deployed in support of such demands.

[47] Id at 678–79.

[48] See, for example, Gould at 170–73 (cited in note 38); Craver at 138–39, 148 (cited in note 38).

union efforts to organize—an obstacle that, like the other two, imposed values not expressed in the NLRA to defeat rights declared in the Act. That ruling is the subject of the next section.

III. Unlocking the Doors to Union Organization: Town & Country

A. PRELUDE: THE SUPREME COURT'S LOCKING OF THE GATES PRIOR TO THE 1995 TERM

One of the Court's interpretations of the NLRA that has received the most consistent academic condemnation has been its repeated rejection of the Board's efforts to provide union organizers access to the employer's property to talk with the employees they are seeking to organize.[49] The Act confers upon employees a "right" to "form [and] join" labor unions,[50] and forbids employers to "interfere" with the exercise of that right.[51] As early as 1943, the Board declared that the workplace is a "uniquely appropriate" place for organizing activities, and that no other forum provides as meaningful an opportunity for employees to learn the advantages of unionism.[52] To that end, the Board ruled that (1) an employer could not invoke its prerogatives as a property owner to forbid employees to discuss unionization on the employer's premises, so long as those discussions did not occur when the employees were supposed to be working, and (2) an employer could not invoke its prerogatives as a property owner to bar union organizers from the nonworking areas of the premises (such as parking lots) when such access was necessary for employees to have meaningful communication with the organizers. In the Board's words, "the employer's right to control his property does not permit him to deny access to *persons whose presence is necessary there to enable the employees effectively to exercise their right to self-organization and collective bargaining.*"[53]

---

[49] See, for example, Cynthia L. Estlund, *Labor, Property and Sovereignty after Lechmere*, 46 Stan L Rev 305 (1994); Gould at 23–25, 157–58 (cited in note 38); Craver at 29–30, 141–42 (cited in note 38); Atleson at 60–62, 93–94 (cited in note 38).

[50] Section 7 of the NLRA, 29 USC § 157.

[51] Section 8(a)(1), 29 USC § 158(a)(1).

[52] *Republic Aviation Corp.*, 51 NLRB 1186, 1195 (1943). See also *Babcock & Wilcox Co.*, 109 NLRB 485, 486 (1954).

[53] *Le Tourneau Co.*, 54 NLRB 1253, 1259–60 (1944).

In 1945, in *NLRB v Republic Aviation*,[54] the Court, quoting and approving this passage,[55] upheld a Board ruling that an employer had violated the Act by forbidding employees to talk to each other in nonworking areas of the plant. But in 1956, in *NLRB v Babcock & Wilcox*,[56] the Court held that the Board could not require an employer to permit nonemployee union representatives to enter the employer's parking lot to communicate with employees. Although acknowledging that the "right of self-organization depends in some measure on the ability of employees to learn the advantages of self-organization from others,"[57] and that, on the facts of this case, the employer's parking lot was "much more effective a place for communication of information" than attempting to reach employees at their homes,[58] the Court nonetheless declared that the Board had "failed to make a distinction between rules of law applicable to employees and those applicable to nonemployees":[59]

> Organization rights are granted to workers by the same authority, the National Government, that preserves property rights. Accommodation between the two must be obtained with as little destruction of one as is consistent with the maintenance of the other.[60]

Thus, the Court said, "when the inaccessibility of employees makes ineffective the reasonable attempts by nonemployees to communicate with them through the usual channels, the right to exclude from property has been required to yield to the extent needed to permit communication of information on the right to organize."[61] But the employer may invoke its property rights to bar union organizers "if reasonable efforts by the union through other available channels of communication will enable it to reach the employees with its message."[62]

---

[54] *Republic Aviation Corp. v NLRB*, 324 US 793 (1945).

[55] Id at 802 n 8.

[56] *NLRB v Babcock & Wilcox Co.*, 351 US 105 (1956).

[57] Id at 113.

[58] Id at 107. The Court noted the Board's finding that, absent access to the parking lot, there was no way the union organizers could talk to the employees near the workplace as most employees drove directly into the employer's parking lot, id at 107.

[59] Id at 113.

[60] Id at 112.

[61] Id.

[62] Id.

This passage can be read as suggesting that unions are entitled to access upon a showing that efforts to reach employees elsewhere have been unavailing, but it was evident from two other aspects of the Court's opinion that that is not what it intended. First, the examples it gave of circumstances where unions would be entitled to access were those in which the employees lived on the employer's premises, that is, situations where access to the employees in their homes literally was impossible without entering the employer's premises.[63] Second, the Court ruled that the union in *Babcock* had not made a sufficient showing to entitle it to access,[64] even though it recited the Board's factual findings that the employees' homes were scattered over a thirty-mile radius,[65] and despite massive efforts, the union had been able to communicate with only 20% of the employees.[66]

The Court in *Babcock* took a right unqualifiedly granted by the statute and subordinated it to an interest nowhere declared in the statute, the property rights of employers. Unlike the Board, which had held that employers could limit the time, place, and manner of union access to assure conformity with legitimate *operational* concerns, the Court approved a right to deny access that did not depend to any extent upon the employer showing that it would suffer any interference (apart from increased risk of unionization) from the union organizers' appearance. It was the employer's naked property right—the right to exclude without the need to show inconvenience—that defeated the right declared in the statute.

In *Babcock*, the employer had not itself used its premises to campaign *against* the union. Two years later, however, in *Nutone*,[67] the Court extended its holding to permit employers to bar union organizers even when the employer was using its facilities to wage a campaign against the union. Over the dissent of Justices Black and Douglas, the Court held that the Act does not entitle "labor organizations" to use a medium of communication "simply because the employer is using it."[68]

---

[63] Id at 113–14.

[64] Id at 113.

[65] Id at 106.

[66] Id at n 1.

[67] *NLRB v United Steelworkers (Nutone and Avondale)*, 357 US 357 (1958).

[68] Chief Justice Warren also dissented, but on a narrower ground. He would not allow unions access to employer premises simply because the employer is using those premises

Two decades later, the emerging ubiquity of shopping centers brought new attention to the question of organizers' access to the workplace. Because the general public is invited to enter shopping centers, unions argued that the refusal of employers (or of shopping center owners acting at the behest of employers) to permit union organizers to talk with employees in the common areas of shopping centers should be looked at differently. Dicta in Supreme Court opinions during the 1970s hinted that the Court might be receptive to such arguments and, indeed, that it might even be receptive to recasting the balancing test of *Babcock* with respect to workplaces generally.[69] The Board picked up on these hints and developed a new balancing formula to weigh the employer's interest in the undisturbed enjoyment of its property against the employees' interest in being informed about the advantages of unionism:

---

to campaign against the union, but thought that such access is warranted when, as in the case before him, the employer has committed unfair labor practices that unlawfully weakened the union's cause. Id at 369–70. This narrower notion took root decades later, when the Board began to order employers to grant unions limited access to employers' premises as a *remedy* in cases where employers had engaged in widespread illegal campaigns of terror—usually, firing pro-union employees and threatening to punish workers if they selected a union. See *United Steelworkers v NLRB*, 646 F2d 616 (DC Cir 1981) (describing cases); *United States Serv. Indus., Inc.*, 319 NLRB 231 (1995); Note, *NLRB Orders Granting Unions Access to Company Property*, 68 Cornell L Rev 895 (1983). The Board reasoned in these cases that without such access, the union would be unable to dissipate the effects of the illegal conduct. (Notice, again, the Board's appreciation that other means of communication are inferior.) The Supreme Court has not ruled on the permissibility of this remedy.

[69] *Central Hardware Co. v NLRB*, 407 US 539 (1972); *Hudgens v NLRB*, 424 US 507 (1976). Both were cases in which the NLRB had held the union entitled to access to public areas of shopping centers, relying at least in part on a perception that the First Amendment, as construed in *Food Employees v Logan Valley Plaza, Inc.*, 391 US 1601 (1968), entitled the union to such access. In each, the Court held the First Amendment inapplicable, limiting the sweep of *Logan Valley* in the first, and expressly overruling it in the second, and remanded with instructions that the case be decided solely on the basis of the NLRA. And in each, the terms of the remand hinted at the availability of a balancing test that took account of the unions' lack of success in attempting to reach its audience elsewhere. Thus, in *Central Hardware*, the Court indicated that the court of appeals' task was to assess whether there was substantial evidence on the record as a whole to support the Trial Examiner's conclusion that "no reasonable means of communication with employees were available to the non-employee Union organizers other than solicitation in Central's parking lots . . ." 407 US at 547–48. In *Hudgens*, the Court gave this spin to the passage in *Babcock* that had talked of the Board's obligation to "accommodate" the employer's property rights and the employee's rights to receive the union's communications:

> The locus of that accommodation . . . may fall at differing points along the spectrum depending on the nature and strength of the respective § 7 rights and private property rights asserted in any given context. In each generic situation, the primary responsibility for making this accommodation must rest with the Board in the first instance.

424 US at 522.

> [I]n all access cases our essential concern will be the degree of impairment of the [employees' organizational] right if access should be denied, as it balances against the degree of impairment of the private property right if access should be granted. We view the consideration of the availability of *reasonably effective* alternative means as especially significant in this balancing process.[70]

The courts of appeals that reviewed this formula uniformly approved it, reasoning that the dicta in the Court's 1970s decisions had recast *Babcock* to take account of the union's inability to reach employees elsewhere.[71]

In 1992, however, the Supreme Court rejected the Board's formulation as impermissibly pro-union. In *Lechmere*,[72] in an opinion authored by Justice Thomas, the Court declared that the Board had misunderstood *Babcock*, which contemplated access for union organizers only when the employees "are isolated from the ordinary flow of information that characterizes our society."[73] That isolation occurs only when "the employees . . . reside on [the employer's] property."[74] Thus, the Board may not grant union organizers access to the employer's premises merely because the union's efforts to reach the employees via mailings, phone calls, or home visits prove unavailing. Such access, the Court explained, is not a "necessary element" of "reasonably effective communication."[75] It was enough in *Lechmere* that "signs (displayed, for example, from the public grassy strip adjoining Lechmere's parking lot) would have informed the employees about the union's organizational efforts."[76]

Justice White, joined by Justices Blackmun and Stevens, dissented, insisting that the right to self-organization conferred by the Act had to be implemented with realism, not formalism, and that *Babcock*, especially as it had been construed in the dicta in the

---

[70] *Jean Country*, 291 NLRB 11, 14 (1988).

[71] *Lechmere Inc. v NLRB*, 914 F2d 313, 320–21 (1st Cir 1990), rev'd 502 US 527 (1992); *Laborers' Local 204 v NLRB*, 904 F2d 715, 717–18 (DC Cir 1990); *Emery Realty, Inc. v NLRB*, 863 F2d 1259, 1264 (6th Cir 1988).

[72] *Lechmere Inc. v NLRB*, 502 US 527 (1992).

[73] Id at 540.

[74] Id.

[75] Id.

[76] Id.

1970s shopping center cases, should be understood to allow access whenever efforts to reach employees elsewhere proved ineffective in practice.[77] They argued that it subverted the statutory scheme to relegate unions to communicating via signs that must be read by passing drivers: "Actual communication . . . not mere notice that an organizing campaign exists, is necessary to vindicate [employees' organizational] rights."[78] When it is demonstrated that reasonable efforts to reach employees via other means have not "permit[ted] *proper* communication with employees," access to the employer's premises must be allowed.[79]

The impact of *Lechmere* on unions' prospects for organizing is devastating. Most of the employees whom unions seek to organize work in places where organizers cannot speak to the employees without coming on the premises; the workplaces are in shopping centers with their own parking lots or on industrial properties into which employees drive. Waving signs from the public roadway as employees drive into work is the only worksite-proximate form of communication left to unions. But, as Justice White observed, this is hopelessly inadequate.

Employees selecting a union are making a fateful step; they are surrendering their autonomy over their terms and conditions of employment to an exclusive bargaining representative, one whose responsibility runs to the entirety of the workforce and that may not, therefore, champion their particular views.[80] Sensible persons are likely to be hesitant to confer such trust upon an unknown institution whose only personification is an awkward stranger waving a sign as one drives past to work. Employees are likely to have innumerable questions about the union that require detailed answers. What's more, the potential benefits of unionism in our

---

[77] Id at 543–45.

[78] Id at 543.

[79] Id. Unions have not always been lucky in their Supreme Court litigation, and in this instance the timing could not have been more unfortunate. If this issue had arrived at the Court just a couple of years earlier, when Justices Brennan and Marshall were still on the Court, it is a virtual certainty that Justice White's interpretation would have prevailed. Both those Justices were on record as believing that access to employer premises was warranted unless unions were able in fact to engage in meaningful communications with employees elsewhere. *Central Hardware Co. v NLRB*, 407 US at 532–34; *Hudgens v NLRB*, 424 US at 548–49. Both their successors (Justices Thomas and Souter) voted otherwise.

[80] *JI Case Co. v NLRB*, 321 US 332 (1944); *Vaca v Sipes*, 386 US 171 (1967); *Emporium Capwell Co. v Western Addition Community Org.*, 420 US 50 (1975).

modern era are subtle and complicated, and may require extended elaboration.[81]

Compounding employee reluctance to unionize, the usual response of employers to an organizing drive is to use the workplace to attack the union as corrupt, undemocratic, incompetent, and likely to cost the employees their jobs. The employer is permitted to deliver "captive audience" speeches, instructing the employees to stop work and assemble to receive the employer's message.[82] Against this background, an organizing drive is, in significant part, an effort to build trust and to persuade employees that the union is not the evil or dangerous institution the employer has described. This cannot be accomplished on a picket sign.

The exclusion of union organizers is also a strongly negative symbol. It sends a message of weakness that is not likely to engender employee confidence. If the union can't even enter the premises, how will it be able to represent the employees effectively? Under the law, unions are entitled to access to the extent necessary to perform their representational functions[83] *once they are selected*

---

[81] Unorganized workers are likely to view unions as proffering economic muscle in support of demands for higher pay and benefits. These are doubtful of accomplishment in an era in which striking is such a dangerous proposition. See text accompanying notes 34–43. But unions offer a range of other services that are not fraught with danger: expertise in dealing with complicated legal and contractual entitlements (such as benefit programs), a mechanism for addressing "collective goods" problems, and a representational role in dealing with management on a host of day-to-day problems that arise. Michael H. Gottesman, *In Despair, Starting Over: Imagining a Labor Law for Unorganized Workers*, 69 Chi Kent L Rev 59, 79–83 (1993).

[82] The Board will set aside an election if the employer delivers a captive audience speech less than 24 hours before the Board-conducted election, but there are no restrictions respecting the employer's use of captive audience speeches prior to that 24-hour window. *Peerless Plywood Co.*, 107 NLRB 427, 429 (1953).

[83] *NLRB v Holyoke Water Power Co.*, 778 F2d 49, 52–53 (1st Cir 1985); *NLRB v National Broad. Co.*, 798 F2d 75, 77 (2d Cir 1986); *NLRB v American Nat'l Can Co.*, 924 F2d 518, 524 (4th Cir 1991); *NLRB v C.E. Wylie Constr. Co.*, 934 F2d 234, 239 (9th Cir 1991). A common formulation of the standard controlling entitlement to access appears in *American National*, 924 F2d at 524:

> [A] union is not automatically entitled to access to an employer's premises to obtain information simply because the information has been shown to be relevant to the union's proper performance of its representational duties. The right of employees to be responsibly represented by a labor union must be balanced against the right of the employer to control its property and ensure that its operations are not interfered with. . . . [I]n a given case the Board [must] determine whether responsible representation of employees can be achieved by any means other than entry onto the employer's premises. If the Board finds that alternative means exist, the union may properly be denied access. On the other hand, when it is found that responsible representation requires union access to the employer's premises,

as bargaining agent, but that's not something employees are likely to know.[84]

Unions can attempt to communicate with the employees they seek to organize at locations away from the workplace, by calling rallies or by phoning or visiting them in their homes, or by writing to them. These, however, are inadequate counters to the employer's workplace propaganda—indeed, far more inadequate today than they were at the time *Babcock* was decided in 1956. Few employees want to spend their free time attending union rallies, especially at the outset of an organizing campaign when they have no commitment to the union. And although a union can phone, visit, or write to employees if it knows their identities, it is not entitled to this information unless it already has cards signed by at least 30% of the employees declaring their interest in an election.[85] Of course, the union may attempt to compile a list of employees by drawing on the knowledge of its initial supporters within the workforce, but except in the smallest of workplaces, this rarely generates more than a fraction of the employees' names.[86]

Moreover, even when the union knows the employees' names and addresses, communication by telephone, mail, or home visits is unlikely to prove satisfactory. In this era of multiple phone solic-

---

the employer's property rights must yield to the extent necessary to achieve this end without unwarranted interruption of the employer's operations.

In addition, the statute requires that the employer "meet at reasonable times and confer in good faith" with the union which has been selected as exclusive bargaining representative, Section 8(a)(5), 29 USC § 158(a)(5), albeit such meetings need not be on the employer's premises.

[84] Unions engaged in organizing campaigns avail themselves of the rule that entitles employees to communicate on-premises about the union. See text accompanying notes 54–55. The union can ask early employee-supporters to distribute its literature within the workplace, and to answer questions that other employees have about the union. But even the most capable employee is unlikely to have the institutional knowledge about the union needed to provide well-informed responses to those questions. While unions regularly "debrief" their employee-sponsors and prepare new literature to respond to the questions that were asked of those sponsors, these written responses are not a wholly satisfactory means of communication: they are belated, many employees are not as facile at comprehending through reading as they are through oral communication, and, in any event, employees without prior exposure to the union are less likely to credit answers when they cannot see and judge the credibility of the speaker.

[85] *Excelsior Underwear Inc.*, 156 NLRB 1236 (1966), approved in *NLRB v Wyman-Gordon Co.*, 394 US 759 (1969) (union entitled to list within seven days after Board directs election); 29 CFR § 101.18(a) (Board will not direct election unless union has submitted authorizations by at least 30% of the employees).

[86] For example, in *Babcock*, after a massive effort, the union had been able to locate only 20% of the employees. See text accompanying note 66.

itations each day, those answering rarely stay on the line to hear out the caller. Similarly, the reaction of most recipients to junk mail renders it unlikely that letters from the union will be read. Home visits are even less promising, given the reaction of most people today to a stranger's knock on the door.

B. THE COURT HANDS UNIONS A KEY TO THE WORKPLACE

If unions are to make a comeback, they must be able to communicate with prospective members. The Court's decision last term in *Town & Country* validated a circuitous route by which unions can infiltrate their organizers onto the employer's premises: by getting them hired by the employer so that they can exercise the organizing rights of employees.

In the 1970s, a few unions resolved to take advantage of the dichotomy the Court had created in *Republic Aviation* and *Babcock*: While nonemployee union organizers could be denied access to the employer's premises, employees were entitled to use those premises to communicate about the union. These unions began sending union organizers to apply for jobs with the employer so that, if hired, they could exercise their rights as "employees" to solicit other employees' support for the union.

These efforts were not greeted enthusiastically by employers, who labeled these job applicants Trojan Horses[87] and their efforts "salting"—after the phrases "salting a mine" (introducing foreign substances into a mine), and "salting the books" (falsifying accounts).[88]

Of course, employers will not want to hire paid union organizers, even if, as often will be the case, they offer work skills superior to other applicants.[89] But the NLRA forbids "discrimination in regard to hire . . . to . . . discourage membership in a labor organization,"[90] and, while the Act's protections extend only to "employ-

---

[87] The paid union organizer's "presence in the workplace is reminiscent of the Trojan Horse whose innocuous appearance shields a deadly enemy." *Sunland Constr. Co.*, 309 NLRB 1224, 1232 (1992) (concurring opinion of Board Member Clifford Oviatt).

[88] *Tualatin Elec., Inc.*, 312 NLRB 129, 130 n 3 (1993) (ALJ opinion).

[89] Union organizers often are graduates of work in the industry they are seeking to organize. As skilled and experienced employees, they often will be better qualified than the other candidates seeking employment.

[90] Section 8(a)(3), 29 USC § 158(a)(3).

ees," the Supreme Court early on approved the Board's position that a job applicant is an "employee" entitled to this protection— "for otherwise the Act's prohibition of 'discrimination in regard to hire' would serve no function."[91] The issue, then, is whether paid union organizers who seek employment for the purpose of organizing-from-within would, if hired, be "employees" within the meaning of the Act; if so, employers cannot discriminate against them at the hiring gate.

Employers mounted a two-prong attack against this result, arguing that paid union organizers are not "bona fide" employees because (1) otherwise employers will lose the "right" that *Babcock* conferred upon them to deny union organizers access to the premises, and (2) the organizers' allegiance to the union will compromise their loyalty to the employer.

The Board rejected these contentions and held that the refusal of employers to hire organizer-applicants, if motivated by a desire to resist organizing-from-within, violates the Act. The courts of appeals, however, divided on this issue.[92] Courts rejecting the Board's position accepted one of the other of the two arguments proffered by employers. The Fourth Circuit, for example, drew the lesson from *Babcock* that employers have a "right" to keep union organizers off their premises, a right that can be vindicated only by holding that union-paid applicants are not employees and that employers are thus entitled to reject them on this ground.[93] Taking the alternative approach, the Eighth Circuit reasoned that union organizers are not bona fide employees because they would owe their primary allegiance to the union and thus would have conflicted loyalty respecting the employer.[94]

In *Town & Country*, a nonunion building contractor advertised for workers to begin a new project. Among the small number of applicants responding to the ad were two full-time salaried union

---

[91] *Phelps Dodge Corp. v NLRB*, 313 US 177, 185–86 (1941).

[92] Three circuits upheld the Board's position. *Willmar Elec. Serv., Inc. v NLRB*, 968 F2d 1327 (DC Cir 1992), cert denied, 507 US 909 (1993); *Escada (USA) Inc. v NLRB Local 138*, 970 F2d 898 (3d Cir 1992), enf'g w/o opinion, 304 NLRB 845, 848 (1991); *NLRB v Henlopen Mfg. Co.*, 599 F2d 26, 30 (2d Cir 1979). Cases rejecting the Board's position are cited in notes 93–94.

[93] *HB Zachry Co. v NLRB*, 886 F2d 70, 74 (4th Cir 1989).

[94] *NLRB v Town & Country Elec., Inc.*, 34 F3d 625, 629 (8th Cir 1994) (hereinafter *Town & Country II*).

organizers and nine long-term union members who were unem-
ployed and had been promised by the union that it would pay them
to conduct organizing activities on premises if they sought and
obtained jobs with the employer. The employer, although desper-
ately in need of skilled workers, refused to consider the union-paid
applicants.[95] The Board ruled that the employer's refusal to hire
these applicants because of their union connection was prohibited
by the Act, and ordered the employer to hire them with back pay.[96]

The Eighth Circuit reversed,[97] and the Board sought and obtained certiorari. All six of the Justices who had slammed the gates
on union access in *Lechmere* four years before were still on the
Court. Employers could reasonably hope that these Justices would
not allow the Board to "exalt form over substance."[98] But that
hope was misplaced. The Court unanimously held that paid union
organizers are "employees" entitled to the Act's protection against
"discrimination . . . in regard to hire."

Justice Breyer's opinion for the Court framed the issue this way:
"Can a worker be a company's 'employee,' within the terms of the
National Labor Relations Act, . . . if, at the same time, a union
pays that worker to help the union organize the company? We
agree with the National Labor Relations Board that the answer is
'yes.' "[99] Indeed, the Court declared the issue easy: While the
Board's interpretations of the statute are entitled to "a degree of
legal leeway," "the Board needs very little leeway here to convince
us of the correctness of its decision."[100]

The Court offered six considerations in support of its
interpretation:

1. "The ordinary dictionary definition of 'employee' includes
any person who works for another in return for financial or other
compensation."[101]

---

[95] The employer refused to interview ten of them. The eleventh was hired before the
employer learned he was union-paid, but was fired as soon as this was discovered. Id at
626–27.

[96] *Town & Country Elec.*, 309 NLRB 1250, 1280 (1992) (hereinafter *Town & Country I*).

[97] *Town & Country II*, 34 F3d 625.

[98] *HB Zachry Co. v NLRB*, 886 F2d at 73.

[99] *NLRB v Town & Country Elec.*, 116 S Ct 450, 451 (1995) (hereinafter *Town & Country
III*).

[100] Id at 453–54.

[101] Id at 453 (quoting *American Heritage Dictionary* 604 (3d ed 1992)). A similar definition
from *Black's Law Dictionary* was also invoked.

2. The statute defines "employee" as "any employee," signifying that a broad interpretation was intended.[102]

3. The Act's definition of employee includes a list of exceptions (e.g., independent contractors, agricultural laborers, domestic workers, and railroad and airline employees covered by the Railway Labor Act), "but no exception applies here."[103]

4. The legislative history is "consistent" with the Board's broad interpretation, for sponsors of the NLRA had stated that the term "employee" "means someone who works for another for hire" . . . [and] "includes every man on a payroll."[104]

5. The Court in prior cases had given the term "employee" an expansive definition, interpreting it to include undocumented aliens, job applicants, and certain confidential employees.[105]

6. When the statute was amended in 1947 as part of the Taft-Hartley Act, Congress inserted an unrelated provision that recognized that an employee might receive payment from a union and an employer at the same time.[106]

None of these considerations, however, offers a convincing account of why a Congress that insisted that employers have a right to keep union organizers out of their parking lots—what the Court in *Babcock* and *Lechmere* insisted Congress had mandated as the "rule of law"—would in the same statute command that employers afford union organizers nondiscriminatory consideration for hire, a command that would require employers to *pay* union organizers to come onto their premises to organize the employees.

The Court's opinion does not acknowledge, let alone answer,

---

[102] Id at 454.

[103] Id.

[104] Id.

[105] Id (citing, respectively, *Sure-Tan, Inc. v NLRB*, 467 US 883, 891 (1984); *Phelps Dodge*, supra note 91; *NLRB v Hendricks County Rural Elec. Membership Corp.*, 454 US 170, 189–90 (1981)).

[106] Id. The provision, Section 302(c)(1), 29 USC § 302(c)(1), forbids an employer from making payments to union officials and union employees (in effect, bribes), but exempts payments made to such persons for work done for the employer. Its probative value for the issue the Court was deciding in *Town & Country* is questionable. Once a union is elected as bargaining representative, in-plant employees are likely to be paid a stipend to assist in carrying out some of the union's representational functions (e.g., processing grievances at the lower levels, or serving as a local union official). It was this phenomenon that Congress had in mind when it inserted the exemption in 302(c)(1). There is no evidence that Congress envisioned that full-time professional union organizers would seek employment at the workplaces they were seeking to organize.

the contention that Congress could not have entertained these two conflicting objectives in the same statute. The only passage that even elliptically addresses the conflict appears in the middle of the litany of mechanical points listed above:

> [T]he Board's broad, literal interpretation of the word 'employee' is consistent with several of the Act's purposes, such as protecting the 'right of employees to organize for mutual aid without employer interference', *Republic Aviation Corp. v. NLRB.* . . .[107]

This invocation of *Republic Aviation*—the pre-*Babcock* decision that held that *employees* are entitled to engage in organizational activities in the workplace—is remarkable. The "employees" whose rights the Court is championing in this passage surely are not paid union organizers, but *other* employees who might benefit from the organizers' message. The Court seems to be saying that those employees' organizational rights are served by receiving the union organizers' communications in the workplace. But that is precisely the consideration that had prompted the Board to hold pre-*Babcock* that union organizers were entitled to come onto employer premises—a consideration the Court in *Babcock* held insufficient to justify an invasion of the employer's property rights. The Court in *Town & Country* did not explain why this consideration was sufficient to support Trojan horses, but insufficient to accord union organizers access to an employer's parking lot.

The interpretative approaches adopted in *Babcock* in 1956 and *Town & Country* in 1996 could not have been more dissimilar. The Court in *Babcock* did not consult the dictionary; if it had, it would have sustained the Board's ruling that organizers are entitled to come onto the parking lot because banning such access clearly "interfered with" the employees' "right to organize," as the Court readily acknowledged in its opinion.[108] Instead, the Court in *Babcock* embraced a chestnut of nineteenth-century formalism—the property owner's unqualified right to exclude trespassers—and attributed to Congress a nowhere-stated intention that that chestnut would trump the statutory language. It is hard to believe that the

---

[107] Id.

[108] See text accompanying notes 57–58.

Court in *Babcock* would have allowed the loophole of "salting" to erode the employer's vaunted property right to exclude union organizers.

Town & Country thus stands as an implicit indictment of the interpretative approach employed in *Babcock* and *Lechmere*. But it does not overrule those decisions. To the contrary, in a passage explaining that employers are not rendered totally helpless by its ruling, the Court ticked off a number of rights they still retain: They can fire union organizers who don't perform well; they can call the police if union organizers engage in unlawful activity on the premises; "[a]nd, of course, *an employer may as a rule limit the access of* non*employee union organizers to company property.*"[109]

What is puzzling is not that Justice Breyer, who was not on the Court when *Lechmere* was decided, upheld a loophole that eviscerates employers' property rights, but that the six Justices who formed the *Lechmere* majority joined Breyer's opinion in *Town & Country*.

If there is a moral to this story, it is perhaps that two wrongs *can* make a right. It was wrong for the Court in *Babcock* to import formalist notions of property rights to hobble a statute that was quintessentially an instance of legal realism intended to overcome those notions, and it was wrong for the Court in *Town & Country* to derive that statute's meaning by consulting the dictionary. The end result, however, is that unions now have a second-best mechanism (just how far inferior to the best will be explored shortly) for achieving what Congress plainly intended when it enacted the NLRA: communication with employees at the workplace.

The Court in *Town & Country* also had to address the employer's contention (and the Eighth Circuit's holding) that paid union organizers are not bona fide employees because they owe their primary allegiance to the union, rather than the employer. In support of this proposition, the employer argued that the common law definition of employee excludes one who has a conflict of interest. The Court elided the question whether it would uphold a Board interpretation that conflicted with the common law,[110] for it concluded that "the Board's interpretation of the term 'employee' is

---

[109] *Town & Country III*, 116 S Ct at 457 (citing *Babcock* and *Lechmere*).
[110] Id at 455.

consistent with the common law," as there is no conflict of interest in an employee's organizing on behalf of a union.[111]

The Court cited the Restatement (Second) of Agency for the proposition that "a person may be the servant of two masters . . . at one time as to one act, if the service to one does not involve abandonment of the service to the other."[112] The statute, by entitling employees to engage in organizational activities on the employer's premises, established as a matter of law that there is no conflict between serving one's employer and organizing a union.[113] The employer's concern that the paid union organizers might subordinate the employer's interests to the union's was unsupported in the record;[114] indeed, the Board had observed that it was in the union's interest that the paid organizers do their jobs for the employer well, for otherwise the employer would have an excuse to fire them and defeat the union's objective of organizing from within.[115] The Court ruled that employers cannot discriminate against union adherents based on fears of disloyalty that are attributed to nothing more than their union connection.[116]

One cannot help but wonder at the relativity of values embraced and rejected in *Babcock* and *Town & Country*. The inconvenience to an employer of allowing union organizers in the parking lot is trivial compared to the uncertainty whether a union organizer

---

[111] Id at 456.

[112] Id (citing Restatement (Second) of Agency, § 226). The Court gave as an example a detective on the city police force who gets hired by a restaurant as a waiter so that he can surveil the restaurant's customers. His food delivery serves the restaurant, his surveillance serves the city, and neither duty conflicts with the other.

[113] Id.

[114] Id.

[115] *Town & Country I*, 309 NLRB at 1257.

[116] *Town & Country III*, 116 S Ct at 456. An employer could refuse to hire an employee who had demonstrated disloyalty on a prior job, for that would be a legitimate basis for rejection and not discrimination based on the one criterion forbidden by the NLRA. It is thus very much in a union's interest to select "salts" who have unblemished records with prior employers.

The employer had also argued that it was inappropriate to have paid union organizers in the workforce, as they will have a financial inducement to vote in favor of the union in the Board election that culminates the organizing drive. The Court did not find this a legitimate ground for refusing to hire a union-paid applicant; the appropriate solution, if this is deemed a problem, is to disqualify the employee from inclusion in the union's bargaining unit, not from the job. Id at 457. See also *Town & Country I*, 309 NLRB at 1256–57.

may turn out to be a disloyal or disobedient employee. It is hardly plausible that Congress would reject access to the parking lot, but mandate nondiscriminatory consideration for hire in the same statute.

C. EPILOGUE: WILL THE KEY FIT?

No one familiar with labor relations could believe that employers will all give nondiscriminatory consideration to union-paid applicants simply because the Supreme Court ruled as it did in *Town & Country*. At least some employers, perhaps most, will resort to one of three strategies to prevent the "Trojan horse" from entering their premises. Whether *Town & Country* ultimately provides access for union organizers will depend upon how the Board and the courts respond to these strategies.

1. *Neutral criteria that coincidentally disqualify union-organizer applicants.* The Act forbids only refusals to hire that are discriminatory, that is, that are motivated by the forbidden criterion of union adherence. Thus, the deployment of a neutral criterion ordinarily does not violate the Act even though the person disqualified happens to be a union adherent.

Some neutral criteria, such as a rule against employing persons who will engage in "simultaneous employment" for another employer, would by definition disqualify all paid union organizers. Similarly, a ban on hiring persons who will "moonlight," that is, work after hours for another employer, would disqualify paid organizers who are expected to work for the union away from the employer's premises.[117]

Much will depend upon whether the Board holds, as it should, that such rules cannot be applied to treat as disqualifying conduct which is specifically protected by the Act. It is a settled principle that employers cannot invoke "neutral" criteria to forbid conduct that the Act specifically protects. For example, because employees have a right to engage in union solicitation on the employer's

---

[117] One of the Board members, in a concurring opinion in the companion case to *Town & Country*, had listed these as devices that would be available to employers to avoid the bite of the Board's ruling in that case. *Sunland Constr.*, 309 NLRB 1224, 1232–33 (1992) (Member Roudabaugh, concurring).

premises so long as it does not interfere with their work,[118] the employer cannot invoke a general "no solicitation" rule to forbid union solicitation even though it regularly enforces the rule against all other types of solicitation.[119] Similarly, an employer may not refuse to hire a job applicant because she intends to engage in union solicitation at work, notwithstanding the existence of a general no-solicitation rule.The question, then, is whether an employee's solicitation of union support on the employer's premises loses its protected status if the employee is paid by the union to do it. The Board historically has held that employees who engage in union solicitation at work enjoy the Act's protection even though they receive stipends from the union for doing so.[120] This makes sense, for whatever the employer's interest in prohibiting in-plant solicitation by its employees, there are no legitimate reasons why, once the right to engage in the activity is conferred by statute, it should make any difference that the employee is paid to do what she is statutorily entitled to do. Nor is there any reason why the rule should be different for a professional union organizer than for an ordinary employee who is paid by the union. Thus, a ban on "simultaneous employment" should not lawfully be a ground for refusing to hire a paid union organizer, whose only intended "simultaneous employment" is to engage in activities on the employer's premises that are protected by the NLRA.

Similar considerations would invalidate an employer's refusal to hire a paid union organizer because she will "moonlight" after hours. The Board and the courts have construed the Act to protect a wide array of employee activities away from the workplace—including most of the activities that would constitute the workload of a professional union organizer. Among these are off-premises organizing and representational activities on behalf of the employees,[121] activities supporting the job-related efforts of employees of

---

[118] See text accompanying notes 54–55.

[119] See *Republic Aviation*, 324 US at 805.

[120] *Elias Bros. Big Boy, Inc.*, 137 NLRB 1057, 1073–75 and n 16 (1962), enf'd in pertinent part, 325 F2d 360 (6th Cir 1963); *Elias Bros. Big Boy, Inc.* 139 NLRB 1158, 1164–65 (1962); *Holbrook Knitwear, Inc.*, 169 NLRB 768, 771 (1967).

[121] See, e.g., *Walls Mfg. Co.*, 137 NLRB 1317 (1962), enf'd, 321 F2d 753 (DC Cir 1963), cert denied 375 US 923 (1963) (reporting health violations to state health department); *Altex Ready Mixed Concrete Corp. v NLRB*, 542 F2d 295, 297 (5th Cir 1976), enf'g 223 NLRB 696 (1976) (filing workplace-related lawsuit).

other employers,[122] lobbying activities,[123] campaigning for election of public officials supportive of union interests,[124] and participating in union governance or internal union activities.[125] Because these activities are protected, employers cannot discriminate against employees for engaging in them, nor may they discriminate against job applicants because they intend to do so.[126] These holdings, therefore, support the proposition that a full-time union organizer could not lawfully be refused employment or fired pursuant to a "no-moonlighting" rule, so long as her off-premises responsibilities to the union would be protected if engaged in by an ordinary employee.

Even if the Board were to conclude that being paid by a union to exercise Section 7 rights withdraws their protected status, there are two other thresholds an employer would have to satisfy before being able to apply a neutral rule to forbid such paid activities (and, hence, to refuse to hire employees who declare their intention to engage in them). The employer would have to show that the rule was not adopted *for the purpose* of stifling union activities,[127] and

---

[122] Section 7 protects activities of employees "in support of employees of employers other than their own." *Eastex, Inc. v NLRB*, 437 US 556, 564 (1978) (citing *Phelps Dodge Corp. v NLRB*, 313 US 177, 191–92 (1941)); see also *Baker v General Motors Corp.*, 478 US 621 (1986) (supporting employees on strike at another plant of the same employer); *Yellow Cab, Inc. v NLRB*, 210 NLRB 568, 569 (1974) (supporting striking employees of *other* employers); *NLRB v Peter Cailler Kohler Swiss Chocolates Co.*, 130 F2d 503, 506 (2d Cir 1942) (L. Hand, J) (same); *Washington State Serv. Employees v NLRB*, 188 NLRB 957, 959 (1971) (participating in sit-in demonstration in support of another employer's employees).

[123] *Eastex* at 569 (cited in note 122) (urging employees to write their state legislators opposing state right to work law, and criticizing presidential veto of a bill increasing the minimum wage); *Bethlehem Shipbuilding Corp. v NLRB*, 114 F2d 930, 937 (1st Cir 1940), dismissed on motion of petitioner, 312 US 710 (1941), enf'g 11 NLRB 105 (1939) (appearing before legislative committees); *Kaiser Eng'rs v NLRB*, 538 F2d 1379, 1384–85 (9th Cir 1976), enf'g 213 NLRB 752 (1974) (lobbying legislators).

[124] *Eastex* at 570 (cited in note 122).

[125] *Metropolitan Edison*, 460 US 693, 698, 700–01 (1983) (holding union office); *Fort Wayne Corrugated Paper Co. v NLRB*, 111 F2d 869, 873–74 (7th Cir 1940), enf'g *Cayuga Linen and Cotton Mills, Inc.*, 14 NLRB 1, 4–5 (1930) (engaging in activities as district union official).

[126] Indeed, the Supreme Court's decision in *Metropolitan Edison* (cited in note 125) implicitly supports this proposition. The Court there held that an employer could not discriminate against employees who hold union office. While the Court's opinion does not mention whether the union officers received a salary for their position, most such positions are salaried. The Court's failure to inquire signifies that it thought the fact irrelevant to the existence of statutory protection.

[127] *State Chem. Co.*, 166 NLRB 455 (1967); *NLRB v Roney Plaza Apartments*, 597 F2d 1046 (5th Cir 1979).

the employer would have to apply the rule uniformly to all activities, and not merely selectively to union activities.[128]

The rule against improperly motivated neutral rules would be a serious obstacle to implementing either of the rules discussed above, for an employer who did not see the need for such rules prior to *Town & Country* would be hard-pressed to persuade fact-finders that its sudden interest in such a rule was not motivated by a desire to inoculate itself against the danger of a union salting. The rule against discriminatory application also would be troublesome for "no-moonlighting" rules in this era of multiple job-holding, for the employer would have to exclude from its labor pool a significant proportion of prospective candidates. What is more, the employer might have to fire all incumbent employees who did not abandon their moonlighting jobs, a step that would likely deter adoption of such a rule.[129]

2. *Cheating, hoping not to be caught. Town & Country* does not give paid union organizers a right to be hired. It merely gives them a right not to be discriminatorily passed over because of their union allegiance. Even if employers cannot find neutral rules to disqualify them, it is likely that some employers will simply "cheat," proffering pretextual explanations for failing to hire each such applicant (e.g., that other candidates appeared to be better qualified). The burden will be on the Board's General Counsel to prove discriminatory animus, and that can be difficult.

Unions, if they are wise, will proffer candidates who are skilled and experienced at the jobs they are seeking and who have good work records with prior employers. Many union organizers will possess these credentials. In such circumstances, the contrast with

---

[128] See, for example, *Restaurant Corp. of Amer. v NLRB*, 827 F2d 799 (DC Cir 1987). Thus, the Supreme Court in *Babcock* noted that an employer who allowed other outsiders to solicit on its premises could not invoke the right it otherwise would possess to bar nonemployee union organizers. 351 US at 112 (employer's rule banning nonemployee distribution on behalf of unions is valid "if [it] does not discriminate against the union by allowing other distribution").

[129] Employers might argue that "grandfathering" existing employees at the time a "no-moonlighting" rule is adopted should not be considered discriminatory application, especially if the employer declares itself prepared to tolerate paid union "moonlighting" activity by existing employees. (Existing employees would not likely be sophisticated union organizers, so this is a trade-off employers might be willing to make.) But even if the Board were to accept such a distinction, the employer would have the troublesome task of convincing the Board that its motivation was not pretextual given the vast amount of moonlighting it would be tolerating via the grandfathering.

other applicants may be striking. Moreover, unions undertaking "salting" programs sometimes have resorted (as did the union in *Town & Country*) to sending several highly qualified applicants, making it harder for an employer who rejects them all plausibly to contend that it was not improperly motivated.[130]

3. *Cheating, knowing one will be caught.* Finally, some employers may refuse to hire paid union organizers even if they expect that their proffered reasons for preferring others will be found to be pretextual. One of the saddest stories about the NLRA is that the remedies for discriminating against union adherents are insufficient to deter employer violations; it is cheaper to pay backpay and offer reinstatement years later than to suffer the costs of unionization that would be attendant upon obeying the Act's commands.[131] If the Board relies on the ordinary remedial scheme, *Town & Country* will fail in its promise of providing on-premises communication between employees and union organizers, and instead will simply be a revenue-enhancing mechanism for union organizers; they can apply for jobs at nonunion firms, file NLRA charges when passed over, and collect backpay years down the road.

But the Board has statutory authority to seek immediate injunctions to compel employers to desist from violating the Act.[132] Although the Board historically has invoked this authority only infrequently, the Board recently has greatly increased its resort to injunctive remedies.[133] The true promise of *Town & Country* likely will be realized only if the Board exercises that power regularly in "salting" cases, and courts issue prompt injunctions.

Thus, the path from *Town & Country* to full realization of the opportunity it provides will be a difficult one. Some employers will obey the law and others may be brought to heel by 10(j) injunctions. At the least, *Town & Country* is the first Supreme Court decision, sixty years after the Act's enactment, to afford a means

---

[130] As the Supreme Court noted in *International Brotherhood of Teamsters v United States*, 431 US 324, 342 n 23 (1977), the "inexorable zero," in that instance, zero blacks hired as over-the-road drivers, is telling evidence of discriminatory motivation.

[131] The definitive discussion of this phenomenon is Weiler, *Promises* (cited in note 1). A House-passed bill in 1978 to strengthen the remedies for discriminatory behavior was squelched in the Senate by a 19-day filibuster. Id at 1770 n 1.

[132] Section 10(j) of the Act, 29 USC § 160(j).

[133] In fiscal year 1994, the Board authorized 126 injunctions, compared with 26 and 42 in the two prior fiscal years. BNA, Daily Labor Report 181 (Sept 18, 1996): E-5.

by which unions can hope to obtain on-premises communication with the employees they seek to organize.

IV. Removing Disincentives: Brown v Pro Football

Town & Country has opened the door to easier communication between unions and the employees they seek to organize, but the organizers still have to convince the employees that they should opt for unionization. That task is formidable enough, but the Court of Appeals for the District of Columbia Circuit issued a decision in *Brown v Pro Football* that would have made it harder.[134] That court held that employees, by unionizing, forfeit the Sherman Act's protection against conspiracies between employers to cap the wages paid their employees.

A legal regime that attached forfeiture of Sherman Act protection as the price for unionizing would be a powerful deterrent to unionization.[135] Accordingly, it is significant that the Supreme Court rejected the court of appeals' theory, and instead ruled that Sherman Act protection is lost only if, and only so long as, the union elects to engage in *multiemployer* bargaining, that is, bargaining with multiple employers with the goal of reaching a single agreement applicable to all.[136] Multiemployer bargaining is consensual, and a union is free to insist upon bargaining separately with each employer.[137] Thus, the Court has left control of the Sherman Act's applicability in the union's hands.

Brown arose on these facts. The National Football League Players Association was the exclusive bargaining representative of the players for each of the clubs comprising the National Football League. The union had always negotiated with the clubs as a group, entering into a single agreement applicable to all players on all clubs. In 1987, the existing agreement was coming to an end, and the parties were in multiemployer negotiations looking toward a successor agreement.

The existing agreement prescribed a minimum salary, but left each player free to negotiate with his club for a salary above the

---

[134] *Brown v Pro Football, Inc.*, 50 F3d 1041 (DC Cir 1995) (hereinafter *Brown II*).

[135] See discussion in text accompanying notes 154–60.

[136] *Brown v Pro Football, Inc.*, 116 S Ct 2116 (1996) (hereinafter *Brown III*).

[137] *Charles D. Bonanno Linen Serv. v NLRB*, 454 US 404, 412 (1982).

minimum. Under this arrangement, players on the clubs' "developmental squads"—a corps of up to six players per club who did not suit up on game day but who practiced with the regular players during the week and waited in the wings for activation should a regular player become injured—had individually negotiated salaries well above the stipulated minimum.

The NFL clubs, seeking to contain player salaries, proposed that the successor agreement prescribe a fixed salary for all developmental players of $1,000 per week. The union rejected the proposal, insisting that it would not surrender the right of each player to negotiate individually for the highest salary he could obtain. After some time had elapsed and the union's intransigence on this issue was manifest, the clubs declared that the parties were at an impasse on the issue and proceeded to do what the NLRA authorizes employers to do once an impasse is reached; to implement "unilaterally" (i.e., without the consent of the union) the last offer that was made to the union. Thus, during the following season, in which no collective bargaining agreement was in effect, each developmental player received the fixed $1,000 weekly salary that the clubs had agreed upon among themselves.

The affected players sued, contending that the clubs had violated the Sherman Act by conspiring to eliminate what until then had been a competitive market for developmental squad players—a market in which clubs competed on the basis of salary to attract players.[138] The players conceded that the "nonstatutory labor exemption" to the Sherman Act privileges fixed salaries *if the union has agreed to them*. (The "nonstatutory labor exemption" was crafted by the Court to harmonize the Sherman Act with the later-enacted NLRA. In essence, any conduct that is clearly mandated by the NLRA is deemed exempt from the Sherman Act.[139] Because the NLRA contemplates that unions may opt to negotiate jointly with multiple employers for a single agreement, perforce it allows the fixing of salaries pursuant to such an agreement.) But the players argued in *Brown* that, in the absence of union agreement, the Sherman Act forbids separate firms to agree upon a common salary that each will pay its employees.

---

[138] Developmental squad players were free agents, and thus not limited to one team. *Brown III*, 116 S Ct at 2119.

[139] Id at 2120–21.

The clubs defended as lawful their combining to fix the salary of developmental squad players on three separate grounds:

First, the clubs argued that the Sherman Act does not condemn conspiracies between employers to fix salaries in the absence of a resultant injury to the product market. Here, the NFL's product market—the provision of football games for the entertainment of sports fans—was not injured by the agreed-upon salary cap; indeed, by holding down the cost of fielding teams, it relieved the pressure to raise admission prices and thus benefited the fans.

Second, the clubs maintained that even if the Sherman Act forbids the fixing of salaries by agreement among *nonunion* employers, the nonstatutory labor exemption kicks in the moment employees unionize, so that an agreement among *unionized* employers to fix salaries is not unlawful.

Finally, the clubs contended that even if unionized employers who bargain separately with the union cannot agree among themselves to fix salaries, if the union elects to engage in multiemployer negotiations seeking a single agreement applicable to all the employers, the nonstatutory labor exemption permits the employers to act in concert not only in negotiating toward a joint agreement but also in implementing their last offer if the union rejects it and bargaining reaches an impasse.

The district court rejected all three arguments and entered a judgment that the clubs had violated the Sherman Act and a damage award exceeding $30 million—treble the difference between the $1,000 salary per week per player that was paid in 1989 and the salaries the players likely would have received in the absence of the fixed salaries (in the prior year, without the salary cap, players had averaged several thousand dollars per week).[140] The clubs renewed all three arguments on their appeal to the D.C. Circuit, and again in their brief to the Supreme Court.[141]

The clubs' first argument—that the Sherman Act does not forbid an agreement among separate employers to fix salaries so long as there is no resultant injury in the product market—was rooted in two sources. The first is Section 6 of the Clayton Act, which declares in its first sentence that "the labor of a human being is not a commodity or article of commerce." If that is so, the clubs

---

[140] *Brown v Pro Football, Inc.*, 782 F Supp 125 (DDC, 1991) (hereinafter *Brown I*).

[141] Brief for Respondents at 8–49, *Brown v Pro Football* (No 95-388).

argued, then fixing wages cannot be a "conspiracy in restraint of trade or commerce" unless it has an injurious impact on the product market that *is* commerce. The second source is Chief Justice Stone's opinion for the Court in *Apex Hosiery* in 1940,[142] which is said to have embraced this conception. Dicta in *Apex Hosiery* declared that:

> • a restraint does not violate the Sherman Act "unless the restraint is shown to have or is intended to have an effect upon prices in the market or otherwise to deprive purchasers or consumers of the advantages which they derive from free competition;"[143]
> • eliminating "that part of such competition which is based on differences in labor standards . . . has not been considered to be the kind of curtailment of price competition prohibited by the Sherman Act;"[144] and
> • the proper interpretative approach requires "an impartial application of the Sherman Act to the activities of industry and labor alike"[145] (an approach that the clubs contended legitimates agreement among employers upon a common salary scale because *employees* are entitled to combine to seek a common salary; in the words of *Apex Hosiery*, the second sentence of Section 6 of the Clayton Act makes "plain that restraints on the sale of the employee's services to the employer, however much they curtail competition among employees, are not in themselves combinations or conspiracies in restraint of trade or commerce under the Sherman Act").[146]

These sources have persuaded a number of scholars—including Archibald Cox and Theodore St. Antoine—that an agreement among employers to fix the salaries of their employees does not violate the Sherman Act, unless there is a consequent injury in the employers' "product market."[147] Ordinarily, holding *down* the

---

[142] *Apex Hosiery Co. v Leader*, 310 US 469 (1940).

[143] Id at 500–01.

[144] Id at 503–04.

[145] Id at 512.

[146] Id at 503.

[147] Archibald Cox, *Labor and the Antitrust Law—A Preliminary Analysis*, 104 U Pa L Rev 252, 254–55, 262–64 (1955); Theodore St. Antoine, *Connell: Antitrust Law at the Expense of Labor Law*, 62 Va L Rev 603, 606, 608 (1976); Robert H. Jerry and Donald E. Knebel, *Antitrust and Employer Restraints in Labor Markets*, 6 Indus & Lab Rel Rev 173 (1984); Gary R. Roberts, *Reconciling Federal Labor and Antitrust Policy: The Special Case of Sports League Labor Market Restraints*, 75 Georgetown L J 19, 26–58 (1986).

price of an input to production would not portend injury to the ultimate product market, and indeed in the instant case the court of appeals found that there was no such injury.[148]

Despite its academic proponents, however, this theory has been rejected by most lower federal courts.[149] The courts have found unpersuasive the two predicates upon which the no-violation thesis is based:

1. The first sentence of Section 6 of the Clayton Act, however inartful its wording, had a very specific and limited purpose: to liberate *employees* from the risk that, by unionizing and demanding a common wage, *they* would be found to be conspiring to fix the price at which they sold *their* "product" (i.e., their labor). One cannot support workers' rights to unionize without exempting their combined efforts from the antitrust laws. That this sentence was intended to protect only workers' combinations is confirmed by the second sentence of Section 6, which expressly declares that the activities of unions, when acting alone, are not to be enjoined, but extends no similar protection to the activities of employers.

2. *Apex Hosiery*'s dictum that the Sherman Act is limited to effects upon "purchasers or consumers" was overtaken a few years later by the Court's decision in *Mandeville Farms*, holding that a conspiracy by sugar refiners to cap the price they would pay farmers for sugar cane violated the Sherman Act: "It is clear that the agreement is the sort of combination condemned by the [Sherman] Act, even though the price fixing was by purchasers, and the persons specially injured . . . are sellers, not customers or consumers."[150] While *Apex Hosiery* was a labor case and *Mandeville Farms* was not, the declaration in *Apex Hosiery* was not predicated on anything unique to labor terms, but rather on a narrow conception of the Sherman Act. That conception was repudiated in *Mandeville Farms*.

The rejection by most lower courts of the theory that the Sherman Act does not condemn salary-fixing has been endorsed by

---

[148] *Brown II*, 50 F3d at 1058.

[149] See, for example, *Cordova v Bache & Co.*, 321 F Supp 600 (SDNY 1970); *Mackey v National Football League*, 543 F2d 606, 617 n 22 (8th Cir 1976), cert denied, 434 US 801 (1977); *Brown II*, see text accompanying note 152. See also Lee Goldman, *The Labor Exemption to the Antitrust Laws as Applied to Employers' Labor Market Restraints in Sports and Non-Sports Markets*, 19 Utah L Rev 617, 622–35 (1989) (discussing cases).

[150] *Mandeville Island Farms v Sugar Co.*, 334 US 219, 235 (1948).

Phillip Areeda and his colleagues in their treatises on antitrust law.[151]

In *Brown v Pro Football*, the Court of Appeals for the District of Columbia Circuit declared that, even in the absence of resultant injury in a product market, the NFL clubs' agreement to fix salaries would violate the Sherman Act unless saved by the nonstatutory labor exemption. Indeed, the Court explained, if the union was decertified, the players would regain protection against a fixing of salaries by agreement among the employers, for in the absence of a union, the nonstatutory labor exemption would be inapplicable.[152]

But the court of appeals then proceeded to embrace the clubs' second contention, that the mere act of unionizing conferred upon the clubs an exemption from the Sherman Act. The court of appeals explained:

> We recognize, of course, that, as a general matter, the antitrust laws may apply to restraints on competition in non-unionized labor markets. . . . However, we think the inception of a collective bargaining relationship between employees and employers irrevocably alters the governing legal regime.
>
> * * *
>
> [W]e conclude that injecting antitrust liability into the system of resolving disputes between unions and employers would both subvert national labor policy and exaggerate federal antitrust concerns.
>
> * * *
>
> In our view, the nonstatutory labor exemption requires employees involved in a labor dispute to choose whether to invoke the protections of the NLRA or the Sherman Act. If employees wish to seek the protections of the Sherman Act, they may forego unionization or even decertify their unions.[153]

The court of appeals reasoned that this approach was necessary to prevent unionized employees from gaining an unfair advantage over their employers: "Injecting the Sherman Act into the collective bargaining process would disrupt this balance [of power under

---

[151] Phillip Areeda and Donald F. Turner, *Antitrust Law*, Vol III, ¶ 229d, pp 198–202 (1978); Phillip Areeda and Herbert Hovenkamp, *Antitrust Laws*, Rev Ed, Vol III, ¶ 377c, p 312 (1995).

[152] *Brown II*, 50 F3d at 1054–55.

[153] Id at 1054, 1056–57.

the NLRA] by giving unions a powerful new weapon, one not contemplated by the federal labor laws."[154]

From the perspective of unions hoping to organize, this is dangerous stuff. Ironically, the clubs' first argument, which the court of appeals rejected, might have driven workers *into* unions, because if that argument had been accepted, collective economic power might then have been seen by workers as the only feasible response once salary-fixing destroyed a competitive market for labor. But the combined effect of the court of appeals' rejection of the first argument and adoption of the second would predictably drive workers *out of* unions (and certainly deter new workers from joining).

Any doctrine that takes legal protections away from employees as the consequence of their unionizing is likely to be a substantial deterrent to unionization. Recognizing this, the Supreme Court recently struck down, as preempted by the NLRA, a state's effort to confine a mandated benefit to nonunion workplaces. Although the state was motivated by a desire to avoid interfering with collective bargaining, the Court reasoned that withholding the benefit from unionized workers might have the unintended effect of deterring unionization.[155] The Court explained that "[a] state rule predicating benefits on refraining from conduct protected by federal labor law poses special dangers of interference with congressional purpose. . . . This unappetizing choice . . . cannot ultimately be reconciled with a statutory scheme premised on the centrality of the right to bargain collectively. . . ."[156]

The court of appeals' ruling in *Brown* would have complicated unions' efforts to organize. It would have furnished employers an additional "talking point" to discourage employee interest in unionization. Although employers are not permitted to threaten employees with retaliation if they select a union, they *are* permitted to inform employees of the legal consequences that may attend unionization.[157] For example, it is commonplace for employers to tell employees contemplating unionization that the employer is permitted by law to seek to reduce the existing wages and benefits

---

[154] Id at 1052.

[155] *Livadas v Bradshaw*, 114 S Ct 2068 (1994).

[156] Id at 2074–75; see also id at 2081–82.

[157] See text accompanying notes 158–59.

in negotiations with a union,[158] and to permanently replace the employees should they strike in support of the union's demands.[159] Under the court of appeals' ruling in *Brown*, this litany could be expanded to include the report that "you will lose your protections under the Sherman Antitrust Act if you vote for a union."

This warning would forecast a real injury, although the nature of the injury would vary depending on the employment conditions in the industry. Consider first those industries where there is a viable competitive market for labor—one in which employers seek to outbid one another to attract the best workers. In this environment, employees would not likely contemplate unionization merely to increase their bargaining power—the market furnishes them bargaining power without a union. Still, they might opt for unionization for a host of other reasons—to address collective goods problems (benefit plans, safety and health, etc.), to secure representation with respect to day-to-day grievances, or to monitor the employer's compliance with legal obligations owed employees. In an industry of this sort, the court of appeals' ruling in *Brown* could significantly reduce the incentives for unionizing. In such an industry, the union would not likely attempt to equalize salaries across the industry; quite the contrary, the union would want to maintain the competitive labor market. But if unionization triggered forfeiture of Sherman Act protection, it would provide the employers an opportunity not otherwise available to conspire to eliminate the competition between them to attract labor. Thus, the court of appeals' rule would likely fence unions out of industries characterized by high-skill jobs.

Another environment—the one typical of the major industries that were the backbone of organized labor in its heyday—is one in which employees individually lack bargaining power, and employers compete by attempting to achieve lower labor costs than their competitors. Here, the union is likely to strive to equalize wages between employers in order to remove the incentive for employers to race to the bottom. In this context, the union might

---

[158] *International Paper Co.*, 273 NLRB 615 (1984).

[159] *Gino Morena*, 287 NLRB 1327 (1988); *John W. Galbreath & Co.*, 288 NLRB 876 (1989); *Larson Tool and Stamping Co.*, 296 NLRB 895 (1989). As these decisions make clear, if the employer tells employees of its right to permanently replace strikers, it must also advise them that if permanently replaced they will enjoy preferential entitlement to recall opportunities, see note 36.

opt for multiemployer bargaining. But, alternatively, it might opt for bargaining individually with each employer, attempting to secure a good package from the most vulnerable employer and then "whipsawing" the other employers into meeting the package (else confronting a strike while the first-settling employer continues to operate). In this environment, the employees would be best served by a legal regime in which the union is entitled (as Section 6 of the Clayton Act clearly provides) to seek equalized wages, but in which employers are forbidden to conspire with each other to drive the package down. If the Sherman Act forbids employer conspiracies in this context, unions will enjoy a one-way ratchet and thus can offer a modicum of additional bargaining power to workers.

Against this backdrop, let us examine the Supreme Court's disposition of the issue in *Brown*. Although the Court affirmed the court of appeals' holding that the nonstatutory labor exemption shielded the salary-fixing from Sherman Act invalidation, it did so on a ground that has no impact on unions that abstain from multiemployer bargaining. The Court declared that "we do not interpret the [nonstatutory] exemption as broadly as did the Appeals Court."[160] The Court explained that what triggered the exemption's applicability in this case was the union's choice to engage in multiemployer bargaining—a choice that entitled the employers, pursuant to the NLRA, to conspire (*a*) to formulate and bargain for common terms, and (*b*) to implement those terms once bargaining reached an impasse.[161] But the Court suggested that the employers' exemption would disappear if the parties no longer were in a multiemployer bargaining relationship.[162]

Curiously, although the Court expressly disapproved the court of appeals' interpretation, it did not explain why it disapproved that interpretation. There are two possibilities. First, the logic of the Court's opinion suggests that the exemption comes into play only when it is necessary to lubricate a form of bargaining authorized by the NLRA. There is no body of decisional law recognizing a right of employers who negotiate separately with a union to conspire to reach a common set of terms and conditions. Second, as

---

[160] *Brown III*, 116 S Ct at 2119.

[161] Id at 2123–24, 2127.

[162] Id at 2127.

Judge Wald observed in her dissenting opinion in the court of appeals, a holding that mere unionization forfeits the protection of the Sherman Act would chill unionism and thus threaten "the central purpose of our labor laws of promoting collective bargaining. . . ."[163]

Unlike the court of appeals' opinion, the Supreme Court's ruling will not chill unionism. Employers will not be able to tell their employees that by selecting a union they will forfeit Sherman Act protection. In industries with viable competitive markets for labor, employees will be able to unionize without fear of losing the benefits of that market. In industries without competitive labor markets, employees may hope that the additional bargaining power they acquire by unionizing cannot be offset by employer conspiracies to resist whipsawing.

The qualification in the preceding sentence—unions may "hope" that employers cannot conspire to resist whipsawing—reflects a lingering doubt about the ultimate sweep of the holding in *Brown*. On its face, *Brown* appears to state that, absent multiemployer bargaining, employers do not enjoy the benefit of the nonstatutory labor exemption, but the Court was not contemplating the implications of that statement for situations in which the union *seeks* a common wage and invokes whipsawing tactics to achieve its end. Long before *Brown*, Professors Areeda and Turner had suggested that the exemption should apply in such circumstances.[164] It would be incautious to conclude that the Court's rejection of the court of appeals' definition of the exemption's sweep forecloses further inquiry in future cases. And even if the exemption is confined to the multiemployer context, there would remain the question whether employers confronting a whipsaw might vali-

---

[163] *Brown II*, 50 F3d at 1059 (Wald, J, dissenting).

[164] Professors Areeda and Turner advocated that "*regardless of the dimensions of the normal bargaining unit*," that is, even when the union negotiates separately with each employer, the exemption should protect the activities of "an employer combination that is no broader than the union." Areeda and Turner (cited in note 151), ¶ 229d, at 200. "We are discussing only those instances in which wage policy direction on the employees' side embraces at least the combining employees (and perhaps more). Thus the existence of separate locals would be irrelevant when policy is substantially determined in a larger unit such as the regional or national headquarters of such a union." Id at 200 n 39. The authors cited a decision exempting from antitrust review a conspiracy between two Detroit newspapers to reach the same economic settlement in separate negotiations with the same union. *Newspaper Drivers Local 372 v NLRB*, 404 F2d 1159 (6th Cir 1968), cert denied sub nom *Newspaper Drivers Local 371 v Detroit Newspaper Publishers Assn.*, 395 US 923 (1969).

date their "salary-fixing" pursuant to the "rule of reason" that is available to actors who enjoy no exemption from the Sherman Act.

While there is thus room for continuing argument on behalf of employers who confront a union whipsaw despite the absence of multiemployer bargaining, there is no gainsaying that, from the vantage of unions contemplating a renewed effort at organizing, *Brown* represents a bullet dodged. The immediate negative consequences of the court of appeals' ruling have been erased. Employers cannot tell employees that unionization forfeits their Sherman Act protection, and employees in industries with competitive labor markets need not fear that unionization will trigger an end to that competition. With respect to industries without competitive labor markets, *Brown* does not increase (relative to the state of the law prior to *Brown*) the probability that employers confronted with union whipsaws will combine in response. Indeed, if anything, it makes their task harder by nominally withdrawing access to the nonstatutory labor exemption. In any event, in these industries, as in the case of multiemployer bargaining, unions hold the key. Unionization alone will not trigger an entitlement of employers to combine; at worst, unions may bring that on by electing to proceed in a manner that is within their control.

V. Conclusion

The labor movement is stirring. Whether it will succeed in reinvigorating America's workers and in expanding its now precarious position in the private sector is surely in doubt. At best, its task is formidable. Many observers attribute the labor movement's fall during the past quarter century in part to the Court's unsympathetic interpretations of the National Labor Relations Act.[165] Those interpretations remain as substantial barriers to the labor movement's resuscitation.

In the 1995 term, however, the Court took modest but noteworthy steps that will facilitate the unions' efforts at revival. For the first time in the sixty-year history of the NLRA, the Court has construed the Act to provide a means (however circuitous) by which union organizers may be able to communicate with employ-

---

[165] Atleson (cited in note 38); Gould (cited in note 38); Craver (cited in note 38).

ees on employer premises. Further, the Court has overturned a ruling that would have freighted the employees' choice to unionize with the loss of protections under the Sherman Act.[166]

One should not draw the lesson that the current Justices have a secret passion for unionism. To the contrary, six of them have participated in decisions in past years that are quite unsympathetic to unions.[167] But at a time in which unions need any help they can get, the 1995 term was a welcome step in the right direction.

---

[166] The interests of unions were upheld in each of the other three decisions in the 1995 Term involving the rights of unions. See note 28 supra. However, the stakes in those cases were so small that they are unlikely to influence the prospects for success in unionization efforts (except that *Holly Farms* entitles a particular class of chicken processor employees to the NLRA's protections in seeking to unionize).

[167] *Lechmere*, described in text accompanying notes 72–78; *Trans World Airlines*, described in text accompanying note 37; *NLRB v Health Care & Retirement Corp. of Am.*, 114 S Ct 1778 (1994) (licensed practical nurses who direct less skilled employees in providing patient care are supervisors and thus not "employees" entitled to NLRA coverage).

PAUL D. CARRINGTON AND
PAUL H. HAAGEN

CONTRACT AND JURISDICTION

Introduction

Over the last dozen years, the Supreme Court has rewritten the law governing commercial and employment arbitration in the United States. So bold has the Court been that its work in this field could be said to exemplify the indeterminacy of American law, confirming the hypothesis of Critical Legal scholars that our judges (or at least our Justices) are uncontrolled by legal texts or precedents and free to decide cases according to their own political predilections.[1]

This article is a comment on five cases decided by the Court in the 1994 and 1995 Terms, all of them presenting issues of commercial arbitration law.[2] The field of arbitration is sufficiently ar-

Paul D. Carrington is Chadwick Professor of Law, Duke University. Member, Board of Directors, The Private Adjudication Center, Inc., since 1983; President, 1989–1994, Chairman since 1994. The Center is a nonprofit corporation providing dispute resolution and continuing education services and conducting research in the field of dispute resolution. His work on this article was supported by the E. T. Bost Fund of the Law School and Cannon Trust III. Paul H. Haagen is Professor of Law, Duke University.

AUTHORS' NOTE: The authors express gratitude to Deborah DeMott and Ian Macneil for helpful comments and to Traci Jones, David Azar, Soo Im, and Welly Tontano for research help.

[1] For example, Joseph William Singer, *The Player and the Cards: Nihilism and Legal Theory*, 94 Yale L J 1 (1984).

[2] *Doctors' Associates, Inc. v Casarotto*, 116 S Ct 1652 (1996); *Allied-Bruce Terminix v Dobson*, 115 S Ct 834 (1995); *First Options of Chicago, Inc. v Kaplan*, 115 S Ct 1920 (1995); *Mastrobuono v Shearson Lehman Hutton, Inc.*, 115 S Ct 1212 (1995); *Vimar Seguros y Reaseguros, S.A. v M/V Sky Reefer*, 115 S Ct 2322 (1995). For additional comment, see Jean R. Sternlight, *Panacea or Corporate Tool? Debunking the Supreme Court's Preference for Binding Arbitration*, 74 Wash U L Q 637 (1996); Jeffrey W. Stempel, *Reflections on Judicial ADR and the Multi-*

cane that these cases are not likely to have been closely observed by any but *cognoscenti.* But what the Court has done in these cases and in recently antecedent cases has significant implications for much American law and offers instruction to students of the Court about the character of that institution at the end of the twentieth century.

The Court's aggression has been the product of two worthy but overindulged impulses. One impulse has been to encourage international trade by enforcing dispute resolution provisions in international commercial contracts. The second has been to conserve scarce judicial resources by encouraging citizens to resolve disputes by private means. Few readers of this Review would quarrel with either of these impulses, and we do not. But to elevate them, as the Court has, to the rank of imperatives is to disregard serious risks of injustice and lawlessness sometimes attending the enforcement of such provisions. It was suggested that Great Britain acquired its empire in the nineteenth century in a "fit of inadvertence"; that term may be equally useful as an account of the Court's remaking of arbitration law.

Three features of the law emerging from the Court's decisions animated by these impulses of internationalism and privatization are striking. First, the Court has enforced arbitration clauses that were until recently deemed invalid impairments of rights conferred by Congress in its regulation of commerce, thereby weakening enforcement of the national law.[3] Second, the Court has completely federalized a body of law that was until recently regarded as an appropriate subject for the exercise of state sovereignty,[4] thereby substantially disabling states from effective regulation of commercial and employment transactions.[5] Third, the Court appears to be

---

Door Courthouse at Twenty: Fait Accompli, Failed Overture, or Fledgling Adulthood, 11 Ohio St J on Disp Resol 297 (1996); and see Thomas E. Carbonneau, *Arbitration and the U.S. Supreme Court: A Plea for Statutory Reform,* 5 Ohio St J on Disp Resol 231 (1989).

[3] For example, *Rodriguez de Quijas v Shearson/American Express,* 490 US 477 (1989); *Vimar,* 115 S Ct 2322.

[4] This action of the Court had an antecedent in *Prima Paint Corp. v Flood & Conklin Mfg. Co.,* 388 US 395 (1967), when for the first time the Court held that the 1925 Act was an exercise of the commerce power, not as previously believed an exercise of the power of Congress over the federal courts. But the Court in that case stopped far short of sweeping preemption of state law.

[5] For example, *Southland Corp. v Keating,* 466 US 1 (1984); *Dobson,* 115 S Ct 834; *Casarotto,* 116 S Ct 1652.

transforming a dispute-resolving process traditionally regarded in this country as nonlegal into a process more nearly resembling that of a court of law.[6] This legalizing transformation is an almost inevitable if unforeseen consequence of the two previously stated features of the new national arbitration law the Court has crafted; its potential effect is to deprive commercial arbitration of its traditional virtues of efficiency and dispatch.

Those who have been prejudiced by the Court's handiwork include many American consumers, patients, workers, investors, shopkeepers, shippers, and passengers. Those whose interests have been served include all those engaged in interstate or international commerce deploying their economic power to evade enforcement of their contractual duties or the lash of those state or federal commercial laws that are privately enforced.

We present these developments as evidence that when the Court turns to the task of constructing broad national policies, it is capable of doing quite a bad job. In a time when we are prone to discredit Congress and the political process, it is well to keep in mind that the Court is not necessarily a superior source of wise political leadership.[7] James Bradley Thayer's historic dictum to that effect[8] remains sound. For all its shortcomings, Congress remains the legitimate source of national policy. The people share responsibility for its misdeeds, but have no responsibility for bad law made by Justices with life tenure, and are entitled to resent an institution taking it upon itself to construct law that is in so many ways injurious to their interests.

THE COURT AND FREEDOM OF CONTRACT

Before turning to the perplexing technicalities of arbitration law, we note that the phenomenon we observe may be seen as an aspect of a larger feature of the Court's work. Both the impulse to superinternationalism and the apparent passion for ADR can be

---

[6] For example, *Mitsubishi Motors Corp. v Soler Chrysler-Plymouth, Inc.*, 473 US 614 (1985); *Vimar*, 115 S Ct 2322.

[7] We join Neil Komesar in acknowledging that all our institutions are imperfect. See Neil K. Komesar, *Imperfect Alternatives: Choosing Institutions in Law, Economics, and Public Policy* (Univ of Chicago Press, 1994).

[8] James Bradley Thayer, *The Origin and Scope of the American Doctrine of Constitutional Law*, 8 Harv L Rev 129, 144 (1893).

attributed to the Court's simple faith in freedom of contract. Cass Sunstein has called attention to the enduring vitality of that faith,[9] and Richard Shell has found it to be in recent times a pervasive influence on the Court.[10] In its sometimes uncritical acceptance of the importance of freedom of contract, the Court curiously ignores the national experience in this century, and even its own misadventures.

The unwisdom of blind commitment to freedom of contract was forcefully depicted by Roscoe Pound in 1909[11] and has been re-marked many times since. Contract is not merely a source of eco-nomic power, but it is also a deployment of that power[12] that can effect a transfer of wealth from the weak to the strong. The Pro-gressives recognized this potential and used the police power of the state and federal governments to limit predations by those with economic power over workers, consumers, tenants, insureds, shop-keepers, shippers, and passengers.[13] Much of that legislation re-stricted freedom of contract and much of it was directed at im-posed contracts.

In 1919, Edwin Patterson, commenting on recent developments in state courts, introduced into our legal vocabulary the term "con-tract of adhesion."[14] The term applied to agreements that are not the result of bargaining.[15] An early paradigm was the contract made with customers by Thomas Hobson, a seventeenth-century Lon-don liveryman; his name is still associated with nominal choices that are in reality not choices at all.[16] Patterson noted that in such

---

[9] Cass Sunstein, *Lochner's Legacy*, 87 Colum L Rev 873 (1987).

[10] G. Richard Shell, *Contracts in the Modern Supreme Court*, 81 Colum L Rev 431 (1993).

[11] Roscoe Pound, *Liberty of Contract*, 18 Yale L J 454 (1909).

[12] Richard A. Posner, *Economic Analysis of Law* 29 (Little Brown, 3d ed 1986).

[13] See generally Richard A. Hofstadter, *The Age of Reform: From Bryan to F.D.R.* (Knopf York, 1955).

[14] Edwin Patterson, *The Delivery of a Life-Insurance Policy*, 33 Harv L Rev 198, 222.

[15] For a more elaborate definition, see Todd D. Rakoff, *Contracts of Adhesion: An Essay of Reconstruction*, 96 Harv L Rev 1174 (1983). His definition would exclude franchise agree-ments that provide many of the cases discussed here, but he recognized them as contracts of adhesion "at least in situations in which the franchisee is also a lessee." Id at 1178 n 15.

[16] Hobson's customers were required to take the horse nearest the door. *Cincinnati En-quirer* (July 30, 1995), p D5. Another example is provided by Henry Ford's dictum regard-ing the Model A Ford—the buyer could choose any color he liked so long as it was black.

transactions, " 'freedom of contract' rarely exists," and courts therefore "strain the language out of its clear meaning"[17] to protect the party who casually or inadvertently assents to a very improvident term. While such adhesion contracts are contracts in form, they lack the characteristics traditionally providing the moral justification for enforcing the promises they contain.[18]

Thirty years before Patterson wrote, the Supreme Court itself explained the difficulty. On March 12, 1880, *Montana*, en route from New York to Liverpool, ran aground in Holyhead Bay, Wales, and lost much of its cargo. The owner of the cargo sued for negligence; the carrier's defense relied on a clause in the bill of lading exempting the carrier from liability for negligence. The Court noted that the term was not the product of free exercise of the right to make enforceable promises; to the contrary, a shipper "prefers to accept any bill of lading, or to sign any paper, that the carrier presents; and in most cases, he has no alternative but to do this, or to abandon his business."[19] When a contract is imposed in this fictive manner, the Court held, it should be enforced only if its terms are "just and reasonable."

That decision was prescient in foretelling the development of contract law. In many situations exemplified by the bill of lading, our law proceeds from the premise that the instrument was not read or understood by the party on whom its terms are imposed.[20] The Restatement (Second) of Contracts assumes that parties using standardized, printed forms do not expect their customers to read or understand what they are required to sign.[21] Sometimes, as with insurance policies, the purchaser may not have an opportunity to read or sign because the written instrument is delivered after the transaction has been made.[22]

---

[17] Patterson, *The Delivery of a Life-Insurance Policy* at 222 (cited in note 14).

[18] Lewis A. Kornhauser, *Unconscionability in Standard Forms*, 64 Cal L Rev 1152 (1976).

[19] *Liverpool Steam Co. v Phenix Ins. Co.*, 129 US 397, 441 (1889).

[20] Rakoff, *Contracts of Adhesion* at 1179 (cited in note 15).

[21] Restatement (Second) of Contracts § 211, comment B ("A party who makes regular use of a standardized form of agreement does not ordinarily expect his customers to understand or even to read the standard terms.").

[22] W. David Slawson, *Mass Contracts: Lawful Fraud in California*, 48 S Cal L Rev 1, 12 (1974). See also Friedrich Kessler, *Contracts of Adhesion—Some Thoughts About Freedom of Contract*, 43 Colum L Rev 629, 632 (1943).

While thus suspect as true contracts embodying a meeting of minds, contracts of adhesion such as printed bills of lading serve useful social functions.[23] They are perhaps inevitable in an economy dominated by mass production and mass distribution.[24] They permit businesses to reduce juridical risk, being "an important means of excluding or controlling the 'irrational factor' in litigation,'"[25] and reduce transaction costs.[26] But as Patterson and Kessler and many courts have recognized, they can be abusive. While the reaction of American courts to such "contracts" has, as Kessler noted more than fifty years ago, been sometimes "highly contradictory and confusing," what has emerged in the Restatement (Second) of Contracts[27] and gained expression in the Uniform Commercial Code[28] is a conception of contracts of adhesion widely understood and applied that permits courts to respond flexibly to the social realities underlying imposed contracts.

A lucid explanation of the prevailing view was provided by Karl Llewellyn, the draftsman of the Code:

> Instead of thinking about "assent" to boiler-plate clauses, we can recognize that so far as concerns the specific, there is no assent at all. What has in fact been assented to, specifically, are the few dickered terms, and the more broad type of the transaction, but one thing more. The one thing more is a blanket assent (not a specific assent) to any not unreasonable or indecent term the seller may have on his form, which do not alter or eviscerate the reasonable meaning of the dickered terms. The fine print that has not been read has no business to cut under the reasonable meaning of those dickered terms which constitute the dominant and only real expression of agreement, but much of it commonly belongs in.[29]

---

[23] Arthur Allen Leff, *Contract as Thing*, 19 Am U L Rev 131, 143–44 (1970).

[24] Kessler, *Contracts of Adhesion* at 631 (cited in note 22). Kessler believed that adhesion contracts were associated with the tendency of mature capitalism to move toward monopoly. Writing forty years later, Rakoff demonstrated that they are useful even in the absence of oligopolistic power. *Contracts of Adhesion* at 1218 (cited in note 15).

[25] Kessler, *Contracts of Adhesion* at 632 (cited in note 22).

[26] Leff, *Contract as Thing* at 143–44 (cited in note 23).

[27] See, e.g., Restatement (Second) of Contracts §§ 205, 211.

[28] See, e.g., id § 2-302.

[29] Karl Llewellyn, *The Common Law Tradition: Deciding Appeals* 370 (Little Brown, 1960). On the relation between this idea and the Code, see Richard Danzig, *A Comment on the Jurisprudence of the Uniform Commercial Code*, 27 Stan L Rev 621 (1975).

Those who resisted Progressive politics a century ago often celebrated the sanctity of contract as a precept of constitutional law.[30] That sanctification resonated with the social Darwinism infecting the thinking of many Americans in the earlier period of industrialization, when both legislatures and courts backed away from laws to protect workers, consumers, or even merchants from the overbearing conduct of nascent industry.[31] Reflecting the constitutional law of that earlier era was the work on contracts of Samuel Williston, who disregarded the distinctive features of adhesion methods, and treated them as true contracts.[32]

The Court abandoned freedom of contract as constitutional doctrine when the federal government began to regulate the national economy in the second and fourth decades of this century. From the mid-1930s, states as well as the federal government were free to impose restraints on freedom of contract in order to protect the weak from the strong.[33] Thus, state legislatures as well as Congress have added to the list of those needing protection from overbearing contracts those thousands of small businesses operating as franchisees, often of multinational corporations owning trademarks that by means of modern media have become almost essential to success in many otherwise local enterprises.[34]

Despite these developments in constitutional law and the law of contracts as administered by state courts, the Court may now be seen as a born-again Willistonian believer in freedom of contract.[35] In the days of *Lochner*, the Court as the champion of freedom of

---

[30] For example, Christopher Tiedemann, *A Treatise on the Limitations of Police Power in the United States* (Thomas Law Book, 1886).

[31] Herbert Spencer, *Social Statics; or, The Conditions Essential to Human Happiness Specified and the First of Them Developed* (Williams & Norgate, 1872), an English work, was perhaps the most noted expression of this view. William Graham Sumner was the leading American exponent of social Darwinism, having derived many of his ideas from Herbert Spencer. See Jonathan H. Turner, *Herbert Spencer: A Renewed Appreciation* (Sage, 1985). For an account of the relation between their extreme individualism and the constitutional doctrine of that era, see Richard Hofstadter, *Social Darwinism in American Thought, 1860–1915* (Beacon, 1944); Les Benedict, *Laissez-Faire and Liberty: A Re-evaluation of the Meaning and Origin of Laissez Faire Constitutionalism*, 3 L & Hist Rev 293 (1985).

[32] See, e.g., Samuel Williston, 1 *A Treatise on the Law of Contracts* § 35 (W. Jaeger, 3d ed 1957); Restatement (First) of Contracts § 70 (1932).

[33] Stephen A. Gardbaum, *Why the New Deal Was Not a Nationalist Revolution in Constitutional Terms*, U Chi L Rev (forthcoming, 1997).

[34] See generally William Laird Siegel, *Franchising* (Wiley, 1982); and *Franchising 1987: Business Strategies and Legal Compliance* (Practicing Law Institute, 1987).

[35] The reference to Williston is explained in the text at note 34.

contract was employing its power of judicial review to strike down Progressive legislation as unconstitutional restraints on freedom of contract;[36] in these days of greater judicial restraint, the Court is not invalidating Progressive regulation of economic power, but is more subtly effecting similar results by favoring the freedom of those having sufficient economic strength to contract out of effective private enforcement of regulations adverse to their interests. Herbert Spencer's *Social Statics*, so long lost from constitutional law,[37] has been found by the Court to be alive and well and residing in the Federal Arbitration Act of 1925.

It is possible to find in this development a moment of triumph for the academic movement identified in recent decades as law-and-economics.[38] Those imbued with its dogma tend to believe that efficiency, the mother of all worthy values, is best served by the unseen hand of the market, and hence that "rational choice does not mean conscious choice."[39] If that were so, then there would be no reason to distinguish contracts of adhesion from real contracts,[40] or to be concerned for a party who unconsciously and improvidently submits to an adverse choice of forum for the enforcement of his rights because the market will always provide him with all that he deserves. Whether the development we depict is a triumph for such thinking is open to doubt. There is meager evidence of such a victory in the Court's opinions.

An alternative explanation is that the Court is so absorbed in matters of seemingly greater public moment that its members have failed to attune themselves to the values and the realities of private law. While some members of the Court, notably Justice Stevens, have at times seemed to be conscious of what the Court has been doing, a majority have generally been content to rest their decisions on formal grounds, falsifiable assumptions, or sweeping doc-

---

[36] For a contemporaneous account, see Ernst Freund, *The Police Power: Public Policy and Constitutional Rights* (Callaghan, 1904).

[37] *Lochner v New York*, 198 US 45, 75–76 (1905) (Holmes, J, dissenting).

[38] See, e.g., Richard A. Epstein, *Unconscionability: A Critical Reappraisal*, 18 J L & Econ 293 (1975); James A. Brickley et al, *The Economic Effects of Franchise Termination Laws*, 34 J L & Econ 101 (1991).

[39] Richard A. Posner, *The Ethical Significance of Free Choice: A Reply to Professor West*, 99 Harv L Rev 1431, 1439 (1986).

[40] Daniel A. Farber, *Contract Law and Modern Economic Theory*, 78 Nw U L Rev 303 (1983).

trines derived not from the actual texts of the controlling statute and treaty (and sometimes at odds with those texts) but from cosmic purposes mistakenly attributed to the legislators who made them.

The field of commercial arbitration, it must be said, is not an easy one to master. The statute is brief, but dense. The treaty governing recognition of foreign awards, like many, is vaporous. The relationship between private and public institutions is complex, and the illumination of that relationship provided by counsel is often dim. In any case, the Court's opinions seem more the product of underattention to practical consequences than to overattention to grand theory.

THE FEDERAL ARBITRATION ACT OF 1925

There is no need here fully to recount the history of the Federal Arbitration Act of 1925. It has been quite accurately reported by Justice O'Connor,[41] and more recently and fully by Ian Macneil.[42] But for readers who are not familiar with arbitration law, it may be helpful to summarize.

A principle widely accepted by American courts in the nineteenth century, and still the law in some states, is that a clause providing for arbitration of a nonexisting dispute is non binding. Contrary to a frequently expressed shibboleth,[43] this principle was not necessarily the product of hostility to arbitration. While there was a strand of thought derived from English precedent guarding judicial jurisdiction against "ouster" by contract,[44] arbitration was widely favored in America.[45] Awards of arbitrators were as enforceable in federal and most state courts as were judicial judgments.[46]

---

[41] *Southland Corp. v Keating*, 465 US 1, 21 (1984) (O'Connor, J, dissenting).

[42] Ian R. Macneil, *American Arbitration Law: Reformation, Nationalization, Internationalization* 15–133 (Oxford, 1992).

[43] For example, *Kulukundis Shipping Co. v Amtorg Trading Corp.*, 126 F2d 978, 985 (2d Cir 1942). (Jerome Frank, J) quoted by Justice Blackmun in *Mitsubishi*, 473 US at 623.

[44] Paul L. Sayre, *Development of Commercial Arbitration Law*, 37 Yale L J 595 (1927); A. W. Brian Simpson, *Contracts for Cotton to Arrive: The Case of the Two Ships* Peerless, 11 Cardozo L Rev 287, 322 (1989).

[45] Macneil, *American Arbitration Law* at 19 (cited in note 42).

[46] For example, *Hamilton v Liverpool, London & Globe Ins. Co.*, 136 US 242 (1890); *Red Cross Line v Atlantic Fruit Co.*, 264 US 109 (1924).

It was, however, perceived by at least some courts that the existence of genuine mutual assent was suspect when parties agreed to arbitrate a future dispute, and that a dispute resolution clause could be a trap for the unwary. As one court put it: "[b]y first making the contract and then declaring who should construe it, the strong could oppress the weak, and in effect so nullify the law as to secure the enforcement of contracts usurious, illegal, immoral, or contrary to public policy."[47] This view of commercial reality (a view roughly corresponding to that expressed by Llewellyn in the passage quoted above) led to the opinion that the best way to assure true assent to arbitration was to afford a party having promised to arbitrate a future dispute an opportunity to withdraw assent when a real dispute has arisen and the revoking party is at last likely to be attentive to the hazards of dispute resolution and well-advised.

Revocability (or, more accurately, rescindability), while thus justifiable as an application of elementary contract doctrine requiring comprehending mutual assent, proved to be an impediment to commerce in the age of railroads and industrialization. When parties began to make contracts with people whom they did not know and who resided in distant jurisdictions whose courts might reasonably be feared as xenophobic, it became more important to provide for future disputes.[48] Well-advised parties unwilling to expose themselves to the risks of suit in the other party's court could sometimes make deals if both were assured of a neutral arbitral forum. Irrevocability was needed to give that assurance and foster interstate commerce.

For this reason, many states, often but not always by legislation, moved away from the principle of revocability and began to enforce arbitration clauses contained in commercial contracts. An early New York case conceded that arbitration clauses

> induced by fraud, or overreaching, or entered into unadvisedly through ignorance, folly or undue pressure, might well be refused a specific performance or disregarded, when set up as a defense to an action. But when the parties stand upon an equal

---

[47] *Parsons v Ambos*, 121 Ga 98, 48 SE 696 (1904). Compare *Cocalis v Nazlides*, 308 Ill 152, 139 NE 95 (1923); *W. H. Blodgett Co. v Bebe Co.*, 190 Cal 665, 214 Pac 38 (1923). And see *Handbook, National Conference of Commissioners on Uniform State Laws* 60–73 (1924).

[48] Simpson, *Contracts for Cotton* at 321–24 (cited in note 44).

footing, and intelligently and deliberately, in making their executory contracts, provide for an amicable adjustment of any difference that may arise, either by arbitration or otherwise, it is not easy to assign at this day any good reason why the contract should not stand, and the parties made to abide by it, and the judgment of the tribunal of their choice.[49]

By 1920, a widespread effort was afoot to modify arbitration laws in all states to secure better enforcement of arbitration agreements. This movement to "modernize" arbitration law was driven by those engaged in interstate trade; its oft-stated purpose was to "make the benefits of arbitration generally available *to the business world.*"[50]

There was, however, opposition to the enactment of state statutes aiming to assure the arbitrability of future disputes. As late as 1924, both the National Conference of Commissioners on Uniform State Laws and the American Bar Association took positions firmly in opposition to what was perceived by some to be an idiosyncrasy of New York law, that is, the enforcement of arbitration clauses contained in printed contracts.[51] Macneil quotes as illustrative the statement of one opponent:

> Under the New York Act you are called upon to agree in advance through a clause that is in the contract, most often in small type, that all controversies of any nature, kind, or description are to be taken out of the courts and are to be submitted to an arbitrator either named then or to be named later. It is felt by the great majority of the [ABA] committee that this is wrong in principle, to call upon men to agree in advance to arbitrate any difficulties that might arise, particularly in view of the fact that that would be done in most instances without any realization on the part of the contracting parties as to what they were really doing. Of course, we all agree that men ought to know what they are doing when they are signing contracts, but we all know from a practical experience that the fine type of contracts whilst entirely binding, is seldom read, and we do feel that is a giving up rights that the American people really regard as sacred and they shouldn't be called upon to do so.[52]

---

[49] *President, Managers, and Comp. of Delaware & Hudson Canal Co. v Pennsylvania Coal Co.*, 50 NY 250 (1872); cf *Henry v Lehigh Valley Coal Co.*, 215 Pa 448, 64 Atl 635 (1906).

[50] *Robert Lawrence Co. v Devonshire Fabrics, Inc.*, 271 F2d 402, 407 (2d Cir 1959) (citing S Rep No 536, 68th Cong, 1st Sess at 3) (italics supplied).

[51] Macneil, *American Arbitration Law* at 49–51 (cited in note 42).

[52] Id at 51.

Reflecting this opposition, the Uniform Arbitration Act of 1924 did not provide for the enforcement of agreements to arbitrate future disputes.[53]

However, that Act was adopted in only four states, and the "modern" reformers succeeded over the next four decades in securing legislation in all but three states providing for the enforcement of such arbitration clauses.[54] Instrumental in that effort was the "modern" Uniform Arbitration Act of 1955,[55] which was enacted in over thirty states, often with significant modifications, but always with provisions for the specific enforcement of arbitration clauses. The prevailing view was that as between contracting parties of reasonably equal strength and sophistication, there is no substantial public interest to be served by precluding parties from so moderating the rights they create by their contract, and ample reason to enforce agreements to arbitrate claims asserting such rights. Yet, in 1991, the Supreme Court of Nebraska held that Nebraska's "modern" legislation was in violation of the Nebraska constitutional provision assuring that "all courts shall be open, and every person, for any injury done him in his goods, person, or reputation shall have a remedy by due course of law, and justice administered without denial or delay."[56] That holding set off a major effort of "modern" reformers to amend Nebraska's constitution, an effort that appears at the moment to have been successful.[57]

It was in the context of this prolonged debate over the reform of state law that Congress was in 1925 importuned to act. The "modern" law, particularly that of New York, had been disregarded in federal litigation in admiralty and diversity cases. An influential 1915 opinion of Judge Hough exclaimed that federal

---

[53] Uniform Arbitration Act of 1925, § 1.

[54] Macneil, *American Arbitration Law* at 55–57 (cited in note 42).

[55] Uniform Arbitration Act of 1955, 7 Unif Laws Ann 1 (1996). Maynard Pirsig, *Some Comments on Arbitration Legislation and the Uniform Act*, 11 Bus Law 44 (1956). For an account of the current state legislation, see George K. Walker, *Trends in State Legislation Governing International Arbitrations*, 17 NC J Intl L & Comm Reg 419 (1992).

[56] *State v Nebraska Association of Public Employees*, 239 Neb 653, 477 NW2d 577, 580 (1991); but see *Dowd v First Omaha Securities Corp.*, 242 Neb 347, 495 NW2d 36 (1993) (holding Nebraska law preempted).

[57] Nebraska voters approved an amendment in May 1996, but there is pending litigation contesting the adequacy of the notice to the voters of the content of the amendment. *Omaha World Herald* (May 19, 1996), at 14B.

courts were powerless to compel arbitration because it was too well settled as a matter of federal equity that an arbitration agreement could not be specifically enforced.[58] The damages remedy for breach being ineffective, a party seeking to evade an arbitration agreement could find a refuge in the federal admiralty or diversity jurisdictions. Congress was asked to eliminate this refuge from state law by authorizing federal courts to specifically enforce arbitration clauses valid under the controlling state law of contracts.

No one suggested in 1925 that Congress ought to consider enacting a law creating a federal right to enforce an arbitration clause. Had such a right been created, it would surely have provided, as all other federal rights do, an independent ground for federal jurisdiction, something the Act clearly did not do. On the widely shared understanding that the Act was intended merely to accommodate federal courts deciding diversity and admiralty cases to local state law, opposition to the 1925 Act was slight.[59] Unopposed were those members of the ABA who had just taken a position favoring the revocability of arbitration clauses, but who had no objection to federal court enforcement of New York law foreclosing revocation. The federal legislative aim of 1925 was made largely redundant by the decisions of the Court in *Erie*[60] and *Guaranty Trust v York*,[61] holding that a federal court in a diversity case must supply the same remedies for the enforcement of state-created rights as the local state courts would provide.

The ultimate victory of "modern" reformers in state legislatures and in state courts was incomplete even in those many states in which they prevailed. Many, perhaps most, state legislatures recognized arbitration clauses as a potential means of economic oppression; accordingly, they qualified their arbitration laws in diverse ways responsive to the concern stated in 1924 by the opponents of enforcement of arbitration clauses. The states regulated arbitration clauses both substantively and procedurally.[62] Many state legislatures specified substantive categories of cases that are not subject

---

[58] *United States Asphalt Refining Co. v Trinidad Lake Petro. Co.*, 222 Fed 1006, 1012 (S D NY 1915).

[59] Macneil, *American Arbitration Law* at 115–17 (cited in note 42).

[60] *Erie R. R. v Tompkins*, 304 US 64 (1938).

[61] *Guaranty Trust Co. v York*, 326 US 99 (1945).

[62] Macneil, *American Arbitration Law* at 69–71 (cited in note 42).

to arbitration. Some state courts interpreted other laws of their states to create rights that could not be put at risk by arbitration clauses. Other states restricted the use of arbitration clauses to weaken substantive rights by imposing special requirements for the procedure by which agreements to arbitrate are made. Most required that arbitration agreements be in writing, thus extending the principle of the statute of frauds to such agreements. Many imposed additional requirements designed to assure that a party signing another party's form fully understands the import of the arbitration clause.

Congress has never considered the possibility that any of these state laws might be inconsistent with federal policy, nor has it considered the possible uses of arbitration to diminish or nullify rights that it has conferred on citizens. Arbitration as practiced in 1925 between merchants engaged in interstate and marine commerce was not a means of diverting from courts disputes arising in the enforcement of Progressive legislation regulating business to limit economic power and protect the weak from the strong. And Congress could not in 1925 foresee its use for that purpose because it was enacting law then applicable primarily to admiralty and diversity cases in federal courts, that is, cases generally involving the enforcement of rights that the parties themselves created by contract.

Commercial arbitration, at least as it is practiced in America, is a method of dispute resolution, but not necessarily a method of enforcing legal rights.[63] It has been a nonlegal process, often conducted by nonlawyers working under the aegis of trade associations or the American Arbitration Association, a body founded and supported by merchants and traders.[64] As Justice Black remarked in 1967, arbitrators may be "wholly unqualified to decide legal is-

---

[63] See generally Ian R. Macneil, Richard E. Speidel, and Thomas J. Stipanowich, *Federal Arbitration Law: Agreements, Awards and Remedies and the Federal Arbitration Act* § 4.07 (Little Brown, 1994). Edward A. Dauer, *Manual of Dispute Resolution, ADR Law and Practice* (McGraw Hill, 1994); Edward Brunet, *Questioning the Quality of Alternate Dispute Resolution*, 62 Tulane L Rev 1, 13–31 (1987); Judith Resnik, *Many Doors? Closing Doors? Alternative Dispute Resolution and Adjudication*, 11 Ohio St J on Disp Res 211 (1995); Jack B. Weinstein, *Some Benefits and Risks of Privatization of Justice Through ADR*, 11 Ohio St J on Disp Res 241, 247–64 (1996).

[64] For a brief account of institutional arbitration, see Martin Domke, *The Law and Practice of Commercial Arbitration*, § 2.01 (G. Wilner ed, Callaghan, 2d ed 1968); on the freedom of arbitrators to do equity and nurture amiability, see id §§ 1-01-1.03; and see Kenneth S. Carlston, *Theory of the Arbitration Process*, 17 L & Contemp Probs 631, 633–47 (1952).

sues."[65] And if qualified, the arbitrator has been under no duty to resolve a dispute in compliance with the parties' legal rights. A Latin phrase sometimes employed to describe the spirit of much American commercial arbitration is *ex aequo et bono*—a resolution is sought that is equitable, minimizes harm to either party, and enables potential adversaries to maintain a valuable commercial relationship; the role of such an arbitrator is said in Europe to be that of an *amiable compositeur.* It is said of the American commercial arbitrator that he "may do justice as he sees it, applying his own sense of the law and equity to the facts as he finds them to be and making an award reflecting the spirit rather than the letter of the agreement."[66] Many awards resulting from such proceedings might also be described as Solomonic, halving the objects in dispute.

In 1970, the United States acceded to the United Nations Convention on Recognition and Enforcement of Foreign Arbitral Awards,[67] which had been opened for signing in 1958.[68] The purpose of the treaty was to facilitate recognition of awards made by arbitrators outside the United States and thus to facilitate international trade. A second chapter was added to Title 9 to align the enforcement of foreign awards with the enforcement of domestic awards,[69] and federal jurisdiction was conferred on actions "falling under the Convention."[70] Contrary to the usual American practice, some foreign awards are the product of a process designed to enforce legal rights. The rules of the International Chamber of Commerce in Paris,[71] and the UNCITRAL Rules,[72] often incorporated

---

[65] *Prima Paint Corp.*, 388 US 395, 407 (Black, J, dissenting).

[66] *Silverman v Benmor Coats, Inc.*, 61 NY2d 299, 308, 461 NE2d 1261, 1266 (1984).

[67] 84 Stat 692, Pub L No 91-368 § 1 (1970).

[68] On the history of the accession, see S Rep 702, 91st Cong, 2d Sess (1970); George Aksen, *American Arbitration Accession Arrives in the Age of Aquarius: United States Implements United Nations Convention on the Recognition and Enforcement of Foreign Arbitral Awards,* 3 Sw U L Rev 1 (1971). In 1990, the United States acceded to the Inter-American Convention on International Commercial Arbitration, which closely resembles the earlier UN Convention, and Chapter 3 of Title 9 of the United States Code was added to make provision for the enforcement of this treaty. 9 USC §§ 301 et seq (1994).

[69] 9 USC §§ 201–08 (1994).

[70] 9 USC § 203 (1994).

[71] International Chamber of Commerce Rules of Arbitration, Art 13(4) (1988). L. Craig, W. Park, and J. Paulson, *International Chamber of Commerce Arbitration* 312–13 (Intl Chamber of Commerce, 2d ed 1990).

[72] United Nations Commission on International Trade Law Arbitration Rules, Art 33(2) (1976). On the meaning of the terms in this context, see Henry J. Brown and Arthur L.

into international commercial agreements forbid arbitrators to proceed *ex aequo et bono* or in the role of *amiable compositeur* except by agreement of the parties. Nevertheless, authority for such proceedings is not rare in commercial contracts in many countries,[73] and there are many foreign awards that are like typical American awards in that they are results of procedures that are not intended to assure fidelity to law.

Whether the arbitration is domestic or foreign, and whatever duty foreign law might or might not impose on arbitrators to apply controlling law, there is inherent in the institutions of private dispute resolution an endemic disinclination to enforce legal rights rigorously. Even International Chamber of Commerce arbitrators are dependent for their careers, to a degree that no judges are, on the acceptability of their awards to the parties, and perhaps especially on their acceptability to parties who are "repeat players." This circumstance creates pressure on arbitrators to appear to be considerate of the interests of all parties, even those who have sorely abused the rights of others. For this reason, while there are doubtless many courageous arbitrators and many weak judges, reluctant parties have cause to believe that their legal entitlements will be more squarely observed in court than in an arbitral tribunal, even an International Chamber of Commerce tribunal.

This disinclination of arbitrators to observe legal entitlements is most likely to manifest itself in regard to those rights that are not created by the contract from which they derive their jurisdiction. For the reason that their own status is linked to the contract, parties may reasonably expect arbitrators to tend to uphold and enforce a contract, sometimes even at the expense of rights existing independently of that contract.

The assessment that arbitrators are less likely to enforce rights is further reinforced by contrasts in accountability. Given the non-legal informality of traditional arbitral proceedings and awards, judicial review of the merits of awards was rightly viewed as not merely aimless, but a serious intrusion on a process designed not to protect rights but to resolve disputes quickly, efficiently, with civility and dispatch. With this consideration in mind, the FAA

Marriott, *ADR Principles and Practice* 63 (Sweet & Maxwell, 1993). See also UNCITRAL Model Law on International Commercial Arbitration, Art 28(3) (1985).

[73] Gary B. Born, *International Commercial Arbitration in the United States: Commentary and Materials* 135 (Kluwer, 1994).

limits judicial review of awards to narrow grounds such as fraud, bias, or serious misconduct by the arbitral tribunal.[74] As Richard Speidel has emphasized, nonreviewability is a "core ingredient" giving arbitration its advantage over litigation.[75] Seemingly precluded by the FAA is judicial review of awards to correct errors of law or even egregiously mistaken findings of fact.[76]

Indeed, the FAA does not require arbitral tribunals to explain their decisions or even to record the evidence on which they are based, so that it is often impossible to detect whether a particular award is or is not a faithful application of the controlling law. The relation between the recording of evidence and the possibility of effective review to assure fidelity to law has been well understood at least since the time of Justice Story.[77] In part, the absence of this requirement in arbitration reflects another traditional aim that is of signal importance to many who use private ADR: privacy.[78] Making a transcript of evidence presented at a hearing, and requiring statements of reasons that can circulate, threaten public exposure of evidence that it may be the legitimate aim of the parties to escape. This consideration is most appropriate where matters such as trade secrets are at issue, but also suggest a reason for concern when matters of legitimate public concern are diverted from courts to arbitral tribunals.

In contrast to customary American practice, the International Chamber of Commerce Rules, rooted in the vision of arbitration

---

[74] 9 USC § 10 (1994).

[75] Richard Speidel, *Arbitration of Statutory Rights Under the Federal Arbitration Act: The Case for Reform*, 4 Ohio St J on Disp Resol 157, 191 (1989).

[76] There have been occasional suggestions that an award might be set aside if it were found to be in "manifest disregard of the law." Justice Frankfurter, dissenting in *Wilko v Swan*, 346 US 427, 440 (1953), asserted that "Arbitrators may not disregard the law. . . . [T]heir failure to observe the law 'would constitute grounds for vacating the award' . . . " citing dicta of Chief Judge Swan in the same case, 201 F2d 439, 445 (2d Cir 1953). Compare *In re I/S Stavborg v National Metal Converters*, 500 F2d 424 (2d Cir 1974); *Merrill Lynch Pierce Fenner & Smith v Jaros*, 70 F3d 418 (6th Cir 1995). More accurate is the statement in *Bernhardt v Polygraphic Co. of America*, 350 US 198, 203 n 4 (1956): "Whether the arbitrators misconstrued a contract is not open to judicial review." The same may also be generally the result if arbitrators misapply a statute. See *Merrill, Lynch, Pierce, Fenner & Smith v Bobker*, 808 F2d 930 (2d Cir 1986); *Rostad & Rostad Corp. v Investment Management & Research, Inc.*, 923 F2d 694 (9th Cir 1991); *R. M. Perez & Assocs v Welch*, 960 F2d 534 (5th Cir 1992). Judge Haight concluded that such review is especially inappropriate when the court is asked to confirm a foreign award. *Brandeis Intsel Limited v Calabrian Chemicals Corp.*, 656 F Supp 160 (S D NY 1987).

[77] *Parsons v Bedford*, 3 Pet 433 (1830).

[78] Soia Mentschikoff, *Commercial Arbitration*, 61 Colum L Rev 846, 849 (1961).

as a legal process, do require a statement of reasons, and an award issued under Chamber auspices is reviewed by its International Court of Arbitration before it is regarded as final.[79] This of course adds materially to the cost and delay of the proceeding, but it lends credence to the otherwise very questionable assumption that arbitration is a means of enforcing the law. The UNCITRAL Rules likewise require a statement of reasons unless the parties waive the requirement,[80] but there is no provision for review to consider whether the reasons stated are sound or even plausible. Such "speaking awards" are also common in labor arbitration practice in the United States, but are not associated with judicial review for errors of law or fact.[81] In the industrial context, speaking awards by labor arbitrators serve to create a "law of the shop."

The FAA confers a subpoena power on arbitrators,[82] but otherwise makes no provision for discovery. Given the date of its enactment thirteen years before promulgation of the Federal Rules of Civil Procedure, it would be remarkable if the Act had made provision for lawyers to exercise the prerogatives conferred on them by Rules 26–37 of the 1938 Rules. American arbitrators may employ their subpoena power to accomplish many of the aims of the discovery rules,[83] but the absence of such a provision marks an important difference between arbitration under the FAA or in international practice and adjudication in a federal court. While discovery may be regarded as a mixed blessing at best, because of its costs, it cannot be doubted that the availability of discovery assures that courts are in general more effective than arbitral tribunals in detecting wrongdoing and enforcing the rights of victims, whether of securities fraud, price-fixing conspiracies, race or gender discrimination, or environmental misdeeds. Because discovery is a unique feature of American civil procedure, it is unsurprising that no provision is made for it in the international rules generally in use. Indeed, in arbitrations conducted in other countries, it is not unlikely that the parties will not only have no opportunity to dis-

---

[79] International Chamber of Commerce Rules of Arbitration, Art 32 (1988).

[80] UNCITRAL Rules, Art 32(3).

[81] David E. Feller, *Relationship of the Agreement to External Law*, in Christopher A. Barreca et al, eds, *Labor Arbitrator Development* (Bureau of National Affairs, 1983).

[82] 9 USC § 7 (1994).

[83] Macneil et al, *Federal Arbitration Law* at § 34-2 (cited in note 63).

cover documents or other evidence, but will have no opportunity to see witnesses, much less cross-examine them.[84] In some countries, arbitrators have no subpoena power; and in some it may be a crime for an arbitrator to attempt to put a witness under oath or otherwise expose him or her to the hazard of perjury. The one assurance given by the FAA is that each party must have an opportunity to be heard by the arbitrators,[85] but even with that assurance, some courts have questioned whether there is any constitutional requirement of procedural due process applicable to arbitration.[86]

Despite the many and manifest limitations of arbitral tribunals as institutions for the enforcement of legal rights, the Court has insisted that the "streamlined procedures of arbitration do not entail any consequential restriction on substantive rights."[87] No matter how frequently the Court may insist on this view, it is, for the reasons stated, simply false doctrine. Whatever its strengths as a means of resolving disputes, traditional arbitration[88] is inferior to adjudication as a method of enforcing the law, as Congress and the state legislatures have consistently understood.

The FAA does not authorize a court to compel a party to arbitrate any matter in the absence of an explicit agreement to do so. Where a party denies having agreed to submission, the Act acknowledges and affirms the right to jury trial, except in admiralty cases, on the issue.[89] It specifies that in admiralty, the issue of whether there is a contract to arbitrate shall be decided by the court. It also allows revocation of an arbitration clause "upon such

---

[84] Arthur Marriott, *Evidence in International Arbitration*, 5 Arb Intl 280 (1989).

[85] 9 USC § 10(c).

[86] For example, *Stroh Container Co. v Delphi Industries, Inc.*, 783 F2d 743 (8th Cir), cert denied 476 US 1141 (1986). See generally Edward Brunet, *Arbitration and Constitutional Rights*, 71 NC L Rev 81 (1992).

[87] *Shearson/American Express Inc. v McMahon*, 482 US 232 (1987).

[88] The one significant exception may be the "Rent-a-Judge" system in California which employs retired judges and provides for application of judicial procedures and appellate review. For an account, see Anne S. Kim, Note, *Rent-a-Judges and the Cost of Selling Justice*, 44 Duke L J 166 (1994).

[89] 9 USC § 4 (1994). This section reads in pertinent part:

If the making of the arbitration agreement or the failure, neglect or refusal to perform the same be in issue, the court shall proceed summarily to the trial thereof. If no jury trial be demanded by the party alleged to be in default, or if the matter in dispute is within admiralty jurisdiction, the court shall hear and determine such issue.

grounds as exist in law or equity for the revocation of any contract."[90] These provisions left ample room for federal courts to administer state contract law with appropriate sensitivity to the possible abuses of arbitration agreements by strong parties to diminish the rights of weaker ones by applying the widely accepted principle expressed by Llewellyn.[91]

The FAA does not state or imply that the issue of the revocability of an arbitration clause could be decided by the arbitral tribunal. Inasmuch as the issue is one "in law or equity," it would seem to imply that the decision, like that of whether an agreement to arbitrate was made, should be decided by a law court, not the arbitral tribunal. A consideration supporting this reading is that the arbitral tribunal forfeits jurisdiction, and hence compensation for its members, when it decides in favor of revocation, and so has a conflict of interest in deciding that issue. On the other hand, if a party seeking to revoke can defer arbitration by, for example, claiming fraud in the inducement to sign the contract containing the arbitration clause, the hope for a quick, amiable disposition of a contract dispute is significantly diminished. Impressed more by the dangers to the integrity of arbitration posed by delay than it was by the potential conflict of interest in permitting arbitrators to decide the scope of their jurisdiction, the Court in 1967 held that parties might by broad terms in an arbitration clause confer on the arbitral tribunal the jurisdiction to decide issues of revocability such as fraud in the inducement.[92]

WAIVING ACCESS TO COURTS

A party in control of the drafting process is, of course, not limited to the mandatory arbitration clause in its efforts to use

---

[90] 9 USC § 2 (1994):

> A written provision in any maritime transaction or a contract evidencing a transaction involving commerce to settle by arbitration a controversy thereafter arising out of such contract or transaction, or the refusal to perform the whole or any part thereof, or an agreement in writing to submit to arbitration an existing controversy arising out of such a contract, transaction, or refusal, shall be valid, irrevocable and enforceable, save upon such grounds as exist at law or in equity for the revocation of any contract.

[91] Quoted in text at note 31.

[92] *Prima Paint Corp*, 388 US 395, following *Robert Lawrence Co. v Devonshire Fabrics Inc.*, 271 F2d 402 (2d Cir 1959).

contract to undermine the enforceability of rights potentially threatening to it. Perhaps the most extreme example of such a use of contract is the cognovit note. Such a note waives the constitutional right of the promisor to notice of a suit filed to enforce the note, and authorizes the promisee in the event of a default on the note to take a default judgment against the promisor without prior notice. The cognovit note does not destroy the ability of the defaulter to secure relief from the judgment. The judgment cannot be executed without prior notice, giving the promisor an opportunity prior to execution to secure relief from the judgment if he or she can prove nonliability. The cognovit does, however, reassign the burden of going forward with litigation and the burden of proof. While far short of a total abrogation of the promisor's rights not to be held liable for a promise that he or she did not make or had already performed, it is effectively a significant diminution of those rights because the promisee holding a cognovit note has the whip hand in proceedings to resolve disputes over such defenses. The power gained by the promisee is so great, in fact, that most states do not allow the device.[93] The Supreme Court of the United States, while upholding its use between two sophisticated corporate parties, noted that Charles Dickens had denounced the practice[94] and cautioned that its use in less appropriate circumstances might constitute a taking of property in violation of the Due Process Clause of the Fourteenth Amendment.[95]

Another device inviting comparison to the arbitration clause is the forum selection clause designating the courts of a named jurisdiction as those in which the contract or other rights arising out of the contract may be enforced.[96] Such clauses were long disfavored by American courts, who suspected that such clauses were devices to deprive weaker parties of their rights by making it too difficult to assert them.[97] Even the Court deciding *Lochner* ac-

---

[93] H. Ward Classen et al., *A Survey of the Legality of Confessed Judgment Clauses in Commercial Transactions*, 47 Bus Law 729, 731 n 6, 758–72 (1992).

[94] Charles Dickens, *The Posthumous Papers of the Pickwick Club* ch 47, 750–52, 754 (1837, Robert L. Patten ed; Penguin, 1972).

[95] *D. H. Overmyer Co. v Frick Co.*, 405 US 174, 177 (1972). Compare *Peralta v Heights Medical Center, Inc.*, 485 US 80 (1988).

[96] *Scherk v Alberto-Culver Co.*, 417 US 506, 516 (1974).

[97] Linda S. Mullenix, *Another Choice of Forum, Another Choice of Law: Consensual Adjudicatory Procedure in Federal Court*, 57 Fordham L Rev 291, 308 (1988).

knowledged the power of Congress to create rights of workers that cannot be waived in their contracts of employment,[98] and that decision was followed by a holding that an employer cannot impose on a worker a disadvantageous choice of a forum in which such rights must be asserted.[99]

But forum selection clauses can facilitate transactions, especially in international trade. On that account, the National Conference of Commissioners on Uniform State Laws in 1968 approved a Model Act giving limited sanction to these clauses,[100] and in 1971, the American Law Institute approved the enforcement of such clauses when not "unfair or unreasonable."[101] The next year, the Supreme Court of the United States in *M/S Bremen v Zapata Offshore Co.*[102] held that such agreements may be enforceable in federal courts exercising admiralty jurisdiction, but cautioned against too broad a reading of its holding, emphasizing that the agreement under consideration in that case was made at arm's length between sophisticated corporations.

The forum chosen in *Bremen*, the courts of the United Kingdom, was, the Court noted, a suitably neutral ground for the resolution of a dispute between German and American corporations, each of whom might be reasonably fearful of subjecting its claims or defenses to the national courts of the other contracting party. It may also have been relevant that the claim asserted by the party invoking the clause was one arising under the agreement, and thus no public regulatory policy aimed at protecting one party against the power of the other was compromised by having the dispute resolved by a British court.

The lower federal courts applying *Bremen* have demonstrated varying degrees of receptivity to forum selection clauses in adhesion contracts. Some have enforced them with apparently little concern for the fact that they were buried in fine print,[103] and,

---

[98] *Philadelphia, Baltimore & Washington Railroad Co. v Schubert*, 224 US 603 (1912) (applying provision in Federal Employers Liability Act of 1906 making workers' rights under the statute nonwaivable).

[99] *Boyd v Grand Trunk Western Ry. Co.*, 338 US 263 (1949).

[100] Willis M. Reese, *The Model Choice of Forum Act*, 17 Am J Comp L 292 (1969).

[101] Restatement (Second) of Conflict of Laws § 80 (1988).

[102] 407 US 1 (1972).

[103] For example, *General Eng'g Corp. v Martin Marietta Alumina, Inc.*, 783 F2d 352 (3d Cir 1986); *Bryan Elec. Co. v Fredericksburg*, 762 F2d 1192 (4th Cir 1985); *Lien Ho Hsing*

rejecting the Restatement rule requiring reasonableness, despite manifest inconvenience to the party against whom they were enforced.[104] One court emphasized that "no one deterred [the party] from getting his glasses and reading the contract."[105] Other courts, however, have been wary of enforcing such clauses and declined to enforce them absent evidence that the party against whom the clause is invoked was aware of the clause and its consequences,[106] or where in light of the circumstances at hand the choice of forum was "unreasonable."[107]

The courts have also demonstrated varying degrees of willingness to enforce forum selection clauses where the forum selected would not enforce the rights asserted by the party against whom the clause was invoked. Some, going beyond *Bremen*, have enforced clauses in which the parties designated foreign fora in which parties would be unable to protect rights conferred on them by federal law.[108] Others, including all who have considered cases in which Americans would have been required to assert claims in the courts of the Islamic Republic of Iran,[109] have refused on the ground that such a clause would be unreasonable.

In 1967, the Second Circuit en banc held that a forum selection

---

Steel Enter. Co. v Weihtag, 738 F2d 1455 (9th Cir 1984); *Norman Sec. Sys. v Monitor Dynamics Inc.*, 740 F Supp 1364 (N D Ill 1990).

[104] For example, *In re Diaz Contracting*, 817 F2d 1047 (3d Cir 1987); *Coastal Steel Corp. v Tilghman Wheelabrator*, 709 F2d 190 (3d Cir 1983). The level of inconvenience needed to invalidate a forum selection clause generally has been treated as a question of fact to be determined by the trial court.

[105] *Hoffman v National Equipment Rental, Ltd.*, 643 F2d 987, 991 (4th Cir 1981); see also *Mercury Coal & Coke v Mannesmann Pipe & Steel Corp.*, 696 F2d 315 (4th Cir 1982); *Gaskin v Stumm Handel GmbH*, 309 F Supp 361 (S D NY 1975).

[106] *Colonial Leasing Co. of New England v Pugh Brothers Garage*, 735 F2d 380 (9th Cir 1984); *Couch v First Guaranty Ltd.*, 578 F Supp 331 (N D Tex 1984); *Quick Erectors, Inc. v Seattle Bronze Corp.*, 524 F Supp 351 (E D Mo 1981); *Cutter v Scott & Fetzer Co.*, 510 F Supp 905 (W D Wis 1981); *Peterson v Zochonis (U.K.) Ltd. v Compania United Arrows S.A.*, 493 F Supp 626 (S D NY 1980); *Kolendo v Jerell, Inc.*, 489 F Supp 983 (S D W Va 1980).

[107] For example, *Copperweld Steel Co. v Demag-Mannesmann-Bohler*, 578 F2d 953 (3d Cir 1978); *Calzavara v Biehl & Co.*, 181 So2d 809 (La App 1966); *Cerami-Kote, Inc. v Energywave Corp.*, 116 Idaho 56, 773 P2d 1143 (1989).

[108] For example, *Bense v Interstate Battery System of America Inc.*, 683 F2d 718 (2d Cir 1982); *Medoil Corp. v Citicorp*, 729 F Supp 1456 (S D NY 1990).

[109] For example, *McDonnell Douglas Corp. v Islamic Republic of Iran*, 758 F2d 341 (8th Cir 1985); *Rockwell Intl Sys., Inc. v Citibank N. A.*, 719 F2d 583 (2d Cir 1983); *Harris Corp. v National Iranian Radio & Television*, 691 F2d 1344 (11th Cir 1982). For other cases, see Gregory C. Lehman, *Comment, Mandatory Forum Selection Clauses and Foreign Sovereign Immunity: Iran's Litigation Problems in United States Courts*, 12 Brooklyn J Intl L 553 (1986).

clause in an ocean bill of lading contravenes the provision of the Carriage of Goods by Sea Act[110] invalidating clauses that relieve the carrier of liability for negligence or that might "lessen" such liability.[111] That holding was reaffirmed in 1981 by the Fourth Circuit, the court distinguishing *Bremen* as a case not subject to COGSA and its nonwaiver provision. Both courts of appeals noted that the selection of a distant forum could substantially deny the shipper any effective relief for negligence by the carrier.[112] A stellar example was provided by the facts of the 1967 case, which involved a claim for rust on a barrel of nails. The carrier sought to require the plaintiff to sue in Oslo, as required by the clause in its printed bill of lading. The settlement value of a claim of a New York plaintiff for rust in one barrel of nails is effectively reduced to zero if that claim can be asserted only in Oslo, so the clause did as a practical matter not merely lessen, but eliminated the liability of the carrier for its negligence.

More recently, in a much-criticized decision,[113] the Court in *Carnival Lines v Shute*[114] held that a federal court in the state of Washington was obliged to enforce a forum selection clause contained in the fine print of a cruise ticket; the clause required all litigation between passenger and cruise line over a personal injury alleged to have occurred aboard ship to be conducted in Florida. The Court reaffirmed its earlier statement that such clauses are "subject to judicial scrutiny for fundamental fairness," but found the designation of the ship's home port as fundamentally fair, at least as long as the home port is in another state of the United States that will presumably give effect to any applicable law of Washington. The Court acknowledged but chose not to apply Section 183 of the Limitation of Vessel Owner's Liability Act explic-

---

[110] 46 USC § 1300 et seq.

[111] *Indussa Corp. v S. S. Ranborg*, 377 F2d 200 (2d Cir 1967) (en banc).

[112] *Union Insurance Society of Canton, Ltd. v S. S. Elikon*, 642 F2d 721 (4th Cir 1981).

[113] Patrick J. Borchers, *Forum Selection Agreements in the Federal Courts After Carnival Cruise: A Proposal for Congressional Reform*, 67 Wash L Rev 55 (1992); Linda S. Mullenix, *Another Easy Case, Some More Bad Law: Carnival Cruise Lines and Contractual Personal Jurisdiction*, 27 Tex Intl L J 323 (1992); Edward A. Purcell, *Geography as a Litigation Weapon: Consumers, Forum-Selection Clauses and the Rehnquist Court*, 40 UCLA L Rev 423 (1995); and see *Northwestern Nat'l Ins. Co. v Donovan*, 916 F2d 372, 376 (7th Cir 1990) (Posner, J) ("If ever there was a case for stretching the concept of fraud in the name of unconscionability, it was *Shute*; and perhaps no stretch was necessary.").

[114] *Carnival Cruise Lines, Inc. v Shute*, 499 US 585 (1991).

itly invalidating any agreement between the owner of a vessel and a passenger that limits liability for personal injury or purports to "lessen" or "weaken" the right of a personal injury claimant to "trial by a court of competent jurisdiction,"[115] a statutory provision very similar to that contained in COGSA.

The Court did not find it necessary to explain how there could be mutual assent to a clause contained in a ticket delivered after the passage had been booked and paid for, a problem that other courts in other contexts might well have found insurmountable.[116] Had the contract, for example, been governed by the Uniform Commercial Code, the onerous provision added so belatedly might well be deemed outside the contract and invalid.[117] In the specific context of the cruise ticket, the passenger will normally have planned a vacation and made a heavy emotional investment in that plan before learning of the clause, diminishing the possibility that he or she will view critically the new terms inserted into the contract as embodied in the ticket. Finally, the cruise ticket was on its face nonrefundable, so the passenger would have had to consult a lawyer in order to know that he or she might reject the ticket and secure a refund.

The court of appeals held the clause to be revocable by the Shutes. Applying the standard expressed in *Bremen* and the Restatement, it held that a forum selection clause in a contract of adhesion such as a passenger ticket is not enforceable because it has not been negotiated.[118] The Supreme Court reversed this holding, concluding that Florida was in the circumstances a reasonable choice of forum. Among the reasons given were that the forum selection clause usefully eliminated the issue of jurisdiction, thus sparing the parties the expense of disputing that issue, and that "it stands to reason that passengers who purchase tickets containing a forum selection clause like that at issue in this case benefit in the form of reduced fares reflecting the savings that the cruise line enjoys by limiting the fora in which it may be sued."[119]

This benefit stands to reason only if one makes assumptions that

---

[115] 46 USC § 183c.

[116] See Restatement (Second) of Contracts § 237, Comment f.

[117] See USC § 2-207.

[118] *Shute v Carnival Cruise Lines*, 897 F2d 377, 388–89 (9th Cir 1990).

[119] *Carnival Cruise*, 499 US at 594.

are demonstrably false.[120] The term is not negotiated, the specific market is noncompetitive, the issue of forum choice is of trivial importance to an individual passenger ex ante, and the unadvised passenger cannot be expected to assign a suitable value to the clause; hence, the savings resulting from the enforcement of the clause went straight to the bottom line of Carnival Lines. In offering its unrealistic analysis of economic effects, the Court did on this one occasion pay its respects to neo-Spencerian law-and-economics.[121] It recalls uncomfortably the 1842 opinion of Chief Justice Shaw that engineers voluntarily undertook risks as demonstrated by the fact that they received higher rates of pay than machinists.[122]

Turning to the nonwaiver provision in the Limitation of Vessel Owner's Liability Act, the Court in *Carnival Lines* asserted that the forum selection clause in the ticket did not "take away" the right to trial.[123] But the Act forbids the vessel owner not merely to insert any clause taking away rights, but also from inserting a clause purporting to "lessen, weaken, or avoid" the "right of the claimant to a trial by court of competent jurisdiction." It seems evident that the Shutes claims would command a higher price in a settlement negotiation if they were free to litigate in the courts of Washington than they would if limited to proceedings in courts so distant from their homes. In that essential respect, the Shutes' rights were clearly "lessened" by the operation of the clause. While conceptually they were not deprived of their rights by the clause, in reality, as the court of appeals noted,[124] they were.

In concluding, the Court emphasized that the Limitation of Liability Act was aimed at arbitration clauses. "There was no prohibition of forum selection clauses" that allow a judicial resolution of the Shutes' claims.[125] It did not note, as it might have, that the

[120] Lee Goldman, *Public Policy: My Way and the Highway: Law and Economics of Choice of Forum Clauses in Consumer Form Contracts*, 86 Nw U L Rev 700 (1992).

[121] For example, Richard A. Posner, *Economic Analysis of Law* 102 (Little Brown, 3d ed 1986).

[122] *Farwell v Boston & Worcester Railroad Corp.*, 45 Mass (4 Met) 49, 57.

[123] *Carnival Cruise*, 499 US at 596.

[124] 897 F2d 377, 387 ("Dismissal of this suit from Washington effectively may prevent the Shutes from obtaining relief.").

[125] Id.

forum selected was the court of a state, and not of a foreign country where enforcement of the applicable American law might fail to be enforced.

One point made by the Court may have somewhat greater force. As the Court noted, a bad accident at sea could, if the clause is not enforced, result not only in high legal costs caused by the need repetitively to defend the ship in the courts of every place from which an injured passenger came. Worse, perhaps, than the cost would be the unevenness in the enforcement of the rights of passengers and the duties of shipowners. The possibility of unevenness may be an especially appropriate consideration given the tradition of admiralty law, manifested for example in the law of general averaging,[126] which strives to distribute the risks of disaster evenly among those sharing risk. If the forum selection clause were invalid, the ship's liability to its passengers for a disaster would differ radically according to the jurisdiction from which they came. Co-passengers suffering identical injuries in a common accident might receive vastly different settlements. This consideration would seem to warrant some form of procedural accommodation, whether by enforcing a forum selection clause or by other means, such as transfer,[127] class action,[128] or interpleader.[129] The weakness of this argument as applied to the Shutes is that their claim arose from an isolated event involving no other passengers. Nevertheless, the admiralty tradition offers a basis for distinguishing *Carnival Lines* in future cases in which consumers find inside their new washing machines or electric shavers a warranty certificate containing a clause mandating a distant forum for enforcement of the warranty.

Both Supreme Court cases enforcing forum selection clauses arose in the exercise of the admiralty jurisdiction. In neither case was there any reference to state law. In routine diversity litigation, the law controlling the validity of contract clauses is, of course,

---

[126] Grant Gilmore and Charles L. Black, *The Law of Admiralty* 244–71 (West, 2d ed 1975). On maritime law as a distinct tradition, compare *Hodes v SNC Achille Lauro*, 858 F2d 905, 909 (3d Cir 1988).

[127] 28 USC §§ 1404, 1407.

[128] FRCP 23.

[129] 28 USC § 1335. For example, *State Farm Fire & Cas. Co. v Tashire*, 386 US 523 (1967).

state law. Some lower federal courts have assumed to the contrary
with respect to forum selection,[130] despite the clearly controlling
principle of *Erie*.[131] Where, as in *Bremen*, the transaction is one in
international commerce, it is at least barely plausible to contend
that the enforcement of the forum selection clause bears on international relations and is therefore a proper subject of federal common law,[132] but none of the cases creating a federal common law of
international relations have involved matters of such slight political
consequence as the exercise of jurisdiction over a dispute between
parties to a commercial transaction, and no federal court to date has
rested a decision enforcing a forum selection clause on the premise
that federal law controls in matters other than admiralty. The Court
has held that the weight to be given a forum selection clause by a
federal court when considering a possible transfer of venue for "fairness and convenience" is an issue of federal law, being governed by
Section 1404,[133] but no court of appeals has applied that holding when
the issue arises on a motion to dismiss.[134]

One reason the issue whether state or federal law is being applied has seldom arisen is that *Bremen*, if not *Carnival Lines*, is
conventional in its analysis and result, applying the doctrine stated
in the Restatement (Second) of Conflict of Laws.[135] State courts
confronting forum selection clauses have generally cited *Bremen*,[136]
whether the transaction was interstate or international,[137] and have

---

[130] *In-Flight Devices Corp. v Van Dusen Air, Inc.*, 466 F2d 220, 234 n 24 (6th Cir 1972);
Wellmore Coal Corp. v Gates Learjet Corp., 475 F Supp 1140, 1143 (W D Va, 1979); *Public
Water Supply Dist. No. 1 of Mercer County, Mo. v American Ins. Co.*, 471 F Supp 1071, 1072
(W D Mo 1979).

[131] *Erie*, 304 US 64.

[132] Compare *Banco Nacional de Cuba v Sabbatino*, 376 US 398 (1964) (act of state doctrine)
and *Zschernig v Miller*, 389 US 429 (1968). See David Westin and Gary B. Born, *The
Aerospatiale Decision: Its Foundation and Application in State Court Proceedings*, 26 Colum J
Transnatl L 901 (1988); Daniel C. K. Chow, *Limiting Erie in a New Age of International
Law: Toward a Federal Common Law of International Choice of Law*, 74 Iowa L Rev 165 (1988);
A. M. Weisburd, *State Courts, Federal Courts and International Cases*, 20 Yale J Intl L 1
(1995).

[133] *Stewart Org., Inc. v Ricoh Corp.*, 487 US 22 (1988).

[134] For example, *Alexander Proudfoot Co. World Headquarters L. P. v Thayer*, 877 F2d 912,
918 n 12 (11th Cir 1989).

[135] Restatement (Second) of Conflict of Laws § 80 (1988).

[136] As of July 1996, Bremen had been cited 228 times by state courts.

[137] For example, *Abadou v Trad*, 624 P2d 287 (Alaska, 1981); *Societe Jean Nicholas et fils,
J. B. v Mousseux*, 123 Ariz 59, 597 P2d 541 (1979); *Smith, Valentino & Smith, Inc. v Supreme
Court*, 17 Cal3d 491, 551 P2d 1206, 131 Cal Rptr 374 (1976).

exercised varying degrees of rigor in scrutinizing the reasonableness of a selected forum. But some state courts have rejected *Bremen* and continued to hold that forum selection clauses are not
enforceable, at least in cases involving American litigants.[138] Some
legislatures have expressed themselves on the question, Nebraska
enacting a statute that may be more favorable to enforcement than
the opinion of the Court in *Bremen*,[139] and Montana enacting a
statute that provides:

> **Restraints upon legal proceedings void.** Every stipulation
> or condition in a contract by which any party thereto is re-
> stricted from enforcing his rights under the contract by the
> usual proceedings in the ordinary tribunals or which limits the
> time within which he may thus enforce his rights is void. This
> section does not affect the validity of an agreement enforceable
> under Title 27, chapter 5 [Montana Uniform Arbitration
> Act].[140]

There is no visible basis on which the Supreme Court could
legitimately require Montana or other state courts to enforce forum selection clauses in cases not involving international litigants,
and it has so far refrained from suggesting that its decisions on
such matters have any applicability to state court litigation even
when international litigants are involved.

Forum selection by contract may be achieved by implication. An
example is provided by *Burger King v Rudzewicz*.[141] That case was
brought in Florida by Burger King against a Michigan franchisee
for alleged breach of the franchise agreement. That agreement
contained a clause describing the contract as one made and to be
performed in Florida and governed by Florida law. While there
were other factors present,[142] the Court relied in important part
on that clause as a submission by the franchisee to the jurisdiction
of Florida courts.[143] The Court was untroubled that the franchisee's defense rested in part on the Michigan Franchise Investment

---

[138] For example, *Redwing Carriers Inc. v Foster*, 382 So2d 554 (Ala, 1980); *Davenport Mach. & Foundry Co. v Adolph Coors Co.*, 314 NW2d 432 (Iowa, 1982); *Fidelity Union Life Ins. Co. v Evans*, 477 SW2d 535 (Texas, 1972).

[139] See *Haakinson & Beaty Co. v Inland Ins. Co.*, 216 Neb 426, 344 NW2d 454 (1984).

[140] Mont Code Ann § 28-2-708 (1995).

[141] 471 US 462 (1985).

[142] Id at 466–67, 479–80 (noting that McShara trained in Florida).

[143] Id at 482.

Law,[144] an enactment intended to protect local franchisees from the overbearing exercise of economic power by franchisers such as Burger King. The enforcement of that law was left to the mercies of courts sitting in Florida. The Court did not suggest that the clause precluded suit by the franchisee in a Michigan court to obtain rights conferred by the Michigan law, but in the circumstances of the case, such an action might have been premature,[145] so that the clause as interpreted operated as a practical matter to "oust" the Michigan courts of the opportunity to enforce the state's law. However, because the Court did not regard the clause as an overt forum selection clause, it did not find it necessary, in the manner of its *Bremen* opinion, to defend the selection of Florida as a fair and reasonable choice. It bears notice that if the Court had read the franchise agreement written by Burger King in the same spirit in which insurance contracts are read,[146] the choice of law clause could have been read as a disavowal of any purpose of the contract to effect a selection of forum; if Burger King wanted a Florida forum, it could have said so in language as plain as that in which it expressed its preference for Florida law, and its failure to do so could therefore be taken as a concession that any litigation would be conducted in Michigan, but pursuant to Florida law, except insofar as Michigan might disallow such a choice of law.[147]

As the Court in *Bremen* acknowledged, and as both state and federal courts have had frequent occasion to observe, any forum selection clause (whether explicit or implicit) potentially threatens to diminish the value of substantive entitlements. This is so for at least two reasons. One is the potential transaction cost of asserting a claim or defense in a distant forum where one must employ unfamiliar counsel and bear special costs of transport and communication. The other is the risk that the forum selected will be unreceptive to the claim or defense at issue. Unreceptivity may result from ethnocentric choice of law, reduced competence to under-

---

[144] Id at 489.

[145] On requirements of ripeness in Michigan courts, see 1 David J. Lanciotti, Jacqueline E. Lanciotti, and William B. Murphy, *Michigan Pleading and Practice* § 215 (Callaghan, 1996 rev).

[146] See John Alan Appleman and Jean Appleman, 13 *Insurance Law and Practice* § 7401 (West, 1976).

[147] Pamela J. Stephens, *The Single Contract as Minimum Contacts: Justice Brennan "Has It His Way,"* 28 Wm & Mary L Rev 89, 110 (1986).

stand the law on which the claim or defense is asserted, the un-
availability of discovery, or xenophobia in the evaluation of testimony, among other causes.

To the extent that the rights jeopardized by a disadvantageous
forum selection clause are those created entirely by the contract
of which it is a part, there is diminished public interest in the protection of the rights so exposed to risk, and hence less reason for
close scrutiny of the reasonableness of the choice made. On the
other hand, where Congress has conferred a measure of inalien-
ability on rights not created by the parties themselves, as with the
Carriage of Goods by Sea Act or the Limitation of Vessel Owner's
Liability Act, there is every reason for a court to take scrupulous
care to disallow a forum selection that will impede the assertion
of that right. Contrary to the clearly expressed purpose of Congress to assure full enforcement of the rights of shippers and passengers, claims brought under either of those statutes will settle
for fewer dollars than they would have had the Court been more
attentive to the use of forum selection to evade the national law
and frustrate the policy it expresses.

ARBITRABILITY IN FEDERAL LAW[148]

The 1925 Act contained one provision comparable to those
in state legislation designed to protect weaker parties from the loss
or diminution of their rights through arbitration conducted pursuant to contracts of adhesion. That was the exclusion from the Act's
coverage of "contracts of employment of seamen, railroad employees, or any other class of workers engaged in foreign or interstate
commerce."[149] Section 2 of the Act conferred validity and irrevocability only on arbitration clauses in writing set forth in a maritime
or commercial transaction.[150] Those conditions met, a federal court
having jurisdiction over a dispute was directed to compel performance of an agreement to arbitrate "an existing controversy arising
out of such a contract [or] transaction" unless the arbitration
clause is revocable "upon such grounds as exist in law or in equity
for the revocation of any contract."

---

[148] See generally Macneil et al, *Federal Arbitration Law* at § 15.1 (cited in note 63).

[149] 9 USC § 1 (1994).

[150] Ch 213, § 2, 43 Stat 883 (1925) (current version at 9 USC § 2 (1994)).

An issue of arbitrability did not reach the Court until 1953. That year, in *Wilko v Swan*[151] the Court held that an arbitration clause is not binding on a plaintiff seeking a recovery under the Securities Act of 1933.[152] The Court relied on the language of the Securities Act declaring void any "condition, stipulation, or provision binding any person acquiring any security to waive compliance with any [of its] provision[s]."[153] The Court noted that the entire Act had the purpose of protecting unsophisticated investors from savvy brokers by affording them more accessible judicial remedies for fraud. It concluded that "the intention of Congress concerning the sale of securities is better carried out by holding invalid . . . an agreement for arbitration of issues arising under the Act."[154] In reaching this conclusion, it followed the position taken by the Securities and Exchange Commission in its amicus brief.[155]

The court of appeals in *Wilko* was more prescient than the majority of the Court. It held that claims arising under the Act were arbitrable, but that the failure of the arbitrators to observe and enforce the provisions of the Securities Act "would constitute grounds for vacating the award pursuant to Section 10 of the Federal Arbitration Act."[156] Justice Frankfurter, dissenting, agreed with the assumption made by the court of appeals, concluding that "appropriate means for judicial scrutiny must be implied in the form of some record or opinion, however informal, whereby such compliance will appear."[157] He also noted that the plaintiff had not proved that "in opening an account [he] had no choice but to accept the arbitration stipulation"; had such proof been tendered, then Justice Frankfurter stood ready to regard the clause as "unconscionable and unenforceable."[158] There was thus no member of the Court in 1953 willing to enforce a boiler-plate arbitration clause against a party asserting a nonwaivable right conferred by

---

[151] 346 US 427 (1953).

[152] Id at 434–35.

[153] Section 14 of the Securities Act of 1933, 15 USC § 77 n (1988).

[154] *Wilko*, 346 US at 438.

[155] Id at 428, 435.

[156] 201 F2d 439, 445 (1953).

[157] *Wilko*, 346 US at 440 (Frankfurter, J, dissenting).

[158] Id.

Congress for the public purpose of deterring fraud in securities transactions, but there was opinion favoring the transformation of the arbitral process to make it accountable for its fidelity to law.

Wilko won acceptance and approval.[159] The Second Circuit, sitting in New York and comprised of judges familiar with traditional commercial arbitration in that city, applied *Wilko* to invalidate arbitration clauses in bills of ladings,[160] just as it had earlier invalidated forum selection clauses in ocean bills of lading. It also held that claims arising under the antitrust laws of the United Sates are not arbitrable pursuant to adhesive clauses.[161] In the latter case, there was no statutory text in the Sherman Act from which the court could derive authority, but it reasoned that the aim of the law was to protect those with less economic power from those with more, and that this purpose would be partly frustrated if the stronger party could impose on the weaker an agreement to arbitrate future antitrust claims in a forum not accountable for its fidelity to the law.

The UN Convention and the implementing legislation ratified and enacted in 1970 stop far short of being a full faith and credit clause for foreign awards. Articles V and XIV of the Convention enumerate eight grounds on which a court of a signatory nation may decline to enforce a foreign award; these include that the court finds that "(a) The subject matter of the difference is not capable of settlement by arbitration under the law of that country; or (b) The recognition or enforcement of the award would be contrary to the public policy of that country."[162] The principle of *Wilko* was thus explicitly acknowledged by the Convention, and it was never suggested that acceding to it would disable Congress or state legislatures from protecting weaker parties from overbearing use of arbitration by those endowed with economic power. Indeed, other signatory nations had asserted that foreign awards presuming

---

[159] See Note, *Arbitration Under the Securities Act of 1933*, 49 Nw U L Rev 101 (1954); Note, *Securities Act*, 66 Harv L Rev 1326 (1953); see also Note, *Enforceability of Arbitration Agreements in Fraud Actions Under the Securities Act*, 62 Yale L J 985 (1953) (urging the Court's result prior to the Court's ruling).

[160] In the Matter of *AAACON Auto Transport, Inc.*, 537 F2d 648 (2d Cir 1976).

[161] *American Safety Equipment Corp. v J. P. Maguire & Co., Inc.*, 391 F2d 821 (2d Cir 1968).

[162] Art V, para 2.

to adjudicate liabilities under their regulatory laws would not *pro tanto* be recognized in their courts.[163]

It was perhaps a misfortune that the first case to reach the Court after accession to the Convention was *Scherk v Alberto-Culver Co.*[164] In that case, a substantial American manufacturer of toiletries sought to assert rights under the Securities Exchange Act of 1934 against a German who sold it trademarks alleged by the plaintiff to have been subject to undisclosed encumbrances. It sought to enjoin arbitration in France pursuant to the arbitration clause in the contract of sale, invoking the no-waiver provision of the 1934 Act, and citing *Wilko.* This was scarcely a situation in which arbitration threatened a right conferred on a weak party by a paternal Congress; indeed, it was not clear that any American law was applicable to the transaction. A majority of the Court thought *Wilko* distinguishable, and emphasized, as one difference, the international character of the transaction at bar.[165] Four Justices dissented, Justice Douglas protesting in their behalf that

> [T]he international aura which the Court gives this case is ominous. We now have many multinational corporations in vast operations around the world—Europe, Latin America, the Middle East, and Asia. The investments of many American investors turn on dealings by those companies. Up to this day, it has been assumed by reason of *Wilko* that they were all protected by our various federal securities Acts. If these guarantees are removed, it should take a legislative enactment. I would enforce our laws as they stand, unless Congress makes an exception. . . . [166]

Scherk set the stage for *Mitsubishi Motors Corp. v Soler Chrysler-Plymouth, Inc.,*[167] the 1985 decision in which the Court set itself firmly on the course that it has since taken. Soler was a dealer in Puerto Rico for automobiles manufactured by a Tokyo firm that

---

[163] Justice Stevens cites Belgian, Italian, and German examples in *Mitsubishi*, 473 US at 660–61, nn 35–36; and see Gary B. Born, *International Commercial Arbitration in the United States: Commentary & Materials* 527 (Kluwer, 1994). With respect to the enforceability of adhesion contracts, even in international commerce, compare Civil Code of Italy, Arts 1341–42.

[164] 417 US 506 (1974).

[165] Id at 513–16.

[166] Id at 533 (Douglas, J, dissenting).

[167] 473 US 614 (1985).

was a joint venture of Mitsubishi Heavy Industries and Chrysler.
A dispute arose over Soler's refusal to pay for cars that it was alleged to have ordered. Mitsubishi initiated arbitration pursuant to
the dealership agreement, which provided for arbitration in Japan
of all disputes arising between the parties, and brought an action
in the federal court in Puerto Rico to compel Soler to arbitrate.
Soler counterclaimed for defamation and violation of the Sherman
Act, the Federal Automobile Dealer's Day in Court Act,[168] the
Puerto Rico competition act,[169] and the Puerto Rico Dealers' Contracts Act.[170] The counterclaims were also asserted against
Chrysler, Soler's principal supplier who had mediated the transaction with Mitsubishi, and who had not imposed an arbitration
clause on its own contract with Soler. At issue in the Supreme
Court was only the order compelling Soler to arbitrate its antitrust
claim against Mitsubishi in Japan.

The Court affirmed the order, Justice Blackmun explaining that
international arbitration fostered international trade: if arbitral
tribunals

> are to take a central place in the international legal order, na-
> tional courts will need "to shake off the old judicial hostility
> to arbitration," and also their customary and understandable
> unwillingness to cede jurisdiction of a claim arising under do-
> mestic law to a foreign or transnational tribunal. To this extent
> at least, it will be necessary for national courts to subordinate
> domestic notions of arbitrability to the international policy of
> favoring commercial arbitration.[171]

This superinternationalism brought a strong dissent from Justice
Stevens and others:

> The Court's repeated incantation of the high ideals of "in-
> ternational arbitration" creates the impression that this case
> involves the fate of an institution designed to implement a for-
> mula for world peace. But just as it is improper to subordinate
> the public interest in enforcement of antitrust policy to the
> private interest in resolving commercial disputes, so it is
> equally unwise to allow a vision of world unity to distort the

---

[168] 15 USC § 1221 et seq.

[169] P R Laws Ann Tit 10, § 257 et seq (1976).

[170] P R Laws Ann Tit 10, § 278 et seq (1976 & Supp 1983).

[171] *Mitsubishi*, 473 US at 638–39 (quoting *Kulukundis Shipping Co.*, 126 F2d 978, 985).

importance of the selection of a proper forum for resolving this
dispute. Like any other mechanism for resolving controversies,
international arbitration will only succeed if it is realistically
limited to tasks it is capable of performing well—the prompt
and inexpensive resolution of essentially contractual disputes
between commercial partners. As for matters involving the political passions and the fundamental interests of nations, even
the multilateral convention . . . recognizes that private international arbitration is incapable of achieving satisfactory results.[172]

The majority responded to the dissent with the promise tendered
by Justice Frankfurter in *Wilko*. It undertook to assure that the
arbitration in Japan would faithfully enforce the Sherman Act, cal-
culating that the task for the Japanese arbitrators was not different
from that performed by federal courts discerning foreign law in
the manner provided by Federal Rule 44.1.[173] A transcript would
be made, the Court assured itself, an opinion would be prepared
by the three Japanese arbitrators, and their award would be reviewed by the federal court in Puerto Rico for errors of law.[174]
As it happens, proceedings in the Japan Commercial Arbitration
Commission may be conducted in English,[175] but the Court manifested no interest in that fortunate circumstance.

In so deciding *Mitsubishi*, the Court appeared to lose sight of at
least two foreseeable consequences. One of these was the plight
of Soler in presenting its counterclaim to arbitrators in Tokyo. It
is, of course, true, as the Court pointed out,[176] that judges sometimes apply foreign law, and that Japanese arbitrators may be
equally capable of doing so. It is, however, a commonplace observation that even judges are prone, when in doubt, to apply the law
they know, and may be more prone to err when they try to apply
unfamiliar law. Moreover, even assuming utmost good faith and
professionalism on the part of Japanese arbitrators, the logistics
were in Soler's case prohibitive, given the stakes. Effective presen-
tation would require the participation of an American lawyer to
attend the hearing. The hearing would almost certainly be con-

---

[172] Id at 665.

[173] FRCP 44.1.

[174] *Mitsubishi*, 473 US at 634 n 18.

[175] Japan Commercial Arbitration Association Rule 52(1) provides that "The language or
languages to be used in arbitral proceedings shall be Japanese or English or both."

[176] *Mitsubishi*, 473 US at 634 n 18.

ducted discontinuously in the manner of Japanese civil litigation,[177] requiring Soler's lawyer to cross the Pacific perhaps numerous times.[178] In addition, Soler would in 1985 have needed a Japanese *bengoshi* to address the arbitrators.[179] Perhaps the evidence could be entirely documentary; if not, the transport of parties and witnesses would also be required. Of course, Soler's counterclaim would, like most claims, be settled. But its settlement value, whatever its merit, was reduced to a peppercorn.

Second, the Court appeared to give no consideration to the implications of its decision for domestic manufacturers and franchisers. If Mitsubishi is to be permitted thus to evade the Sherman Act, are its American competitors to be allowed to do the same? It almost surely had to follow that General Motors could require its Puerto Rico dealers to come to Detroit or New York, or perhaps even Japan if its cars contain Japanese parts, to arbitrate any claims they might have under the Sherman Act. But to the extent that General Motors must afford its dealers a more convenient forum than does Mitsubishi, competition in the automobile business is a somewhat less than level playing field, for Mitsubishi is less inhibited by American law in its business practices and dealer relations than are its American competitors.

Mitsubishi foretold reconsideration of the arbitrability of securities fraud claims. In 1987, the Court held that such claims arising under the Securities Exchange Act of 1934 are arbitrable[180] even though the Act contained a nonwaiver provision very similar to that held in *Wilko* to preclude enforcement of the clause requiring arbitration of a future dispute.[181] The Court distinguished *Wilko* on the entirely formal ground that it interpreted the 1933 rather than the 1934 Act,[182] a distinction long and universally rejected by lower federal courts[183] and dismissed as merely "colorable" by the

---

[177] Takaaki Hattori and Dan Fenno Henderson, *Civil Procedure in Japan* 7-59 to 7-78 (Mathew Bender, 1985). This problem is not limited to Japan, but is also a feature of arbitration in Europe as well. Born (cited in note 163) at 86.

[178] For example, *Fotochrome, Inc. v Copal Co., Ltd.*, 517 F2d 512 (1975).

[179] Japanese law was revised in 1996 to permit foreign lawyers to appear in international arbitral proceedings. Foreign Legal Consultants Law of Japan, Art 58-2.

[180] *Shearson/American Express*, 482 US 220.

[181] See Securities Exchange Act of 1934 § 29, 15 USC § 78.

[182] *Shearson/American Express*, 482 US at 228–29.

[183] Macneil et al, *Federal Arbitration Law* at § 16.23 (cited in note 63).

Court itself in *Scherk*. Its more cogent point was that the Securities Exchange Commission in 1987 favored arbitration of fraud claims, contrary to its position at the time of *Wilko*. One could dismiss this change of position as merely a reflection of changing presidential politics: a Commission appointed by President Reagan could be expected perhaps to sympathize with securities brokers and firms having a distaste for securities fraud litigation. But it was true that the Commission had in the intervening years acquired a role in the oversight of arbitration in the securities industry and had taken steps to assure the disinterest, economy, and effectiveness of the process. Moreover, Congress did in 1975 enact legislation favoring self-regulation in the industry.[184] That legislation reflected a not unfounded belief that the securities industry, perhaps more than any other, has a large stake in the effectiveness of its own regulation. If it allows the public to perceive that fraud goes unredressed, the theory goes, everyone with a stake in the market will suffer the consequences.[185] That theory may be correct, and if it is, then brokers accused of committing fraud on their clients may have even more to fear from arbitration than from trial by jury.

The claim under the 1934 Act was joined with another under the Racketeer Influenced and Corrupt Organizations Act,[186] which the Court also held to be arbitrable. RICO contained no non-waiver provision comparable to Section 14 of the Securities Act, but did provide for the recovery of treble damages, a feature of the antitrust laws that lower courts had taken as a sign that plaintiffs enforcing the legislation serve as private attorneys general whose function should not be subject to subversion by means of contract terms diverting their claims into inefficient or ineffective forums.[187] By the standards of an earlier day, contract clauses requiring arbitration of future RICO claims would not have been enforceable, and this holding cast doubt on the principle hitherto so well established in the lower courts with respect to antitrust claims,[188] at least in the absence of an international transaction.

---

[184] 29 USC § 19.

[185] S Rep No 94-75 (1975); H R Conf Rep No 94-229 (1975).

[186] 18 USC § 1961 et seq.

[187] *Shearson/American Express*, 482 US at 241–42.

[188] See, e.g., *Kotam Electronics, Inc. v JBL Consumer Products, Inc.*, 93 F3d 724 (11th Cir en banc 1996), overruling *Cobb v Lewis*, 488 F2d 41 (5th Cir 1974).

In 1989, the Court explicitly overruled *Wilko* and enforced a clause requiring arbitration of a future claim under the 1933 Act.[189] The Court was on firm ground in describing its 1987 decision as indistinguishable. But four Justices dissenting were on equally firm ground in stating that when the lower courts have relied for thirty-five years on a decision giving "a statutory provision concrete meaning, which Congress elects not to amend" for that period, it is the duty of the Court to respect the judgment of Congress.[190] Congress had revised the act many times without expressing the least doubt about the correctness of *Wilko*.

The Court took yet another questionable step in 1991. In *Gilmer v Interstate/Johnson Lane Corporation*,[191] it held that a claim arising under the Age Discrimination in Employment Act[192] is arbitrable. The Court justified its disregard of the provision of Section 1 of the FAA excluding employment contracts from the coverage of the Act by reference to the fact that the applicable clause was not in a contract but in an application seeking registration as a broker. The application was made on a printed form entitled "Uniform Application for Securities Industry Registration or Transfer," and the arbitration clause was mandatory under Rule 347 of the New York Stock Exchange.

The Court pointed out that there was no explicit language in the ADEA forbidding enforcement of arbitration agreements,[193] and that the Act favored informal methods of conciliation,[194] but failed to observe the large difference between mandatory, binding arbitration of the sort required by Rule 347 and voluntary, non-binding conciliation of the sort envisioned by ADEA. The Court also concluded that private enforcement of the Act was unimportant, that it can be adequately enforced by the Equal Employment Opportunity Commission without the aid of bounty-hunting private plaintiffs. The Court distinguished three of its own earlier decisions holding that employment discrimination claims arising under Title VII of the Civil Rights Act are not subject to binding

---

[189] *Rodriguez de Quijas*, 490 US 477.

[190] Id at 486 (Stevens, J, dissenting).

[191] 500 US 20.

[192] 29 USC § 621 et seq.

[193] *Gilmer*, 500 US at 29.

[194] Id.

arbitration foreclosing access to either courts or the Commission[195] on the ground that arbitrators serving pursuant to collective bargaining agreements, as were those involved in those three cases, have no authority to decide civil rights claims, but are restricted to enforcement of the contract conferring their authority. The implication of the distinction is that an arbitration clause in an individual contract of employment can extend arbitral jurisdiction to Title VII claims despite the FAA's explicit exclusion of employment contracts.

Justices Stevens and Marshall, dissenting, contended that the FAA does not apply to employment disputes whether the clause is in a contract or in a registration application; that because arbitration can afford no broad injunctive relief extending to the protection of the plaintiff's co-workers, it is not consistent with the legislative scheme of ADEA fostering class remedies; and that the means by which ADEA is enforced is no business of the New York Stock Exchange, whose provisions should be read to be inapplicable to civil rights disputes. The latter point may have warranted even greater emphasis; while it is arguable that the securities industry can be trusted to regulate itself to prevent fraud, there is no reason to assume that its arbitrators will faithfully enforce civil rights laws in actions against major investment banking firms.[196] This was not the kind of self-regulation of the industry that Congress had had in mind in 1975. The dissent also did not note, as it might have, that the ADEA (even more than RICO) was written at a time when it would have been almost unthinkable that any federal court would have enforced an agreement subjecting otherwise justiciable civil rights claims to arbitral jurisdiction. The dissent aptly concluded, however, that "the Court has put to one side any concern about the inequality of bargaining power between an entire industry, on the one hand, and an individual customer or employee, on the other."

Gilmer has been faithfully applied by lower federal courts to claims of individual brokers alleging other forms of discrimina-

---

[195] *Alexander v Gardner-Denver Co.*, 415 US 36 (1974); *Barrentine v Arkansas-Best Freight System, Inc.*, 450 US 728 (1981); *McDonald v City of West Branch*, 466 US 284 (1984).

[196] Securities industries arbitrators are not selected for their experience and judgment in civil rights matters. Steven A. Holmes, *Arbitrators of Bias in Securities Industry Have Slight Experience in Labor Law*, New York Times (April 15, 1994) at B-4.

tion.[197] Some courts have also enforced arbitration clauses in individual employment contracts to compel former employees to arbitrate wrongful discharge or sexual harassment claims, notwithstanding the exclusion of employment disputes from the coverage of the FAA.[198] One court of appeals, encouraged by *Gilmer*, has gone so far as to read the FAA as applicable to clauses in all employment agreements except for those of workers "actually engaged in the movement of goods in interstate commerce."[199] And at least one has suggested that *Gilmer* overrules *Alexander v Gardner-Denver*.[200] On the other hand, another court of appeals has held that an individual broker was not bound to arbitrate pursuant to a clause in a contract that she was not allowed to read before signing, that contained a reference to a manual she was not provided, and that made no explicit reference to Title VII discrimination claims.[201] The court in the latter case stands out as one of the few in recent years that has noticed how adhesive prehiring arbitration clauses can be; as Katherine Stone depicts them, they are "today's 'yellow-dog contracts.' "[202]

This extension of arbitration into employment law has generated not merely criticism,[203] but resistance. In 1994, a Special Task Force created by the leaderships of the National Academy of Arbitrators, the American Bar Association, the American Civil Liberties Union, the Federal Mediation and Conciliation Service, the Society of Professionals in Dispute Resolution, and the National Em-

---

[197] For example, *Mago v Shearson Lehman Hutton, Inc.*, 956 F2d 932 (9th Cir 1992).

[198] For example, *Matthews v Rollins Hudig Hall Co.*, 72 F3d 50 (7th Cir 1995); *Metz v Merrill, Lynch, Pierce, Fenner & Smith*, 39 F3d 1482 (10th Cir 1994); *De Gaetano v Smith Barney*, 1996 WL 44226, 70 FEP Cases 401, 68 Empl Prac Dec, ¶ 44,024; *Gulenia v Bob Baker Toyota*, 915 F Supp 201 (S D Cal 1996), enforced an arbitration clause in an employment contract in an age discrimination case. Compare *Pritzker v Merrill Lynch Pierce Fenner & Smith, Inc.*, 7 F3d 1110 (3d Cir 1993); *Saari v Smith, Barney, Inc.*, 789 F Supp 155 (D NJ 1992).

[199] *Asplundh Tree Expert Co. v Bates*, 71 F3d 592 (6th Cir 1995); but see *Acre v Cotton Club of Greenville, Inc.*, 883 F Supp 117 (N D Miss 1995).

[200] For example, *Nghiem v NEC Electronics*, 25 F3d 1437, 1441 (9th Cir 1994). See also *Austin v Owens-Brockway Glass Container, Inc.*, 78 F3d 875 (4th Cir 1996).

[201] *Prudential Ins. Co. of America v Lai*, 42 F3d 1299 (9th Cir 1994), cert denied 116 S Ct 61 (1995).

[202] Katherine Van Wezel Stone, *Mandatory Arbitration of Individual Employment Rights: Agreements to Arbitrate or Conceding to Capitulation?* (forthcoming).

[203] See Christine Godsil Cooper, *Where Are We Going with Gilmer? Some Ruminations on the Arbitration of Discrimination Claims*, 11 SLU Pub L Rev 203 (1992).

ployment Lawyers Association proposed a protocol for the arbitration of statutory discrimination claims providing an equal role for the employee in selecting the arbitrator, discovery, and review for errors of law.[204] The Judicial Arbitration and Mediation Service announced its withdrawal from employment cases unless its standards of due process were met by the arbitration clauses they were asked to enforce.[205] The National Employment Lawyers Association, an organization of over two thousand attorneys representing employees, announced a boycott of dispute resolution service providers taking employment cases pursuant to clauses not meeting that organization's standards.[206] The United States Equal Employment Opportunity Commission has also expressed its opposition to the use of arbitration to circumvent the Commission's authority to enforce the civil rights laws, and in 1996 issued its own National Enforcement Plan.[207] In at least one case in 1995, the Commission secured the invalidation of an arbitration clause requiring the employee to pay half the cost of the arbitration.[208] Similarly, the National Labor Relations Board compelled an employer to reinstate an employee fired for refusing to agree to arbitrate unfair labor practice claims.[209] The American Arbitration Association also adopted National Rules for the Resolution of Employment Disputes that reserve the right to the Association of refusing to administer cases under contracts not meeting "due process standards."[210]

In 1995, the Court in *Vimar Seguros y Reaseguros, S. A. v M/V Sky Reefer*[211] applied its newly reconstructed FAA to a case in which a shipper sought to avoid an arbitration clause as a violation of the provision in the Carriage of Goods by Sea Act invalidating contract terms "lessening" the liability of carriers.[212] The Court

---

[204] Arnold M. Zack, *Arbitration as a Tool to Unclog Government and the Judiciary: The Due Process Protocol as an International Model*, 7 World Arbitration & Mediation Rep 10 (1996).

[205] 6 World Arbitration & Mediation Rep 240 (1995).

[206] Id.

[207] 7 World Arbitration & Mediation Rep 51 (1996).

[208] *EEOC v River Oaks Imaging*, 1995 WL 264003 (S D Tex 1995).

[209] *Arbitration: Accord Reached on Unfair labor Practice Case Involving Mandatory Arbitration Pledge*, 1996 Daily Labor Reporter (BNA) 96 d15.

[210] 7 World Arbitration & Mediation Rep 123 (1996).

[211] 115 S Ct 2322 (1995).

[212] Id at 2325.

relied in part on *Carnival Lines*[213] as authority that mere cost and inconvenience in the assertion of a claim does not "lessen" liability. It disregarded the distinction emphasized earlier by the Court in *Carnival Lines*[214] that the forum chosen by the cruise ticket was not an arbitral tribunal, but a court of law in a state of the United States.[215] The Court discussed and rejected the analysis of numerous courts of appeals cases holding that a forum selection clause may be invalid as a "lessening" of liability.[216] With exquisite formalism, it explained that the arbitration clause did not diminish the theoretical liability of the carrier; in part because the arbitral tribunal will be obligated to enforce COGSA, the Court found that there was no conflict between COGSA and FAA.

The case before the Court involved a loss of over a million dollars in damage to fruit in transit from Morocco to Massachusetts. The printed bill of lading provided for arbitration in Tokyo. The insurer who paid the bulk of the loss sued in the federal court in Massachusetts and secured a stay of arbitration. It argued, inter alia, that the Japanese arbitrator would apply the Japanese rules exculpating the shipper for the blunder of Moroccan stevedores in mispacking the fruit. The Court held that the stay was premature. Citing *Mitsubishi*,[217] the Court gave comfort to the insurer that the district court would retain jurisdiction to ascertain whether the Japanese arbitrator applied COGSA. If he did not, then it would be time to set the award aside. The Court also echoed *Mitsubishi* in expressing sentiments of superinternationalism. Referring to the UN Convention, it explained that:

> If the United States is to be able to gain the benefits of international accords and have a role as a trusted partner in multilateral endeavors, its courts should be most cautious before interpreting its domestic legislation in such manner as to violate international agreements. That concern counsels against construing COGSA to nullify foreign arbitration

---

[213] 499 US 585 (1991).

[214] *Vimar*, 115 S Ct at 2327–28.

[215] Emphasizing the importance of this distinction is Elizabeth A. Clark, *Foreign Arbitration Clauses and Foreign Forum Selection Clauses in Bills of Lading Governed by COGSA*, 1996 BYU L Rev 483.

[216] *Vimar*, 115 S Ct at 2326.

[217] Id at 2329–30.

clauses because of inconvenience to the plaintiffs or insular distrust of the ability of foreign arbitrators to apply the law.[218]

Again, the Court seems to have overlooked readily visible consequences of its decision. In relying on *Carnival Lines* and disregarding the difference between forum selection clauses and arbitration clauses, the Court implied that a forum selection clause could be set forth in ocean bills of lading without regard for the choice of location or the willingness or ability of the foreign court selected to apply controlling American law. If this is indeed the case, then the qualifications expressed in the Court's opinion in *Bremen* are no longer operative. It will be recalled that the Court in *Bremen* emphasized the equality of the parties, the arms-length character of the bargain, and the reasonableness of the choice of a neutral turf. In *Vimar*, it appears that the Court would now enforce a clause in a bill of lading issued by a carrier bearing a Liberian or Panamanian flag (as many do) requiring shippers to assert any claims against the carrier in the courts of Liberia or Panama, however worthless that requirement might render the rights not "taken away" but reduced to a merely theoretical existence.

The Court seems also to have been unaware of the consequences of its holding for the shipping market. COGSA was a part of a prolonged multilateral effort to harmonize national laws regulating the terms of bills of lading.[219] It sought to impose equal burdens of duty on all carriers bringing goods to the United States without regard for the national flags they might fly. As the Act has now been read by the Court, that purpose has been substantially frustrated. Shippers will again be well advised to note the flag of the carrier before placing their goods in the holds of ships unless they are fully insured against loss resulting from the carrier's negligence, in which case insurance companies expecting to subrogate to claims for such losses should consider charging higher premiums for insurance on cargo in the holds of foreign ships, especially those bearing flags of nations whose courts are distant and unlikely to enforce COGSA effectively.

Perhaps more significant was the Court's failure to take realistic account of the international consequences of what it did. While

---

[218] Id at 2329.

[219] Michael F. Sturley, *The History of COGSA and the Hague Rules*, 22 J Marit L & Comm 1, 4–6 (1991).

few would wish the United States to be other than a trustworthy partner in multilateral endeavors (or guilty of "insular distrust"), it seems unlikely that international relations will in the long run be advanced by a procedure sending international parties to Japan to arbitrate (or Liberia to litigate) an issue of American law only to deny recognition of the award (or judgment) when it appears that the arbitrator (or judge) did not correctly apply American law. We will return to the problem of judicial review of awards in a later section of this article. But this is the place to observe that the Court's eager internationalism in sending claimants of rights conferred by American law to foreign tribunals is misplaced for at least three reasons.

First, in the global economy, the predatory conduct of those with greater economic power is seldom inhibited and is generally uncontrollable by any transnational regulatory mechanism. No world government protects consumers, patients, workers, passengers, shippers, or franchisees. This is one reason that the global economy is a mixed blessing—a boon to those who sell sophisticated goods and services and a bust to those in the lower reaches of the economic hierarchy whose vulnerability is made even greater by globalization. As national governments bend to exploit the opportunities of the global economy, they yield some of their ability to protect the weak from the strong. When the Court preempted, as it many times did, state regulatory law inconsistent with more comprehensive national regulatory laws, it was not leaving the weak unprotected, but was putting their protection in other governmental hands. But when the Court preempts both state and federal protections in favor of unregulated freedom of contract in the global economy, it leaves weaker parties quite without the possibility of governmental protection from predators in a position to impose contractual terms upon them. The result can be described as regulatory arbitrage. If courts of all nations were to join the Court in generous, unquestioning enforcement of arbitration clauses made in the course of international trade, the result would be to strip weaker parties everywhere of the protections afforded by privately enforced national laws.[220] Because American law relies so heavily on enforcement by private actions, it is especially impor-

---

[220] Jay R. Sever, *The Relaxation of Inarbitrability and Public Policy Checks on U.S. and Foreign Arbitration: Arbitration Out of Control?* 65 Tulane L Rev 1661, 1663 (1991).

tant in this country that multinational firms be constrained from using their economic power to impede adjudication of rights provided American consumers, workers, shippers, passengers, and franchisees. There is not a syllable in the Convention from which one might reasonably infer a duty of national courts to allow the use of arbitration clauses in international contracts to subvert national law in that way. To the contrary, as we have noted, Article V of the Convention, as quoted above, affords ample room to subordinate foreign awards to the need to protect weaker parties to bargains from timidly or inadvertently waving their rights under applicable American law.

A second consideration weighing against enthusiastic extension of international legal texts by the Court is that international treaties and conventions are the appropriate object of intermittent negotiation by the executive branch of the government. When courts extend special courtesies to foreign litigants or overenforce foreign arbitral awards, they may not only disadvantage American litigants, but they may also deprive the Department of State of a bargaining chit. Special concessions to international interests could and should be exchanged for comparable courtesies to Americans interests.[221] Courts cannot bargain, so nothing is received in exchange for what they give away. For this reason, as Jay Westbrook has observed, the only hope for the establishment of agreed, effective transnational regulation of abusive practices in international trade is aggressive regulation by each sovereign.[222]

A third reason for scruples against overextension of the UN Convention is to give appropriate protection to the political role of the United States Senate in ratifying treaties and conventions not presented to it as substantial modifications of American law.[223] The UN Convention, like others advanced under the auspices of the Hague Conference on Private International Law,[224] and like

---

[221] Hans Smit, *Recent Developments in International Litigation*, 35 S Tex L Rev 215, 220–23, 226–28, 239–42 (1994) (arguing against the Hague Service and Evidence Conventions as against the interests of the United States).

[222] Jay Westbrook, *Extraterritoriality, Conflict of Laws and the Regulation of Transnational Business*, 25 Tex Intl L J 71, 85, 92–96 (1990).

[223] For broader discussion, see Martin A. Rogoff, *Interpretation of International Agreements by Domestic Courts and the Politics of International Treaty Relations: Reflections on Some Recent Decisions of the United States Supreme Court*, 11 Am U J Intl L & Pol'y 559 (1996).

[224] For example, The Hague Convention on the Taking of Evidence Abroad in Civil and Commercial Matters, 23 UST 2555, 28 USC § 1781 (1994); The Hague Convention on

friendship treaties the United States has made with many na-tions,[225] was presented to the Senate and the public as serving the American national interest by conceding equal status, not special status, for foreign nationals or foreign awards in our courts. Such treaties and conventions are of course proposed for ratification by the Department of State with the support of international inter-ests, many of whom are among the most adept and well-financed lobbies in Washington. There was no lobby opposing the Conven-tion or other treaties of the sort described. Of course, no such treaty or convention would be ratified if it were disclosed to the Senate that it would adversely affect the rights of American con-sumers, patients, workers, shippers, passengers, or franchisees. It was never imagined by any Senator that the UN Convention would enable foreign manufacturers to require their American franchises to arbitrate their antitrust claims in Beijing, or their American employees' age discrimination claims in Paris.

There is now substantial evidence that international litigants fare better in our courts than Americans do.[226] The Court's super-internationalist treatment of the UN Convention suggests one rea-son this may be so. But it is not merely discrimination against American litigants or American arbitral awards that has resulted. Instead, to prevent such discrimination, the Court has diminished the effectiveness of privately enforced American law, making it in important respects as weak as the nonexistent international law that is unavailable to regulate business conducted in the global economy. Only marginally do international litigants benefit more from that weakness than do our own powerful enterprises.

In light of *Mitsubishi, Rodriguez de Quijas, Gilmer,* and *Vimar,* it is not clear that there remains any private claim of federal right that cannot be diverted into an arbitral tribunal. Even the explicit exclusions set forth in the FAA may be substantially inoperative. The national law constraining fraud in our investment markets, monopolization and other abuses of open markets, and even much of our civil rights laws can now be diverted by adhesion contracts

---

the Service Abroad of Judicial and Extra-Judicial Documents in Civil and Commercial Mat-ters, 20 UST 361, 28 USCA FRCP 4 (West, 1992).

[225] See, e.g., Japan-United States Friendship Treaty, 22 USC cf 44 § 1901 et seq.

[226] Kevin Clermont and Theodore Eisenberg, *Commentary: Xenophilia in American Courts,* 109 Harv L Rev 1120 (1996).

from the courts that have enforced them and be entrusted to arbitral forums that are not infrequently erected by the very parties whom those laws were enacted to regulate and that are in any case not bound to enforce substantive rights.

The Court has not so far allowed employers to require job applicants to agree to arbitrate any claims they might someday have to be paid the minimum wage required by the Fair Labor Standards Act.[227] And one awaits with interest how the Court will deal with the Automobile Dealer's Day in Court Act. As the title to the latter Act suggests, that statute had as its only purpose the dispatch of the federal courts on the errand of correcting the imbalance in bargaining power between automobile dealers and automobile manufacturers. Its substance is a vaporous declaration that manufacturers shall not act other than "in good faith."[228] What good faith means in this context was plainly intended by those who drafted and enacted the statute to be, in at least some circumstances, a jury issue.[229] How indeed will the Court explain its likely holding that even a claim under that act can be diverted to arbitration if a dealer such as Soler should in the dealership agreement submit to a broad arbitration clause written by the manufacturer and requiring arbitration in Tokyo?

One vestige of revocability of arbitration clauses may have been identified by the Ninth Circuit. In *Graham Oil Co. v Arco Products Co.*,[230] that court invalidated an arbitration clause in a distributorship agreement. The claim arose under the Petroleum Marketing Practices Act,[231] a rough analogue to the Automobile Dealer's Day in Court Act protecting fuel distributors and service station owners

---

[227] Compare *Donohue v Susquehanna Collieries Co.*, 138 F2d 3 (3d Cir 1943). And see *Lambdin v District Court for the 18th Judicial District of Arapahoe*, 1995 Colo LEXIS 662, 903 P2d 1126 (1995).

[228] 15 USC §§ 1221 et seq § 1222 provides that "an automobile dealer may bring suit . . . and shall recover damages by him sustained and the cost of suit by reason of the failure of said automobile manufacturer . . . to act in good faith in performing or complying with any of the terms or provisions of the franchise, or in terminating, canceling, or not renewing the franchise with said dealer; Provided, That in any such suit the manufacturer shall not be barred from asserting in defense of any such action the failure of the dealer to act in good faith."

[229] *Woodard v General Motors Corp.*, 298 F2d 121 (2d Cir 1962); *Bateman v Ford Motor Co.*, 302 F2d 63 (3d Cir 1962); *Studebaker Rambler Sales, Inc. v American Motors Corp.*, 375 F2d 932 (5th Cir 932); *Hanly v Chrysler Motor Corp.*, 453 F2d 718 (10th Cir 1970).

[230] 43 F3d 1244 (4th Cir 1994).

[231] 15 USC §§ 2801–06.

from predation by major oil companies. The court acknowledged that claims under the act are generally arbitrable, but found that, in the specific context of this transaction, the arbitration clause was invalidated by its connection to other overreaching provisions by which the distributor was required to waive rights conferred by the Act, including the right to punitive damages and attorneys' fees, and by a foreshortening of the time within which a claim might be brought from one year to ninety days. The court could have saved the arbitration clause and deleted only the three offending provisions, but it found arbitration to be so closely related to the illicit waivers that it, too, should be deemed invalid, and the claim should be permitted to go forward in court.

PREEMPTION

As we have seen, arbitration law was well developed in every state, and often expressed in carefully drafted and politically tested legislation balancing considerations of free markets and freedom of contract against the need to protect weaker parties, especially those who were cast for the role of private attorneys general. The differences in state law were sufficiently ample to excite the enthusiasm of Justice Brandeis for the use of the states as laboratories for legal experiments.[232] After 1938 and the Court's decision in *Erie*, the interesting and troublesome question was whether the FAA could have any application in diversity cases, or whether it was limited in applicability to admiralty and federal question cases.[233]

Almost sixty years after it was enacted, the Court began to regard the FAA as applicable in state courts displacing state arbitration law. This belated application of the preemption doctrine was imposed by a Court that was otherwise inclining in the direction of devolving power to the states and avoidance of implied preemption.[234] The first indication by the Court that the FAA might have

[232] *New State Ice Co. v Leibmann*, 285 US 262, 311 (1932).

[233] For example, *Bernhardt v Polygraphic Co. of America, Inc.*, 350 US 198 (1956); *Prima Paint Corp.*, 388 US 395.

[234] For a useful summary of preemption law, see Appellate Judges Conference, American Bar Association, *The Law of Preemption* (ABA, 1991). On the declining use of implied preemption, see S. Candice Hoke, *Preemption Pathologies and Civic Republican Values*, 71 Boston U L Rev 685, 738–47 (1991); Stephen A. Gardbaum, *The Nature of Preemption*, 79 Cornell L Rev 767, 806–07, 811–12 (1994). And see *Lividas v Bradshaw*, 114 S Ct 2068 (1994); *Hawaiian Airlines v Norris*, 114 S Ct 2239 (1994).

some substantive implications came in 1967.[235] That the FAA had preemptive effect was first confirmed in the 1983 holding in *Moses H. Cone Mem. Hospital v Mercury Construction Co.*[236] The Court there held that a federal court had abused its discretion in staying a diversity action to compel arbitration pending the outcome of a state court action in which a preliminary injunction had been issued staying the arbitration. To reach that conclusion, the Court had necessarily to find that there was a federal right to arbitrate that a state court was obliged to observe, and that a federal court having subject matter jurisdiction was obliged to enforce.

In the next term, the Court in *Southland Corp. v Keating*[237] invoked the Supremacy Clause to invalidate California law treating certain state law claims as inarbitrable. The claims in question arose under the California Franchise Investment Law,[238] which explicitly invalidated arbitration clauses in franchise agreements that would "oust" the state's courts of jurisdiction to enforce the disclosure requirements in its law. As Professor Macneil and Justice O'Connor have amply demonstrated, the opinion of the Court was an extraordinarily disingenuous manipulation of the history of the 1925 Act.[239] Everyone associated with that legislation, pro or con, assumed that it had no application to state courts. The decision

---

[235] *Prima Paint*, 388 US at 395, held that the FAA was controlling in a diversity action in federal courts, notwithstanding possibly contrary state law. The Court's opinion spoke of the FAA as prescribing "how federal courts are to conduct themselves," indicating that the Court then took the statute to be procedural legislation. Id at 405. Seen thus, the FAA could be compared to the Rules Enabling Act, 28 USC § 2072, in its constitutional status. The Court was, it ought to be acknowledged, vexed by the task of making sense out of the FAA in a post-*Erie* world. On its facts, the case involved a thoroughly negotiated contract for the sale of a business that had been substantially performed before the dispute arose. One of the parties then sought to escape the arbitral forum by alleging fraud in the inducement. Most states limiting the power of revocation would not have recognized such a ground as an acceptable one, and it was not certain that the applicable New York law conflicted with the federal principle created and invoked in *Prima Paint*. The Court emphasized that the FAA made arbitration clauses "as enforceable as other contracts, but not more so." 388 US 404 n 12. It also gave assurance that "categories of contracts otherwise within reach of the Arbitration Act but in which one of the parties characteristically has little bargaining power are expressly excluded from the reach of the Act," citing Section 1. 388 US 403 n 9.

[236] 460 US 1.

[237] 465 US 1 (1984).

[238] Cal Corp Code § 31000 et seq.

[239] The bogus history had antecedents in the opinion of Judge Harold Medina in *Robert Lawrence*, 271 F2d at 410–23, and in *Prima Paint*, 388 US at 402–05. In his dissent in the latter case, Justice Black vigorously denounced the rewriting of the statute, 388 US at 410–23. One can scarcely imagine what he might have said about its subsequent extensions.

made Title I of the FAA unique: it became the only federal law creating substantive entitlements enforceable only in state courts, for the text of the Act cannot support federal jurisdiction over arbitration litigation, as cases "arising under" federal law.[240]

In *Southland*, as in other cases considered here, the Court seemed in its zealous devotion to private dispute resolution to be oblivious to consequences. Indeed, the Court relied almost wholly on its bogus legislative history, and made no effort to analyze the practical consequences of preempting state law, perhaps in part because they were not fully briefed on them.[241] The California law at issue was no different in its aim than Section 14 of the Securities Act of 1933 upheld in *Wilko*. At the time of *Southland*, *Wilko* was still the federal law. Even today the Court has not gone so far as to deny Congress the power to invalidate arbitration or other forum selection clauses when they diminish the effectiveness of privately enforced federal legislation. No reason was given why California should not be allowed to do as Congress may clearly do and designate classes of potential plaintiffs as private attorneys general and also assure them a judicial forum for the litigation of rights that it confers. The Court, ignoring the assurance it had given in *Prima Paint*,[242] in effect held that the California legislature could not prevent a party with superior bargaining power from using an arbitration clause to block its private attorneys general from access to its courts. And the Court said nothing in *Southland* about the possibility that a state court might retain jurisdiction (in the manner approved in *Mitsubishi* and in *Vimar*) to review an award to ensure that the arbitrator was faithful to the Franchise Investment Law, as a federal court might do to assure fidelity to the federal antitrust laws in *Mitsubishi* or COGSA in *Vimar*.

Perry v Thomas[243] followed *Southland* and foretold *Gilmer*. Like *Gilmer*, it involved a dispute between a stockbroker and his employer and so was subject to arbitration under the rules of the New York Stock Exchange. But California law explicitly provides that

---

[240] FAA § 4 and 28 USC § 1332. It will support federal jurisdiction to enforce a foreign award. § 203.

[241] This is Justice Breyer's partial explanation of *Southland*. *Allied Bruce Terminix*, 115 S Ct at 837–39.

[242] 388 US 403 n 9, quoted in note 235.

[243] 482 US 483 (1987).

an action to recover wages may be maintained "without regard to the existence of any private agreement to arbitrate."[244] The Court brushed aside the California law, again holding the FAA preemptive. Given the explicit exclusion of employment contracts from Section 1 of the Act, it is hard to see how the policy of the FAA requires the displacement of congruent state law.

While the Court in *Mitsubishi* and *Vimar* explicitly directed lower federal courts to review arbitral awards to assure their fidelity to the federal antitrust laws and COGSA, it made no similar accommodation to state courts reviewing awards to assure their fidelity to state law. Neither in *Southland* nor in *Perry* did the Court suggest or imply that a California court might be free to set aside or amplify an award if it found that an award was in manifest disregard of the California Franchise Investment Law or if it determined a wage earner was awarded less than he was legally entitled to be paid. But it is at least possible that the Court will allow California to enforce its public policy by setting aside an award that is manifestly contrary to its law. Such a result would not be easy to square with the text of Section 10 of the FAA, anymore than are *Mitsubishi* and *Vimar*, but would serve to alleviate the harm done to the enforcement of state law by the extensive preemption imposed by the Court.

The Court carried preemption to the full limits of Congress's power to regulate interstate commerce in *Allied-Bruce Terminix Companies, Inc. v Dobson*.[245] It there enforced an arbitration clause in a contract to remove termites from a private home in Alabama. It held that such a contract was one "involving commerce" within the meaning of Section 1 of the FAA, and hence the FAA preempted Alabama law invalidating predispute arbitration clauses.[246] In that small-stakes case, the attorneys general of twenty states appeared as amici to implore the Court to overrule *Southland*. As they explained, the *Southland* principle was a serious impediment to the enforcement of state law, empowering parties with bargaining power, as it did, to move claims against them into a forum less likely to enforce rights and duties created by the states.[247] The

---

[244] Cal Lab Code § 229.

[245] 115 S Ct 834 (1995).

[246] Ala Code § 8-1-41(3).

[247] Brief Amici Curiae of the Attorneys General of the States of Alabama, Alaska, Arkansas, Colorado, Florida, Hawaii, Illinois, Mississippi, Missouri, Montana, Nebraska, Nevada,

Court did not deny the premise of the argument. It responded that the *Southland* Court had recognized the preemption issue as difficult, that the issue had been resolved, that private parties had now written contracts in reliance upon the decision, and that Congress had tinkered with the FAA without overruling *Southland*, so that it must be treated as settled law. This is hardly a compelling justification for what the Court has done, given that the law now settled by *Southland* is even yet no more settled than was the principle of state law on inarbitrability when it was belatedly preempted, or than was *Wilko* for over thirty years. The attorneys general did, however, persuade Justice Scalia, who announced in dissent his readiness to overrule *Southland*.[248]

Justice Breyer, in an almost apologetic opinion of the Court, offered the attorneys general additional comfort by reminding them that the states can still regulate arbitration clauses "upon such grounds as exist in law or in equity for the revocation of any contract."[249] "What States cannot do," he affirmed, "is decide that a contract is fair enough to enforce all its basic terms (price, service, credit), but not fair enough to enforce its arbitration clause."[250] The statutory text on which the Court relied for support of this statement has been quoted above and provides that an arbitration *clause* may be held invalid or revocable upon any ground sufficient to support the invalidation or revocation of a contract. The "plain language" of the Act thus seems to say that if a contract can be revoked for the reason that it is unconscionable, then an unconscionable clause should be equally and independently revocable. It may well be that it is the arbitration clause alone that makes a contract as a whole unconscionable in the contemplation of applicable state law; that might be so (pursuant to conventional contracts law) where its practical effect is to require the weaker party to submit claims of right under a state franchise law or a

New Hampshire, New Jersey, North Dakota, South Carolina, Utah, and Vermont; and the Commonwealths of Massachusetts and Pennsylvania, in support of respondents G. Michael Dobson and Wanda C. Dobson, 115 S Ct 834 (1995) (No 93-1001).

[248] 115 S Ct at 844. Justice Thomas joined in Justice Scalia's opinion. Unfortunately, Justice O'Connor was no longer willing to stand by her *Southland* dissent, being dissuaded wholly by "considerations of stare decisis." Justices Stevens and Rehnquist, who also dissented in *Southland*, nevertheless joined to majority in *Allied Bruce Terminix*.

[249] 9 USC § 2 (1994).

[250] *Allied-Bruce Terminix*, 115 S Ct 834, 843.

state antitrust law to an expensive private forum that is free to disregard those laws. But a court of equity refusing to enforce a partially performed franchise agreement or termite removal contract it deems unconscionable because of an unconscionable arbitration clause would generally salvage as much of the bargain as may be consistent with the conscience of the court. The Uniform Commercial Code explicitly permits a court finding in "any clause [in a commercial contract] to have been unconscionable at the time it was made" to "enforce the remainder of that contract without the unconscionable clause."[251]

Responding to the attorneys general in *Allied-Bruce Terminix*, the American Arbitration Association appeared as an additional amicus to explain how efficient arbitration can be in handling small claims such as those involving termite damage. The AAA is of course correct that arbitration can be expeditious and economic. But so can adjudication.[252] Arbitration is not in all circumstances more efficient. There are in many states small claims courts; these sometimes resemble traditional trade association arbitration in being quick, cheap, and loose in their fidelity to the law.[253] AAA arbitration is seldom as cheap as small claims courts. The AAA charges an administrative fee for its services that is generally higher than court filing fees,[254] and one is not invited to proceed *in forma pauperis* in AAA arbitration.[255] Moreover, while arbitrators may agree to serve without compensation as an act of loyalty to a trade association, most must be paid by the parties, sometimes at handsome hourly rates.

The AAA as amicus argued that arbitration is cheaper than litigation and generally regarded as fair by counsel.[256] The AAA did not explicitly argue, as the Court did in *Carnival Lines*, that the

---

[251] § 2-302.

[252] For a review of the empirical evidence, see Thomas J. Stipanowich, *Rethinking American Arbitration*, 63 Ind L J 425, 452–76 (1988).

[253] For a description, see John A. Goerdt, *Small Claims and Traffic Courts: Case Management Procedures, Case Characteristics, and Outcomes* in 12 Urban Jurisdictions (1992).

[254] See Macneil et al, *Federal Arbitration Law*, App IV at 20–22 (cited in note 63).

[255] Compare 28 USC § 1915.

[256] Brief of American Arbitration Association as Amicus Curiae in Support of Petitioners, 93-1001 (1994). For an earlier unqualified proclamation that arbitration is cheaper than litigation, see William A. Rehnquist, *A Jurist's View of Arbitration*, Arb J (March 1977) at 1.

cost saving would be reflected in the price of termite removal; because there is price competition in that field, it is more likely that any cost saving would be reflected in the price of the service than it was with respect to the clause in the cruise ticket. On the other hand, the operative effect of the clause in the termite removal contract was to deny many homeowners having small claims access to any forum at all. In Llewellyn's terms, the arbitration clause may well "eviscerate" the warranty that is a major selling point offered by Terminix.

If the purpose of the clause was to serve the interests of homeowners, the termite company could as a special inducement have offered an arbitration clause providing a genuinely accessible forum for their future claims; or it could have offered two contracts at different prices, one with and one without the more expensive arbitration. Or it could have awaited the assertion of a claim for breach of contract before offering arbitration as a means of saving both sides the allegedly greater cost of litigating. The most effective way to assure that the arbitration is fair to both parties is the traditional way that Alabama followed, making the arbitration clause revocable and thus renegotiable by the parties at a time when the dimensions of their dispute are known and both have consulted counsel. The AAA to the contrary notwithstanding, one need not be hostile to arbitration to prefer the Alabama law to that imposed on Alabama by the Court, which allows Terminix to immunize itself against small and medium-size claims of homeowners disappointed with the quality of their service.

Yet another extension of the preemption of state law occurred in 1996 in *Casarotto v Doctors' Associates*,[257] invalidating a provision of the Montana Uniform Arbitration Act requiring prominent notice to persons signing standard contracts containing arbitration clauses. In light of *Southland, Perry* and *Allied-Bruce Terminix*, this outcome was eminently foreseeable, but the case extended preemption by depriving state legislatures of the power to regulate the procedure by which arbitration agreements are formed. As noted above, a common form of state arbitration legislation has sought to assure that the weaker party does in actual fact assent to arbitration. In this respect, legislation requiring special notice of an arbi-

---

[257] 116 S Ct 1652 (1996).

tration clause is a specific form of a larger category of legislative intrusions on freedom of contract to assure that parties to adhesion contracts know and understand the terms to which they are formally assenting.

It is true that the FAA requires only that arbitration clauses be in writing and makes no provision for warning those who sign printed contracts that they may be diminishing the enforceability of their rights. A reason may be that those who drafted and enacted the Act had no cause to envision that it would apply in state courts or to claims arising under federal law. Where the arbitration clause is inserted in a commercial agreement between businessmen (the sort of transaction envisioned by the drafters of FAA) for the purpose of resolving disputes arising in the performance of the contract, there is little reason for a special caution to weaker parties. But when a party is being invited to reduce the enforceability of rights conferred on that party by legislation, the need for fair warning is enhanced. The franchise agreement containing the arbitration clause applied in *Casarotto* was not a consumer or employment contract, nor was the claim asserted by the Casarottos one conferred by a legislature solicitous of their economic vulnerability. Possibly *Casarotto* might be distinguished in later cases involving workers or consumers asserting claims under civil rights or antitrust laws. As noted above, the Ninth Circuit did in one case refuse to compel arbitration of a civil rights claim partially on the ground that the clause did not give adequate notice to a party who might reasonably have supposed that the clause conferred jurisdiction limited to matters of private law.[258] It might seem more appropriate to the Court if Montana law required the franchiser to specify any public laws, federal or state, that it intended by the agreement to submit to arbitration. There is, however, nothing in the Court's opinion to suggest such a limitation on the holding.

An issue not briefed in *Casarotto* nor treated in the Court's opinion is one raised by the designated location of the arbitration proceeding.[259] The Casarottos claimed that they were induced to invest in a Subway franchise in Great Falls, Montana, by the promise that they would have the opportunity to invest in a preferable loca-

---

[258] *Prudential Ins. Co.*, 42 F3d 1299.

[259] The issue was noted in *Doctor's Assocs., Inc. v Stuart*, 85 F3d 975, 979 (2d Cir 1996).

tion in that city when it became available. Their claim was filed in a state court in Great Falls. The defendants' response was a motion to compel arbitration in Bridgeport, Connecticut, in conformity with the franchise agreement. Bridgeport is the home office of the defendant, and the contract written by the defendant called for the application of Connecticut law. This was marvelously convenient for Subway (Doctors' Associates) for it enabled them to resolve all their disputes with franchisees across the continent most efficiently, using a single law firm intimately familiar with its affairs and without need of consultation on the law of any other jurisdiction. On the other hand, the Casarottos live in Great Falls; the contract was negotiated and was to be performed in Great Falls; and the facts in dispute pertain to events and circumstances in Great Falls. So far as appears, the Casarottos were never in Bridgeport and were not amenable to the personal jurisdiction of a Connecticut court. As the Supreme Court of Montana explained, the arbitration clause was massively inconvenient for them, so inconvenient that it effectively extinguished their right to the promised location if such a promise was made:

> Regardless of the amount in controversy between these parties, the arbitration clause in the Subway Sandwich Shop Franchise Agreement requires that the Casarottos travel thousands of miles to Connecticut to have their disputes arbitrated. Furthermore, it requires that they share equally in the expense of arbitration, regardless of the merits of their claim. Presumably, that expense could be substantial, since under the Commercial Arbitration Rules of the American Arbitration Association (1992), those expenses would, at a minimum, include the arbitrator's fees and travel expenses, the cost of witnesses chosen by the arbitrator, the American Arbitration Association's administrative charges, and a filing fee of up to $4000, depending on the amount in controversy. For a proceeding involving multiple arbitrators, the administrative fee alone, for which the Casarottos would be responsible is $150 a day. In addition, since the contract called for the application of Connecticut law, the Casarottos would be required to retain the services of a Connecticut attorney.
>
> In spite of the expenses set forth above, the procedural safeguards which have been established in Montana to assure the reliability of the outcome in dispute resolution are absent in an arbitration proceeding. The extent of pretrial discovery is within the sole discretion of the arbitrator and the rules of

evidence are not applicable. The arbitrator does not have to
follow any law and there does not have to be a factual basis
for the arbitrator's decision.[260]

The opinion of the Court in *Casarotto* manifests no concern for
these practical considerations. One might wonder whether the
Court would see a problem if the clause had merely provided that
the Casarottos must bear all the costs of any arbitration (or litigation) arising from the franchise relationship, whatever the outcome. The Court's opinion in *Allied-Bruce Terminix* indicates a
negative answer, that because the other terms of the franchise
agreement are unobjectionable, nothing can be done about an unreasonable arbitration clause, but presumably the Court did not
really mean what it said.

It bears notice that a clause requiring the Casarottos to sue Subway only in a Connecticut court would be void under the explicit
and unpreempted Montana statute quoted above.[261] By clothing an
otherwise unlawful forum selection in the garb of an arbitration
clause, Subway successfully evaded Montana's effort to protect
weaker parties from precisely this form of predation by stronger
ones. The Court could have allowed enforcement of the unpreempted Montana law on forum selection clauses by permitting the
Montana court to compel arbitration in Great Falls instead of
Bridgeport. The change of venue would have made the clause a
reasonable one, consistent with conventional contract law, but
would of course have deprived Subway of the unjust advantage that
it was the purpose of the clause to secure.

Casarotto could have been explained as an application of Darwin-
ian law-and-economics. The Court could have said that Subway
franchisees should unite in gratitude that their disputes with the
franchiser will all be conducted in a forum most congenial to the
franchiser, because the market assures them that the price of their
franchises is less on that account. Perhaps in some minds, that
"stands to reason," but no person conscious of the practical realities of dispute resolution would be deceived by that academized
theory, and the Court did not advance it.

It is not clear that there is anything a well-advised state can do
to redeem the effectiveness of its private attorneys general other

---

[260] *Casarotto v Lombardi*, 51 Mont 1350, 886 P2d 931 (1994).

[261] See text at note 143.

than address their grievance to Congress. In a time when Congressmen on both sides of the aisle are advocating the devolution of the police power back to the states, it is certainly imaginable that Congress would respond to such an initiative, although it would be opposed by the AAA and by those endowed with economic power who enjoy their ability to partially immunize themselves against enforcement of some state laws.

Although *Terminix* and *Casarotto* leave very little room for the exercise of state sovereignty to protect weaker parties or to arm private attorneys general to enforce state law and policy, states might consider other possible legislative responses. One possibility might be to broaden application of the principle of unconscionability, perhaps by making section 2-302 of the Uniform Commercial Code applicable to services-consumer and employment contracts and to franchise agreements, thus authorizing its courts to review terms in such contracts and delete those it deems unconscionable. It seems possible that if the Montana court had employed its equitable powers to allow revocation of the clause in the Casarottos' franchise as unconscionable, thereby invoking a ground on which Montana equity might allow revocation of any contract, the Court would have had nothing to say about it. A possible flaw in the Montana law that attracted the Court's attention may have been that it was expressed in legislation entitled as a Uniform Arbitration Act, something Montana is apparently not allowed to have.[262]

Possibly, as a variation on the extension of the unconscionability principle, the Montana legislature might enact the following response to *Casarotto* as a revision of the statute quoted above:

> **Restraints upon legal proceedings void.** Every stipulation or condition in a contract by which any party thereto is restricted from enforcing his rights under the contract *or rights conferred on that party by the laws of this state or by the laws of the United States* by the usual proceedings in the ordinary tribunals or which limits the time within which he may thus enforce his rights is void. This section does not affect the validity of an agreement ~~enforceable under Title 27, chapter 5 [Montana Uniform Arbitration Act]~~ *by which a party consciously agrees to arbitrate or litigate in a specified judicial forum, provided that the arbitration or litigation is to be conducted in a place and manner*

---

[262] Macneil et al, *Federal Arbitration Law* at § 10-5 (cited in note 63).

> *that assures the just, speedy, and inexpensive enforcement of rights*
> *created by the contract or conferred on a contracting party by the*
> *laws of this state of by the laws of the United States. The courts of*
> *this state shall upon request enjoin any proceeding in any forum*
> *brought in violation of the restraints imposed by this Act. Any party*
> *may demand trial by jury to determine whether there was an agree-*
> *ment of the parties that the dispute later arising between them would*
> *be arbitrated or litigated in a specified judicial forum.*

The purpose of this revision is to situate the appropriate restraints on arbitration clauses among the parallel restraints on other contract clauses designed to oppress the weak or trap the unwary, and thus to confirm them as "grounds [that] exist at law or in equity for the revocation of any contract."[263] In essence, it extends the principle applied to forum selection clauses by the Restatement of Conflict of Laws to commercial arbitration. The reader will likely have noted that the aim of "just, speedy, and inexpensive" dispute resolution is drawn from Rule 1 of the Federal Rules of Civil Procedure.[264] If such law had been in force in Michigan, Rudzewicz might have secured a Michigan injunction against a Florida adjudication of his rights under the Michigan Franchise Investment Law. If in force in Montana, it might have assured that the arbitration was conducted in Great Falls.

The suggested text treats the making of a contract as potentially an issue of fact.[265] A Montana jury might have found as a fact that the Casarottos did not know of, and hence did not assent to, the clause binding them to arbitration in Bridgeport. Treating contract as fact is not incompatible with the text of FAA; to the contrary, it tracks Section 4 of that act.[266] Thus, a California court has recently found that a passenger on a Carnival Cruise line did not in the particular circumstances assent to the forum selection clause that bound the Shutes.[267] And the Michigan court has held that an employee handbook is not a contract.[268] In circumstances such as those existing in *Casarotto*, *Gilmer*, *Terminix* or *Carnival Lines*,

---

[263] 9 USC § 2 (1994).

[264] See Patrick Johnston, *Problems in Raising Prayers to the Level of Rule: The Example of Federal Rule of Civil Procedure 1*, 75 Boston U L Rev 1325 (1995).

[265] Leff, *Contract as Thing* at 144–55 (cited in note 23).

[266] The text is quoted in note 89.

[267] *Carnival Lines v Superior Court*, 286 Cal Rptr 323 (Ct App 1991).

[268] *Heurbetise v Reliable Business Computers, Inc.*, 550 NW2d 243 (Mich 1996).

findings that there was no assent to the clause would seem eminently plausible.

An alternative solution for the states is to substitute public agencies for private attorneys general. The demerits of that alternative need not be rehearsed here. It will suffice to note that insurance contracts are closely regulated in every state.[269] For this reason, insurance policies do not contain provisions requiring insureds and beneficiaries to present their claims to distant fora that are not accountable for their fidelity to the law. Perhaps the Montana insurance commissioner should have his or her jurisdictions enlarged to regulate terms in all consumer or individual employment contracts or franchise agreements made or to be performed in that state. Such a jurisdiction would clearly extend to the contracts of multinational firms such as Mitsubishi.

CHOICE OF LAW CLAUSES

The relation between contractual selection of forum and contractual selection of controlling law has been perplexing, as the *Burger King* example illustrates. The autonomy of parties to determine the controlling law by contract, like their autonomy to designate a forum, has never been unqualified. Restatement black letter law[270] precludes Burger King from opting out of the Michigan Franchise Investment Law by the simple gesture of making its franchisees agree that Florida law shall control, because the application of Florida law "would be contrary to a fundamental policy of [Michigan] which has a materially greater interest" in the determination of the rights of Michigan franchisees.[271]

In the course of its aggressive effort to rewrite arbitration law, the Court has twice encountered troublesome choice of law clauses. In *Volt Information Sciences, Inc. v Board of Trustees of Leland Stanford Junior University*,[272] the Court was confronted with a construction contract containing both an arbitration clause and a

---

[269] *Appleman and Appleman*, at § 10391 et seq (cited in note 146).

[270] Restatement (Second) of Conflict of Laws § 187(2)(b)(1988).

[271] *Modern Computer Systems, Inc. v Modern Banking Systems*, 858 F2d 1339 (8th Cir 1988); *Winer Motors Inc. v Jaguar Rover Triumph Inc.*, 208 N J Super 666, 506 A2d 817 (1986); *Young v Mobil Oil Corp.*, 85 Ore App 64, 735 P2d 654 (1987).

[272] 489 US 468 (1989).

clause designating California law as the controlling law. Volt sought to compel arbitration; the university sought to stay arbitration pending resolution of related litigation involving third parties who had not agreed to arbitration. The California court granted the stay pursuant to an explicit provision of the California arbitration legislation,[273] over the objection that the stay was not authorized by the FAA. The Court affirmed. It commenced its explanation by observing that "the interpretation of private contracts is ordinarily a question of state law, which this Court does not sit to review,"[274] and, pointing to Sections 3 and 4 of the FAA that are explicitly applicable only in federal courts, it concluded that the Act "does [not] reflect a congressional intent to occupy the entire field of arbitration."[275] It assessed the California provision at issue and concluded that it was not at odds with the FAA because a stay of arbitration pending the outcome of related litigation does not "undermine the goals and policies of the FAA."[276] It then concluded with the observation that the purpose of the FAA and of the Court was to enforce the intent of the parties as expressed in the contract, and the parties appeared to have intended to incorporate into their agreement the California arbitration law authorizing the stay.[277] The dissent noted that the FAA is the law of California (as it is the law in all states) and argued that states cannot allow parties by contract to "nullify a vital piece of federal legislation."[278]

The decision in *Volt* was a tacit acknowledgment by the Court that private dispute resolution is not always efficient, but the Court did not fully elucidate the reason that it would have been inefficient in the case at hand. If the arbitration had preceded the litigation, the contractors litigating with the university would have sought to employ arbitral findings adverse to the university (if announced) as issue preclusive in the later litigation, thereby claiming the benefit of the arbitration without exposing themselves to its hazards. It is uncertain whether such a preclusion would or should

---

[273] Calif Code Civ Pro § 1281.2(c).

[274] *Volt*, 489 US at 474.

[275] Id at 477.

[276] Id at 478.

[277] Id at 479.

[278] Id at 492. There is irony in this expression, given the Court's interpretation of FAA as an act allowing parties by contract to nullify many vital pieces of state legislation.

be allowed.[279] Hence some and perhaps all the issues arbitrated would be relitigated in court. On the other hand, if a court selected by the defendant university made findings adverse to it, it would be reasonable and likely that an arbitral forum would take the findings as preclusive in arbitration, thus eliminating the prospect of reconsideration of the issue. The FAA makes no provision for a stay of arbitration in such circumstances, in part no doubt because the law of issue preclusion is largely a post-1925 development.

The opinion in *Volt* was a step back from the full-throttle surge of the Court toward arbitration. It suggested the possibility that other state laws bearing on arbitration and not too directly at odds with the Court's policy favoring arbitration might be permitted to escape preemption, but, as we have seen in *Casarotto*, that was not to be. *Volt* remains, however, a potentially significant precedent in cases involving choice of law clauses. It calls attention to the ambiguity of simple choice of law provisions that fail to specify how much of the chosen jurisdiction's law is to be applied; a choice of law provision may, or may not, be taken to include the curial law of the jurisdiction, that is, the law governing the relations between courts and arbitral tribunals, or to include that jurisdiction's rules of arbitral practice and procedure.[280]

Volt was, however, later distinguished on grounds suggesting that its holding may have very narrow application. The Court in 1995 was confronted with a choice of law clause having the apparent purpose of evading the lash of otherwise applicable Illinois law. *Mastrobuono v Shearson Lehman Hutton, Inc.*[281] involved yet another printed brokerage agreement containing an arbitration clause and a clause designating the law of New York as controlling. Illinois investors sued their brokers, alleging mishandling of their account and claiming both compensatory and punitive damages. The brokers secured a stay pending arbitration pursuant to the FAA. When the arbitrator awarded compensatory and punitive damages, the brokers moved to vacate the punitive award as contrary to New York law. The brokers were successful in the lower federal courts, but the Supreme Court reversed.

---

[279] Macneil et al, *Federal Arbitration Law* at § 39.3. And see id § 39.5 (cited in note 63).

[280] Born, *International Commercial Arbitration* at 25–26, 161–81 (cited in note 163).

[281] 115 S Ct 1212 (1995).

The brokers and the lower courts relied on a New York decision holding that an arbitral tribunal cannot be empowered by contract to award punitive damages.[282] The New York holding rested on the premise that punishment is a role for the state alone, that a party cannot submit to private punishment nor by waiver diminish the power of the state of New York to impose it. It is thus the law of New York that while parties may bargain for private resolution of claims for compensation, their claims for punitive damages are not extinguished by the arbitration clause, but may be pursued separately in court, unless perhaps an award finding no liability might preclude a claim in court for punitive damages.[283] The brokers, however, sought to invoke the choice of law clause as a waiver of any right to punitive damages, a result that would have been at odds with the New York law they invoked.

The Court rightly perceived that the lower courts, although faithful to the Court's precedents, had produced an incorrect result. It surely ought not be that Illinois investors signing a printed brokerage agreement forfeit substantive rights conferred by Congress and the Illinois legislature to protect them from the misdeeds of the author of the contract simply because the agreement contains an obscure choice of law clause. The Court escaped this result by reading the choice of law clause as not embracing any limitations that New York might impose on the power of arbitrators.[284] It distinguished *Volt*, perhaps somewhat disingenuously, on the ground that in that case, the Court had deferred to an interpretation of California law by California courts. It must therefore be concluded that as things stand, choice of law clauses have little if any limiting effect on the jurisdiction of arbitral fora.

Not considered by the Court is the possibility that the New York law in question has been preempted by the FAA. Given *Southland*, *Perry*, and *Allied-Bruce Terminix*, it seems at best questionable whether New York can preclude arbitrators in cases af-

---

[282] *Garrity v Lyle Stuart, Inc.*, 40 NY2d 354, 353 NE2d 793, 386 NYS2d 831 (1976), followed in *Merrill Lynch Pierce Fenner & Smith, Inc. v Cornell*, 7 World Mediation & Arbitration Rep 76 (New York Supreme Court, Feb 14, 1996).

[283] *Dicenci v Lyndon Guaranty Bank of New York*, 807 F Supp 947, 953–54 (S D NY 1992) (severing and staying further arbitral proceedings on punitive damages); *Mulder v Donaldson, Lufkin & Jenrette*, 611 NYS2d 1019, 1021–22 (1994).

[284] *Mastrobuono*, 115 S Ct at 1217.

fecting commerce from deciding punitive damage claims.[285] The
Court circumnavigated preemption in *Volt* by finding that the California law at issue was not inconsistent with the FAA. Although
the preemption question appears to be unresolved in *Mastrobuono*,
it is not easy to see how the New York rule on punitive damages
can be reconciled with the sweeping effect the Court has imparted
to the FAA. This is unfortunate if New York had it right. Punishment is not consonant with the amiability that traditional commercial arbitration has sought to engender, and the administration of
punishment should be the outcome of a legal process in which the
procedural rights of the accused are amply protected, with appropriate review to assure that the punishment is proportional and
consistent with substantive law and with due process of law.[286]
These are not the conditions of commercial arbitration. On the
other hand, the New York rule would be very unjust if applied to
an arbitration conducted pursuant to a contract of adhesion having
the effect of requiring a consumer or employee to split his or claim
between arbitral and judicial tribunals.

JUDICIAL REVIEW OF AWARDS

    Among its very recent cases, the Court made one decision
that can be viewed by reductionists as anti-arbitration. In *First Options of Chicago, Inc. v Kaplan*,[287] the Court affirmed a court of appeals decision reversing the earlier decisions of an arbitrator and
of a district court determining that the Kaplans had agreed to submit the issue of arbitrability to the arbitrator. The facts require
attention. The Kaplans were trading options in the name of their
wholly owned corporation. When the account went in the red, a
workout was arranged. The broker, First Options, demanded that
the Kaplans personally pay the deficiency. When they failed to do
so, First Options demanded arbitration pursuant to the workout
agreement executed by the corporation. When the arbitrators met,
the Kaplans filed an objection to any consideration of their liability

---

[285] Holding that the New York law has been preempted is *Mulder v Donaldson, Lufkin &
Jenrette*, 1996 N Y App Div LEXIS 9920 (Oct 8, 1996).

[286] See *Honda Motor Corp. v Oberg*, 114 S Ct 639 (1994).

[287] 115 S Ct 1920 (1995).

on the ground that they had not personally signed the workout agreement containing the arbitration clause and that they had therefore conferred no jurisdiction on the arbitrators to decide even whether they had agreed to arbitrate. The arbitrators ruled against them and made an award favoring First Options. The district court confirmed the award.

In reversing, the Third Circuit asserted that the courts were obliged "independently [to] decide whether an arbitration panel has jurisdiction over the merits of any particular dispute."[288] Characterizing the ruling of the district court as one of law, it reviewed that holding *de novo*. The Supreme Court unanimously affirmed. For the Court, Justice Breyer acknowledged that parties might agree to submit even the arbitrability issue to an arbitral tribunal for decision. Whether they have done so in a particular instance, however, is an issue to be resolved according to state law governing the formation of contracts, which in this case "requires the court to see whether the parties objectively revealed an intent to submit the arbitrability issue to arbitration."[289] And the court "should not assume that the parties agreed to arbitrate arbitrability unless there is 'clear and unmistakable' evidence that they did so." The Court distinguished *Mitsubishi* and other cases indicating a presumption in favor of arbitration as cases involving the arbitration of the merits and not arbitration of the threshold issue as to whether the parties had made a contract to arbitrate. The Court also brushed aside the argument of First Options that by presenting their objections to the arbitrators the Kaplans had conferred authority on them to decide whether those objections were well-founded.[290]

The unanimity of the Court in *First Options* may indicate that the period of its intoxication with arbitration may be coming to an end. Plausible arguments were made for the contrary result, but persuaded no member of the Court. On the other hand, little can be made of this. In *Casarotto*, the case decided in its most recent term, the Court was almost equally unanimous in holding that Montana law on the procedure for forming an arbitration agreement was preempted.

---

[288] 19 F3d 1503, 1509 (3d Cir 1994).

[289] *First Options*, 115 S Ct at 1924.

[290] Id at 1924.

Perhaps of greater significance is the strength this decision may lend to the suggestion advanced above that the threshold issue of arbitrability may be treated by state law as fact-bound, and in some circumstances ripe for decision by a jury, something that the Kaplans did not demand. Presumably, a party denying the authority of its officer to agree to an arbitration clause would also be entitled to adjudicate the authority of the agent who ostensibly bound it to arbitrate a future dispute. By the same token, what is most troubling about the decision is the prolixity of the process approved. It is a pity that the jurisdictional issue could not have been resolved before the arbitral tribunal conducted a hearing and made a decision on merits that it had no authority to evaluate. A more orderly and efficient resolution would have resulted if arbitrability were resolved by the court in an action to enjoin the arbitration, as California state law and the state statute suggested above provides. In failing to pursue that course, the Kaplans got not one, but three forums repetitively to consider their objections.

The Court in *First Options* made it clear that its holding had no application to judicial review of the substantive merits of arbitral awards. As we have seen, the UN Convention explicitly allows a rigorous judicial review of foreign arbitral awards. It would not have been ratified by so many nations were it otherwise, for many have long traditions of reviewing awards for errors of law,[291] thus precluding use of arbitration to evade duties imposed by law that are independent of the duties created by the contract. But the FAA, in contrast, as we have also seen, makes no provision for review of the merits of an award.

While there have been occasional suggestions that an American award might be set aside for "manifest disregard of law," lower federal courts have almost uniformly eschewed any such power or responsibility.[292] One reason for this restraint is that commercial awards are seldom "speaking awards," that is, awards that are ac-

---

[291] Danish courts, for example, traditionally review arbitral awards for "clear and significant error"; this necessarily implies a requirement of speaking awards. Joseph M. Lookofsky, *Transnational Litigation and Commercial Arbitration: A Comparative Analysis of American, European and International Law* 622 (Tranational Juris Pub, 1992). For a case holding that a foreign award rendered in India is enforceable under the Convention even though it is still subject to pending judicial review on the merits in an Indian court, see *Fertilizer Corp. of India v IDI Management, Inc.*, 517 F Supp 948 (S D Ohio 1981).

[292] See cases cited in note 66; see also Macneil et al, *Federal Arbitration Law* at § 40.7 at 40:80–40:96 (cited in note 63).

companied with a reasoned explanation of the result. Effective review of the merits requires not only such a reasoned explanation, but also access to the proof on which the reasoned explanation rests. In short, review on the merits requires arbitration that conforms in some way with Federal Rules 43[293] and 52[294] requiring that a judge in deciding cases make findings of fact and state conclusions of law that are based on a record of the testimony and exhibits. Absent such requirements, review for manifest disregard of the law is merely a caution to the arbitral tribunal not overtly to thumb its nose at the controlling law.

In *Mitsubishi* and in *Vimar*, as we have seen, the Court sent American businessmen to Tokyo to arbitrate their disputed claims arising under American law, but promised them that their rights under American laws would be respected in the arbitration and that the lower federal courts would see that this was done. This was precisely what Justice Frankfurter had in mind doing with the Securities Act claim in *Wilko*.[295] Because this form of review is at odds with the text of Section 10 of the FAA, its use must rest on inferences from other federal statutes, COGSA in *Vimar* and the antitrust laws in *Mitsubishi*. If so, then the review of awards may not be available to state courts as a means of assuring fidelity of awards to such laws as the California Franchise Investment Law. On the other hand, if a state court should set aside an award for disregard of state law protecting consumers or employees who arbitrated pursuant to an adhesive arbitration clause, the Court would be forced in review to recognize the consequences of what it has done to the states' abilities to govern, and might recede from some of its excesses.

There is little experience with this form of litigation. The lower federal courts have been slow to scrutinize the fidelity of arbitrators to controlling law.[296] Illustrating the difficulties to be encountered is *PPG Industries, Inc. v Pilkington*.[297] A district court there compelled arbitration of an antitrust claim in London, but added that

[293] FRCP 43.

[294] FRCP 52.

[295] *Wilko*, 346 US at 440 (Frankfurter, J, dissenting).

[296] *Kotam Electronics, Inc.*, 93 F3d 724.

[297] 825 F Supp 1465 (D Ariz 1993).

the Court may, and certainly will, withdraw the reference to
arbitration if U.S. antitrust law does not govern the substantive
resolution of PPG's claims. In addition, the court directs that
any damages determination, or arbitral award, made by the arbitrators shall be determined according to U.S. antitrust law
irrespective of any conflict that may exist between those laws
and the laws of England. Finally, the court will retain jurisdiction over this matter in order to ensure that the arbitration
directed by this order is conducted in accordance with this
order.[298]

This appears to be precisely what the Court had in mind in *Mitsubishi* and *Vimar*, but the result is to transmogrify the arbitral process, making it a joint venture between the court and the arbitral
tribunal and requiring of the tribunal a formal record and a speaking award based on the record that justifies the award as an application of the Sherman Act. In other words, the district court has
implicitly imposed much of Rule 52 of the Federal Rules of Civil
Procedure on an English arbitration forum. While the court does
not in its order specify that it will review the arbitrators' legal analysis de novo, there is nothing in the opinion to suggest that the
"clear error" standard, much less the "manifest disregard" standard, will qualify the scrutiny given by the court to any award.
While this violence to Section 10 of the FAA can be explained as
a necessary implication of the antitrust laws and readily reconciled
with either clause of paragraph 2 of Article V of the UN Convention,[299] this is surely not a process that the authors and ratifiers of
that Convention intended to foster.

Thus, while Pilkington contended mightily for its right to arbitrate an antitrust claim in London, it seems probable that when
the day is done, counsel will wonder whether this was a useful
course. Perhaps they hoped to wear PPG down by thus prolonging
the resolution of the antitrust dispute. Perhaps their profit margin
is sufficiently high that any delay of proceedings is a net gain to
Pilkington, however much is spent to secure the delay. But except
for counsel motivated by one or the other of these unworthy motives, it would seem likely that most firms drafting similar agreements in the future will, if well advised, draft their arbitration
clauses narrowly to preclude arbitration of future claims arising

---

[298] Id at 1483.

[299] Quoted in text at note 162.

under the antitrust laws of the United States. Those who fail to do so may well find their otherwise arbitrable contracts disputes delayed and metastasized with marginal and spurious claims of federal right that the arbitral tribunal will be unable to resolve with finality but which will linger on as subjects of relitigation in court.

It is difficult to see that any identifiable public policy has been usefully served by this transformation. The movement for commercial arbitration, now attired in the name of the ADR movement, is not well served by an arbitration law that thus transposes the simple, efficient, expeditious, and civil process for resolving disputes between business associates into a complex, redundant, dilatory, and combative process for keeping commercial disputes in lawyers' offices for years. It is equally difficult to see what this does for international relations. True, the district court in *Pilkington* is intruding only in a private proceeding, not one conducted by Her Majesty's court, distinguishing it from those in which American courts have recoiled from exercising continuing jurisdiction over matters being litigated in foreign courts.[300] Still, the making of truly bargained contracts in the global economy is not likely to be encouraged by the sight of *Pilkington*. Those who benefit from the process the Court has created are those who have the expectation that they can wear their adversaries down in prolonged litigation or who are financially so favored by the law's delay that they can afford whatever its costs. Those who are harmed are American consumers, workers, patients, shippers, passengers, and franchisees whose rights are diminished by the added burden imposed on their assertion.

All that can be said for this procedure is that it is preferable to the alternative of allowing stronger parties to use arbitration clauses altogether to escape the lash of privately enforced laws designed to protect weaker parties to contracts from predation. Sadly, even this much protection of statutory rights is denied to weaker parties who would invoke rights under state statutes, all of which seem to have been preempted. As we noted, the *Pilkington* procedure is not thus far clearly open to state courts enforcing state law because it is derived by inference from the federal antitrust law, to which the Court's reconstructed FAA must make

---

[300] For example, *In re Union Carbide Corp. Gas Plant Disaster*, 809 F2d 195 (2d Cir 1987).

some concession. Indeed, it is not yet clear that the *Pilkington* procedure is available when the arbitration is conducted in an American rather than a foreign arbitral tribunal, although there is no apparent reason to distinguish between them.

CONCLUSION

As architecture, the arbitration law made by the Court is a shantytown. It fails to shelter those who most need shelter. And those it is intended to shelter are ill-housed. Under the law written by the Court, birds of prey will sup on workers, consumers, shippers, passengers, and franchisees; the protective police power of the federal government and especially of the state governments is weakened; and at least some and perhaps many commercial arbitrations will be made more costly while courts determine whether arbitrators have been faithful to certain federal laws.

Better law would rest firmly on recognition that arbitration and forum selection clauses *in contracts of adhesion* are sometimes a method for stripping people of their rights. Better law would distinguish cleanly those rights that cannot be impaired by that method and those that may be put at risk in order to secure the undoubted benefits of commercial arbitration. Better law would empower state governments to draw some of those lines for the purpose of assuring faithful execution of their privately enforced regulatory laws. Better law would observe the Restatement's requirements that contractual choices of forum and of law be fair and reasonable, applying that same standard to adhesive arbitration clauses designating remote or unreasonably expensive tribunals. Except where Congress or a treaty otherwise explicitly directs, better law would assure all international litigants in American courts of a level playing field, and provide all foreign awards with recognition equal to that given to domestic awards, but never more. Better law would not compel informal arbitration proceedings designed merely to resolve disputes to become formal quasi-judicial proceedings designed to be accountable for the enforcement of legal rights. Alas, there seems to be no possibility that the Court can rebuild the shantytown it has made into such a city on a hill. To extricate itself and the nation from the morass it has created, the Court would have to overrule *Moses Cone, Mitsubishi, Southland, Perry, Carnival Lines, Vimar, Terminix,* and *Casarotto,* and belatedly limit the holding in *Prima Paint*. If we are to have sound arbitration law, there is no place to look for it except in the halls of Congress.

Compassion and respect for the honored membership of the Court who have done their day's work dictate that humble authors having no responsibility except that of criticism ought be fully satisfied, having chastised the Court so meanly for its shortcomings as professional craftsmen. But we do not stop there, for there is a greater impropriety than mere negligent craftsmanship. What the Court has done was a trespass on the institutions of democratic government. Our city on the hill is not a mythic place, but the one that Congress planned. Had the Court in making commercial arbitration law been more faithful to the controlling legal texts, it would not have built the ugly habitation for which it alone is responsible.

A question the Court might have employed, but did not, was to ask itself whether the texts as it interpreted them could have been enacted. It seems clear to us that if the UN Convention had been presented to the Senate, or if the FAA had been presented to Congress, as legislation having the effects ascribed to them by the Court, neither would have been assured of a single vote of approval. It is hard to imagine any officer accountable to an electorate who would openly avow the purpose of enabling those with economic power to diminish the enforceability of rights conferred by Congress and state legislatures on consumers, patients, employees, investors, shippers, passengers, franchisees, and shopkeepers. Nor would any officer of the United States or any state government admit having deliberately enacted law favoring foreigners in their disputes with Americans. But the Court forgot its duty to interpret legislation as legislators and the people would have it interpreted, and conformed the texts to the elitist sentiments of its members. That has been a more serious mischief than making bad law.[301]

---

[301] See generally William N. Eskridge, *Dynamic Statutory Interpretation* (Harvard, 1994); Francis Lieber, *Legal and Political Hermeneutics; or, Principles of Interpretation and Construction in Law and Politics* (1837; 2d ed, Little Brown, 1838, F. H. Thomas, 3d ed 1880; republished in 16 Cardozo L Rev 1883 (1995)).

ARTHUR D. HELLMAN

THE SHRUNKEN DOCKET OF THE REHNQUIST COURT

From 1971 through 1988, the United States Supreme Court was hearing and deciding an average of 147 cases each Term.[1] There were only three Terms during that period in which the number fell below 140. "One hundred fifty cases per year" came to be regarded both as a maximum and a norm for the plenary docket.[2]

In the 1989 Term, the number of plenary decisions dropped to 132. That alone would not necessarily have signaled any change. But in 1990 the number dropped still further, to 116. Thereafter, with one trivial exception, the plenary docket continued to shrink. The 1995 Term, which came to an end in July 1996, yielded only 77 plenary decisions—half the number that the Court was handing down a decade earlier.[3]

A 50% decline in the decisional output of the nation's highest court would be remarkable under any circumstances. It is even more so when considered against the background of two other developments. One is the volume of cases brought to the Court for

Arthur D. Hellman is Professor of Law at the University of Pittsburgh.

AUTHOR'S NOTE: Thanks to Michiel Kohne for helpful comments on an earlier draft. Ira S. Nathenson provided speedy, reliable research assistance.

[1] For discussion of the plenary docket before 1971, see Arthur D. Hellman, *The Business of the Supreme Court Under the Judiciary Act of 1925: The Plenary Docket in the 1970's*, 91 Harv L Rev 1709 (1978).

[2] See Peter L. Strauss, *One Hundred Fifty Cases Per Year: Some Implications of the Supreme Court's Limited Resources for Judicial Review of Agency Action*, 87 Colum L Rev 1093 (1987).

[3] The plenary docket comprises all cases that receive full briefing and oral argument, including the handful that are dismissed or disposed of by per curiam opinions after argument. The numbers used here are thus slightly larger than those found in analyses that count only signed opinions.

review. In the 1971 Term, the number of new filings was 3,643. In the 1995 Term, the number was 6,595.[4] Thus, during the period when the Court was cutting its decisional output in half, the input came close to doubling.

Even more dramatic is the increase in the work of the federal courts of appeals, the principal source of the Supreme Court's docket. In the 1970s, when the Supreme Court was giving plenary consideration to 150 cases a Term, the courts of appeals were deciding about 10,000 cases on the merits annually. Today the number of merits decisions by the courts of appeals exceeds 25,000 each year.[5]

How can we explain the Supreme Court's shrunken docket? One possible source of enlightenment is the Justices themselves. From time to time, members of the Court have offered their views about why the Court is taking so few cases. Justice David H. Souter has been particularly voluble in suggesting hypotheses; Chief Justice William H. Rehnquist and Justice Anthony M. Kennedy have also offered theories to explain the Court's diminished level of activity.

Experience has shown, however, that the Justices do not always have an accurate picture of the Court's practices.[6] Nor can we rely on the impressions or speculations of those who watch the Court from the outside. If we want to know why the docket has shrunk so drastically, we must identify the changes that have taken place in the cases selected for plenary review and analyze them in a systematic fashion.

That is the approach taken in this article.[7] Specifically, I shall compare the composition of the plenary docket during the three most recent Terms (1993 through 1995) with the docket 10 years earlier, during the height of the 150-case era.[8] Using these data,

---

[4] These figures are taken from the statistical reports issued by the Court at the end of each Term. The reports are reproduced in United States Law Week (BNA).

[5] Statistical information about the work of the courts of appeals can be found in the annual reports of the Director of the Administrative Office of United States Courts. Each year, Table B-1 gives detailed figures on dispositions.

[6] See Arthur D. Hellman, *Conference on Empirical Research in Judicial Administration, Foreword: Exploring the Mysteries of the Least Known Branch*, 21 Ariz St L J 33, 34 (1989).

[7] Unless otherwise indicated, all data on the Court's work are based on my own analysis of the cases.

[8] Each Term, a few cases are dismissed or remanded after the grant of review but before oral argument. Generally this occurs because the parties have settled or the case has become

I shall test five hypotheses that have achieved special prominence, either because they have been cited frequently by outside observers or because they have been endorsed by one or more Justices. They are:

>1. The virtual elimination of the Supreme Court's mandatory appellate jurisdiction allows the Court to deny review in some cases that would have received plenary consideration under the pre-1988 regime.
>2. After the retirement of its three most liberal Justices, the Court took fewer cases in which lower courts had upheld convictions or rejected civil rights claims.
>3. Twelve years of Reagan-Bush judicial appointments brought greater homogeneity to the courts of appeals, resulting in fewer intercircuit conflicts that the Supreme Court had to resolve.
>4. The Federal Government was losing fewer cases in the lower courts and therefore filed fewer applications for review in the Supreme Court.
>5. The 12 years of Reagan-Bush appointments made the courts of appeals more conservative, resulting in fewer "activist" decisions of the kind that a conservative Supreme Court would choose to review.

As will be seen, none of these theories fully explain why the Court is accepting only half as many cases for review as it did a decade ago. But they do offer clues. And a comprehensive analysis of the plenary docket of today, compared with that of the 1983–85 period, suggests that while external developments have played a part, the principal agent of change has been internal—a shift in the Supreme Court's own view of its role in the American legal system.

I. THE BUSINESS OF THE SUPREME COURT

The Supreme Court exercises two kinds of jurisdiction: original and appellate. Cases within the original jurisdiction generally involve disputes between states. The decisions are sui generis, with little connection to the rest of the docket. They are few in

---

moot. The number of cases that washed out before argument was about the same in each of the two periods of the study—13 in 1983–85 and 11 in 1993–95. These cases will not be considered further here.

number; in an entire decade, they accounted for only 13 plenary opinions. The analysis here will therefore be limited to the Court's exercise of its appellate jurisdiction.[9]

In the three Terms 1983 through 1985, the Supreme Court handed down a total of 457 plenary appellate decisions. In the three most recent Terms, the total was 249. Thus, in the course of a decade that brought increased judicial business everywhere, the Supreme Court reduced the number of cases it was hearing from an average of 152 per Term to an average of 83.[10]

To understand the Court's behavior, it is useful to divide the appellate docket into two broad segments.[11] The first segment encompasses cases that adjudicate the limits of governmental powers. Included here are cases involving the Bill of Rights and the Fourteenth Amendment as well as the division of powers between state and national governments and the separation of powers within the Federal Government. The issues may be substantive—that is, can a particular unit of government act in a particular way?—or they may involve remedies or procedural questions such as the choice of forum.

All other issues of federal law fall within the second segment. This portion of the docket encompasses issues of antitrust law, admiralty, copyright, ERISA, employment discrimination, and other federal "specialties." Also included are issues of procedure and jurisdiction, both civil and criminal, that do not turn on constitutional interpretation or the resolution of conflicts between federal and state law. For convenience, I shall refer to this as the "statutory" segment of the docket.

In the 1983–85 period, cases involving issues of governmental powers totaled 291, accounting for just under two-thirds of the Court's plenary decisions. A decade later, there were only 139 such cases, a drop of more than 100%. Meanwhile, the statutory seg-

---

[9] For a comprehensive account of the Court's handling of its original jurisdiction, see Vincent L. McCusick, *Discretionary Gatekeeping: The Supreme Court's Management of Its Original Jurisdiction Docket Since 1961*, 45 Me L Rev 185 (1993).

[10] Here and throughout this article, two or more cases decided by a single opinion or order are treated as one "case" or "decision."

[11] Prior research has shown that the Court applies significantly different criteria in selecting cases for the two segments of the docket described in the text. See Arthur D. Hellman, *Case Selection in the Burger Court: A Preliminary Inquiry*, 60 Notre Dame L Rev 947 (1985).

ment of the docket also shrank, but on a much more modest scale—from 166 cases to 110.

Before turning to the various theories that have been offered to explain these developments, it will be helpful to provide a more detailed framework for analyzing the two broad segments of the docket. For the governmental powers cases, I begin with three objectively defined variables: the court of origin (state or federal), the level of government whose power is being challenged (state or federal), and whether the court below ruled for or against the challenger's claim. Building upon these variables, we can divide the cases into six categories, each of which reflects a different facet of the Court's role as arbiter of the limits of governmental power in the American political system. These in turn can be grouped into "activist" and "counteractivist" grants of review.

Activist *decisions* are those that expand judicial power over other branches of the national government or over state governments.[12] From the perspective of the Supreme Court, an activist *grant* is one that fosters activism by accepting review of a decision that rejected a constitutional or Supremacy Clause claim. Activist grants encompass three familiar categories of cases:

> **Supremacy**: state-court cases in which the state court rejected a challenge based on federal law to an assertion of power under state law.
> **Checking**: federal-court cases in which the federal court rejected a constitutional challenge to an exercise of power by the Federal Government.
> **Vindication**: federal-court cases in which the federal court upheld an exercise of state power and rejected a federal claim or defense.

A counteractivist grant is one that accepts review of an activist decision by the court below. Counteractivist grants can be of three kinds, each corresponding to one of the categories of activist grants, but with a contrary result in the court below:

> **Overreading**: state-court cases in which the state court ruled in favor of a federal claim or defense and in opposition to an exercise of state power.[13]

---

[12] See Richard A. Posner, *The Federal Courts: Crisis and Reform* 208–11 (Harvard University Press, 1985).

[13] See Preble Stolz, *Federal Review of State Court Decisions of Federal Questions: The Need for Additional Appellate Capacity*, 64 Cal L Rev 943, 971 (1976): "Occasionally a state court will over-read Supreme Court precedents and invalidate state statutes or official action on federal grounds when the Supreme Court itself would not do so."

Restraint: federal-court cases in which the federal court ruled in favor of a constitutional challenge to federal official action.[14]

"Our Federalism": federal-court cases in which the federal court ruled in favor of a federal claim or defense and in opposition to an exercise of state power.[15]

For the statutory segment of the docket, two variables come into play: the nature of the litigation and the identity of the party bringing the case to the Court. These variables give us five categories of cases:

Government: The United States Government (generally represented by the Solicitor General) is the petitioner.

Individual: Review was sought by an individual or entity with the United States as respondent.

Defendant: Review was sought by the defendant in a private civil suit, and the legal rule in question would favor either plaintiffs or defendants as a class. Areas of law in which such issues predominate include antitrust, employment discrimination, securities regulation, and maritime personal injury.

Plaintiff: Review was sought by the plaintiff in a private civil suit, and the legal rule in question would favor either plaintiffs or defendants as a class.

Other: Any case not falling within any of the preceding categories.

Of course, there are other ways of classifying the Court's cases. But these are best considered in the course of testing the various theories.

II. REPEAL OF THE MANDATORY JURISDICTION

Until 1988, certain kinds of cases could be brought to the Court by appeal rather than by certiorari. If a case came to the

---

[14] See *United States v Butler*, 297 US 1, 78–79 (1936) (Stone dissenting): "[W]hile unconstitutional exercise of power by the executive and legislative branches of the government is subject to judicial restraint, the only check upon our own exercise of power is our own sense of self-restraint." In theory, both "checking" and "restraint" cases could come from state courts, but there were no such grants during either of the two periods studied. Nor is this surprising. Suits challenging federal official action, if brought in state courts, would almost invariably be removed to federal court.

[15] See *Younger v Harris*, 401 US 37, 44 (1971).

Court on appeal, the Court had no choice but to decide it on the merits. The decision would then become a binding precedent for all lower courts.[16] To be sure, the Court did not have to accord plenary consideration to an appeal case; it could summarily affirm the decision below.[17] But, as the Justices themselves explained in a letter urging Congress to eliminate the mandatory jurisdiction, "there is no correlation between the difficulty of the legal issues presented in a case and the importance of the issue to the general public."[18] Thus, in order to avoid summary affirmance of a judgment that might be in error, the Court often felt obliged to call for full briefing and oral argument in appeal cases that did not raise issues of broad significance.

In 1988, Congress responded to the Justices' pleas and eliminated virtually all of the remaining elements of the mandatory jurisdiction. Two members of the Court, as well as outside observers, have suggested that this change is responsible for at least part of the shrinkage of the docket in the 1990s. For example, Justice Anthony M. Kennedy commented at the House appropriations hearings in 1996, "We had mandatory jurisdiction over cases that were unimportant. We calculated that there were 35 to 40 of these a year. We told the Congress, please take those cases away from us, and the Congress did. And in part what you see after 1988 is a drop which we projected . . . ."[19]

To test this hypothesis, it is necessary to look separately at the three classes of cases that fell within the mandatory jurisdiction before 1988 but not after.[20] Not coincidentally, each constitutes

---

[16] See *Hicks v Miranda*, 422 US 332, 343–44 (1975).

[17] In cases from state courts, the Court could dismiss "for want of a substantial federal question." This form of disposition was tantamount to affirmance. See Arthur D. Hellman, *Error Correction, Lawmaking, and the Supreme Court's Exercise of Discretionary Review*, 44 U Pitt L Rev 795, 812–20 (1983).

[18] See HR Rep No 660, 100th Cong, 2d Sess 27 (1988) (letter signed by all nine sitting Justices), reprinted in 1988 USSCAN 766, 781.

[19] The record of the 1996 appropriations hearings has not been published. Here and elsewhere in this article, I have used a transcript based on the C-Span broadcast. Minor infelicities of expression have been silently corrected.

[20] The 1988 legislation made no change in the law providing for a direct appeal in cases required to be heard by a three-judge district court. The latter category is confined primarily to reapportionment and Voting Rights Act cases. Appeals from three-judge courts have been excluded from the analysis in the text.

a subclass of one of the categories of governmental powers cases identified earlier:

> **supremacy** cases in which a state court upheld a state statute challenged as "repugnant to the Constitution, treaties, or laws of the United States" (former §1257(2)).
>
> **restraint** cases in which a federal court, in a civil case, held a federal statute unconstitutional (former §1252).
>
> **"Our Federalism"** cases in which a federal court of appeals held a state statute unconstitutional (former §1254(2)).

The three broad categories of cases—supremacy, restraint, and "Our Federalism"—all dropped off sharply from the 1980s to the 1990s. To that extent, the data are consistent with the hypothesis that the 1988 legislation was responsible, at least in part. More detailed analysis, however, casts doubt on this explanation. As shown in Table 1, the appeal cases in the 1983–85 period were limited (with a single exception) to civil suits.[21] If the elimination of the mandatory jurisdiction were one of the causes of the shrinkage in the three categories of cases, we would expect the decreased level of activity to be more pronounced on the civil side than in criminal prosecutions. In fact, civil and criminal cases diminished to approximately the same degree. Indeed, the sharpest decline came in criminal (i.e., habeas corpus) cases in the federal courts of appeals—a subcategory that was barely affected by the mandatory jurisdiction repeal.

Other evidence casts further doubt on the "mandatory jurisdiction repeal" hypothesis. In a lecture delivered a few months after the enactment of the 1988 legislation, Justice Antonin Scalia called attention to the fact that "a high proportion of [the Court's] Commerce Clause cases . . . involved appeals rather than petitions for certiorari."[22] He ventured a "guess (or perhaps it is just my hope)" that the Court's Commerce Clause jurisprudence "will be considerably less extensive" in the future, "when these cases can be avoided without determining that there is no substantial federal question involved."[23]

---

[21] For purposes of this analysis, habeas corpus cases in the federal courts, which technically are civil suits, are treated as part of the criminal docket.

[22] Antonin Scalia, *The Rule of Law as a Law of Rules*, 56 U Chi L Rev 1175, 1185–86 (1989).

[23] Id at 1186.

TABLE 1

Effect of Mandatory Jurisdiction Repeal

	Civil Cases				Criminal and Habeas Cases			
	1983–1985			1993–1995	1983–1985			1993–1995
	Appeal*	Certiorari	Total	Total	Appeal	Certiorari	Total	Total
Supremacy	30	12	42	26	0	20	20	10
"Our Federalism" (courts of appeals)	26	48	74	13	1	30	31	2
Restraint	18	12	30	12	0	15	15	5

* Excludes three-judge court cases.

Thus far it does not appear that Justice Scalia's prediction has proved accurate. In the 1983–85 Terms, the Court heard five Commerce Clause cases from state courts. All came up by appeal. In the 1993–95 Terms, with state-court appeals relegated to the history books, the number of Commerce Clause cases was seven, not including one decision on the retroactivity of a Commerce Clause ruling. The picture is essentially the same if we compare the 1981–85 Terms with the 1991–95 Terms.[24] In short, with the elimination of the appeal jurisdiction, the Supreme Court's Commerce Clause jurisprudence has become more, not less, extensive.

It is always difficult to prove a negative. We have no way of knowing whether, among the denials of certiorari in the 1993–95 Terms, there were cases which, if they had come up by appeal, would have received plenary consideration. But, on the available evidence, I conclude that the elimination of the mandatory jurisdiction played no more than a minuscule role in the shrinkage of the plenary docket in the 1990s.

III. Retirement of the Liberal Justices

Between the mid-1980s and the mid-1990s, the composition of the Supreme Court changed substantially. In particular, the three stalwarts of the liberal wing of the Burger Court—Justices William J. Brennan, Thurgood Marshall, and Harry A. Blackmun—all retired within a period of four years. Some observers have seen a connection between their departure and the shrinkage of the plenary docket. For example, one commentator, summarizing "reasons [that have been offered] for the slowdown," has suggested that "the Court has no active liberal faction inclined to reach out to take on new issues. When [the three liberal Justices] sat together, they frequently provided three of the four votes necessary to accept cases, and they often agreed to hear claims of civil rights or civil liberties that had been rejected by lower courts."[25]

---

[24] In the 1981–85 Terms, the Court heard eight Commerce Clause cases from state courts, all but one of which came to it by appeal. In the 1991–95 Terms, the number was 11, all of which were certiorari cases.

[25] David B. Savage, *Docket Reflects Ideological Shifts: Shrinking Caseload, Cert Denials Suggest an Unfolding Agenda*, ABA J, Dec 1995, at 40. See also Glen Elsasser, *High Court Chooses Not to Decide; Justices Examine Lowest Number of Cases Since 1960s*, Chicago Tribune (July 3, 1994), News Section, at 7 (available on NEXIS, NEWS library) (quoting Professor Lawrence Marshall): "If Brennan and Marshall would see an unfair conviction or an unfair

TABLE 2

"Liberal" Grants on the Plenary Docket, 1983–85 and 1993–95 Terms

Category	Review Sought By	1983–85	1993–95
Supremacy	Criminal defendant	18	10
Checking	Criminal defendant	7	10
Vindication	Habeas petitioner	6	10
Vindication	Section 1983 plaintiff	16	9
Total	....	47	39

If this hypothesis is correct, the effects would be felt in four categories of cases, each a subclass of one of the categories of activist grants. They are:

> **supremacy** cases in which the state court rejected the federal claims of a state criminal defendant;
> **checking** cases in which the federal court rejected the constitutional claims of a federal criminal defendant;
> **vindication** cases in which the federal court ruled against a state criminal defendant seeking habeas corpus; and
> **vindication** cases in which the federal court ruled against a plaintiff in a civil rights suit under section 1983.[26]

Table 2 presents the data on these four subclasses. As can be seen, the Court did accept fewer petitions from state criminal defendants and from civil rights plaintiffs in the 1990s than it did in the 1980s. But the number of grants in the other two subcategories actually increased.

In any event, the more telling figure is the total number of "liberal" grants in the 1983–85 Terms. That number is so small—little more than 10% of the plenary appellate docket—that any decline could not possibly have played a major role in the reduction in the overall level of plenary activity. We must therefore look elsewhere for the explanation.

---

denial of a claim in a civil rights context, they would be moved to take the case even if it didn't quite meet the [Court's] general criteria for granting review."

[26] This category is considerably more problematic than the others. Should a case be characterized as a "liberal" grant when the section 1983 plaintiff is a white male challenging an affirmative action program? When the plaintiff is a corporation arguing that state regulation has been preempted by federal law? To maximize objectivity, the figures in Table 2 include all cases brought to the Court by losing litigants in section 1983 cases, irrespective of whether their claims might appeal to "liberal" Justices. In view of the conclusions stated in the text, it is not necessary to fine-tune the category further.

IV. INTERCIRCUIT CONFLICTS AND THE PLENARY DOCKET

One of the principal functions of the Supreme Court is to resolve conflicts between federal judicial circuits.[27] In remarks at the House appropriations hearing, Justice David H. Souter suggested that one reason the Court was taking fewer cases is that the incidence of intercircuit conflicts had declined. As Justice Souter explained, 12 years of appointments by Presidents Reagan and Bush "resulted in a greater degree of [philosophical] homogeneity in the courts of appeals than you're likely to find in many judicial epochs."[28] That homogeneity meant that there were "fewer conflicts in the courts of appeals than historically" has been the case. The result was a shrinkage in the plenary docket.[29]

On its face, Justice Souter's hypothesis is not a particularly plausible one. To begin with, it is rather surprising to find Justice Souter taking for granted the "philosophical homogeneity" of the Reagan-Bush appointees. Justice Souter himself was appointed by President Bush; so was Justice Clarence Thomas. Does Justice Souter really view Justice Thomas as his philosophical soulmate? It seems unlikely.[30]

But even if we accept Justice Souter's initial assumption, the connection between philosophical homogeneity—or the lack of it—and intercircuit conflicts is attenuated at best. Differences in philosophy play out primarily in cases involving governmental powers. Intercircuit conflicts are typically generated by issues of statutory construction. Many of these are narrow or technical; of all cases, they are the least likely to divide judges along ideological lines.[31]

There is a further difficulty. Justice Souter seems to assume that

---

[27] See Arthur D. Hellman, *By Precedent Unbound: The Nature and Extent of Unresolved Intercircuit Conflicts*, 56 U Pitt L Rev 693, 698–701 (1995).

[28] See note 19.

[29] Justice Souter offered the same hypothesis, in almost the same language, one year earlier in remarks at the Third Circuit Judicial Conference. See Shannon P. Duffy, *Inside the Highest Court: Souter Describes Justices' Relationship, Caseload Trend*, Pa L Weekly (Apr 17, 1995), at 11 (available on NEXIS, NEWS library).

[30] In fact, Justice Souter has disagreed with Justice Thomas more often than he has disagreed with any other member of the current Court. See *The Supreme Court, 1994 Term: Statistics*, 109 Harv L Rev 111, 351 (1995).

[31] See Arthur D. Hellman, *The Proposed Intercircuit Tribunal: Do We Need It? Will It Work?* 11 Hastings Const L Q 375, 431 (1984).

conflicts are created when panels in two or more circuits address the same issue at roughly the same time. That is one pattern, but it not the only one. A more likely scenario (especially if we accept Justice Souter's initial premises) is that a panel in the 1990s, dominated by Reagan-Bush appointees, would reject a decision rendered by another circuit during the era of domination by liberal appointees of President Jimmy Carter.

Notwithstanding these considerations, it would be just as wrong to reject the "homogeneity" hypothesis on the basis of speculation as it would be to accept it on that basis. Rather, we must subject the theory to empirical scrutiny. To do so, I analyzed the cases in which the Supreme Court reviewed decisions of the federal courts of appeals. Cases were classified as "conflict grants" if they met any of the following criteria:[32]

> The Supreme Court stated that it granted review to resolve an intercircuit conflict.
> The Court's opinion, although not specifying conflict as the reason for granting review, pointed clearly to the existence of an intercircuit disagreement.
> The conflict was explicitly acknowledged by one or more courts of appeals in a case that was brought to the Court's attention before review was granted.[33]

Table 3 presents data on the court of appeals cases that received plenary consideration during each of the two study periods (1983–85 and 1993–95). In the governmental powers segment of the docket, the data lend some support to Justice Souter's hypothesis: cases presenting intercircuit conflicts did decline in number between the 1980s and the 1990s. But the diminution in conflict

---

[32] The term "conflict grant" is to some degree a shorthand, and it should not be misunderstood. We can be quite confident that some of the cases in this group would have received the four votes necessary for plenary review even in the absence of a contrary ruling by another circuit. But ordinarily we have no way of knowing which they are. Rather than speculate about the Justices' thinking, I have relied on the objective criteria set forth in the text. Of course, if there is affirmative evidence of the Court's reasons for accepting a case, I do take that into account.

[33] Whether a "conflict" has been "explicitly acknowledged" is not always beyond dispute. I emphasize, therefore, that a substantial majority of the "conflict grants" were classified as such on the basis of characterization by the Supreme Court. Among those that were based solely on acknowledgment by a lower court, there were only a handful in which the court did not reject another circuit's precedent in clear and unmistakable language. For a discussion focusing on conflict cases the Court did not review, see Hellman, 56 U Pitt L Rev 693 (cited in note 27).

TABLE 3

FEDERAL COURT OF APPEALS CASES ON THE PLENARY DOCKET,
1983–85 AND 1993–95 TERMS

CATEGORY	1983–85			1993–95		
	Conflict	Other	Total	Conflict	Other	Total
Checking	9	3	12	10	6	16
Vindication	13	15	28	12	13	25
Restraint	14	15	29	9	8	17
"Our Federalism"	32	73	105	14	11	25
Total governmental powers	68	106	174	45	38	83
Government	39	34	73	18	9	27
Individual	19	9	28	24	4	28
Defendant	13	16	29	13	2	15
Plaintiff	4	6	10	11	2	13
Other	8	17	25	21	5	26
Total statutory	83	82	165	87	22	109
Total court of appeals cases	151	188	339	132	60	192

grants is modest compared with the shrinkage in cases that did not involve intercircuit conflicts. Indeed, the single most substantial reduction came in "Our Federalism" cases that did not present conflicts—from 73 in the earlier period to only 11 in the more recent.

In the statutory segment of the docket, the data squarely contradict Justice Souter's theory. The number of conflict grants actually increased, albeit only by four cases. Meanwhile, the number of plenary decisions that did not involve conflicts declined quite substantially, from an average of more than 25 per Term to an average of fewer than eight per Term.

It is important to note the limits of these data. They do not tell us whether intercircuit conflicts became more or less numerous in the 1990s than they were in the 1980s. Nor do they enable us to draw any conclusions about homogeneity (or the lack of it) in the courts of appeals. What the data do tell us is that the Supreme Court is taking somewhat fewer conflict cases than it did in the 1980s, but that the reduction in conflict grants accounts for only a small part of the overall shrinkage in the plenary docket. Thus, in seeking an explanation for the diminished level of plenary activity, we must investigate other aspects of the case selection process.

V. THE GOVERNMENT AS PETITIONER

Historically, the United States Government, represented by the Solicitor General, has been the most frequent litigator in the United States Supreme Court. At the certiorari stage, the Government generally appears as respondent or appellee, arguing that the decision below is correct and does not warrant further review. Our interest, however, lies in the cases that the Government brings to the Court as petitioner or appellant. When the Government seeks review of an adverse ruling, its applications are granted at a rate that generally exceeds 60% and sometimes is substantially higher.[34] Some commentators have suggested that one reason for the shrinkage in the plenary docket is that the Government has been losing fewer cases in the courts of appeals and therefore filing fewer applications for review in the Supreme Court.

The data provide some support for this theory. In the 1983–85 Terms, the plenary docket included 123 cases in which the certiorari petition or jurisdictional statement was filed by the Federal Government. A decade later, Federal Government cases numbered only 46. That represents a shrinkage of nearly two-thirds. And it accounts for nearly 40% of the overall reduction in the level of plenary activity. But counting the number of Federal Government cases granted is only the first step in the analysis. Ultimately, we would like to know: why did the numbers fall so dramatically?

One possibility, of course, is that the Government continued to file petitions at the same rate, but the Court applied a more rigorous standard in determining whether to grant them. To test this hypothesis, I identified all cases in both periods in which the Government petitioned for review without success.[35] I discovered that

---

[34] See Eric Schnapper, *Becket at the Bar—the Conflicting Obligations of the Solicitor General*, 21 Loyola LA L Rev 1187, 1211–13 & n 68 (1988). A principal reason for the Government's success is that the Solicitor General carefully screens the cases in which the Government has lost in the court below. Further, "in selecting the cases in which review will be sought, [he] generally attempts to apply the same standards which the Court itself utilizes in passing on petitions." Id at 1213.

[35] The cases in the most recent period were identified by perusing the "Subject Matter Summary of Cases Recently Filed" in volumes 62 through 64 of United States Law Week (BNA). Unsuccessful Federal Government petitions in the 1983–85 Terms were identified through perusal of volumes 52 through 54.

in all three of the most recent Terms there were only 28 Government cases in which review was denied.[36] Even if every one had been accepted, the total number of Federal Government cases on the plenary docket would still be far below what it was a decade ago. Further, the number of denials in the 1993–95 Terms was about the same as it was in the 1983–85 period.

The evidence thus rules out the hypothesis that the shrinkage in Government cases came about because the Supreme Court tightened the standard that it was applying to the Government's petitions. Rather, the Government cut back sharply on the number of cases it has been bringing to the Court. But why? Is it because the Government has been losing fewer cases in the courts of appeals? Because the Solicitor General has been seeking review in fewer of the cases that the Government has lost? Or does the answer lie in some combination of these circumstances?

It might seem unlikely that the Solicitor General would cut down on the number of cases he was taking to the Supreme Court if the courts of appeals were continuing to hand down adverse rulings at the same rate as in the past. However, at a recent hearing of the Senate Judiciary Committee, witnesses and committee members raised questions about the zeal of Drew Days, whose tenure as Solicitor General coincided almost exactly with the three most recent Terms of the Supreme Court. In particular, the senators suggested that General Days "declined to press for rehearing in criminal cases . . . in which the government had lost."[37]

Unfortunately, there are no published data on the Federal Government's win-loss rate in the courts of appeals. Thus, it is impossible to determine whether the Government was losing fewer cases in the 1990s than it was in the 1980s—let alone whether there were fewer cases that might have warranted an additional level of review. In any event, two facts are clear. The reduction in the number of petitions filed by the Solicitor General does account for a substantial part of the shrinkage of the plenary docket in the 1990s. But the decline in cases heard at the behest of other classes

---

[36] Some of these were protective petitions that were denied review after the Court rejected the Government's position in a case that did receive plenary consideration. See generally Arthur D. Hellman, *The Supreme Court's Second Thoughts: Remands for Reconsideration and Denials of Review in Cases Held for Plenary Decisions*, 11 Hastings Const L Q 5 (1983).

[37] Eva M. Rodriguez, *Senators Train Sights on Solicitor General*, Legal Times of Washington (Nov 20, 1995), at 19 (available on NEXIS, NEWS library).

of litigants was even greater. Thus, the mystery of the shrunken docket is far from solved.

VI. CONSERVATISM IN THE LOWER COURTS

Between 1980 and 1992, Presidents Ronald Reagan and George Bush appointed 115 judges to the federal courts of appeals.[38] By 1992, the Reagan-Bush appointees accounted for more than 60% of the circuit judges in active service.[39] Nominees of the two Republican Presidents constituted a majority of the active judges in all 13 federal judicial circuits.[40]

The Reagan-Bush judges are generally regarded as "conservative" in their judicial philosophies. The Supreme Court, too, is widely viewed as having shifted to "the right." Some commentators believe that this convergence goes far toward explaining the shrinkage of the plenary docket in the 1990s. The essence of the theory is that, by the late 1980s, the courts of appeals were handing down fewer of the liberal activist decisions that a conservative Supreme Court would see as worthy of review.

The assumptions underlying this theory are themselves open to debate,[41] but for present purposes I will not question them. Rather, I will attempt to determine whether the theory provides a valid explanation for the trimmed-down plenary docket of the 1990s. To do so, I will focus on three categories of cases, each a subset of one of the categories of counteractivist grants identified earlier. If the theory is correct, we would expect to find a sharp decline in each of these subsets. They are:

> **restraint** cases in which a federal court of appeals ruled favorably to the constitutional claim of a federal criminal defendant;
> **"Our Federalism"** cases in which a federal court of appeals

---

[38] Sheldon Goldman, *Bush's Judicial Legacy: The Final Imprint*, 76 Judicature 282, 293 (1993) (Table 4). President Reagan appointed 78 judges; President Bush, 37.

[39] Id at 295 (Table 6).

[40] In the largest circuit, the Ninth, the majority was very thin. Further, the "limited en banc" used in the Ninth Circuit meant that the majority did not necessarily control the law of the circuit even when cases were heard en banc. See Arthur D. Hellman, *Dividing the Ninth Circuit: An Idea Whose Time Has Not Yet Come*, 57 Mont L Rev 261, 281 (1996).

[41] For some confirmatory data, see Robert A. Carp et al, *The Voting Behavior of Judges Appointed by President Bush*, 76 Judicature 298 (1993).

ruled in favor of a state criminal defendant challenging his conviction or sentence through federal habeas corpus;

"Our Federalism" cases in which a federal court of appeals ruled in favor of an individual or entity pursuing a civil rights claim under 42 USC 1983.

Table 4 presents data on these categories during the two periods of the study. For purposes of comparison, data are also given on two other classes of cases that are in some respects analogous: "Our Federalism" grants other than those arising under the habeas corpus statute or section 1983, and cases in which a *state* court ruled favorably to the constitutional claim of a state criminal defendant.

In all three of the grant categories that we might view as reacting to liberal outcomes in the courts of appeals, the data support the theory: the number of plenary cases declined sharply from the 1980s to the 1990s. Of particular note, habeas corpus cases brought to the Court by state prosecutors dropped from 31 in the 1983–85 Terms to only two in 1993–95. But there was also a reduction in "Our Federalism" cases that did not arise under the habeas corpus statute or section 1983. While some of these cases reflected lower-court activism that produced liberal outcomes, others involved issues—such as federal preemption of state law— where activism generally serves ends that would be regarded as "conservative."

The more telling datum, however, is that in the 1990s the Court also cut back on its grants of review of liberal criminal-law decisions from *state* courts. State courts, of course, would not have been affected by the Reagan-Bush appointments.

These data do not refute the "conservative judges" thesis, but they do suggest caution in embracing it. In particular, the fact that the same patterns can be seen in state-court cases as in the corresponding group of cases from federal courts raises the possibility that the crucial change took place not at the court of appeals level but in the behavior of the Supreme Court.

That possibility cannot be tested by analyzing the plenary decisions alone. Rather, we must examine the totality of the Court's treatment of a benchmark set of activist rulings from state as well as federal courts. The best way to do this is to study the cases brought to the Court by state prosecutors—habeas corpus cases from the federal courts of appeals and direct criminal appeals from

TABLE 4

Counteractivist Grants on the Plenary Docket, 1983–85 and 1993–95 Terms

Category	Type of Court	Type of Case	Review Sought By	1983–85	1993–95
Restraint	Court of appeals	Criminal	Federal Government	29	5
"Our Federalism"	Court of appeals	Habeas	State prosecutor	31	2
"Our Federalism"	Court of appeals	Section 1983	State official	51	14
"Our Federalism"	Court of appeals	Other	Defender of state law	23	9
Overreading	State court	Criminal	State prosecutor	23	3

the state courts. For the most part, the two classes of cases involve the same kinds of constitutional issues.[42] Further, the issues are ones that, as much as any, produce a high correlation between judicial activism and liberal outcomes.

To pursue the inquiry, we must look at the cases in which review was denied as well as those that received the four votes required for plenary consideration.[43] We must also take account of two less common forms of disposition, the summary reversal and the "GVR." The first is a reversal without oral argument or full briefing, but accompanied by a per curiam opinion.[44] It is reserved (at least in theory) for lower-court decisions that are plainly contrary to controlling law but do not present issues of precedential significance.[45] The GVR is an order that grants certiorari, vacates the judgment below, and remands for reconsideration in light of an intervening Supreme Court decision.[46]

Table 5 presents complete data on the petitions filed by state prosecutors that received final disposition in the two periods of the study. In the three Terms 1983 through 1985, there were 120 cases in which a federal court of appeals had ruled favorably to a state criminal defendant seeking habeas corpus. As already reported, the plenary docket included 31 such cases. Two additional rulings were summarily reversed, and 16 were "GVR'd." In the

---

[42] There is one exception: under the Supreme Court's decision in *Stone v Powell*, 428 US 465 (1976), search and seizure claims by state prisoners generally cannot be litigated on federal habeas corpus. To be sure, habeas corpus cases often involve procedural issues unique to habeas jurisprudence, but the state-court cases have their counterpart in disputes over whether a state court decision rests on a state-law ground that is independent of federal law and adequate to support the judgment favoring the defendant. See, for example, *Arizona v Evans*, 115 S Ct 1185 (1995).

[43] Again, the cases in which review was denied were identified through perusal of United States Law Week.

[44] The Court can also affirm by summary order, but that mode of disposition is generally confined to appeal cases. There were no summary affirmances in cases brought to the Court by state prosecutors during either of the study periods.

[45] The summary reversal with opinion has always been controversial, and its use has declined substantially since its peak in the 1970s. See Hellman, 44 U Pitt L Rev at 825–36 (cited in note 17). (This form of disposition should not be confused with the summary reversal without opinion, which was common during the Warren Court years, but not thereafter. See id at 821–25.)

[46] For discussion of the "GVR," see Hellman, 11 Hastings Const L Q 5 (cited in note 36). The Court itself uses the abbreviation as a verb. See, for example, *Lawrence v Chater*, 116 S Ct 604, 608 (1996) ("this Court's well established practice of GVR'ing"). There are other kinds of GVRs, but they do not come into play here.

TABLE 5

State Prosecutors' Petitions in the Supreme Court, 1983–85 and 1993–95 Terms

	Plenary Review	Summary Reversal	GVR Order	Cert Denied	Total	Acceptance Rate (%)
Federal court cases (habeas):						
1983–85	31	2	16	71	120	26
1993–95	2	5	1	55	63	3
State court cases (direct review):						
1983–85	23	5	9	87	124	20
1993–95	3	1	6	97	107	3

remaining cases, 71 in all, the Court simply denied review.[47] Thus, the acceptance rate for petitions in this subcategory was 26%.[48]

As it happens, the number of petitions filed by state prosecutors from decisions of state courts during this first period was almost identical; the total was 124. The Court accorded plenary consideration to 23, reversed five with summary opinions, and GVR'd nine. The remaining 87 were denied review. The acceptance rate for the "overreading" cases was thus just under 20%.

Ten years later, the number of petitions filed by state prosecutors challenging habeas rulings by federal courts decreased to 63. Two received plenary consideration, and five were reversed summarily. One was GVR'd; the remaining 55 were denied review. The acceptance rate was thus 3%.

Meanwhile, on the state-court side, the number of petitions declined only modestly, to 107. One was reversed summarily, and six were GVR'd. Only three of the prosecutors' petitions were granted, leaving 97 that were denied review. The acceptance rate was therefore 3%—exactly what it was for the habeas cases from federal courts.

These data strongly suggest that the explanation for the

---

[47] In one case, the Court granted review but dismissed the petition after the defendant died. See *Mintzes v Buchanon*, 471 US 154 (1985).

[48] Measuring the "acceptance rate" in this way involves a slight distortion, because some of the cases that receive plenary consideration during a given Term will have been accepted for review in the preceding Term, while some of the cases accepted in that Term will not be heard until the following Term. However, when the object is to compare two three-Term periods, the distortion is de minimis.

shrunken docket of the 1990s does not lie in the supposedly conservative predilections of the Reagan-Bush appointees to the federal courts of appeals. To be sure, the findings do support the proposition that the courts of appeals became somewhat more conservative than they were in the 1980s, at least in the realm of criminal law. In the 1983–85 period, state prosecutors filed 120 petitions in habeas cases; a decade later, the number dropped to 63. We have no reason to think that prosecutors, as a group, became less zealous in challenging adverse rulings by lower courts; thus it is reasonable to infer that the incidence of such rulings declined. The inference is strengthened by the fact that although the number of prosecutors' petitions from state courts also decreased, the reduction was much smaller.

Still, even if the court of appeals judges did become more conservative, that does not explain the sharp decline in the *rate* at which the Supreme Court agreed to review their activist rulings. Further, among the petitions that were denied in the more recent period, there were at least some that went beyond applying settled law to particular facts.[49] Thus, the conclusion that begins to emerge is that the Justices of the 1990s were scrutinizing these petitions with a more skeptical eye than were the Justices of the 1980s.

The conclusion is reinforced by the Court's handling of the "overreading" cases from state courts. Although the number of petitions filed by state prosecutors remained at almost the same level as in the 1980s, the number that received plenary consideration dropped precipitously, from 23 to three. The result, as already noted, was an acceptance rate identical to that found in the habeas cases—and much lower than the corresponding rate in the 1980s.

It is possible, of course, that the petitions filed by state prosecutors in the 1993–95 Terms were so far inferior in overall quality to those filed a decade earlier that the Justices of the 1980s would have granted no more than the handful that their successors found to be certworthy. But that hypothesis runs up against the fact that in the 1980s the Court accepted at least some prosecutors' peti-

---

[49] See, for example, *Blazak v Ricketts*, 1 F3d 891 (9th Cir 1993), cert denied, 114 S Ct 1866 (1994); *Hamilton v Vasquez*, 17 F3d 1148 (9th Cir), cert denied, 114 S Ct 2706 (1994). The Court denied review in at least nine cases in which a federal court of appeals set aside a death sentence affirmed by the state courts.

tions that did not even purport to raise issues of precedential significance.[50] Thus, the more plausible explanation is that the Justices of the 1990s have been applying a different—and more rigorous—standard in deciding whether to hear the cases. And if that new rigor characterized the case selection process generally, it would go far toward explaining why the number of cases accepted for review has declined so dramatically.

VII. A BALANCED DOCKET

None of the narrowly focused theories fully explains the shrinkage in the plenary docket. However, analysis of the Court's handling of petitions filed by state prosecutors suggests that in that segment of the docket the Justices of the 1990s were applying a more rigorous standard than their predecessors of the preceding decade. The next question is whether this pattern manifested itself elsewhere in the Court's work. To find out, we must look more broadly at the changes in the cases selected for plenary consideration. Table 6 encapsulates the Court's work in the realm of governmental powers; Table 7 presents data on the statutory segment of the docket.

Looking at the composition of the docket of the 1980s, one leitmotif stands out. With a single exception—governmental powers cases from state courts—case selection was skewed in what would generally be viewed as a conservative direction. Grants implicating judicial restraint in the oversight of Federal Government action substantially outnumbered those that fostered the "checking" function. For every case the Court accepted from a litigant challenging a federal court decision that upheld state power, there were four in which the exercise of state power was struck down. In the statutory segment of the docket, government petitions outnumbered those filed by individuals challenging government action by a ratio of almost three to one. Three to one was also the ratio, in private litigation, of petitions filed by defendants to petitions filed by plaintiffs.

I hasten to acknowledge that not every grant of review in the dominant categories of the 1980s responded to a lower-court rul-

---

[50] See Hellman, 60 Notre Dame L Rev at 1037–38 & n 477 (cited in note 11).

TABLE 6

Governmental Powers Cases in the Supreme Court, 1983–85 and 1993–95 Terms

Category	Definition	1983–85			1993–95		
		Criminal	Civil	Total	Criminal	Civil	Total
Supremacy	Cases in which a state court upheld an exercise of state power and rejected a federal claim or defense	20	42	62	10	26	36
Checking	Cases in which the court below (generally a federal court) rejected a constitutional challenge to federal official action	7	6	13	10	10	20
Vindication	Cases in which a federal court upheld an exercise of state power and rejected a federal claim or defense	6	23	29	11	17	28
Total activist grants		33	71	104	31	53	84
Overreading	Cases in which a state court ruled in opposition to an exercise of state power on the basis of a federal claim or defense	23	9	32	3	6	9
Restraint	Cases in which the court below (generally a federal court) ruled in favor of a constitutional challenge to federal official action	15	32	47	5	12	17
"Our Federalism"	Cases in which a federal court ruled in opposition to an exercise of state power on the basis of a federal claim or defense	31	77	108	2	27	29
Total counteractivist grants		69	118	187	10	45	55
Total governmental powers cases		102	189	291	41	98	139

TABLE 7

The Statutory Segment of the Plenary Docket, 1983–85 and 1993–95 Terms

Category	Description	1983–85			1993–95		
		Criminal	Civil	Total	Criminal	Civil	Total
Government	Petition filed by the United States or one of its agencies, or by any other litigant represented by the Solicitor General	10	64	74	8	19	27
Individual	Case in which the United States is the respondent	11	17	28	17	11	28
Defendant	Petition filed by a defendant in a private civil suit and the legal rule in question would favor either plaintiffs or defendants	N.A.	29	29	N.A.	17	17
Plaintiff	Petition filed by a plaintiff in a private civil suit and the legal rule in question would favor either plaintiffs or defendants	N.A.	10	10	N.A.	14	14
Other	Petition not falling into any of the preceding categories	N.A.	25	25	N.A.	24	24
Total		21	145	166	25	85	110

ing that would be deemed "liberal." But for the last several decades it has generally been true that judicial activism correlates with liberal outcomes, and in the governmental powers segment of the docket most of the cases conformed to the stereotype. On statutory issues, activism does not come into the picture, but, far more often than not, a decision adverse to the Federal Government or to a civil defendant would be viewed as liberal in result.[51] The imbalance in the statutory segment of the docket thus can be seen as sharing the predominantly conservative orientation of the governmental powers segment.

The plenary docket of the 1990s presents a dramatically different picture. In every category of federal-court litigation, "liberal" and "conservative" grants appear in numbers that are virtually equal. This pattern can be seen in the governmental powers segment of the docket; it also holds true for issues of statutory interpretation.

The only imbalance is found in state-court cases involving governmental powers. But the imbalance favors litigants asserting federal rights, not those defending state official action. Further, this is the one class of litigation in which activist grants outnumbered counteractivist grants even in the 1980s, when conservatism otherwise held sway. In this respect, however, the Court is simply going back to its roots. From the earliest days of the nation's history, no function of the Court has ranked higher than the protection of federal rights from hostility or misunderstanding on the part of state courts.[52] We would not expect the Court to break with that tradition, and it has not.

These data suggest that the pattern revealed by the analysis of the prosecutors' petitions was not an anomaly but a manifestation of a broader trend in the Court's handling of its docket. The Court no longer leans to "the right" in selecting cases for plenary consid-

----

[51] As explained in Part I, a case is categorized as a "defendant's petition" only when the legal rule in question would favor either plaintiffs or defendants as a class. Cases of this kind typically arise under statutes like the Sherman Act or Title VII of the 1964 Civil Rights Act, where outcomes favoring plaintiffs would almost universally be regarded as "liberal."

[52] In the oft-quoted comment of Justice Holmes, "I do not think the United States would come to an end if we lost our power to declare an Act of Congress void. I do think the Union would be imperiled if we could not make that declaration as to the laws of the several states." Oliver Wendell Holmes, *Collected Legal Papers* 295–96 (Harcourt, Brace, 1920) (speech delivered in 1913).

eration; rather, it has moved close to complete neutrality. Indeed, apart from maintaining the Court's traditional role of overseeing compliance with federal law by state courts, the docket reflects a balance that may well be unique in the Court's modern history.

VIII. A NEW COURT AND A NEW PHILOSOPHY

What explains the new approach to case selection? One obvious possibility is that the Court of today is not the Court of 10 years ago. Six of the Justices who sat on the Court in the 1983–85 period have retired, and one of the remaining three serves as Chief Justice rather than as an Associate Justice.

I have already considered the theory that the shrinkage of the docket can be attributed to the departure of the Court's most liberal members. The data do not support that hypothesis, at least if we assume that those Justices would have concentrated their efforts on securing review of cases that rejected civil liberties claims. But there is good reason to believe that other personnel changes had substantially greater effect on the case selection process.

During the 1970s and the first half of the 1980s, Warren E. Burger served as Chief Justice of the United States. Burger's public statements leave no doubt that he zealously supported Supreme Court review of activist decisions by lower courts, especially those that favored the constitutional claims of criminal defendants.[53] When the late Chief Justice retired at the end of the 1985 Term, counteractivist petitioners lost what was probably their most reliable vote for certiorari.

Justice Byron R. White, although not particularly ideological in his approach to case selection, took an expansive view of the Court's role in providing doctrinal guidance to the lower courts.[54] Justice White retired at the close of the 1992 Term and was succeeded by Ruth Bader Ginsburg. Justice Ginsburg has expressed little sympathy for the idea that every doubtful issue of federal law should be resolved by a national court.[55] Almost certainly, she votes to grant certiorari far less often than did her predecessor.

---

[53] See Hellman, 11 Hastings Const L Q at 434–35 (cited in note 31).

[54] See Hellman, 56 U Pitt L Rev at 705–06 (cited in note 27) (describing Justice White's dissents from denial of certiorari).

[55] See Ruth Bader Ginsburg and Peter W. Huber, *The Intercircuit Committee*, 100 Harv L Rev 1417 (1987).

As an Associate Justice, William H. Rehnquist articulated a view of the Court's role that appears close to that of Chief Justice Burger and Justice White.[56] Since he became Chief Justice, he has moved away from that interventionist approach. He is now willing to deny review in cases whose outcomes or reasoning he disagrees with, but which present no issues of precedential importance.[57]

Finally, Justice Antonin Scalia, who was appointed to Justice Rehnquist's seat when Chief Justice Burger retired, has provided the most detailed jurisprudential justification for a stripped-down plenary docket.[58] Justice Scalia explicitly disavowed the common-law approach of "gradually closing in on a fully articulated rule of law by deciding one discrete fact situation after another until . . . the truly *operative* facts become apparent."[59] Rather, he would extend "the law of *rules* . . . as far as the nature of the question allows," then leave the rest to the lower courts, even if this means "tolerat[ing] a fair degree of diversity" in the rules' application.[60]

In short, the Justices who have joined in the Court in the last 10 years take a substantially different view of the Court's role in the American legal system than the Justices of the 1980s.[61] They are less concerned about rectifying isolated errors in the lower courts (except when a state-court decision threatens the supremacy of federal law), and they believe that a relatively small number

---

[56] See William H. Rehnquist, *The Changing Role of the Supreme Court*, 14 Fla St U L Rev 1, 10 (1986) (suggesting that review by a national tribunal should be available whenever the petitioner "raises [an] important federal question[] not foreclosed by any decision of [the Supreme] Court."); see also Arthur D. Hellman, *Preserving the Essential Role of the Supreme Court: A Comment on Justice Rehnquist's Proposal*, 14 Fla St U L Rev 15, 26–27 (1986) (analyzing Justice Rehnquist's dissents from denial of certiorari).

[57] In the 1983 through 1985 Terms, Associate Justice Rehnquist dissented from denial of certiorari in 28 cases. In the three most recent Terms, Chief Justice Rehnquist dissented only three times. The Chief Justice has been quoted as saying that he no longer votes to take a case just because it is "interesting." See Joan Biskupic, *The Shrinking Docket: Attorneys Try to Make an Issue Out of the Dramatic Decline in High Court Rulings*, Washington Post (March 18, 1996), at A15 (available on NEXIS, NEWS library).

[58] See Scalia, 56 U Chi L Rev 1175 (cited in note 22). This article was based on a speech that Justice Scalia delivered shortly before the Court began to cut back substantially on the number of cases in which it was granting review. We have no way of knowing whether Justice Scalia was articulating a philosophy that he ultimately persuaded his colleagues to share.

[59] Id at 1178 (emphasis in original).

[60] Id at 1186–87 (emphasis in original).

[61] Comments by Justices Anthony M. Kennedy and David H. Souter at the 1996 House appropriations hearings indicate that they too are satisfied with the new approach.

of nationally binding precedents is sufficient to provide doctrinal guidance for the resolution of recurring issues.[62]

The influence of this philosophy can be seen most readily in the statutory segment of the docket. In the three Terms 1993 through 1995, the Court decided 110 cases involving statutory issues. In 88 of these, the need for precedential guidance was signaled in the clearest possible way: by an intercircuit conflict. Of the remaining 22 cases, nine were brought to the Court by the Federal Government, and five were filed by private parties with the support of the Government. Thus, in this segment of the docket, the Court relies almost entirely on two strong indicia of the need for a nationally binding decision: the presence of an intercircuit conflict or an assertion of importance backed by the unique credibility of the Solicitor General.

In the governmental powers segment of the docket, the Court's criteria are somewhat more flexible, but, outside the realm of the Supremacy Clause, the emphasis remains on articulating rules rather than on filling in the interstices of existing doctrines. Of the 139 cases in the 1993–95 Terms, 48 involved conflicts between circuits. In 10 cases, the Court resolved other kinds of intercourt disagreements—conflicts between state courts or between a state court and a federal court of appeals. Federal Government petitions that did not present conflicts accounted for 12 decisions, and petitions supported by the Solicitor General accounted for three more.[63] The docket also included 27 supremacy grants that did not involve conflicts.

These categories encompass all but 39 cases in the three Terms. Some of the 39 cases involved little more than disagreement over the application of previously articulated rules, but they are in the minority. Rather, what stands out about the cases in this group is their importance to the development of the law, the operation of governmental institutions, or both. Here we find constitutional challenges to Acts of Congress or to executive practices of broad applicability.[64] Here, too, are several opinions that explicitly repu-

---

[62] The latter point was explicitly made by Justice Kennedy at the 1996 House hearings.

[63] For purposes of this analysis, I have not distinguished between certiorari cases and appeals. There were only seven appeal cases in all three Terms, and all but two were filed or supported by the Solicitor General.

[64] See, for example, *Colorado Republican Fed. Campaign Committee v FEC*, 116 S Ct 2309 (1996) ("Party Expenditure Provision" of Federal Election Campaign Act); *Adarand Con-*

diate the implications or the holding of a recent precedent.[65] Here also are controversial rulings on emerging issues of public policy such as homosexual rights, term limits for members of Congress, and the use of computer technology in law enforcement.[66]

In both segments of the docket, the patterns I have described demonstrate a substantial narrowing of the criteria that the Court applied during the 1980s. In the 1983–85 Terms, the number of statutory cases that received plenary consideration in the absence of either a conflict or the support of the Solicitor General was not eight but 41. The number of residual grants involving governmental powers was not 39 but 84—and that is only the certiorari cases. If appeals are included, the current figure represents a shrinkage of almost two-thirds from that of the earlier period.[67]

The new philosophy is also reflected in the 1995 revision of the Supreme Court's rules.[68] For example, in describing the criteria for a grant of certiorari, the rules now tell petitioners that the existence of an intercourt conflict, without more, is not sufficient; the conflict must involve a question of importance. In addition, for the first time, the rules explicitly state that a petition "is rarely granted when the asserted error consists of . . . the misapplication of a properly stated rule of law."

IX. An Olympian Court?

From Taft and Hughes onward, the Justices of the Supreme Court have emphasized that the Court's function is not to correct errors in the lower courts, but to "secur[e] harmony of decision and the appropriate settlement of questions of general importance."[69] Under Chief Justice Rehnquist, the Court has moved

---

structors, Inc. v Pena, 115 S Ct 2097 (1995) (race-based presumptions in subcontractor compensation clauses).

[65] See, for example, *44 Liquormart, Inc. v Rhode Island*, 116 S Ct 1495, 1511 (1996) (plurality opinion); *Lewis v Casey*, 116 S Ct 2174, 2181 (1996); *Sandin v Conner*, 115 S Ct 2293, 2300 & n 5 (1995); *Adarand*, 115 S Ct at 2113.

[66] See *Romer v Evans*, 116 S Ct 1620 (1996); *U.S. Term Limits, Inc. v Thornton*, 115 S Ct 1842 (1995); *Arizona v Evans*, 115 S Ct 1185 (1995).

[67] In the 1983–85 Terms, the residual group was composed of 108 cases, including 24 appeals. In the 1993–95 Terms, the 39 residual cases included two appeals.

[68] See Bennett Boskey and Eugene Gressman, *The Supreme Court's New Rules—Model 1995*, 164 FRD 80, 89–90 (1996).

[69] See Hellman, 91 Harv L Rev at 1718 (cited in note 1) (quoting Supreme Court Justices).

closer than at any time in its history to acting upon that vision.
It resolves direct conflicts between circuits; it responds to pleas by
the Solicitor General that vital interests of the Federal Government are at stake; and it guards the supremacy of federal law
against apparent violations by state courts. The Court also addresses issues of obvious importance in the realm of governmental
powers. Beyond that, with only occasional exceptions, the Court
stays its hand.[70]

Many judges and lawyers will see this as a positive development.
They share the concern of Justice Ginsburg that centralization of
judicial authority tends to carry the "'imperial' judiciary to its logical limits."[71] In this view, the Court can best serve the needs of
the national law by laying down broad principles, leaving their application and elaboration largely to the federal courts of appeals
and the state appellate courts. Nor is there any need for the Supreme Court to iron out every wrinkle of statutory interpretation,
even some that give rise to apparent intercircuit conflicts. From
this perspective, the shrunken docket of the Supreme Court can
be seen as the judicial counterpart to the devolution that is taking
place in the political branches of the national government.

But there is also a less benign way of viewing this development.
The Court, if not imperial, has now become Olympian. The Justices seldom engage in the process of developing the law through
a succession of cases in the common-law tradition. Rather, Court
decisions tend to be singular events, largely unconnected to other
cases on the docket and even more detached from the work of
lower courts.

This approach may pose a threat to the effective performance
of the Court's functions that is no less serious than that created
by an "imperial judiciary." At the simplest level, the Court runs

---

[70] Outsiders have no way of knowing the extent to which this regime can be attributed
to the leadership of the present Chief Justice, but it is certainly consistent with what we
know of his personality. Chief Justice Rehnquist has little patience for extended discussion
at the Court's conferences. See William H. Rehnquist, *The Supreme Court; How It Was,
How It Is* 290–93 (William Morrow, 1987). His opinions for the Court often manifest an
impatience with nuances of doctrine or policy. See, for example, *Albright v Oliver*, 510 US
266 (1994) (plurality opinion); *Barnes v Glen Theatre, Inc.*, 501 US 560 (1991) (plurality
opinion); *Calder v Jones*, 465 US 783 (1984). It would not be surprising if he were equally
impatient with the common-law approach of "gradually closing in on a . . . rule of law"
and preferred to provide doctrinal guidance through a small number of decisions that are
as definitive as a majority can be mustered for.

[71] Ginsburg and Huber, 100 Harv L Rev at 1417 (cited in note 55).

the risk that the paucity of decisions will leave wide gaps in the doctrines governing important areas of law. Consider, for example, the recurring question of the preemptive effect of section 301 of the Labor-Management Relations Act on state-law claims by individual employees. The Court's jurisprudence on the subject consists primarily of two unanimous decisions handed down three years apart. One decision found preemption;[72] the other did not.[73] The Court itself has said, with some understatement, that "the Courts of Appeals have not been entirely uniform in their understanding and application of the principles set down in [the two decisions]."[74] But the Court has passed up several opportunities to clarify those principles in cases presenting the issue in conventional settings.[75] Instead, the Court accepted review of a complex case in which section 301 was invoked only peripherally and "nonpreemption under 301 [was] clear beyond peradventure."[76] Variations on this pattern can be seen in the Court's jurisprudence on the discretionary function exception to the Federal Tort Claims Act,[77] the government contractor defense,[78] and personal jurisdiction over nondomiciliaries.[79]

Some will see these gaps as symptomatic of a larger problem

---

[72] *Allis-Chalmers Corp. v Lueck*, 471 US 202 (1985).

[73] *Lingle v Norge Division of Magic Chef, Inc.*, 486 US 399 (1988).

[74] *Livadas v Bradshaw*, 114 S Ct 2068, 2078 n 18 (1994).

[75] See, for example, *Berda v CBS, Inc.*, 881 F2d 20 (3d Cir 1989), cert denied, 493 US 1062 (1990); *White v National Steel Corp.*, 938 F2d 474 (4th Cir), cert denied, 502 US 974 (1991).

[76] *Livadas*, 114 S Ct at 2078 n 18.

[77] See Donald N. Zillman, *Congress, Courts and Government Tort Liability: Reflections on the Discretionary Function Exception to the Federal Tort Claims Act*, 1989 Utah L Rev 687.

[78] The Court's jurisprudence on the government contractor defense consists essentially of a single decision—the case in which the Court first recognized the availability of the defense. That case involved a design defect claim against a military contractor. See *Boyle v United Technologies Corp.*, 487 US 500 (1988). All other questions relating to the scope and availability of the defense have been left to the lower courts. See, for example, *Carley v Wheeled Coach*, 991 F2d 1117, 1119 (3d Cir) (noting "significant split in authority" in cases involving nonmilitary contractors), cert denied, 114 S Ct 191 (1993).

[79] In *Asahi Metal Indus. Co. v Superior Court*, 480 US 102 (1987), the Justices divided evenly over the question whether the "stream of commerce" theory can be invoked to support personal jurisdiction over nondomiciliaries. Since then, some lower courts have said that the theory is good law; others have said that it is not. The Supreme Court has denied review to cases on both sides of the issue. Compare *Lesnick v Hollingsworth & Vose Co.*, 35 F3d 939 (4th Cir 1994) (jurisdiction improper), cert denied, 115 S Ct 1103 (1995), with *Barone v Rich Bros. Interstate Display Fireworks Co.*, 25 F3d 610 (8th Cir) (jurisdiction proper), cert denied, 115 S Ct 359 (1994).

in the legal system: an insufficient number of nationally binding precedents.[80] Others will argue that when it comes to expounding the national law, more is not necessarily better. Certainly it is not difficult to find areas and issues that have received sustained attention from the Court, but which continue to generate confusion and conflict.[81]

In any event, the Court's Olympian stance raises concerns that go beyond the adequacy of the doctrinal guidance that the decisions provide. Quite apart from any gaps in precedent, paring the docket may impair the quality of the Court's work in the cases that it does take. When the Court addresses a particular statute or doctrine only in isolated cases at long intervals, the Justices may not fully appreciate how the particular issue fits into its larger setting.[82] They may lose sight of the practical aspects of adjudication that emerge only when judges actually apply their rules to resolve disputes in a variety of factual contexts.[83] The cases that attract the Court's attention may well be ones that involve extreme facts or idiosyncratic lower-court rulings. The resulting decisions, if not tempered by precedents deriving from more routine controversies,

---

[80] A decade ago, when the Supreme Court was hearing 150 cases a Term, the debate over the "national appellate capacity" centered on proposals for a new tribunal that would assist the Justices in resolving recurring issues of federal law. See Hellman, 11 Hastings Const L Q 375 (cited in note 31). Today, the focus has shifted to ideas for increasing the number of nationally binding precedents at the court of appeals level. See, for example, Joseph F. Weis, Jr., *Disconnecting the Overloaded Circuits—a Plug for a Unified Court of Appeals*, 39 St Louis U L J 455 (1995). The theory, in essence, is that substituting a "law of the Nation" for a "law of the circuit" would make the law more coherent and outcomes more predictable. That question is the subject of a research project now in progress. See Arthur D. Hellman, *Precedent, Predictability, and Federal Appellate Structure* (forthcoming).

[81] A good example is Indian law. Over the last 15 years, the Court has issued more than 30 opinions interpreting statutes and treaties governing the rights of Indians. Most of the cases have involved preemption of state law. Here, if anywhere, the Court's decisions should have closed in on a rule or set of rules that would require little additional elaboration. Yet basic and recurring issues of tribal court jurisdiction remain controversial and difficult for the lower courts. See, for example, *A-1 Contractors v Strate*, 76 F3d 930 (8th Cir) (8–4 en banc decision rejecting a Ninth Circuit precedent), cert granted, 117 S Ct 37 (1996).

[82] To be sure, the Court will often get help from amicus briefs, including those submitted by the Solicitor General. But there is a difference between acquiring background information on issues that are not actually before the Court and mastering the record and arguments on issues that must be decided.

[83] For example, the Court has often been criticized for adopting multifactor tests or open-ended standards for recurring issues. See, for example, *BMW of North America, Inc. v Gore*, 116 S Ct 1589, 1617 (1996) (Ginsburg dissenting); *Commissioner v Soliman*, 506 US 168, 180 (1993) (Thomas concurring). Would the Court be so enamored of that approach if the Justices themselves had to apply tests of that kind in numerous cases?

may skew the law in a way that would be avoided if the Court regularly adjudicated cases in that area.[84]

Detachment from the work of lower courts gives rise to concerns of a different kind. A prime illustration of the phenomenon is the decision last Term in *Whren v United States.*[85] The Court held that a traffic stop supported by probable cause does not violate the Fourth Amendment even if the police officer stopped the vehicle as a "pretext" to investigate more serious crimes "as to which no probable cause or even articulable suspicion exist[ed]."[86] No Justice dissented, and no Justice wrote separately. Nothing in the Court's opinion even hinted that any court or judge had ever viewed the issue differently. A reader might wonder why the Court had granted review in a case whose resolution was so self-evident.[87] In fact, the issue had generated a conflict of long standing among the lower courts,[88] with strongly worded opinions rejecting the position that is now the law of the land.[89]

The Supreme Court need not acknowledge the work of lower courts in every one of its decisions, or even most of them. Nor need the Court attempt to replicate the common-law method in all of the many areas of its jurisprudence. But if the Court recurrently ignores the efforts of lower-court judges to address the issues on its docket, while remaining aloof from the day-to-day operation of the rules it lays down, two consequences can be anticipated.[90] Lower-court judges will no longer feel the spirit of

---

[84] The suggestions in this paragraph are admittedly speculative; unfortunately, they do not readily lend themselves to empirical testing. For example, the Rehnquist Court has been far more active in the realm of bankruptcy law than it has been in matters involving intellectual property. Are the Court's bankruptcy decisions superior to those dealing with intellectual property? How would one go about making that determination? Yet even if the questions are ultimately unanswerable, it is important that the legal community give attention to the qualitative consequences of a shrunken docket—consequences that, to some extent, are the inevitable product of the limited capacity of our one supreme court.

[85] 116 S Ct 1769 (1996).

[86] Id at 1773.

[87] The Court affirmed the decision below.

[88] See *Cummins v United States*, 502 US 962 (1991) (White dissenting from denial of certiorari).

[89] See, for example, *United States v Ferguson*, 8 F3d 385, 397 (6th Cir 1993) (en banc) (Jones dissenting); *State v Haskell*, 645 A2d 619, 621 n 1 (Me 1994). Other recent opinions that give no hint of the lower-court disarray that presumably led the Court to grant certiorari include *Exxon Co. v Sofec, Inc.*, 116 S Ct 1813 (1996); and *O'Connor v Consolidated Coin Caterers Corp.*, 116 S Ct 1307 (1996).

[90] There is evidence that the Court has distanced itself from the lower courts in yet another way: by adopting rules or modes of analysis that no other court has endorsed.

goodwill and cooperation that comes from participation in a shared enterprise. Without that spirit, it is hard to see how a hierarchical judiciary can function effectively. What is worse, the Justices themselves, engaged in work that is increasingly distinct from that of other courts, will have ever greater difficulty in adhering to the line that separates the judicial role from the legislative. The result, ironically, may be a Court that is even more "imperial."

The Court has already moved in that direction. During the same period that the Justices have reduced their role as a source of precedential guidance for lower courts, they have cut a wide swath through controversial issues of public policy, enhancing judicial power and setting at naught the resolutions reached through majoritarian processes. It is a telling fact that although the 1995 Term brought fewer plenary decisions than any previous Term in this century,[91] four of those decisions held Acts of Congress unconstitutional. Four other Acts of Congress were struck down in the 1994 Term.[92] One must go back 60 years to find two consecutive Terms in which eight discrete federal statutes met their doom at the hands of the Court.[93]

Decisions exemplifying this phenomenon include *Gustafson v Alloyd Co.*, 115 S Ct 1061 (1995); *Heck v Humphrey*, 114 S Ct 2364 (1994); *Central Bank of Denver v First Interstate Bank of Denver*, 511 US 164 (1994); and *Ratzlaf v United States*, 510 US 135 (1994). As Professor Kitch has written, "There may be occasions when it is best for the Court to craft an approach that is uniquely its own, but it needs to aware that when it does so it casts off the safeguards provided when it is adopting a position that has already been considered and analyzed by other informed and thoughtful people." Edmund W. Kitch, *Gustafson v Alloyd Co.: An Opinion That Did Not Write*, 1995 Supreme Court Review 99, 123.

[91] The 1953 Term produced fewer signed opinions than the 1995 Term, but the number of argued cases was higher. For data on the 1927 through 1976 Terms, see Hellman, 91 Harv L Rev at 1731 (cited in note 1). Data on earlier Terms do not seem to be readily available, but there is no doubt that the number of argued cases was substantially higher than it is today. See Felix Frankfurter and James M. Landis, *The Supreme Court Under the Judiciary Act of 1925*, 42 Harv L Rev 1, 5 (1928) (caseload data for 1923 through 1927 Terms).

[92] In the same pair of Terms, the Court also struck down two state constitutional amendments and several state statutes. The state statutes include redistricting measures that had been approved by the executive branch of the national government as well as by the state legislature. See, for example, *Bush v Vera*, 116 S Ct 1941, 1950–51 (1996) (redistricting plan approved by Texas Legislature and precleared by United States Department of Justice).

[93] In the 1934 and 1935 Terms, the Court handed down no fewer than 11 decisions holding federal statutes unconstitutional. (Included in this array, of course, were the decisions that prompted President Roosevelt's Court-packing plan.) In the 1967 and 1968 Terms, there were eight such rulings, but two of these were companion cases involving different portions of the same statutory scheme. See *Marchetti v United States*, 390 US 39 (1968); *Grosso v United States*, 390 US 62 (1968). For a listing of the cases through 1990, see Lee Epstein et al, *The Supreme Court Compendium: Data, Decisions, and Developments* 96–99 (Congressional Quarterly 1994).

Plainly, the Court is not going to withdraw from the arena of public policy; however, the era of shrinkage in the plenary docket may be ending. As the 1996 Term began, the number of cases the Court had accepted for review was substantially higher than it was a year earlier, though still well below the levels of the 1980s. Perhaps the Justices have begun to sense that the Court cannot entirely escape its common-law roots, and that a docket devoted solely to making law may not make law in the most effective way.

CHRISTOPHER L. EISGRUBER

JOHN MARSHALL'S JUDICIAL RHETORIC

The modern judgment upon John Marshall's judicial opinions is paradoxical. On the one hand, Marshall's work is regarded as the greatest the American judiciary has produced: forcefully written resolutions to some of the most difficult constitutional problems facing a new nation. On the other hand, Marshall is held to have committed technical errors that would shame a first-year law student: he omitted crucial premises and neglected applicable precedents, even when those precedents were cases he himself had decided.[1] Marshall's opinions are frequently praised but rarely, if ever, emulated.

Scholars have attempted to explain the supposed weaknesses in Marshall's otherwise great opinions by reference to his circumstances or personality. Some commentators have pointed to the absence of a well-developed reporter and citation system,[2] to fail-

Christopher L. Eisgruber is Professor of Law, New York University School of Law.

AUTHOR'S NOTE: I am grateful to Richard Bernstein, Sandy Levinson, Eben Moglen, Bill Nelson, Jeff Tulis, and the New York University Law School's Law and History Colloquium for helpful comments on earlier drafts. They saved me from numerous errors; the ones that remain are my fault. I am also grateful to the Filomen D'Agostino and Max E. Greenberg Faculty Research Fund, which provided generous financial support for this research.

[1] David P. Currie writes that Marshall's opinions are characterized by "rhetorical flourish, bare assertion, plentiful dicta, multiple holdings, inattention to favorable precedent, and emphasis on the undesirable consequences of an interpretation at variance with his own." David P. Currie, *The Constitution in the Supreme Court: The First Hundred Years 1789–1888* 125–26 (Chicago, 1985) ("*The First Hundred Years*"). Currie also remarks that "it is difficult to find a single Marshall opinion that puts together the relevant legal arguments in a convincing way." Id at 197. For discussion of Marshall's attitude toward precedent, see id at 69–70 & n 44, and at 196.

[2] Id at 163 ("the indexing of cases was not what it is today").

ings of Marshall's memory,[3] and to the "immaturity" of the American legal system.[4] Others have attributed the Chief Justice's rhetoric to a concern with political rather than legal issues, and have agreed that Marshall chose wisely in electing to use his office in a statesmanlike, rather than merely judicial, fashion.[5]

This article argues that John Marshall's constitutional style was neither a reflection of judicial practices dominant in his age, nor the result of personal idiosyncrasy, carelessness, or a rejection of law in favor of politics. Robert Faulkner, in his meticulous and illuminating study of Marshall, captures some of the truth: because Marshall wished to defend his conclusions against future critics, Marshall avoided precedent, "whose justice and appropriateness might always be challenged," and relied instead on " 'safe and fundamental principles' " which, he hoped, would persuade more people.[6] That is only part of the story, however. Marshall's rhetorical practice resulted chiefly from a distinct theoretical focus. Modern adjudicative styles reflect a concern with the legitimacy of counter-majoritarian features of American politics, including both judicial review and, to a lesser extent, the Constitution. Judges today assume that elected officials enjoy presumptive authority to speak on behalf of the people about political conflicts, and that judicial impositions upon legislative authority require special justification. As a result, judges often hide their own political judgments behind technical arguments about legal precedent. Marshall, by contrast, had to address the legitimacy of American law in general, including

---

[3] Id (speculating that "nobody remembered" the relevant precedent).

[4] Richard Posner has written

A . . . characteristic of Marshall's opinions, remarkable in our legal culture, is the absence of citations to previous decisions, American or English (and there were plenty he could have cited); also . . . remarkable . . . is Marshall's avoidance of legal jargon. Whether such a style remains possible in a mature legal system is a matter of doubt; in any event Marshall has had no successful imitators. He had, of course, the advantage of interpreting the Constitution while it was still fresh. Although he required (and fortunately possessed) great political wisdom, he did not face as severe an interpretive problem as his successors did. Nor did he have the modern judge's burden of negotiating a minefield of authoritative precedents.

Richard A. Posner, *Law and Literature: A Misunderstood Relation* 290 (Harvard, 1988).

[5] See, e.g., G. Edward White, *The American Judicial Tradition* 33–34 (Oxford, 1976); William E. Nelson, *The Eighteenth-Century Background of John Marshall's Constitutional Jurisprudence*, 76 Mich L Rev 893, 956–60 (1978).

[6] Robert Kenneth Faulkner, *The Jurisprudence of John Marshall* 220 (Princeton, 1968). The internal quote is unattributed.

statutory law. The early judiciary's claim to speak for the American people was contested, but so too were the claims of Congress and the state legislatures. Marshall accordingly approached the legitimacy of judicial review from a different perspective than the one adopted by modern judges: rather than trying to convince people that the judiciary posed no threat to majoritarian institutions, Marshall tried to convince people that national institutions, including the federal judiciary, would govern well. As we shall see, Marshall's theoretical perspective, and his rhetorical style, may have more to offer modern judges than is commonly thought.

I. Law in Marshall's America

In the United States today, the rule of law is hard to define but not much in doubt. To be sure, polemicists occasionally lambast administrative discretion or judicial activism as departures from the very idea of law. Yet, even these critics make their arguments by drawing unfavorable comparisons between their targets and other, uncontroversial examples of American law. In mainstream legal circles, nobody believes that congressional lawmaking, for example, poses any threat to rule of law ideals.

Marshall's day was different. It was an open question how Americans could define for themselves a concept of law, if law was to be something different and better than commands from the powerful. The possibilities for mob rule, pervasive corruption, majority tyranny, popular rebellion, and general breakdown were real and alarming.

In a well-known passage in *Federalist* 1, Publius observes that

> it seems to have been reserved to the people of this country, by their conduct and example, to decide the important question, whether societies of men are really capable or not of establishing good government from reflection and choice, or whether they are forever destined to depend for their political constitutions on accident and force.[7]

This observation is today frequently cited in order to demonstrate the founding generation's faith in the "new science of politics" and the ability of reason to govern American politics.[8] Yet Publi-

---

[7] Federalist 1 (Hamilton) in Clinton Rossiter, ed, *The Federalist Papers* 33 (Mentor, 1961).

[8] See, e.g., Paul W. Kahn, *Legitimacy and History: Self-Government in American Constitutional Theory* 13–16 (Yale, 1992); Sotirios A. Barber, *The Constitution of Judicial Power* 62 (Johns Hopkins, 1993).

us's remark is deeply ironic. If Publius was right that a national government is essential, then Americans had no choice but to establish a government from reflection and choice. The apparent alternative to a chosen constitution—a constitution founded upon custom and tradition—was inapplicable to the American situation. The country's great size, and the disparate histories of the groups who settled it, left the new nation without a homogenous culture. And much of what was shared among its diverse citizens was inherited from the English political tradition and thus rendered subject to challenge by the recent revolution.[9] The founding generation put its faith in reason and choice because it had no other choice.

The American recourse to, and enthusiasm for, scientific government thus should not be confused with unwavering confidence. On the contrary, American politics in the decades following the founding reflected persistent doubts about how and whether a government from reason and choice could be a government of laws. The idea of law, as understood in England, was bound up with the idea of custom. Custom, not science, distinguished law from will and gave it legitimacy. As Robert Ferguson observes,

> Immersed in the legitimacy of the unwritten and immemorial common law (the *jus non scriptum* rooted in custom predating recorded history), the American lawyer of 1787 suddenly found himself crafting a written constitution with only the vaguest theoretical claim upon the remote past. Arguably, there *was* no past to support the common law in America because the legal definition of custom beyond memory required origins preceding the reign of Richard the First. As St. George Tucker pointed out in his Virginia edition of Blackstone's *Commentaries*, North America had been settled four hundred years too late to qualify. The legitimacy of American law obviously required more immediate sources. And yet every lawyer in America quailed at the thought of a definitive constitution born of a single convention.[10]

The problem was even worse than Ferguson reports. The idea of creating "a definitive constitution" in order to make the concept of law applicable to the American nation not only was alarming, but itself required, as Suzanna Sherry has argued, a revision of

---

[9] See G. Edward White, *The Marshall Court and Cultural Change, 1815–1835*, 112–14, 118–19 (Macmillan, 1988); Julius Goebel, Jr., *Antecedents and Beginnings to 1801* 114–18 (Macmillan, 1971).

[10] Robert Ferguson, *Law and Letters in American Culture* 21 (1984). Footnotes omitted.

legal concepts.[11] And the creation of a written constitution in turn generated new problems about the postconstitutional authority and content of previously honored common law rules.[12]

The status of Blackstone's *Commentaries* among early American lawyers illustrates the difficulties facing them. The *Commentaries*, as Ferguson points out, had the advantage of lucidity and clear organization.[13] Blackstone's ability to systematize convincingly the vast content of English law offered hope that the new American polity might similarly draw order from complexity. Blackstone for this reason directly inspired the efforts of early America's great legal scholars, including St. George Tucker, James Kent, and Joseph Story.[14] Perhaps as importantly for the purposes of the new, vast nation, Blackstone had compressed nearly all of the common law into a package small enough to fit within the saddle bags of a lawyer or judge who had to ride long distances to reach court and clients. Yet Blackstone stressed again and again that England's laws owed their legitimacy to custom. He had little faith in the power of reason and science to govern human affairs. Blackstone himself denied the authority of common law in America.[15] Blackstone's anglocentrism rendered reliance on his *Commentaries* problematic in the new American legal order.

Nor could early Americans solve the problem of legal legitimacy by turning from English to state law. Ardent antifederalists might have hoped that the states, which were more homogenous than the Union as a whole, could legitimate their laws by reference to local customs.[16] The American states in 1787, however, were already too large and too heterogenous to function as republican enclaves, and they were only getting bigger. Moreover, the despotism of the state governments was one of the precipitating causes of the Constitution.[17] Whatever appeal it may have had for others,

---

[11] Suzanna Sherry, *The Founders' Unwritten Constitution*, 54 U Chi L Rev 1127, 1146–55 (1987).

[12] See, e.g., Goebel, *Antecedents and Beginnings* at 109–12.

[13] Ferguson, *Law and Letters in American Culture* at 30–32.

[14] White, *The Marshall Court and Cultural Change* at 81–111.

[15] William M. Blackstone, 1 *Commentaries* *107–08.

[16] Nelson, 76 Mich L Rev at 902–24 (cited in note 5).

[17] Gordon S. Wood, *The Creation of the American Republic 1776–1787* 466–67 (North Carolina, 1969). Jack Rakove goes so far as to maintain that the "central conviction" at the heart of James Madison's constitutional analysis was that "neither state legislators nor their constituents could be relied upon to support the general interest of the Union, the

the legitimacy of state law could not provide a stable foundation for the arguments of Federalists, including Marshall, who aimed to legitimate a powerful and supreme national government.

The issue of judicial review reflected early America's need to remake the idea of legal legitimacy. On the one hand, judicial review promised a solution to the problems of a nation that lacked a customary law and so might have to rely upon statutory enactments. The rash impulses of the legislature could be checked by the judiciary. Put more affirmatively, the judiciary could legitimate the enactments of the legislature and thereby establish them as being law rather than mere products of majority power. Yet on the other hand, judicial review threatened to give to judges the same lawless power it took from the legislature. If the sources of legal legitimacy were unwritten, why should the judiciary be any more likely than the legislature to perceive those sources accurately, or to adhere to them? And if the sources of legal legitimacy were within the newly written Constitution, why should that document be regarded as less suspect than the written enactments of a legislature—and, again, why should the judiciary be a better interpreter than the legislature?

Viewed in this way, the problem of judicial review takes on aspects quite different from its character today. In modern constitutional theory, judicial activism is discussed in terms of whether judicial government is, substantively or procedurally, worse than legislative government—that is, whether judicial activism produces bad results or is antidemocratic.[18] In the decades that followed the founding, these problems about the *quality* of judicial and legislative government were supplemented by concerns about how *either* judges or legislatures in the United States could create or announce anything that deserved the name of law at all, much less do so well.

---

true public good of their own communities, or the rights of minorities and individuals." Jack N. Rakove, *Original Meanings: Politics and Ideas in the Making of the Constitution* 47 (Knopf, 1996). See also id at 216–17 (describing widespread crisis of confidence in state assemblies). Rakove's characterization of Madison is controversial; Lance Banning, the other leading student of Madison's thought, portrays Madison as more sympathetic to state government. Lance Banning, *The Sacred Fire of Liberty: James Madison and the Founding of the Federal Republic* 370 (Cornell, 1995). Yet, even Banning concedes that a concern with the failures of state government was fundamental to Madison's constitutional theory. Id at 120.

[18] See, e.g., Alexander M. Bickel, *The Supreme Court and the Idea of Progress*, 107–08, 112, 175–76 (Harper & Row, 1970). I do not mean to endorse this focus; indeed, I have criticized it in the past—Christopher L. Eisgruber, *Justice and the Text: Rethinking the Constitutional Relation Between Principle and Prudence*, 43 Duke L J 1, 3–9 (1993)—and I do so again in Section V of this article.

Marshall and his brethren thus had to confront the problem of showing not only that their decisions were right, but that their decisions were law. Moreover, they could not solve that problem merely by assimilating constitutional law to statutory law or common law. Statutory and common law had problems of their own. On the other hand, if the Constitution's legitimacy were established, then the rest of American law—or at least federal law—might be legitimated by reference to it.

II. Marshall's Adjudicative Style

1. *Marshall's constitutional theory.* John Marshall faced the task of demonstrating that crucial and difficult constitutional questions could be resolved without leaving American politics subject to the undisciplined play of either legislative or judicial discretion. An important part of Marshall's response was tactical. First, Marshall established the Court's practice of issuing a majority opinion—most often authored by Marshall himself, and without dissent—rather than seriatim opinions.[19] Doubts about the possibility of lawful decision making in America might be inflamed by the spectacle of multiple and inconsistent reasoning from the various Justices, even where those Justices reached the same result; Marshall realized that doing away with seriatim opinions would both enhance the power of the Court and allow him to construct a clear and determinate constitutional doctrine.[20] Moreover, the practice of issuing unanimous opinions left Marshall greater control over what issues would be raised in a case.[21] Second, Marshall aggressively took advantage of political circumstances to deflect attacks upon the Court and to secure useful precedents.[22] The most fa-

---

[19] See, e.g., Donald G. Morgan, *Justice William Johnson, The First Dissenter: The Career and Constitutional Philosophy of a Jeffersonian Judge* 168–81 (South Carolina, 1954) ("*The First Dissenter*"); White, *The Marshall Court and Cultural Change* at 186–92 (cited in note 9).

[20] Morgan, *The First Dissenter* at 175–76; White, *The Marshall Court and Cultural Change* at 189–99.

[21] Morgan, *The First Dissenter* at 176–77 (commenting on Marshall's willingness to reach for issues that might be left undecided). It was also true, however, that Marshall at times may have had to sacrifice his own views in favor of preserving unanimity. Id at 176 n 34. See also White, *The Marshall Court and Cultural Change* at 191–92.

[22] See White, *The Marshall Court and Cultural Change* at 165–73 (discussing Marshall's active role in getting *Martin v Hunter's Lessee*, 14 US 304 (1816), before the Court); Faulkner, *The Jurisprudence of John Marshall* at 214 (cited in note 6).

mous example is, of course, *Marbury v Madison*,[23] where the Chief Justice coupled his argument for judicial review to an effective maneuver: he exercised judicial review to strike down a law that would have augmented the judicial power and enabled the Federalist judiciary to protect a Federalist appointee.[24] Not only did the outcome placate the Court's republican opponents, but the Court's willingness to impose constitutional limits on its own power made it appear a more trustworthy exponent of the power it claimed.

These tactics were essential adjuncts to Marshall's rhetoric and constitutional theory. By themselves, however, the tactics were inadequate; they provided no means for conceptualizing the foundations of American law. Marshall's theoretical task had an obvious starting point: the well-known Federalist theory about constitutional legitimacy which maintained that the Constitution was law because it was the work of the sovereign people. Yet, as Edmund S. Morgan points out, the doctrine of popular sovereignty poses "a continuing problem of authentication. . . . In reality the people themselves, if such an entity can be said to exist at all, can act only through representatives, and one set of representatives can be superior to another only by our willingness to accept them as such."[25] Federalist constitutional theory maintained that the people had acted when state conventions ratified the proposals issued from Philadelphia. That was not obviously correct. "The calling of the Constitutional Convention came about without any visible popular demand, its members were not popularly elected, and ratification was achieved in several state conventions by dubious means, including the conversion of delegates pledged to vote against it."[26]

Of course, once the state conventions had assembled and acted, few statesmen were disposed to denounce their authority. Nevertheless, questions about their legitimacy implicitly surfaced with each dispute about the Constitution's meaning. When the Constitution was ambiguous, one could not determine what the conventions had done except by asking what they should have done—

---

[23] 5 US 137 (1803).

[24] See, e.g., Edward S. Corwin, *The Doctrine of Judicial Review* 9–10 (Princeton, 1914); Robert G. McCloskey, *The American Supreme Court* 40–44 (Chicago, 1960).

[25] Edmund S. Morgan, *The Fiction of "The People,"* NY Rev Books 46 (April 23, 1992).

[26] Id at 48.

since, when the Constitution was ambiguous, there was no clear evidence that they had done anything less. And figuring out what a convention should have done meant, in turn, figuring out how a convention would behave if it were truly speaking on behalf of the sovereign people.

To complete the Federalist defense of the Constitution, then, one had to develop criteria to determine what decisions bore the imprimatur of the sovereign people. As we shall see, Marshall's theory was simple: the Constitution was an authentic expression of the people if and only if it conduced toward their happiness and prosperity. If Marshall could show that his reading of the Constitution would produce good government, then it would be natural to think both that the Constitution was the work of the popular sovereign and that he had faithfully interpreted it: after all, isn't good government what the people want? By their fruits shall you know them, one might say.[27]

This theory defined Marshall's rhetorical strategy. Marshall needed to reinforce the conviction that the Constitution spoke for the people. His task was to persuade others that, as Marshall himself believed, the Constitution was in fact a reliable means to good government. To do that, Marshall had to make practical arguments about likely results; references to the process that created the Constitution merely begged the question, and, as we have seen, analogies to statutory and common law could provide no aid.

Marshall's key rhetorical tactic, which both explains the peculiar force of his opinions and their departure from conventional legal style, was to avoid arguing the unarguable. Practical arguments about likely results inevitably depend upon controversial empirical claims. Does judicial review produce good government? That depends, in part, upon whether judges are prudent and reliable decision makers—and that is an empirical question. Would Americans be better off if congressional powers were broadly construed? That depends, in part, upon the extent to which Americans were enough alike to share a common interest—and that, again, is an empirical question. When Marshall's arguments required a controversial empirical claim, and invariably they did, he would merely assert it or

---

[27] Modern government substituted the people for God as the ultimate source of political authority (see Morgan, NY Rev Books at 46), but it could not improve on the old acid test.

even imply it without trying to prove it. He would spin out the implications of his premises rigorously and emphatically but leave the premises themselves unjustified and sometimes unstated. Less is sometimes more, as every lawyer knows. When claims are contestable, piling on reasons only calls attention to them and makes them suspect. John Marshall knew precisely when to stop arguing.

Instead of concocting elaborate proofs for contestable propositions, Marshall sought to put his readers in the right frame of mind to make the relevant judgments themselves.[28] Roughly speaking, he tried to stand them in the shoes of the framers; put more precisely, he engaged in a rhetorical recreation of the founding perspective. Marshall reminded readers of the political crisis that precipitated the framing and ratification of the Constitution. He demanded that readers consider the needs of the new nation in light of that crisis. But he said relatively little to justify his own practical judgments about how best to serve American interests. Marshall knew that many readers would, ultimately, reach judgments inconsistent with his own, but he also knew that pages of argument would do little to convince those who disagreed with him and might instead plant doubts among potential allies.

2. *McCulloch.* Perhaps the best example of Marshall's art is *McCulloch v Maryland.*[29] Nearly the entire opinion is a reflection upon the axiom that constitutional meaning flows from the purposes of the constitutional project: by considering the practical obstacles to that project, and the means that a practical people could use to overcome those obstacles, one can ascertain the extent of the new government's powers. Yet Marshall's characterization of the constitutional project was remarkably abstract. He stressed its importance and its difficulty rather than its content. The following paragraph typifies the opinion:

> The subject is the execution of those great powers on which
> the welfare of a nation essentially depends. It must have been

---

[28] Paul Kahn argues that Marshall's rhetoric flowed from a conviction that "[t]he Constitution embodies the principles of republican government, which are deducible as a matter of science." Paul Kahn, *Legitimacy and History* at 28 (cited in note 8). To some extent, my account of Marshall is consistent with Kahn's: both Kahn and I draw attention to Marshall's insistence that the Constitution was well formulated to achieve good government. In my view, however, Kahn's emphasis upon "science" and "deduction" is misleading; I believe that Marshall's reasoning was self-consciously constructed on the basis of numerous contingent, practical judgments.

[29] 17 US 316 (1819).

the intention of those who gave these powers, to insure, so far as human prudence could insure, their beneficial execution. This could not be done by confiding the choice of means to such narrow limits as not to leave it in the power of Congress to adopt any which might be appropriate, and which were conducive to the end.[30]

Marshall's discussion of constitutional purposes was similarly abstract elsewhere in the opinion. Congress must be able to "perform the high duties assigned to it, in the manner most beneficial to the people."[31] Congress alone can be entrusted with respect to "measures which concern all."[32] The obstacles to success are numerous: the impossibility of providing a complete code describing the government's powers,[33] the difficulty of dealing with uncooperative or hostile state governments,[34] and the great size of the country.[35]

Though Marshall avoided specifying constitutional purposes concretely, he was emphatic about certain aspects of the constitutional project. The people of the Union are both the authors of the Constitution and the beneficiaries of its creation.[36] The Constitution is intended to endure,[37] and to be comprehensible to the public mind.[38] The purposes the Constitution serves are important—they are purposes upon "which the happiness and prosperity of the nation . . . vitally depends."[39] These claims combine to provide a basis for ascribing broad powers to the national government. If the people of the United States are a single people sharing a single common interest, and if they have founded the new national

---

[30] Id at 415.

[31] Id at 421.

[32] Id at 431.

[33] Id at 407.

[34] Id at 406, 431.

[35] Id at 408.

[36] "The government of the Union, then (whatever may be the influence of this fact on the case), is, emphatically and truly, a government of the people. In form and in substance it emanates from them. Its powers are granted by them, and are to be exercised directly on them, and for their benefit." Id at 404–05.

[37] "This provision is made in a constitution intended to endure for ages to come. . . ." Id at 415.

[38] The framers could not specify comprehensively the government's powers, since doing so would result in a legal code so lengthy that it "would probably never be understood by the public." Id at 407.

[39] Id at 408.

government in recognition of the importance of that interest and in order to secure it, a prudent interpreter of the Constitution will construe the national government's powers broadly.[40] Marshall devoted his opinion to tracing the implications of these crucial premises—a task he executed admirably well—but the premises themselves stand for the most part as assertions.

Marshall did defend against one possible challenge, the argument that the Constitution derived its authority not from the people of the Union but from the states.[41] Yet as Spencer Roane realized, Marshall's reasoning on this point does more to distract attention from the strongest argument against Marshall's position than to respond to that argument. Roane, in a series of anonymous newspaper columns criticizing the *McCulloch* opinion, forcefully pointed out that the people who authorized and approved the Constitution might not be "the people of the Union" so much as the peoples of the states. In other words, one may concede Marshall the claim that the people, not the state governments, created the Constitution, without conceding his ultimate claim that the Constitution united the American population into a single people with a single common good.[42] The new federal republic might instead be an alliance of peoples with disparate interests, defining themselves within disparate collectivities. If so, the people of the United States—the peoples of the several states—might indeed have authored the Constitution for their own benefit while confiding to their own state governments the powers upon which their "happiness and welfare vitally depend."[43] Marshall handled the ultimate question in *McCulloch* by assertion.

---

[40] For further reflections upon Marshall's theoretical commitment to the unity of the American people, see Christopher L. Eisgruber, *The Fourteenth Amendment's Constitution*, 69 S Cal L Rev 47, 66–70 (1995); William F. Harris III, *The Interpretable Constitution* 73–83, 193 (Johns Hopkins, 1993).

[41] 17 US at 403–04.

[42] This old debate received a surprising revival in *U.S. Term Limits v Thornton*, 115 S Ct 1842 (1995), where Justice Thomas deployed Roane's distinction against Justice Stevens. Id at 1878 (dissenting opinion). Thomas wrongly claimed that Marshall was on his side. Id at 1877. Whatever one might think of the historical merits of the debate between Stevens and Thomas, it is odd to think that Roane's view should enjoy any enduring force after the Civil War and Reconstruction. See Eisgruber, 69 S Cal L Rev at 71–73 (cited in note 40). In *U.S. Term Limits*, only Justice Kennedy acknowledged the significance of the Reconstruction Amendments. Id at 1874–75 (concurring opinion).

[43] Spencer Roane, *Hampden Letter IV* (June 22, 1819), reprinted in Gerald Gunther, ed, *John Marshall's Defense of McCulloch v Maryland* 138, 140–48 (1969). The quoted phrase is from *McCulloch*, and appears above in the text accompanying note 39 of this article.

What else could he have done? Whether or not there existed a single, united American people, capable of sharing a common good, was a complex issue—partly philosophical, partly empirical, and wholly contestable. The problem was not, at least in Marshall's view, that there was "no right answer"; on the contrary, Marshall adamantly insisted Americans formed one united people. Nor was the problem that "reasons ran out" or that there was nothing to say. There were reasons aplenty. Marshall could, for example, have quoted or reiterated John Jay's observations published in *Federalist* 2.[44] It would be more accurate to say there were too many reasons. Roane and his friends could offer reasons as plausible as Jay's for the opposite conclusion. By adducing reasons in support of his position, Marshall would only call attention to the intractable character of the issue upon which his argument depended.[45]

Instead, Marshall engaged in a rhetorical recreation of the founding perspective. He reminded readers of the needs and crises confronting the founders. His point was not originalist. Marshall did not ask what the framers (or the people) intended, but rather what they *must have intended* in order to launch a successful Constitution. Marshall tried to get readers to ask the same question—a question about what it took to make the Constitution a practical instrument for just governance. He hoped that, once focused upon the right question, they (or enough of them, at any rate) would make the same judgments he had made himself.

In *McCulloch*, Marshall supplemented his recourse to the founding perspective by discussion of the constitutional text, particularly

---

[44] Federalist 2 (Jay) in *The Federalist Papers* 38–39 (cited in note 7).

[45] Marshall's great rival took the same tack. The nub of Spencer Roane's argument in *Hunter v Martin* was that if the state courts became subject to review by the United States Supreme Court, then the principles justifying that power of review would, whenever a question of American law arose in a case tried in India, "equally make the Supreme Court of Calcutta, a part of the judicial system of the United States." 18 Va 1, 39 (1814) (opinion of Roane). This argument, of course, is utterly specious. The fact that the state courts but not the Calcutta court are within the borders of the American nation, or the fact that state court judges but not the Indian judges have sworn to uphold the federal constitution, are obviously sufficient to distinguish the two cases. But Roane was attacking, rhetorically rather than logically, the foundations of the legitimacy of national judicial review. Roane realized that the Marshall Court's claim to be engaged in a lawlike process of judicial interpretation depends upon its claim to be an authoritative interpreter of an authoritative speech by the national people. He attacked this claim at its roots: he implicitly denied the existence of a national people; there was instead a collection of peoples, all of whom spoke through their states. Roane did not offer reasons for his empirical claim that there was no national people—but in that respect he was no different from Marshall.

the Necessary and Proper Clause,[46] the Supremacy Clause,[47] and the Preamble.[48] Marshall's use of the text can beguile even the most careful readers. Robert Faulkner, who recognizes that in "difficult and interesting cases" Marshall's reasoning would "turn upon an understanding of the law's ends," nevertheless insists that Marshall "always beg[an] his decisions with a consideration of the fundamental law itself, not with the country's goals as such." Faulkner says that Marshall's "reasonings were based upon careful examination of the particular words of the provision in question; he sought to distill, as he put it, their 'natural and common import.'"[49] That assessment is misleading. In *McCulloch*, the Chief Justice did not begin, in either the logical or the temporal sense of that term, from the words of the text, nor did he derive his conclusions from the text. Both the Necessary and Proper Clause and the Supremacy Clause become meaningful only as the result of an antecedent construction of the Constitution. The scope of the powers necessary and proper to carry out constitutional tasks depends upon what powers have been granted the national government and what ends those powers serve. Besides, Marshall admitted that his interpretation of the Constitution would have been no different had the Necessary and Proper Clause been omitted.[50] Likewise, the Supremacy Clause, absent some independent claim about the scope of national powers, may simply be a conflict-of-laws provision upholding the enforceability, but not necessarily the practical efficacy, of the narrow range of laws that the national government might legitimately enact. Marshall's use of the reference to "the People" in the Preamble is vulnerable to Roane's arguments.[51]

The textual references in Marshall's opinions are not, however, a diversion. They refashion key terms of the Constitution to reflect the premises of Marshall's own argument.[52] The Necessary and

---

[46] 17 US at 411–20.

[47] Id at 405–06, 432.

[48] Id at 403–04.

[49] Faulkner, *The Jurisprudence of John Marshall* at xiii (cited in note 6).

[50] 17 US at 419.

[51] Roane's arguments are discussed above, in the text accompanying notes 41–43.

[52] See White, *The Marshall Court and Cultural Change* at 8 (cited in note 9) ("the words replaced nontextual sources of principles and were packed with nontextual meanings").

Proper Clause comes to represent Marshall's premise that the Constitution is a practical document designed to effectuate the purposes of the Founding. The Supremacy Clause comes to stand not for a mere conflict-of-laws provision, but for the greater dignity and importance of the national government. The Preamble's attribution of authorship comes to represent the unity of the American populace within a single collectivity.[53]

By integrating into his political argument about the character of the nation an interpretive argument about particular phrases, Marshall redefines those phrases in a way useful to political and legal argument. Later interpreters may grasp Marshall's perspective upon Constitutional meaning through the phrases that he reconstituted as images of his own political premises. Marshall's refashioning of language does not proceed by stipulation; it is rather a redefinition by careful composition, in the way described by James Boyd White.[54] Marshall's way of giving meaning to, for example, the phrase "necessary and proper" depends upon a precise understanding of the limited range of meanings that phrase might convincingly reflect. But, still, to say Marshall's opinion is textual in this way—to say, in other words, that Marshall understood the rhetorical and political limits of the text—is far different from claiming that Marshall drew his argument from the text.

3. *Marbury.* As a second, equally classic example of Marshall's practice, consider *Marbury.* Marshall's argument for judicial review is famous, and famously incomplete. Because "those who have framed written constitutions contemplate them as forming the fundamental and paramount law of the nation, . . . the theory of every such government must be, that an act of the legislature, repugnant to the Constitution, is void." Do courts have the power to deter-

---

[53] Marshall's rhetorical reformulations of the ideas of "the people" and "supremacy" are both nicely illustrated by the following passage, wherein Marshall is discussing the consequences of accepting Maryland's argument allowing states to tax creations of the federal government:

> We shall find it capable of arresting all the measures of the government, and of prostrating it at the foot of the states. The American people have declared their constitution and the laws made in pursuance thereof, to be supreme; but this principle would transfer the supremacy, in fact, to the states.

17 US at 432.

[54] James Boyd White, *When Words Lose Their Meaning: Constitutions and Reconstitutions of Language, Character and Community* 217–18 (Chicago, 1984). White applies his insights to *McCulloch* in id at 247–74.

mine whether a particular statute is void? They must, said Marshall, because "[i]t is emphatically the province and duty of the judicial department to say what the law is."[55]

As the eminent Pennsylvania jurist John Bannister Gibson pointed out some twenty years later, Marshall proved his conclusion by assuming it. The judiciary's job is to decide cases; at issue in *Marbury* was whether the judiciary should decide cases on the basis of its own best judgment about constitutional meaning, or whether it instead had to respect Congress's judgment as final. Marshall had to establish that the judiciary has the power "to say what the law is"; he did so by using that proposition as a premise.

Nevertheless, despite this circularity, Marshall's opinion implicitly supplies a standard by which to test the judiciary's power, a standard that returns us, as his opinion in *McCulloch* did, to the founding perspective. In a paragraph too often dismissed as mere ornamentation, Marshall wrote:

> That the people have an original right to establish, for their future government, such principles as, in their opinion, shall most conduce to their happiness is the basis, on which the whole American fabric has been erected. The exercise of this original right is a very great exertion; nor can it, nor ought it to be frequently repeated.[56]

The people, Marshall said, have laid down principles (not mere rules, like the one specifying that each state should have two senators); moreover, they cannot repeat this exertion often, so somebody, or some institution, must interpret and enforce those principles for them. Presumably the people delegated that sensitive responsibility to whatever institution (or institutions) was best suited to handle it—after all, their purpose was to establish principles conducive to their happiness, and vesting authority in the wrong institution would hardly tend toward that end. It makes sense to conclude that the judiciary has authority to interpret the Constitution only if the judiciary is likely to do a good job figuring out what principles the people laid down. In short, judicial review is defensible only if it produces good results.[57]

---

[55] 5 US 137, 177 (1803).

[56] Id at 176.

[57] I have proposed this interpretation of *Marbury* elsewhere. Christopher L. Eisgruber, *The Most Competent Branches: A Response to Professor Paulsen*, 83 Geo L J 347, 351 (1994).

What *Marbury* needed, but lacked, was an argument in favor of judicial competence. Marshall surely knew that; as Robert Faulkner points out,[58] Marshall followed Alexander Hamilton's argument in *Federalist* 78, and Hamilton included reasons for believing that the judiciary would do a good job interpreting the Constitution—he observed, for example, that life tenure insulated judges from political pressure, and that if judges were good at interpreting other kinds of laws then the same skills would help them interpret the Constitution as well.[59] Marshall omitted these arguments. Why?

The question Marshall ducked was, once again, empirical and contestable. Hamilton's reasons were sound enough, but there were equally plausible things to be said on the other side. Life tenure, for example, is a double-edged sword; it might free statesmen to act on principle or liberate zealots to disregard the interests of the people. The latter prospect was real rather than imaginary to observers of the Marshall court; all they had to do was fix their attention upon Samuel Chase. Through a quirk of casebook editing, constitutional lawyers today remember Chase as a natural lawyer, an impression based upon excerpts from his opinion in *Calder v Bull*.[60] When read as a whole, however, *Calder* reveals Chase to be simply a jurist out of control, an exemplar of unconstrained will who made concrete the fear that American government could not be lawful government. The sixth paragraph of Chase's opinion might lead one to think that Chase was a natural lawyer,[61] but later

---

[58] Faulkner, *The Jurisprudence of John Marshall* at 211 (cited in note 6).

[59] Federalist 78 (Hamilton), in *The Federalist Papers* 468–70 (cited in note 7).

[60] 3 US 386 (1798). For the conventional casebook treatment of *Calder*, see, e.g., Geoffrey R. Stone, et al, *Constitutional Law* 71–72 (Little, Brown, 3d ed 1996).

[61] He wrote,

> I cannot subscribe to the *omnipotence* of a *State Legislature*, or that it is *absolute and without controul*; although its authority should not be *expressly* restrained by the *Constitution*, or *fundamental law*, of the State. . . . The purposes for which men enter into society will determine the *nature* and *terms* of the *social* compact; and as *they* are the foundation of the *legislative* power, *they* will decide what are the *proper* objects of it: The *nature*, and *ends* of *legislative* power will limit the *exercise* of it. . . . There are certain *vital* principles in our *free Republican governments*, which will determine and over-rule an *apparent and flagrant* abuse of *legislative* power; as to authorize *manifest injustice by positive law*; or to take away that security for *personal liberty*, or *private property*, for the protection whereof the government was established. An ACT of the Legislature (for I cannot call it a *law*) contrary to the *great first principles* of the *social compact*, cannot be considered a *rightful exercise* of *legislative* authority.

3 US at 387–88 (emphasis in the original). Even in this passage, Chase was quite ambiguous on the question whether the "fundamental law" is natural or positive.

in the same opinion Chase (in a passage usually omitted by case-book editors) provided a ringing affirmation of positivism.[62] The opinion is mired in hopeless confusion. It was out of control sub-stantively, rhetorically, and (at least as reprinted in the United States Reports) typographically. Chase alluded first to the necessity of judicial supervision of the legislature, and then to the necessary supremacy of positive law within an American government of laws. If these two necessities are reconcilable, they must be delicately joined by the judiciary, and the Supreme Court in particular. But here the Supreme Court is represented by Justice Chase, who could not give decent order to his own opinion, much less a com-plex polity. None of Chase's political theory was of obvious rele-vance to his treatment of the case; his organization was unintelligi-ble; he sprinkled his opinion with references to Coke on Littleton, Lord Raymond, Oliver Cromwell, and King Louis XVI of France; and he eventually treated in eight pages a problem that three of his brethren addressed in a combined total of seven.

Calder was not an isolated incident. Chase detested the Jefferson administration, loudly criticized it, was given to emotional out-bursts, and had a turbulent past.[63] Chase's partisan charge to a Baltimore jury in 1803, the same year *Marbury* was decided, led to his impeachment; he barely survived the trial.[64] Marshall

---

62

> It seems to me, that the *right of property*, in its origin, could only arise from *compact express, or implied*, and I think it the better opinion, that the *right*, as well as the *mode*, or *manner*, of acquiring property, and of alienating or transferring, inher-iting, or transmitting it, is conferred by society; is regulated by *civil* institution, and is always subject to the rules prescribed *by positive law*. When I say that a *right* is vested in a citizen, I mean, that he has the *power* to do *certain actions*; or to possess *certain things, according to the law of the land*.

Id at 394 (emphasis in the original). Chase provided an even more emphatic endorsement of positivism in a controversial jury charge that he delivered in Baltimore. In the jury charge, Chase alleged that recent reforms to the Maryland state constitution and to the federal Judiciary Act threatened to precipitate tyranny or anarchy. Chase continued on to deride theories of natural right that he held responsible for the assault upon political order and to attack, in barely veiled fashion, the Jefferson administration. The charge is reprinted in 2 *Trial of Samuel Chase* v–viii (DeCapo, 1970) (originally printed 1805).

[63] Richard B. Lillich, *The Chase Impeachment*, 4 Am J Legal Hist 49, 49–53 (1960); James Haw, et al, *Stormy Patriot: The Life of Samuel Chase* 176 (Maryland Historical Society, 1980).

[64] Chase escaped conviction by a mere four votes. For extensive accounts of the impeach-ment trial, see generally Raoul Berger, *Impeachment: The Constitutional Problems* 224–51 (Harvard, 1973); Peter Charles Hoffer and N. E. H. Hull, *Impeachment in America, 1635–1805* 228–55 (Yale, 1984); and Richard B. Lillich, *The Chase Impeachment*, 4 Am J Legal Hist 49 (cited in note 63); see also Ralph Lerner, *The Supreme Court as Republican Schoolmas-ter* 1967 Supreme Court Review 127, 129–34, 148–55.

feared that the Chase impeachment was only the beginning of a more general assault upon the independence of the federal judiciary.[65]

Whether future federal judges might be so reckless and partisan as Chase was an empirical question. It was far from obvious that the judiciary would attract better men; Supreme Court Justices bore the onerous burden of riding circuit, and Marshall himself held the Chief Justiceship only because John Jay had refused to take it for a second time.[66] If future Chases were to populate the bench, the fact that they enjoyed life tenure could hardly serve to increase confidence in their performance. The competence of the judiciary to discern justice, and hence to carry out the Constitution, was very much in doubt. When your prudence is in doubt, praising it yourself is an especially ineffective form of self-serving testimony. Marshall understood that, and in *Marbury*, rather than lauding the judiciary's good judgment in general, he exhibited his own.

III. Disdain for Precedent

No aspect of Marshall's style so rankles twentieth-century commentators as does his flagrant disdain for precedent. In *Cohens v Virginia*,[67] for example, Marshall examined issues of federal jurisdiction which his loyal and able ally, Joseph Story, had treated at length in *Martin v Hunter's Lessee*.[68] Only in the concluding sentence of his constitutional argument, after forty-eight pages of discussion, did Marshall even mention *Martin*.[69] Marshall also neglected opinions he had written himself. In *Osborn v Bank of the United States*,[70] he revisited two points he had previously argued in *Cohens:* first, that the Eleventh Amendment was not a correction

---

[65] Albert J. Beveridge, 3 *The Life of John Marshall* 178–79 (Houghton Mifflin, 1919).

[66] See, e.g., Faulkner, *The Jurisprudence of John Marshall* at 231 (cited in note 6).

[67] 19 US 264 (1821).

[68] 14 US 304 (1816).

[69] Marshall must have had a twinkle in his eye when at last he acknowledged Story's labors in *Martin*, for what he said was that "the subject was fully discussed and exhausted in the case of *Martin v Hunter*." 19 US at 423. Not fully enough to exhaust Marshall, apparently.

[70] 22 US 738 (1824).

of an erroneous Court decision in *Chisholm v Georgia*,[71] but a practically necessary attenuation of a sound constitutional principle;[72]
and, second, that a broad reading of the Supreme Court's jurisdiction is essential to prevent individual states from frustrating the
exercise of national powers.[73] A modern jurist would almost certainly have cited *Cohens* in *Osborn* on both points. Marshall does
not cite it at all.

Marshall's treatment of precedent was neither accidental nor the
product of historical vogue. To be sure, the doctrine of *stare decisis*
in the late eighteenth century was looser than later versions. One
scholar remarks, "What we can say . . . about case-law at the end
of the eighteenth century is that certainly there was a practice of
following precedents, which it was regarded as important to protect. But the doctrine of *stare decisis* was a *principle* of adhering to
decisions, not a set of rules."[74] Nevertheless, the variations within
Marshall's own practice, and between his practice and those of his
contemporaries, provide clear evidence of a self-conscious choice
about how to weigh the significance of past cases.

Marshall himself sometimes discussed precedent extensively.[75]
He defended the use of English cases to resolve common law is-
sues[76] and rejected their relevance to constitutional questions.[77]
Marshall used American constitutional precedents carefully and

---

[71] 2 US 419 (1793). Marshall never mentions *Chisholm* in either opinion.

[72] *Cohens*, 19 US at 405–07. *Osborn*, 22 US at 850.

[73] 19 US at 385–90; 22 US at 847–49. The two arguments have numerous parallels. In
both instances, Marshall raises the threat that a state might penalize a federal officer for
carrying out federal duties, suggests that individual states might thereby arrest the activity
of the nation, and admits that his examples are extreme while arguing that the line between
the present case and the extreme one is only a matter of degree.

[74] Jim Evans, *Change in the Doctrine of Precedent during the Nineteenth Century*, in Laurence
Goldstein, ed, *Precedent in Law* 45 (Clarendon, 1987). See also Rupert Cross, *Precedent in
English Law* 22–23 (Clarendon, 3d ed 1977).

[75] See, e.g., *The Venus*, 12 US 253, 288, 298–317 (1814) (Marshall dissenting in part)
(maritime prize case).

[76] *Livingston v Jefferson*, 15 F Cases 660, 664–65 (Va Cir Ct 1811).

[77] *Osborn*, 22 US at 851:

> If this question were to be determined on the authority of English decisions, it
> is believed that no case can be adduced where any person has been considered as
> a party, who is not made so in the record. But the Court will not review those
> decisions, because it is thought a question growing out of the constitution of the
> United States requires rather an attentive consideration of the words of that instru-
> ment, than of the decisions of analogous questions by the Courts of any other
> country.

strategically. For example, *Osborn*, like *McCulloch*, dealt with a state tax on the national bank; Marshall acknowledged that *McCulloch* directly governed the constitutionality of the Ohio regulation at issue in *Osborn*.[78] Marshall, however, chose to "review" the question decided in *McCulloch*.[79] Yet Marshall's review of the state power to regulate federal instruments had a character different from his original discussion in *McCulloch*. The difference is revealed in Marshall's claim in *Osborn* that the "whole opinion of the court, in the case of *McCulloch v The State of Maryland*, is founded on, and sustained by, the idea that the bank is an instrument which is 'necessary and proper' for carrying into effect the powers vested in the government of the United States."[80] As we have seen, this idea is better described as an effect of, rather than the foundation for, the opinion in *McCulloch*. Marshall does however use this idea as the foundation for his opinion in *Osborn*, which offers at most a faint echo of the grand arguments from the founding perspective that dominated *McCulloch*. Instead, the *Osborn* opinion stays closer to the issues raised by the bank in particular. In doing so, Marshall relies on the success of his general project in *McCulloch* even as he reviews its specific conclusion.

The comparison between Marshall and other judges is even more telling. Some of Marshall's most famous rivals shared his attitude toward precedent. In their most notable statements on federal judicial power, Spencer Roane[81] and John Bannister Gibson[82] pointedly argued that precedent had limited relevance in con-

---

[78] Id at 859.

[79] Id.

[80] Id at 860.

[81]

> Throwing out of view, all these opinions . . . except so far as I may think them correct, and use them for the purpose of illustration, and taking for my guide the constitution, which cannot err, I will examine these important questions. I will also avail myself of such principles, as all the enlightened friends of liberty concur in, as essential to preserve the rights and promote the harmony of both governments.

Martin v Hunter, 18 Va 1, 29 (opinion of Roane) (1814). See also id at 27 ("I shall never hold myself bound, by the opinions of any *individuals*, further than they appear to me to be correct").

[82]

> Now, in questions of this sort, precedents ought to go for absolutely nothing. The constitution is a collection of fundamental laws, not to be departed from in practice nor altered by judicial decision, and in the construction of it, nothing would be so alarming as the doctrine of *communis error*, which offers a ready justi-

stitutional jurisprudence. The opinions they wrote were comparable in style to Marshall's own. Gibson's opinion in *Eakin v Raub*[83] is especially interesting because one of his colleagues took a much more modern approach. Gibson's opinion was short on citation, though not so short as Marshall's work. Gibson mentioned, early in the portion of the opinion dealing with the constitutional issue, both *Marbury* and Justice Patterson's jury charge, delivered while riding circuit, in *Vanhorne v Dorrance*.[84] But Gibson mentioned these cases only to dismiss them on the ground that first principles, not precedents, should control an issue so fundamental as the power of judicial review.[85] Later, Gibson cited a Pennsylvania case for the proposition that the Constitution was to be construed according to principles different from those applicable to a common deed.[86] He eventually distinguished away two cases, a Pennsylvania case, *Austin v The University of Pennsylvania*,[87] and the *Vanhorne* case.[88] Gibson also invoked as support for his position the opinions of Blackstone and Dr. William Paley, a contemporary philosopher frequently invoked by lawyers.[89] Finally, when Gibson reached the ultimate substantive constitutional issue in the case—the validity of the challenged law, rather than the legitimacy of judicial review—he cited and follows *Calder v Bull*.[90]

These are the only citations in a fifteen page opinion, and all of these, with the exception of the last one, could be omitted without much altering Gibson's argument. By contrast, Gibson's colleague on the Pennsylvania bench, Judge Thomas Duncan, man-

---

fication for every usurpation that has not been resisted *in limine*. Instead, therefore, of resting on the fact, that the right in question has universally been assumed by the *American* courts, the judge who asserts it ought to be prepared to maintain it on the principles of the constitution.

Eakin v Raub, 12 Sergeant & Rawle 330, 346 (Pa 1825) (Gibson dissenting).

[83] Id.

[84] 2 Dallas 304 (Pa Cir 1795).

[85] 12 Serg & Rawle at 346.

[86] Id at 349. The case cited is *The Farmers and Mechanics' Bank v Smith*, 3 Serg & Rawle 63 (Pa 1817).

[87] 1 Yeates 260 (Pa 1793).

[88] 12 Serg & Rawle 355–56.

[89] Id at 348 (Blackstone), 347 (Paley). For a discussion of Paley's significance, see Christopher L. Eisgruber, *Justice Story, Slavery, and the Natural Law Foundations of American Constitutionalism*, 55 U Chi L Rev 273, 302 n 85 (1988).

[90] 12 Serg & Rawle at 358.

aged to deploy a vast array of citations, in a manner that would please a law clerk today, while discussing the same issues Gibson resolved by recourse to first principles.

On the other hand, Justice Joseph Story, although a loyal ally to Marshall on the Court and an enthusiastic admirer of the Chief Justice, invoked a rhetorical style significantly different from Marshall's. Story sought legitimation of his judicial opinions by application of the same principles that guided his scholarly efforts: the idea that the integrity of law in the American polity depended upon making that law scientific and rational.[91] Story advocated a form of legal reasoning that was characterized by employment of "close and systematical logic"; grounded in natural law and immutable principles of right and wrong; and productive of a carefully systematized body of rules and precedents.[92] It was this faith in the ability of reason to make law scientific, and the ability of science— rather than, as was the case in Marshall's work, political justice— to legitimate judicial power, that determined the rhetorical structure of Story's opinions.

Dartmouth College v Woodward provides an especially clear example of the contrast in the judicial styles of the Court's two most prominent Federalists. In *Dartmouth College*, Story concurred while Marshall wrote the opinion of the Court.[93] Story wrote a highly detailed mini-treatise on the status and characteristics of public and private corporations in American law. He chastised counsel for conceptual sloppiness: "[w]hen, then, the argument [of counsel] assumes, that because the charity is public, the corporation is public, it manifestly confounds the popular, with the strictly legal sense of the terms."[94] Story then gave a precise exposition of the "legal sense of the terms," documented with copious citations to Anglo-American authorities. Story's opinion differs in both form and content from Marshall's, who avoided legal authorities and relied instead upon a discussion of the general goals and purposes of corporate law.

Story's opinion in *Martin v Hunter's Lessee* provides a less obvi-

---

[91] G. Edward White, *The Marshall Court and Cultural Change* at 145–54 (cited in note 9).

[92] Id at 149–50.

[93] 17 US 518, 666–713 (1819) (Story concurring).

[94] Id at 671.

ous but ultimately more interesting example. In *Martin*, Story invoked and defended many of the constitutional principles dearest to Marshall: that the government was ordained and established by the people, not the states;[95] that the words of the Constitution must be given their "natural and obvious sense";[96] that the Constitution was intended to be permanent;[97] that the national government was to be supreme;[98] and that the Court's disposition of the case is essential to averting "great mischief" and disorder.[99]

Story's treatment of these points is, however, influenced by his scientific conception of the law. The *Martin* opinion is a careful, point-by-point elaboration of the logic of federal jurisdiction. Story considered, with meticulous attention to detail, whether Congress must act to confer jurisdiction to the federal courts,[100] over which cases Congress must confer jurisdiction,[101] and the extent of the appellate jurisdiction.[102] The first two topics are largely irrelevant to the substantive issue[103] but of great significance to Story's rhetorical project: put together, the opinion makes up another mini-treatise, this time on federal jurisdiction, which manifested its legal character in its precision, detail, and organization.

Thus, although Story's opinion is, like many of Marshall's, nearly devoid of citation,[104] his style is considerably different. Indeed, Story expressly declared the irrelevance to his interpretation of the necessity or wisdom of the principles he expounds.[105] Marshall could not have included this declaration within one of his opinions without undermining the persuasiveness of his argument, which was always based upon the idea that the people wanted, and had through their Constitution effectively established, good gov-

---

[95] 14 US at 324.

[96] Id at 326.

[97] Id.

[98] Id at 328.

[99] Id at 342, 347, 348.

[100] Id at 328–33.

[101] Id at 333–37.

[102] Id at 337–52.

[103] See Currie, *The First Hundred Years* at 94–95 (cited in note 1).

[104] Story does cite one case, *Smith v State of Maryland*, 10 US 286 (1810), to support his arguments that jurisdiction to review federal questions decided in state court implies jurisdiction to review antecedent questions of fact. 14 US at 359.

[105] Id at 347.

ernment.[106] Moreover, although the various themes that make up Marshall's recourse to the founding perspective are individually present in Story's opinion in *Martin*, those themes are scattered through paragraphs of detail. Nowhere does one find the short, compelling, integrated conceptualization of the Union that was characteristic of Marshall's great opinions. The contrast is especially clear in light of Marshall's rhetoric in *Cohens*, which ranks, along with *Marbury* and *McCulloch*, among his most forceful opinions.[107] Marshall may have perceived a need to provide such an integrated image in order to facilitate comprehension of his own (and Story's) more particular arguments, and that perception may have been one reason for his unwillingness to rely upon *Martin* in *Cohens*.[108]

---

[106] Paul Kahn makes a similar point. Kahn, *Legitimacy and History* at 38, 41 (cited in note 8) (distinguishing between Marshall's "science of politics" and Story's "science of law").

[107] In *Cohens*, Marshall, while asserting the Supreme Court's appellate jurisdiction over cases to which a state is a party, reiterates—in both form and substance—much of his argument from *McCulloch* dealing with the supremacy of the federal government, the constitutional authority of the "American people," and the threat of state hostility to national action. *Cohens*, 19 US at 380–90. Consider in particular the passages in id at 380–81, where Marshall says in part,

> The American States, as well as the American people, have believed a close and firm Union to be essential to their liberty and to their happiness. They have been taught by experience, that this Union cannot exist without a government for the whole; and they have been taught by the same experience that this government would be a mere shadow, that must disappoint all their hopes, unless invested with large portions of that sovereignty which belongs to independent states. Under the influence of this opinion . . . the American people, in the conventions of their respective States, adopted the present constitution.
>
> . . . . The general government, though limited as to its objects, is supreme with respect to those objects. . . .
>
> To this supreme government ample powers are confided; and if it were possible to doubt the great purposes for which they were so confided, the people of the United States have declared, that they are given "in order to form a more perfect union . . . [quoting the entire Preamble]."

Here, in quick succession, Marshall rehearses several themes recognizable from *McCulloch*: the importance of the Constitution's objects, the authority and unity of the people, the significance of the Supremacy Clause and the Preamble, and the danger that a weak government might be practically inadequate to carry out the tasks set for it.

[108] There is another important reason for Marshall's willingness to reargue the points raised in *Martin*, however. *Cohens* was a case that developed largely as a result of widespread antagonism to *Martin* in Virginia. Despite Story's efforts, the *Martin* decision was under attack as a partisan exercise of power. White, *The Marshall Court and Cultural Change* at 504–10 (cited in note 9). The Court might conceivably have defended itself simply by citing *Martin* and standing its own ground, but Marshall apparently calculated that his own rhetoric was powerful enough, and the prestige of the Court low enough, to warrant another, independent defense of the Court's jurisdiction.

While Story was perhaps Marshall's most loyal ally, Justice William Johnson was the Chief Justice's most able critic on the Court. Johnson endorsed the view that the Constitution was at least in part established by the states, rather than, as Story and Marshall both contended, entirely by the people.[109] Because he regarded the document as a kind of contract, the problem of constitutional interpretation reduced for Johnson to ascertaining the intent of the contractors and the content of the antecedent restrictions, if any, on the capacity of the contractors. What results is, in other words, a jurisprudence founded upon the actual (as opposed to idealized, as was the case with Marshall) original intent of the framers, as modified by the natural law constraints.

We can see one side of Johnson's style in his opinion in *Gibbons*, which begins with a historically documented account of the founding, complete with a discussion of the convention debates.[110] He goes on to construe the Constitution according to what he identifies as the historical purpose of the clause: "If there was any one object riding over every other in the adoption of the constitution, it was to keep the commercial intercourse among the states free from all invidious and partial restraints."[111] *Fletcher v Peck* illustrates the other side of Johnson's adjudicative style. Johnson, unlike Marshall, rested his disposition of the case not on the Contracts Clause but "on a general principle, on the reason and nature of things: a principle which will impose laws even on the deity."[112] The principle is drawn from a discussion of the norms that control national sovereignty and the "supreme power of a country."[113]

---

[109] *Martin*, 14 US at 373 (Johnson concurring):

> the constitution appears, in every line of it, to be a contract, which, in legal language, may be denominated tripartite. The parties are the people, the states, and the United States. It is returning in a circle to contend, that it professes to be the exclusive act of the people, for what have the people done but to form this compact? That the states are recognized as parties to it is evident from various passages, and particularly that in which the United States guaranty to each state a republican form of government.

See also *Gibbons v Ogden*, 22 US at 223 (Johnson concurring) (arguing that the principal means adopted by the Constitution was that of protecting "the independence and harmony of the states, that they may better subserve the purposes of cherishing and protecting the respective families of this great republic").

[110] 22 US at 223–36.

[111] Id at 231.

[112] 10 US at 143 (Johnson concurring).

[113] Id at 143–44.

Johnson had no patience with Story's attempts to legitimate American law by scientific method. He dismissed Story's painstaking analysis in *Martin* with the comment that "I have seldom found much good result from hypercritical severity, in examining the distinct force of words."[114] When textual and historical arguments failed to dispose of issues, Johnson was ready to invoke natural law arguments, as in *Fletcher*, or what were apparently policy arguments, as in *Martin*.[115] On Johnson's theory of the Constitution, legitimacy for federal law rested ultimately upon state law, and constitutional interpretation was the construction of a particular contract which derived its force from the participation of the state sovereigns. As the Constitution did not generate a distinct, and certainly not a supreme, source of sovereignty, there was neither need nor justification for independent legitimation of federal law.

* * *

Comparing Marshall's opinions to those of his contemporaries makes clear that Marshall's disdain for precedent was not dictated by historical circumstance. Comparing Marshall's opinions to one another makes clear that Marshall was keenly aware of what he and other Justices had done in the past; he adjusted his rhetoric in light of past decisions even when he did not cite them. However one might judge Marshall's use of precedent, it was calculated rather than unthinking or hasty.

Marshall's attitude toward precedent was of a piece with his more general constitutional theory and the rhetorical strategy that it sponsored. Marshall believed that the Constitution's claim to speak for the people depended upon its connection to justice and the common good. To defend his controversial interpretations of the Constitution, Marshall had to persuade people that his reading of the document was likely to produce good government. Citing precedents, especially controversial precedents, was not an effective means to do that; adhering to bad precedents would entrench bad government. Marshall preferred to buttress precedents with additional argument rather than building on their uncertain foun-

---

[114] 14 US at 374. While Johnson regarded Story's opinion as "hypercritical" in its examination of language, Story apparently thought Johnson's opinions were "wanting in exactness." White, *The Marshall Court and Cultural Change* at 360 n 341 (cited in note 9).

[115] 14 US at 377–82 (discussing the benefits of state-federal comity in areas of joint jurisdiction).

dation. Marshall believed that the Constitution required the Court to exercise judgment, and, unlike modern Justices, who frequently cite "binding" precedents to prove that they are not themselves exercising judgment at all, Marshall's ambition was to prove that the Court was not only exercising judgment but doing it well.

IV. The Contracts Clause Cases

Marbury, *Cohens*, and *McCulloch* are the three purest exemplars of Marshall's adjudicative style, but he employed similar rhetorical strategies in other constitutional cases, including the Commerce Clause cases.[116] In his lone constitutional dissent, however, Marshall made striking departures from the practices that characterized most of his constitutional jurisprudence. Because of its exceptional status, *Ogden v Saunders*[117] clarifies the connection between Marshall's adjudicative style and his constitutional theory.

The *Ogden* dissent came at the end of a line of Contracts Clause cases. The first of these cases, *Fletcher v Peck*,[118] though largely consistent with Marshall's standard rhetorical paradigm, foreshadowed what was to come. The Court had to decide the constitutionality of a Georgia law purporting to annul a grant of lands by an

---

[116] *Gibbons v Ogden*, 22 US 1 (1824); *Brown v Maryland*, 25 US 419 (1827); *Willson v Black Bird Creek Marsh Co.*, 27 US 245 (1829). The founding perspective figures in these cases to differing degrees. It is most explicit in *Brown*, where Marshall wrote

> The oppressed and degraded state of commerce previous to the adoption of the constitution can scarcely be forgotten. . . . It may be doubted whether any of the evils proceeding from the feebleness of the federal government contributed more to that great revolution which introduced the present system, than the deep and general conviction that commerce ought to be regulated by Congress. . . . To construe the power so as to impair its efficacy, would tend to defeat an object, in the attainment of which the American public took, and justly took, that strong interest which arose from a full conviction of its necessity.

25 US at 445–46. *Willson*, on the other hand, is a terse opinion in which Marshall upheld an exercise of state power with almost no explanation and without citing either *Gibbons* or *Brown*. Marshall had no incentive to provide a lengthy discourse on the need for state police power. By falling back on the American lawyer's practice of categorization—a practice born out of Blackstone's much admired systematization of English law and nurtured by the American exponents of scientific reasoning in law (see, e.g., White, *The Marshall Court and Cultural Change* at 81–95 (cited in note 9))—Marshall was able to decide *Willson* on its facts without sacrificing legitimacy.

[117] 25 US 213 (1827). The case provoked one of only six dissents written by Marshall during his thirty-four years on the Court, and his only dissent in a constitutional case. See Morgan, *The First Dissenter* at 189, 220 (cited in note 19).

[118] 10 US 87 (1810). The other cases preceding *Ogden* were *Sturges v Crowninshield*, 17 US 122 (1819), and *Trustees of Dartmouth College v Woodward*, 17 US 518 (1819).

earlier, corrupt legislature and to strip ownership rights from a third party purchaser of the lands that had been granted. The case turned upon the question of whether the legislative grant was a contract within the meaning of Section 10, Article I of the Constitution, providing that "no state shall pass any . . . law impairing the obligation of contracts."

Marshall's treatment of this question displayed a combination of common law reasoning and recourse to the founding.[119] Marshall opened by quoting the relevant constitutional provision and stating Blackstone's definition of a contract. In light of Marshall's view that English precedent is relevant to common law issues but not constitutional ones, his reliance upon Blackstone is not surprising: Marshall plausibly viewed the Contracts Clause as incorporating a common law term of art. Marshall then parsed the constitutional text, emphasizing the terms of its positive provision protecting contracts.[120] To a greater extent than in opinions like *McCulloch*, Marshall in *Fletcher* did begin from the constitutional text. Perhaps Marshall realized, as we shall see presently, that the Contracts

---

[119] Far too much has been made of Marshall's remarks that

> If the legislature of Georgia was not bound to submit its pretensions to those tribunals which are established for the security of property and to decide on human rights, if it might claim to itself the power of judging in its own case, yet there are certain great principles of justice, whose authority is universally acknowledged, that ought not to be entirely disregarded,

Fletcher, 10 US at 133, and that

> Georgia was restrained, either by general principles, which are common to our free institutions, or by the particular provisions of the constitution of the United States, from passing a law where by the estate of the plaintiff in the premises so purchased could be constitutionally and legally impaired and rendered null and void.

Id at 139. Some commentators have taken these passages to indicate that Marshall is drawing conclusions from natural law to the derogation of positive law. See Sherry, 54 U Chi L Rev at 1170–71 (cited in note 11) (citing references).

Yet from the context of the first quotation, it is at least possible that the "great principles of justice" Marshall had in mind were the common law rules of contract, providing that a third party purchaser for value from the holder of a voidable title secured a good title. See 10 US at 133–34. The vague reference to "general principles" in the second passage may again be a reference to common law rules, or to the various political principles Marshall used to interpret the Constitution. In any event, neither sentence is sufficiently important to Marshall's reasoning or rhetoric to turn *Fletcher* into a "natural law" opinion.

[120] As already noted, Marshall in cases like *Marbury* and *McCulloch* does spend extensive amounts of time discussing constitutional language, but that textual work depends in many respects upon Marshall's discussion of the founding project. See text accompanying notes 46–54 supra. Here, by contrast, the attempt at legal definition of the idea of contract seems capable of standing on its own as a basis for Marshall's resolution of the case.

Clause would eventually present severe difficulties for his standard rhetorical method and constitutional theory.

Nonetheless, Marshall supplemented his first argument with a recourse to the founding perspective that characterized his approach in *Marbury*, *McCulloch*, and *Cohens*. Marshall assimilated the ends of the Contracts Clause to the constitutional project's more general aim of securing the polity against lawlessness and unruled passion:

> . . . it is not to be disguised that the framers of the constitution viewed with some apprehension, the violent acts which might grow out of the feelings of the moment; and that the people of the United States, in adopting that instrument, have manifested a determination to shield themselves and their property from the effects of those sudden and strong passions to which men are exposed. The restrictions on the legislative power of the states are obviously founded in this sentiment; and the constitution of the United States contains what may be deemed a *bill of rights for the people of each state*.[121]

Marshall thus depicted the Contracts Clause as a specific provision aimed at the more general constitutional end of avoiding undisciplined and impassioned government. In one respect, Marshall's strategy was quite sensible. American history from before the Constitution and into the twentieth century bears out the need for the people to design constitutional protections against improvident state policies. There was, however, a problem lurking within Marshall's argument. As Marshall may have known, Madison had struggled unsuccessfully in Philadelphia to give Congress a veto over state laws.[122] Unfortunately, Madison failed. What the Constitution provided was (absent a very bold construction of the Contracts Clause) rather modest: "No state shall pass any bill of attainder, *ex post facto* law, or law impairing the obligation of contracts."[123] And thus the difficulty: if the Constitution needed to provide "a bill of rights for the people of each state" in order

---

[121] 10 US at 137–38 (emphasis supplied).

[122] On Madison's struggle to give Congress "a negative *in all cases whatsoever* on the legislative acts of the states," see Rakove, *Original Meanings* at 47–54, 81–82, and 197–98 (cited in note 17). The quoted phrase is from Madison's letter to George Washington, written on April 16, 1787, and quoted by Rakove, *Original Meanings* at 51.

[123] US Const, Art I, § 10. As a historical matter, the Philadelphia Convention substituted the Supremacy Clause for Madison's proposed veto. Rakove, *Original Meanings* at 81.

to secure justice and good government, then the Constitution was defective. This problem, avoided in *Fletcher*, would become more apparent as Marshall applied his method to later Contracts Clause cases.

These difficulties came to a head in *Ogden*, where the Court had to decide whether states could enact regulations excusing bankrupt parties from the performance of those contracts that were made after the regulations were passed.[124] The Court held the regulation constitutional, and Marshall, joined by Story and Duvall, dissented.

The Justices voting to uphold the law argued that the rule discharging the obligations of bankrupts did not impair the obligation of contracts, but rather altered the forms of permissible contracts by inserting an implied term operative in the event that one of the parties became insolvent. The discharge provision was analogized to statutes of limitation and various rules regulating commercial bonds.[125] Marshall based his response in large part on a state-of-nature theory designed to show that contractual rights flow not from political grant but from pre-political rights not subject to legitimate government control.[126] By a sustained examination of man's conduct in "the rudest state of nature," Marshall purported to show, with a series of examples involving hunters and barter for animal skins, that "the right to contract, and the obligations to created by contract, . . . exist anterior to, and independent of society."[127] Therefore, Marshall reasoned, the right to contract could derive from government grant only if people had surrendered to government their right to contract, and then had received that right back from the government. Marshall argued that

> [a]s we have no evidence of the surrender, or of the restoration of the right; as this operation of surrender and restoration would be an idle and useless ceremony, the rational inference seems to be, that neither has ever been made; that individuals do not derive from government their right to contract, but bring that right with them into society; that obligation is not

---

[124] The Court had already held that no such regulation could excuse bankrupt parties from obligations created by contracts formed prior to passage of the regulation. *Sturges v Crowninshield*, 17 US 122 (1819).

[125] 25 US at 256–58, 261 (opinion of Washington).

[126] Id at 344–47.

[127] Id at 345.

conferred on contracts by positive law, but is intrinsic, and is conferred by the act of the parties.[128]

This chain of reasoning "is, undoubtedly, much strengthened by the authority of . . . writers on natural and national law,"[129] and, Marshall added later, "[w]hen we advert to the course of reading generally pursued by American statesmen in early life, we must suppose that the framers of our constitution were intimately acquainted with the writings of [these] wise and learned men."[130]

This argument is a remarkable departure from the other Marshall opinions we have examined. First, Marshall here made recourse not to the founding perspective, but to a controversial and abstract theory of government, which may or may not have been held by the American founders, and which at any rate is in no way particularly drawn to fit American circumstances and in no way essential to the project of establishing lawful government in the American polity. Second, Marshall now makes recourse to the private opinions of the constitutional draftsmen—he in fact reasons from the reading lists of those men—rather than to the public perspective shared by individual framers and the American people. This, in my view, is Marshall's one exercise in originalist constitutionalism. Third, Marshall's natural law theory is substantively naive. State-of-nature theory, in its more sophisticated versions, is not a historical thesis, but rather a device for making plain the elements of human nature upon which political societies are founded.[131] In *Ogden* Marshall relied on a somewhat laughable, apparently historical account, containing the twin claims that barbarian hunters contracted with one another before the founding of political society, and that there was no identifiable "ceremony" in which people and government engaged in a reciprocal surrender of power over contracts.

The effort to assimilate the Contracts Clause to the more general project of the founding, somewhat successful in *Fletcher*, thus collapsed entirely in *Ogden*. Marshall did make some references to the need to create an enduring Constitution, and to the need, dis-

---

[128] Id at 346.

[129] Id at 347.

[130] Id at 353.

[131] For a synopsis of the idea of a "state of nature" in political philosophy, see Allan Bloom, *Justice: John Rawls vs. the Tradition of Political Philosophy*, 69 Am Pol Sci Rev 648, 651–53 (1975).

cussed in greater length and with more subtlety in *Fletcher*,[132] to make contracts and property secure in order to guarantee "the prosperity and harmony of our citizens."[133] He also observed, with some force, that a legal theory incorporating into contracts as an implied term any prospective law would gut the Contracts Clause, for legislatures might enact a prospective law making all future contracts subject (by implied term) to retrospective alteration.[134] This observation, coupled with the sort of concerns raised in *Fletcher*, might have provided the ground for a sounder and less openly speculative argument. By themselves, however, the premises of *Fletcher* and the attack upon the theory of the Justices who made up the majority fail to provide a determinate interpretation of the Contracts Clause. Marshall's opinion concentrated on the search for such a determinate rule, trying not only the wild natural law theory, but also a textual argument,[135] a historical argument raising the possibility that the derogation of contracts might "sap the morals of the people, and destroy the sanctity of private faith,"[136] and a somewhat extended discussion of the dangers of "insane" state governments.[137] To modern readers, Marshall's opinion in *Ogden* cannot help but conjure up images of *Lochner v New York*;[138] unlike Marshall's other work, *Ogden* exacerbates concern about the capacity of the Court to speak for the people.

What are we to make of Marshall's dissent? Is it merely an example of a slip by a great master, or does it carry any deeper significance? Certainly in many respects the *Ogden* opinion was a mistake. Marshall's attempt to justify theoretically his ultimate political judgment upon the Contracts Clause is at odds with the rhetorical genius of his opinions in cases like *McCulloch* and *Marbury*. Marshall's arguments in those cases rested on various unjustified and sometimes unarticulated political judgments—about the unity of the American people, the ability of the judiciary to recover

---

[132] See quotation at note 121 above.

[133] 25 US at 339.

[134] Id.

[135] Id at 355–57 (arguing that if the Contracts Clause did not control prospective limitations upon contractual form, then the word "retrospective," or a synonym, would have appeared in the clause).

[136] Id at 355.

[137] Id at 351–53.

[138] 198 US 45 (1905).

the founding perspective, and the substantive supremacy of the national government. A justification of those judgments might well have led Marshall into the theoretical thickets he did enter in *Ogden*. But rather than providing such a justification, Marshall engaged in a detailed and reassuring examination of the consequences of his premises. He might have done the same in *Ogden*. Perhaps his rare station on the losing side caused him to believe that recourse to ultimate justification was essential. If so, he erred: Marshall's positions in dissent might eventually have been vindicated by later politics (perhaps influenced by his persuasive efforts) even in the absence of a justifying theory, just as Marshall's positions for the Court might have been rejected by later politics despite his victory in the case before the Court.

On the other hand, Marshall's opinion in *Ogden* does reveal a more fundamental problem with Marshall's constitutional theory, and so with the rhetorical paradigm it sponsored. Marshall's constitutional theory maintained that because the purpose of the Constitution was to enable the people to govern themselves well, it should be interpreted, insofar as possible, in ways that were conducive to the happiness of the American people. His rhetorical strategy attempted to show that the Constitution was the work of the American people by showing that it was conducive to the happiness of the American people. Viewed from these twinned perspectives, however, the Constitution had two (likewise connected) defects: it made real concessions to state sovereignty, thereby sacrificing the interests of the American people to the interests of the state governments, and it accommodated slavery.[139] Both defects showed up in the failure of the Constitution to provide adequate protection against state invasions of personal liberty. Marshall tried to press the Contracts Clause into that role. But the Contracts Clause was too narrow and rigid to bear such responsibility. The Reconstruction Congress would eventually remedy the defect,[140] but not in time to help Marshall. The difficulties that precipitated his dissent in *Ogden* were partially his fault but principally the fault of Ameri-

---

[139] Eisgruber, 69 S Cal L Rev at 70–71 (cited in note 40).

[140] Id at 71–74. Rakove suggests that the Reconstruction Amendments may be the most Madisonian elements of the Constitution, because only through them did "the federal government acquire the authority that Madison sought for it in 1787: to act as an umpire mediating the various forms injustice that he expected to flourish within the states." Rakove, *Original Meanings* at 337–38 (cited in note 17).

ca's flawed founding: one cannot demonstrate the goodness of a profoundly defective Constitution.[141]

V. The Modern Style

It is generally assumed that Justices today could not, and should not, write the way Marshall did. Certainly they do not. And certainly much has changed since Marshall's time. The modern Court's docket is heavier.[142] Through its decisions, the Court supervises a massive bureaucracy of state and federal judges. It would be fruitless, and next to impossible, for the Justices to return to first principles each time they determined whether police officers failed to honor a suspect's request for counsel or whether a state had created a public forum. In most of the Court's work today, precedent and doctrine have to play a more prominent role than they did in John Marshall's jurisprudence.[143]

On the other hand, we should not exaggerate the effect of these changes. Each term, the Court gets a handful of landmark cases. In these cases, the plentiful citations to precedent rarely illuminate the issues at stake. For example, the Justices seem almost incapable of deciding an Equal Protection Clause case without rehashing and remaking their doctrine about tiers of scrutiny;[144] these formulae would be obscure even if the Court never changed them, and it

---

[141] Compare Faulkner, *The Jurisprudence of John Marshall* at 224–25 (cited in note 6) ("It appears that Marshall died knowing full well that to a considerable degree he, and in a deeper sense the Constitution, had failed"). Faulkner appears to blame this failure on democracy, rather than on slavery and antebellum federalism. Id at 225.

[142] G. Edward White reports that, between 1815 and 1835, the Marshall Court handled an average of forty cases per year; the modern Court has handled more than three times that number in a single term. White, *The Marshall Court and Cultural Change* at 159 (cited in note 9). As White suggests, however, it would be a mistake to make too much of this difference; the early Justices had no support staff and substantial additional duties, including riding circuit. Id at 159–63. On the other hand, the modern Court, unlike Marshall's, has an enormous certiorari docket—in the October 1995 Term, for example, it disposed of more than 6,500 petitions. 65 USLW 3100 (1996).

[143] Douglas Laycock has offered similar observations about the causes of the modern style of opinion writing. Douglas Laycock, *Notes on the Role of Judicial Review, the Expansion of Federal Power, and the Structure of Constitutional Rights*, 99 Yale L J 1711, 1742–43 (1990).

[144] A short tour of the crooked path might include *San Antonio v Rodriguez*, 411 US 1 (1973); *Regents of University of California v Bakke*, 438 US 265 (1978); *Craig v Boren*, 429 US 190 (1976); *Plyler v Doe* 457 US 202 (1982); *City of Cleburne v Cleburne Living Center*, 473 US 432 (1985); *Metro Broadcasting, Inc. v FCC*, 497 US 547 (1990); *Adarand Constructors, Inc. v Pena*, 115 S Ct 2097 (1995); *United States v Virginia*, 116 S Ct 2264 (1996); and *Romer v Evans*, 116 S Ct 1620 (1996).

is hard to believe that lower courts or anybody else can benefit from the tiresome charges and countercharges about whether the Court has modified its test.

Conventional wisdom puts much of the blame upon law clerks,[145] and there is some truth to this accusation. By virtue of their schooling and inexperience, law clerks have a persistent desire to document the self-evident and demonstrate the indemonstrable—usually, in both cases, by a string-cite.[146] They also think that every case they work on is a landmark and so cannot comprehend the idea that different rhetorical and interpretive styles might suit different cases.

Yet, whatever the deficiencies of law clerk writing, it is implausible to think that modern judges would justify themselves in the way Marshall did if deprived of their staffs. To be sure, without clerks, judges would have to write shorter opinions with fewer footnotes.[147] As Richard Posner has recognized, however, law clerks' affection for length and citation is a symptom of a deeper problem. Clerks, he says, are "timid jurists" who want to "conceal novelty and to disguise imagination as deduction" because "[t]hey do not yet fully understand that in any case involving a novel issue . . . the most important thing is not the authorities, which by defi-

---

[145] For discussion, see, e.g., Richard A. Posner, *The Federal Courts: Crisis and Reform* 102–19 (1985).

[146] As Posner says,

> Law clerks . . . do everything they can to conceal novelty and to disguise imagination as deduction—hence the heavy reliance in opinions drafted by law clerks on string citations for obvious propositions (where they are superfluous) and novel propositions (for which they are inaccurate); on quotations (too often wrenched out of context) from prior opinions; on canons of statutory construction that were long ago exploded as clichés; on truisms; on redundant adjectives and adverbs ("unbridled discretion," "inextricably intertwined," "plain meaning"); and on boilerplate of every sort.

Id at 109.

[147] Posner presents data indicating that the length of federal appellate opinions has more than doubled since 1960, id at 114, and it is hard to believe that judges could sustain such an output if they had fewer clerks. Nevertheless, as Posner points out, "Nineteenth-century Supreme Court justices sometimes wrote opinions of staggering prolixity" without benefit of law clerk assistance. Id at 108. If modern Justices believe that good opinions should be long and heavily documented, then they might well devote their time to authoring ponderous opinions in important cases. The average opinion would become shorter, but landmark opinions would continue to resemble quasi-scientific scholarship of the sort that Story, but not Marshall, aspired to produce. See text accompanying notes 91–108 supra. If, on the other hand, modern Justices believe that good opinions should be short, it is hard to see why they do not adopt the simple expedient of imposing page limits upon their clerks.

nition do not determine the outcome of the case, but the reasoning that connects the authorities to the result."[148] Posner accordingly blames clerks for the lack of candor in judicial opinions, but that diagnosis is, in my view, mistaken. Judges have been terse and obfuscatory at the same time. One need not spill much ink or waste much paper to mask a value behind a textual reference,[149] a common law precedent,[150] or a historical claim.[151]

The influence of law clerks is neither necessary nor sufficient to explain why Supreme Court Justices prefer not to talk about justice in hard cases. The crucial change to the Supreme Court's environment has been conceptual, rather than material, technical, or administrative. When Marshall served on the Court, congressional legitimacy was problematic; Marshall and other Federalists had to legitimate national law in general, not just judicial review. After the Civil War, that was no longer so. People disagreed about how much power Congress had and how it should be used, but congressional legislation was well on its way to becoming the para-

---

[148] Id at 108–09.

[149] People often assume that textual references usefully constrain judicial discretion. In cases about individual rights, I think that almost precisely the opposite is true. As I have written elsewhere, "specific clauses are to lawyers what the brier patch was to Brer Rabbit: Protected by a thicket impenetrable to pursuers, they move about more freely than in an open field." Eisgruber, 69 S Cal L Rev at 90 (cited in note 40).

For patent examples of judicial efforts to hide a judgment behind a clause, see *Rochin v California*, 342 US 165, 175 (1952) (Black concurring) ("I think a person is compelled to be a witness against himself not only when he is compelled to testify, but also when as here, incriminating evidence is forcibly taken from him by a contrivance of modern science"); *Stanley v Georgia*, 394 US 557, 565 (1969) ("If the First Amendment means anything, it means that a State has no business telling a man, sitting alone in his own house," whether he may watch an obscene film). Whatever the contributions of law clerks to Black's concurrence in *Rochin* or Marshall's majority in *Stanley*, it bears notice that neither opinion is lengthy, scholarly, or festooned with citations. I have elsewhere criticized these opinions and the Court's more general obsession with specific clauses. Eisgruber, 69 S Cal L Rev at 90–95; Christopher L. Eisgruber, *Political Unity and the Powers of Government*, 41 UCLA L Rev 1297, 1330–35 (1994).

[150] Felix Frankfurter rested his opinion in *Rochin*, which gave us the "shocks the conscience" test, upon "the compelling traditions of the legal profession," 342 US at 171, and the foundations of "English jurisprudence." Id at 170 n 4. Again, I have criticized the Court's use of common law precedent to hide political judgment at greater length elsewhere. Eisgruber, 69 S Cal L Rev at 84–89.

[151] For discussions of how Justices have used (or misused) history to cloak political judgments, see, e.g., Alfred H. Kelly, *Clio and the Court: An Illicit Love Affair*, 1965 Supreme Court Review 119; John G. Wofford, *The Blinding Light: The Uses of History in Constitutional Interpretation*, 31 U Chi L Rev 502, 508–09 (1964). Both articles predate the explosion in the length of judicial opinions which Posner attributes to law clerk influence. Posner, *The Federal Courts* at 112.

digmatic example of law against which other exercises of political power could be measured (for their legitimacy, though not necessarily for their wisdom). For the twentieth-century Supreme Court, the dominant intellectual problem has been legitimating itself by comparison to elected national officials, particularly Congress but also, increasingly, the President.

That development is no accident; it is the inevitable consequence of successfully founding a government upon the idea of popular sovereignty. In principle, the sovereign people is an abstraction not reducible to any corporeal group. As Edmund Morgan says, "Individual people or groups of people could be seen, heard, touched, smelled, and could act, do things, and cause a lot of trouble, but *the* people, in the sense of all those who were to be governed and who could authorize government, could not."[152] Or, in the words of William Harris, the Constitution is "a symbolization of the whole people who have no other immanent identity."[153] These ideas, however precise as a matter of political theory, are too subtle to be politically marketable. People, told that they govern, reasonably expect the sovereign authority to connect up in some tangible way to actual people. And if the actual people are sovereign, and they disagree with one another, then the majority must govern (because the alternative is allowing the minority to govern). Hence the problem that has transfixed the Supreme Court for most of this century: neither the judiciary nor the Constitution is a majoritarian institution, and their claim to speak for the sovereign people is thereby cast into doubt.

It was both Marshall's chief problem and his chief advantage that, in his day, the claims of the states deprived the national majority of the presumptive legitimacy it now enjoys. Some institution had to exercise judgment on behalf of the people, and no institution had an unproblematic claim to do so. Marshall had to legitimate both national supremacy and judicial review. To do that he had to avoid identifying the American people with the national majority: national majorities were frightening to state peoples who

---

[152] Morgan, NY Rev Books at 46 (cited in note 25).

[153] William F. Harris, *The Interpretable Constitution* at 193 (cited in note 40). See also id at 77 ("the term 'popular sovereignty' does not aptly refer to the power of the dominant part of a segmentable voting population to select incumbents to hold office in the institutions of the Constitution").

might be national minorities. Marshall defended the national government and, more specifically, the Supreme Court on the basis of their ability to produce good results. By contrast, in the twentieth century, elected officials appear to be the natural representatives of the people. If somebody must exercise judgment on behalf of the people, then, it might seem, they should do so. The non-Marshallian tropes of twentieth-century judicial rhetoric—originalism, tradition, precedent, and doctrinal manipulation—serve to legitimate the Court's power by minimizing the appearance of independent judgment.[154] Law clerks facilitate a certain version of these tropes, a version that generates long opinions which resemble law review articles. But the decision to deploy clerks in this way is a judicial choice that reflects judges' ideas about what an opinion should look like.

There is something distinctly odd about the assumptions that underlie the modern adjudicative style. To begin with, nobody really doubts the legitimacy of judicial review any more. *West Coast Hotel v Parrish*[155] is receding into, by American standards, ancient history; during the last fifty years, the Court's greatest failures have come when it declined to act (e.g., *Korematsu v United States*,[156] *Dennis v United States*,[157] and *Naim v Naim*[158]), and its greatest moments have come when it intervened most boldly (e.g., *Brown v Bd. of Education*,[159] *Reynolds v Sims*,[160] and *New York Times v United*

---

[154] Professor Laycock also argues that the Court's tendency to "hide the ball" in tough cases is the result of prevailing theories about judicial legitimacy, not structural changes in the adjudicative process. Laycock, 99 Yale L J at 1743 & n 177 and 1747 (cited in note 143). My diagnosis differs from Laycock's in two respects. First, Laycock tethers his claims to a particular view, which I do not share, about the analytic structure of constitutional rights. Id at 1743–46 (arguing that constitutional rights take the form of "sweeping prohibitions subject to implied exceptions for reasons of necessity" and therefore compel courts to engage in balancing). Second, Laycock seems to blame academic commentators for the Court's lack of candor about its judgments. See, e.g., id at 1747 ("Too many critics have said the Court is not supposed to decide which goals are legitimate and which are important"). I think Laycock is partly correct, but, as the text preceding this note should make clear, I believe that the academy's error has a constitutional source: in a government founded upon the idea of popular sovereignty, there is a predictable tendency to exaggerate the authority of majoritarian institutions.

[155] 300 US 379 (1937).

[156] 323 US 214 (1944).

[157] 341 US 494 (1951).

[158] 350 US 891 (1955), 985 (1956) (per curiam).

[159] 347 US 483 (1954).

[160] 377 US 533 (1964).

States[161]). *Roe v Wade*[162] has now been on the books for nearly twenty-five years, and the skies have not fallen; unlike *Scott v Sandford*[163] or *Lochner v New York*,[164] Roe cannot be associated with a Civil War or a Great Depression. Indeed, three Justices appointed by Ronald Reagan and George Bush reaffirmed the abortion right, saying that even if *Roe* wasn't precisely correct, it certainly wasn't catastrophic.[165]

It should be no surprise, then, that Felix Frankfurter has no disciples on today's Court. During the Court's October 1995 Term, every Justice joined the majority in either *Romer v Evans*[166] or *Shaw v Hunt*.[167] In the October 1994 Term, every Justice joined the majority in either *United States v Lopez*[168] or *U.S. Term Limits v Thornton*.[169] The Court's most prominent "conservatives"—Antonin Scalia and William Rehnquist—show no reluctance to make judgments about what constitutes an appropriate electoral district or a defensible exercise of the Commerce power, inquiries that surely would have made Frankfurter's skin crawl.[170] Nobody on the Court really believes in judicial restraint any more.[171]

It could be, of course, that judicial review is uncontroversial pre-

---

[161] 403 US 713 (1971).

[162] 410 US 113 (1973).

[163] 60 US 393 (1856).

[164] 198 US 45 (1905).

[165] See generally *Planned Parenthood v Casey*, 505 US 833 (1992) (opinion by O'Connor, Kennedy, and Souter); see especially id at 853 ("the reservations any of us may have in reaffirming the central holding of *Roe* are outweighed by the explication of individual liberty we have given combined with the force of stare decisis"); at 855 ("Although *Roe* has engendered opposition, it has in no sense proven 'unworkable' "); and at 856 ("for two decades . . . people have organized intimate relationships and made choices that define their views of themselves and their places in society, in reliance on the availability of abortion in the event that contraception should fail").

[166] 116 S Ct 1620 (1996).

[167] 116 S Ct 1894 (1996).

[168] 115 S Ct 1624 (1995).

[169] 115 S Ct 1842 (1995).

[170] I leave readers to judge whether Frankfurter remained true to his faith. Compare *West Virginia v Barnette*, 319 US 624, 647 (1943) (Frankfurter dissenting) (urging Court to defer to the legislature in flag salute controversy) with *Rochin v California* 342 US 165, 172 (1952) (promulgating the "shocks the conscience" test) and *United States v Kahriger*, 345 US 22, 37 (1953) (Frankfurter dissenting) (arguing that federal tax on bookies exceeded the scope of Congress's enumerated powers).

[171] Louis Michael Seidman makes a similar observation in *Romer's Radicalism: The Unexpected Revival of Warren Court Activism* (unpublished manuscript on file with the author).

cisely because everybody—or some relevant set of people—believes that it involves no exercise of independent judgment. Supreme Court Justices occasionally say that. In *Casey v Planned Parenthood*, for example, Antonin Scalia maintained that "As long this Court thought (and the people thought) that we Justices were doing essentially lawyers' work up here—reading text and discerning our society's traditional understanding of that text—the public pretty much left us alone. Texts and traditions are facts to study, not convictions to demonstrate about."[172] But who really believes this?[173]

Today's jurisprudential debate is not ultimately about whether judges should exercise judgment, or about whether they should enforce constitutional limits on legislatures, but rather about how they should do so—in particular, about how their job requires them to balance moral principle and historical tradition. To settle that question, judges must reconcile their responsibilities with the American faith in popular sovereignty; in particular, they must find some way to recognize the people on whose behalf they act. One way to do that is to give a historical interpretation to the popular sovereign, identifying *the* people with actual, tangible majorities from the past.

Marshall's jurisprudence suggests an alternative strategy. The people are recognizable by their desire for justice and good government, and any majority which betrays those objectives is a false representative of the people. On this understanding, when the Constitution is ambiguous, the interpretive task of judges is to figure out what justice requires. Their rhetorical task will have two parts: first, to defend their conception of justice, and, second, to identify this conception with the actual, tangible American people, thereby enhancing the plausibility of the idea that a desire for justice is the true signature of the sovereign people.[174] Judicial opin-

---

[172] *Casey v Planned Parenthood*, 505 US at 1000 (dissenting opinion).

[173] Surely the public does not think the way Scalia supposes. If it did, the Court's decision in *Griswold v Connecticut*, 381 US 479 (1965), protecting the use of contraception under the Due Process Clause, would be more controversial than *Texas v Johnson*, 491 US 397 (1989), protecting flag burning under the First Amendment. The electorate, at least, reacts to the substance of the Court's decisions, and knows little about its methods.

[174] On the capacity of judicial rhetoric to identify constitutional goals with the American people, see generally Christopher L. Eisgruber, *Is the Supreme Court an Educative Institution?* 67 NYU L Rev 961 (1992).

ions would thus have a historical character, but, as with Marshall's own opinions, the historical details would be selected and presented for a rhetorical purpose—to reinforce the conviction that the American people want whatever is in fact just and so established their Constitution to achieve justice.

I leave it to readers to decide whether Marshall's theory is an attractive one; whether it is more practicable today, when judicial review is relatively secure, than it was earlier in this century; and whether Marshall's rhetorical strategy might explain the Supreme Court's references to the founding better than do more conventional theories, such as originalism. Whatever one's judgment upon these questions, I think it clear that today's departures from Marshall's adjudicative style reflect theoretical choices, not technical "progress." If we think Marshall's approach inapplicable today, it must be because we think his constitutional or rhetorical judgments mistaken. It is not clear to me that he was wrong about either. To be sure, we might hope that judges would admit their judgments more candidly than Marshall did, particularly since judicial authority is no longer so precarious in our day as it was in his. But even Marshall's rhetorical misdirection seems preferable to the irrelevant citations—to precedent, tests, and intentions—that judges today favor as a means for hiding their judgments.[175]

VI. Conclusion

Summed up most simply, John Marshall's constitutional theory flowed from the premise that what Americans wanted was, ultimately, justice. For that reason, thinking about what justice required was a sound means for figuring out what the people wanted—and what they had done when they established the Constitution. Applied to the structural issues that loomed largest on his Court's agenda, Marshall's theory entailed that insofar as the Constitution was ambiguous, it should be construed to reflect whatever allocation of political authority would best serve justice.

In Marshall's day, as today, it was far from obvious that Americans were truly committed to justice. The coincidence of justice

---

[175] See Ronald M. Dworkin, *Freedom's Law: The Moral Reading of the Constitution* 37 (Harvard, 1996) (recommending that "judges . . . construct franker arguments of principle that allow the public to join in the argument).

and popular sovereignty in the United States is both philosophi-
cally and empirically contestable. It is also politically undeniable;
politicians who tell the people they are unjust will lose their office.
"One does not preach democracy's limitations to democrats and
expect thus to leaven democracy," wrote Faulkner to explain why
Marshall did not state his premises more bluntly in *Marbury*.[176]
Ironically, one might well hope to leaven democracy by exaggerat-
ing its virtues. A presumed coincidence between democratic will
and justice is a good excuse for the people's agents to do justice.
That may be constitutional democracy's saving grace; it is, in any
event, the strategic fulcrum of John Marshall's constitutional
jurisprudence.

---

[176] Faulkner, *The Jurisprudence of John Marshall* at 211 (cited in note 6).